THE *Course* OF *American Diplomacy*

*f*rom the
revolution to
the present

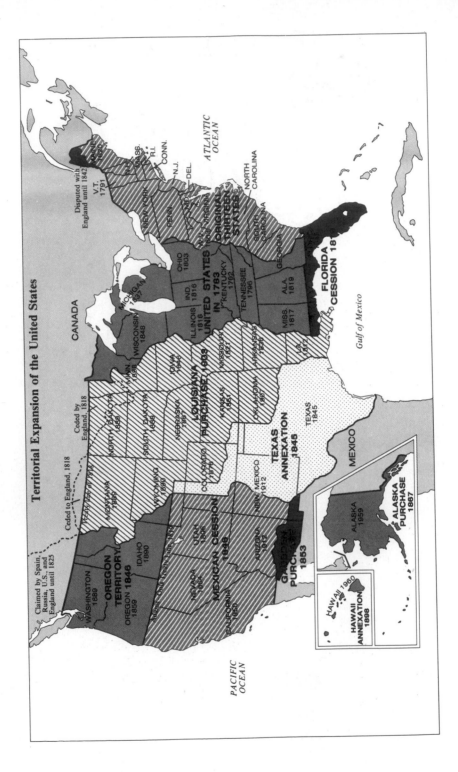

Territorial Expansion of the United States

THE *Course* OF *American Diplomacy*

*f*rom the revolution to the present

HOWARD JONES
The University of Alabama

Second Edition

The Dorsey Press
Chicago, Illinois   60604

Acquisitions editor: David Follmer
Developmental editor: Leslie Abramson
Project editor: Waivah Clement
Production manager: Charles J. Hess
Designer: Keith J. McPherson
Photo researcher: Diane Hamilton
Cartography: Mapping Specialists, Ltd.
Cover designer: Jame A. Riley
Compositor: P&M Typesetting, Inc.
Typeface: 10/12 Palatino
Printer: The Book Press

ISBN 0-256-06088-6

Library of Congress Catalog Card No. 87–72023

Printed in the United States of America

1 2 3 4 5 6 7 8 9 0 BP 5 4 3 2 1 0 9 8

Preface

This work focuses on the personalities, security interests, and expansionist tendencies behind the formulation of America's foreign policy. It rests on the premise that the most effective foreign policy results when the two themes of idealism and realism run parallel in methods and goals. Should a choice become necessary, as it often did, decisionmakers nearly always recognized that the wiser course was to protect America's vital interests rather than adopt an idealistic policy that risked national security in the name of morality. Washington's leaders have been consistent in pursuing the national interest as they perceived it. Though at times lapsing into naive pronouncements virtually impossible to fulfill, they usually worked within the bounds of reality, seldom wavering from the central objective of safeguarding the nation. Whereas European diplomats commonly talked of power relationships, economic interests, and imperialism, Americans voiced concern over the following ideals: natural rights; the republican ideas of popular rule, free trade, neutral rights, and freedom of the seas; the separation of political and economic concerns in foreign policy; and freedom from Old World political and military entanglements. At the same time, however, they realized that these ideals were related to issues of power.

This study has other emphases. It illustrates the intimate relationship between foreign and domestic policy. It does not dwell on twentieth-century American foreign policy at the expense of virtually ignoring its historical antecedents. And it relies primarily on the natural chronology of events to organize and narrate the story as the nation's leaders saw it. Policymaking in any area of the world cannot occur in a vacuum. Events occurred concurrently and day after day, only at times appearing to be manageable. One cannot discuss the Oregon question of the 1840s without considering the Texas issue with Mexico and the onset of war in 1846. Nor can one understand pre–Pearl Harbor relations with Japan without recognizing that European events affected the actions of both Japan and the United States. To compartmentalize each topic in thematic chapters may impose a design onto foreign affairs that did not exist. Such a topical approach can create the illusion that history takes place in a well-ordered fashion, making policymakers vulnerable to unwarrantable criticisms for failing to see alleged "patterns" in history. Should readers recognize that events are largely uncontrollable, they will begin to understand the plight of policymakers who daily encounter a kaleidoscopic array of problems rarely susceptible to simple analysis and ready solution. If readers come to realize that the outcome of events is not inevitable and that the complexity of history makes decisionmaking a difficult process, this book will have served its purpose.

Hopefully this work will stand on the strengths of readability, organization, and accuracy. My intention was to write a straightforward, balanced, and comprehensive account of the major events in the nation's foreign policy, from the American Revolution to the present. The writer recognizes that history is complex—that any event results from many causes and is seldom predictable. Rather than making judgments that might reflect the times in which I have lived, I have drawn conclusions based on an attempt to understand the times in which policymakers lived. The narrative concentrates on mainstream events because they occupied the presidential administrations' attention and most affected the national interest. Readers wanting more detailed accounts should examine the many fine articles and monographic studies cited in the "Selected Readings" sections following each chapter. For these and numerous other historical works, they should consult the superb *Guide to American Foreign Relations since 1700*, edited by Richard Dean Burns.

This study is the product of several people's labors. It has profited from the readings of friends in the profession as well as from three anonymous readers who served as referees. Robert H. Ferrell read the manuscript, giving it that special "treatment" that so many of his former students have been fortunate to receive. Two of my colleagues were especially helpful. Forrest McDonald (along with his wife Ellie) read the manuscript and offered countless suggestions regarding thematic unity, style, and content. John Pancake shared his vast knowledge of the American Revolutionary period by giving Chapter 1 a careful reading. Randall Woods read some of the early chapters, making numerous useful recommendations. Pete Maslowski read the chapter on the Polk period and offered considerable help and encouragement. The manuscript also benefited from the comments of graduate students in my two-semester seminar in American foreign policy. For reading all or parts of the manuscript, I want to thank the following class members: Mark Boazman, Bob Browning, Paul Clark, Danny Cooper, Carol Jackson, Tim Johnson, Thornton Miller, Patrick Moore, Jim Parker, Guy Swanson, Lynn Wesson, and Don Williams. To Guy, Mark, and Tim, I owe a special debt for showing continued interest in my work, sharing ideas that have sharpened my thinking on several issues, and displaying an enthusiasm for history that is infectious.

There were other forms of encouragement. The University of Alabama granted a sabbatical leave that allowed me to complete a major portion of this manuscript, along with a considerable amount of work on another book-length project concerning the Truman Doctrine. A fellowship from the Earhart Foundation in Ann Arbor, Michigan, furthered my work on the Truman era, while affording time for the diplomatic survey as well. Also of assistance were Will Davison, Ruth Kibbey, Susan Peck, and Kitty Sassaman.

In this, the second edition, I have likewise profited from the assistance of numerous people. David C. Follmer, publisher at The Dorsey Press, has contributed in so many ways that it would be impossible to list them. Others at the press were especially helpful, including Leslie Abramson, Waivah Clement, and Bob Cunningham. I also want to express appreciation for careful readings by Robert A. Divine, Joseph A. Fry, and Gaddis Smith. Inspiration, advice, and encouragement came from still another group of graduate students at the University of Alabama: Jim Birdseye, David Bucy, Bill Caulkins, Paul Grass, James Griffin, John Griffiths, Jim Head, Wesley Hughes, Fred Nusbaum, Marilyn Peebles, Howard Potts, George Prewett, Don Rakestraw, Hugh Terry, Ruth Truss, Enbao Wang, Buford Williams, and Mark Zimmerman.

Finally, this book would not be complete without the following dedication. My deepest gratitude goes to those who most understand the sacrifices involved in research and writing: my parents, who have agonized over this work as much as I have; Mary Ann, my spouse and closest friend; and my children, Debbie, Howie, and Shari. If this book has any value, it is due to their inspiration.

Howard Jones

Contents

List of Maps

List of Illustrations

Chapter 21

Chapter 22

Chapter 23

Chapter 24

Chapter 25

Chapter 26

Chapter One

The Revolutionary Beginnings of American Foreign Policy, 1775–1789

IDEALISM AND REALISM: THE COLONIAL BACKGROUND

American foreign policy has always been difficult for outsiders to understand. Policymakers in most other countries are straightforward in following a single principle, that of furthering national self-interest as they perceive it. Americans, by contrast, adhere to the same principle, but are moved by a curious mixture of idealism and realism, and one can never be sure which set of ingredients is likely to prevail in a given set of circumstances. In 1812 they went to war against Great Britain partly for the high-minded goal of defending the principle of freedom of the seas, but also for the less exalted purpose of taking land. Later in the century they engaged in wars of expansion against Mexico and Spain, and yet afterward insisted upon paying for the territories they conquered. In the twentieth century they fought one war to "make the world safe for democracy," another to make it safe against fascism, and two more in part to defend small nations from communism.

The ambivalence of the United States in dealing with other nations is rooted in its colonial past. One form of idealism was evident from the beginning. When the early Puritans proclaimed that they were establishing a new Zion, a "city on a hill" which would be a model for the corrupt Old World to follow, they established the basis for isolationism, the American ideal of nonentanglement in European political affairs. For the next hundred years the relative isolation of American settlements gave that ideal a large measure of reality. Even until the middle of the twentieth century the fortunes of geography gave the United States free secu-

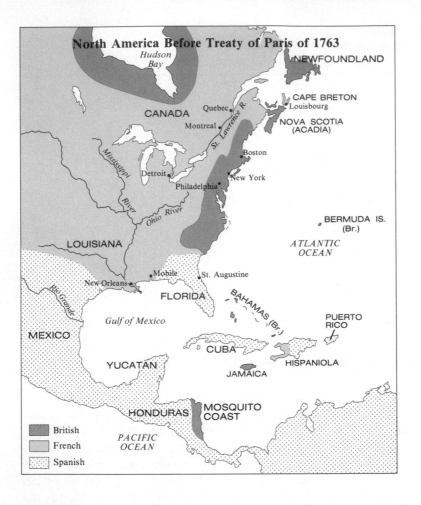

MAP 1 (above) and MAP 2 (opposite)

The most striking difference between the maps is the almost total absence of France from North America. This humiliation at the peace table helped encourage the French to join the Americans in the Revolutionary War against England.

rity, which permitted an adherence to idealism without endangering the country's independence and territorial integrity. During the eighteenth century American contact with Europe became more frequent; and yet, though European leaders increasingly directed their craft toward the pursuit of power and profit, the Americans came to believe in a God-given "law of nations" that governed—or ought to govern—international relations. From English political writers, mainly John Locke, they learned natural rights' theory; from the French and Scottish Enlightenments they learned to despise and distrust what they perceived to be the deceit and

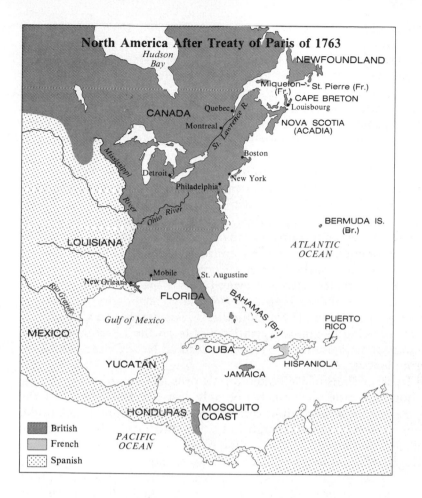

trickery of formal diplomacy. Americans also learned to believe in free trade, freedom of the seas, and peaceful intercourse among nations. These so-called ideals were a part of real American interests.

Self-interest was also there from the beginning. Even the seventeenth-century Puritans admitted that they emigrated to America in search of economic opportunity as well as in hope of saving their souls. The one thing British North America had in abundance which attracted Europeans throughout the colonial period was rich land. It mattered little to settlers that Indians happened to occupy that land; newcomers simply took what they wanted and when the Indians resisted, the colonists resorted to the same pattern of trickery and force as did most diplomats of Old Europe. Land hunger and territorial expansionism developed side by side with isolationism and idealism.

During the colonial and early national periods of American history the prime determinants of international relations were not what Americans thought and did, but what Europeans did. Between 1689 and 1815 the nations of Europe, especially Britain and France, were locked in almost continuous struggle, and in that struggle the American colonies were little more than pawns. During that long period Spain, Austria, Prussia, and other powers shifted sides, and America broke imperial ties and fought its first two wars as a nation; but through it all, the central antagonists remained England and France. They fought each other seven times in that era, and in so doing engulfed much of the world in sixty years of warfare.

The last of the colonial wars—variously known as the French and Indian War, the Seven Years' War, and the Great War for the Empire—left Britain in command of North America and, on paper at least, the most powerful country in the Western world in 1763. The war won Canada from France along with all of France's claims to land east of the Mississippi River, and upon securing Florida from Spain (France's ally in the war), Britain completed control of the entire eastern half of North America from the Hudson Bay to the Gulf of Mexico. In addition, Britain retained a number of West Indian islands captured during the war. Of a once vast empire, France was able to keep only three large islands in the West Indies and two small ones off Newfoundland. Spain received Cuba in exchange for agreeing to grant navigation rights on the Mississippi to the British, and as compensation for Florida it secured New Orleans and Louisiana from France.

The Treaty of Paris of 1763 offered little prospect for an end to Anglo-French hostilities, for the French not only lost the war, they lost the peace. To the French who could recall their nation's magnificence under King Louis XIV, it was bad enough to be humbled on the battlefields; to be humiliated at the peace table was too much to bear. The elder William Pitt of England had stirred the drive for empire, however, and the diplomats at Paris responded with severe peace terms. The French burned with desire for revenge, and a resumption of the Anglo-French war was nearly predictable.

Meanwhile, the removal of France from North America encouraged a feeling of commonality among Americans and served as the prelude to independence. The colonists believed they no longer needed the protection of the British Empire, while the government in London could no longer ignore the colonists' violations of imperial regulations. Thus, Englishmen at home sought to tighten the bonds of empire—and require the colonists to share the burden of maintaining it—at precisely the time when the colonists ceased to regard it as necessary. In the pre-Revolutionary decade of the 1760s colonial Americans behaved in characteristic fashion. On one hand, they tried to avoid paying taxes and obeying the law. On the other, they defended their position with ringing appeals to the "rights of Englishmen" and "rights of man."

In the course of the American colonists' first venture in international affairs, they more fully realized that the Western world remained a group of predatory nation-states, monarchical and committed to mercantilism or commercial domination through the acquisition of colonies. The law of nations exercised only partial restraints. Despite the Enlightenment's call for fundamental rights, the Old World continued its timeless preparations for war and the building of empire. The resumption of the Anglo-French struggle drove home this truth during the formative era of the United States.

THE FRENCH ALLIANCE

Americans quickly became acquainted with the realities of world politics in the period following the French and Indian War. In the words of William Pitt, France was a "vulture hovering over the British empire, and hungrily watching the prey that she is only waiting for the right moment to pounce upon." From 1764 through the beginning of the War for Independence, the French engaged in secret activities designed to avenge the humiliation of the Treaty of Paris. They disrupted English commercial and colonial policies, secretly supported Americans in their protests against unpopular pieces of legislation, and led them to believe that a break with the mother country would bring military assistance. French hopes rose with the furor over the Stamp Act of 1765, the Tea Act and Boston Tea Party of 1773, the Intolerable Acts of the following year, and the outburst of fighting at Lexington and Concord in 1775. By that time the French were ready to take advantage of the impending collapse of the British Empire.

The French foreign minister, Étienne-François duc de Choiseul, was especially eager for revenge. His instructions to French agents denounced England as evil and urged those in America to encourage rebellion against the crown. He warned that the expulsion of France from North America had not satiated Britain's hunger for empire; it now craved the remainder of Spain's New World holdings as well. Choiseul complained to King Louis XV that England "is, and will ever be, the declared enemy of our power, and of your state. Her avidity in commerce, the haughty tone she takes in the world's affairs, her jealousy of your power, the intrigues which she has made against you, make us foresee that centuries will pass before you can make a durable peace with that country which aims at supremacy in the four quarters of the globe." The fiery foreign minister fell from grace in 1770, in part because the king feared that his continual scheming could lead to premature war with England.

Choiseul's removal did not stem official hatred for the English, for in 1774 the new foreign minister under King Louis XVI, Charles Gravier comte de Vergennes, made it clear that the French attitude had not changed. Though debonair and outwardly calm, Vergennes quietly seethed with anger. At one point he declared that "England is the natural enemy of France; and she is a greedy enemy, ambitious, unjust and treacherous: the unalterable and cherished object of her policy is, if not the destruction of France, at least her degradation and ruin." The "duty" of France, he continued, was to "seize every possible opportunity to re-duce the power and the greatness of England." He tempered his hatred for the English with the realization that the British Empire was the strong-est power in the Western world.

Vergennes's opportunity for striking at England came through the machinations of Pierre Augustin Caron de Beaumarchais, poet, musician, playwright author of the comedies, *The Barber of Seville* and *The Marriage of Figaro*, celebrated maker of a watch so small that Madame de Pompa-dour, the French king's mistress, could wear it in a ring on her finger. Beaumarchais, working as secret agent for the crown, had talked with Virginian Arthur Lee in London about the massive unrest in the British colonies, and in early 1776 suggested to his French government that it en-courage a rebellion in America by extending secret military aid. His argu-ments were persuasive. Bolstered by a matching contribution from King Charles III of Spain, French aid to America began in May 1776 through a front organization called Rodrigue Hortalez and Company, even though Finance Minister Baron Turgot warned that such drains upon the French treasury would add to the heavy burden of a general French military and naval buildup and lead to bankruptcy. Thus, before the Declaration of In-dependence and even prior to the arrival of American emissaries in Paris, Hortalez and Company sent America muskets, cannons, cannon balls and powder, bombs, mortars, tents, and enough clothing for 30,000 men.

French (and Spanish) assistance kept American hopes alive during the crucial spring of 1776; and in June of that year, when Richard Henry Lee introduced in the Continental Congress his resolution for independence, he also proposed the immediate negotiation of treaties of alliance with Britain's principal enemies. On the face of things, the Americans' eager courting of European monarchs seemed to contradict their professed ideals and their aversion to foreign entanglements. Indeed, in the pam-phlet *Common Sense*, the most widely read document of the American Revolution except the Declaration of Independence itself, Thomas Paine argued that independence was the only way to avoid such entangle-ments. "Any submission to, or dependence on, Great Britain," he wrote, "tends directly to involve this Continent in European wars and quarrels, and set[s] us at variance with nations who would otherwise seek our friendship, and against whom we have neither anger nor complaint." American foreign policy, he declared, should be independent of Old World political alliances and built on the doctrine of freedom of the seas. "Our plan is commerce, and that, well attended to, will secure us the peace and friendship of all Europe." But some Americans were realistic enough to know that they could not win their independence from Britain without French help, and idealistic enough to believe that they could ben-efit from such assistance without incurring long-lasting obligations.

To secure outside assistance, the Continental Congress appointed John Adams as head of a committee to draft a Model Treaty to guide for-mal negotiations with France and other interested nations. As principal

Thomas Paine

The author of Common Sense, *he urged Americans to push for independence from England and to refrain from political entanglements with the Old World.* (A 1793 engraving by William Sharp; Library of Congress)

architect of the Plan of Treaties (September 1776), Adams issued a warning similar to Paine's: Americans should shun entangling political alliances. "I am not for soliciting any political connection, or military assistance, or indeed naval, from France," he wrote an acquaintance. "I wish for nothing but commerce, a mere marine treaty with them." His Model Treaty called for the separation of political and economic concerns, recognition of the principles of "free [neutral] ships, free [neutral] goods," and freedom of the seas based on reciprocal commercial "rights, liberties, privileges, immunities and exemptions." Adams refused to offer France any political concessions for fear that Vergennes would ask for Canada and the fisheries of Newfoundland; he proposed instead to entice the French with the prospect of ending English commercial control of North America. Like Paine, Adams wanted to draw all of Europe into the American market, on the theory that by establishing commercial ties with several nations the United States could avoid the danger of dependence on a single nation. In the spirit of the Enlightenment, Adams sought to establish a peace based on world economic interdependence. Thus his treaty guide was idealistic in conception and self-serving in purpose.

While it offered France trading opportunities in the New World which then belonged to England, it guaranteed America commercial advantages without political obligations. The Model Treaty exemplified the finest form of foreign policy—idealism balanced with realism.

Meanwhile the Continental Congress in Philadelphia prepared to implement the Model Treaty by sending a three-man delegation to France. Some months earlier Congress had asked Arthur Lee, the same American who had talked with Beaumarchais, to report on European attitudes toward the growing unrest in America. Congress, not aware of Beaumarchais's secret preparations for aid, had also dispatched Connecticut Congressman Silas Deane to Paris to seek military assistance. It now appointed Benjamin Franklin and Lee to join Deane in France. Only Franklin had to make the trip, for Deane and Lee were already in Paris.

If Lee and Deane were "militia diplomats," as new to the world of diplomacy as the American militia was to war, through sixteen years in England Franklin had long since become master of the trade. Plain-spoken, simply dressed, and deceptively humble, Franklin was capable of arranging the truth as it suited him, and he had one great advantage when

Benjamin Franklin

Regarded by many in Europe as the Enlightenment personified, he was instrumental in negotiating the Franco-American Treaties of 1778 and the Treaty of Paris of 1783 ending the Revolutionary War. (Painting ca. 1789; Historical Society of Pennsylvania)

he arrived in Paris in December of 1776: the French regarded him as the embodiment of the Enlightenment in America. Inventor of the lightning rod, a stove, harmonica, bifocals; author of the immensely popular and internationally read *Poor Richard's Almanack*; natural philosopher who, like Thomas Jefferson, had won a place in the French Academy—these were a few of the achievements accredited to the seventy-year-old Franklin by the French *philosophes* who revered science and reason. The image as much as the reality of this wealthy, wily, colorful, and extraordinarily gifted man was instrumental in convincing the French court, intellectuals, and common people that aid to America would not only bring down the lofty British, but would further the cause of humanity.

Despite Franklin's favorable effect on the French, and despite the consuming French desire to humble the British, the Vergennes ministry held back on formal recognition of the United States and official extension of military aid. Such decisions could not be taken lightly, for they would entail war with England. In a memorandum to the French king, Vergennes wrote that France should avoid becoming more deeply involved until the Americans established themselves with a decisive victory on the field of battle. Such victory was long in coming: in the dreary months which followed the brief exultation of July 1776, American prospects for success dimmed as the Continental Army lost to Sir William Howe's forces at Brandywine and Germantown in the autumn of 1777, and subsequently set up winter quarters at Valley Forge.

Yet the tide had already begun to turn in that autumn of 1777. The British continued their major offensive from the north, designed to divide New England from the rest of the colonies and take Philadelphia. From New York City, Howe was to go up the Hudson River to Albany, where he would join General John Burgoyne approaching from Canada. Unaccountably, Howe did not follow these plans. He moved south by himself and took the capital of Philadelphia, while Burgoyne went on to defeat in upper New York near a little village called Saratoga, on October 17. Burgoyne urged leaders in London to seek immediate peace.

America's victory at Saratoga was an epoch-making event in world history. The news arrived in France early in December and set off waves of enthusiasm for the Americans, while in England a distraught Lord North immediately moved for conciliation. A secret agent, Paul Wentworth, made his way to the Americans in Paris to offer assurances of fair treatment if their cohorts across the ocean would resume their rightful place within the empire. Finding his audience unreceptive, in early January Wentworth impatiently declared that England would continue the war for another decade before granting independence. "America," Franklin crisply replied, "is ready to fight fifty years to win it." In the meantime he placed additional pressure on Vergennes by leaking news of the British offer to the French. The foreign minister may already have gathered this information from the spies following Wentworth; in any event, two days after Franklin's conversation with the British agent, a French official asked

Franklin how to prevent America from settling with England on anything other than total independence. Franklin deftly responded: "The immediate conclusion of a treaty of commerce and alliance would induce the Deputies to close their ears to any proposal which should not have as its basis entire liberty and independence, both political and commercial." That day, January 8, 1778, Franco-American negotiations began in Paris, and less than a month afterward, on February 6, two treaties were concluded.

The treaties only partly adhered to Adams's Plan of Treaties. The first, the Treaty of Amity and Commerce, followed the idealistic guidelines of the Plan of 1776. It signified French recognition of the United States; called for a restricted list of contraband or illicit goods which did not include naval stores and foodstuffs; endorsed the rights of neutrals to trade with belligerent or warmaking nations; recognized the principle of "free ships, free goods," in that no confiscation of nonmilitary materials could take place when a ship showed neutral colors; and implemented the "most favored-nation-clause," which provided that if either nation allowed commercial benefits to others, each signatory to the treaty would share in those same privileges.

The second agreement, the Treaty of Alliance, reflected the realities of the international situation. Colonial experience, Thomas Paine, and Model Treaty notwithstanding, the American negotiators in Paris agreed to a military pact that would become effective in the event of war between France and England. The United States and France promised not to make peace until American independence was "formally or tacitly assured," and neither party would enter a separate "truce or peace" with the British without "formal consent of the other." Article XI of the Treaty of Alliance would have troublesome implications in the future, for in it the United States and France mutually guaranteed their claims to territory in North America, "from the present time and forever against all other powers."

The negotiations between France and America, though secret, were known to the British within two days of the treaties' signatures because Benjamin Franklin's personal secretary, Dr. Edward Bancroft, was a spy. When Silas Deane first arrived in Paris as agent of the Continental Congress in July 1776, he had been delighted to find his old friend Bancroft working with the American delegation. Not knowing that Bancroft was also in the private employ of the British, Deane permitted him to serve as interpreter during the discussions with Beaumarchais concerning the delivery of French goods to the American armies. Deane eventually shared so many official secrets with Bancroft that King George III moaned that the days were not long enough to read all of them. During the treaty talks of 1778 Bancroft kept a steady stream of information flowing to London—including copies of the treaties themselves.

Bancroft's reports persuaded the British government to try to stop America's ratification of the French alliance by sending a mission to America, headed by Lord Carlisle, to offer local autonomy and restoration of the empire as it was in 1763. Unfortunately for the British the treaties reached Philadelphia before the Carlisle mission did, and on May 4, just two days following their arrival, Congress approved the twin pacts. A month later Carlisle's group arrived, only to find that Congress would not meet with the men until they agreed to discuss British evacuation of America and recognition of American independence. After five months of arguments, threats, and attempted bribery, the mission failed and returned home.

The Treaty of Alliance filled Americans with such exhilaration that, for the moment, they forgot all talk of model treaties. General George Washington declared from Valley Forge that the alliance "chalk[ed] out a plain and easy road to independence," and even John Adams regarded it as a major triumph for the United States. Despite earlier pronouncements about isolationism, the fate of America had become enmeshed in European political affairs.

On June 17, 1778, the French and English navies clashed in the English Channel, and the strange military alliance of monarchy and republic went into effect. The Franco-American Treaty of 1778 became the first entangling alliance with Europe entered into by the United States, and it would be the last until 1949, when the nation became part of the North Atlantic Treaty Organization.

DIPLOMACY OF WAR

Encouraged by its success with France, the United States tried to build alliances with Spain, Russia, and the Netherlands as well. Though French desire for vengeance had overcome their own realistic considerations, other countries were uncomfortable with America's revolutionary principles, fearful of British retaliation if the Franco-American effort failed, and more concerned with commercial and territorial goals than the independence and integrity of the United States. These nations found it safer to stand behind the shield of neutrality—at least until the verdict of the war became clear.

Americans first tried to persuade the Spanish to increase their secret aid, but the government in Madrid had become more hesitant about helping the rebels. Spain's King Charles III certainly wanted England brought to its knees: the English had taken both Gibraltar and Florida from Spain in the not too distant past. Yet the Spanish recognized the danger of example. Could the monarchy assist republicans engaged in revolution and not expect to encourage a similar eruption among its own colonies in New Spain? Would an independent United States confine itself east of the Appalachian Mountains and not threaten Spain's interests in the Mississippi Valley? The truth is that Spain's decision to send war matériel to the Americans was attributable to its desire to see the English and the Americans exhaust each other in battle. A Spanish diplomat best expressed his country's fears: the American "republic has been born as it were a pigmy.

But a day will come when it will be a great, a veritable awe-inspiring co-lossus in these regions." After the battle of Saratoga, the Spanish cut back assistance to the young nation.

After the signing of the treaties of 1778 France exerted enormous pres-sure on Spain to help the Americans, for Vergennes was convinced that success against Britain depended on the support of the Spanish navy. He was negotiating from a tenuous position because, in his zeal to defeat the British, he had severely strained relations with Spain by supporting Beaumarchais's secret aid plan in 1776, without first getting Spain's ap-proval. Nonetheless, on April 12, 1779, Vergennes secured the secret Treaty of Aranjuez, whereby Spain agreed to join France in military oper-ations against the British. To obtain this pact he engaged in double-deal-ing that violated the spirit of the French treaties with the United States. For one thing, he accepted Spain's refusal to extend the alliance to include the United States, or even to recognize American independence. More important, Vergennes gave in to Spain's demand that France refrain from signing a separate peace with the British until the Spanish had won back Gibraltar. Thus the fortunes of the United States became irrevocably at-tached to a European political matter.

Unaware of the intricacies of the Franco-Spanish Treaty, the Ameri-cans were elated when Spain declared war on England on June 21, 1779, and they immediately moved toward securing a formal alliance and fi-nancial assistance from the government of Madrid. In September, Con-gress sent thirty-four-year-old John Jay of New York to Spain to seek recognition of American independence and a $5 million loan. Jay, who had come from a long line of wealthy French-Dutch merchants and had gone to King's College (later Columbia) before becoming involved in revo-lutionary politics, had had no experience that could have prepared him for the treatment he received in Spain. Things began to go awry from the moment he landed in that country in January 1780. He and his wife bat-tled fleas, bugs, terrible roads, and high-priced innkeepers on their inland trip to the Spanish court. Soon after arriving in Madrid their infant daughter suddenly took ill and died. To make matters worse, Jay found the king too preoccupied with hunting to bother with affairs of state, and the foreign minister, Count de Floridablanca, was not interested in seeing him. Jay suffered the further indignities of Spanish officials intercepting and reading his correspondence, of spies trying to hear his conversations, and of his money running out because Congress, confident that its emis-sary would secure a financial agreement in Madrid, had incurred mone-tary obligations that it now could not meet.

By the summer of 1781 Congress so desperately felt the need for Spanish aid that it authorized Jay to forgo claims to the Mississippi River. Though British military fortunes in the south were on the rise, the con-gressional decision to drop demands for the river was suspect. Not only did Jay's offer sacrifice the only bargaining position the United States had, but if accepted it would have undercut America's potential for expansion.

For this concession the Spanish were to help the Americans preserve "all their respective territories"—which at the time did not include lands west of the Alleghenies. Floridablanca turned down this attractive deal, probably in hope that his soldiers would solidify their hold on the Floridas and, without American ties, move on to acquire the vast region between the river and mountains.

After more than two years of frustration and embarrassment, Jay had secured only sufficient funds from Floridablanca to see him through daily expenses, but he had acquired enough hostility toward European diplomacy to last him the rest of his life. He had never been officially received. After one stormy session with Spanish officials Jay angrily declared to the French ambassador that he had come to Madrid "to make *propositions*, not *supplications*." Furthermore, he suspected the French of undermining American expansionist aims by privately assuring Spain of territories west of the Appalachian Mountains. The Spanish foreign minister eventually agreed to give Jay about $175,000, a paltry sum that placed the United States in the uncomfortable position of receiving enough assistance to instill a flickering hope that more was forthcoming, but not enough to call the mission a success. Jay's humiliating experience left him embittered though more knowledgeable about Old World craftiness. The Spanish court, he complained, had "little money, less wisdom, no credit, nor any right to it."

While Jay underwent his trials in Spain, Americans turned for assistance to the new League of Armed Neutrality, organized in 1780 by Catherine the Great of Russia to defend freedom of the seas. The empress had opposed Britain's restrictions on Russian trade in the Baltic Sea, and had invited Sweden and Denmark-Norway to ally in defense of neutral rights. Though later joined by Prussia, the Holy Roman Empire, the Kingdom of the Two Sicilies, and Portugal (normally a British ally), the League, Catherine admitted, was an "armed nullity" of small-navy nations too weak to challenge British supremacy at sea. Yet it managed to close the Baltic to belligerents, and to cut off Britain's chances for European allies. More important to Americans, its goals were similar to those contained in the Plan of 1776.

The Continental Congress resolved to support the League's ideals and dispatched Francis Dana of Massachusetts to the Court of St. Petersburg in a futile attempt to negotiate a treaty permitting America's participation. Despite two years of effort, Dana never persuaded Catherine to welcome him on an official basis. How could a belligerent ally with a neutral? Was it certain that America would remain independent? The Russian empress had to ponder the costs of recognizing America. War with England was out of the question.

America's hopes for foreign aid again rose in 1780 when British relations with the Netherlands seriously deteriorated and resulted in war. Dutch merchants had been engaged in a prosperous carrying trade to Europe and America which relied on their small West Indies island of St.

Eustatius as a way station; during one year in the war over 3,000 ships, including some from Hortalez and Company, had operated out of the island and thus threatened England's effort to put down the American revolt. An Anglo-Dutch treaty of 1678 had stipulated that each power would come to the assistance of the other if threatened by a third party. Instead, the Dutch had allied with the League of Armed Neutrality. England proposed a deal: if the Dutch would forgo the trade in naval materials to France, it would not invoke the treaty of 1678. The Dutch refused the offer and sent armed escorts for their commercial vessels. The anticipated exchange of fire took place, and the English declared war on the Netherlands in late 1780.

Earlier in the summer of 1780, when it appeared that England and the Netherlands would soon be at war, the Continental Congress had transferred John Adams from Paris to Amsterdam to secure a treaty of assistance. He met stubborn resistance, for the Dutch preferred the profit of the carrying trade to extending aid to the Americans and risking war with England. It was like negotiating with a "school of sharks," Adams bitterly complained. Finally, in April 1782, he won Dutch recognition of American independence, and in June secured a large loan from bankers in Amsterdam. The following October, too late to affect the outcome of the war, he negotiated a treaty of amity and commerce. Adams's mission was a success.

Throughout much of the diplomacy of the war Americans felt secure with France, yet several factors suggest that their European ally was more dangerous than Mother England. In 1780–81 Vergennes supported an Austro-Russian attempt to mediate the war which, if successful, would have come too early to guarantee America's independence. He then managed to reconstitute America's peace delegation in Paris. Fearing that the headstrong John Adams was not subject to manipulation, Vergennes used the talents of his minister in the United States (including bribery of members of Congress) to secure four additional members to the commission: two Francophiles, Franklin and Jefferson, and two of French descent, Jay and Henry Laurens of South Carolina. In the meantime Vergennes arranged a revision of America's peace demands. The new directives of 1781 stipulated that the commissioners were "to undertake nothing in the negotiations" without France's "knowledge and concurrence." As fate would have it, the war saved the Americans from their ally.

DIPLOMACY OF THE PEACE

At a Virginia hamlet called Yorktown on October 19, 1781, a band struck the tune "The World Turned Upside Down," while British soldiers in bright red uniforms stacked their weapons before the American Revolutionary Army. Earlier that day General Lord Charles Cornwallis had surrendered his 7,000 regulars to a combined force of 9,000 Americans under

General Washington and 8,000 French soldiers under General Comte de Rochambeau. The Marquis de Lafayette, who was also at Yorktown, declared, "The play is over . . . . The fifth act has just ended." Upon hearing the news Franklin proclaimed: "The infant Hercules has now strangled his second serpent that attacked him in his cradle." In England Lord North repeatedly stammered, "Oh God! It is all over!"

The dramatic defeat at Yorktown intensified the widespread desire in England to end the fighting. The American war, never popular in England, was steadily depleting the nation's resources, steering it into conflict with most of the Western world, eroding its maritime supremacy in the English Channel, and threatening to expose the country itself to invasion. Would it not be wiser to trade with the Americans than to fight them? Though British forces would go on to later victories, popular attention focused instead on recent reverses in the Caribbean and on the mounting national debt. By early March 1782 Parliament resolved to bring a close to the war, and shortly afterward the Marquis of Rockingham, leader of the Whig opposition and pledged to end the fighting, replaced Lord North as minister. In early April Richard Oswald, a wealthy, elderly Scottish merchant, former slave trader, friend of Franklin's, and onetime resident of Virginia, embarked for Paris to discuss peace with the Americans. Before the talks could begin Rockingham died, and Lord Shelburne, longtime advocate of Anglo-American peace, free trade, and commercial ties between the Atlantic peoples, became prime minister. Though he hoped to hang onto the colonies, for the first time peace seemed to be in sight.

In the initial discussion of mid-April, Franklin moved to take advantage of Britain's troubles. Oswald was inexperienced in diplomacy and indiscreetly admitted that his country had become "foolishly involved in four wars," making peace "absolutely necessary." Franklin saw the opening and suggested that the cession of Canada would smooth Anglo-American relations. He then called for British recognition of American independence and favorable boundaries and, according to some accounts, suggested the feasibility of a separate peace. Franklin had learned much from his long service abroad. Though Vergennes was aware of Oswald's mission, of course, he never heard about either Franklin's Canada proposal or his hint of a separate peace.

The need for political adjustments in England delayed the attempted negotiations for a few weeks and gave Franklin a chance to ask Adams and Jay to join him in Paris. While the government in London debated the direction of foreign affairs, Franklin was stricken with a serious attack of the gout and a disabling kidney disease that kept him in bed for over three months. He needed help in the long hours ahead. Though Laurens would not arrive until the last stages of the negotiations and Jefferson never made it at all, Adams returned to Paris in late October and found Jay already there; Jay had arrived in Paris the previous June after a welcome departure from Madrid.

Jay was deeply suspicious of European diplomacy after his experiences in Spain, and immediately agreed with Franklin's refusal in August to enter formal talks until Oswald got his instructions changed. The Shelburne ministry, however, refused to recognize American independence prior to the signing of a peace treaty, and directed Oswald to negotiate with "the said colonies or plantations." Continued protests from Franklin and Jay persuaded the British cabinet in late August to agree in principle to preliminary recognition of the United States if the Americans first insisted that the king recommend that Parliament pass such a resolution. After this face-saving measure Shelburne offered a type of compromise whereby he authorized Oswald to meet with representatives of the "thirteen United States."

Jay's worst fears were reserved for the French. Shortly after his arrival in Paris he had discussions with the Spanish ambassador and a representative of Vergennes, which confirmed his suspicions that the French intended to help the Spanish keep the Americans out of the Mississippi Valley. He was already indignant over Vergennes's attempt to dismiss the wording of Oswald's August instructions as a technicality, and he was not assured by the French foreign minister's declaration that the important point was British recognition of American independence in the final treaty. Franklin was satisfied, but Jay remained concerned. His anxiety deepened when he received a copy of a communication sent from the French chargé d'affaires in the United States to Vergennes that called on the foreign minister to oppose the American request for fishing rights off Canada. If this was not convincing evidence of French duplicity, Vergennes's private secretary, Joseph de Rayneval, clinched the case in early September by informally proposing to Jay that England receive the area above the Ohio River, with Spain and the United States dividing the region below.

These developments fitted Jay's direst apprehensions about France. Its interest in keeping Spain in the war, he thought, had caused Vergennes to offer America's western claims; Jay could not have known that the real reason was the French foreign minister's failure to deliver Gibraltar. While mutual Spanish and American distrust kept them occupied, only the British would stand in the way of France's control of North America. Jay realized these were high stakes, but he also knew that empires had been won and lost about as often at the peace table as on the battlefield.

Jay's fears seemed substantiated when he learned that in early September Vergennes sent Rayneval to London on a secret mission—probably, Jay thought, to satisfy Spanish demands in North America. The French foreign minister, indeed, had instructed his secretary to inform the British that generous concessions to the Americans were inadvisable and unnecessary. It is impossible to be sure, but Vergennes had apparently left the door ajar for a separate Franco-British peace that would provide concessions to Spain at the expense of the United States. Shelburne gathered from Rayneval's statements that the French supported America's claims to independence, but preferred limited national boundaries and no American fishing rights off Newfoundland. Perhaps momentarily bewildered, he shrewdly commented to the king that the French appeared "more jealous than partial to America."

Jay believed that his most trying task would be to persuade Franklin to set aside French sentiments and act in the American interest. "Let us be grateful to the French for what they have done for us," he advised Franklin, "but let us think for ourselves. And, if need be, let us act for ourselves." This was wise counsel. Though Franklin initially downplayed Jay's alarm, Adams (who had just arrived in Paris) recognized the French danger and worked to bring Franklin to their side. Vergennes, Adams remarked, meant "to keep his hand under our chin to prevent us from drowning, but not to lift our heads out of water." Perhaps Franklin's sickness kept him from arguing the issue with his younger colleagues; more likely, he privately agreed with their alarm about France and only reluctantly turned on the country he loved. In any case, Jay was already taking the initiative. Without telling either Franklin or Adams, he notified Shelburne that he would talk with Oswald about terms, and in October the shift was under way toward separate peace negotiations.

The military aspects of the war worked with diplomatic maneuverings to determine the path of the preliminary peace talks in Paris. Oswald had received instructions in early September 1782 to accept America's demands for a boundary north to the Nipissing line (the southwestern tip of Quebec prior to the Quebec Act of 1774), and *not* to seek the return of prewar debts or confiscated Loyalist property. But soon after the delegates in Paris initialed this draft treaty on October 5 and sent it to London, news arrived that the three-year siege of Gibraltar was over and that the massive rock fortress still belonged to England. Shelburne tightened his stipulations. He now required restitution for English creditors and Loyalists, and even made an eleventh-hour attempt to salvage the Old Northwest. Though the prime minister may have made this last proposal only to achieve satisfaction on the other two points, Franklin considered it too much. The British, he complained, "wanted to bring their boundary down to the Ohio and to settle the Loyalists in the Illinois country. We did not choose such neighbors."

The Americans eventually made concessions on their boundary expectations. On the northeast boundary they retreated from the St. John River to the St. Croix, while in the west they gave up the Nipissing line and consented to a border following the St. Lawrence River and Great Lakes, and then to the Lake of the Woods before dropping to the Mississippi River. Britain and the United States signed the preliminary peace treaty on November 30, 1782, with the understanding that it would not go into effect until the French and English had settled their differences.

Vergennes complained about the United States's separate peace talks with England, but in reality he knew they had saved him from a weblike situation with Spain. Strictly speaking, the discussions did not constitute a violation of the Franco-American Treaty of 1778 because the resulting preliminary pact was not to take effect until Britain and its other antagonists had also signed peace treaties. Yet Vergennes was caught in a dilemma. Though freed from his secret Gibraltar obligation to Spain, he would now have to deal with bitter Spanish criticism for America's independent course. After considerable thought he decided to explain to the government in Madrid that America had violated the Treaty of Alliance and left the war, and that the French had no choice but to bow out.

Franklin applied the coup de grâce to the separate-peace controversy when he secretly implied to Vergennes that further French protests could drive the Americans into an alliance with England. The foreign minister had first congratulated the Americans on their successful negotiations, but two weeks afterward he sent a face-saving note to Franklin which was suprisingly mild in tone:

> I am at a loss, sir, to explain your conduct and that of your colleagues on this occasion. You have concluded your preliminary articles without any communication between us. . . . You are about to hold out a certain hope of peace to America without even informing yourself on the state of the negotiation on our part.
>
> You are wise and discreet, sir; you perfectly understand what is due to propriety; you have all your life performed your duties. I pray you to consider how you propose to fulfill those which are due to the King?

Franklin explained that the agreements were only preliminary to the final treaty and apologized for failing to notify the French government before entering the talks, but he assured Vergennes that his lapse was not due to "want of respect to the King, whom we all love and honor." Franklin then salved Vergennes with a master stroke: *"The English, I just now learn, flatter themselves they have already divided us.* I hope this little misunderstanding will therefore be kept secret, and that they will find themselves totally mistaken."

In the same letter Franklin had the audacity to ask for another French loan; even more amazing, the financially strained French government, probably out of fear of American collapse, approved the request.

Franklin's private exchange with Vergennes did not remain secret from the British for long. Bancroft had become secretary to the full American peace delegation and had already furnished considerable information to the British about the negotiations. Their knowledge of the Franco-American rift helps to explain the transparent effort by British agents in

---

MAP 3

That America survived as a nation against the French, English, and Spanish was a tribute to the abilities of the Founding Fathers.

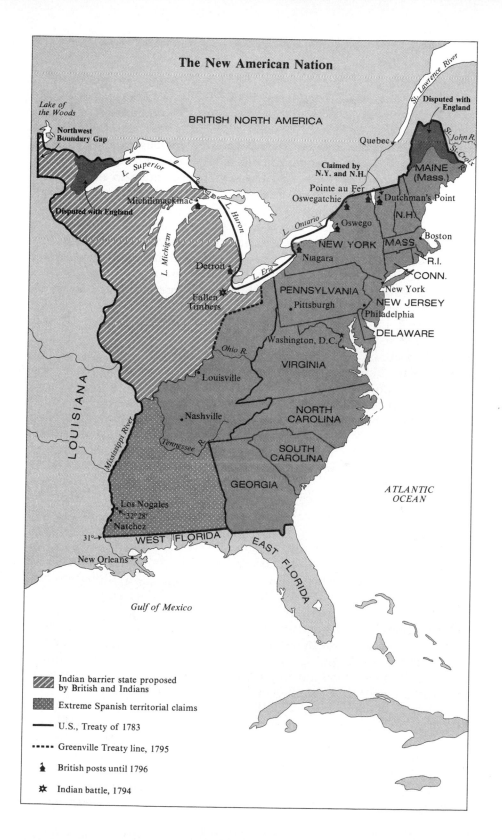

The New American Nation

Lake of the Woods

Northwest Boundary Gap

BRITISH NORTH AMERICA

St. Lawrence River

Disputed with England

Quebec

St. John R.

St. Croix

Claimed by N.Y. and N.H.

MAINE (Mass.)

L. Superior

Michilimackinac

Pointe au Fer
Oswegatchie

Dutchman's Point

Disputed with England

L. Huron

L. Michigan

Oswego

L. Ontario

N.H.

Detroit

L. Erie

Niagara

NEW YORK

MASS.

Boston

R.I.

Fallen Timbers

CONN.

PENNSYLVANIA

New York

NEW JERSEY

Pittsburgh

Philadelphia

DELAWARE

Ohio R.

Washington, D.C.

Louisville

VIRGINIA

LOUISIANA

Nashville

Mississippi River

NORTH CAROLINA

Tennessee R.

SOUTH CAROLINA

GEORGIA

ATLANTIC OCEAN

Los Nogales
32° 28'
Natchez

31°→

WEST FLORIDA

EAST FLORIDA

New Orleans

Gulf of Mexico

Indian barrier state proposed by British and Indians

Extreme Spanish territorial claims

U.S., Treaty of 1783

Greenville Treaty line, 1795

British posts until 1796

Indian battle, 1794

Paris to establish an amicable relationship with the Americans. London intended to undercut French interests in the New World.

On September 3, 1783, England and the United States affixed their signatures to the "Definitive Treaty of Peace," the Treaty of Paris officially ending the American Revolutionary War. The general settlement incorporated a British pact signed with France and Spain the previous January, along with a treaty with the Netherlands. Except for Spain receiving the Floridas, the provisions were identical to those of the preliminary treaty of 1782. The British agreed to withdraw military and naval holdings "with all convenient speed," and to recognize that use of the Mississippi River was to be forever "free and open to the subjects of Great Britain, and the citizens of the United States." On paper, America's independence seemed final.

Upon learning the provisions of the Anglo-American pact, Vergennes remarked that "the English buy the peace more than they make it." The treaty terms, in fact, were more liberal than America's military victories had earned, and undoubtedly contributed to Shelburne's fall from power. Some Englishmen accused him of abandoning both the Loyalists and the Indians of the Northwest, while others denounced him for virtually relinquishing Britain's navigation rights on the Mississippi by allowing America's northern boundary to lie above the source of the river. The British prime minister, however, was an advocate of the free-trade gospel espoused by his friend Adam Smith, and desired above all to replace the Franco-American alliance with Anglo-American commercial ties. Indeed, he had widened the gap between France and the United States by recognizing America's independence and agreeing to its boundary demands. Even so, one parliamentary member declared that Shelburne had "certainly proved himself a great Christian, for he had not only parted with his cloak to America, but he had given his coat likewise."

But all was not harmonious among the peace delegates in Paris, for disagreements developed over other matters after settlement of the larger questions of independence and national boundaries. The British wanted exclusive fishing rights off Newfoundland's Grand Banks, as well as sole use of the Canadian coastal areas for drying and curing their catch. John Adams staunchly defended the interests of fellow New Englanders. A compromise of sorts was the result, by which the Americans won the "liberty" but not the "right" to fish in waters off both Newfoundland and Canada. Decades of controversy followed during which one Adams descendant after the other attempted to resolve the matter.

Heated exchanges also took place over two other issues—the Loyalists and private debts owed by Americans to Britons. The crown sought reparations for property losses sustained by the many colonists who had left their homeland rather than join the rebellion. Though Franklin's son had remained loyal to the British after serving as royal governor of New Jersey, the elderly diplomat in Paris vehemently resisted appeals for light treatment. "Your ministers," he burst out to the British delegates, "require that we should receive again into our bosom those who have been our bitterest enemies, and restore their properties who have destroyed ours; and this while the wounds they have given us are still bleeding." On the debt problem, the British were incredulous when the Americans, who had incurred heavy financial obligations before 1775, now argued that the war had wiped them from the record.

Adams eventually emerged with a settlement. The American delegates agreed to "earnestly recommend" that the states return properties taken from "real British subjects" during the war, and British business leaders would "meet with no lawful impediment" in attempting to collect money from Americans. Little hope for satisfaction existed on either count. The debt issue remained a source of argument, whereas most Loyalists were born in America and did not fit the treaty's classification, and the central government established under the Articles of Confederation in 1781 lacked the power to tell the states what to do.

Despite some discontent, the treaty was a good peace for both the United States and England. Though the Americans were novice diplomats in an experienced European world, they had stayed clear of political involvement in continental affairs while using Europe's problems to advantage. The Americans in Paris had seen the right moment to violate instructions and break French ties; Shelburne had discerned the time to accept the demise of mercantilism and release the American colonies. Both Atlantic nations understood that a chief advantage in furthering economic ties was that they could shut out the French from North America.

Ironically, France emerged as the major casualty of its victory over the British. Vergennes's shifting diplomatic efforts had cost an American ally, the loyalty of Spain, and, most serious, the world's recognition of Britain's defeat. He had failed to reverse the outcome of the Seven Years' War in 1763, for the British had not been humbled and France still had no foothold on the North American continent. On paper, France stood victorious in 1783, much as Britain had reigned triumphant twenty years earlier. Yet in both instances outward appearances obscured the reality. As in 1763, the defeated parties in Paris walked away with fewer obligations and could maneuver for position in both North America and other places. The major difference in the latter war was that the French had no rich colonies to share the financial burden. The revolution that followed in France in 1789 was profoundly more critical than the one faced by the British in 1776: it tore down the nation from within and ultimately wrapped the succeeding Napoleonic empire in a series of disastrous world wars that culminated in another humiliation—this one at Waterloo in 1815.

CONFEDERATION–CONSTITUTION

The form of government established in 1781 also demonstrated the opposition between those who affirmed and those who denied that idealism was an effective way of securing America's interests. The Articles of Confederation was a loose gathering of thirteen sovereign states held together by the demands of war. The exultation that came with the end of British control was bitter-sweet. In ridding itself of the mother country, the new nation threw off imperial protection and now lay exposed to Old World powers whose intention was to encourage the republic's collapse. The national government under the Articles lacked the coercive power to resolve the social, political, and economic problems left by the Revolution and by the war.

If the Confederation Congress could have enforced the powers granted it, the Founding Fathers might not have met in Philadelphia as early as 1787. But Congress could not pass laws that bound individuals, and found it nearly impossible to deal with states which retained their "sovereignty, freedom and independence." Reverence for states' rights was understandable after years of royal rule, and when Congress attempted to formulate national policies the states did not follow them. In the meantime the defense structure of the nation was dangerously weak, and John Jay as new secretary of the Department of Foreign Affairs lacked the means of enforcing the powers he possessed.

Events since the guns were first fired at Lexington and Concord had not brought economic liberation from England: by 1790 nearly half of America's exports and 90 percent of its imports were with the mother country. Furthermore, the diffused nature of the Articles of Confederation assured each state of its own tariff and customs regulations, and the result was competition among Americans themselves. America's prime avenue into the British commercial system had been through Lord Shelburne, but his generous peace terms had already driven him from office. A widely read pamphlet written by Lord Sheffield in 1783 better expressed the British attitude about trade with the Americans. No need existed for commercial reciprocity, he declared, for the new government under the Articles would not be able to halt the deluge of cheaper British goods that would hit the American markets after the war. The long tradition of mercantilism did not terminate with either the writings of Adam Smith or the knell rung at Yorktown.

The British posed another obstacle to the American nation when they refused to evacuate the northwest territory immediately after the war. The day before formal ratification of the Treaty of Paris, April 8, 1784, the London government secretly decided to instruct the governor general in Canada not to relinquish a series of forts strung from Lake Champlain to Lake Michigan. When pressed later, the English explained that America's failures to fulfill treaty obligations relating to British creditors and Loyalists had led to the refusal to leave. Yet the decision to keep the forts came *before* the Americans had had an opportunity to violate the treaty. They were convinced that the British wanted to preserve the fur trade and were arming the Indians to encourage them to resist further migration of Americans into the area.

Soon other problems developed with England. The physical characteristics of the North American hinterland did not correspond with the descriptions contained in the Treaty of Paris, and this fact caused confusion over the Canadian-American boundary. Southerners complained about having received no compensation for slaves taken by British soldiers leaving America after the war. Stories spread along the North American frontier that the British had offered commercial use of the St. Lawrence River to Vermont (not yet part of the United States) if its people pursued their separatist plans. In the meantime Virginia and Maryland violated the Paris Treaty by forbidding their courts from helping British subjects to collect debts. When John Adams, America's first minister to London in 1785, inquired why the British had not reciprocated with a representative to the United States, they scoffed and wondered whether *thirteen* would be necessary.

The postwar situation with Spain was little better. By the end of 1784 nearly 50,000 Americans had moved into the trans-Allegheny west and endangered Spanish claims to the area. Perhaps part of the confusion was due to British manipulations at Paris in 1783. The settlement allowed Americans free use of the Mississippi River "from its source to the ocean," while Britain's pact with the Spanish did not mention this guarantee. A similar problem existed with the northern boundary of Florida. Americans understood it to be the 31st parallel, whereas the British gave Spain the right to "retain" West Florida—without specifying its boundaries. The Spanish claimed the same border established by England in 1764—the junction of the Mississippi with the Yazoo River, or the line of 32°28'. Combined with Indian problems, secessionist sentiment, and a decision by Spain to close the Mississippi River to American shipping, Spanish-American relations approached crisis intensity by 1784.

The Spanish had only a few hundred soldiers in Louisiana and attempted to negotiate a settlement with the United States. In 1785 they sent Don Diego de Gardoqui to talk with Secretary John Jay in New York about the possibility of conceding the Mississippi River to Spain in exchange for a commercial treaty and favorable boundary adjustments. Gardoqui spoke excellent English; he had been in charge of shipping Spanish munitions to America during the war; and he had made a favorable impression on Jay during the latter's disastrous stay at the court in Madrid. Armed with a ready smile and a sack of money used for social occasions as well as to bribe members of Congress, Gardoqui offered lavish compliments to both the secretary and his wife that they thankfully received, while he played on the northeast's apprehensions over the west's rapid commercial development. Though the Spanish emissary's motives were transparent, he almost succeeded.

A year of painful discussions led only to frustration. In early August 1786 fellow New Yorkers and other northeastern mechants exerted pressure on Jay to consider a trade agreement that permitted American access to Spain's home ports and those in the Canary Islands, if he would persuade Congress to "forbear" use of the Mississippi River for perhaps twenty-five years. A stormy debate followed in Congress, during which sectional alliances within that body barely forestalled the concession. Late in August a majority in Congress—seven northern states—voted in favor of the suggestion, but five southern states did not. Some westerners talked of secession and an alliance with either Spain or England, while others discussed taking New Orleans. Land speculators, along with southerners holding territorial claims in the southwest, joined the growing number of commercial interests and others who accused Jay of being willing to sell out America's interests. Jay dropped the issue when he realized the impossibility of lining up the nine states necessary to ratify an agreement.

France also presented serious difficulties to the postwar United States. Though the treaty of 1778 bound both nations to protect each other's possessions "forever," Paris did not offer support when England and Spain threatened America's claims in the trans-Appalachian west. Jefferson, new minister to France when Franklin returned home in 1784, secured only limited commercial access to the West Indies because, the French complained, the United States first had to repay war debts. The French, hurting from within and stung by Britain's refusal to act the part of the vanquished, waited for another renewal of the struggle for North America.

Another foreign problem involved the Barbary coast pirates of northern Africa. While the Americans were colonists, the British Empire provided protection against piracy in the Mediterranean—primarily through payment of money to the pirates. With the restraints of mercantilism lifted, the advantages of the system likewise came to a close. Americans found it difficult to fill the monetary demands of Morocco, Algiers, Tunis, and Tripoli, mainly because of embarrassing financial shortages. Finally, in 1787, the United States negotiated a treaty with Morocco, but still lacked means for halting the raids by the other Barbary states. Such was the Mediterranean situation in May 1787 as fifty-five delegates gathered in Convention Hall in Philadelphia.

America's foreign and domestic difficulties provided an atmosphere conducive to constitutional reform. Using the Articles of Confederation as foil, the delegates emerged four months later with a new document that seemingly strengthened the central government while safeguarding the rights of the states and the American people. Human beings had a propensity toward evil, the Founding Fathers believed, and the remedy lay in spreading governmental powers and establishing a system of checks and balances. In addition to correcting numerous domestic flaws, the United States Constitution placed the executive branch of the national government in charge of foreign policy and made the Constitution and treaties "the Supreme Law of the land." Besides the president having the power to make appointments and welcome foreign dignitaries, he could conclude treaties with other nations, provided that two-thirds of the senators present gave their "advice and consent." Though the two-thirds provision probably reflected southern and western distrust for the east caused by the Jay-Gardoqui negotiations, Americans overlooked these signs of sectional discontent to exalt the unity afforded by the new Constitution. They could now agree with the forecast made by the American geographer Jedidiah Morse in 1789: "We cannot but anticipate the period, as not far distant, when the AMERICAN EMPIRE will comprehend millions of souls, west of the Mississippi."

The Constitution, ratified in 1788 and put into operation the year afterward, established the nation on a firm domestic and foreign policy base, and set the machinery in motion for George Washington to become first president of the United States in 1789. Indeed, the embarrassments thrust upon the country by foreign hostilities during the Confederation period were vital to the creation of a constitution that comprised a balance of idealism and realism.

THE NEW NATION AND FOREIGN POLICY

Despite the ideals expressed in the Model Treaty, the success of the young nation's first foreign policy was largely attributable to French military assistance in the Revolutionary War. After the jubilation of victory had culminated in the Constitution, Americans realized that their original foreign policy based on Enlightenment ideals had been altered to accommodate the compromises necessitated by the realities of world politics. The repercussions of the French Treaty of Alliance, the outbreak of France's own revolution in 1789, and the onset of still another round of Anglo-French wars made both an American defense network and involvement in European political affairs virtually inescapable. The timing of the new nation's completion was fortunate in view of the French Revolution and the rise of Napoleon. The last chapter of the long Anglo-French struggle for world control was about to unfold. And in the course of the unfolding, the United States would repeat its good fortune during 1775–83, this time not by securing national independence but by doubling the national territory.

Selected readings

Bemis, Samuel F., *The Diplomacy of the American Revolution*. 1935.

Clark, Ronald W., *Benjamin Franklin: A Biography*. 1983.

Dull, Jonathan R., *A Diplomatic History of the American Revolution*. 1985.

———, *The French Navy and American Independence: A Study of Arms and Diplomacy, 1774–1787*. 1976.

Gilbert, Felix, *To the Farewell Address: Ideas of Early American Foreign Policy*. 1961.

Hutson, James H., *John Adams and the Diplomacy of the American Revolution*. 1980.

Kaplan, Lawrence S., ed., *The American Revolution and "A Candid World."* 1977.
———, *Colonies into Nation: American Diplomacy, 1763–1801.* 1972.
Lang, Daniel G., *Foreign Policy in the Early Republic: The Law of Nations and the Balance of Power.* 1985.
Mackesy, Piers, *The War for America, 1775–1783.* 1964.
Middlekauff, Robert, *The Glorious Cause: The American Revolution, 1763–1789.* 1982.
Morris, Richard B., *The Peacemakers: The Great Powers and American Independence.* 1965.
Nordholt, Jan Willem Schulte, *The Dutch Republic and American Independence.* 1982. Originally published in the Netherlands in 1979. Translated by Herbert H. Rowen.
Palmer, Robert R., *The Age of the Democratic Revolution: A Political History of Europe and America, 1760–1790.* 1959.
Pancake, John S., *1777: The Year of the Hangman.* 1977.
Savelle, Max, *The Origins of American Diplomacy: The International History of Anglo-America, 1492–1763.* 1967.
Stinchcombe, William C., *The American Revolution and the French Alliance.* 1969.
Stourzh, Gerald, *Benjamin Franklin and American Foreign Policy.* 1954.
Tucker, Robert W., and David C. Hendrickson, *The Fall of the First British Empire: Origins of the War of American Independence.* 1982.
Van Alstyne, Richard W., *Empire and Independence: The International History of the American Revolution.* 1965.
———, *The Rising American Empire.* 1960.
Varg, Paul A., *Foreign Policies of the Founding Fathers.* 1963.

Chapter Two

The Federalist Era and the Wars of the French Revolution, 1789–1801

WASHINGTON THE PRESIDENT

As the tall, august Virginian walked onto the balcony of Federal Hall in New York City, he probably took for granted the pomp accorded an American president. Perhaps on this day, April 30, 1789, George Washington wished he had declined the honor in favor of quiet retirement at Mount Vernon. Yet the people demanded his services a third time and, charismatic statesman that he was, Washington agreed to become the nation's first chief executive. He would set precedents in domestic and foreign affairs, and he would direct the United States toward political and economic stability, the latter a double-edged feat that required wisdom, patience, and tact. Washington realized that in foreign policy no clear lines existed between external and internal affairs. The American people preferred simple, idealistic solutions to complex problems, and yet, as president he had to make complex, realistic decisions.

The Constitution only vaguely outlined the machinery of foreign policy. It did not establish an office for the purpose, although Congress filled that void in July 1789 by creating the Department of Foreign Affairs, which in two months became known as the Department of State and was comprised of five members. Confusion hampered the relations of the branches of government, especially in regard to the treaty process. The Constitution stipulated that the executive was to seek the "advice and consent" of the Senate in making treaties, and President Washington and Secretary of War Henry Knox arrived in that body's chambers on a Saturday morning in 1789 to ask its advice and consent on seven proposals re-

George Washington

*As commander of the Continental Army and later president of the United States,
Washington became both man and monument in American history.* (Charles Wilson Peale;
Library of Congress)

lating to negotiations with the Indians. The clatter of wagons outside the
building drowned out Washington's first attempt to be heard. Trying two
more times to speak above the noise he became irritated, and Vice President John Adams asked for the president's papers, read the proposals,
and on each point asked the senators: "Do you advise and consent?"
Only a few at first gathered what was going on. As more understood,
they thought Washington wanted them to discuss each proposal at
length. This drove the president to anger. Already upset because he regarded senators as subordinates, his face reddened and he sprang to his
feet to exclaim that "this defeats every purpose of my coming here."
Eventually an understanding developed that the president should seek
both the advice and consent of the Senate *after* he had already taken action.

Washington's appointments of Alexander Hamilton as secretary of
the treasury and Thomas Jefferson as secretary of state did not lessen the
problems of determining a foreign policy. Rather, the rivalry between the
two men led to a bitter struggle that helped the formation of America's

Alexander Hamilton

As secretary of the treasury, he advocated a strong central government and a pro-British foreign policy that attracted followers known as Federalists. (Charles Wilson Peale; Library of Congress)

first political party system. Their differences in background, philosophy, personality, and temperament would soon divide the administration over foreign as well as domestic matters.

Hamilton, born into a financially troubled family in the British West Indies, was outgoing, brash, charming, elitist, conservative, pro-English, and an advocate of implied powers and strong central government; Jefferson, reared by his wealthy Virginia plantation family, was a philosopher in manner, humble in spirit, liberal in thought, pro-French, and a staunch protector of states' rights. Though Jefferson was in charge of foreign affairs, Hamilton conceived his role as being similar to that of the prime minister of England: control of the treasury entitled him to delve into foreign matters. When at one point Jefferson wrote a 17,000-word paper protesting England's violations of the Treaty of 1783, Hamilton privately assured the British minister to the United States that this view did not represent that of the Washington administration. Hamilton's financial plan of 1790–91 further encouraged political division because, among other issues, it urged commercial ties with England and an increased role of the national government. Jefferson countered with warnings against British interests in the New World and calls for decentralized government. After considerable infighting, those who followed Hamilton became known as Federalists, while supporters of Jefferson allied with fellow Virginian James Madison and called themselves anti-Federalists, or Republicans.

The first major diplomatic test of the Washington administration came in 1789 when England and Spain got involved in a dispute over Nootka Sound that had the fortunate outcome for America of encouraging better relations with Britain. Spain had earlier declared exclusive control over this small strip of land along the west coast of Vancouver Island. In the summer of 1789, however, British traders tried to establish a post in Nootka Sound and were seized by the Spanish. Both countries prepared for war, which caused a serious problem for the Washington administration. What if England asked permission to cross American territory in striking at Spanish possessions in Louisiana and Florida? Or worse, what if it crossed *without* asking permission? Hamilton advised the president to grant approval, while Jefferson feared British intentions and opposed this stand. The first choice could mean war with Spain, the second war with England. Before Washington's advisers could reach agreement, Spain capitulated to England. Spain had called upon its French ally for help, but France's own revolution precluded any assistance. The ensuing Nootka Sound Convention of 1790 required Spain to return property taken from England and permitted English traders and settlers to enter these territories, once exclusively Spanish.

The Nookta crisis awakened England to the possibility of Americans taking advantage of its troubles elsewhere to seek concessions from London. By no coincidence did England in 1791 send its first minister, George Hammond, to the United States.

The diplomacy of Washington's presidency was inseparable from the French Revolution of 1789, for that domestic struggle grew into a world war that almost pulled in the United States before the Virginian left office eight years later. America's relations with France were uneasy before Washington became president. The first minister from Paris to the United States in 1787, Count de Moustier, lasted only a year because of some personal difficulties, compounded by his indiscreet expressions of French interest in Spanish Louisiana. America's desire to trade with both England and France provided the basis for a neutral stance in the wars that began in 1793, but the Washington administration feared that France might invoke the Treaty of Alliance of 1778 by requesting American military aid. Idealism suggested the possibility of declaring neutrality and enjoying commercial prosperity; reality dictated that this was unlikely.

THE FRENCH REVOLUTION

In July 1789 French mobs stormed the Bastille in Paris and set off the revolution. Americans rejoiced that the insurgents' ideals coincided with theirs of the previous decade, for the French renamed streets after their cry of "Liberty, equality, and fraternity," and called for a Declaration of the Rights of Man similar to the Declaration of Independence. Jeffersonians raised liberty poles, wore liberty caps, called each other "citizen" and "citizeness" to correspond with new titles in France denoting equality, and praised the Girondin political party for its republicanism. But after France declared itself a republic in September 1792, the romance of the revolution gave way to an ugly phase when European monarchs joined the exiled French nobility in an attempt to restore King Louis XVI to the throne. In response, the National Convention in January 1793 voted 361 to 360 to behead the king, and similar executions followed that included Queen Marie Antoinette and 20,000 others. Americans asked whether a reign of terror and the abolition of godly worship were legitimate costs for the establishment of republicanism. Most thought not. Many agreed with Jefferson, however, who wrote: "My own affections have been deeply wounded by some of the martyrs to this cause, but rather than it should have failed I would have seen half the earth desolated; were there but an Adam and an Eve left in every country, and left free, it would be better than it now is."

In February 1793 France declared war on England, Spain, and the Netherlands, and thereby caused a debate in the United States over what its policy should be if the government in Paris invoked the treaties of 1778. Differences between Federalists and Republicans hardened, the former accusing the Republicans of planning to drag the United States into the war on the side of anarchy, the latter charging the Federalists with opposing French revolutionary ideals and conspiring to end liberty at home. During the debates among the president's advisers, Hamilton declared that, since the collapse of the monarchy changed the form of government in France and since treaties were between governments and not between peoples, America's obligations under the pacts of 1778 had been canceled. He added that the treaties were "defensive" in nature and that *France* had declared war on England. Should the United States support the revolution and end up on the wrong side, Hamilton warned, a new king would come to power, America would have alienated all monarchies in Europe, and France's intentions of reestablishing its empire in North America would have renewed hopes. Jefferson countered with an argument for *de facto* recognition—that King Louis XVI had acted only as a representative of the French nation and that a change in the form of government did not abrogate treaties. The nation and its government *in fact* remained. Yet Jefferson did not favor American aid to France. He suggested that if the French asked for help under the treaties of 1778, the United States could decline on the ground that the French had not offered assistance when the British refused to evacuate the northwest fur posts.

The president's advisers focused their discussions on whether he should issue a proclamation of neutrality. Jefferson, supported by Attorney General Edmund Randolph, stood in opposition on the constitutional ground that only Congress could declare war and therefore only it could declare neutrality. The secretary of state also argued against a declaration of neutrality without first securing trading privileges from the belligerents. Hamilton, backed by Secretary of War Knox, warned that the use of neutrality to wrest concessions from England could lead to involvement in the war. Congress had not declared war, Hamilton concluded, and the president's duty was to keep the peace. He could proclaim neutrality and continue trade.

On April 22, 1793 President Washington accepted Hamilton's argument and proclaimed neutrality. Out of deference to Jefferson, he did not mention the word *neutrality*, but urged Americans "to pursue a conduct friendly and impartial" toward the nations at war. Refusal to obey would lead to prosecution for any transgression of "the law of nations" that took place "within the cognizance of the courts of the United States." Congress eventually followed with the Neutrality Act of June 1794, which made the United States a leading proponent of neutral rights.

Trouble had already developed around a young French emissary sent to the United States, Citizen Edmond Charles Genet. Brash, charming,

Edmond Charles Genet

"Citizen" Genet from France became the focal point of domestic and foreign policy divisions in the United States when he attempted to seek help from Americans during his country's war with England and Spain. (Library of Congress)

multitalented, an idealistic advocate of worldwide revolution for human freedom, he unleashed a popular storm which threatened to draw the United States into France's war with England. Genet's letter of accreditation was a forecast of the problems he would face in America. His superiors addressed it to Congress, not to the president, because of their erroneous belief that the legislature, like the National Convention in Paris, embodied the sovereignty of the country. Genet's instructions were clear: negotiate a "national pact" with America to spread republicanism to all humanity; "germinate" a liberation movement in Louisiana, Florida, and Canada; secure advance payments on the Revolutionary War debt; request free passage of privateers (privately owned ships licensed by the government to raid enemy vessels) and prizes (which France alleged was implicit in the provision of the Treaty of Amity and Commerce of 1778, since it forbade such privileges to France's enemies). Genet did not invoke the Treaty of Alliance, but he intended to use the United States as a base of operations against England and Spain.

Genet arrived in the United States on April 8, 1793, not in Philadelphia (the new capital since 1790) but in Charleston, South Carolina. Charleston was a hotbed of republican sentiment, which Genet kindled into a crisis for the Washington administration. The governor of the state, William Moultrie, was openly favorable to France. In addition to recalling French help during the Revolutionary War, like many South Carolinians Moultrie held frontier claims that would rise in value if Spain were removed from Florida and the Mississippi Valley. Genet persuaded the governor to permit the commissioning of more than a dozen privateers, which eventually captured more than eighty prizes in the war. French consuls in the United States, following Genet's instructions, set up admiralty courts that condemned and sold the prizes. Though the United States Supreme Court declared these actions illegal a year later, that was no help in 1793. Meanwhile Americans served on the privateers in violation of the neutrality proclamation, but when several of them were arrested, pro-French juries found them innocent. Some captures occurred in American territorial waters, eliciting vigorous protests from British Minister Hammond. When Genet was unsuccessful in securing advance payments on the debt the United States owed France, he prepared to wrest New Orleans from the Spanish by commissioning an expedition of Americans led by the aged George Rogers Clark, of Revolutionary War fame. This scheme failed, but Genet was undaunted. The envoy began an anti-administration propaganda campaign, arranging the publication of pro-French editorials in Philadelphia's newspapers that urged Americans to disregard the president's posture of neutrality.

America's greatest concern—that Genet might call for its intervention in the European war—did not materialize, for he knew that the United States had no navy and that it was more advantageous to seek help for France's trade in the Caribbean. Numerous times British naval commanders seized American ships with French goods aboard and escorted them into prize courts where the cargoes were condemned. The British argued that the absence of an Anglo-American treaty guaranteeing the rights of neutrals permitted Royal Navy officers to confiscate goods on board these ships. To counter these losses, Genet offered liberal trade concessions to American merchants willing to carry food and naval stores from the French West Indies to Europe.

Genet angered the Washington administration by his actions and by his delay in arriving in the nation's capital. The president's decision in March to receive the French envoy, though he stipulated "without too much warmth or cordiality," was tacit recognition of the French treaties and acceptance of Jefferson's arguments for *de facto* recognition. But the neutrality proclamation had upset Genet, and he took twenty-eight days to make a normal week-long journey through Republican backcountry from Charleston to Philadelphia. There he encountered a president visibly angered by this affront to the Executive Office. The president's icy reception caused Genet to charge that "old Washington" envied his fame. Francophilic Americans joined in criticizing the president, and Genet attended a banquet in the capital during which 200 guests toasted the guillotine while artillery battery outside fired rounds of approval. Woodcuts soon appeared, attributed by some to Genet, which showed Washington a victim of the blade.

Jefferson agreed with the president that Genet had gone too far. He informed the emissary that granting military commissions in American territory was an insult to the nation, and cited various authorities on international law in declaring that a belligerent's fitting of privateers was a violation of neutrality. Genet nonetheless licensed as privateer a recently seized British ship and ordered it, with Americans aboard and under French colors, down the Delaware River to take Louisiana from Spain. To protests from Jefferson and the governor of Pennsylvania, Genet indignantly replied that he would appeal to Congress and to the American people for a popular ruling on America's obligations to France under the treaties of 1778. Genet believed that the division in the United States afforded opportunity to liberate it from "aristocratic" control, and he refused to listen to Jefferson's protests. Nor would he accept Jefferson's arguments that the president had a constitutional right to interpret treaties. Genet's intentions to defy the president led Jefferson to term his actions "disrespectful and even indecent." Washington lashed out: "Is the minister of the French Republic to set the acts of this Government at defiance *with impunity?*" He continued, "What must the World think of such conduct, and of the Government of the United States submitting to it?"

Genet had a legitimate basis for several of his claims, but he misread the situation in the United States. Since the Treaty of Commerce of 1778 denied certain privileges to France's enemies in war, this was an implication that France should enjoy these same privileges. Furthermore, before France intervened in the Revolutionary War, it had permitted privileges to Americans which President Washington now refused to France. Moreover, the neutrality proclamation constituted a break with European practice: according to standard usage, the United States, as France's ally, could have declared a "friendly" neutrality instead of a "strict" neutrality. But the Frenchman failed to understand that President Washington followed a course of neutrality not to hurt France but to protect America's interests.

Providential intervention, as some have called it, saved the United States from internal upheaval and war with France. Vice President John Adams, for one, was worried that the "terrorism" caused by Genet would lead to anarchy in the United States, as it had done in France. But during the height of the Genet crisis in late summer of 1793, yellow fever swept the nation's capital and scattered Philadelphians into the countryside. At the cost of over 4,000 lives among a population of 55,000, the epidemic dispersed the mobs and, Adams believed, saved the city and nation from revolution.

Washington ended the episode in August by securing unanimous support from his advisers for Genet's recall. In the meantime the French arranged the departure of America's minister in Paris, Gouverneur Morris, for interfering in French affairs in behalf of the king and his supporters. Genet's Girondin party, however, had lost power to Maximilien Robespierre and the radical Jacobins, and the ensuing consignment of republicans to the gallows moved Genet to ask Washington if he could remain in the United States. The president gave in, with the stipulation that Genet retire from public life. His successor, Jean Fauchet, arrived in February 1794 with orders to restore amicable relations with the United States and to arrest Genet and send him home for trial and probable execution. Instead, Genet married the daughter of Governor George Clinton of New York, became a naturalized citizen, and lived a quiet, prosperous life until his death in the 1830s. But he never understood Washington's constitutional role in foreign policy or the adulation Americans felt for him after the Revolutionary War. Genet remained under the delusion that he had failed because Jefferson had prevented him from calling upon the American people to help him achieve his objectives.

JAY'S TREATY

As America's relations with France improved, those with England deteriorated in almost direct proportion. The Definitive Treaty of Peace of 1783 had become a mockery by the spring of 1794. British soldiers remained in the northwest fur posts. Indians were armed with British weapons. The United States had rejected British efforts to mediate the conflict between the Indians and the Americans in the Ohio Valley; the British plan called for the establishment of a "neutral, Indian barrier state" that was to be derived from American territory and was obviously designed to protect Britain's fur trading interests. At sea the problems were equally serious. The English had already captured over 250 American merchant vessels in the French West Indies. James Madison and others in Congress believed that American products were vital to England's war effort and pushed through a sixty-day embargo on goods bound for foreign ports. Only the tie-breaking vote of Vice President Adams prevented the Senate from passing a nonintercourse bill against the English, but Congress called out 80,000 militia and authorized the defense of America's harbors. Danger awaited those who opposed this wave of Anglophobia; in Baltimore and Norfolk, mobs tarred and feathered Americans who spoke favorably of the mother country.

At the outset of the French wars in 1793, the British introduced maritime restrictions which curtailed America's freedom of the seas and violated its honor. Within a year three Orders-in-Council, which were based on recommendations from the privy council, the advisory body to the king, ignored the principle of "free ships, free goods" and prohibited neutrals from carrying contraband or illegal war matériel to France and its islands in the Caribbean. One justification, the British explained, was the Rule of 1756, which they had arbitrarily proclaimed during the Seven

John Jay

He became one of the nation's most vilified diplomats after negotiating a treaty with England in 1795 that did not achieve what Americans expected. (Begun by Gilbert Stuart ca. 1783 and completed ca. 1804–8 by John Trumbull; National Portrait Gallery)

Years' War. The rule held that ports not open in peacetime remained closed in war. Another justification was the doctrine of "continuous voyage," which permitted British cruisers to seize American vessels moving from the French West Indies, even if en route home, on the ground that their ultimate destination was the enemy—France. In 1793, to stop desertions, the British asserted the right to search American ships and "impress" or force runaways back into the Royal Navy. This practice of impressment violated America's rights at sea, and British naval officers ultimately removed Americans as well as Englishmen. The United States was in a precarious position. To insist on neutral rights could mean war with England, failure to do so permitted affronts to honor and violated the treaties of 1778 with France.

Federalists feared war and, in mid-April, Hamilton and a few allies persuaded the president to appoint John Jay, then chief justice of the Supreme Court, as special emissary to England to resolve problems between the nations. Experienced in European diplomacy after his time in Madrid and Paris during the Revolution, veteran of the abortive negotiations with Gardoqui, the secretary of foreign affairs under the Articles of Confederation, Jay also had disadvantages in that he was a Federalist and pro-English. Furthermore, he was to seek concessions from a country at war and hated by Americans. Jeffersonians were unable to block Jay's approval by the Senate. The bitterness of the battle caused President Washington to depart from the established procedure of discussing a diplomat's instructions with the Senate. Instead, he asked Edmund Randolph (who had succeeded Jefferson as secretary of state) to draft secret instructions. Jay himself had misgivings about the appointment: "[No] man could frame a treaty with Great Britain without making himself unpopular and odious."

Jay's assignment was extremely difficult. Ninety percent of America's imports came from England, and his general instructions were to avoid war at nearly any cost. Specifically, he was to seek reparations for British violations of American shipping, negotiate an agreement whereby neither nation would furnish arms to the Indians for use against each other, settle all Anglo-American problems since the treaty of 1783, and negotiate a commercial agreement. Randolph overcame Hamilton's objection and included a warning to England that failure to comply with America's requests could cause the United States to join the League of Armed Neutrality, the alliance of small-navy nations formed in 1780. Hamilton, believing that such a threat would lead to war, took care of that problem privately. Before Jay arrived in London in June, Hamilton secretly informed British Minister Hammond that the isolationist tenets of the Washington administration precluded joining the alliance. Hamilton's action was of questionable propriety, but it had no effect on the negotiations. The British considered the League too weak to challenge Britain's supremacy at sea. Moreover, evidence shows that Hamilton was not telling Hammond anything new. The government in London had secured a copy of Jay's correspondence with the Department of State and realized that an American alliance posed no danger. And yet, though the odds were against him, Americans expected Jay to hold fast to the French treaties of 1778, win commercial rights in the British West Indies, and gain recognition of national honor.

Jay received a warm welcome in London, one quite different from what he had grown accustomed to during his days in Madrid. In fact, the British were so cordial that he decided not to inform people back home for fear that they might think he had sold out to England. This was sound reasoning, for when Americans learned that he had followed English custom and kissed the queen's hand, they accused him of prostrating America before the English—and probably for gold. The London government played upon Jay's well-known vanities. A private report in the hands of Lord Grenville, the British foreign secretary, outlined the procedure he intended to follow during the negotiations:

> He [Jay] can bear any opposition to what he advocates provided regard is shown to his ability. He may be attacked by good treatment but will be unforgiving if he thinks himself neglected. . . . He certainly has good sense and judgement. . . . But almost every man has a weak and assailable quarter, and Mr. Jay's weak side is *Mr. Jay*.

Jay's overriding concern for peace prevented him from exploiting the biggest advantage he had: England's realization that war would hurt its campaign against France and close its largest commercial outlet—the United States.

Jay and Grenville signed a Treaty of Amity, Commerce, and Navigation on November 19, 1794, which offered measured satisfaction on issues affecting North America but did not contain the maritime concessions that Americans had hoped for. The British agreed to evacuate the northwest fur posts by June 1, 1796, but with the stipulation that traders and citizens of either nation, with the exception of the British Hudson's Bay Company, could "pass and repass by land or inland navigation, into the respective territories and countries of the two parties, on the continent of America . . . and to navigate all the lakes, rivers and waters thereof, and freely to carry on trade and commerce with each other." Such provisions, Jay and Grenville hoped, would calm people along the border. The Mississippi River remained open to England, although Jay resisted Grenville's effort to expand control south to present-day Minneapolis. America won economic privileges in the British West Indies and most-favored-nation status in the British Isles. But the British West Indies remained closed to American ships more than seventy tons in size. In exchange for this limited concession, Jay agreed that American vessels would not export cotton, sugar, and other staples from the islands to any port other than in the United States. The other problems—reparations for maritime violations, pre–Revolutionary War debts, the northeast boundary of present Maine—would be resolved by joint Anglo-American arbitration commissions.

Jay did not achieve everything Americans wanted. His treaty contained no mention of impressment, no guarantee of neutral rights, no end to paper or nonenforceable blockades, and no indemnification for slaves taken from America by departing British soldiers in 1783. Jay recognized that under certain conditions the British could confiscate American food headed for France, with compensation, and agreed that French goods on American vessels were subject to seizure, and permitted the British to treat naval stores as contraband. Thus he violated the treaties of 1778 with France. In a transparent effort to conceal these mutually exclusive treaty provisions, the signatories in London attached an assurance that no part of their treaty would "operate contrary to former and existing public treaties with other sovereigns or States."

President Washington received the treaty shortly after Congress adjourned in March 1795, leading him to call the Senate into special session, to meet in June. Meanwhile he kept its terms secret, which fanned the fears of Republicans and Francophiles, who mounted an intense propaganda campaign against a treaty they had not seen. The Senate debated it in secret session with the Federalists managing to save it by the minimum two-thirds vote of 20 to 10. All New Englanders except two voted for it, and the entire South stood in opposition. The Senate consented to the pact only after rejecting the restrictive terms relating to America's trade with the British West Indies.

During the debate a Republican senator informed the newspapers of the treaty's contents, and that set off a raging public battle. Republicans hanged and burned Jay in effigy for failing to gain a renunciation of impressment, reciprocal commercial privileges with the British, and recognition of America's freedom of the seas. Southerners, less concerned with principles than with economic interests, denounced the absence of compensation for their confiscated slaves, and the possibility of having to pay the debts they had incurred before the Revolution. An angry crowd in Charleston toppled the statue of William Pitt, who in pre-Revolution years Americans had regarded as their spokesman in England. In New York City a heckler stoned Hamilton when he spoke for ratification of the treaty, and someone remarked that Jay could have crossed the country at night by the light of his burning effigies. The author of *An Emetic for Aristocrats* described the negotiations in Biblical style, complete with the devil:

> One John, surnamed Jay, journeyed into a far country, even unto Great Britain. 2.   And the word of Satan came unto him saying, Make thou a covenant with this people, whereby they may be enabled to bring the *Americans* into bondage, as heretofore: 3.   And John answered unto Satan, of a truth . . . let me find grace in thy sight, that I may secretly betray my country and the place of my nativity.

An anonymous writer scrawled his wrath on a fence: "Damn John Jay! Damn every one that won't damn John Jay!! Damn every one that won't put lights in his windows and sit up all night damning John Jay!!!" On the Federalist side, the ablest defense of the treaty was a series of twenty-eight articles signed "Camillus" but written by Hamilton. So persuasive were these pieces that Jefferson complained to Madison, "Hamilton is really a Colossus to the anti-Republican party. Without numbers, he is an host within himself."

President Washington considered Jay's most important achievement the maintenance of peace, yet when he signed the treaty on August 18, 1795, he had serious reservations, not all of them the product of Republican propaganda. He had objected to the restrictive West Indian clause which the Senate deleted, and he had doubts about other commercial provisions. A feature that might have made the treaty attractive—the removal of the British from the northwest fur posts—had been made inconsequential by General Anthony Wayne's defeat of the Indians at the battle of Fallen Timbers. The ability of the British to hold the posts depended on Indian support, but in August 1794, when they failed to back the Indians against Wayne, the Indians became disillusioned with the British. In the ensuing Treaty of Greenville of 1795, Wayne forced the Indians to agree to leave Ohio country and that made it impossible for the British to remain there, irrespective of Jay's Treaty.

But the treaty made it possible to avoid war. Jay emphasized to the president that Britain, as a nation at war, could not make concessions injurious to its cause. England would never "admit principles, which would impeach the propriety of her conduct in seizing provisions bound to France, and enemy's property in neutral ships." The president had no alternative but to sign the treaty. He could not take a divided country, having almost no army and under a limited and still experimental government, into a war that would expose it to both Indians and Spanish along the western frontier and the powerful British navy on the seas. War with England was out of the question.

The treaty fight was partisan and sectional. Republicans in the House of Representatives made one last attempt to block the pact by refusing to appropriate money for its implementation. The debate reached a climax in the spring of 1796, when the president turned down a House request to hand over official materials relating to the treaty on the ground that such a move would violate the constitutional provision that the treaty power rested only with the Executive Office and the Senate. The atmosphere became so heated that one Republican who spoke in behalf of the appropriation was stabbed by his brother-in-law, also a Republican. In April the House voted 51 to 48 to approve the funds. Most yeas came from Federalist-dominated New England and New Jersey, while the nays came from the Republican South.

Jay's Treaty was important for several reasons. Britain's signature on the document and the territorial concessions contained within it reconfirmed America's sovereignty. The treaty marked the beginning of a ten-year Anglo-American rapprochement or harmonious relationship that permitted America's trade with England to triple and allowed the United

States to solidify its status as a nation. The joint-commission approach to international disputes encouraged the use of arbitration in diplomacy, which itself was a major breakthrough in international relations. And, by putting English and American relations on a more friendly footing, the treaty necessarily changed America's relations with Spain and France.

In regard to Spain, the changes effected by Jay's Treaty were highly advantageous. The Spanish foreign minister, Don Manuel de Godoy, had initiated a move toward negotiations when he learned in July 1794 that Jay was preparing to depart for England. He suggested to the Washington administration that Spain was amenable to an agreement regarding the Florida boundary and the Mississippi River. After some delay the president directed the South Carolina Federalist Thomas Pinckney, then minister to London, to leave for Madrid as special envoy. By the time he arrived in June 1795, conditions were favorable to a settlement. Spain had pulled out of the European war, on the way to switching sides from England and allying with France. Spanish leaders did not know the terms Jay had negotiated with England, but the mere existence of an Anglo-American pact was frightening. In July Spain signed the Treaty of Basle with France, in violation of Spain's agreement of 1792 with England. Fearful of British retaliation, Godoy assumed the worst when he heard of Jay's negotiations.

Godoy was concerned about areas west of the Appalachians, for Jay's Treaty, as far as he knew, might have authorized an Anglo-American force to take Spain's possessions in North America. Moreover, the Spanish had failed to foment separatism and Indian uprisings in the west, and the Americans' westward movement threatened Spain's holdings on the continent. Perhaps western concessions along with his treaty with France would delay America's migration west, for he knew that the French hoped to restore their imperial interests in North America. A clash between the Americans and the French could preserve the Spanish empire and restore Godoy's popularity to the point that he could again appear in public. Thus Pinckney's Treaty resulted from Godoy's effort to win American favor and stave off an Atlantic alliance against his country.

Pinckney sensed his advantages. In the palace monastery at San Lorenzo, he asked for and received the following concessions: free navigation of the Mississippi River; the "right of deposit" (permitted Americans to store goods while waiting for shipment) at New Orleans for three years, renewable there or at some other port; a northern boundary of Florida at the 31st parallel, which constituted a considerable retreat from Spain's previous demands for a line almost a hundred miles north at 32°28'; a mutual pledge not to stir the Indians against each other; Spain's approval of America's definition of neutral rights; and the establishment of mixed commissions to resolve Americans' damage claims for depredations committed by the Spanish navy during the European conflict. Godoy convinced the Spanish Council of State that the possibility of war with England prevented a refusal of Pinckney's requests.

In October 1795 Pinckney's Treaty was signed, securing everything America's minister had sought, though in fact Spanish forces did not pull out of the disputed area above Florida for three years. The treaty caused a surge of nationalism in the United States by opening the river, restraining the Indians, and ending Spain's separatist efforts in the southwest. It also had a reciprocal effect on Jay's Treaty. Southerners and westerners in the House of Representatives realized that their support of the treaty with England would guarantee passage of the agreement with Spain. In March 1796 the Senate unanimously approved Pinckney's Treaty.

In regard to France, news of Jay's negotiations had an unsettling effect. America's relations with France had improved since James Monroe, Virginia Republican and ardent Francophile, had arrived in Paris as minister in 1794. Before the National Convention Monroe passionately supported the revolution and, amid cheers, received the customary fraternal kiss signifying the bonds between the countries. Despite Washington's proclamation of neutrality, Monroe implied that America's sympathies lay with the French. During the excitement over Jay's mission, he promised that his country would not violate the Treaty of Alliance. President Washington, Monroe assured the French, would not ratify the treaty.

When Washington did sign the treaty, Monroe's efforts could not stop the rapid decline in Franco-American relations. In the summer of 1796 the Paris government renounced the rights of neutrals defined in the treaties of 1778, and in late August the president became exasperated with Monroe's behavior and called him home. When Washington sent Charles Cotesworth Pinckney of South Carolina (brother of Thomas Pinckney) to succeed Monroe, the French Directory refused to receive him and warned that failure to leave the country would lead to his arrest. Pinckney left for the Netherlands. The French minister in Philadelphia, Pierre Adet, who had brought pressure on members of Congress to vote against the House appropriations bill for Jay's Treaty, cast support for Thomas Jefferson in the presidential election of 1796, hinting darkly that only Jefferson's election would prevent France from making war on the United States. By the end of the year war with France seemed imminent.

Relations with France and England had an impact on Washington's Farewell Address, published in the Federalist newspaper *American Daily Advertiser* of Philadelphia, in September 1796. The president had decided against a third term, and with Hamilton as coauthor of his last public declaration, he recommended that the nation "steer clear of permanent alliances with any portion of the foreign world." Ideas expressed earlier by Thomas Paine and John Adams permeated the document. The Atlantic Ocean, Washington asserted, separated the United States from the Old World, allowing Americans to stand clear of "the ordinary vicissitudes of her politics or the ordinary combinations and collisions of her friendships or enmities." America's economic expansion should have little relation to its "political connection," for Europe's interests were different from those of the United States. Americans should permit only "temporary alliances for extraordinary emergencies." The president also warned that party division "opens the door to foreign influence and corruption" by subjecting "the policy and the will of one country . . . to the policy and will of another." In a statement reflecting America's encounters with France and England, the president concluded that "history and experience prove that foreign influence is one of the most baneful foes of republican government." His Farewell Address was not a call for isolationism, but a plea for noninvolvement by Europe and America in each other's political affairs.

Even though war seemed on the horizon when Washington left office, his achievements in foreign relations had been outstanding. Perhaps during the Washington administration circumstance deserves more credit than the man, but Washington had dignified the office of presidency without following the tempting paths toward monarchy. He had held the nation together and in so doing had set precedents for a restrained policy. The United States had finally realized the assurances contained in the Treaty of 1783. It was on secure economic footing, had maintained neutrality during the French wars, was in control of the Mississippi River, and could look forward to settling the areas north of Spanish Florida.

ADAMS THE PRESIDENT

By an electoral vote of 71 to 68, John Adams defeated Thomas Jefferson for the presidency in 1796. The closeness of his victory and the strange circumstance of Jefferson as runner-up becoming vice president, augured ill for the Adams administration. Washington's popularity had declined, and with it had gone the strength of the Federalist party. His legacy to Adams included troubles with Hamiltonians in the party as well as the growing troubles with France. The popular base of the Republican party had widened while that of the Federalists had stagnated, for its democratic ideals attracted immigrants and other nonelites of American society. Adams's personal traits added to his tribulations, for he was an anachronism in a nation moving toward greater popular participation in government. Sixty-two years of age and vice president for eight years, he was vain, humorless, cold, and puritanical; and these personal flaws mitigated against his better traits of a fervent nationalism, strong will, and deep intellect. Finally he faced a problem within the administration. Partly because he did not wish to seem presumptuous, but mainly because he could not find able men willing to serve in the existing political climate, Adams retained Washington's entire cabinet. That was an ill-advised decision, for these men were friends and admirers of Hamilton's, and Hamilton and Adams were far from friends and admirers of one another. Given all this, and given the French problem, the question was which realm of America's affairs would explode first—the domestic or the foreign.

While the breach in the Federalist party threatened to wreck the administration, Adams had more pressing problems with France. In 1797 the French declared that American vessels carrying enemy cargo of any

John Adams

President of the United States during the Quasi-War with France, he earlier headed the committee to draft the Model Treaty in 1776 and helped to negotiate the Treaty of Paris of 1783. (Library of Congress)

kind were subject to capture, and warned that French officers would treat everyone aboard as pirates. By June France had seized more than 300 American ships in the West Indies. In one instance, the commander of a French privateer tortured an American in a vain effort to convince him to say the cargo he carried was English and subject to confiscation. Adams followed the example of his predecessor and dispatched a special mission to France to resolve these difficulties.

The president's decision to negotiate with France was his best option in 1797, but he was not dealing from a position of strength. He appointed a nonpartisan, three-man delegation comprised of Charles Cotesworth Pinckney, still in the Netherlands; John Marshall, a Federalist from Virginia, distant cousin of Jefferson's, and later chief justice of the Supreme Court; and Republican Elbridge Gerry of Massachusetts, the president's longtime friend who accepted after Jefferson and Madison turned down the invitation. In October the delegation was introduced to European diplomacy by Charles Maurice de Talleyrand-Périgod, former bishop of the Roman Catholic Church during the *ancien régime* and now foreign minister. Talleyrand had lived in exile in the United States during the early stages of the French Revolution, and had become convinced that the new American nation was so weak that the mere threat of commercial restrictions would force adherence to the treaties of 1778. He hoped that protracted negotiations would hurt Adams's chances for reelection and bring in a Republican administration favorable to France. This would afford time for Talleyrand to work toward the acquisition of Louisiana from Spain and the reestablishment of the French empire in North America.

The timing of the American mission was unfortunate, for the European war had tipped in France's favor. The young Corsican, General Napoleon Bonaparte, had secured the Treaty of Campo Formio with Austria in mid-October and won several battles in Italy. Talleyrand was in no mood for concessions and displayed a haughtiness insulting to America. He hoped to widen political divisions in the United States, and either destroy the republic from within or force a treaty that could have the same devastating result by pulling it into the war with England.

The episode took a mysterious and ominous twist when three Frenchmen entered the anteroom where the American delegation waited. Claiming to speak for Talleyrand, they demanded an apology for disparaging remarks Adams had made about France in his recent message to Congress, and called for a payment of $250,000 and a loan of $12 million as prerequisites to negotiations. "No; no; not a sixpence," Pinckney replied to the suggested bribe. To sweeten the proposal, Talleyrand sent a woman to persuade the Americans to submit to French requests.

Many would like to think that the American diplomats turned down French demands for money because they believed such action morally wrong, but the truth was that Pinckney, Marshall, and Gerry knew that the use of bribes—money and women—was standard procedure in European diplomacy. Besides, the United States had sent large amounts of money to the Barbary states of North Africa to prevent piracy of American commercial vessels in the Mediterranean. The problem was that the three Americans' instructions did not authorize payment of such a huge sum, for a major loan to France would have violated neutrality and caused war with England. The risks were too great, especially when the Americans would gain only the right to negotiate. After months of frustration, Pinckney and Marshall demanded their passports. Talleyrand, who believed that continued negotiations would prevent an American war he did not want, urged Gerry to remain; but soon afterward the Adams government called him home.

News of the diplomatic exchanges in Paris arrived in America in early 1798 and stirred a popular demand for war. President Adams appeared before Congress in May to report that attempts at peace had failed and that he was preparing to defend the United States against France. Frantic, disbelieving Republicans in the House denounced the president for pushing unnecessarily for war and demanded to see the official correspondence from the delegation to France. Adams broke Washington's precedent and complied, after changing the names of Talleyrand's three agents to X, Y, and Z. Upon reading the dispatches, the Republicans realized their mistake and tried to block the release of the papers to the pub lic. Adams, however, ordered the printing of 10,000 copies of the XYZ dispatches and whipped emotions to such a pitch that many Americans called for war. Newspapers claimed that when X, Y, and Z demanded the bribes, Pinckney roared: "Millions for defense but not one cent for tribute!" Though he repeatedly denied having said those words, they became permanently attached to him during his lifetime and followed him to his grave, to be emblazoned on a tablet over his tombstone in Charleston. Americans chanted the phrase to stir the fainthearted into joining a war for honor. The song "Hail Columbia" was written to heighten nationalism, while President Adams, torn between his predecessor's advice to shun war and the popularity that was his for the first time, assured Americans that he would not send another minister to France until that government promised to receive him as "the representative of a great, free, powerful, and independent nation."

By the summer of 1798 the United States had taken several steps toward war, short of a formal declaration. Congress approved a war loan, authorized a "Provisional Army" of 10,000 men to supplement 3,500 regulars along the frontier, created a marine corps, established a Navy Department (formerly an adjunct of the War Department) and allowed an increase in the number of ships from three to twenty-seven, authorized the arming of merchant vessels and commissioning of privateers, and abrogated the treaties of 1778 on the ground that French maritime seizures had already violated their provisions. Adams attempted to persuade Washington to become general of the armies, but the Virginian refused until Hamilton, Adams's archenemy, became his second in command and took charge of field operations. Adams was unable to contain his wrath. Hamilton dreamed of leading armies into Louisiana and Florida, and favored Anglo-American cooperation in removing Spain and France from the Caribbean and South America, in line with the aims of Francisco de Miranda and other Latin American revolutionaries.

The combination of patriotism and distrust of French sympathizers in the United States set off a national frenzy in 1798. Suspicion of fellow Americans as well as French and Irish aliens in the country became so rife that leading Republicans, including Vice President Jefferson, were watched for treasonous behavior. One of the milder Federalist comments about waffling Republicans was that they reminded him of the "weak dupe who finds himself compelled to turn an unfaithful wench out of doors, stopping her at the threshold to whine over their former loves, and to remind her of past joys." From their pulpits ministers denounced godless France, while other Americans warned that anarchy was about to sweep the United States—perhaps in the form of slave uprisings. Adams's supporters wore black badges, fights broke out over the XYZ Affair, and the president rode the wave of xenophobia by dramatically declaring: "The finger of destiny writes on the wall the word: War."

Federalists in Congress responded that same year with a series of laws aimed more at the Jeffersonians than at subversion. Justifying them as "wartime" measures, Congress passed the Naturalization Act, which raised residency requirements for citizenship from five to fourteen years and slowed the growth of the Republican party; the Alien Act, which permitted the president to crack down on dissent by arresting and deporting "dangerous" aliens; the Alien Enemies Act, authorizing the deportation of enemy aliens in time of war; and the Sedition Act, which forbade "any false, scandalous and malicious writing" against the government, and led to the indictment of twenty-five Republican newspaper editors, ten of whom were tried and convicted by Federalist-dominated juries. That summer George Logan, a Philadelphia Quaker, traveled to Paris as an unauthorized emissary for peace and received a warm welcome from the Directory. This enraged the secretary of state, Timothy Pickering. At his urging the Federalists in Congress rammed through the Logan Act, which prohibited diplomatic involvement by private citizens under penalty of a $5,000 fine or a year in prison, or both. These measures by Congress confirmed the Republicans' worst fears. More than party strife was involved. Jefferson warned: the republic was at stake because the Federalists were conspiring to establish monarchical rule.

Jeffersonians attacked these acts with the Virginia and Kentucky Resolutions. Secretly written by Jefferson and Madison in 1798 and 1799, the resolutions employed the "compact theory" of government to justify criticism of the Alien and Sedition Acts as violations of the First Amendment to the Constitution. The states, they proclaimed, must mediate between the people and the central government to protect liberty. Both writers appeared to advocate interposition as remedy, but their solution would be a Republican victory at the polls in 1800.

President Adams meanwhile changed his stand and decided to resist the popular clamor for war. Indeed, he reversed himself upon learning that Hamilton was to be second in command—and mainly for that reason, though in fact it was a prudent decision. He shocked fellow Federalists by refusing to ask Congress for a declaration of war, and left its members to explain the reasons for their new laws. Adams soon faced rebellion within his party. Maritime incidents did continue for over two years, during which the American navy seized nearly a hundred French armed ships in what became known as the Quasi-War. But neither nation declared war.

President Adams overcame the pressure for war and sent another mission to France to resolve the countries' differences. He had learned from three sources—William Vans Murray, American minister to the Netherlands, John Quincy Adams, representing his father in Berlin, and Talleyrand—that France wanted to settle its disputes with America. Adams appointed an all-Federalist delegation comprised of Murray, Oliver Ellsworth, chief justice of the Supreme Court, and William R. Davie, former governor of North Carolina. The Senate approved and the men left for Paris in March 1800.

By autumn of that year the delegation had taken advantage of a changed situation in the European conflict to negotiate an end to the Quasi-War. Napoleon, having seized control of the French government, needed a break in the war with England to enable him to solidify his position, and he worked with Talleyrand to offer terms to the Americans. The two Frenchmen had revived their designs on North America, for Louisiana might become a granary to feed the French sector of Santo Domingo, and the island could provide sugar for France. Such a scheme would also avenge the humiliations of the 1763 Treaty of Paris. Enthusiastic reports of the economic and military value of the Ohio and Mississippi valleys convinced Napoleon and Talleyrand to reach a settlement with the United States that would facilitate French acquisition of Louisiana from Spain. A French empire in North America necessitated a truce in the war and a resolution of difficulties with the United States. The time was right for Americans to profit again from troubles in Europe.

Negotiations with France stretched seven months, for Talleyrand fell ill and Napoleon was often gone during the war in Italy; but in September 1800 the two countries signed the Convention of 1800. The pact upheld the maritime principles sought by Americans in the Plan of 1776. Both nations agreed to follow "the privileges of the most favored nation" in trading with one another, and they agreed to return ships taken during the Quasi-War. When the Americans sought indemnification for violations of the treaties of 1778, however, the spokesman for the French, Napoleon's brother Joseph, countered that the United States had abrogated the treaties and could not seek reparations under them. Further discussions postponed the matter to "a convenient time." After more complications, the French agreed to cancel the treaties if the Americans gave up their damage claims stemming from recent maritime seizures. The United States assumed the claims and eventually settled (but not until the early 1900s) $20 million in damages to its citizens. But this was a small price for release from the French Alliance of 1778.

At Joseph Bonaparte's country estate at Môrtefontaine, Napoleon held a huge party to celebrate the treaty-signing ceremony. Unknown to the Americans, the first consul and Talleyrand had already moved toward planting a new French empire in North America. That same day (though it was dated the following day, October 1), the French secretly concluded the Treaty of San Ildefonso, which awarded territory in Italy to Spain in exchange for Louisiana.

The Convention of 1800 marked an end to America's first era in foreign policy. It substantiated the principles of the Plan of 1776, confirmed the wisdom of Washington's Farewell Address, sealed the fate of the Federalist party, and, most important, freed the republic of its entangling alliance of 1778. Washington and Adams had placed the United States on a Federalist course, and had kept the country out of war without sacrificing honor. Trade was increasing because of the rapprochement with England brought by Jay's Treaty and America's problems with France; Americans were pushing westward because of the treaties with Spain and the Indians; and the nation had an independent foreign policy. Adams asked to be remembered in posterity for preventing war with France, yet one has mixed feelings about the epitaph he arranged to have inscribed on his tombstone: "Here lies John Adams, who took upon himself the responsibility of the peace with France in the year 1800." Adams's policies had unnecessarily taken the nation close to war. Nor can he escape blame for many of his party's troubles at home. His uncertain French policy administered a near lethal dose to a staggering political party. Adams helped to bequeath the Republicans' victory in 1800.

ACHIEVEMENTS OF THE FEDERALIST ERA

By the end of the Federalist era the United States had formulated a realistic foreign policy built upon political and economic interests. Hamilton's financial plan brought economic order, and Jefferson's arguments established a precedent for *de facto* recognition of foreign governments. Washington's policies were sometimes unpopular, but they were always in line with the national interest. The controversies between Hamilton and Jefferson, though divisive, helped the president make decisions based on diverse points of view. The Neutrality Proclamation, Jay's Treaty, Pinckney's Treaty, the Treaty of Greenville, the Convention of 1800—all were monuments to a realistic diplomacy which helped the United States secure the guarantees contained in the Treaty of 1783 ending the Revolutionary War.

The Federalists' successes were tempered by the realization that Adams's French policies had helped wreck the party. A proud people proclaimed vindication of independence and national integrity in 1800 by electing Jefferson over Adams as president. Labeled idealist and pacifist, Jefferson and his successor eight years later, friend and ally James Madison, would venture into diplomatic paths avoided by Washington and Adams, and take the nation into war with England.

Selected readings

Ammon, Harry, *The Genet Mission*. 1973.

Bemis, Samuel F., *Jay's Treaty: A Study in Commerce and Diplomacy*. 1923; 1962.

———, "Washington's Farewell Address: A Foreign Policy of Independence." *American Historical Review* 39 (1934): 250–68.

———, *Pinckney's Treaty: America's Advantage from Europe's Distress, 1783–1800*. 1926; 1960.

Bowman, Albert H., *The Stuggle for Neutrality: Franco-American Diplomacy during the Federalist Era*. 1974.

Boyd, Julian P., *Number 7: Alexander Hamilton's Secret Attempts to Control American Foreign Policy*. 1964.

Burt, Alfred L., *The United States, Great Britain and British North America*. 1940.

Charles, Joseph, *The Origins of the American Party System*. 1956.

Chinard, Gilbert, *Honest John Adams*. 1933.

Combs, Jerald A., *The Jay Treaty: Political Battleground of the Founding Fathers*. 1970.

Darling, Arthur B., *Our Rising Empire, 1763–1803*. 1940.

DeConde, Alexander, *Entangling Alliance: Politics and Diplomacy under George Washington*. 1958.

——, *The Quasi-War: Politics and Diplomacy of the Undeclared War with France, 1797–1801*. 1966.

Gilbert, Felix, *To the Farewell Address: Ideas of Early American Foreign Policy*. 1961.

Hutson, James H., "Intellectual Foundation of Early American Diplomacy," *Diplomatic History* 1 (1977): 1–19.

Jensen, Merrill, *The New Nation: A History of the United States during the Confederation, 1781–1789*. 1950.

Kaplan, Lawrence S., *Colonies into Nation: American Diplomacy, 1763–1801*. 1972.

——, *Jefferson and France*. 1967.

Kurtz, Stephen G., *The Presidency of John Adams: The Collapse of Federalism, 1795–1800*. 1957.

McCoy, Drew R., *The Elusive Republic: Political Economy in Jeffersonian America*. 1980.

McDonald, Forrest, *Alexander Hamilton: A Biography*. 1979.

——, *The Presidency of George Washington*. 1974.

Marks, Frederick W., *Independence on Trial: Foreign Affairs and the Making of the Constitution*. 1973.

Miller, John C., *Alexander Hamilton: Portrait in Paradox*. 1959.

——, *The Federalist Era, 1789–1801*. 1960.

Perkins, Bradford, *The First Rapprochement: England and the United States, 1795–1805*. 1955.

Ritcheson, Charles R., *Aftermath of Revolution: British Policy toward the United States, 1783–1795*. 1969.

Stinchcombe, William C., *The XYZ Affair*. 1980.

Varg, Paul A., *Foreign Policies of the Founding Fathers*. 1963.

——, *New England and Foreign Relations, 1789–1850*. 1983.

Whitaker, Arthur P., *The Mississippi Question, 1795–1803*. 1934.

——, *The Spanish-American Frontier, 1783–1795*. 1927.

White, Leonard D., *The Federalists: A Study in Administrative History*. 1948.

Chapter Three

Jeffersonian Diplomacy, 1801–1809

International conditions at the time of Thomas Jefferson's inauguration as president in March 1801 were not auspicious for the Republican administration. Problems remained with England, France, and Spain, and soon Jefferson and Secretary of State James Madison would become deeply involved in the Napoleonic Wars in Europe. During the election campaign the Federalists castigated Jefferson because of his pro-French stand, and because of his collaboration with Madison in a theory of government that accepted the premise that, if necessary, an end to the state was preferable to giving up individual liberty. Many Americans feared that Jefferson, author of religious freedom in Virginia, sought to abolish godly worship, while others assailed the writer of the Declaration of Independence as a dangerous radical who would destroy the nation before seeing his ambitions deterred. In his inaugural address he asserted that "we are all Republicans, we are all Federalists," and called for "peace, commerce, and honest friendship with all nations, entangling alliances with none." The irony is that during twelve years of perilous times the Federalists had kept the United States out of war, while within the same amount of time the Republicans took the nation into a naval conflict in the Mediterranean and into a war with the British that could have ended America's independence.

THE BARBARY WARS

President Jefferson's international problems did not concern only England, France, and Spain, for as mentioned in the previous chapter, independence also brought difficulties with the pirates of the Barbary coast of

Thomas Jefferson

Before becoming president in 1801, Jefferson wrote the Declaration of Independence and, while secretary of state under Washington, advocated a decentralized form of government that became a basic principle of the anti-Federalists or Republicans. (Charles Wilson Peale; Library of Congress)

North Africa. Since 1776 America's merchant marine was no longer under British protection and found its passage into the Mediterranean blocked by the vessels of Algiers, Morocco, Tripoli, and Tunis. Bribery was less costly than war, and the Washington and Adams administrations soon joined Britain and other European nations in paying tribute to the Barbary states. The United States bought its first treaty in the mid-1780s from Morocco, but the other three states continued to raid American shipping and to enslave seamen. In the following decade Congress authorized the construction of six frigates to escort commercial vessels through the Mediterranean; but before they were ready, the dey (pasha or ruler) of Algiers negotiated a treaty with the United States, by which his country received money plus yearly naval stores. The American government soon purchased similar treaties with Tripoli and Tunis, but the raids went on. The most insulting incident came in October 1800, when the dey of Algiers forced the captain of the warship *George Washington* to lower the Stars and Stripes, raise Algerian colors, and transport that country's ambassador and gifts to the sultan in Constantinople. Although Americans had praised Charles Cotesworth Pinckney for allegedly declaring to the

French "Millions for defense, but not one cent for tribute," the United States sent money to pirates.

Two months after Jefferson's inauguration, the pasha of Tripoli declared war on the United States. The president did not ask Congress for a similar declaration but acted on the constitutional provision authorizing him to be commander-in-chief of the country's armed forces. He immediately sent a squadron to the Mediterranean and sought a buildup of the navy. In June 1805, after some minor skirmishes, the United States claimed victory over Tripoli and signed a treaty that temporarily eased problems in the Mediterranean. The United States paid a ransom for imprisoned American seamen, and agreed that new consuls would bear gifts for the pasha. In 1807, during America's maritime crisis with England, President Jefferson ordered the navy home from the Mediterranean, and for nearly a decade which included the War of 1812, America's commercial vessels fended for themselves against pirates. Finally, in March 1815, Congress approved the use of force against Algiers, whose dey had declared war on the United States. During the summer the American navy repeatedly battered the Barbary states of Algiers, Tripoli, and Tunis. Help from European warships ended the tributes and the piracy.

LOUISIANA PURCHASE

Jefferson's first major decision in foreign affairs concerned the Louisiana Territory, the vast area west of the Mississippi River to the Rocky Mountains, which involved the competing interests of France, Spain, and England. Jefferson had always advocated American migration west. After becoming chief executive he spoke to James Monroe of the time when the United States would encompass the entire continent. Access to the oceans, he envisioned, necessitated a canal through Central America. At present, the country had other problems and the areas bordering its western frontiers fortunately belonged to a weak Spain. With patience, he declared, the United States could take the area "piece by piece."

The Spanish had long been apprehensive that America's westward movement would drive them from North America. In 1794 the Spanish governor of Louisiana pinpointed the mainspring of American expansionism:

> Their method of spreading themselves and their policy are so much to be feared by Spain as are their arms. Every new settlement, when it reaches thirty thousand souls, forms a state, which is united to the United States, so far as regards mutual protection, but which governs itself and imposes its own laws.

Pinckney's Treaty of the following year unleashed a drive toward northern Louisiana and the eastern bank of the Mississippi River. Americans in Tennessee, Georgia, and the Mississippi Territory, realizing that the Floridas controlled river entrances into North America, regarded West

Florida as the key to the Gulf of Mexico. Although some day the United States would have to have New Orleans and the Floridas, its leaders were not worried as long as the areas were in Spain's hands. As Jefferson wrote in July 1801, "We consider [Spain's] possession of the adjacent country as most favorable to our interests, and should see with an extreme pain any other nation substituted for them."

France upset this comfortable relationship with Spanish Louisiana. For years rumors had circulated that the French intended to regain the territory lost to Spain during the Seven Years' War. The French minister to the United States during the late 1780s openly speculated about a restored empire in North America. Genet's efforts to wrest New Orleans from Spain were fresh in Americans' minds, and when France and Spain signed the Treaty of Basle in 1795, stories spread in the United States that the French had tried to acquire Louisiana as part of the agreement. Though France failed in this venture, it completed control of Santo Domingo by securing the Spanish part of the island—an acquisition which stimulated interest in Louisiana as a granary for feeding the slaves on the sugar-rich Caribbean island. During the presidential campaign of 1796 Federalists accused Republicans of conspiring with the French to fuse areas west of the Appalachians with Louisiana. More than 100,000 Americans who had crossed the mountains by 1790 had reason to worry, for Talleyrand, now foreign minister under Napoleon, had dreams of reestablishing the French empire in the New World.

On the same day of the Convention of 1800 between the United States and France, Napoleon negotiated the secret treaty of San Ildefonso with Spain, which provided for the retrocession of Louisiana. Though many believed that the French had forced Spain to give up the territory, the truth was that the government in Madrid had been anxious to sell because Louisiana had become a burden. The colony's revenue totaled only a fifth of the costs of holding onto it. Britons and Americans along the river were engaged in a thriving smuggling trade, and the Spanish had lost control over the right of deposit in New Orleans. As early as 1797 Spain's foreign secretary, Don Manuel de Godoy, remarked that "you can't lock up an open field." In a letter to the French of June 22, 1800, four months before the retrocession, he admitted that the area was too costly to keep. According to the treaty of 1800, France promised an Italian kingdom for King Charles IV's nephew, the prince of Parma, in exchange for six warships and Louisiana. Napoleon's efforts to attach the Floridas failed. Talleyrand assured the Spanish king that French Louisiana would be "a wall of brass forever impenetrable to the combined efforts of England and America." Spain had seemingly secured a buffer between the Americans and its possessions on the continent, for Napoleon assured Spain that he would never sell Louisiana.

Rumors of a deal between France and Spain regarding Louisiana began drifting into Washington early in Jefferson's first administration. Signs of French activity in the New World had appeared in 1801 when

French soldiers arrived in the Caribbean to put down a slave insurrection that had begun in Santo Domingo six years earlier. These fears seemed confirmed when America's minister to London, Federalist Rufus King of New York, informed Secretary of State Madison in late March 1802 that France had promised an Italian kingdom to Spain, probably in exchange for Louisiana and the Floridas. The following November the British government, hoping to block French expansion in the New World, handed the American minister a copy of a Franco–Spanish treaty of March 1801 (the Convention of Aranjuez), by which the Spanish king's nephew was to become king of Tuscany, later called Etruria. The treaty did not mention Louisiana, but the pieces of information so far received pointed to that area as the prize.

Jefferson reacted in several ways to the rumored sale of Louisiana to the French. He secured authorization from Congress to federalize 80,000 state militiamen for duty along the Mississippi River; he warned French and Spanish diplomats in Washington of the anger of western Americans; and he publicly associated with the British chargé in Washington. The charade had effect. The French chargé declared to his home government: "I am afraid they may strike at Louisiana before we can take it over." Through a long-time friend then in Washington, Pierre Samuel duPont de Nemours, the president sent two letters to Paris, one addressed to America's minister, Robert Livingston of New York. Dating it April 18, 1802, Jefferson declared that French ownership of Louisiana

> reverses all the political relations of the United States and will form a new epoch in our political course. . . . There is on the globe one single spot, the possessor of which is our natural and habitual enemy. It is New Orleans, through which the produce of three-eighths of our territory must pass to market. . . . France, placing herself in that door, assumes to us the attitude of defiance. . . . The day that France takes possession of New Orleans . . . we must marry ourselves to the British fleet and nation.

Jefferson left the note unsealed, intending that DuPont read it and make known its contents to the French court. In a covering letter the president warned that the reestablishment of France in North America would be "the embryo of a tornado."

A few days later, May 1, the president instructed Livingston to attempt to buy New Orleans and the Floridas. Though the minister was aged, nearly deaf, and unable to speak French, he was so persistent that his French counterpart in the negotiations remarked afterward that the American ought to receive a certificate honoring his performance. The New Yorker, first secretary for foreign affairs under the Articles of Confederation, knew the value of patience and persistence in diplomacy. Though Talleyrand denied that France had acquired Louisiana, Livingston ignored the denial. He continually reminded the French that control of Louisiana was meaningless without the Floridas. He labeled New Orleans and the surrounding area "a desert and an insignificant town" and a "distant wilderness," and questioned whether the entire province would bring either wealth or power. In a suggestion that constituted the first official American interest in lands beyond the Mississippi, he declared that if the United States owned the territory above the Arkansas River, it would serve as a buffer between French possessions below the river and British interests in Canada. Livingston also tried to tie in the reparations claims left unpaid by the Convention of 1800. A settlement regarding Louisiana, he insisted, should clear the air by including French reparations for damages incurred by American shippers during the Quasi-War of the late 1790s.

As Livingston hammered away, the United States learned that in October 1802 Spain's acting intendant (fiscal officer) in New Orleans, Juan Ventura Moralès, had suspended America's right of deposit. The move caused alarm, for it violated Pinckney's Treaty and appeared to confirm fears that France had regained Louisiana. A British observer declared that "scarcely any thing has happened since the Revolution which has so much agitated the minds of all Descriptions of People in the United States as this decree." Americans had reason for concern. Their wartime markets in Europe and the West Indies had grown tremendously by the late 1790s. Sugar, flour, and cotton from the Mississippi Valley entered the world market not only because of the right of deposit, but also because an ongoing slave rebellion in Santo Domingo wrecked the island's sugar industry and left a vacuum filled by Americans. In 1796 exports down the Mississippi River were small, but by 1802 they were valued at $2 million. Cotton shipped through New Orleans had increased forty times over in three years, and by 1803 American shipping on the river was more than double that of the Spanish and French combined. The order suspending the right of deposit did not prevent Americans from unloading their flatboats directly onto outgoing vessels, but many inhabitants of the Mississippi Valley thought this was Napoleon's first step toward closing the river to American commerce. If rumors were correct that he had secured the Floridas, the French could seal off the Gulf of Mexico.

Fiction was more dangerous than truth in this instance, for the French had had nothing to do with suspending the right of deposit. Moralès had followed a secret directive of July 1802 from Madrid, which instructed him to declare that under Pinckney's Treaty he could not extend the privilege of using New Orleans without approval of the Spanish king. The motive was clear: Spain intended to preoccupy France and the United States with one another and forestall American encroachments on Spanish territories in North America.

While irate westerners waited for Jefferson to act, the Federalists saw the opportunity for political gain and blasted the administration for failing to protect America's interests along the Mississippi River. In the Senate, Federalist James Ross of Pennsylvania demanded $5 million to finance an expedition to take New Orleans. Alexander Hamilton also urged the Republicans to occupy the city and the Floridas before attempting to discuss the matter with France. The objects of the Federalists' strategy were clear: Jefferson either would ask Congress for war with France, or he would refuse to do so and betray the west. Jefferson instead followed the advice of his friend DuPont, who had arrived in Paris and warned in December 1802 that a hardline policy would worsen matters. Unaware of Livingston's efforts, DuPont recommended that the United States offer to buy New Orleans and the Floridas. Even if the effort failed, it would quiet the Federalists and convince westerners of the president's loyalty to their interests. The United States could not go to war with France. Jefferson again turned to diplomacy.

In January 1803 the president nominated fellow Virginian James Monroe as "minister extraordinary" to France and Spain to assist Livingston in buying New Orleans and the Floridas. It was a wise political move. Monroe was popular among agrarians of the South and West, partly because he owned land in the West and had been a longtime advocate of free navigation of the Mississippi River. He would also have a favorable reception in Paris because of his pro-French stance during his ministerial stay there during the 1790s. Should France refuse to negotiate, or should it close the Mississippi River, Monroe was to leave for England to negotiate an alliance. After the Senate narrowly approved his appointment, a House committee recommended an appropriation of $2 million for use in the negotiations, and stipulated free navigation of the Mississippi River and access to all waterways in the Floridas which emptied into the Gulf. "If we look forward to the free use of the Mississippi, the Mobile, the Apalachicola, and the other rivers of the West," Jefferson insisted, "New Orleans and the Floridas must become a part of the United States, either by purchase or by conquest." In a striking move he privately authorized Monroe to go as high as $10 million for New Orleans and the Floridas. Shortly after the Ross resolution for taking the port city met narrow defeat in the Senate, the special envoy left for France in early March 1803.

During the political controversy in Washington, important changes on the diplomatic front worked to benefit the United States. In March Napoleon decided to break the Peace of Amiens of 1801 and resume the war against England. This required money for the European campaign and for expected problems in the New World. Without French control of the Floridas, the British navy could seize New Orleans and close Louisiana. In the winter of 1802–3 Napoleon had planned to seize Louisiana, but the army he assembled in the Netherlands for this purpose was iced in at port and later kept from the sea by storms. He had failed to soothe American fears of his intentions in the New World, and he now worried that uneasy Franco-American relations could lead to an Anglo-American alliance.

Failure to acquire the Floridas had weakened France's position by exposing Louisiana to the British, but a more immediate threat to Napoleon's New World plans was his inability to put down the slave insurrection in Santo Domingo. The island, rich in sugar, coffee, indigo, and cotton, was to become the commercial center of a restored French empire in the New World. After the French had secured control over the entire island in 1795, a former slave and spokesman for the blacks, Toussaint L'Ouverture, had at first claimed loyalty to France, but that same year led an insurrection against white control. In November 1801, a month after a preliminary peace with England, Napoleon sent a first detachment of 20,000 men under command of his brother-in-law, General Victor Leclerc, to end the rebellion. But everything went wrong for the French. In 1802, 24,000 soldiers died in the fighting and from yellow fever. Leclerc tricked L'Ouverture into captivity that year and shipped him to France where he died in prison of bad treatment and pneumonia. The insurrection, however, raged on. In one instance, 173 of 176 black captives hanged themselves. Leclerc estimated that another 70,000 men were necessary and proposed the following approach:

> We must destroy all the mountain Negroes, men and women, sparing only children under twelve years of age. We must destroy half the Negroes of the plains, and not allow in the colony a single man who has worn an epaulette. Without these measures the colony will never be at peace, and every year, especially deadly ones like this, you will have a civil war on your hands which will jeopardize the future.

A month later Leclerc died of yellow fever. Notified of his brother-in-law's death, Napoleon disgustedly decided to abandon his American plans: "Damn sugar, damn coffee, damn colonies," he declared. With Santo Domingo gone (along with 50,000 French soldiers), the mainstay of the French empire in the New World had slipped from Napoleon's hands and with it passed the need for Louisiana.

On April 11, 1803, Talleyrand shocked Livingston in Paris by asking whether the United States would like "to have the whole of Louisiana?" Taken aback, Livingston managed to reply: "No, our wishes extended only to New Orleans and the Floridas." But he would discuss the matter with Monroe, who was en route from Washington. Several considerations affected France's decision to sell, but the basic one was Napoleon. The previous day he had notified two of his ministers that he intended to part with Louisiana, and shortly before the offer to the Americans he informed his minister of finance, François Barbé-Marbois. Though money for the war with England was vital, his most important objectives were to prevent British control of Louisiana and to diminish the danger of an Anglo-American alliance.

Two days after Talleyrand's offer to sell Louisiana, Monroe arrived in Paris and Livingston informed him of the changed situation. Neither man had authority to deal for territory beyond the Mississippi, but they quickly decided to approve the sale. After considerable dickering over the price, the United States agreed to pay $11,250,000 for Louisiana, and to assume responsibility for $3,750,000 in reparations due to American citizens for some of the claims arising from the Quasi-War. In the treaty signed on May 2 but antedated to April 30, France ceded "the colony or province of Louisiana, with the same extent that it now has in the hands of Spain, and it had when France possessed it; and such as it should be after the treaties subsequently entered into between Spain and other states." Inhabitants of the province were to become American citizens, and the United States guaranteed France and Spain access to Louisiana's ports for twelve years with the same regulations that applied to Americans.

Hardly able to contain their excitement, Livingston and Monroe waited until they signed the treaty to ask the dimensions of the territory. Did it include West Florida? Livingston asked Talleyrand. The wily French foreign minister replied in a statement certain to stir unrest: "I can give you no direction. You have made a noble bargain for yourselves, and I suppose you will make the most of it." When the Americans persisted in their inquiries, Marbois asked Napoleon and he remarked: "If an obscurity did not already exist, it would perhaps be good policy to put one there." It is possible that Livingston and Monroe wanted a vague boundary description in the treaty to enable the United States to claim West Florida. Whatever the truth, the United States had bought a huge territory containing thousands of Indians and countless inhabitants of French and Spanish lineage.

Jefferson's celebration of the Louisiana Treaty was short-lived, for several constitutional and legal questions troubled him. The Constitution of the United States did not authorize the president to purchase land, nor did it permit him to convert a territory's residents into American citizens. He also had qualms about Napoleon's right to hand over Louisiana, for the Spanish minister in Washington emphasized that France had not yet transferred territories in Europe to Spain in accordance with the retrocession of 1800. No change of title to Louisiana had taken place and it still belonged to Spain, he told Jefferson. Furthermore, the Spanish minister noted that Napoleon had promised the king of Spain that no third power would own Louisiana. But Jefferson's major worry was whether the United States had the constitutional right to make the purchase.

Jefferson considered a constitutional amendment to justify the purchase. After Congress approved the treaty and paid for the area, he thought, it "must then appeal to *the nation* for an additional article to the Constitution. . . . The legislature, in casting behind them metaphysical subtleties and risking themselves like faithful servants, must . . . throw themselves on their country for doing for them unauthorized what we know they would have done for themselves had they been in a situation to do it." Albert Gallatin, secretary of the treasury, had sent a memorandum to Jefferson noting a constitutional justification for acquiring land as a means for expanding the republic. "The existence of the United States as a nation," Gallatin wrote, "presupposes the power enjoyed by every nation of extending their territory by treaties, and the general power given to the president and Senate of making treaties designates the organs through which the acquisition may be made." By the doctrine of im-

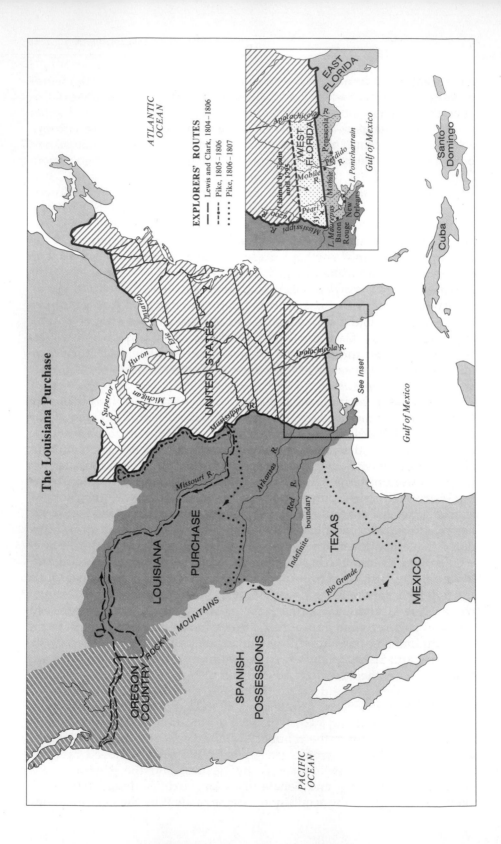

The Louisiana Purchase

EXPLORERS' ROUTES
Lewis and Clark, 1804–1806
Pike, 1805–1806
Pike, 1806–1807

ATLANTIC OCEAN

EAST FLORIDA

WEST FLORIDA

Apalachicola R.

Pensacola

Claimed by Spain until 1795

Perdido R.

L. Pontchartrain

Mobile

Mobile R.

Pearl R.

L. Maurepas

Baton Rouge

New Orleans

Mississippi R.

Gulf of Mexico

See Inset

Apalachicola R.

UNITED STATES

L. Superior

L. Michigan

Huron

L. Erie

L. Ontario

Mississippi R.

Missouri R.

Arkansas R.

Red R.

LOUISIANA

PURCHASE

ROCKY MOUNTAINS

OREGON COUNTRY

SPANISH POSSESSIONS

Indefinite boundary

TEXAS

Rio Grande

MEXICO

Cuba

Santo Domingo

PACIFIC OCEAN

Gulf of Mexico

plied or inherent powers, long rejected by Jefferson, Gallatin argued that in times of national need the president or Congress may go beyond the strict letter of the Constitution for the good of America.

Jefferson hesitated, but finally decided to forgo his rigid interpretation of the Constitution in the interest of the nation. In Paris, meanwhile, Livingston had warned that Napoleon might back out of the deal. The president received a letter from the minister in August declaring that France was "sick of the bargain," that Spain was "much dissatisfied," and that the "slightest pretense" could cause Napoleon to cancel the treaty. To Madison, Jefferson advocated overcoming the constitutional problems "*sub silentio*." The president forwarded the treaty to the Senate, explaining that his purpose was "to secure a good which would otherwise probably be never again in reach." A "strict observance to the written laws is doubtless one of the *high* duties of a good citizen, but it is not the *highest*. The laws of necessity, of self-preservation, of saving our country when in danger, are of a higher obligation." Years afterward Jefferson agreed with Madison that the United States would become an "empire for liberty" because it had joined freedom with expansion and was based on a Constitution that promoted "extensive empire and self-government."

The laws of politics dictated a battle over the treaty's approval. Federalists denounced the purchase because it authorized too much money for land the country did not need. They attacked its constitutionality and objected to admitting Louisiana into the Union as one or more states equal to the others. Yet these were masks for their concern that new western states would ally with the South to damage New England's political position in the nation. One Federalist senator sincerely concerned about the constitutionality of the purchase was John Quincy Adams, son of the former president, who asked whether the Constitution's treaty-making power permitted the involuntary addition of non-Americans to the Union. An amendment was necessary, he insisted. But when his motion to establish a committee for this purpose failed, Adams was the only Federalist to vote with the Republicans and the treaty won approval in October 1803 by a tally of 24 to 7.

On December 20, 1803, in a small ceremony at the Place d'Armes in New Orleans, the United States doubled in size when the French formally made the transfer of Louisiana, less than three weeks after receiving the province from Spain. In the presence of a few Americans and no French soldiers, the Stars and Stripes replaced French colors over American Louisiana.

MAP 4

Clearly Jefferson's outstanding achievement as president, the purchase of Louisiana doubled the size of the United States and pointed the way to a continental empire.

Livingston had been correct in urging the president to approve the purchase without delay. Napoleon had acted illegally. He had not upheld his deal with Spain in 1800, for no nations recognized Etruria and his soldiers still remained in the kingdom. By transferring Louisiana to a third power, he broke his promise to Spain and violated the French constitution of 1799 by selling territory without the legislature's approval. Similarly, as Napoleon violated his word, his treaties, and his country's constitution, President Jefferson departed from his understanding of the American Constitution in accepting the territory in the national interest.

Later, in 1828, the United States Supreme Court implicitly approved the constitutionality of the Louisiana Purchase in the case of *American Insurance Company* v. *Canter*. The nationalistic Chief Justice John Marshall, Jefferson's cousin but no friend or political ally, ruled (in regard to the purchase of Florida) that the government's treaty and warmaking authority gave it "the power of acquiring territory [which]'. . . becomes a part of the nation" and permitted its inhabitants to be "incorporated into the Union of the United States." Louisiana had already become the first state cut out of the vast territory; it was admitted into the Union in 1812.

The Louisiana Purchase laid the basis for an American empire, even though past treaties gave the United States no rightful claim to West Florida as part of the sale. "From this day," Livingston declared, "the United States take their place among the powers of the first rank." The treaty affirmed the imprecision of the boundaries, for it defined Louisiana as "the same extent it now had in the hands of Spain and that it had when France possessed it [before the Treaty of Paris of 1763]." Livingston's efforts to determine the borders revealed that French and Spanish markings were different. Louisiana under French control before the 1760s was larger than when Spain owned it. French Louisiana enveloped all areas east along the Gulf shores to the Perdido River, including Mobile. Spanish Louisiana stretched east from the Mississippi River only along the Iberville River and Lakes Maurepas and Pontchartrain. Lands between the Iberville and Perdido rivers, or much of West Florida, went to England in 1763 and were returned to Spain by the Treaty of Paris two decades later. The Louisiana dealt by Spain to France in 1800, and which Napoleon sold to the United States three years later, did not include West Florida.

America's claim to West Florida was unfounded for other reasons as well. It is doubtful that, at the outset of the negotiations, Livingston considered either of the Floridas part of Louisiana. He wrote Madison that he favored exchanging Louisiana for the Floridas, since the latter were more important. Yet after the negotiations, Livingston seems to have convinced himself that Napoleon had unwittingly included the Floridas in the sale to the United States. Jefferson must have recognized the weakness of this argument. After the negotiations in Paris, Monroe left for Madrid where he attempted to deal for the Floridas. This move indicated that the Louisiana Treaty did not include them. Yet the ambiguity of the boundary provisions permitted the United States to make what it claimed was a legitimate argument for West Florida. Livingston and Monroe recommended that President Jefferson assume control over all lands between the Mississippi and Perdido rivers. Despite claims by both France and Spain that Louisiana's eastern border was the Mississippi and the Iberville, the United States asserted that the purchase included all of West Florida west of the Perdido, and that the port of Mobile belonged to America.

Without legal or historical claim to the Gulf coast east of the Mississippi River, Jefferson engaged in several schemes to establish American control over West Florida. In February 1804 Congress took the first step toward this objective by passing the Mobile Act. It authorized the president to exert jurisdiction over Mobile and set up customs controls on the bay, though this was Spanish territory. Protests from Madrid caused Jefferson to move the customs district inland to Fort Stoddard on the Mobile River, in American territory north of the 31st parallel. The following April President Jefferson sent Monroe to join Charles Cotesworth Pinckney, now American minister in Madrid, to persuade Spain to sell the Floridas. The timing seemed propitious, for Spain was allied with France in war against England. The two Americans sought East Florida and the Perdido River as the boundary of West Florida, but Spain was backed by France and refused to sell. In May 1805 Monroe and Pinckney proposed to Secretary of State Madison that the United States simply take the Floridas as indemnity for damage claims against Spain, stemming from the Quasi-War of the 1790s and its decision to close the port at New Orleans in 1802. In Jefferson's message to Congress in 1805 he tried to force Spain into an agreement by warning of the possible use of 300,000 soldiers.

Napoleon dropped his support for Spain's position on the Floridas when once again he needed money for the European wars. In 1805 he intimated to the United States that he might persuade Spain to sell the provinces for $7 million. Sensing the opportunity, the president convinced Congress in February 1806 to authorize a secret sum of $2 million to begin the process of acquiring the Floridas. But when the war shifted in Napoleon's favor, he withdrew the offer and the negotiations never got under way. The Jefferson administration had one more chance in January 1808, when Napoleon tried to draw the United States into the war against England in exchange for the Floridas. But French armies seized Spain, and he again changed his mind when his brother Joseph, occupying the Spanish throne, opposed giving them up. Jefferson's hopes for acquiring the Floridas ended when an insurrection in Spain was followed by similar uprisings in its New World colonies.

The Louisiana Purchase, even without West Florida, was of monumental importance. The United States had acquired 828,000 square miles of territory for three cents an acre. The negotiations had possibly prevented war with France and an alliance with England. The new territory had widened the agrarian base of the Republican party and deepened western loyalties to the Union. The purchase had established a pattern for acquiring territories and people. And, the questionable chapters in the Louisiana story did not dampen America's territorial drive, as witnessed by its continuing interest in acquiring West Florida. Some expansionists even interpreted the Louisiana Treaty to include Texas, which they saw as a stepping-stone toward California, Oregon, and the Pacific Ocean. The deal of 1803 was indicative of the Anglo-American tradition of absorbing territories by linking freedom with expansion.

Jefferson fostered American expansion in another important way. Less than a week after Monroe agreed to join Livingston in France, the president asked Congress to authorize an expedition by Meriwether Lewis and William Clark to explore the regions beyond the Mississippi River. Lewis and Clark departed in the spring of 1804 and returned more than two years later with a claim to the continental interior stretching from the Mississippi to the Pacific coast. Meanwhile Jefferson sent army Lieutenant Zebulon Pike on two explorations. In 1805–1806 Pike failed to locate the source of the Mississippi River, but returned with information on British influence in the surrounding area. He led another group southwest in 1806–7, ostensibly to find the headwaters of the Arkansas and Red rivers, but probably under secret orders to determine Spanish strength in northern Mexico. These three explorers established America's overland ties with the Pacific coast and the Spanish southwest, and helped to fulfill Jefferson's expansionist objectives in America. Meanwhile, by 1805, steadily worsening relations with England turned attention to Atlantic affairs.

DETERIORATING ANGLO–AMERICAN RELATIONS

Resumption of the Anglo-French war in 1803 involved the United States because of its commercial interests and because of its efforts to protect neutral rights at sea. British naval supremacy barred French and Spanish vessels from transporting goods to and from the Caribbean, and these two countries permitted Americans to take over the carrying trade. At first, in the early 1790s, Britain had sought to prevent this traffic by invoking the "Rule of 1756," which arbitrarily declared that ports closed in peacetime could not be opened in wartime. Since 1794, however, Britain had in effect waived the rule for American shippers by allowing the doctrine known as the "broken voyage" to open ports on the continent. According to this doctrine, if carrier commanders "broke" a voyage from French or Spanish islands in the Caribbean by paying duties or posting bond in an American port, they changed the status of the cargo to "neutral" or "American" before reexporting it to Europe. The British Admiralty Court confirmed the doctrine in the *Polly* decision in 1800. As a consequence, between the early 1790s and 1807, American exports increased fourfold and imports doubled. Even so, President Jefferson and Secretary of State Madison, not content with the flimsy protection of the broken voyage, wanted more: they insisted on the principle that "free ships make free goods."

Instead, they were about to get less. Upon the renewed outbreak of war, Royal Navy officers complained that America's trade with Britain's enemies was harming the British war effort and depriving their merchants of profits. Moreover, they claimed that Americans were using the doctrine of the broken voyage fraudulently by not actually removing cargo while in an American port and by receiving a refund or drawback on the duties substantiating the conversion of the goods.

The beginning of the end of America's "first rapprochement" with England came with the *Essex* decision of 1805, which attempted to rectify the problems of the broken voyage concept by reversing the *Polly* case. British naval commanders seized the *Essex*, an American merchant vessel out of Barcelona, Spain, as it moved toward Havana after "breaking" the voyage in Salem, Massachusetts. The British Admiralty Court ruled that mere claim of duty payment no longer proved that the voyage had been "broken." Evidence later showed that British suspicions were correct: the captain of the *Essex* had paid $5,278 in duties and received a refund of $5,080 before leaving for Havana. The stopover in Salem, the judge declared, had not "neutralized" the goods because the captain had not made a bona fide payment of duty. The voyage was "continuous" and a violation of the Rule of 1756 because its final destination was another enemy port.

The problems caused by the *Essex* case were attributable more to implementation of the decision than to the decision itself. Most nations recognized a belligerent's right to confirm a neutral's status and to search for contraband, but the special irritant here was that the government in London gave no advance notice that the *Essex* decision had changed policy. The Royal Navy was to take suspicious ships to Halifax, Nova Scotia, for trial by an admiralty court already infamous for confiscating cargo or delaying shipment. British commanders stopped American vessels carrying French or Spanish goods headed toward either the Caribbean or Europe. Their decision to station warships near America's ports constituted a virtual blockade that enraged Americans.

Other events in 1805 also signified that British policy had hardened toward neutrals. In October the navy, under Lord Admiral Horatio Nelson, defeated the combined French and Spanish fleets near Trafalgar and established British control of the seas; two months later the French armies rolled over Austrian and Russian forces at Austerlitz, leaving Napoleon in control of Europe. The war stalemated and the battle scene shifted to efforts to inflict injury by control of trade. On the same day of Nelson's victory, October 21, a pamphlet in London gained instant popularity by urging England to clamp down on maritime restrictions. Sir James Stephen, a lawyer specializing in admiralty matters and an acquaintance of several British political leaders, wrote *War in Disguise; Or, the Frauds of the*

Neutral Flags, which argued in behalf of the *Essex* decision and Britain's right to regulate the seas. Taxation, licensing, blockades, searches for contraband, impressment—*any* measures were justified to restrict neutral activity. The United States would not fight, Stephen insisted. Within a year the government in London used the *Essex* decision, Nelson's victory, and Stephen's ideas to try to shut off neutral trade to France.

The United States was soon caught between the belligerent powers. In May 1806 the British announced the first of a series of Orders-in-Council that proclaimed a blockade of Europe from Germany's Elbe River to the French town of Brest. Napoleon retaliated with the Berlin Decree, which declared British ports closed. Americans denounced both measures as "paper blockades" and in violation of international law. Early the following year the British announced two more Orders-in-Council which ruled that trade carriers had to stop in England and pay duties on cargo before entering French ports. Napoleon countered with the Milan Decree of December, which warned that anyone submitting to Britain's rules would become a "British" possession subject to capture. His "Continental System" did not close all European ports, for Spain, Sweden, and Russia kept trade lanes open; but from 1807 to 1812 the French captured more American vessels than did the British. Thus the British confiscated those ships not abiding by the rules, while the French seized those who did. Europe was a "great madhouse," moaned President Jefferson.

England's supremacy at sea made it the main object of America's complaints. The Royal Navy patrolled American waters and met American protests with ill-concealed arrogance, whereas the French could only stop ships in their ports or in the Caribbean; and besides, though they never paid reparations, the French usually implied that they were going to do so by apologizing for their seizures as "mistakes." England's licensing system was an affront to neutral rights, which Americans only grudgingly accepted because they profited from the sale of goods to the British Isles.

After 1803 Britain's return to impressment became the most emotional issue between the Atlantic nations. Desertions from the Royal Navy increased as the war progressed; by 1801, Nelson reported, 42,000 sailors had jumped ship. Many publicly denounced their officers and encouraged British impressment gangs to be less discriminating in rounding up runaways. Abominable working conditions, wretched food, and miserable wages drove nearly 2,500 a year from British ranks. Many signed with American ships because treatment on board was more humane and wages far higher than on English vessels. Between 1793 and 1812 British commanders impressed nearly 10,000 seamen from American vessels, 6,000 of whom came after 1808. Many were native Americans. The London government claimed that by 1812, 20,000 of its people were on American ships, about half the total on their rolls. The Royal Navy needed 10,000 additional men a year. A British commander had declared in 1797: "It is my duty to keep my Ship manned, and I will do so wherever I find men that speak the same language with me." Americans offered to bar British deserters from American vessels in wartime in exchange for the renunciation of impressment. The British refused.

The impressment issue was complex. Few questioned Britain's right to stop desertions, but America claimed that its naturalization process for granting citizenship protected former Englishmen from capture. The British argued for perpetual allegiance—"Once an Englishman always an Englishman"—which meant that a person born in England could not change citizenship. Impressment, they declared, was a prerogative of the crown built upon common law and supported by acts of Parliament. Jefferson disagreed. "I hold the right of expatriation [renunciation of allegiance] to be inherent in every man by the laws of nature."

Some enterprising Americans exacerbated the situation by falsifying naturalization or "protection" papers and selling them for a small price. Britain's First Lord of the Admiralty, Lord St. Vincent, complained that "every Englishman . . . may be made an American for a dollar." Deserters bribed American consuls and others in responsible positions and received bogus citizenship papers in return. The British never claimed the right to remove natural-born Americans, but refused to recognize naturalized Americans and made mistakes in distinguishing between Englishmen and native Americans. These mistakes, Americans bitterly declared, were often in proportion to the number of men needed to fit the British ship in question. The British offered to free those captives who could prove they were bona fide Americans, but such a process required time and included no provision for reparation.

The question of sovereignty was central to the impressment controversy. Americans believed that their ships were an extension of their country, protected by the flag overhead. Madison considered "a neutral flag on the high seas as a safeguard to those sailing under it." To this assertion, British Foreign Secretary Lord Harrowby replied in 1804 that the "pretension advanced by Mr. Madison that the American flag should protect every individual sailing under it on board of a merchant ship is too extravagant to require any serious refutation." The British denied that this doctrine applied to private vessels, and claimed the right to visit and search on the seas. Sovereignty rested in *naval* vessels, they admitted, but a merchant ship was not a piece of American territory simply because it flew the American flag.

The two opposing arguments were nonnegotiable because of what was involved on each side. The British regarded it as a matter of vital national interests: renunciation of impressment would invite desertions, threaten supremacy at sea, and jeopardize the war effort with France. The Americans saw it as a matter of national integrity: impressment of either naturalized or native Americans was an infringement of the flag and sovereignty and a demeaning of national honor. Had Americans been willing to accept something less than renunciation of the practice—perhaps Britain's adoption of extreme precautionary measures to prevent mistakes and indemnification for those made—they might have resolved the issue. Had the British been amenable to American assurances that deserters would not be welcome on merchant vessels, the two parties might have found grounds for settlement. But each side distrusted the other. British commanders eventually gave up trying to distinguish between native Americans and sailors born in England. They regarded all naturalization papers as forged or illegal under British law and arbitrarily selected those seamen deemed traitors and fit for duty. Mistakes occurred, and even when evidence convinced the British Foreign Office that American citizens had been victimized, no reparation was available upon their release.

JEFFERSON'S POLICIES

In 1801 President Jefferson wrote that American economic pressure would force England and France to respect neutral rights. "Our commerce is so valuable to them that they will be glad to purchase it when the only price we ask is to do us justice. I believe we have in our hands the means of peaceable coercion." In truth, Jefferson's only choice was economic. His desire to cut taxes had restricted the navy to small, single-gun ships which were expected to safeguard the Atlantic coast. Gunboats, he wrote, were the "only *water* defense which can be useful to us, and protect us from the ruinous folly of a navy." He considered drydocking ships-of-war near Washington, and in times of crisis replacing them with gunboats manned by voluntary militia. The results of Jefferson's economic measures were evident in the country's lack of military and naval power. Commercial pressures were of little value without military leverage; gunboats were no match against warships.

The lack of military strength highlighted two other shortcomings in Jefferson's policy. America's trade was *not* vital to England, as Jefferson thought, and Americans were in no mood to make sacrifices for the administration's economic policies. Successful negotiations depended upon military and economic strength. Power without willingness to negotiate leads to tyranny, while negotiations with no means of support lead to protracted discussions that can bring frustration, defeat, and ultimately war. Jefferson's policies pointed toward the latter course.

In late 1806 Jefferson turned to a special mission to resolve maritime difficulties with England, when he sent Maryland attorney William Pinkney to join Minister James Monroe in London. Congress had passed a nonimportation act the previous April, calling for restrictions on specified British goods after November 1, but the president withheld its implementation pending negotiations with England. Monroe and Pinkney had instructions impossible to fulfill. The president and Madison wanted England to renounce impressment and to renew the maritime provisions in Jay's Treaty, due to expire in October 1807. Neither objective was possible in wartime.

In the negotiations, Pinkney and Monroe proved more flexible than their superiors in Washington. They gave up the principle of "free ships, free goods" in exchange for relaxed enforcement of the Rule of 1756. Britain assured a return to the broken voyage concept of the *Polly* decision and agreed to permit American ships into French ports if they first entered a home port of the United States. Foodstuffs were exempted from contraband, England allowed American ships to pass into European ports not under blockade, and the United States agreed to end nonimportation for a ten-year period. Negotiations over impressment were less promising. Britain agreed only to attach a note to the treaty which pledged greater care in removing seamen and assured reparation for injuries. In practice these expedients would have alleviated the problem; in theory they did not. Monroe and Pinkney signed the treaty on December 31, 1806 and forwarded it to the president, who refused to send it to the Senate because the terms included no disavowal of impressment. Thus the impressment question ended the possibility of a treaty settlement and soon became the central issue in Anglo-American relations.

On June 22, 1807, America seemed headed for war when a crisis occurred that Jefferson considered the most serious since Lexington. An American naval vessel, the frigate *Chesapeake*, was en route from Norfolk to the Mediterranean. Its commodore, James Barron, had been in a hurry to leave the United States and had not prepared his guns or crew for action. The men were not at battle stations and the gun deck was strewn with naval stores to be put away while at sea. Ten miles off the Virginia shore, near Cape Henry, Captain Salusbury P. Humphreys of the British frigate *Leopard* signaled the *Chesapeake* for a request. Would the Americans be willing to carry diplomatic correspondence to the Mediterranean? Barron agreed to the request but did not follow the prescribed naval procedure of readying his men for battle when moving alongside a foreign ship-of-war.

A British officer boarded the *Chesapeake* and asked permission to search for and remove deserters, in pursuance of orders from Vice Admiral George C. Berkeley in Halifax. The 375-man crew of the *Chesapeake* included a number of Englishmen, or so rumor claimed. In fact, the previous February, some crew members from a British ship had escaped into Virginia and signed on board the American ship. Barron refused to permit the search.

Before Barron could prepare his men for action after the British officer's return to the *Leopard*, Captain Humphreys ordered three broadsides fired into the *Chesapeake*. The Americans managed a single return shot, but within ten minutes their ship lay helpless, three men dead and eighteen wounded, including Captain Barron. Surrender followed, and British sailors came aboard and seized four deserters, three of whom were native Americans.

The British had impressed Americans from a *naval* vessel, and the result was explosive. They had searched naval vessels before. In 1798 the British had stopped the *Baltimore* near Havana, and in 1805 they had searched a gunboat and removed three deserters. But when the *Chesapeake* limped back into Norfolk, a mob called for revenge and angrily destroyed a huge supply of water headed for British sailors in Lynnhaven Bay. President Jefferson could have had a declaration of war from Congress, but the military weakness of the United States precluded such a request. He convened his cabinet and proclaimed that despite Jay's Treaty, Britain could no longer use American ports for provisioning. He asked the states' governors for 100,000 militia, and prepared the army and navy to defend the coast. These actions were smoke and not fire, however, for he did not call Congress into session until October, nearly four months after the *Chesapeake* affair. Jefferson demanded an apology from England and informed the French minister in Washington that if the British made no reparations, the United States would seize Canada. Independence and honor were at stake, declared Secretary of the Treasury Gallatin.

Given America's military weakness, Jefferson's only recourse was what he had termed "peaceable coercion." Britain's minister in Washington, David Erskine, warned his London office of the widespread anger in the United States and the British appeared ready to apologize, but not to renounce impressment. They recognized that Captain Humphreys of the *Leopard* had overstepped bounds, and they seemed amenable to removing him from command, returning the impressed Americans, making reparations, and agreeing to leave American warships alone. But most of these concessions came years afterward—too late to atone for this violation of national honor.

On December 22, 1807, after Jefferson implemented nonimportation, Congress replaced it with a stronger measure called the Embargo Act. It closed America's ports to foreign vessels and restricted American ships to the coastal trade. Madison explained: "We send necessities to her [England]. She sends superfluities to us. Our products they must have. Theirs, however promotive of our comfort, we can to a considerable degree do without." The Jefferson administration authorized the confiscation of cargo and ships involved in illicit trade, required government approval before loading goods, and stipulated that captains involved in the coastal trade had to post bond twice the value of their cargoes to guarantee compliance with the law. By the following year the country's outgoing goods were a fifth of what they had been before the act, while goods from England dropped more than half.

These police measures failed. Shippers accused of breaking the law were usually released, especially by New England courts where jurors disliked the administration's policies. Jefferson had called for a national sacrifice without instilling a sense of patriotic duty. Bitter denunciation of the Embargo Act came from New Englanders, whose commercial prosperity had declined at the hands of a Republican administration, and some were talking of secession. Such behavior was treason, complained Jefferson, author of the Declaration of Independence and the Virginia Resolutions. Americans disregarded the embargo as smugglers sold goods in Spanish Florida, took them across Lake Champlain or overland into Canada (subsequently declared illegal), and claimed that winds had blown their ships off course into Canada or the West Indies, and even to Europe.

The Embargo Act threatened to revive the Federalist party. To dramatize the situation, Federalists in Boston exaggerated the hardships by building soup kitchens for starving sailors. They accused the president of taking sides with the French. The Embargo Act was unconstitutional, they claimed, because the government could only regulate trade, not stop it. They argued that the measure augmented Napoleon's Continental System by preventing American merchants from carrying goods to Europe. The South and West, Republican strongholds, did not protest as hotly because the British blockade had hurt their trade and economic retaliation seemed appropriate.

The Federalists were correct in their assessments: the Embargo Act damaged America more than England. In the United States, foreign commerce virtually came to a halt as businesses shut down, seamen lost their jobs, prices for manufactured goods soared, and farmers who relied on the export trade were ruined. The act hurt British manufacturers who imported American cotton and tobacco, but British merchants took over America's carrying trade with the Continent. They sold products to Spain, whose people had rebelled against Napoleon, and to its colonies in Latin America. The embargo did damage to the British West Indies and Newfoundland, both dependent upon American foodstuffs, and the lack of American cotton forced some English textile mills to close. But the effects on British ruling circles were not sufficient to change maritime policy. Those in England who suffered most lacked the franchise and had no influence on the government. The harvest of 1808 was plentiful and helped to offset food problems caused by the embargo. Jefferson believed the act stimulated American manufacturing by reducing dependence on English goods. Doubt exists about this assertion. Albert Gallatin's *Report on American Manufacturers* in 1810 admitted that money went into industry, but warned that the public outcry against the administration and the costs in unemployment and trade outweighed any impetus to manufacturing. Evidence suggests that American manufacturing would have grown faster without the Embargo Act.

Napoleon welcomed the act because it hurt England and caused Anglo-American difficulties. In April 1808 he ordered the capture of vessels under American colors found in French ports, on the specious ground that they had to be British because of the embargo. By mid–1809 the French had seized $10 million of American ships and goods. A Massachusetts Federalist disgustedly declared: "Mr. Jefferson has imposed an embargo to please France and to beggar us!"

Had the embargo remained in effect a while longer, rising food prices and declining industrial sales might have forced the British to reconsider their maritime policy. But Americans were in no mood for sacrifice and demanded its repeal.

The Embargo Act, strange to say, was both idealistic and realistic in conception. To be sure, it was idealistic to expect Americans to support their government's wishes if such an act meant compliance with a self-destructive law, and it was a miscalculation to hope that England would feel its effects before the United States did. While the ports of other nations were open to British merchants, the president expected Americans to shut out *all* foreign trade. And yet the act had realistic undertones in that Jefferson had no alternative to economic pressure. His longtime opposition to armed force dictated peaceful measures, for his other choice was submission. Had it been possible to limit the embargo to England and France, he might have eased the financial burden on American merchants, focused grievances on British (and French) infractions of neutral rights, and inspired loyalty to government policy. Had violations continued, the United States might then have scaled its restrictions upward. Anything was wiser than asking Americans to accept a policy more harmful to them than to those the act intended to coerce. The embargo bought time for the United States by keeping it out of the European war, but time is valuable only if those in power use it to advantage.

On March 1, 1809, three days before Madison became president, Congress replaced the embargo with the Nonintercourse Act. It opened the export trade with all countries except England and France, but provided that if either nation offered to respect America's rights at sea, trade would resume with it immediately. That scarcely improved the situation, since most of America's commerce was with the two countries at war, and the United States was still caught between them. Thus Jefferson's legacy for Madison was nearly certain war with England.

Selected readings

Adams, Henry, *History of the United States during the Administrations of Jefferson and Madison*. 9 vols. 1889–91.

Brant, Irving, *James Madison: Secretary of State, 1800–1809*. 1953.

Burt, Alfred L., *The United States, Great Britain and British North America*. 1940.

DeConde, Alexander, *This Affair of Louisiana*. 1976.

Egan, Clifford L., *Neither Peace nor War: Franco-American Relations, 1803–1812*. 1983.

Kaplan, Lawrence S., *Jefferson and France: An Essay on Politics and Political Ideas*. 1967.

Lyon, E. Wilson, *Louisiana in French Diplomacy, 1759–1804*. 1934.

McDonald, Forrest, *The Presidency of Thomas Jefferson*. 1976.

Malone, Dumas, *Jefferson the President: First Term, 1801–1805*. 1970.

———, *Jefferson the President: Second Term, 1805–1809*. 1974.

Mannix, Richard, "Gallatin, Jefferson, and the Embargo of 1808," *Diplomatic History* 3 (1979): 151–72.

Perkins, Bradford, *The First Rapprochement: England and the United States, 1795–1805*. 1955.

———, *Prologue to War: England and the United States, 1805–1812*. 1961.

Sears, Louis M., *Jefferson and the Embargo*. 1927.

Smelser, Marshall. *The Democratic Republic: 1801–1815*. 1968.

Spivak, Burton, *Jefferson's English Crisis: Commerce, Embargo, and the Republican Revolution*. 1979.

Varg, Paul A., *Foreign Policies of the Founding Fathers*. 1963.

———, *New England and Foreign Relations, 1789–1850*. 1983.

Walters, Raymond, Jr., *Albert Gallatin: Jeffersonian Financier and Diplomat*. 1957.

Whitaker, Arthur P., *The Mississippi Question, 1795–1803*. 1934.

White, Leonard D., *The Jeffersonians: A Study in Administrative History, 1801–1829*. 1951.

Chapter Four

Anglo-American Difficulties and the War of 1812, 1809–1817

Historians have disagreed over the causes of the War of 1812 with England, but many have found a unifying theme in the defense of national honor. In a real sense it was America's "Second War for Independence," because the new republic was still trying to convince other countries (especially England) that it deserved a respected place in the family of nations. Disputes developed over maritime matters—impressment, search, paper blockades, freedom of the seas—expansion into Canada and the Floridas, and Indian troubles along the frontier; bitter rivalries existed over the relationship between internal political direction of the country and international affairs. But the basic issue was America's desire to protect the republic against external and internal peril. In 1812 Republicans under President James Madison believed the United States was in danger of collapse. As Madison saw things, the country had only two options: submit to Britain's violations of America's rights, and lose the people's support to Federalists who were determined to subvert republicanism in favor of a monarchical form of government; or go to war to protect liberty at home and abroad, but at the risk of almost certain defeat. The Madison administration chose the latter course.

MADISON'S POLICIES

Madison's inauguration as president in March 1809 seemed to indicate that American foreign policy would continue to be as irresolute as it had been under Jefferson. Despite his keen intellect and stubborn will, Madi-

James Madison

President of the United States for two terms, he was commander-in-chief of American forces during the War of 1812. (T. Sully del/D. Edwin, ca. 1810; Library of Congress)

son was an unimpressive figure of a man—five-feet-four-inches tall, a scant hundred pounds in weight, self-effacing and seemingly indecisive. His vivacious wife, Dolley, was a head taller and called him "my darling little husband"; the writer-diplomat Washington Irving referred to him as "poor Jemmy" and "a withered little apple-john." Moreover, Madison owed his election to the Republican party caucus and the state party organizations, and was bound to the party's "resistance-far-short-of-war" position. His Federalist opponents, for their part, appeared willing to capitulate to British pressure. Thus it seemed unlikely that Madison would change America's policy toward Britain unless the frustrations bequeathed by Jefferson continued to mount, leaving as the only choice either abject submission or war. Appearances, however, were deceiving: but for the arrival of a new British minister, Madison might have been ready to go to war in 1809. Indeed, some months before taking office he declared that as president he would call Congress into special session "with an understanding that War will then be the proper course, if no immediate change abroad shall render it unnecessary." But then the new president was encouraged about prospects for peace by Britain's new minister to the United States, David Erskine, who was married to an American and had friends there. Erskine opposed war and suggested that his government drop the Orders-in-Council in exchange for America's maintaining the Nonintercourse Act only against France. Under certain conditions British Foreign Minister George Canning was amenable. He required the United States to reopen trade with Britain, adhere to the Rule of 1756, and permit the Royal Navy to help America enforce the Nonintercourse Act against France. Canning even spoke of settling the *Chesapeake* affair with an "honorable reparation for the aggression."

Canning's stipulations were impossible and Erskine knew it. Britain's participation in enforcing the Nonintercourse Act would imply American subservience to the mother country because British warships would be capturing American vessels trading with France. Erskine disregarded his instructions and in April worked out a pact with Secretary of State Robert Smith—without incorporating Canning's restrictions. Madison announced the end of the Nonintercourse Act against Britain on June 10, the day Parliament was to repeal the Orders-in-Council, and nearly 600 American ships left for England as the Erskine Agreement went into effect.

The celebration was short. Canning read the agreement, denounced Erskine as a "Scotch flunkey," called him home in disgrace, and repudiated the agreement, though he did allow American ships already at sea to enter English ports. Madison, feeling tricked and embarrassed, reinstated the Nonintercourse Act against Britain on August 9. An angry national mood prevailed. Americans thought the foreign minister's actions confirmed his well-known animosity for the United States, for they did not realize that Erskine had violated his instructions. Negotiations over the *Chesapeake* came to an end, and disillusionment and bitterness characterized Anglo-American relations afterward.

Relations with England further deteriorated when Canning replaced Erskine with Francis James Jackson. Nicknamed "Copenhagen" because of his earlier participation in Britain's destruction of Denmark's navy and bombardment of its capital city, Jackson lacked Erskine's calm and trusting manner and quickly alienated nearly everyone in Washington. He arrived in Boston in September 1809 with eighteen servants and a wife who was an arrogant Prussian baroness, and he indiscreetly visited leading Federalists on his way to Washington. His contempt for Americans was undisguised. The president was a "rather mean-looking man," Dolley was "fat and forty, but not fair," and Americans were "all alike, except that some few are less knaves than others." He referred to Erskine as a "fool" for negotiating the treaty and implied that President Madison was a liar for denying having known of Canning's conditions for an agreement. Jackson received a number of threatening letters and in April 1810 Madison demanded that he be recalled, which he was, but not until the end of the period for which he had been paid. Jackson returned home with honor, and the British waited almost a year to send a successor.

Relations with France were likewise on the verge of collapse. Napoleon complained that the Nonintercourse Act discriminated against the French, and countered with two additional decrees—both announcing the resumption of seizures of American ships in French harbors. The second decree, the Rambouillet Decree of March 1810, ultimately led to the confiscation of $10 million of American possessions and the imprisonment of hundreds of American seamen.

When the Nonintercourse Act expired in early 1810, Congress followed with an unusual measure called Macon's Bill Number Two. The first effort at a new approach had failed to pass Congress. It would have allowed American trading vessels to enter any port, while keeping American harbors closed to Britain and France until one of them terminated its maritime restrictions. But by 1810 few British vessels entered American waters and no French ships did. The alternative, Number Two, went into effect on May 1, 1810. It opened America's trade with all nations but stipulated that if either Britain or France agreed to recognize America's neutral rights at sea, the president could then reinstate the Nonintercourse Act against the other, after a three-month period of grace.

The Madison administration's attempt at European-style diplomacy resulted in an unorthodox approach to foreign policy that is almost as difficult to explain as it was to implement. The measure was ill-advised because in an effort to preserve American honor it clumsily smacked of extortion. Worse, it opened the door for Napoleon. He considered Macon's Bill Number Two a capitulation to England because its navy controlled the seas and any concessions under the law could come only from London. He had nothing to offer—unless he could convince Madison that he had ended French restrictions on American shipping. In so doing, Napoleon could determine whether the president was serious.

Napoleon in August 1810 directed his foreign minister, the Duc de Cadore, to inform the American minister in Paris that he would repeal the Berlin and Milan decrees against the United States if Americans "shall cause their rights to be respected by the English." Napoleon stipulated that either the British must repeal their Orders or the United States must force them to respect America's rights at sea. Either way he won. Repeal of the Orders would open the sea lanes for American commerce—even those leading to France. Nonrepeal would mean war with England and by implication an alliance with France. Napoleon concluded with a transparent attempt at flattery that in less trying times would have received the inattention it deserved: "His Majesty loves the Americans. Their prosperity and their commerce are within the scope of his policy. The independence of America is one of the principal titles of glory to France." On November 2 Napoleon announced that his government would end its restrictions on American shipping.

The president was not fooled by Napoleon's assurance and more than likely used it to justify a decision already made. He waited the promised three months before reimposing the Nonintercourse Act against Britain on February 2, 1811. The British complained that Napoleon had lied. Indeed, the French were shrewd. Seizures by the Royal Navy totaled more than 900 from 1803 to 1812; French violations numbered 560. But after the episode involving the Cadore letter, the number of incidents dropped dramatically to 34. The new secretary of state, James Monroe, denounced Britain for trying to control American trade and defame its honor. Retaliatory action was in order. Perhaps Madison acted hastily, for Napoleon had not halted all confiscations of American ships. But one must note that the president did not like Macon's Bill because it surrendered control over American trade to England. The Cadore letter permitted a way out. Madison used Napoleon's duplicity as leverage to persuade England to retract the Orders-in-Council. He informed his attorney general that the Cadore letter provided an opportunity to escape either a "mortifying peace" or war with England *and* France. England could rescind the Orders or accept the possibility of war with the United States. In February 1811, when the Nonintercourse Act went back into effect against England, America's minister in London, William Pinkney, returned home after five years of frustration.

Within three months another Anglo-American crisis developed at sea. In the evening hours of May 16, 1811, the American frigate *President* came upon a smaller British ship, the *Little Belt,* near the Virginia capes. Someone fired a shot, the origin of which is uncertain. Americans suddenly found an outlet for their pent-up emotions over the *Chesapeake* and other violations of honor. When the firing stopped, the *Little Belt* lay barely afloat with nine dead and twenty-three wounded. Only one American was injured in the fray, and it appeared that the United States had atoned for the *Chesapeake*.

Though many Englishmen talked of war, London's major concerns were its own domestic crises and Napoleon, and hopes for peace lay in a new minister en route to the United States, Augustus Foster. He arrived in Washington during the summer of 1811 prepared to make belated indemnification for the *Chesapeake*, but found Americans preoccupied with the *Little Belt* affair and talking of seizing Canada. Foster did not understand that the president's warnings about British behavior were sincere and that war was a possibility. He befriended the Federalists, repeated that Napoleon had not revoked his decrees, and demanded that the United States reopen trade with his country. Monroe defended Napoleon and demanded that London repeal the Orders-in-Council. Neither gave in. Foster secured the return of two of the three Americans impressed from the *Chesapeake* (the other had died in jail), and arranged for reparations. Americans considered these gestures to be too little and too late, and grew increasingly incensed that the British did not take their grievances seriously.

At this crucial juncture in Anglo-American relations, several events forced the British to concentrate on internal affairs. Near the end of 1810 King George III went insane after his favorite child died, and a drawn-out political controversy developed over the rise to power of the prince regent. During the summer of 1812 shock again swept the nation when an assassin killed Prime Minister Spencer Perceval in the lobby of the House of Commons. The British government postponed the long-planned parliamentary discussion over repeal of the Orders. Signs were apparent throughout England that the ministry was moving unsteadily toward ending maritime restrictions on America, but Pinkney's departure and a poor understanding of Britain's mood by the American chargé in London led the Madison administration to believe that it should prepare to defend the nation's honor.

Meanwhile, the elections of 1810 in the United States had brought to Congress a young and outspoken group of nationalists who picked up the name "War Hawks." Among them were Henry Clay of Kentucky (by 1812 speaker of the House of Representatives), John C. Calhoun of South Carolina, and Felix Grundy of Tennessee. They were not warmongers as such, but like many Americans they were angered by British insults and considered war the only alternative to humiliation. Clay valued the "honor and independence of the country" above an "ignominious peace." He asked, "What nation, what individual was ever taught in the schools of ignominious submission, the patriotic lessons of freedom and independence?"

Another problem was that many Americans believed the British were inciting the Indians of the Northwest to resist American migration to the area. Crown officials in Canada kept the Indians supplied in case of an American attack on the province. But if the British policy was defensive, a fine line existed between providing Indians with matériel for defense and expecting them not to use it for halting American expansion. Americans interpreted British involvement as an effort to stir the Indians against them. Two Shawnee brothers, Tecumseh and Tenskwautawa (known as the Prophet), organized an Indian confederacy throughout the vast region between the Appalachians and the Mississippi River to stop white expansion into the Ohio Valley. Americans attributed these frontier problems to the British, who, according to popular belief, were paying bounties to the Indians for the scalps of white people. The British actually wanted to avert war between Indians and whites and tried to buy the Indians' allegiance with nonmilitary gifts. But the frontier was alive with rumor. In 1809 Governor William Henry Harrison of the Indiana Territory, using whisky and vague land markings, secured treaties with the Indians that opened 3 million acres of land to Americans and pushed the Indians to the Wabash River. When Tecumseh asked Harrison to return the land, the governor refused.

The long-expected battle began when Harrison led a thousand men to the capital of the Indian confederacy at Prophetstown, a village where Tippecanoe Creek empties into the Wabash River near present-day Lafayette, Indiana. At dawn on November 7, 1811, the Indians, without Tecumseh (who was then in the South), attacked the encamped American force. Harrison barely won the Battle of Tippecanoe, but his men inflicted numerous Indian casualties. Retreating Indians left weapons on the battlefield that bore the British monogram.

News of the Battle of Tippecanoe ignited Americans. A Kentucky newspaper called the Indian war along the Wabash "purely British," and Andrew Jackson sought to avenge the bloodletting caused by "the secret agents of Britain." Canada was headquarters for Britain and the objective of their anger, for the American navy was too weak to challenge England at sea. Matthew Clay of Virginia declared: "We have the Canadas as much under our command as she [England] has the ocean; and the way to conquer her on the ocean is to drive her from the land." Some Americans talked about taking Florida, for it belonged to Britain's ally Spain, and provided refuge for Indians who had attacked Americans in the South. Besides, Britain might use Florida as a base of operations against the United States. Henry Clay agreed with Jefferson that taking Canada was "a mere matter of marching." Its acquisition would further American control of the fur trade with the Indians, provide access to the St. Lawrence River, furnish farmland, end troubles with the Indians, and rid the continent of England. Some western Americans believed that Canada could serve as a "hostage" for forcing the British to leave the Indians alone and to relax maritime restrictions. Shortly after the Battle of Tippecanoe, Monroe told Congress: "Gentlemen, *we must fight*. We are forever disgraced if we do not."

The president emphasized in his annual message of November 1811 that his concern was to maintain national honor. London's maritime restrictions had "the effect of war on our lawful commerce" and violated "rights which no independent nation can relinquish." Moreover, Americans considered the Orders-in-Council only the *symbol* of Britain's willingness to trample their flag and national honor. The British had to change their attitude toward the United States. Furthermore, President Madison had paid a British secret agent $50,000 for a packet of letters which allegedly proved British collusion with the Federalists of New England. Though the charges were unfounded, Madison further inflamed emotions by releasing the letters to the public in March. The following month he proposed a sixty-day embargo on all ships in port, an action normally considered preparatory to war. Congress extended the embargo to ninety days.

Ironically, though the administration in Washington did not know because it had no minister in London, America's economic policies were just then beginning to have their desired effect in England, and succeeding events proved Jefferson and Madison correct in arguing that economic coercion would ultimately have forced repeal of the Orders-in-Council. Depression hit England by the spring of 1812, and the combination of poor grain yields, threatened mob action, and the Nonintercourse Act caused British manufacturers to push for reopening trade with the United States. In Birmingham a petition fifty feet long and bearing 20,000 signatures urged revisions in maritime policies. The groups which had previously backed the maritime laws—shippers and planters with interests in the West Indies—were now among those urging repeal.

In April 1812 the London government declared that it would repeal the Orders-in-Council if the French rescinded the Berlin and Milan decrees. Within a month the American minister to Paris, poet Joel Barlow, received a copy of a decree from the French foreign minister asserting that Napoleon had dropped the decrees more than a year and a half earlier. The date on the new decree from St. Cloud was April 28, 1811. The paper was a fake and Barlow knew it. But he used it to persuade the British to withdraw the Orders-in-Council. The new foreign minister in London, Lord Castlereagh, favored better relations with the United States and informed Parliament on June 16, 1812, that his government had suspended the Orders as they applied to the United States. Back in Washington the day before, another sign appeared that Britain was easing its policy. The British minister informed the Madison administration: "If you can at any time produce a full and unconditional repeal of the French decrees . . . we shall be ready to meet you with a revocation of the Orders-in-Council."

But it was too late: Congress had already declared war on Great Britain on June 18. Lack of speedy communications permitted this seemingly bizarre situation, but the causes of America's decision went beyond the Orders-in-Council. The British expected Madison to suspend the move for war due to repeal of the Orders, but he refused to do so because impressment and other trespasses upon the nation's honor remained. The causes of the War of 1812 were evident in the president's message to Congress on June 1. Violations of America's rights at sea dominated the grievances, and impressment headed the list. Madison declared that Americans had been "dragged on board ships of war of a foreign nation" and forced to fight for their "oppressors." Confiscation of American goods and the proclamation of paper blockades infringed upon America's maritime freedoms. The Orders-in-Council were attempts to monopolize the ocean lanes for British merchants. Madison closed with a denunciation of the British for inciting the Indians along the frontier. In a private communication the president emphasized that America went to war to protect its sovereignty.

Disputes still continue over the causes of the War of 1812. Some writers note that Madison's emphasis on maritime factors did not coincide with the pattern of voting in Congress: those for war were almost exclusively Republicans from the agrarian West and South, while all Federalists in the mercantile New England and Middle Atlantic states were opposed. This apparent paradox is capable of explanation: British naval actions hurt western and southern grain and cotton sales and brought a depression in agriculture, while commercial interests profited from the wartime trade despite British restrictions. The voting distribution roughly corresponded with that of the presidential election of 1812. Madison's 128 electoral votes came primarily from the West and South (and Pennsylvania, whose resi-

dents were concerned about national honor and the welfare of the Republican party), while Federalist DeWitt Clinton's 89 votes came from the
commercial New England and Middle Atlantic states. Federalists accused
westerners and southerners of entering an arrangement whereby they
would maintain political control in Congress by securing Canada for the
West and Florida for the South. But no evidence has appeared to support
this allegation, and it seems more likely that those concerned about these
areas wanted to use them to force England to stop insulting American
honor. British infractions at sea hurt the United States economically, but
the thread holding Americans together was widespread concern for their
nation's sovereignty.

Americans came close to declaring war on France also. The Senate argued for days before the Federalists failed by two votes in their move to
bring about a joint declaration of war on both England and France. Some
members of the opposition explained that they wanted to fight the belligerents one at a time and that France would be next after England's defeat.
The Federalists' accusations that Madison had worked with Napoleon in
pushing for war with England were unsubstantiated; Jefferson explained
that the British were a more immediate danger to America's integrity than
the French. Only the Royal Navy had patrolled within American waters
and helped bring on American deaths. Only the British had stirred the
Indians into taking American lives. Only Britain's attitude was conde-
scending. Another factor was important. President Madison realized that
the United States could have help from France without having to reciprocate. Napoleon would open ports to Americans and furnish free protection against the British.

America's second war with the mother country comprised another
chapter in the long struggle between England and France. The English
were concerned about Napoleon and incensed that Americans did not
recognize the evil in Paris. At the moment of America's entry into the European war, the French were sending over half a million men into Russia,
and England was preparing for the final phase of the war. The American
theater was thus peripheral to the grand scheme of the European war.
The United States nonetheless had to establish its place in the world and
to safeguard its share of the hemisphere from European intervention.

On another level, the war with England threatened the nation by endangering the republican form of government as well as the American political party system at home. The Jeffersonians' political experiences in the
past decade had convinced them that the Federalists intended to undercut
the Republican party, disrupt republicanism, and establish a monarchical
government. Perhaps Jefferson and Madison used the threat for political
gain, but many Americans feared that the republican experiment would
collapse if the nation did not preserve the Republican party by safeguarding national honor. As Jefferson and Madison saw it, national honor and
the Republican party were inseparable, and the existence of the United
States as an independent republic was at stake. The choice was submis-

sion to England and the return of the Federalists to power, or war with England and the salvation of America from mother country and Federalists. War was the only alternative to a return to colonial status.

It was an unusual time in America's history, for politics had become synonymous with national destiny. The ideal meshed with reality, and the Madison administration chose war.

WAR

The War of 1812 was widely unpopular among Federalists and their supporters in the United States. Opposition was so strong in New England that Americans loaned money to the enemy, aided British soldiers as they invaded the country, and traded with Canada and England during the war. Commanders of the Royal Navy reciprocated by looking the other way as merchant vessels broke the blockade and headed toward London or Liverpool, and the government in London avoided actions that could alienate the northern states. Federalists called it "Mr. Madison's War," accused Virginia of conspiring to destroy New England, and talked of secession. Strife was so severe that during the controversy over the war declaration in the summer of 1812, a mob of Madison's supporters stormed a gathering of Federalists in Baltimore and killed and mutilated a number of them.

The Madison administration faced immense problems in raising money and an army. The charter for the Bank of the United States had been allowed to expire in 1811, and state banks were unable to handle wartime needs. Congress raised the tariff and levied taxes on states and individuals, but still had to borrow by issuing treasury notes and bonds. The effects of Jefferson's military cutbacks became apparent in the early stages of the war. The army's rolls included 35,000 names, yet those in the field numbered no more than 10,000, many untrained and spread along the frontier. The United States was not able to field its full force of 35,000 men until 1814. American officers were inept. Few capable leaders appeared until Generals Jacob Brown, Winfield Scott, and Andrew Jackson came along late in the war. Of 700,000 state militiamen supposedly ready for action, only 10,000 responded to the president's call for 100,000 in 1812. Many refused to fight outside their home states and hardly any considered leaving the country. Taking Canada and Florida became less important than preventing the British from taking the United States.

Yet the popular cry for expansion prodded the American army into a series of attacks on Canada during the summer of 1812. President Madison favored a drive to Montreal, which could have broken Britain's water connection between the St. Lawrence River and the Great Lakes and endangered its holdings in North America. But Americans were unable to amass such an assault. Invasion attempts through Lake Champlain, Niagara, and Detroit ended in the surrender of two American armies because of incompetent military leadership and the refusal of militias to fight.

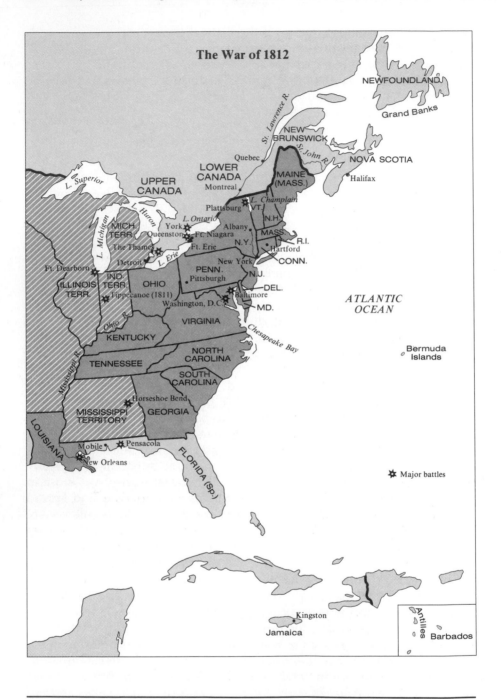

MAP 5

Though the war ended in a stalemate, the United States could claim a victory in that it had overcome both internal and external perils to stay intact.

General William Hull briefly took part of Canada when he headed beyond Detroit, but he lost his belongings and private papers to the British during the march, which cost him his rank and almost cost him his life afterward. The governor of Upper Canada, General Isaac Brock, allied with Tecumseh to force Hull's surrender in Detroit in August. Court-martialed and sentenced to hang for failure to fight, Hull received a presidential pardon because of his service during the Revolutionary War. Brock meanwhile repulsed American forces at Niagara under General Stephen Van Rensselaer. Though Brock died in an engagement at Queenston, Canada, New York militiamen refused to enter Canada to help the American army, and British forces rallied to drive the invaders back into the United States.

The following two years of the war were little better for the expansionists. In 1813 General William Henry Harrison's forces regained Detroit and at one time held Canadian territory after defeating the British at the Battle of Thames in October. A fourth campaign in Canada the next year had similar results. The Americans seized a small spot of Canada near Detroit, but were unable to launch an offensive. Enthusiasm for expansion southward had diminished, for shortly after the declaration of war and again in early 1813, northern members of Congress—Federalists and Republicans—defeated a bill that authorized the president to seize Florida. The United States took Mobile in 1813, which it claimed was part of Louisiana, and Andrew Jackson defeated the Creek Indians, allies of Britain and Spain, at Horseshoe Bend in present-day Alabama in March 1814. But that was the extent of America's expansionist achievements. Northerners blamed southerners for failure to take Canada; southerners accused northerners of preventing the acquisition of Florida.

On the naval front the British blockade stretched from New England to the outlet of the Mississippi River, and even into Chesapeake Bay and up the Delaware and Susquehanna rivers, and the Royal Navy received assistance from bases at Halifax, the Bermudas, Barbados, and Jamaica. The 170 American gunboats along the Atlantic coast were worthless; on one occasion, a storm tossed a gunboat out of the water and into a field. The navy, however, was in better shape than the army. It had sixteen seaworthy ships in 1812, including seven frigates. And American naval officers had gained experience during the Quasi-War with France and the war in the Mediterranean against the Barbary pirates of North Africa.

America had surprising success at sea in the early part of the war. The United States frigate *Constitution* won several battles, including the seizure of the British frigate *Guerriere*. Commodore Oliver Hazard Perry defeated the British navy on Lake Erie and took Detroit in 1813. In one-on-one encounters, American ships outmaneuvered British vessels, winning most of the initial engagements. Nearly 500 American privateers ran the blockade, seized about 1,400 British commercial vessels (some even in the English Channel), and inflicted great damage on British shipping.

Yet as the war dragged on, Britain's naval superiority became apparent. The Royal Navy began to minimize losses by using convoys to escort merchant ships through the ocean lanes; it avoided engagements unless outnumbering the Americans by comfortable margins; it tightened the blockade to confine American merchants, privateers, and naval vessels to shore. At war's end America had three warships left of the original sixteen.

The British carried out a holding operation in North America until Napoleon's defeat in Russia and his exile to Elba in 1814. This strategy was changed during the summer of that year, when they landed thousands of battle-seasoned troops from the duke of Wellington's command and prepared for a three-pronged attack on the United States. One section was to hit the Atlantic coast at Chesapeake Bay and move inland to Washington and Baltimore; the second was to enter the St. Lawrence River and march toward Niagara and Lake Champlain and the Hudson Valley; the third was to launch an invasion through the Mississippi River at New Orleans.

None of the British invasions succeeded. The first force took the nation's capital city in September 1814 and burned the White House, the Capitol, other public buildings, and a few homes en route to Baltimore. The president escaped by boat to Virginia after his wife had run from the White House clutching the huge portrait of George Washington. But American forces held the line at Fort McHenry outside Baltimore, despite an all-night bombardment. During the battle Washington lawyer Francis Scott Key, then captive on a British vessel, immortalized the American flag by adapting new words to an English drinking song that eventually became "The Star-Spangled Banner." The second British contingent also met defeat. The Americans stopped the redcoats in Niagara, while on Lake Champlain in September 1814, Lieutenant Thomas McDonough drove back the British at Plattsburgh, New York. The third British force, 8,000 veterans led by General Sir Edward Pakenham (Wellington's brother-in-law), marched into New Orleans, where they encountered General Andrew Jackson and a ragtag force of 3,500 men consisting of army regulars, militia, frontiersmen, Indians, black slaves, Louisiana French, and river pirates. After a two-week assault the British retreated on January 8, 1815 with numerous casualties, including the death of Pakenham. Some observers have dismissed the importance of the Battle of New Orleans because poor communications allowed it to take place two weeks after the United States and England had signed a peace treaty in Europe. They argue that the British wanted to end the war in 1814 because of growing internal problems combined with the improved European situation, and that they would not have fought after New Orleans unless the United States went after Canada or refused to ratify the treaty. Yet Americans could not have known this. As far as they were concerned, the pact had not been ratified and a British victory at New Orleans might have hardened their position and led to territorial demands as a prerequisite to peace. Americans have sanctified the battle with reason.

PEACE

The Anglo-American peace negotiations were unusual in several respects. They began simultaneously with the onset of war, which meant that the tone of the discussions rose and fell with news from the battlefield. Until the British won the war in Europe, they would seek no peace in North America and would only frustrate the negotiations. Thus the failure of either antagonist to win a decisive battle prolonged discussions over matters that had no direct bearing on the causes of the war. The talks did not center on neutral rights, impressment, Canada, Florida, or national honor; they swirled around secondary issues such as boundaries and fishing and navigation rights in North America. The end of the war in Europe in 1814 made the causes of the War of 1812 academic, for no war would have occurred with England had the English not been at war with the French. The irritants that encouraged Anglo-American conflict were pique, anger, frustration, accusations of treachery, and mutual distrust. Once these emotions spent themselves and exhaustion from the Napoleonic Wars set in, the English and Americans realized the senselessness of war and worked toward ending it short of victory for either. The treaty was ultimately an armistice by two countries that realized their interests lay in peace.

The first call for negotiations in the Anglo-American war had come in the winter of 1812–13, through an offer of mediation from Czar Alexander I of Russia. Napoleon had just taken Moscow, and the czar wanted the United States out of the war to enable his English ally to save Russia. He also wanted American commercial goods. The Russian foreign minister, in September 1812, made the mediation proposal to the American minister in St. Petersburg, John Quincy Adams, and when President Madison learned of it the following March, he immediately showed interest. He asked Secretary of the Treasury Gallatin to join James Bayard, Federalist senator from Delaware, in meeting Adams in Russia to negotiate an end to the war. But Madison had made a tactical mistake. With the war going poorly for the United States, he accepted mediation without first notifying England. Lord Castlereagh refused to participate, claiming that he wanted to negotiate only with the United States. In actuality, London was not on good terms with the Russians because they shared the Americans' views on neutral rights. Prime Minister Lord Liverpool did not trust the czar and called him "half an American."

After some anxious months, Castlereagh notified the United States in November 1813 that he was ready to negotiate, but without the Russians. The president added Henry Clay, speaker of the House, and Jonathan Russell, former chargé to London and now minister to Sweden, to the Adams, Gallatin, and Bayard mission. They prepared to meet a three-man British delegation in Ghent, a Flemish town in the Lowlands across the channel from England, which was garrisoned by British soldiers.

The British team arrived in Ghent on August 6, 1814, and the talks began two days afterward. The three men Castlereagh sent to Ghent were Lord Gambier, a naval officer; Henry Goulburn, a minor government official; and William Adams, a lawyer specializing in admiralty matters. The men were capable but lacked distinction. They had little authority and had to send all matters to London, where Castlereagh kept close control over the talks. Castlereagh's main concern was the ongoing conference in Vienna, a fact the Americans realized. The foreign minister also wanted to wait for British military victories in the United States to solidify his position.

Conflicts had already developed among the American negotiators. Cramped quarters and the presence of five strong personalities caused trouble. Clay proved to his colleagues that he deserved his reputation for gambling, card playing, and drinking, and in so doing caused hard feelings with Adams, who like his father preferred work to whiling away time with idle amusements. Adams found it annoying that at 5 A.M., when he began his workday with a reading from the Bible, he heard Clay's card-playing partners rattling around the room next door on their way home. Adams also became exasperated when Clay dozed during the day's lengthy peace discussions. Only Clay's charm, Gallatin's tact, Adams's work, and Bayard's congenial humor managed to keep the delegation together.

When the negotiations got under way in early August, both sides' demands ensured that the talks would be long and arduous. Secretary of State Monroe had originally instructed his delegates to demand British renunciation of impressment, cession of Canada, acceptance of the American definition of neutral rights, indemnification for properties confiscated or damaged under authority of the Orders-in-Council, and the return of black slaves taken by the British. But the United States was not negotiating from a position of strength. It had no money, no allies, and virtually no military force. By the summer of 1814 President Madison and his cabinet had put off the matter of impressment. In the evening of August 8, after the first day of talks, revised directives arrived in Ghent. The Americans shelved interest in Canada and Florida and sought peace on the principle of *status quo ante bellum,* a return to conditions before the war.

Britain's terms almost wrecked the negotiations because they suggested the attitude of a nation victorious in war. London's newspapers demanded submission from the United States. British negotiators were flushed with victories in Chesapeake Bay and expected America to withhold military installations on the Great Lakes, permit Britain's free use of the Mississippi River and Great Lakes, and give up land in eastern Maine, upper New York, and the northern sector of the Mississippi River near Lake Superior. Between Quebec and the St. John River, the British planned to build a military road, which would wind through New Brunswick before reaching the Atlantic. The British negotiators also wanted concessions for renewed fishing privileges off Grand Banks and Newfoundland, which they claimed had terminated during the war. Goulburn even exceeded his instructions when he renewed the call for an Indian buffer state derived from American territory in the northwest. When Adams seemed amenable to allowing British use of the Mississippi River as a *quid pro quo* (an equivalent) for American fishing rights off the Atlantic coast, Clay heatedly refused and Gallatin convinced the British to postpone both matters for future consideration.

The talks deadlocked when Clay urged refusal of all the British demands rather than surrender American sovereignty and honor. Castlereagh eventually relented on the Indian neutral zone and all questions involving the Great Lakes, but offered peace on the principle of *uti possidetis*, that each belligerent would keep lands won during the war. Britain's invasion of Washington and occupation of territories in the northern part of the United States made this proposal unacceptable.

Events in America combined with those in Europe to break the impasse in the Ghent negotiations. News of America's victory at Plattsburgh on Lake Champlain and the defense of Baltimore encouraged the delegates to demand again the *status quo ante bellum*, even though Britain still retained upper Maine and parts of the northern Mississippi Valley. President Madison had also made the English people wonder if their government were merely engaged in a war for territory when, in violation of customary diplomatic procedure, he made public the original demands of the British delegation. On the European side Castlereagh's dream of constructing a lasting peace in Vienna seemed to be shattering as Russia and Prussia insisted upon territorial concessions.

Financial and economic problems in England and increasing talk in France about returning Napoleon from Elba necessitated a reassessment of the situation. The ministry sought the opinion of Wellington, who told Parliament that the war in America was unwinnable. Britain's failure to win decisively did not warrant a demand for territorial concessions, he emphasized. Exhausted by the war with Napoleon and fearing that the American war could wear on endlessly, in November 1814 the British government accepted Wellington's recommendation to agree to terms of *status quo ante bellum*. On Christmas Eve the two delegations signed the Treaty of Ghent, which ended the War of 1812.

The settlement was favorable to America even though it did not touch upon the issues raised by President Madison's war message. The country was intact. Factors beyond its control had again worked to advantage, for the biggest stimulus to ending the conflict was the defeat of Napoleon and the close of the European war. Continuation of Anglo-American hostilities made no sense when both sides wanted peace and a resumption of trade. Impressment and neutral rights automatically disappeared from the debate, for they could not be issues in peacetime. Except for Mobile, the British and Americans returned all territories occupied during the war, granted amnesty to Indians no matter which side they had supported, and called for the establishment of joint commissions to resolve boundary problems in the northeast around Maine and in the northwest between Lake Superior and the Rocky Mountains. The Treaty of Ghent did not resolve the questions of armaments on the Great Lakes and of fishing rights in the North Atlantic, but it confirmed the independence of the United States. On February 17, 1815, the Senate unanimously approved the treaty and the following day the war with England was officially over. John Quincy Adams spoke the feelings of Americans: "I hope it will be the last treaty of peace between Great Britain and the United States."

An unusual event occurred near the end of the war that encouraged Americans to believe that they had emerged victorious: the peace treaty arrived in Washington at the same time as the news of Jackson's victory at New Orleans. The repulsion of the British seemed to have direct connection with the Ghent proceedings, for Americans considered the Battle of New Orleans to be retribution for the burning of Washington and the major factor in bringing the enemy to terms. The narrow line between stalemate and defeat escaped Americans. They were under the impression that ill-trained militia were sufficient to defend the country, and hailed Jackson as a living legend.

The confirmation of America's independence and honor enabled most Americans to dismiss the discontent in New England as unimportant. Representatives from Connecticut, Rhode Island, and Massachusetts had gathered in Hartford, Connecticut, in December 1814 to draw up constitutional amendments requiring a two-thirds vote of each House of Congress to declare war (except in case of invasion) or to pass an embargo. Extremists urging secession failed to win control of the convention, but the delegates approved several other amendments designed to protect the states from the federal government. The end of the war and the appearance of victory dampened this threat to the Union, and President Madison ignored their proposals.

REFLECTIONS ON THE TREATY OF GHENT

The Treaty of Ghent ended another era in America's foreign policy. Two times in the short history of the republic, outside forces had threatened its independence. Peace in Europe calmed the controversies over freedom of the seas and by the time Madison left office in 1817, Americans could concentrate on domestic development and expansion westward. The war with England had taken the lives of 2,260 Americans and cost the nation $105 million. But British troops had withdrawn from American soil; Indian problems diminished both in the northwest and in the southeast; Americans boasted of their victories at sea and called for a larger navy; impressment and violations of neutral rights came to an end, and Anglo-American commercial relations seemed guaranteed. Some Englishmen were unhappy that the war had failed to secure concessions from America, but most welcomed the easing of taxes and the reestablishment of trade. British opposition to the peace settlement virtually disappeared by March 1815, when news arrived of Jackson's victory at New Orleans and of Napoleon's return to Paris from exile.

Skeptics have argued that the war and treaty were meaningless because they failed to resolve the causes of the war, yet those issues had ceased to exist once the fighting ended in Europe. The war made Americans aware of the need for a transcontinental network of defense that entailed expanding the nation's borders from ocean to ocean. It was also symbolically important in helping to establish respect for the United States both inside and outside the country, and thus in solidifying the nation. The War of 1812 preserved the republic as the Jeffersonian Republicans saw it, affirmed America's character and independence, caused a surge of nationalism that stilled sectional division, and left the National Anthem as a monument to these successes.

Selected readings

Adams, Henry, *History of the United States during the Administrations of Jefferson and Madison*. 9 vols. 1889–91.

Brant, Irving, *James Madison: Commander in Chief*. 1961.

———, *James Madison: The President, 1809–1812*. 1956.

Brown, Roger, *The Republic in Peril: 1812*. 1964.

Burt, Alfred L., *The United States, Great Britain and British North America*. 1940.

Campbell, Charles S., *From Revolution to Rapprochement: The United States and Great Britain, 1783–1900*. 1974.

Coles, Harry L., *The War of 1812*. 1965.

Egan, Clifford L., *Neither Peace nor War: Franco-American Relations, 1803–1812*. 1983.

Engelman, Fred L., *The Peace of Christmas Eve*. 1962.

Goodman, Warren H., "The Origins of the War of 1812: A Survey of Changing Interpretations," *Mississippi Valley Historical Review* 28 (1941–42): 171–86.

Horsman, Reginald, *The Causes of the War of 1812*. 1962.

———, *Expansion and American Indian Policy, 1783–1812*. 1967.

———, *The War of 1812*. 1964.

Irwin, Ray W., *The Diplomatic Relations of the United States with the Barbary Powers, 1776–1882*. 1931.

Perkins, Bradford, *Prologue to War: England and the United States, 1805–1812*. 1961.

Pratt, Julius W., *The Expansionists of 1812*. 1925.

Smelser, Marshall, *The Democratic Republic: 1801–1815*. 1968.

Stagg, J. C. A., *Mr. Madison's War: Politics, Diplomacy, and Warfare in the Early American Republic, 1783–1830*. 1983.

Steel, Anthony, "Impressment in the Monroe-Pinkney Negotiations, 1806–1807," *American Historical Review* 57 (1952): 352–69.

Taylor, George R., "Prices in the Mississippi Valley Preceding the War of 1812," *Journal of Economic and Business History* 3 (1930): 148–63.

Varg, Paul A., *Foreign Policies of the Founding Fathers.* 1963.

———, *New England and Foreign Relations, 1789–1850.* 1983.

White, Patrick C. T., *A Nation on Trial: America and the War of 1812.* 1965.

Chapter Five

The Diplomacy of Hemispheric Order, 1817–1825

The presidential administrations of Republican James Monroe of Virginia from 1817 to 1825 embodied the spirit of an awakened American nationalism. The Federalists had become "the party of treason" because of their opposition to the War of 1812 and support for the Hartford Resolutions, and the party's disarray afterward encouraged the nation to believe that to be an American was to be a Republican. Though most citizens rallied around President Monroe in the so-called Era of Good Feelings, Andrew Jackson became the symbol of this new spirit, for his heroics at Horseshoe Bend and New Orleans touched the frontier individualism that glorified the killing of Indians and Englishmen by raw recruits and state militiamen. The young nation had barely escaped calamity by 1815, but this reality was forgotten amidst the exultation over the first genuine sense of freedom from the mother country. America's new status would be short-lived, however, unless it resolved problems with England, Spain, Russia, and France, strengthened northern and southern border defenses, and expanded commerce into Latin America. These objectives necessitated bringing order to the Western Hemisphere and establishing the United States as the New World's guardian against Old World political interference. Among the achievements in this period were smoothened Anglo-American relations, the Adams-Onís Treaty with Spain, and the Monroe Doctrine.

IMPROVED ANGLO-AMERICAN RELATIONS

Anglo-American relations improved after 1815 largely through the efforts of British Foreign Secretary Lord Castlereagh and American Secretary of State John Quincy Adams. Both men understood the importance of trade

James Monroe

He was a two-term president during the postwar Era of Good Feelings, when patriotism ran high and Americans made several foreign policy triumphs. (An 1817 engraving attributed to Stipple; National Portrait Gallery)

in developing trust between the nations. In July 1815 the United States negotiated a commercial convention with England which established reciprocity arrangements for four years, along the lines of Jay's Treaty. But even though the agreement ruled out discriminatory duties, it did not open the West Indies to American vessels because of continuing pressure from British merchants who wanted no competition. Other problems appeared, some of which the Ghent negotiations had only postponed. Boundaries remained uncertain in the northeast around Maine and in the northwest above present-day Minnesota; the status of the Oregon Country was undetermined; questions lingered about the restoration of fishing liberties off British North America; a naval arms race threatened to develop on Lake Champlain and the Great Lakes; complexities arose over the interrelatedness of recognition and commercial matters in Latin America. The Era of Good Feelings was perhaps a misnomer, but Adams and Castlereagh tried to fit international events to the label.

The most immediate problem in foreign affairs was the threat of an arms race on the Great Lakes, which neither the United States nor En-

John Quincy Adams

As secretary of state under Monroe, Adams was integral to several foreign policy
achievements, including the Adams-Onís Treaty and the Monroe Doctrine. (Daguerreotype
portrait; Metropolitan Museum of Art)

gland could afford. Canadians were upset that the Treaty of Ghent had
not granted them control over coastal fishing areas and that it had failed
to guarantee against American invasion. They put pressure on London
for additional border fortifications. On the American side various groups
demanded peace because of the experiences of the Napoleonic Wars, and
Congress sought to cut taxes and the public debt. Both Canadians and
Americans stationed naval vessels on the Great Lakes, and England prepared new programs to stop American smuggling operations along the
frontier and to prevent British military deserters from joining the United
States Army. When an Anglo-American naval race materialized on Lake
Ontario, the Department of State in Washington repeated a suggestion
that had come up before—mutual disarmament. In January 1816 Adams
proposed negotiations, and Castlereagh accepted. The British foreign secretary knew that its location gave the United States the advantage and
that Canada's safety was tied more to good Anglo-American relations
than to an arms buildup. Besides, peace meant trade, and that was eminently more profitable than war.

Talks began in Washington in April 1817 between Acting Secretary of State Richard Rush and British Minister Charles Bagot. The men soon exchanged notes establishing mutual disarmament which the United States Senate approved a year afterward, and the Rush-Bagot agreement became a treaty. Each nation could station one armed vessel on either Lake Champlain or Lake Ontario, and no more than two on the rest of the Great Lakes. No ship could be larger than a hundred tons in size or carry more than a single eighteen-pound cannon. Small armed vessels remained to enforce revenue and customs laws. The treaty had no effect on land fortifications, for navy yards and land defenses stayed on the lakes for years. The Canadian-American border remained a guarded frontier until the resolution of the *Alabama* claims controversy between the United States and England, by the Treaty of Washington in 1871.

The Rush-Bagot Treaty reduced tension along the North American border and facilitated the resolution of other controversies between the nations. It set a precedent for mutual disarmament that resulted primarily from interest in establishing commercial relations and from each government's preoccupation with more pressing problems elsewhere.

The following year the United States and England negotiated the Convention of 1818. Rush, now American minister in London, and Gallatin, who had been sent to England as special emissary, renewed the Anglo-American commercial convention of 1815 for ten years, resolved a controversy over slaves taken by British soldiers after the War of 1812, and granted Americans the "liberty" to fish off British North American coasts "forever." Trade was to be on a reciprocal basis, and the United States won "most-favored-nation" status (any privileges Britain accorded to another nation it also granted to America) in the British West Indies and India, along with limited commercial rights in Canada. The British had argued that the War of 1812 terminated the fishing privileges granted under the Treaty of 1783, and in the period afterward had ordered the seizure of New England fishing boats engaged in the practice. They now proposed a compromise whereby Americans could fish along certain areas of Newfoundland and Labrador and in the waters around Magdalen Island, in exchange for giving up claim to inshore fishing along other parts of the British North American coast. Americans also agreed to restrict drying and curing (important in an era before refrigeration) to unsettled areas along the coast of Labrador and to regions in southern Newfoundland where fishing was allowed.

The remainder of the Convention of 1818 related to the northern boundary of the Louisiana Purchase and to the land beyond the Rocky Mountains. The source of controversy over the boundary east of the Rockies lay in the Treaty of 1783, which set the line from the northwesternmost reach of the Lake of the Woods due west to the Mississippi River. This border, however, was geographically impossible because the source of the river lay below the lake. The Louisiana Treaty of 1803 did not resolve the problem, and three years later, in the treaty that President Jefferson rejected because of the impressment controversy, James Monroe and William Pinkney had drawn the boundary at the 49th parallel from the Lake of the Woods to the Rockies. The Americans at Ghent had called for the same boundary arrangement, but dropped it when the British countered with a proposed *quid pro quo* of access to the source of the Mississippi and free use of its waters. In October 1815 Rush and Gallatin took advantage of England's preoccupation with other problems to draw the boundary of Louisiana south from the northwestern tip of the Lake of the Woods to the 49th parallel and to the Rockies—with no renewal of British navigation of the Mississippi River. But when they suggested extending the line to the Pacific, the British intimated that they preferred the Columbia River from its mouth rather than the 49th parallel, as long as both nations could have commercial use of the river and harbor. England would not give up claims to the Columbia River Basin.

Oregon was not an issue in 1818, but both the United States and England recognized that this vast territory stretching from Alaska to California would not remain quiet for long. Four nations laid claims to the area, although those of Spain and Russia were weak. Anglo-American claims, however, were defensible. British fur trading interests had spread into the Pacific Northwest after the explorations of Captain James Cook and others, thus preceding American claims. Americans based their claims on the voyage of Captain Robert Gray, who in 1792 discovered the mouth of the river named after his ship, the *Columbia*; the Lewis and Clark expedition of 1804–6; and the construction of the fort and trading post at Astoria on the mouth of the Columbia River in 1811. During the War of 1812 the British occupied the fort, but in 1818 turned it back to the United States in line with the Ghent agreements. Castlereagh declared that the restoration of Astoria did not constitute recognition of American control over the mouth of the Columbia, but he did not contest American claims south of the river. Shortly afterward Rush and Gallatin signed the Convention of 1818. They ignored Spanish and Russian claims to Oregon, and under an arrangement known as joint occupation they agreed that the territory would remain "free and open" to Americans for ten years, subject to renewal for the same period.

THE ADAMS-ONÍS TREATY

Improved relations with England made it possible for the United States to concentrate on growing disputes with Spain over the Floridas, Louisiana, and Texas. The Floridas constituted the first major issue, for their control affected the security of the southern coastal regions of the United States as well as the trade through Caribbean waters. Pinckney's Treaty of 1795 had set the 31st parallel as the northern border of the Floridas, and in 1803 Livingston and Monroe had claimed that West Florida to the Perdido

River should belong to the United States on the basis of Louisiana's uncertain boundary. "We shall certainly obtain the Floridas," Jefferson had
predicted, "all in good time."

Madison had tried to make that time come sooner after assuming the
presidency in March 1809. He wanted the Floridas so badly, according to
a French diplomat in Washington, that they were "the object of all of Mr.
Madison's prayers." The president supported a move to separate West
Florida from Spain and bring it into the Union. Most residents of the
province were Americans, and the new secretary of state, Robert Smith,
informed them "that in the event of a political separation from the parent
country, their incorporation into our Union would coincide with the sentiments and policy of the United States." In the autumn of 1810 presidential agents convinced Americans in West Florida to revolt. They seized the
fort at Baton Rouge, raised a blue woolen flag with a single star that proclaimed the "Republic of West Florida," and requested annexation by the
United States.

Within two days of receiving news of the West Florida uprising, President Madison declared that the Louisiana Purchase of 1803 had given him
the authority to extend jurisdiction over the Gulf coast area to the Perdido
River. To substantiate his position, he falsified dates on documents and
ordered the governor of the Louisiana Territory to occupy as much of the
new republic as possible short of confrontation with Spanish soldiers. In
December Americans entered the area west of the Pearl River, carefully
averting a challenge to Spanish forces at Mobile by moving around the
town to the Perdido River. Both Madrid and London protested but could
do nothing because of their involvement in the Napoleonic Wars. The
Russian czar wryly commented to the American minister in St. Petersburg, John Quincy Adams, that it was marvelous how the United States
"keeps growing bit by bit in this world."

Madison sought to use his leverage in West Florida to acquire the
eastern portion as well. American expansionists wanted the Floridas, and
the imminence of war with England made it vital that the United States
take them before they fell into enemy hands. Furthermore, the Spanish
governor at Pensacola had informed Washington of his desire to give
them up. Congress responded with a secret resolution on January 15,
1811, that the United States "cannot, without serious inquietude, see any
part of the said territory [East Florida] pass into the hands of any foreign
power." That same day the legislature secretly authorized the president
to annex East Florida if he met no opposition from local officials; should
a problem develop he would have the army, navy, and $100,000 to safe-
guard the province.

The president prepared to take East Florida. He hired George
Mathews, a seventy-two-year-old veteran of the Revolutionary War and
former governor of Georgia, as a special agent with orders to use the
army and navy, if necessary, to instigate a revolution. Above all, the president warned Mathews, "Hide your hand and mine." In March 1812,

with the assistance of American soldiers and volunteers from his home state, Mathews fomented an insurrection. The American Navy indiscreetly helped his "patriots" take Amelia Island, just below Georgia's border off the Atlantic coast, but Spanish forces prevented him from capturing the fort at St. Augustine. Nonetheless, Mathews established a government, installed a governor, and announced the cession of East Florida to the United States.

If the role of the American government in West Florida's revolution was ill-disguised, at least no proof of complicity appeared; but in East Florida the Americans had engaged in an invasion that constituted an act of war. Madison realized that Mathews had gone too far and recalled him—but not before persuading Congress in the spring of 1812 to annex West Florida, between the Mississippi and Perdido rivers, to the Territory of Mississippi. The president then washed his hands of the affair, just as Mathews prepared to storm St. Augustine. Madison wrote in early April 1813 that he knew of no way to defend Mathews's actions in Florida. The president moaned to Jefferson that Mathews had put the country in "a most distressing dilemma." But war had broken out with England almost a year before, making it too risky to return East Florida to Spain. Ignoring congressional opposition, Madison sent American soldiers to support the "patriots" still in control. The secretary of state, now Monroe, admitted afterward that the revolution in East Florida had embarrassed the United States, and yet the administration could not return the territory to Spain because of fear of England.

After war had begun with England in 1812, Congress empowered the president to seize East Florida, and in West Florida General James Wilkinson took Mobile in April 1813. The following year Andrew Jackson secured the town against the British and attacked the Spanish fort at Pensacola because it had served as Britain's base of operations. Spain demanded reparations for these acts and for Americans opening ports to privateers owned by its rebellious New World colonies. By the time the war ended in December 1814, the United States controlled all of West Florida east to the Perdido River, although it agreed to return East Florida to Spain. The prognosis had changed, however; the government in Madrid recognized that the war and insurrections in its Latin American colonies made it impossible to hold East Florida. The time had come to sell— if Spain could secure a satisfactory boundary between Louisiana and New Spain (Mexico).

The Floridas were in such disarray after the War of 1812 that they were virtually uncontrollable by the Spanish governors in Pensacola and St. Augustine. Amelia Island had become a haven for slave smugglers, adventurers, and pirates, who fitted the Indians with arms. When Indians from East Florida swarmed onto American surveyors near the Georgia border, and some of the renegades on Amelia Island asserted that East Florida belonged to Mexico, President Monroe ordered the island seized in 1817 on the basis of the "no-transfer" idea contained in a congressional resolution of January 1811. Other problems were apparent. Creek Indians who survived Jackson's expedition in 1814 had joined the Seminoles in the Floridas. Supplied by British merchants in East Florida, they and about 800 escaped slaves and a few white outlaws in the northern part of the province raided American settlements, disrupting expansion into Georgia and Mississippi. The United States had to have order in East Florida, and it wanted Louisiana's borders set at the Perdido River to the east (incorporating West Florida) and the Rio Grande to the west. These were extreme claims, but Americans defended them on the basis of the vague boundary provisions of the Louisiana Treaty of 1803 and on Spain's inability to control the Floridas in accordance with Pinckney's Treaty of 1795.

America's negotiations with Spain began in 1817, when Secretary of State Adams met with the Spanish minister in Washington, Don Luis de Onís. Adams was realistic and brilliant, a hardheaded diplomat whose objective was to rid the hemisphere of Old World colonialism and spread American republicanism over North America. He must have recognized some of his own qualities in his talented adversary, for he observed of Onís:

> Cold, calculating, wily, always commanding his own temper, proud because he is a Spaniard, but supple and cunning, accommodating the tone of his pretensions precisely to the degree of endurance of his opponent, bold and overbearing to the utmost extent to which it is tolerated, careless of what he asserts and how grossly it is proved to be unfounded. . . . He is laborious, vigilant, and ever attentive to his duties; a man of business and of the world.

The negotiations took place against a background of hostility toward Spanish colonialism. Adams resisted pressure from Henry Clay to grant *de facto* recognition to Spain's rebellious New World colonies, for he knew that such a move would insult Spain and abort his chances for resolving the Florida question. Adams noted prerequisites to extending recognition to new states. First and foremost, the likelihood of Spain's regaining its possessions had to be "utterly desperate." Second, these governments had to conform to standards of international behavior. Adams knew that a delay in recognition could hurt American commercial interests in Latin America and open the door there to England; yet he realized that a hasty decision could cause war with Spain and arouse help for the Old World empire from antidemocratic European states also having commercial designs on Latin America. Recognition issues had caused war in other instances—much as the French experience had shown in the 1770s. Adams probably agreed with his father, who remarked to him in 1818 that the South American peoples "will be independent, no doubt, but will they be free? General Ignorance can never be free, and the Roman Religion is incompatible with a free government."

American sympathy grew for the Latin Americans. Merchants from the United States carried copies of the Declaration of Independence and

Constitution to the rebellious states and extolled freedom. Clay's oratory in behalf of South America was difficult to counteract. "We behold there," he proclaimed on the House floor, "a spectacle still more interesting and sublime—the glorious spectacle of eighteen millions of people, struggling to burst their chains and to be free." Passage of the Neutrality Acts of 1817 and 1818 failed to dissuade filibustering (private adventuring) and privateering out of New Orleans and Baltimore. In late March of 1818, the Monroe administration won an important battle when Congress overwhelmingly turned down a resolution for recognition of Spain's colonies, supported by westerners hostile to Spain.

Discussions with Onís dragged on as Adams called for the cession of East Florida on the ground that Spanish officials had not stopped the Indian raids in American territory as Pinckney's Treaty had required. He also criticized Spain for failing to return runaway slaves and for aiding England in the War of 1812. Onís countered by demanding that in exchange for East Florida, the United States had to guarantee no interference in the revolts in South America and no recognition of their independence. Adams at first recommended the Rio Grande as the western boundary of Louisiana before agreeing to move northward to the Colorado River midway into Texas, while Onís retreated from his earlier untenable position that the Mississippi River was the western boundary; the state of Louisiana was already part of the Union. In the meantime the Spanish minister warned France and England that if the European powers did not band together, the United States might take all of the Western Hemisphere. But in London Castlereagh rigidly held to his stance of two months before: Spain should give up East Florida in exchange for the best boundary possible between Louisiana and Mexico. The talks might have remained deadlocked had it not been for the dramatic involvement of Andrew Jackson.

The day after Christmas in 1817, President Monroe sent the Tennessean to resolve the Seminole Indian problem in East Florida. Jackson had authorization to cross the international border if necessary, but to stay clear of Spanish forts. He later claimed to have anticipated the president's request. On January 6, 1818, before Jackson's orders arrived in Nashville, he wrote Monroe: "The whole of East Florida [should be] seized . . . and this can be done without implicating the Government. Let it be signified to me through any channel . . . that the possession of the Floridas would be desirable . . . and in sixty days it will be accomplished." The capture of the province would serve as reparations for Spain's violations of America's property. All he needed was some sign of approval from the White House.

In mid-February 1818, Jackson asserted, that sign came while he and his 3,000 men were encamped along the Big Creek River in Georgia. His longtime friend, Representative John Rhea of Tennessee, wrote him a letter which the general later claimed had contained tacit approval from President Monroe to invade East Florida and settle the Indian problem—

even to the point of seizing Spanish towns. Jackson declared that Monroe and Secretary of War John C. Calhoun approved the idea, despite their later denials. No evidence exists, for Jackson asserted that he burned the letter—if there was one—at Monroe's request. Rhea was confused. The elderly man later wondered if he *had* written the letter. By 1818 he admitted to writing a letter which could have left the impression that the government wanted Jackson to take East Florida.

The truth probably lies somewhere between. The president recognized the possibilities in sending the fiery general near a trouble spot inhabited by Indians and Spaniards. Jackson's character did not include the observation of diplomatic niceties in matters injurious to national honor. Monroe must have realized that Jackson would take care of the Indian and Spanish menace in his own way. The timing was opportune, for numerous Spanish forces had moved to South America to put down the insurrections. Jackson assumed his mission was to take East Florida. President Monroe never told him to stay out of the Spanish province. Each man knew what the other wanted without having to say it. In effect, the president and the general were preparing for the possibility of war without consulting Congress.

In March 1818 Jackson's forces marched into East Florida and within two months brought the United States to the edge of war with both Spain and England. His men seized the Spanish garrison at St. Marks in early April, burned a nearby Indian village, executed two Indian prophets, and captured a seventy-year-old Scottish merchant named Alexander Arbuthnot, who was accused of selling arms to the Seminoles. In an Indian camp later on, they seized an English lieutenant suspended from the marines, Robert Ambrister, who also was charged with conspiring with the Indians. A quick court martial in St. Marks found both British subjects guilty. Uncertainty remains about whether Arbuthnot was involved in a dishonest trade, but both men were executed.

Jackson then headed toward Spanish headquarters at Pensacola, where he believed the governor was guilty of helping the Indians. On May 28 he took the town and fort, and the next day confiscated the archives, appointed an American officer as military and civil governor, and activated American revenue laws in East Florida. On May 30 Jackson began the return to Tennessee, perhaps only partly satisfied because he had not taken St. Augustine, and openly regretful that he had not hanged the Spanish governor.

Jackson's actions in East Florida unleashed a fury both outside and inside the United States. The Spanish minister in Washington was livid. When news of Jackson's deeds arrived in July, Onís was at his summer retreat in Pennsylvania, but he returned to the capital early in the morning to interrupt Adams's Bible session and demand reparations and punishment for Jackson's actions. With British support Onís now felt confident of victory in the Florida negotiations. Several times during the following week the two diplomats met, Adams interspersing these heated encounters with almost daily meetings with the cabinet. Secretary of War Calhoun led the cabinet attack on Jackson. Furious that the general had ignored orders, he demanded a court martial. Calhoun even suggested that Jackson had acted in behalf of friends interested in Florida land schemes.

Only Adams defended Jackson in the cabinet. The general's report to Calhoun contained statements that Adams found easy to accept. "I hope," Jackson wrote, "the execution of these two unprincipled villains will prove an awful example to the world, and convince the Government of Great Britain, as well as her subjects, that certain, though slow retribution awaits those unchristian wretches who, by false promises, delude and excite an Indian tribe to all the horrid deeds of savage war." The Florida assault was self-defense, Adams asserted; Jackson was correct in urging the United States to occupy all areas down to the 31st parallel. The Spanish governor of East Florida and the commander at St. Marks deserved punishment. Adams agreed that the United States should return Pensacola, but believed that St. Marks should remain in American hands until the Spanish established control over the Indians. Self-defense, he asserted, was part of the "common sense of mankind." The Spanish had a choice: either meet their international obligations, or cede the province to the United States. In his argument, later sent to Madrid, Adams charged that East Florida "is, in fact, a derelict, open to the occupancy of every enemy, civilized or savage, of the United States, and serving no other earthly purpose than as a post of annoyance to them."

President Monroe was indecisive but not above falsifying the record to justify Jackson's behavior. War was out of the question, he knew, but his only criticism was of the manner in which Jackson carried out the expedition. Monroe said nothing about the results. He thought the posts should revert to Spain, and yet was attracted by the prospect of his administration taking both Floridas if it could escape the stain of aggression. He wrote Jackson that the American case would be defensible if he as president could show that the invasion stemmed from Spanish violations of American rights. If Jackson approved, Monroe offered to alter documentation of the matter:

> You must aid in procuring the documents necessary for this purpose. Those you sent . . . do not, I am satisfied, do justice to the cause. . . . Your letters to the [War] Department were written in haste, under the pressure of fatigue. . . . If you think it proper to authorize the secretary or myself to correct . . . passages, it will be done with care.

Jackson refused the president's proposal. He preferred to present evidence of Spain's misconduct.

In the meantime, Americans hailed Jackson as a hero while his old antagonist, Henry Clay, tried to undercut the Tennessean's growing chances for the presidency by securing a congressional resolution of censure. Horseshoe Bend, New Orleans, and now East Florida—the possibili-

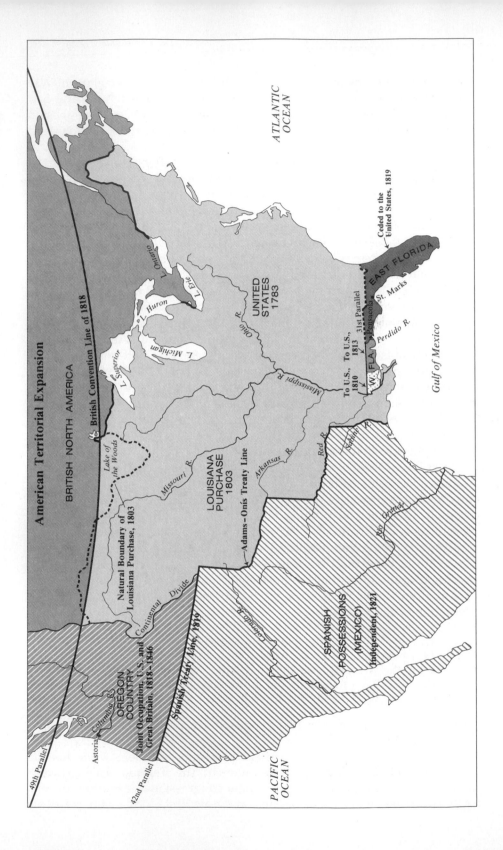

American Territorial Expansion

BRITISH NORTH AMERICA

British Convention Line of 1818

49th Parallel

42nd Parallel

Astoria

Columbia R.

OREGON COUNTRY
Joint Occupation, U.S. and Great Britain, 1818–1846

Continental Divide

Spanish Treaty Line, 1819

PACIFIC OCEAN

Natural Boundary of Louisiana Purchase, 1803

Lake of the Woods

Missouri R.

LOUISIANA PURCHASE 1803

Adams–Onís Treaty Line

Arkansas R.

Red R.

Colorado R.

Rio Grande

SPANISH POSSESSIONS (MEXICO)
Independent, 1821

L. Superior

L. Michigan

L. Huron

L. Erie

L. Ontario

Ohio R.

Mississippi R.

UNITED STATES 1783

Sabine R.

To U.S., 1810

To U.S., 1813

W. FLA.

Perdido R.

31st Parallel

Pensacola

St. Marks

EAST FLORIDA

Ceded to the United States, 1819

ATLANTIC OCEAN

Gulf of Mexico

ties seemed limitless as to what this heroic American frontier Indian fighter would do. Tammany Hall in New York passed a resolution of praise, and Philadelphia and other cities wildly cheered him. Clay led a congressional inquiry into Jackson's conduct that hammered on for three weeks. He also delivered an impassioned three-day speech before a packed House of Representatives in behalf of several resolutions chastising Jackson for the invasion, and for the executions of the British subjects and Indian religious leaders. Even Rome, he declared, respected the "altars and the gods of those whom she subjugated." Those great nations of the past—Greece and Rome—fell because "some daring military chieftain" extinguished their liberties. Such a calamity could happen to America, for "Greece had fallen, Caesar passed the Rubicon."

Jackson swore to "defeat these hellish machinations." Stories circulated, perhaps started by his followers, that he would cut off the ears of anyone who supported a Senate move for censure. Though some senators scoffed, others kept their weapons upon entering the chambers to debate the measure.

In February 1819 Congress decided against censuring Jackson for his conduct. But in so doing, it virtually admitted to having no control over him. Monroe had earlier assured that body that if Jackson entered Spanish territory he would *not* seize Spanish forts. When the general did so, both the president and Congress looked the other way.

Monroe's decision about the Florida episode hinged more on the reaction in England than on popular opinion in the United States. The initial response in England was an angry demand for an apology and reparations for the executions of its subjects. The American minister in London, Richard Rush, warned that the atmosphere was explosive and Foreign Secretary Castlereagh believed that Parliament and the British people were in such an ugly mood that "war might have been produced by holding up a finger." But ameliorative factors were evident. Castlereagh agreed with the United States that Arbuthnot and Ambrister *had* been engaged in illegal gunrunning and deserved no government protection. He was also preoccupied with preserving the peace in Europe and in establishing closer economic ties with the United States. Castlereagh would not interfere on behalf of the two men and England would not support Spain.

Castlereagh's assurances and the popularity of Jackson in the United States eased the president's position. Monroe realized that it would be politically unwise to attack Jackson, and since England posed no danger, he instructed his secretary of state to reject Spain's protests. Adams pre-

---

MAP 6, 1810–1821

The Adams-Onís Treaty, which John Quincy Adams considered his most outstanding accomplishment as secretary of state, was transcontinental in scope and vital to the nation's security.

pared a long paper and attached several documents justifying Jackson's actions as self-defense. Spain's failure to keep its house in order had forced the United States to take action.

Adams reopened negotiations with Onís in October 1818. He first assured the Spanish minister that the United States would return the areas seized by Jackson. Then Adams announced an ultimatum: either maintain order in the Floridas, or cede them to the United States. The atrocities committed by the Indians justified Jackson's decision to execute both Englishmen—without a trial, had he chosen to do so. Adams shocked Onís by demanding punishment of the Spanish officer responsible for the chaos in East Florida and compensation for the expenses of Jackson's expedition. If the United States did not receive satisfaction, Adams seemed to imply, Jackson could ride again. Onís had no rejoinder. His government stood alone and had already instructed him to give up both Floridas. After four months of argument over the Louisiana boundary, Monroe instructed Adams to settle on the Sabine River, dropping claims to Texas and allowing angry westerners to tag the secretary with blame. Spain could not go to war without British support, and it had to concentrate on the insurrections in Latin America. The Spanish found it wiser to pull out with grace—and perhaps with money—than to lose everything in dishonor.

In Washington on February 22, 1819, the secretary of state signed the Adams-Onís Treaty. The negotiators worded the transfer of the Floridas in a manner designed to satisfy each party's argument over whether the area west of the Perdido River had been part of the Louisiana Purchase of 1803. The United States received "all the territories which belong to him [king of Spain], situated to the eastward of the Mississippi, known by the name of East and West Florida." The United States gave up its shadowy claims to Texas based on the Louisiana Treaty, and Spain did the same with equally questionable claims to Oregon. Though the area beyond the Rocky Mountains was not an issue in 1819, Adams recognized the opportunity to solidify his country's argument for the Far West. He had mentioned the 42nd parallel as a boundary, during a conversation with Onís the previous July. Now the two men drew the border in step-like fashion northwest from the mouth of the Sabine River in Louisiana until it reached the 42nd parallel near the Rockies and followed that line west to the Pacific. No exchanges of money took place. Each side dropped damage claims against the other, and the United States agreed to assume its citizens' claims against the Spanish to a maximum of $5 million.

The treaty was a major stride toward Adams's goal of acquiring the Columbia River Basin and building a transcontinental United States. His diary entry for the day of the treaty signing recorded his satisfaction: "The acknowledgement of a definite line of boundary to the South Sea [Pacific Ocean] forms a great epocha in our history. The first proposal of it in this negotiation was my own, and I trust it is now secured beyond the reach of revocation." He continued that "it was, perhaps, the most important day of my life." Adams attributed the triumph to "the work of an intelligent and all-embracing cause."

The slavery question precluded any American interest in acquiring Texas during these negotiations. Unknown to Adams, Onís had received directives from Madrid to forgo Texas by retreating from the Sabine River as the boundary of Louisiana, but Monroe and his cabinet considered the Floridas vital and did not push for the additional territory. Not only did they and many southerners fear that a demand for Texas might hurt the Florida negotiations, but it could lead to serious political repercussions over slavery. Coincidental with these talks, a bitter debate was under way in Congress over the admission of Missouri into the Union as a slave state; its entry would upset the delicate balance between free and slave states in the Senate. A debate over slavery could also unravel the tenuous North-South alliance within Monroe's Republican party. Texas was potentially too dangerous an issue. It remained in Spanish hands, although Onís tied it to Mexico. When Mexico won independence in 1821, it took Texas.

Problems in Spain caused a considerable delay in ratification of the treaty. Some officials in Madrid believed that Onís had not received fair compensation for the land conceded, while others worried about the United States's refusal to agree to withhold recognition of the Latin American insurgents. In 1820 an uprising in Spain forced King Ferdinand VII to accept a liberal constitution, which slowed ratification by requiring legislative approval of treaties. The king also held off ratification because of a dispute over land grants which he had awarded in East Florida after the dates set in the treaty for the termination of such acts. If validated, the grants would have incorporated all unsettled land given the United States by the treaty.

The United States Senate had unanimously approved the treaty, despite criticism from Clay and other western members of Congress for the administration's failure to acquire Texas, and President Monroe had ratified it on February 25. But now Jackson recommended that the United States use "the mouth of the cannon" to close the deal, while Monroe assured Adams that Congress would approve taking the Floridas *and* Texas if Spain did not revoke the royal charters. These drastic measures proved unnecessary. The government in Madrid canceled the grants, and the king ratified the treaty on October 24, 1820. Since the six-month time limit for ratification had expired, the Senate had to vote again on the treaty, and this time approved it with four westerners dissenting on the basis of Clay's cry that "Texas was worth ten Floridas." On February 22, 1821, two years after the original signatures in Washington, the two countries exchanged ratifications and the Adams-Onís Treaty went into effect.

A little over a year later, President Monroe aroused widespread public approval when he recommended that the United States extend recognition to the new republics in Latin America. The temptation to do so had come in June 1821, when Simón Bolívar's forces broke Spain's hold on

Colombia and Venezuela, but Monroe had remained cautious. After more delay he made his move. He assured Congress in March 1822 that the probability of Spain's reestablishing control over its colonies was "most remote." In two months Congress approved Monroe's proposal and authorized $100,000 to establish "such missions to the independent nations on the American continent" as the president should decide.

Acquisition of the Floridas in 1821 had changed the situation in regard to recognition, and self-interest prompted the United States to act. Latin American markets were important and English investors were expanding their interests daily. No guideline existed for determining how long a nation must wait to grant recognition to new states. Still, the United States waited more than a year after the Adams-Onís Treaty to extend recognition. Spain's failure to restore control proved America's actions correct.

The Adams-Onís Treaty was an outstanding achievement in American diplomacy. At virtually no cost, the secretary of state had rounded out the southeastern borders of the United States and had improved the chances for acquiring the Pacific Northwest by reducing the claimants to two. American forces established order on the border between Georgia and East Florida. The people of Mississippi and Alabama were guaranteed access to the Gulf, and cotton fields spread into the rich bottomlands. Furthermore, Adams had raised an issue that would become a matter of debate in international law: whether a nation has the right under self-defense to launch a preemptive strike when a desperate situation existed and no other recourse seemed available. The pattern of American expansionism exemplified by Pinckney's Treaty, the Louisiana Purchase, and now the Adams-Onís Treaty, suggested that interest in Texas and Oregon would not diminish. The only question was which issue would surface first.

THE MONROE DOCTRINE

The Monroe Doctrine of 1823 encouraged the acquisition of Texas, Oregon, and other areas in the transcontinental United States. More than any document of the time, it expressed the mood of an American people bold enough to warn Europe that the Western Hemisphere was no longer open for colonization. It was the first official declaration of America's unique character and a manifesto of political isolationism built upon the natural protection of the Atlantic and Pacific oceans. The new idea contained in the Monroe Doctrine was that the United States assumed the guardianship of the Americas. The genius of the document was its balance between idealism and self-interest. The Monroe Doctrine left the impression that America opposed imperialism and sympathized with the new republics of Latin America, and for those disinterested reasons warned Europe to stay out of the New World. The reality was that the United States did not include itself in the restrictions, for its objectives were territorial and commercial expansion in the Americas.

The history of the Monroe Doctrine primarily started with the Congress of Vienna in 1815, which signaled the end of the Napoleonic Wars. Czar Alexander I of Russia had suggested the establishment of a "Holy Alliance" in September, and within two months Russia, Prussia, Austria, and England renewed the "concert of Europe" or Quadruple Alliance established the previous year. The purpose of the alignment, French Foreign Minister Talleyrand declared, was to stamp out liberalism and restore thrones to governments overturned by constitutional revolutions. By 1818 the organization became known as the Quintuple Alliance when Bourbon King Louis XVIII returned to Paris, and France also became a keeper of order.

The Quintuple Alliance, led by Austrian Foreign Minister Prince Klemens von Metternich, intended to fulfill its mission when popular uprisings led to the establishment of constitutional governments in Naples, Piedmont, Spain, and Portugal. England was reluctant to go along. The ministry in London did not favor liberal revolutions, but sentiments of this type were stirring among its own people and Lord Castlereagh staunchly opposed intervention in European affairs because such a move might cause war. At the Congress of Verona in Italy in 1823, England broke with the European powers, which decided to send French soldiers to return King Ferdinand VII to the Spanish throne. Just before the meeting Castlereagh, in despair over the crumbling peace, committed suicide. His successor, George Canning, also opposed the decision to restore the Spanish monarch.

These events in Europe did not go unnoticed by the United States. The recognition question in Latin America was fraught with danger of Old World interventionism in Spanish America—or so Americans feared. Simón Bolívar, Francisco de Miranda, José San Martín, and Bernardo O'Higgins had launched a series of drives for independence which reached a climax when Mexico broke the Spanish bond in 1821. In the spring of 1822, as indicated earlier, President Monroe extended recognition to the new republics of Latin America, shortly after the last of the Spanish armies pulled out of the New World. Adams and others in Washington sought to establish commercial ties with these new states before they fell under British control. But when France invaded Spain, the Monroe administration became alarmed that the French might try to restore Spanish rule in Latin America—and perhaps march on to the United States. Indeed, Ferdinand urged his European friends to help him regain control over the Spanish colonies in the New World. Rumors were circulating in the United States by the spring of 1823 that an arrangement existed whereby France would receive Cuba in exchange for restoring Spain's empire in Latin America.

These stories had a fortuitous effect on England. When the Latin American rebels threw off the mother country, they opened their ports to British merchants. The administration in Washington could not have known that in late March Canning informed his ambassador in Paris that

England would oppose any French attempts to return Spain's New World possessions.

Canning turned to the United States to secure either a convention or exchange of notes signifying Anglo-American opposition to Europe's intervention in Spanish America. In August 1823 he talked with Rush in London about the French troops in Spain, and the American minister remarked that he was certain the English would not allow the French to do the same in Latin America. Four days later, on August 20, Canning sent an "unofficial and confidential" note calling for a "joint disapprobation" of French intervention. Mutual interests in Latin America's independence pointed toward a cooperative policy. To relieve other nations' suspicions, Canning suggested that both countries take a public stand against territorial acquisitions. Less than a week later he again broached the idea, emphasizing that the two nations had an opportunity to "produce so unequivocal a good and prevent such extensive calamities." England could have enforced this idea without American help, but Canning had other goals.

Canning's motives were self-interest, and Rush knew it. The foreign minister sought to rebuild his country's world influence, hurt badly by the French invasion of Spain, and even a weak ally like the United States would help restore a balance of power vital to peace. Canning also did not want the newly opened markets of Latin America to revert to Spain, and he recognized the economic advantages of drawing closer to the United States; its consumers bought a sixth of England's exports and might exert pressure on Congress to reduce tariffs. Rush maintained a careful composure. He would await instructions from Washington; but if Canning agreed to extend recognition to the new Latin American states, something the United States had sought since 1815, Rush would initial a joint declaration that would "not remain inactive under an attack upon the independence of those States by the Holy Alliance." Conservatives in England opposed recognition, as Rush knew, but he hoped to use Canning's interest in a joint policy to secure a concession long wanted by the United States. The foreign secretary, however, only tentatively offered assurances of recognition. His evasive reply caused Rush to forward the issue to President Monroe.

The Monroe administration was divided in reaction to Canning's proposal. The offer was appealing, but the bearer was not. Canning was infamous for anti-American behavior. Had he not pushed for greater maritime restrictions in the period before 1812? The president asked Jefferson and Madison for advice, and surprisingly both favored acceptance. Jefferson argued that with British assistance the United States could maintain inviolability from the Old World. Madison agreed and recommended that the joint policy encompass a statement in favor of the ongoing Greek revolution against the Turks. The Greeks' drive for freedom had drawn widespread support in the United States, and President Monroe knew that a pronouncement in their behalf would bolster a decision to accept

Canning's invitation. In early November he told the cabinet that he had decided to accept Canning's offer. Adams, however, vigorously protested.

Adams was a realist and expansionist who distrusted the English and warned of strings attached to any "gift" offered by Canning. The secretary of state had no difficulty convincing his colleagues of Canning's character, for they remembered him as the wily diplomat who had recalled his minister to America, the conciliatory David Erskine, in the period before the outbreak of war in 1812. England wanted commercial control of Latin America, Adams reminded fellow cabinet members, and the danger in Canning's proposal rested in the self-denying joint statement, "We aim not at the possession of any portion of them [Spanish states] ourselves." America's signature would constitute a renunciation of claims to Cuba, Texas, and California. Restoration of the Spanish monarchy in September horrified Calhoun, who, according to Adams's diary, was "perfectly moonstruck." Stories were that French ships would soon leave for the New World to restore the Spanish colonies to the crown. To compound matters, Russia's minister in Washington, Baron Tuyll, had informed Adams in mid-October that his country would not recognize the rebellious colonies in Spanish America and was happy with United States neutrality. This apparently signified that Russia would support Spanish and French intervention in Latin America if the United States joined England in a joint declaration of policy.

After several discussions Adams persuaded the president to reject Canning's offer. Adams argued against the danger of European intervention; even if it happened, the United States could rely on the British navy because England had too many economic interests in Latin America to allow anyone to intervene. A joint policy with England would do the United States no good. Latin Americans would thank the English for protection, not the Americans. The United States found it better to act alone than "to come in as a cockboat in the wake of the British man-of-war."

Adams also put down the fear that Russia might intervene in Latin American affairs. Its traders had moved steadily down the northwest coast of North America after the voyages of Vitus Bering in the first half of the eighteenth century. In 1799 the Russian-American Company received a charter granting it sole commercial rights and governing control over the Alaskan area south to 55° north latitude. The company began a string of settlements, and by 1816 had built a trading post above San Francisco Bay in Spanish California. These developments at first did not concern the government in Washington because of preoccupation with England and because of the remoteness of the Pacific coast. But in 1821 the czar issued a ukase (imperial decree) that broadened his country's claims south to the 51st parallel (thereby including much of Oregon) and restricted the waters within about a hundred miles of the coast to Russian vessels. The ukase seemed to be a major step in Russian expansion southward into Oregon. To Calhoun and others, the threat lay in the czar's membership in the Quadruple Alliance. England protested, but the United States acted.

Adams raised the matter in a discussion with the Russian minister in Washington. The United States had received a note from the Russian Foreign Office praising the European alliance and asserting that the czar planned to maintain peace—even if such a move meant preserving Spain's control over its colonies, Tuyll told Adams. The secretary of state did not believe the Russians would intervene. He had seen their domestic problems when he served as minister in St. Petersburg, and it appears that he used the fear of Russia to advance an idea he had been considering for some time. In July 1823 Adams wrote Tuyll that "we should contest the right of Russia to *any* territorial establishment on this continent, and that we should assume distinctly the principle that the American continents are no longer subjects for *any* new European colonial establishments." Adams then sent instructions containing this principle of "noncolonization" to the American ministers in both Russia and England. This idea was not new to England, for over two years before, in January 1821, Adams had stated it in reply to the British minister's question about how far America's claims went in the Columbia River area. "To all the shores of the South Sea [the Pacific]," he declared. When pressed as to whether this affected England's holdings in North America, Adams answered: "No, there the boundary is marked, and we have no disposition to encroach upon it. Keep what is yours, but leave the rest of this continent to us." The secretary's dispatch to London in 1823 was stronger in tone, signifying that he was more apprehensive of England than of Russia.

Adams's stand on noncolonization was hardly defensible, either in practical or theoretical terms. The United States was not strong enough to resist the European nations if they chose to establish colonies in the hemisphere. His colleagues in the cabinet also had doubts about the legal basis for such a pronouncement. European governments had long followed the practice that no country had exclusive claim to unsettled and unexplored areas. Adams knew this. In the Convention of 1818 he admitted to England's joint occupation of Oregon, although it is arguable that this arrangement did not necessarily involve *colonization*. But in 1824 he would agree to Russia's claim to the area above the 54°40' line, and afterward in the same year he accepted the idea of resolving the Oregon boundary controversy by dividing the area along the 49th parallel. Perhaps Adams used the Russian matter to win support for his bid for the presidency in 1824. The opposition had accused him of giving away the West's interests by the treaties of 1818 with England and 1819 with Spain. A strong statement against future European colonization in the Americas might quiet his critics and rally voters around him. This may have been so, but the important point is that a strong declaration aimed at Russia would implicitly warn England that outside interference endangered the American interest.

Canning had not counted on the possibility that the Monroe administration might decline his offer. To solidify his position he applied pressure on the French ambassador in London, Prince Jules de Polignac, to give him a memorandum in early October renouncing his government's intentions to intervene in the Spanish colonies. Canning did not reveal the Polignac memorandum to Rush because he wanted to use the fear of European intervention to secure an American promise not to seek additional territories in the New World.

The question before the government in Washington was how to inform other nations of its stance toward the Latin American republics. Adams wanted to send sternly worded notes to each foreign office, but found no support in the administration. The president suggested including the ideas in his annual message to Congress in December. This approach drew approval and Monroe prepared a draft which he brought before the cabinet on November 21. Adams, however, disliked its defiant tone and opposed the president's intention to warn the leading European powers to stay out of Greece and Spain. Adams wanted to make clear that the United States would be responsible for the western half of the world, and this necessitated mention of Russia's activities along the northwest coast. The message should warn against Old World interference in Latin America and assure that the United States would reciprocate by staying out of European political affairs. Monroe gave in, although he remained convinced that the United States had a mission to spread republican principles. He insisted on expressing concern for the Greeks, but agreed to tone down criticism of French actions in Spain. Adams succeeded in making this an "American cause" that expressed belief in security through isolation on a hemispheric scale.

That part of the president's December 2 message to Congress which later became known as the "Monroe Doctrine" comprised only two pages of a total of thirteen, and was separated into two passages by a long section on domestic matters. The message emphasized the uniqueness of America and the wisdom in political separation of the two hemispheres. The ideas meshed into the central principle of political isolation: "We owe it, therefore, to candor and to the amicable relations existing between the United States and those powers to declare that we should consider any attempt on their part to extend their system to any portion of this hemisphere as dangerous to our peace and safety."

The principles of "noncolonization" and "hands off" associated with the Monroe Doctrine were two component and inseparable parts of America's warning to Europe to stay out of New World political affairs. As pointed out earlier, Adams formulated the noncolonization principle in reaction to the Russian ukase of 1821. The secretary's influence was apparent in the similarity between his note to the Russian minister in Washington during the summer of 1823 and the president's declaration to Congress that "the American continents, by the free and independent condition which they have assumed and maintain, are henceforth not to be considered as subjects for future colonization by any European powers." By not specifying Russia, this section left the implication that it applied to any foreign power—including England—which might consider intervening in the Americas. A corollary of noncolonization was the principle of "no transfer"—that no changes could occur in political control of colonies and once a state became free, it remained so.

The message contained a related assurance by the United States that some have called the "hands-off" principle. Monroe declared:

> With the existing colonies or dependencies of any European power we have not interfered and shall not interfere. But with the Governments who have declared their independence . . . we could not view any interposition for the purpose of oppressing them, or controlling in any other manner their destiny, by any European power in any other light than as the manifestation of an unfriendly disposition toward the United States.

A few months before the congressional message, Adams received word of England's interest in securing Cuba from Spain, and immediately informed the governments of Madrid and Havana that the United States opposed a transfer of ownership. His argument was that a Cuba independent from Spain would attach itself naturally to North America; his fear was England.

The other side of the Monroe Doctrine—the attempted *quid pro quo*—was the principle of abstention, or America's guarantee of noninterference in Old World political affairs. The president drew upon Washington's Farewell Address in stating that "in the wars of the European powers in matters relating to themselves we have never taken any part, nor does it comport with our policy to do so." This was weak leverage, of course, for European powers were not concerned about American interference in their affairs. The Monroe administration realized this, for it left the way open for accepting Canning's proposed joint declaration against the Quadruple Alliance as soon as the State Department could work out a suitable arrangement.

The Monroe Doctrine was a bluff. The European governments had problems of their own and were unlikely to intervene in the Americas. The only teeth in the pronouncement was an implied alliance with England that was based on mutual interest in Latin American independence. A weak United States had to gamble on British help, but it was correct in setting a precedent for the future. The new republics of Latin America tried to band together against outside interference, while the European states decided to build commercial and banking ties without trying to establish political control over the territories. Fortunately for the Western Hemisphere, the European governments were more interested in Asia. These developments furnished time for the United States to mature to the point that it could defend its assertions of 1823.

Latin Americans at first welcomed Monroe's declaration because it seemed to promise United States protection against the Old World, but they quickly realized that deeds did not necessarily follow words. Various liberal thinkers in Latin America approved the message, and five of the new states—Argentina, Brazil, Chile, Colombia, and Mexico—asked Washington for treaties of alliance or assurances of aid should the European countries intervene. Adams turned them down with the admission that the United States would use force only with the help of England. He explained to the representative of Colombia: "The United States could not undertake resistance to them by force of arms, without a previous understanding with those European powers whose interests and whose principles would secure from them an active and efficient cooperation in the cause." Bolívar was skeptical about the president's declaration and recognized that the United States had acted from self-interest. At the Congress of Panama, which he called in 1826 to arrange a common defense against Spain, the United States received only a belated invitation. Because of isolationist sentiment and political difficulties at home, the American Congress so delayed its response that one delegate died before he could leave for the conference and the other arrived after it had adjourned. The Monroe Doctrine proved disillusioning to Latin Americans looking to the United States for assistance.

The Old World was hostile to the president's message because the United States had taken credit for preventing something that never would have materialized. Members of the Quadruple Alliance criticized it as "arrogant" and "blustering." Metternich called it an "indecent declaration" which cast "blame and scorn on the institutions of Europe most worthy of respect," and Czar Alexander claimed it "enunciates views and pretensions so exaggerated, establishes principles so contrary to the rights of the European powers, that it merits only the most profound contempt." The United States could not have known that no member of the alliance seriously considered forcible intervention in Spanish America. The Monroe administration did not learn of France's noninterference guarantees in the Polignac memorandum until Canning revealed them to Rush almost two weeks after the president's message to Congress. The two powers most likely to intervene in Latin America—France and Russia—were not willing to do so. They were aware of Canning's warning to France weeks before the president's message, and they knew that Russia had spread itself too thin with domestic and foreign problems. The Monroe Doctrine probably had little effect on the czar's decisions in 1824 and 1825 to approve two treaties with the United States that withdrew Russia's claims in the northwest to the 54°40′ line, the present southern boundary of Alaska. The president's action did not deter the other European powers; they had already decided *not* to intervene.

The Monroe Doctrine was an implicit warning to England to stay out of New World political affairs. This was not clear at first, for both the British public and Canning thought it supported Latin American independence and hence open markets. The London *Times* noted the similar interests of the United States and England and spoke of cooperative ventures in Latin America. Then the truth sank in. Canning recognized that the message could push the Latin Americans into the American camp and hurt British commercial interests. The United States was receiving praise for what *he* had accomplished with the Polignac memorandum. Furthermore, he realized that the noncolonization principle applied to England as well as Russia and feared that the Monroe administration had designs on Cuba.

To counteract pro-Americanism in Latin America, Canning circulated copies of the Polignac memorandum in the capitals of the Latin American nations, which informed them that *England* had held off the Quadruple Alliance. This effort in the spring of 1824 apparently convinced those already suspicious of America's objectives, but it was not enough to salvage Canning's political standing at home. In December he boasted to Parliament: "I resolved that if France had Spain, it should not be Spain 'with the Indies.' I called the New World into existence to redress the balance of the Old." But Canning's attempt to undermine American prestige in Latin America could not change the fact that the United States had outmaneuvered him. He must have seethed with anger at the caustic remark made by his enemy Lord Charles Grey: "Canning will have the glory of following in the wake of the President of the United States."

The Monroe Doctrine reflected the belief of the president and his secretary of state in national unity, although the document had no legal sanction in the United States and no standing in the international community. Once Monroe rejected Canning's offer, he and Adams put together a paper that satisfied the various sectional and economic divisions in the United States by leaving room for American territorial and commercial expansion southward and westward. They realized that domestic politics were inseparable from foreign policy. The Monroe Doctrine was a broadly based statement of policy that the president hoped any successor to the Oval Office could support. The Republican party, an alliance of planters and merchants, could not quarrel with a policy that called for territorial expansion into the northwest at the same time it advocated the New England merchants' goal of open markets in Latin America. Monroe and Adams knew the nation was vulnerable and tried to turn the European powers against one another. This would give the United States time to build a power base that the Old World would respect. They could not accomplish this with empty threats, but they could take advantage of the European powers' distrust of others.

CONSEQUENCES OF THE MONROE DOCTRINE

The Monroe Doctrine lay dormant for over two decades, when Americans resurrected it to justify the wave of expansion west known as manifest destiny. In the years between the United States did not protest several French ventures in Latin America, nor did it dispute England's annexation of the Falkland Islands or its decision to broaden the borders of British Honduras. During the problems over Oregon and California in the 1840s, President James K. Polk stated what became known as the Polk Corollary of the Monroe Doctrine, when in his first annual address to Congress he announced opposition to new European colonization in North America. The following decade, the Monroe Doctrine got its name. Not until 1895 did a president, Grover Cleveland, again identify American security with the independence of Latin America, and nine years later President Theodore Roosevelt declared that in cases of "chronic wrongdoing," the United States would assume the role of "international police power" in the Western Hemisphere. Nothing was new about the Roosevelt Corollary; President Monroe had set out its ideas more than eight decades before.

Selected readings

Ammon, Harry, *James Monroe: The Quest for National Identity.* 1971.

Bemis, Samuel F., *John Quincy Adams and the Foundations of American Foreign Policy.* 1949.

————, *The Latin American Policy of the United States.* 1943.

Bourne, Kenneth, *Britain and the Balance of Power in North America, 1815–1908.* 1967.

Brooks, Philip C., *Diplomacy and the Borderlands: The Adams-Onís Treaty of 1819.* 1939.

Burt, Alfred L., *The United States, Great Britain and British North America.* 1940.

Campbell, Charles S., *From Revolution to Rapprochement: The United States and Great Britain, 1783–1900.* 1974.

Dangerfield, George, *The Awakening of American Nationalism, 1815–1828.* 1965.

————, *The Era of Good Feelings.* 1952.

James, Marquis, *Andrew Jackson: the Border Captain.* 1933.

Kushner, Howard I., *Conflict on the Northwest Coast: American-Russian Rivalry in the Pacific Northwest, 1790–1867.* 1975.

Logan, John A., Jr., *No Transfer: An American Security Principle.* 1961.

Masterson, William H., *Tories and Democrats: British Diplomats in Pre-Jacksonian America.* 1985.

May, Ernest R., *The Making of the Monroe Doctrine.* 1975.

Patrick, Rembert W., *Florida Fiasco: Rampant Rebels on the Georgia-Florida Border, 1810–1815.* 1954.

Perkins, Bradford, *Castlereagh and Adams: England and the United States, 1812–1823.* 1964.

Perkins, Dexter, *The Monroe Doctrine, 1823–1826.* 1927.

Remini, Robert V., *Andrew Jackson and the Course of American Empire, 1767–1821.* 1977.

————, *Andrew Jackson and the Course of American Freedom, 1822–1832.* 1981.

Tatum, Edward H., Jr., *The United States and Europe, 1815–1823*. 1936.

Varg, Paul A., *New England and Foreign Relations, 1789–1850*. 1983.

Whitaker, Arthur P., *The United States and the Independence of Latin America, 1800–1830*. 1941.

Williams, William A., "The Age of Mercantilism: An Interpretation of the American Political Economy, 1763–1828," *William and Mary Quarterly* 15 (1958): 419–37.

Chapter Six

To the Webster-Ashburton Treaty, 1825–1842

For a few years after the Era of Good Feelings, general calm characterized America's foreign relations because of a preoccupation with internal matters and a time of relative peace in Europe. Perhaps this was fortunate, for the United States entered a new phase in its history when presidents were often inexperienced in foreign affairs. The irony was that John Quincy Adams, the most gifted diplomat of his time, had a disastrous four years as president, even in foreign affairs, and that the fiery Andrew Jackson, his successor in 1828, achieved more in diplomacy than anyone could have predicted. During this era of paradoxes, the American nation reached its greatest heights by 1848 and then proceeded toward the destruction of civil war.

Relations with England dominated America's foreign affairs throughout the period following the Monroe Doctrine. Commercial competition developed in Latin America, and arguments intensified over the trade of the British West Indies, the location of the Canadian-American boundary, and the suppression of the African slave trade. If familiarity breeds contempt, the classic example was Anglo-American relations. The British still seemed reluctant to accept the republic into the family of nations. Bitter resentment remained in England over America's experiments in democracy because the Americans set unwholesome examples for the English masses; on the other side of the Atlantic, Americans viewed with disgust the arrogance of a nation that claimed a monopoly on culture and control over the seas.

The stresses and strains pulling the Atlantic nations apart were countered by economic ties holding them together. The problem was that the bonds were tighter on the American side than on the British. By 1840 the

United States was sending more than half of its exports to the British and receiving more than a third of its imports from them. England was not as dependent on the United States, even though it imported most of its cotton from the South. In 1825 English merchants exported a fifth of their products to the United States, but this fell to a tenth by 1840.

Several factors explain the declining dependence on America. Britain had moved toward free trade, which led to the end of imperial preference; Parliament repealed the Corn Laws, opening the door to other markets; and manufacturers emphasized goods for export. These changes encouraged an ambivalent relationship between the nations. While economic interests held them together, the resulting commercial rivalries threatened to drive them apart. In this atmosphere political disagreements were potential sources of conflict.

ANGLO–AMERICAN RELATIONS UNDER ADAMS AND JACKSON

The presidential troubles of John Quincy Adams began with his close victory over Andrew Jackson in 1824 and extended through four turbulent years. No one received a majority of the electoral votes, and the election went to the House of Representatives, where in a state-by-state ballot Jackson's old nemesis, Speaker Henry Clay, cast his support for Adams. Shortly after his victory the new president appointed the Kentuckian as secretary of state. The outcome resulted from a "corrupt bargain," charged the Jacksonians, a political payoff that stole the election from their hero and guaranteed Clay the presidency as heir apparent. From Adams's first day in office, Jackson's supporters seemed determined to oppose everything the president favored. The accusations and the disappointments in office were particularly difficult for Adams to accept. Like his father, he was often humorless, vain, and puritanical in behavior and outlook; but also like his father, the younger Adams was a devoted public servant and of unquestionable integrity.

In foreign affairs Adams ran into a bitter rivalry with British Foreign Secretary George Canning, who still resented America's independent stance in Latin America, as proclaimed in the Monroe Doctrine. Anglo-American competition over Latin America deepened as the London government extended recognition to the new republics in 1824 and sought control over the markets. "The deed is done," Canning boasted; "the nail is driven, Spanish America is free; and if we do not mismanage our affairs badly, *she is English.*" Adams called the foreign secretary "an implacable, rancorous enemy of the United States."

President Adams's first venture in foreign affairs involved the Pan-American Congress, called by South American hero Simón Bolívar in 1825 to bring the Latin American nations together for protection against Spain and to further their own interests. The United States at first did not receive an invitation, but eventually managed to procure one. Secretary of

Andrew Jackson at the Hermitage

Before serving as president for two terms, Jackson was an Indian fighter and hero of the Battle of New Orleans, who symbolized the frontier individualism of the age. (William S. Pendleton, after painting by R. E. W. Earl; Library of Congress)

State Clay was a longtime advocate of Pan-Americanism and persuaded the president to send delegates. But instead of acting on his own, Adams tried to work through the Senate in securing the appointments and then turned to Congress for funds. The ensuing debate deteriorated into political arguments bearing little relation to the business at hand. In addition, isolationists warned against foreign entanglements, and southerners feared that slavery might appear on the agenda. Northern newspapers supported the conference as conducive to American economic interests in Latin America.

The affair turned into a fiasco that embarrassed the Adams administration. Congress debated for four months before agreeing to fund the expedition to Panama. One envoy died of yellow fever as he made his way through Central America. The other waited for a safer season in which to travel, and the conference ended before he departed. Even if they had made it, Canning had an agent present to discredit the United States. Despite the extreme optimism of the Panama meeting, the Latin American countries never adopted any proposals. No follow-up meetings took place, even though the call for Pan-Americanism would surface again later in the century.

Adams's second effort in foreign affairs was no more successful than the first. American interest in the trade of the British West Indies reappeared as an issue, for after the Napoleonic Wars, America's limited access to the West Indian markets came to an end and the United States spent the next decade trying to gain commercial concessions. The Anglo-American commercial convention of 1815 permitted reciprocal most-favored-nation status in the British East Indies, but not in the West Indies. Castlereagh proposed two years later to allow trade on a restricted basis, but this met resistance from the Congress in Washington, which tried to extract more concessions by repeatedly passing retaliatory trade laws. The United States cut off direct commerce with the British West Indies and obstructed passage of the islands' goods into the United States through New Brunswick, Nova Scotia, Canada, and England. The result was that the legislation hurt American producers and barely bothered the British. But in July 1822 Parliament yielded to pressure from the West Indies lobby and opened the islands to American trade on a limited basis, conditional on the United States allowing British ships into its ports. Adams, then secretary of state, pushed for more concessions, and in March 1823 Congress opened American ports to British vessels with cargo from the West Indies and authorized retaliatory tariffs until America's ships had equal access to the West Indies. The government in London refused to drop its system of colonial preferences, and there the matter rested when Adams became president in March 1825.

Adams ill-advisedly demanded American access to the West Indies as a *right* instead of requesting it as a *privilege*, and this cost him any opportunity he might have had to open the islands to American merchants. Four months after his inauguration, Parliament agreed to open more trade outlets to America in the islands, but with the stipulation that the United States remove its restrictions on British trade. The president refused, hoping the West Indies planters would put pressure on London to give in. But the following July of 1826, Britain shut off the islands to American vessels until Washington agreed to end its retaliatory duties. Adams was unaware of this decision when he sent Albert Gallatin to England to work out a settlement of the issue, based on mutual suspension of restrictive laws. When Gallatin arrived in London, Parliament had closed the islands and George Canning refused to discuss the matter. Furthermore, he chided Gallatin for interfering in Britain's colonial affairs.

Adams's Anglophobia and animosity for Canning had gotten in the way of diplomatic sense. Americans criticized Adams for losing the trade, and even if he was now willing to accept it short of full reciprocity, Congress would not go along. In March 1827 the president adhered to the law and announced the closing of America's ports to vessels arriving from any British possession in the hemisphere. Later that same year he recorded Canning's death in his diary with ill-concealed satisfaction. It was ironic that a man famed as a diplomat should go down to defeat, in his bid for reelection in 1828, at least partly because of his failures in foreign affairs.

Many feared that the new president, Andrew Jackson, would stir up war with England over the West Indies. Yet he surprised Americans by setting aside his distaste for the British and seeking American access to the islands as a privilege, not a right. Jackson worked through Congress and his secretary of state, Martin Van Buren, to open the West Indies. He agreed to repeal discriminatory tariffs even though the British had not ended their colonial preference system. His presidential proclamation of October 1830 threw open American ports to British vessels on an equal trade basis with American ships, and two days after London received news of this change, it granted access to the West Indies on condition that American merchants pay duties levied by London.

This was a major diplomatic victory for the new administration, although it was attributable more to world events than to Jackson. Canning had died, and the new foreign secretary, Lord Aberdeen, was more conciliatory toward the United States. Britain was becoming disenchanted with the navigation system and moving toward free trade. Moreover, people of the West Indies needed American foodstuffs and lumber. Americans overlooked these factors in praising the new president's ability to achieve what his predecessor had failed to secure for four years.

The French claims issue brought out the real Jackson. This matter stemmed from damages inflicted on American merchants by French vessels during the Napoleonic Wars. France afterward paid indemnities to European nations but not to the United States. In July 1831, however, the government in Paris relented and agreed to pay 25 million francs in six annual installments. But when the matter came before the French Chamber of Deputies, that legislative body thought the amount excessive and refused to approve. In February 1833 America's secretary of the treasury drew a draft for the first payment soon due, but the French minister of finance would not honor the request because the Chamber had not set aside the money. The king informed the American minister in Paris that "unavoidable circumstances" had delayed the payment and assured him it would be "faithfully performed." Over a year passed and in April 1834 the Chamber again refused to approve a funding bill. By this time the president was irate. "I know them French," Jackson allegedly bellowed. "They won't pay unless they're made to."

The claims issue soon became a *cause célèbre*. The president took the issue before Congress in his annual message of December 1834 and requested support for sending an ultimatum to France. Jackson proposed "that a law be passed authorizing reprisals upon French property in case provisions shall not be made for the payment of the debt at the approaching session of the French Chamber." Democrats supported this call to arms, but the Whig-led Senate feared commercial losses and refused to follow. The warning was clear to France, however. Talk of war resulted, securities dropped, insurance companies withdrew coverage of merchant houses, and the French government recalled its minister in Washington and suggested that his American counterpart leave Paris. Relations remained tenuous, with only a chargé remaining in the French legation in Washington.

The French could not consider war, but neither could they retreat before the president's demands without risking national humiliation and the fall of their ministry. It was difficult to believe that such a matter could lead to war, but with the mercurial Jackson at the helm, no one could predict which course the ship of state might take. The government in Paris sought an honorable way out of the entanglement. The Chamber appropriated the money, but made payment contingent upon a satisfactory explanation from the president. Jackson refused any statement hinting at an apology, making a diplomatic break seem imminent. In November 1835 the United States closed its legation in France and within two months the French chargé in Washington requested his passports and went home. The following month Jackson told Congress:

> The honor of my country shall never be stained by an apology from me for this statement of truth and the performance of duty; nor can I give any explanation of my official acts except as is due to integrity and justice and consistent with the principles on which our institutions have been framed.

Both nations readied their navies for hostilities.

Fortunately, in January 1836, the government in London offered to mediate the dispute. The British did not want their French ally to go to war and recommended that the French regard the president's reference to the affair in his annual message to Congress of 1835 as an "explanation." By no stretch of the imagination was this an apology, but the government in Paris chose to interpret the address as a recognition of its honor and authorized the claims payments.

The French claims dispute raised questions of national honor and for that reason caused talk of war. Jackson had unnecessarily made an issue of a subject better left to the sedate surroundings of the diplomats' table. This stance was dangerous, for the French government was not in a political position to give in as quickly as he wanted. Jackson got the money, rallied Americans behind him, and probably won some measure of respect in Europe for the United States. But his brash policies had provoked a near confrontation over a matter that, with patience and time, would doubtless have been resolved without leaving such hard feelings.

THE CANADIAN REBELLIONS OF 1837–1838 AND THE *CAROLINE* EPISODE

Jackson's successor, Martin Van Buren, faced several diplomatic issues that threatened to embroil the United States in conflict. The first was Texas, a problem he inherited from Jackson, which will be the subject of discussion in the following chapter. The most pressing matter was the

Martin Van Buren

As president, he helped to defuse a dangerous border situation between the United States and British North America. (Library of Congress)

outbreak of the Canadian rebellions of 1837–38. Dissidents in Upper and Lower Canada, attempting to throw off British rule, attracted considerable interest in the United States by invoking the ideals of 1776. William Lyon Mackenzie and other Canadian rebels aroused strong feelings on both sides of the border. For one thing, the Panic of 1837 had thrown thousands of Americans into the ranks of the unemployed, and they eagerly accepted the promises of cash and land in exchange for fighting the British. A broader consideration was that separation of Canada offered the prospect of American expansion northward and the ultimate expulsion of the British from North America. President Van Buren responded in November 1837 with a proclamation of neutrality that lacked means of enforcement and thus had little effect on events. The following month British loyalists drove Mackenzie out of Upper Canada and into Buffalo, New York, where he raised money and recruits for a "patriot" army to invade his homeland. Headquartered in the Eagle Tavern, he recruited nearly 500 Americans, who gathered under the command of Rensselaer Van Rensselaer of New York at a dilapidated fortress on Navy Island, a small plot of land on the Canadian side of the Niagara River and about a mile above the falls.

Tensions mounted along the border as a forty-five-ton, privately owned American steamer, the *Caroline,* transported American volunteers and war matériel from Buffalo to Navy Island. Exasperated by this open flaunting of American neutrality, a Canadian officer and fifty militiamen determined to destroy the vessel. In the evening hours of December 29, 1837, they made their way to the spot where the *Caroline* was supposed to be moored. But it was not there. This did not stop the men; they crossed the river and found it tied to the dock at Schlosser—in *American* waters. The Canadians boarded the vessel and, after a mild scuffle, took control in less than ten minutes. Only one person was killed, an American named Amos Durfee. The captors forced everyone off the *Caroline,* pulled it to the middle of the Niagara, and set it afire. The *Caroline* sank in flames, just above the falls.

Reaction to the *Caroline* affair along the border was electric. Reports in the newspapers erroneously described the vessel hanging over the lip of the falls, its terrified passengers screaming for help. A poem made a monument of the incident:

> The slumbering genius of freedom woke,
> As over the shelving rocks she broke,
> And plunged in her turbulent grave,
> The slumbering genius of freedom woke,
> Baptized in Niagara's wave,
> And sounded her warning Tocsin far,
> From Atlantic's shore to the polar star.

Coffin-shaped circulars announced the public funeral of Amos Durfee, a grisly spectacle that took place three days later in the city square of Buffalo. Amidst speechmaking and shouts from a mob of 3,000 spectators, the victim's body lay on the courthouse steps, "its pale forehead, mangled by the pistol ball, and his locks matted with his blood!" according to the New York *Herald's* lurid account. The Rochester *Democrat* trumpeted a call for war in the name of national honor.

The matter posed a severe challenge to the diplomats. Secretary of State John Forsyth denounced the destruction of the *Caroline* as an "extraordinary outrage" and demanded an immediate apology and reparations. The British minister in Washington, Henry Fox, called the act self-defense and declared that the rebellions in Canada were a crime and the *Caroline* a pirate subject to destruction in any waters. The government in London refused to accept responsibility for the act. Forsyth countered by asserting that the Canadian rebellions constituted war and that those involved were belligerents. The United States had declared neutrality and the *Caroline* could not have been a pirate.

The British minister detected a flaw in the American argument that for some unexplained reason he failed to exploit. A note to his London office carried striking allusions to Jackson's invasion of Florida in 1817: "If the Americans either cannot or will not guard the integrity of their own soil or prevent it from becoming an arsenal of outlaws and assassins, they have no right to expect that the soil of the United States will be respected by the victims of such unheard of violence."

The Van Buren administration was caught in a dilemma. According to international law, America's neutrality proclamation of 1837 defined the situation in the Canadas as a war between belligerents, which meant that contraband on board a "neutral" vessel was subject to confiscation. If the owners of the *Caroline* knew that it carried war matériel and volunteers for the rebel force (which, in fact, they did know), the boat was no longer "neutral" and should have gone to a prize court. In retrospect the British should have warned the American government that if the *Caroline* continued its activities along the border, they would seize it; if this did not work, they could have disposed of the steamer quietly, not in a burst of flames on the Niagara River.

But hindsight was of no value in early 1838. Americans knew only that the British had invaded American territorial waters, killed an American, and destroyed American property. President Van Buren asked the governors of New York and Vermont to call up their militias, and he dispatched General Winfield Scott to the border to determine what terms each side would accept short of war. The following day, January 5, the president issued another neutrality proclamation, warning Americans that jail awaited those who violated his order. The president's efforts had little effect.

Despite the excitement, the outlook for peace was good. Emotional reaction to the *Caroline* affair diminished as one moved farther from the border, and it aroused little concern even in England. In Parliament the *Caroline* drew only a single reference; members expressed interest in allowing Canada to go on its own because it had become a liability. Americans capable of rational reflection realized that the problems concerning the vessel were frustrating to Britons trying to keep the empire intact, and they also recognized that Canadian officials had overreacted. The *Caroline* was no threat to the British; though making three voyages to Navy Island on the day of the attack, the vessel carried only a small amount of contraband and most trips occurred after the rebellions were nearly over. In March 1838 Congress provided retribution for those involved in border raids, but the president still lacked the power of enforcement. General Scott faced the nearly impossible task of calming the hatred extending along 800 miles of border, but he was impressive in full uniform as he calmed dissidents with the challenge: "Except if it be over my body, you shall not pass this line—you shall not embark."

The British crushed the Canadian rebellions early in 1838, although incidents continued as a rash of secret societies appeared on both sides of the border from Michigan to Vermont. The Canadian Refugee Relief Association of New York called for an invasion of Canada, while another secret organization, the Hunters' Lodges, first appeared in Vermont and boasted a membership of thousands who sought to free North America from British rule. Armed with secret handshakes, signs, and passwords, the Hunters infiltrated Canada and the southern part of the United States, elected leaders of a new Canadian republic, and dubbed the captain of the *Caroline* the "Admiral of Lake Erie."

But these organizations had little chance for success. Two times they failed to invade Canada, and British forces hauled off captives to a penal colony below Australia while remaining members of the societies scattered to their homes. Both Mackenzie and Rensselaer had been arrested, and by the end of 1839 the border was calm. President Van Buren had acted as forcefully as the law and prevailing national mood allowed. He had found it nearly impossible to maintain neutrality because of the vast area involved, the enormous American sympathy with the rebels' goals, the interest in expansion northward, the lax neutrality laws and inadequate federal enforcement, and the large number of Americans hurt by the depression and attracted to the patriot cause by economic inducements. Van Buren did all anyone could have expected.

THE NORTHEASTERN BOUNDARY CONTROVERSY AND THE "AROOSTOOK WAR"

The most perplexing problem in Anglo-American relations since the Paris peace negotiations of 1782–83 was the northeastern boundary that wound along the hump of present-day Maine. Arguments over the boundary's location eventually comprised thirty volumes of evidence. The roots of the controversy lay in the theoretically sound, but practically unsound, wording of the Treaty of Paris ending the American Revolutionary War and allegedly defining the Canadian-American border. The map used by the negotiators (a Mitchell's Map of North America, 1775 edition) was faulty, for it proved impossible to match the words of the treaty with the geographical terrain. But even more important, the diplomats at Paris never intended their maps to show final boundaries. The heavy red lines found on all copies of the maps used in the negotiations were *proposals;* joint commissions were to use these proposals as bases for locating the final boundaries after the war had ended. Because the boundaries discussed in Paris were of a provisional nature only, the diplomats did not attach to the treaty a copy of the map they used. The result was a long history of ambiguity over the northeastern boundary.

The aftermath of the Paris negotiations is a story of continued frustration over the boundary that harried diplomats and threatened to grow into conflict because of the infusion of national honor and Anglophobia. The initial problem was that no river fitted the description of one called the St. Croix in the treaty. Jay's Treaty of 1795 provided for a joint commission to resolve the question. Three years later the commission agreed with the British claim and identified the Schoodic River as the one described in the treaty, not the Magaguadavic River advocated by the United States. But the rest of the line remained uncertain west to the St.

Lawrence River. Anglo-American negotiators at Ghent also provided for mixed commissions; in case of disagreement, the issue would go for arbitration before a third nation, whose decision would be binding. Several attempts failed to resolve the matter, and in the meantime Maine became a state in 1820 (separated from Massachusetts), and it further complicated the situation by insisting on *all* of the territory in dispute.

In 1827 the boundary issue went to the king of the Netherlands, who was to make a decision between the two sides' claims. Four years later he had completed his examination of the opposing maps and arguments and could not consider either stand definitive. He proposed a compromise which divided the land in dispute. The British approved the Netherlands award of 1831, although they pointed out that the king's responsibility was to have accepted one of the two arguments, not to split the territory between them. Maine strenuously objected to any loss of territory, which the Jackson administration recognized would cause major problems in winning Senate approval of the treaty. The president seemed amenable to the proposal, but was hesitant to get involved in an issue politically unpopular in New England, where his Democratic party was trying to build support. Jackson turned over the matter to the Senate without a recommendation, and in June 1832 that body voted against the award 21 to 20, leaving the question unresolved throughout the decade.

At first glance the northeast boundary controversy seemed filled with petty disagreements over pine trees, countless streams, and land basically unsuitable for large-scale farming and habitation; but this was an erroneous conception. Both the British and the Americans had important interests at stake. The British objected to extending the line to the watershed between the St. Lawrence River and the Atlantic Ocean (in accordance with the treaty) because that would cost them direct access to the Atlantic. Such a line would also thrust the tip of Maine between the British provinces of Quebec and New Brunswick and deprive Britain of land for a military road into the Canadian interior. The War of 1812 (reinforced by the Canadian rebellions) made clear that such a road was vital—especially after the St. Lawrence froze over and British soldiers had to march through the area on snowshoes. The British wanted the line below the St. John River, for this would allow a strip of land suitable for a military road to run parallel between the St. Lawrence River and American territory. The line sought by the Americans, however, would have divided the St. John River and isolated the British provinces from one another. The British asserted that their negotiators at Paris in 1782–83 would not have agreed to a boundary that damaged their country's interests. The Americans realized that acceptance of the British claim would forfeit the rich soil of the Aroostook Valley and alienate both Maine and Massachusetts.

In early 1839 mounting exasperation over conflicting boundary claims and mutual distrust between Maine and New Brunswick led to the short-lived and nearly comical "Aroostook War." The government in New Brunswick had extended jurisdiction over the area in dispute and granted land titles to its subjects. When Canadian lumberjacks soon moved into modern upper Maine, that state's legislature sent militiamen to throw out the "invaders." A mild skirmish led to the capture and imprisonment of fifty Americans. Reactions were hot and heavy on both sides of the border. The legislature of Nova Scotia appropriated money for war, New Brunswick sent troops to the troubled area, and the American Congress allotted $10 million and empowered the president to call out 50,000 volunteers to defeat the "Warriors of Waterloo." Senator James Buchanan of Pennsylvania (later president) warned that the choice was "war or national dishonor," and Anglophobia permeated the "Maine Battle Song":

> Britannia shall not rule the Maine,
> Nor shall she rule the water;
> They've sung that song full long enough,
> Much longer than they oughter.

After a few barroom brawls and long hours of drilling and marching, emotions calmed, and General Winfield Scott, again sent by President Van Buren to arrange a settlement, worked out an uneasy truce. Maine and New Brunswick retained the areas then occupied pending final resolution of the boundary. But the brief excitement along the border sent a message to Washington and London that if they did not negotiate a settlement of the boundary problem, the local governments might resolve it by force.

THE CASE OF ALEXANDER McLEOD

In November 1840 a strange case involving a Canadian deputy sheriff named Alexander McLeod caused Anglo-American relations to take a sharp turn for the worse. Troubles left by the Canadian rebellions of 1837–38 threatened to flare up again along the New York border when the story spread that McLeod, a loyalist during the uprisings and from Niagara, Upper Canada, drunkenly boasted in a tavern in Buffalo, New York, that *he* had shot Amos Durfee during the *Caroline* raid. Furthermore, he opened his sheath at his side and thrust forth the still bloodstained sword used in gaining control over the vessel.

It was a fantastic tale, later shown to have no foundation in fact, but given the emberlike atmosphere along the Canadian border, the long-hated McLeod became the symbol of British ruthlessness and the object of bitter attack. New York authorities arrested him for murder and arson during the *Caroline* affair and prepared to bring him to trial. The Canadian government offered bail, but a mob aimed a cannon at the jail and prevented his release. A grand jury from New York indicted him, even though British Prime Minister Lord Palmerston demanded the prisoner's freedom on the basis that he had acted under government orders and could not be held personally responsible. In a statement that reversed England's stand on the *Caroline* affair, the British minister in Washington,

Henry Fox, declared that the vessel's destruction was "the public act of persons obeying the constituted authorities of Her Majesty's Province." The British had earlier refused to accept responsibility for the act, but the situation had changed, and they now found it advantageous to do so and win McLeod's release. President Van Buren and Secretary of State Forsyth were not "aware of any principle of international law, or indeed of reason or justice," granting sanctity to people who "acted in obedience to their superior authorities." They also recognized the limitations on their actions imposed by the states' rights doctrine. But they could not ignore Palmerston's warning that McLeod's execution "would produce war, war immediate and frightful in its character, because it would be a war of retaliation and vengeance." Americans would be guilty of a "judicial murder," Palmerston angrily declared to his minister in Washington.

As tempers rose along both sides of the North American border, the administrations in Washington and London changed hands, brightening chances for a peaceful settlement. The new president (William Henry Harrison had died after a month in office) was John Tyler, and his secretary

Daniel Webster

As secretary of state under Tyler, he negotiated the Webster-Ashburton Treaty with England that resolved several issues, including the longstanding northeast boundary dispute. (From an 1846 daguerreotype; Library of Congress)

of state was Daniel Webster. In April 1841 Webster reversed the stand of the Van Buren administration by agreeing with the British that McLeod had acted under military orders and could not be held responsible; but, like his predecessor, the secretary of state could not arrange the prisoner's release because the federal government had no jurisdiction in the case. His efforts to persuade New York to free McLeod or turn the case over to a federal court had failed, and he later claimed that he was unable to secure a promise of pardon upon conviction from the governor of New York, William H. Seward. The New York Supreme Court refused to grant his release, but agreed to a change of venue from Lockport to Utica. Webster worried about McLeod's safety. "It becomes us to take all possible care that no personal violence be used on McLeod. If a mob should kill him, War w'd be inevitable in ten days. Of this there is no doubt." Meanwhile the Tory ministry of Prime Minister Sir Robert Peel and Foreign Secretary Lord Aberdeen took over the government in London in September 1841 and began working toward a peaceful resolution of the problem.

In an atmosphere rife with threats of violence and lynchings, lawyers furnished by the Canadian government defended McLeod in a surprisingly orderly trial. Alleged witnesses to his participation in the *Caroline* affair did not appear, and McLeod established an alibi that convinced the jury of his innocence. In twenty minutes it returned an acquittal.

The full year of excitement over the McLeod affair suggested that several matters in Anglo-American relations needed rectification. The diplomats had to clear the air of numerous irritants, including the still smoldering *Caroline* matter. It is arguable whether the McLeod episode would have led to war, for the federal government would surely have intervened by force to prevent an execution. Besides, a series of appeals would have moved the case to higher courts and ultimately to the United States Supreme Court, where the federal government could have secured McLeod's release on a writ of habeas corpus since Britain had assumed responsibility for the *Caroline*'s destruction. The lesson nonetheless was clear; the United States had to prevent the states' rights doctrine from interfering with foreign relations. McLeod's personal culpability was not the issue; New Yorkers had placed Great Britain on trial.

THE *CREOLE* AFFAIR

Until the 1830s the American South was not actively involved in the Anglo-American controversies; but as the institution of slavery became an issue both inside and outside the United States, that section of the country became concerned about British behavior. Questions about slavery had not risen to the crisis level because no incident had occurred that brought focus to the matter. Yet a basis for trouble lay in the long-standing disagreements over the suppression of the African slave trade. The stimulus to a major controversy was a slave mutiny on board the American *Creole* in November 1841 as it was engaged in the interstate slave trade from

Hampton Roads, Virginia, to New Orleans. The African slave-trade issue and the *Creole* revolt soon became entangled with each other, threatening to cause a confrontation over slavery.

Early in 1808 both the United States and England had outlawed the international trade in slaves, but only the British proceeded to enforce their laws. Those who took part in slave trading were guilty of piracy, punishable by death. But no provision existed in international law that bound other nations, and no understanding had developed between the Atlantic nations that each could enforce the law against the other's subjects. Article X of the Treaty of Ghent provided that both governments would "use their best endeavors to accomplish" the "entire abolition" of the traffic, and by the Convention of 1824 they agreed to reciprocal rights of search of ships believed to be participating in the slave trade. But memories of impressment led to Senate action forbidding application of the law to North American waters and the convention never went into effect because the government in London would not accept such an amendment. In 1833 Britain abolished slavery in the empire and became leader of the world antislavery movement. The South, supported by northerners such as Senator Lewis Cass of Michigan, vehemently opposed British search of American vessels because the practice smacked of impressment. But by the latter part of the decade, British warships were stopping vessels off the African coast that flew the American flag, and Secretary of State Forsyth of Georgia and America's minister to London, Andrew Stevenson of Virginia, vigorously protested these actions as interference in America's rights at sea.

The British found it difficult to defend the "right of search" in peacetime and tried to draw a distinction between a search and the right to *visit* a ship suspected of involvement in the slave traffic. Palmerston explained that such visiting was necessary to enable British captains to determine whether the colors accurately identified the ship. Britain had signed treaties with several nations of Europe and Latin America, and had to investigate whether slavers were using the American flag as subterfuge. If denied this right of visit, the British could not hope to suppress the African slave trade. Stevenson countered that a "visit" was no different from a "search," and that it was the first step toward inspection of the ship's cargo and perhaps even impressment of American seamen. The United States would not permit a search of its ships, except for contraband in wartime.

By 1840 the United States was the only important seafaring nation which had not joined a treaty authorizing Britain to suppress the slave traffic. The governor of Liberia had declared the year before: "The chief obstacle to the success of the very active measures pursued by the British government for the suppression of the slave trade on the [African] coast is the *American* flag. Never was the proud banner of freedom so extensively used by those pirates upon liberty and humanity as at this season." When the British minister in Washington had asked John Quincy Adams some years before if he, a staunch opponent of slavery, knew of anything more horrible than the slave trade, he replied: "Yes, admitting the right of search by foreign officers of our vessels upon the seas in time of peace; for that would be making slaves of ourselves." The South's complaints about search and impressment perhaps camouflaged its concern over slavery; Adams and Cass were worried about America's rights at sea. All criticized the British.

Thus any incident that focused attention on slavery could inflame the South. That event came in November 1841, when a slave named Madison Washington led eighteen others aboard the *Creole* in revolt, killed one man, and sought safety at Nassau in the British Bahamas. After considerable debate, British officials ultimately released all 135 slaves from the American vessel on the ground that when they entered free territory, they became free. A little over two years before, blacks led by Joseph Cinqué on the Spanish *Amistad* had revolted in Cuban waters and made their way to New York, where U.S. naval officers seized the schooner, blacks, and cargo, and took them all to an admiralty court in New London, Connecticut, for salvage. But authorities placed the blacks under arrest to stand trial for murder. American abolitionists, had meanwhile seen an opportunity to expose the evils of the slave trade and slavery, and arranged a defense based on the natural right of individual liberty. In March 1841, after a lengthy appeal process and just months before the *Creole* revolt, the U.S. Supreme Court declared the *Amistad* blacks free on the ground that their transport from Africa to Cuba had been in violation of laws against the African slave trade. They were kidnapped Africans, entitled to freedom on the basis of self-defense. Though the *Creole* was engaged in the domestic traffic and the blacks aboard were unquestionably slaves by American law, the emotions aroused by the two mutinies did not allow calm analysis. Both caused an uproar in the South. But what made the *Creole* affair more inflammatory was British interference. Southerners demanded the return of their property, but Secretary of State Webster was in no position to comply because the only provision for extradition between the United States and England had been in Jay's Treaty, which had expired in 1807. His only chance for reparations was an appeal to comity (hospitality), which offered little hope for return of the slaves. Thus the South joined the growing number of Americans unhappy with British behavior.

THE WEBSTER–ASHBURTON NEGOTIATIONS

Anglo-American relations by the 1840s were strained and could have tipped either way. It was difficult to determine whether one factor was more dangerous than another, but the basic problem was a lack of trust. Americans remained convinced that the British refused to grant them respect as a nation. However, London's *Edinburgh Review* declared that the American republic was not "undervalued in England." But it admitted that "there is a nation by whom America is anxious to be esteemed—or, to speak more correctly, to be admired and feared—and that is England." America thinks that by adopting a "bold, or even a threatening tone towards England, she will obtain our respect." England disliked America's "swagger or . . . bully."

In a real sense Anglo-American difficulties after 1815 were loose ends left from the period before. Each nation remained suspicious of the other's economic and territorial intentions in the hemisphere, primarily because of commercial rivalries in Latin America, continuing animosities along the Canadian border, disagreements over Texas, and questions concerning Oregon. No single event after the War of 1812 seemed capable of mobilizing the Atlantic peoples into war, but the combination of issues had that potential.

Other irritants made matters worse. Longtime exchanges of insults across the ocean had worn both nations' patience. The writers James Fenimore Cooper and Washington Irving led Americans in defending their country and lamenting British arrogance, while British travelers' accounts denounced American democracy and claimed it generated offshoots of fighting, chewing and spitting tobacco, drinking, stealing, slaving, hangings, and a general chaos brought by rabble rule. Journals in both countries traded vicious jabs in what became known as the "War of the Quarterlies." A London journal acidly remarked that before America "can deserve the name of a wise nation, it must rid itself of its republicanism, its nationalistic 'fourth of July harangues,' [and its] nonsense about 'flying eagles and never setting stars,' . . . and the infinite superiority of the Yankee over all mankind, past, present, and to come." During the Panic of 1837, Americans defaulted on interest payments and on about $150 million in loans from the British that had helped finance new roads, canals, and railroads in the United States. The absence of copyright laws in the United States permitted Americans to "borrow" from British writers without reimbursing them. One writer, Charles Dickens, was bitter on both counts. He had lost money from royalties and from investments in the United States. Dickens received a warm welcome during his visit to the United States in 1842, but he returned home to publish his *American Notes*, which sharply criticized his hosts. For some time social, cultural, and economic ties seemed capable of holding the nations together. But these tenuous relationships needed strengthening by skillful diplomats.

In early 1842 the Peel ministry in London suggested that the two nations negotiate their differences, and the Tyler administration quickly agreed. The British were also concerned about recent problems with France and hoped that better Anglo-American relations might force the French to seek improved British relations. Foreign Secretary Lord Aberdeen appointed Lord Ashburton (Alexander Baring) as special emissary to resolve all matters in dispute. He was an excellent choice. Six feet tall and sixty-seven years old, he was the retired head of the Baring Brothers banking house, which had helped finance the Louisiana Purchase. He also was married to a Philadelphia lady and was known as a critic of British policies toward America before the War of 1812. Though he had had no diplomatic experience, he had sat in Parliament for thirty years and was trusted in international political and financial circles. Americans were flattered by the British decision to send a special mission to the United States, and especially because the envoy had such stature.

Englishmen also were pleased with Ashburton's counterpart in the United States, Daniel Webster. The bushy-browed and robust secretary of state, fifty-nine years old and majestic in appearance, had visited England three years before, where he made many friends, including Ashburton. Webster had served as the Baring Brothers' legal agent in America and spoke for New England mercantile interests. He was also well-known for his desire to become American minister to the Court of St. James in London. An English critic of the United States said of Webster that he was "a living lie, because no man on earth could be so great as he looked." Webster was on thin political grounds because he was the only cabinet member not to resign when President Tyler's policies veered sharply from those of the Whig party. Webster explained that he wanted to complete the northeast boundary negotiations then under way with England; but he probably believed that if he stayed in office he would be in a better position to outmaneuver Henry Clay for the presidency in 1844.

Before the negotiations began, Webster secretly worked to resolve the greatest obstacle to a boundary settlement—the opposition of Maine and Massachusetts to a compromise. He secured permission from President Tyler to use his "secret-service fund," a special annual appropriation from Congress of $17,000, which the executive could draw upon at his discretion in matters affecting foreign affairs. Webster hired a political figure from Maine named Francis O. J. ("Fog") Smith, who circulated newspaper editorials in New England warning that the alternative to a boundary settlement was war. In the meantime Jared Sparks, a Harvard historian, wrote Webster in February 1842 that while doing research in the French archives, he had come across a map containing a heavy red line that Benjamin Franklin had apparently used in drawing the northeast boundary during the Paris peace negotiations of 1782–83. Much to Sparks's surprise the marking supported the extreme British claim to the area in dispute. He returned to his lodging that evening and reconstructed the line from memory on a map of Maine and forwarded it to Webster. The secretary was not surprised; an acquaintance had discovered another map believed to belong to Baron Friedrich von Steuben of Revolutionary War fame, and a red line on it corresponded with that on Sparks's map. Webster momentarily put both of them away, but when the negotiations with England approached, he decided to put them to use. Again with secret-service money, he dispatched Sparks, since returned to the United States, to Augusta, Maine, to convince the state's legislators that refusal to compromise now might be costly; if copies of either red-line map turned up later, the British would have claims to *all* territory in dispute. The completion of Webster's "grand stroke," as he called it, was to persuade both Maine and Massachusetts to send commissioners to the negotiations in Washington.

Ashburton had meanwhile arrived in Washington in April 1842 and had become involved in secret talks of his own. Without notifying his home government, he contacted officials in New Brunswick to determine their stand on the boundary. A secret delegation arrived in Washington sometime later to discuss the matter with Ashburton, and to his regret its demands were more stringent than those of the Peel ministry. Ashburton's lack of diplomatic experience had put him in a precarious position: it enmeshed him in the local interests he sought to avoid. It would be more difficult to reach an amicable settlement now that he had talked with New Brunswick's representatives. He had unknowingly erected another barrier to compromise.

The Webster-Ashburton talks finally got under way in June 1842. The British emissary suggested that the two men dispense with formal diplomatic procedure and hold open, friendly meetings designed to reach a compromise. Webster agreed, and they dropped protocol and exchanged few diplomatic notes. This decision confounded historians who later investigated these proceedings in Washington, but several bits of evidence make it appear that the negotiations did not progress as smoothly and amicably as both men had hoped. Ashburton found the repeated delays, long-winded arguments, and hot and fetid Washington weather almost unbearable. He had come to the United States without his wife because of her poor health, and had hoped to return home in a month. The presence of the Maine and Massachusetts commissioners was especially exasperating. Ashburton never came to understand the practical politics involved in Webster's decision to include them in negotiations between nations, and he refused to talk with them.

After considerable discussion Ashburton retreated on his boundary claims and agreed to a settlement later that month. His instructions were to secure a line as close as possible to that of the Netherlands award of 1831, for that would guarantee enough land for a military road from the Atlantic to the Canadian interior while leaving the Aroostook Valley to the United States. To secure this line, Ashburton conceded free navigation of the St. John River to the United States, along with 7,000 square miles of the 12,000 in dispute. This was about 893 square miles less than the Netherlands award, although the United States received four-fifths of the assessed value of the territory in question, including an important military spot at Rouse's Point at the top of Lake Champlain. To mollify Maine and Massachusetts for consenting to give up part of their land claims, the agreement specified that the United States would pay those states $150,000 each. Finally, the two negotiators also settled another section of the Canadian boundary farther west. Ashburton conceded American claims to 6,500 square miles of territory in the northwest, from Lake Superior to the Lake of the Woods. This was an unexpected bonus for the

United States; in the latter part of the century, Americans discovered that this area (upper Minnesota) was rich in iron ore deposits in the eastern Mesabi Range.

The northeast boundary was the biggest problem facing Webster and Ashburton, but other issues were troublesome. Southerners demanded a favorable settlement of the African slave-trade question and indemnity for the *Creole* affair. Ashburton had told Aberdeen that America's concern was impressment and asked for authorization to renounce the practice. But the foreign secretary could not do this without encouraging desertions and endangering the crown's authority over its subjects. Ashburton nonetheless assured Webster by a note attached to the treaty (but not part of the formal agreement) that impressment in peacetime had "wholly ceased" and would not be "under present circumstances renewed." Webster and Ashburton then tried to remove the necessity for a reciprocal right of search in halting the African slave trade. Article XIII of the treaty established joint-cruising squadrons along the African coast of no less than eighty guns "to enforce, separately and respectively, the laws, rights, and obligations, of each of the two countries, for the suppression of the slave trade." The squadrons would operate independently but with instructions "to act in concert and cooperation, upon mutual consultation, as exigencies may arise."

Webster and Ashburton were unable to reach formal agreement on the *Creole* controversy, but they attached notes to the treaty that contained Ashburton's guarantee that British officials in the islands were to avoid "officious interference" with American ships driven into their ports for reasons beyond their control. In a move to prevent future cases like that of the *Creole* but to placate antislavery groups in the United States and Britain, Webster and Ashburton included a provision in the treaty that established mutual extradition of fugitives accused of seven specified crimes. The list did not include mutiny.

These decisions did not calm the growing controversies over slavery and the slave trade. The United States failed to enforce the joint-squadron clause, largely because of southern influence in key government positions. Until 1857 the British stayed away from ships flying the American flag, but finally again resorted to search tactics in trying to halt the slave traffic. Lewis Cass, then secretary of state, bitterly criticized the "right to visit," and the following year the British agreed to drop the practice in peacetime unless specifically permitted by treaty. In 1862, during the

---

MAP 7

The Webster-Ashburton Treaty resolved two sets of Canadian boundary problems, but the settlement was even more important in establishing a mid-century rapprochement between the United States and England.

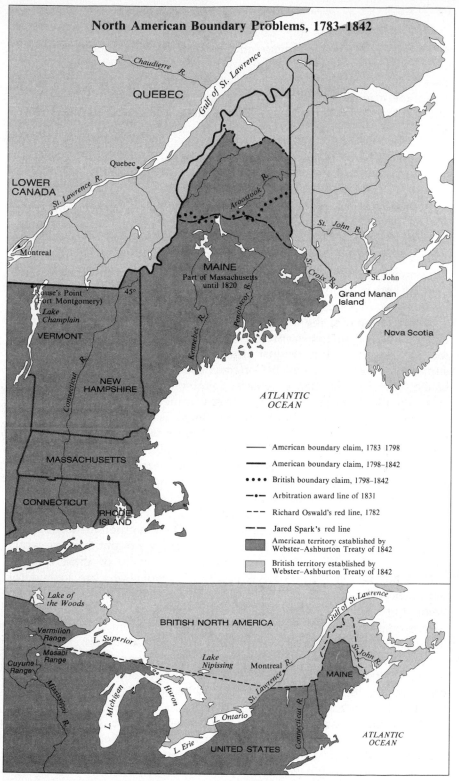

North American Boundary Problems, 1783–1842

QUEBEC

Chaudierre R.

Gulf of St. Lawrence

Quebec

LOWER
CANADA

St. Lawrence R.

Montreal

Aroostook R.

St. John R.

MAINE
Part of Massachusetts
until 1820

St. Croix R.

St. John

Grand Manan
Island

Rouse's Point
(Fort Montgomery)

45°

*Lake
Champlain*

VERMONT

Connecticut R.

Kennebec R.

Penobscot R.

Nova Scotia

NEW
HAMPSHIRE

ATLANTIC
OCEAN

MASSACHUSETTS

CONNECTICUT

RHODE
ISLAND

——— American boundary claim, 1783 1798

——— American boundary claim, 1798–1842

•••• British boundary claim, 1798–1842

–•–• Arbitration award line of 1831

– – – Richard Oswald's red line, 1782

– – Jared Spark's red line

American territory established by
Webster–Ashburton Treaty of 1842

British territory established by
Webster–Ashburton Treaty of 1842

*Lake of
the Woods*

BRITISH NORTH AMERICA

Gulf of St. Lawrence

*Vermilion
Range*

L. Superior

*Mesabi
Range*

Lake
Nipissing

Montreal R.

St. John R.

*Cuyuna
Range*

MAINE

Mississippi R.

L. Michigan

L. Huron

St. Lawrence R.

L. Ontario

Connecticut R.

L. Erie

UNITED STATES

ATLANTIC
OCEAN

American Civil War, the Anglo-American nations signed an agreement allowing mutual search in peacetime. The end of the Civil War brought a close to slavery in the United States and resolved the controversy. In the meantime a joint Anglo-American claims commission in 1853 awarded southerners $110,330 for slaves lost in the *Creole* affair, and that matter was closed.

Webster and Ashburton also resolved the *Caroline* and McLeod affairs. In an exchange of notes attached to the treaty, Ashburton emphasized that on the *Caroline*, "there were grounds of justification as strong as were ever presented in such cases," but he explained that the British intended "no slight of the authority of the United States" in destroying the vessel. He then added a statement that Webster later stretched into an apology: Ashburton expressed regret "that some explanation and apology for this occurrence was not immediately made," and hoped that "all feelings of resentment and ill will, resulting from these truly unfortunate events, may be buried in oblivion, and that they may be succeeded by those of harmony and friendship." Webster made no demands for reparation because he knew that the *Caroline had* been involved in contraband trade. On the McLeod matter Webster expressed regret for the incident, and it too was closed. In late August 1842 the secretary of state, with Tyler's support, drafted a bill which Congress quickly enacted as law; it established federal jurisdiction over cases involving aliens accused of criminal acts committed under orders of their government.

One subject discussed but not considered as an issue was the Oregon country, which sprawled from the southern tip of Alaska to Spanish California, and from the Rockies to the Pacific. Ashburton had instructions to propose the Columbia River as a boundary between the nations, but Webster could not accept this reminder of British imperial days. The secretary of state was not overly concerned about the Pacific Northwest, and as a Whig he was afraid of rapid expansion. In late June 1842 he explained to an acquaintance: "In seeking acquisitions, to be governed as territories, & lying at a great distance from the United States, we ought to be governed by our prudence & caution; & a still higher degree of these qualities should be exercised when large Territorial acquisitions are looked for, with a view to annexation." Ashburton did not believe that American settlement in Oregon would be substantial for some time, and he was willing to postpone the subject for fear that it might interfere with the delicate discussions over the northeast boundary. "It must, therefore, I fear, sleep for the present," he wrote Aberdeen.

Ratification of the Webster-Ashburton Treaty, signed in Washington on August 9, 1842, faced severe obstacles because it got entangled in political battles on both sides of the Atlantic. In the United States, Anglophobe Senators James Buchanan of Pennsylvania and Thomas Hart Benton of Missouri, both Democrats, criticized the settlement for sacrificing part of Maine to Britain. It was a "solemn bamboozlement," Benton proclaimed. Yet within two weeks the Senate approved the treaty by a substantial margin. Most Americans welcomed the news, although people in Maine and Massachusetts were disgruntled until Webster's continued newspaper editorials convinced them that the alternative was war.

The matter was more complicated in Britain. Canadians denounced the treaty, while in England the political "outs," led by Lord Palmerston and his Whig mouthpiece, the London *Chronicle,* bitterly assailed it as a "pitiful exhibition of imbecility" and the "Ashburton capitulation." During the ensuing debates in Parliament in February 1843, news arrived of the Sparks map supporting Britain's boundary claims, and Englishmen unleashed another barrage of criticism of Webster's duplicity and Ashburton's stupidity. Meanwhile, Ashburton uncovered another red-line map in the British Museum (the Richard Oswald or King George III map) which substantiated the claims of the United States, and an embarrassed Aberdeen convinced the American minister in London, Edward Everett, that he had not been aware of the map's existence during the negotiations in Washington. Each side had held maps supporting the boundary claims of its adversary in the dispute. The difference was that Webster knew what he had while Ashburton did not. This discovery took the fire out of the abuse for the treaty—especially when succeeding events showed that *Palmerston* had come across the map some years before and had hidden it in the archives. Parliament approved the treaty with little opposition and voted formal appreciation to Ashburton for his public service.

Lingering suspicions about the Webster-Ashburton Treaty have obscured its contribution toward easing Anglo-American tensions. Some writers still insist that Webster retreated too easily on the northeast boundary; had he held out a while longer, the argument goes, the red-line map discovered in England would have substantiated the American claim. Yet, as noted earlier in this chapter, a careful examination of the Paris negotiations of 1782–83 shows that all maps referred to contained only *proposed* boundaries and that the diplomats' intention was for a joint commission to construct the final markings after the war. Hence the Webster-Ashburton boundary compromise (in which the United States received the better part) was the most feasible route to a settlement. Another controversy has arisen, even more difficult to lay to rest. Some historians have accused Webster of taking money during the negotiations, in exchange for a boundary settlement favorable to Britain. Webster's inexhaustible need for money was well known; but even though this reality has led to hot disputes over his integrity, the charges have never been proved. Webster had bitter political enemies who, in seeking to discredit his performance as secretary of state, have had long-lasting effects on those writers later analyzing his achievements in office. A fair evaluation must take into account all aspects of the negotiations, for the treaty was a package agreement that set forth a compromise in which neither party surrendered vital interests and both achieved their objectives. The Webster-Ashburton Treaty promoted a mid-century rapprochement that helped remove the British obstacle to America's expansion westward. In a broader perspective, the treaty encouraged the formation of an Atlantic friendship having long-lasting ramifications.

Selected readings

Belohlavek, John M., *"Let the Eagle Soar!" The Foreign Policy of Andrew Jackson*. 1985.

Bemis, Samuel F., *John Quincy Adams and the Foundations of American Foreign Policy*. 1949.

———, *John Quincy Adams and the Union*. 1956.

Blumenthal, Henry, *A Reappraisal of Franco-American Relations, 1830–1871*. 1959.

Bourne, Kenneth, *Britain and the Balance of Power in North America, 1815–1908*. 1967.

Campbell, Charles S., *From Revolution to Rapprochement: The United States and Great Britain, 1783–1900*. 1974.

Chitwood, Oliver P., *John Tyler: Champion of the Old South*. 1939.

Corey, Albert B., *The Crisis of 1830–1842 in Canadian-American Relations*. 1941.

Curtis, James C., *The Fox at Bay: Martin Van Buren and the Presidency, 1837–1841*. 1970.

James, Marquis, *Andrew Jackson: Portrait of a President*. 1937.

Jones, Howard, "The Attempt to Impeach Daniel Webster," *Capitol Studies* 3 (1975): 31–44.

———, *Mutiny on the* Amistad: *The Saga of a Slave Revolt and Its Impact on American Abolition, Law, and Diplomacy*. 1987.

———, "The Peculiar Institution and National Honor: The Case of the *Creole* Slave Revolt," *Civil War History* 21 (1975): 28–50.

———, *To the Webster-Ashburton Treaty: A Study in Anglo-American Relations, 1783–1843*. 1977.

Jones, Wilbur D., *The American Problem in British Diplomacy, 1841–1861*. 1974.

———, *Lord Aberdeen and the Americas*. 1958.

Merk, Frederick, *Fruits of Propaganda in the Tyler Administration*. 1971.

Varg, Paul A., *New England and Foreign Relations, 1789–1850*. 1983.

Whitaker, Arthur P., *The United States and the Independence of Latin America, 1800–1830*. 1941.

Chapter Seven

Destiny and Annexation: Oregon, Texas, and the Mexican War, 1842–1848

MANIFEST DESTINY

New York newspaperman John L. O'Sullivan expressed the mood of America in 1845 when he asserted that it was "the right of our manifest destiny to overspread and to possess the whole of the continent which Providence has given us for the development of the great experiment of Liberty and federated self-government entrusted to us." O'Sullivan added that "its floor shall be a hemisphere—its roof the firmament of the star-studded heavens, and its congregation an Union of many Republics, comprising hundreds of happy millions . . . governed by God's natural and moral law of equality." The term *manifest destiny* suggested a mystical, almost religious belief that a higher power mandated American expansionism. Though ostensibly a crusade to civilize backward peoples, it aroused mixed feelings. Opponents of the doctrine derided its arrogant attempt to rationalize aggression and thievery, whereas supporters used it to persuade Britain and others to stand aside for American expansion into Oregon, Texas, California, and the Southwest, moves that led to war with Mexico in 1846. The truth seems to be that manifest destiny was a cloak of idealism that fitted comfortably over realistic territorial objectives. Patterned after Jefferson's "empire for liberty," it was the best of foreign policies in that idealists could support its republican objectives while realists could applaud its expansionist results.

When O'Sullivan wrote his editorials, at first he referred only to Texas but then expanded his claims to include America's "true title" to Oregon. Manifest destiny became the symbol of an age of expansion, when Jackso-

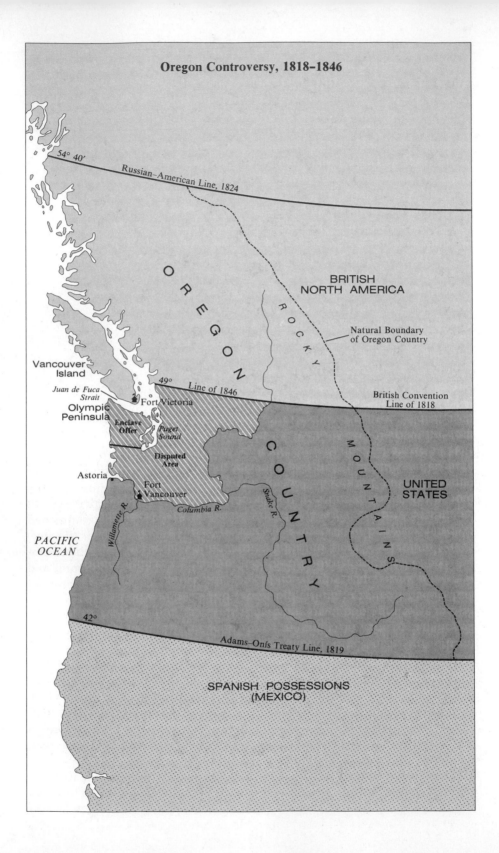

Oregon Controversy, 1818–1846

nian Americans were optimistic about spreading their way of life. Many believed that ever since the Puritans came to the New World, God had ordained them to further a millennial vision having no earthly bounds. At the same time, however, such successes would promote commercial and national security interests. The Webster-Ashburton Treaty eased relations with Britain on the Atlantic side of the continent and allowed America to concentrate on expansion toward the Pacific. The way west would spread the experiment in republicanism, facilitate the exploitation of rich farmland, lead to a plentiful trade in furs that could touch the Orient, and help to safeguard America's security by rounding out its continental borders. Pinckney's Treaty, the Louisiana Purchase, the Adams-Onís Treaty, the Monroe Doctrine—all fitted the pattern, and the decade of the 1840s marked its fulfillment.

OREGON

Oregon captured the imagination of Americans more than other expansionist issues. Americans had first laid claim to that vast area beyond the Rockies in the early 1790s, when Captain Robert Gray discovered the mouth of the Columbia River. The Lewis and Clark expedition of 1804–6 solidified this claim, and in 1811 the New Yorker John Jacob Astor established the fort and fur post called Astoria on the banks of the Columbia River. Two years later he sold Astoria to the British North West Company when it appeared he would lose the post during the War of 1812. The Treaty of Ghent restored Astoria to the United States in 1818, and the following year Spain relinquished claims to Oregon by signing the Adams-Onís Treaty. In 1824 Russia agreed to withdraw north to the 54°40' line. By the 1840s the United States and England were the chief rivals over this one-and-a-half million square miles of territory bounded by the Rockies on the east, the Pacific on the west, the 54°40' line to the north, and the 42nd parallel to the south. The huge area included parts or all of five present states and half of British Columbia.

America's continental expansion had two sides: agricultural and commercial. When Americans spoke of Oregon they primarily meant the Willamette River Valley, a hundred-mile stretch of fertile lowland running north to south below the Columbia. British references to Oregon were to the area above the Columbia, for that area was the site of the headquarters of the Hudson's Bay Company, a parliamentary-supported monopolistic enterprise in furs that had merged with the British North West Company in 1821. Under the leadership of Dr. John McLoughlin it oper-

---

MAP 8

The Oregon Treaty of 1846 was one of President Polk's central achievements, but it came only after threats of war between the United States and England.

ated out of Fort Vancouver and sought to discourage Americans from settling north of the Columbia River. Americans also saw maritime advantages in Oregon. Commercial interests would prosper from the adjoining ocean water's whales, salmon, and fur-bearing animals, whereas Oregon would be a stepping-stone toward Asia.

British claims to Oregon were stronger than those of the United States. Their explorers had entered the waters of the region long before anyone else. Furthermore, they had enhanced their claims by promoting occupation. Sir Francis Drake had sailed along the coast during the sixteenth century, Captain James Cook landed in the northwest during the 1770s, and Captain George Vancouver did the same in the early 1790s. The British did not claim all of Oregon, but preferred an equitable division of the area with the United States. They denied America's argument for the principle of "contiguity," that Oregon was a "natural extension" of the Louisiana Purchase and therefore belonged to the United States, and they rejected the argument for Oregon implied in the Adams-Onís Treaty. The Nootka Sound Convention of 1790, they declared, canceled Spain's right to Oregon and also invalidated American claims because, by the convention, Spain gave up exclusive jurisdiction over the region. On the explorations issue, Britain countered that it had a stronger claim to the land above the Columbia. Both sets of claims seemed to balance, but by 1821 the British had the upper hand because the Hudson's Bay Company was the most powerful economic and political entity in the northwest.

Before the 1840s Americans had little interest in Oregon, except that many were confident that time and American settlers would decide its ownership. Lewis and Clark had not described the area in a way conducive to settlement, and in the 1820s Senator Thomas Hart Benton of Missouri expressed satisfaction with the Rocky Mountains as the "everlasting boundary" of the United States. The Convention of 1818 with England had set up a "free and open" arrangement for ten years which became known as joint occupation, and England later turned down America's suggestion to divide Oregon east and west at the Rockies, instead proposing the Columbia River as boundary. In August 1827 an Anglo-American convention extended joint occupation indefinitely, with the stipulation that abrogation required a year's notice. The British again declined a partition at the 49th parallel, and failed to entice Americans to accept the Columbia River by offering an "enclave," or small piece of land on the Olympic Peninsula, which would have permitted construction of a fort and use of the harbors on Puget Sound. American interest in Oregon remained alive during the late 1830s largely through the efforts of Senator Lewis F. Linn of Missouri, who sponsored resolutions calling for the United States to provide military protection over the road west, and to offer 640 acres of land in Oregon to white males who farmed the tract for five consecutive years. As Congress again debated Linn's bill in 1841, Lord Palmerston warned the House of Commons that passage of that bill "would be a declaration of war." Senator John C. Calhoun of South Carolina temporarily defused the dangerous situation by urging a policy of "wise and masterly inactivity" that would allow the natural course of settlements to resolve the matter.

In 1842 President Tyler proposed a compromise of the Oregon question. Lord Ashburton informally told Webster that Britain still adhered to the Columbia River, and Webster replied that the United States would accept that boundary if Britain persuaded Mexico to sell upper California to the United States and to recognize the independence of Texas. Ashburton had no instructions to accept this "tripartite arrangement" and refused. But that same year the Tyler administration realized that the Columbia River boundary was no longer acceptable. Captain Charles Wilkes of the United States Navy later warned that a dangerous sandbar crossed its mouth and that the river was navigable only to its falls a hundred miles away. The United States had to have the harbors of Puget Sound, and this required a boundary at the 49th parallel.

The Tyler administration's attempt to resolve the matter left a bitter taste with many Americans. Webster and Ashburton chose to drop it, but people in the West and Upper Mississippi Valley had heard rumors of the White House's tripartite proposal and held "Oregon conventions" angrily denouncing the government's willingness to sacrifice the area above the Columbia River. In July 1843, over a hundred representatives from six states gathered in Cincinnati to claim all of Oregon from the 42nd parallel to the 54°40' line. It was, they declared, "the imperative duty of the general government forthwith to extend the laws of the United States over said territory." Their demands went to the president, Congress, and all state governors.

The issue became serious when a burst of expansion west known as "Oregon fever" began in 1843. The Panic of 1837 drove many Americans in search of a new life, while some went simply for adventure. Expansionists spoke of wresting the area from England, staking out the land for American farmers, and acquiring a stepping-stone to the Far East. The area's population in 1841 was about 500, which included fur traders, farmers, and missionaries. About a hundred Americans migrated to Oregon in 1842, but a thousand more went the following year. In 1845 the census showed over 2,000 in Oregon, but after the influx of that year, approximately 5,000 Americans lived below the Columbia, while only 700 British subjects lived above it. In July 1843 the Americans in Oregon established a provisional government, and two years later they passed an amendment with a preamble that the governing provisions would apply "until such time as the United States of America extend their jurisdiction over us." This was an invitation to the government in Washington to act. But despite the Senate's approval of Linn's fortification bill, the House refused support. Representative John Floyd of Virginia and Senator Benton of Missouri, now a converted expansionist, touted the importance of Oregon to Pacific Ocean trade. The Columbia River, Benton declared, was the "North American road to India."

The presidential election of 1844 made western expansionism the central issue of the campaign. Henry Clay of Kentucky captured the Whig nomination, and James K. Polk, a Jacksonian Democrat from Tennessee, became his party's compromise candidate. The Whigs quickly found the answer to their campaign jibe, "Who is James K. Polk?" when he touched the public pulse by calling for expansion. The Democratic platform adopted in Baltimore issued a challenge to Britain by resolving that America's "title to the whole of the territory of Oregon is clear and unquestionable" and calling for the "reoccupation of Oregon and the reannexation of Texas at the earliest practicable period." The Democrats ingeniously linked the two expansionist issues and won the support of southerners interested in Texas for spreading slavery, and northerners and westerners who sought Oregon as a free-soil area. Few Americans laid serious claim to all of Oregon before the election, and no one had connected it with Texas. But the platform satisfied both the slavery and free-soil interests in the party, and the attachment of the prefix "re" to "occupation" and "annexation" furnished the United States a respectable defense against the charges of imperialism. By the time Clay recognized the popularity of the Democratic platform, it was too late. Polk's narrow victory in New York gave him the election. It is difficult to interpret the outcome as na-

James K. Polk

Although president for only a single term, he resolved the Oregon boundary dispute with England, solidified America's claim to Texas, and acquired the great Southwest as a result of the Mexican War. (Nathaniel Currier; National Portrait Gallery)

tional approval for expansion, but the election stirred a British call for arbitration of the Oregon issue and fed the expansionists' cry for territory. In January 1845 Secretary of State Calhoun turned down the British proposal for arbitration, and President-elect Polk hailed the election returns as a mandate for American expansion.

The new president was a realist and an expansionist who skillfully used bluff and the existing Anglophobia in the United States to advantage in foreign affairs. In his inaugural address of March 1845 Polk threw down the gauntlet to London by asserting that America's right to all of Oregon was "clear and unquestionable." The British considered presidential declarations to be official policy statements rather than political pronouncements designed for domestic consumption, and were deeply offended by what one journal called the "*manner*, not the matter in dispute." The London *Times* declared that only war could tear Oregon from Britain. Polk's declaration achieved its desired effect; after fulfilling the Democratic platform's expansionist cry, he prepared to compromise on Oregon.

In July 1845 Polk authorized Secretary of State James Buchanan to inform the British that the United States would accept the 49th parallel as boundary if it received the southern half of Vancouver Island as part of the settlement. When pressed for the reasons for the president's retreat from campaign declarations, Buchanan explained that Polk felt bound by the actions of his predecessors. The British minister in Washington, Richard Pakenham, should have forwarded the proposal to his London office for advice, but he could foresee no change in his superiors' policy and refused it on his own. Pakenham reasoned that Buchanan's offer had not included free British use of the Columbia River, and he was still upset over Polk's previous demand for all of Oregon. The president was irate. He ignored Buchanan's warnings to defuse the issue because of growing troubles with Mexico and in late August again demanded the 54°40' line. In withdrawing his offer of the 49th parallel, Polk declared that "if we do have war it will not be our fault." British Foreign Secretary Lord Aberdeen had meanwhile disavowed Pakenham's unilateral action and his minister twice suggested arbitration, but Polk now insisted on a British concession.

The focus of America's attention in the autumn of 1845 alternated between Oregon and an ongoing crisis with Mexico over Texas, but in December the president again challenged the British presence in the Pacific Northwest. His annual message to Congress clarified America's objectives as Texas, California, and Oregon. Congress should inform Britain that the United States was ready to give the required one year's notice for ending joint occupation in Oregon. In what has become known as the Polk Corollary of the Monroe Doctrine of 1823, he asserted that "the United States cannot in silence permit any European interference on the North American continent, and should any such interference be attempted will be ready to resist it at any and all hazards." Polk applied the noncolonization principle specifically to North America in asserting that "no future European colony or dominion shall with our consent be planted or established on any part of the North American continent." Though he included France and others in the warning, the main focus of concern was England. The president wrote in his diary in early 1846 that "the only way to treat John Bull [England] was to look him straight in the eye."

With the Mexican situation steadily worsening, Polk privately left the door open for a British counterproposal to the 54°40' line. He had to be careful because of political considerations at home. Northern and western expansionists were upset with Calhoun and other southerners, for after Congress admitted Texas into the Union in December 1845, they seemed willing to compromise on Oregon at the 49th parallel. Several Democrats demanded all of the disputed territory to the 54°40' line, and when they thought that Polk was softening on Oregon, Senator Edward Hannegan of Indiana warned: "I shall hold him recreant to the principles which he professed, recreant to the trust which he accepted, recreant to the generous confidence which a majority of the people proposed in him."

Polk was playing a dangerous game, both at home and abroad. A mistake could alienate fellow Democrats who had only narrowly won office in 1844; worse, it could lead to war with Britain. If the Democrats believed the president was not upholding their aims in Oregon, the party would become a shambles and he would be its chief casualty. Pressure on England could have dire consequences. The United States could not afford war, and certainly not concurrently with a probable Mexican conflict. Polk must have been bluffing; he did not make any military preparations during these crisis-ridden months.

The Oregon dispute was susceptible to compromise because it was political in nature rather than military or strategic. The chief concern was not the 54°40' line, but a small triangular shaped territory lying between the Columbia River and the 49th parallel and including Juan de Fuca Strait. In four instances—1818, 1824, 1826, 1844—the British had called for the Columbia River as boundary, but each time the United States argued for the 49th parallel. After the furor over Tyler's tripartite suggestion and the revelations of Wilkes's voyage, the United States could not consider anything less than the 49th parallel. Even Whig commercialists, who opposed Polk's expansionist policies, recognized the necessity of having Juan de Fuca Strait and the harbors of Puget Sound.

Both England and the United States wanted to resolve the Oregon question short of war, but neither could compromise national honor. Aberdeen, like Polk, had to protect his political flanks, and to do so he mobilized the country's military forces. America's minister in London, Louis McLane, was alarmed and brought the matter before Aberdeen. The foreign secretary explained that "the President had determined to discourage any new proposition on the basis of compromise, and to concede nothing of the extreme demand." His country could not take a chance and had to defend Canada, even if that involved "offensive operations."

McLane convinced Polk that he had gone too far. War with Mexico was imminent and conflict with Britain was unthinkable. By return steamer in late February 1846, Buchanan's dispatch informed Aberdeen that even though Polk "would accept nothing less than the whole territory unless the Senate should otherwise determine," he was ready "with reluctance" to "receive and to treat with the utmost respect" a British recommendation for a boundary at the 49th parallel and Juan de Fuca Strait. In the meantime the House passed the bill giving notice of the termination of joint occupation, and forwarded it to the Senate, where that body entered a lengthy, acrimonious debate highlighting manifest destiny and bitter sectional division between northerners and southerners over the Oregon boundary.

The way to compromise in the Senate came from southern Democrats and northern Whigs. Commercial groups from both parties wanted peace, Calhoun joined Webster in calling for an amicable settlement, and the aged Albert Gallatin published a seventy-five-page essay opposing war. The Senate finally passed the House bill announcing the end of joint occupation, but its tone was milder than that found in Polk's message. The original House measure had brusquely instructed the president to announce the notice, while the amended Senate version of late April made no reference to America's "clear and unquestionable" right to the 54°40' line. Instead, it called for "a speedy adjustment" of "the respective claims of the United States and Great Britain." The Senate's approval by a wide margin was an indication that most of its members favored compromise. Within a week of the congressional action, Secretary of State Buchanan sent notice of the treaty's abrogation to Aberdeen, but notified him also of the president's expressed desire for compromise.

Aberdeen likewise wanted a compromise over Oregon at the 49th parallel. Besides problems with France and growing popular feeling against colonialism, his country was dangerously divided by the controversy over repeal of the Corn Laws—the high protective tariff on grain. The potato shortage in Ireland was threatening to become acute, and Britain needed American cotton. Despite these pressures for a settlement, Aberdeen could not leave the appearance of backing down before America's public threats. The only serious concern in the controversy was the Hudson's Bay Company, and it had lost popularity in England because of its high prices on furs. An unexpected coincidence worked to Aberdeen's advantage. By early 1845 the company had decided to move its headquarters from Fort Vancouver on the Columbia River to Fort Victoria on Vancouver Island. The company's spokesmen explained that trappers had cleaned the mainland of fur-bearing animals and that concern was growing about American encroachments from below the river. As late as 1846 fewer than ten Americans lived above the Columbia, but many in the Willamette Valley had a reputation for fighting and seemed ready to overrun the Northwest—especially if that action entailed destroying the Hudson's Bay Company.

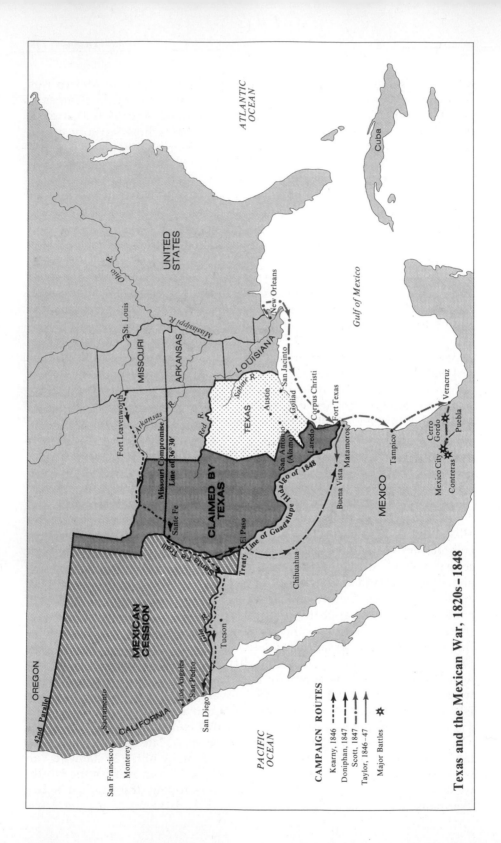

Texts and the Mexican War, 1820s–1848

Aberdeen's treaty proposal on Oregon arrived in Washington in early June. It accepted the 49th parallel as the boundary from the Rockies to the waters around Vancouver Island and the mainland, allowing Britain to retain the island by continuing the line around its southern side. Polk approved these provisions, but did not favor Aberdeen's stipulation that use of the Columbia River from the boundary to its mouth would be "free and open to the Hudson's Bay Company, and to all British subjects trading with the same." But the United States had gone to war with Mexico the previous month and the conciliatory British ministry, Polk realized, maintained only shaky political control. The president followed his cabinet's advice to submit the matter to the Senate for its opinion *before* he accepted or rejected the British treaty. This was a break with the procedure established during the first years of the republic, but the move was good politics and Polk was a good politician. He could escape his campaign vows of 54°40' by allowing the Senate to take the heat.

On June 12 the Senate voted 39 to 12 to advise the president to accept Aberdeen's proposals. The formal signing ceremony for the Oregon treaty took place three days later, and on June 18 the Senate approved it 41 to 14, all of the opposition being Democrats and mostly from the Middle West. The president ratified the treaty the following day. Not all Americans were happy with the settlement. Democratic Senator William Allen of Ohio disgustedly resigned his chairmanship of the Foreign Relations Committee and Benton sarcastically declared: "Why not march up to 'Fifty-four Forty' as courageously as we march upon the Rio Grande? Because Great Britain is powerful, and Mexico is weak." But, Benton seemed unwilling to admit, few Americans demanded *all* of Oregon, and most supported the 49th parallel. War over Oregon was preventable because both the United States and Great Britain were willing to compromise once they convinced constituents that to do so did not violate national honor. Fortunately also, the British again had other more pressing domestic and foreign concerns. If Polk had counted on these developments, he had calculated correctly. The stakes were high, however—perhaps superseded only by the risks. Polk got what he wanted all along—the 49th parallel as boundary and the harbor at Puget Sound—and without war.

THE TEXAS QUESTION

The Mexican War of 1846–48 had its roots in the Texas question, for the annexation of Texas by the United States catalyzed several other issues and ultimately led to conflict. The boundary dispute magnified the central

---

MAP 9

The United States acquired the great Southwest by a war with Mexico that many critics attribute to aggressive imperialism.

issue of annexation: Texans argued for the Rio Grande from its mouth west to El Paso and then north to the 42nd parallel; the Mexican government countered for the Nueces River, over 150 miles north of the Rio Grande and within largely uninhabited territory. The land was not so much the question as it was a series of grievances that grew into questions of honor between the Americans in Texas and the government in Mexico City. Texans believed that the Mexican government had become oppressive, whereas the Mexicans were concerned that in the name of manifest destiny the United States intended to swallow their holdings in the hemisphere. The Texas issue, long-standing damage claims by Americans against Mexico, President Polk's desire for California, manifest destiny—these combined to drive the United States into war with Mexico.

The events in Texas that culminated in the Mexican War began during the 1820s. By the Adams-Onís Treaty of 1819, the government in Washington had given up claims to areas west of Louisiana's border at the Sabine River, but the situation dramatically changed when two years later Mexico won independence from Spain. The Mexican government proved unstable and its empire on paper was so expansive that leaders found it nearly impossible to maintain authority from Mexico City. Mexico spread north and west to Oregon and included thinly populated areas stretching hundreds of miles east to Louisiana. About 60,000 nationals lived in a republic housing six million poor and illiterate Indians and people of mixed nationalities who felt no allegiance to any governing body. Whereas Mexicans of Spanish descent preferred living close to their capital, great numbers of Americans had migrated into the upper provinces of Mexico—Texas, New Mexico, and California.

Like the Spanish before them, the Mexicans used the empresario (contractor) system to attract settlers into Texas. Officials opened the area to anyone, hoping to create a buffer against American encroachments, but proximity dictated that the most rapid influx would be from the United States. Missouri's Moses Austin (who soon died) and his son Stephen were the first empresarios to lead the stipulated 300 families into Texas in 1822. Migrants were to swear allegiance to the Mexican government, pay taxes, convert to Roman Catholicism, and pay ten cents an acre under easy credit terms—a fraction of the going price in the United States of $1.25 cash per acre. The Panic of 1819 had restricted credit arrangements in the United States, and the cheap land in Mexico and its liberal constitution of 1824 brought more than 30,000 Americans into Texas by the mid-1830s. Problems had already developed. Americans maintained their former loyalties, showed little interest in becoming Catholic, and complained when Mexico outlawed slavery, passed tariffs on American imports into Texas, used convicts in its armies, and placed restrictions on further immigration. Moreover, the government had passed into the hands of General Antonio Lopez de Santa Anna, who was elected on a liberal ticket and yet, ironically, suspended the constitution in 1834 and established a military dictatorship. Texans protested infringements of their rights under the constitution and presented a "Declaration of Causes" modeled after America's great document of 1776. By the autumn of 1835 the Texans had had confrontations with Mexican troops, and had established a provisional government and an army under Sam Houston.

Both the government in Washington and its citizens closely followed the growing crisis in Texas. American ministers had tried to purchase Texas on two occasions. During the 1820s Joel Poinsett of South Carolina worked with liberals in the Mexican congress but failed, while President John Quincy Adams authorized his secretary of state, Henry Clay, to try to buy the area. In one of Clay's meetings with the Mexican minister in Washington, he outlandishly argued that the sale of Texas would place the capital city of Mexico closer to the center of the country where all capitals should be. One of President Jackson's appointees, Anthony Butler, was even more blunt. He suggested that the United States follow standard procedure in Mexico and offer a bribe of $500,000. The Washington government's clumsy effort at acquiring Texas forewarned Mexico. Most Americans were discreet: they argued that time and the steady course of American settlement in Texas would decide its fate as these same factors had decided that of the Floridas.

The outbreak of the Texan War for Independence in 1836 caused widespread interest throughout the United States. Despite President Jackson's invocation of neutrality, "Texas meetings" drummed up support for volunteer soldiers and for economic and financial assistance against the Mexican government. During the previous November of 1835 an uprising by a few Texans had forced out the small number of Mexican forces left in the province and caused Santa Anna to lead troops into Texas to reestablish control. He and his large force first engaged the Texans at an old mission in San Antonio called the Alamo. On March 6, 1836, after almost two weeks of fighting, 5,000 Mexican soldiers broke the resistance of Colonel William Travis and 200 companions and killed all survivors, including legendary figures James Bowie and Davy Crockett. Three weeks later James Fannin and 400 Texans, including many volunteers from the United States, surrendered to Mexican forces at Goliad, only to be summarily shot. More Americans joined Houston's army as terrified Texan refugees fled across the Sabine River and into Louisiana to escape Santa Anna's advancing army.

On April 21 at a spot near present-day Houston called San Jacinto, the Texan army of 800 men suddenly attacked the Mexicans, who were then in afternoon siesta. Shouting "Remember the Alamo," Houston's forces charged across an open field and killed over 600 of Santa Anna's men. They found the general disguised in the dress of a common soldier and hiding in a tall clump of grass. On May 14 he signed two treaties with Houston which recognized Texan independence, required Mexican troops to evacuate Texas, and proclaimed the Rio Grande as the western and southern boundary of the new republic. When freed, Santa Anna later disavowed the agreements as made under duress, as did the new government in Mexico City, which had recently overthrown Santa Anna.

The new independent republic of Texas promptly sought annexation by the United States, and with Houston's close friend Jackson in the White House, prospects looked good. As early as April 1836 a proposal was before Congress to extend recognition to Texas, but abolitionists bitterly fought the move as the first step toward annexation and the eventual admission of several slave states. The president understood the warning. Political realities caused him to turn his back on annexation. His Democratic party was a loose alliance of northerners and southerners who could remain united as long as slavery did not become an issue. Abolitionists already accused southerners of conspiring to spread the peculiar institution into Texas, and even though no evidence existed of such a plot, the fact was that the greatest number of migrants into Texas had come from the old South. The president personally favored annexation, but the number of free and slave states in the Union stood balanced at thirteen and it seemed safer to leave matters that way.

As in 1820, when the debate over Missouri's admission raised the issue of slavery and forestalled claims to Texas, the question of territorial expansion again proved complex. In a paradoxical sense, the westward movement was two-headed: it carried the seed of empire while also bearing the seed of self-destruction. The spread of republican institutions was in unhappy wedlock with the extension of slavery. Though they might coexist in precarious balance, the admission of Texas would throw the advantage overwhelmingly to slaveowners because the huge area could be divided into as many as five slave states. Jackson turned his back on a friend, although on the day before he left office, March 3, 1837, he extended recognition to Texas and appointed a chargé d'affaires—almost a year after the Texans won independence at San Jacinto. The following July the United States established diplomatic relations with the new nation, which was under the presidency of Sam Houston.

Continued tensions between Texas and Mexico forced the new republic to turn to Europe for help. The strife-torn government in Mexico City repeatedly warned that it would invade Texas, and twice in 1842 its forces raided areas north of the Rio Grande. Mexico's population outnumbered that of Texas about ten to one, and Texas's military and government needs threatened to sink the country in debt. In August 1837 the Texas minister in Washington had made a formal proposal of annexation, only to withdraw it when the new Democratic president, Martin Van Buren, refused support for the same reasons given by his predecessor. In 1842 Houston returned to the presidency after a brief time out of office, and quickly realized that Texas was in deep financial trouble and in danger of another war with Mexico. The republic had two choices: annexation by the United States, which seemed out of the question, or independence under a British protectorate.

London opposed the American annexation of Texas for several reasons. An independent republic allied with England would halt America's southward expansion, help protect British holdings in the Caribbean, build a balance of power in the hemisphere, encourage division in the United States, and aid British expansion in the New World. Texas would also furnish a source of cotton and a tariff-free market for British goods that might encourage the United States to repeal its duties. British abolitionists hoped for an end to slavery in Texas, which would be an example for the American South. Britain extended recognition to Texas in 1840 and negotiated treaties of commerce and friendship. France likewise shared Britain's feelings about an independent Texas and granted recognition and signed treaties of amity and trade. Britain intervened in 1842 to preserve the uneasy peace between Mexico and Texas.

The Tyler administration tried to bring about the annexation of Texas, even though the slavery question continued to complicate the issue. After Webster resigned as secretary of state in May 1843, his successor, Abel Upshur of Virginia, agreed with the president that Texas should become part of the Union because of the danger of Britain's involvement. In September Upshur informed Houston that the United States was ready for annexation, but the Texan was reluctant to ask again. Yet in mid-February 1844 he wrote Jackson that for the third time Texas would request annexation but warned that another rejection would be a "mortification" of "indescribable" measure that would force it to "seek some other friend." Before Tyler could act, however, Upshur was accidentally killed in an explosion on board the American warship *Princeton*, and the president had to appoint a new secretary. He unwisely chose John C. Calhoun of South Carolina who, unlike Upshur, was not moderate on slavery and immediately revived suspicions of southern intentions. On April 12 Tyler signed the treaty of annexation with Texas and forwarded it to the Senate. But that body then made an unfortunate move. It postponed action until after the political party nominating conventions of May 1844, and Texas became game for the political arena.

Just before the conventions the front-running candidates, Democrat Martin Van Buren of New York and Whig Henry Clay of Kentucky, published statements opposing the quick annexation of Texas, but it became evident that neither man understood the national mood in the United States. As indicated earlier, a dark horse Democratic candidate, James K. Polk of Tennessee, advocated a program of expansion that included Texas, and won him the nomination. The Texas question had become a political issue and less subject to a resolution based on the national interest.

In early June the Senate divided along party lines and voted 35 to 16 against Tyler's Texas treaty. Of twenty-nine Whig senators, all but one opposed annexation; the others came from Van Buren Democrats upset with the nomination of Polk. The outcome was perhaps encouraged by an indiscreet note from Secretary of State Calhoun to the British minister, which an antislavery senator had secured and given to the press. In the note Calhoun advocated the treaty because of British efforts to end slavery in Texas; annexation, he declared in an ill-advised remark, was "the most effectual, if not the only means of guarding against the threatened danger" of abolitionism. He also included a lengthy defense of slavery that cited statistics purporting to prove that liberty for blacks was injurious to their morale and health. Calhoun's defense of slavery infuriated antislavery groups and hurt chances for the annexation of Texas.

While the Texas question smoldered, Americans went to the polls in November 1844 and elected Polk on the Democrats' platform calling for the "reoccupation of Oregon" and the "reannexation of Texas." Thus the Democrats bolstered the belief that Texas at one time belonged to the United States and that John Quincy Adams had returned it to Spain during his negotiations with Onís in 1819. Polk's party interpreted the election results as approval of expansion and prepared to carry out the Democratic platform once he assumed office in March 1845.

The outgoing president did not give up on acquiring Texas. Though without a party and now a lame duck, Tyler decided to act on Texas before he left office. In his annual message to Congress, he reiterated his fears of British and French interests in the republic, and asserted that the election of 1844 showed that a "controlling majority of the people, and a large majority of the states, have declared in favor of immediate annexation." Instead of following the usual path through the Senate, he unleashed a political furor by calling on Congress to annex Texas through the unorthodox procedure of a joint resolution, which meant that approval required only a simple majority in each House rather than a two-thirds vote in the Senate. Whigs in the Senate controlled the Foreign Relations Committee and opposed a joint resolution on the ground that the United States could acquire territory only through a treaty, but Tyler countered by seeking the admission of Texas as a *state*, not a territory, and justified his action by the constitutional provision that "new States may be admitted by the Congress into this Union." The ensuing battle threatened to focus on slavery again, for abolitionists believed that Tyler the Virginian was determined to spread the institution. The truth probably lies somewhere between his wish for political retaliation and his fear of British interference in Texas, with Tyler leaning toward the latter. Piqued with those who had made him a political outcast, he found it easy to favor a bill that denied Jacksonian Democrats the opportunity to acquire Texas and at the same time overcame the Whigs' opposition to it. The independent political status thrust on Tyler permitted him to rise above party and defend annexation as important to the national interest.

Tyler encountered numerous obstacles. John Quincy Adams warned Bostonians that the annexation of Texas would set off a "deadly conflict of arms" between the "spirit of freedom" and the "spirit of slavery." Former President Jackson wrote the newspapers that "you might as well attempt to turn the current of the Mississippi as to turn the democracy from the annexation of Texas. . . . [O]btain it the U. States must—peaccably if we can, but forcibly if we must." Concern also developed over whether Texas would consent to annexation. The province remained under Houston's influence, although he left the presidency in December 1844, and he and fellow Texans were disgruntled over past rejections. In fact, Houston had warned before the last time that if it happened again, Texas would "*remain forever separate*." Tyler and Calhoun tried to soothe his frustrations by sending Jackson's nephew to Texas as chargé d'affaires in August 1844, while Jackson reminded Houston that a good Texan's loyalties lay with the United States and not with Britain. Proponents of the treaty suggested various political plums—including the presidency of the United States—if Houston would support the annexation treaty. He eventually informed Jackson that he would "not interpose any individual obstacle to its consummation."

On January 25, 1845, the House approved the annexation measure 120 to 98 and it went to the Senate, where Benton, a Democrat, recommended an alternate measure which would have permitted that body to regain control over the Texas question. His proposal called for the admission of Texas as a state, but under conditions reached through negotiations with Texas, rather than by those arbitrarily set by the United States. If the proposal was accepted, the president would have to work out an arrangement with Texas that would contain the safeguard of requiring Senate approval. The Missourian later claimed that Tyler had agreed to turn over the matter to President-elect Polk, who offered assurances of accepting Benton's approach.

The political wrangling was still not over. During the night of February 27 the Senate approved the amended version of the House bill by the slim margin of 27 to 25, all Democrats and three southern Whigs voting for it. After the House concurred with Benton's changes, President Tyler signed the bill on March 1. But two days later, the day before Polk took the presidency, Tyler decided to assert presidential authority in the process. Secretary of State Calhoun directed the chargé in Texas to invite Texas into the Union under provision of the House resolution. Benton was infuriated, but the new president eventually went along with his predecessor's decision.

Thus Texas became part of the Union through the unusual procedure of joint resolution. Under the annexation treaty, Texas was to become a state that included "the territory properly included within, and rightfully belonging to the republic of Texas." The United States and "other governments" would resolve any boundary problems. Texas was to send Congress a republican constitution by January 1, 1846, and with Texas's approval, four more states might be created from its territory. Above the Missouri Compromise line of 36°30', no slavery could exist in new states; below it, the people of the states would decide whether to allow slavery. Britain made a last effort to dissuade Texas from accepting the annexation treaty when in May it placed pressure on Mexico to extend recognition.

But that summer Texas opted to join the United States rather than rely on promises from Britain while Mexico prepared for an invasion.

By the time the United States annexed Texas, several countries had extended recognition, including the United States, Britain, France, and the Netherlands. Texas sought annexation as protection against Mexico, even though fears on that score were imaginary because Mexico was incapable of reestablishing control over its former province. The United States made little effort to remain neutral in the period after the Texas revolution of 1836; its laws were too weak to stop Americans in the United States from assisting transplanted Americans in Texas. The government in Washington realized that the longer Texas remained independent, the greater the chances were for trouble with Europe and along the Mexican border. Americans believed it too dangerous and too profitable to turn down the acquisition of Texas. On March 6, 1845, Mexico's minister in Washington secured his passports and returned home.

WAR WITH MEXICO

President Polk's aggressively expansionist policies combined with Mexico's unrealistic stand on Texas to bring war in 1846. The Mexican government had warned of a break in relations if the United States annexed Texas, and yet this position was untenable given Texas's nine years of independence. But Polk had also adopted a provocative stand when he openly favored the province's debatable Rio Grande boundary claim on the basis of the treaties at San Jacinto in 1836. Opponents argued that the treaties were worthless because Santa Anna had signed under pressure and a successor government had repudiated them; proponents countered that nearly all treaties were the result of some form of pressure and that Houston had negotiated with Mexicans representing the regime then in power. Another related point is that the longtime accepted border of Texas had been the Nueces River, located a considerable distance north of the Rio Grande; from 1836 to 1845 neither Mexico nor Texas had attempted to occupy the area between Corpus Christi on the mouth of the Nueces and the Rio Grande. If the area was "disputed," neither nation showed much interest in taking it during Texas's long period of independence. Perhaps the two nations would have been wiser to forgo occupation of the area until they had attempted a negotiated settlement. But Polk's policies hardened the differences and forced a confrontation. He regarded all land above the Rio Grande as part of the United States and worked to solidify that claim. Both nations thus moved toward a war that neither could have wanted had their leaders taken time for reflection.

After Texas agreed to annexation terms during the summer of 1845, Polk escalated pressure on Mexico to surrender areas desired by the United States, either at the tip of a pen or at the end of a gun. In July he ordered General Zachary Taylor and 3,900 regulars to defend the newly acquired American territory against expected Mexican invasion. Trouble was likely, for Taylor had earned the label "Old Rough and Ready" and came from the same temperamental mold as Andrew Jackson. Problems of a political nature soon developed: Taylor was a Whig, and Polk was a cold and aloof Democrat with a devout distrust for Whigs. Polk had not been enthusiastic about sending Taylor, and later events seemed to confirm his suspicions that the general was incompetent, uncooperative, and, most of all, interested in the presidency in 1848. Both men could be invincibly stubborn, and often were—especially in their animosity for one another. Taylor's instructions were to affirm America's title to the disputed territory by moving below the Nueces River and as close to the Rio Grande "as prudence will dictate." He was to take no offensive action and was to avoid areas controlled by Mexican officials. Taylor acted with great restraint, for by August his force was on the west bank of the Nueces at Corpus Christi, where it stayed until March of the following year. That same summer Polk sent agents to Texas who apparently urged its president, Anson Jones, to occupy the disputed area below the Nueces. American military and naval contingents in the region seemingly understood that their "defensive" orders included supporting any attempts by Texas to secure all territory to the Rio Grande. Polk had already secretly dispatched the commander of the Pacific Squadron, Commodore John D. Sloat, to occupy California's major ports if Mexico attacked Texas.

Polk feared British intentions in California—perhaps even more so than in Texas, which by now was fairly safe. America's interest in California had originated before the new president came to office in March 1845. Ten years earlier President Jackson had failed in an attempt to buy San Francisco Bay and Upper California, and the reader will recall that in 1842 President Tyler had offered a tripartite deal whereby the Columbia River would become the boundary of Oregon if Britain could persuade Mexico to sell Upper California to the United States. That same year, in October, Commodore Thomas ap Catesby Jones of the United States Navy received unconfirmed reports that the United States and Mexico were at war and he seized the capital of California at Monterey and annexed the Mexican province. When he learned the next day that war had not been declared, he apologized, returned the harbor to Mexican officials, and received a temporary suspension from command. Secretary of State Webster termed Jones's act "a freak of his own brain" and likewise apologized to Mexico, but that government terminated talks about San Francisco through the tripartite proposal or any other plan.

American involvement in California developed slowly. Settlers had begun to penetrate the vast region off the Oregon trail during the early 1840s, but by that time seafarers, fur traders, and "mountain men" had been there for two decades. In 1845 interest grew in California because of the reports of exploratory expeditions. Charles Wilkes of the United States Navy visited Oregon and California in 1841 and his published accounts lauded San Francisco as having "one of the finest, if not the very best harbour in the world." The Mexican government was weak, he de-

clared, and the area would doubtless become independent and provide a
pathway to the trade of the Pacific and Orient. A second report came
from the famous explorer and son-in-law of Senator Benton, Lieutenant
John C. Frémont of the United States Army's Topographical Corps who
entered California during the winter of 1843–44 and wrote glowing accounts of rich farmland. A third series of reports came from Thomas O.
Larkin of New England, who had lived in Monterey as a businessman
since the early 1830s, and by the opening of the next decade wrote articles
for the eastern press in praise of California. In 1843 he was appointed
the first American consul. Three years later he estimated that close to
1,000 citizens of the United States lived in California, but thought this
would change dramatically if the rapid influx of 1845 was a sign.

Mexico tried to stop American migration into California and to persuade those already there to leave. But as was the case with Texas, local
officials in California were too few to carry out their government's wishes.
As late as 1846 no more than 7,000 people of Spanish lineage lived in California, and Mexico controlled no areas above San Francisco and nothing
farther inland than the coast. Most Spanish settlers were engaged in
sheep and cattle raising, while a few were involved in missionary work.

Polk's California policy was to buy it from Mexico or, failing that, to
encourage its residents to seek annexation by the United States. Consul
Larkin confirmed the president's fears about British intentions in California by uncritically passing rumors to Washington. In mid-October 1845
Polk made Larkin a private agent under orders to encourage separatism
in California and bring about its annexation by the United States. Secretary of State Buchanan ordered Larkin to assure the people of California
that if they won independence from Mexico, "we shall render her all the
kind offices in our power as a sister republic." The United States would
"make no effort and use no influence" to induce California to join the
Union, but if its people chose to do so, "they would be received as breth-
ren, whenever this can be done without affording Mexico just cause of
complaint." Buchanan's letter was an incitement to revolution.

In the meantime Polk inquired whether Mexico would welcome a
minister to discuss the nations' problems, and in mid-October 1845 he
learned that Mexico's president, José Joaquín Herrera, would "receive the
commissioner of the United States . . . to settle the present dispute
[Texas]." Polk, however, ignored Herrera's stipulations of sending a *commissioner* to discuss only the Texas boundary, and appointed Democrat
John Slidell of Louisiana, a known expansionist, as envoy extraordinary
and minister plenipotentiary to open negotiations over Texas, California,
and a longstanding claims issue. Slidell was to recommend a border from
the mouth of the Rio Grande to El Paso and then north to the 42nd parallel and west to the Pacific, which would give eastern New Mexico and
Upper California to the United States. He had authority to pay $25 million
for New Mexico and California, although he could go as high as $40 mil-
lion. The other issue concerned damage claims held by American citizens

that stemmed from the insurrections in Mexico. Slidell's instructions contained flexibility, but the minimum was the Rio Grande border in exchange for the United States's assumption of these damage claims.

Slidell arrived in Mexico City in early December 1845, amid an atmosphere of threatened violence, and Herrera's government could not appear conciliatory without risking its own overthrow. News of Slidell's secret mission had reached Mexico even before he received the appointment, drawing a wrathful reaction in Mexican newspapers. Handbills charged the Herrera government with treason. Moreover, since Slidell's title exceeded commissioner status, dealing with him would have implied the restoration of relations with the United States and Mexico's willingness to accept America's annexation of Texas. In sum, political reality dictated that Mexico could not engage in talks involving Texas or California. Despite its rebuff of Slidell, Herrera's government fell. By March the special envoy assured Buchanan "that nothing is to be done with these people, until they shall have been chastised." War was desirable, he wrote the president. "Depend upon it," he declared; "we can never get along well with them, until we have given them a good drubbing."

After news of Slidell's failure reached Washington, Polk made efforts to establish physical claim to the area below the Nueces River, when on January 13, 1846, he ordered General Taylor to move south out of Corpus Christi and occupy the east bank of the Rio Grande. The president probably intended to force negotiations, but Mexico understandably regarded the move as an act of provocation. After a near skirmish with a small contingent of Mexican cavalry, the American army reached the southern edge of the disputed territory on March 28 and encamped a few miles above the mouth of the Rio Grande at present-day Brownsville, where Taylor established quarters at what became known as Fort Texas. On the other side of the river was Matamoros, a Mexican settlement garrisoned by 3,000 soldiers.

Meanwhile in mid-February a friend of Santa Anna's had approached President Polk with a proposal whereby the former Mexican chieftain, then in exile in Havana, would agree to a boundary satisfactory to the United States if it facilitated his return to power. To persuade the Mexican people to comply, Santa Anna recommended that the American army move to the Rio Grande (which Polk had already arranged), and that Slidell board an American warship at Veracruz and present an ultimatum to the Mexican government. Polk liked the proposal. He presented the idea to his cabinet with the suggestion that if the Mexicans failed to meet its conditions, the Americans were "to take redress into our own hands by aggressive measures." The concurrent Oregon crisis slowed the president's hand, for Buchanan warned against taking any action to provoke Mexico until relations with Britain improved. Polk temporarily shelved the idea of an ultimatum, and instructed Slidell to delay his return to Washington until the Oregon question was resolved. Slidell's rebuff, the president explained, "would produce considerable alarm in the public mind and might possibly exercise an injurious influence on our relations with Great Britain."

Tensions along the Rio Grande exploded into conflict in late April. For almost three uneasy weeks American and Mexican soldiers had glared at each other across the muddy river, and then the Mexicans brought in 2,000 more forces. On April 12 Mexico warned Taylor to pull back to the Nueces River, which in itself seemed to imply approval of Texas's annexation by the United States and reduction of the dispute to the area between the rivers. When Mexico cut off Taylor's access to the Rio Grande, he established a blockade at its mouth which closed the river to Matamoros and constituted an act of war. It was a "defensive precaution," Taylor explained. Less than two weeks later, the Mexican president declared that Taylor's blockade had forced his country into a "defensive war" against the United States, and the following day 1,600 Mexican troops crossed the Rio Grande above Taylor's quarters. That same day Taylor sent a small number of dragoons to investigate a suspected "invasion" of American territory. Though they returned a few hours later with nothing to report, that evening Taylor dispatched another sixty-three men. The next day, April 25, the long-expected confrontation occurred. Mexican soldiers attacked the Americans north of the Rio Grande, killing eleven and taking the rest prisoner. Two days later, in the early morning, Taylor learned of the clash. "Hostilities may now be considered as commenced," he wrote the president.

Before news of the bloodshed reached Washington, President Polk called a cabinet meeting to discuss whether the crisis with Mexico justified war. In his diary he wrote that he assured his cabinet that "we had ample cause of war, and that it was impossible. . . that I could remain silent much longer; that I thought it was my duty to send a message to Congress very soon and recommend definitive measures." All members of the cabinet agreed that the president should ask Congress for a declaration of war, although both the president and Secretary of the Navy George Bancroft noted that an incident along the border would make the American stand clearer. Bancroft explained that "if any act of hostility should be committed by the Mexican forces he was then in favor of immediate war." The president nonetheless retired to his office after the adjournment to write a war message which he would present to Congress the following Tuesday.

Around six P.M. that same evening Taylor's message arrived stating that fighting had taken place on the Rio Grande, and the president immediately reconvened his cabinet. Its members unanimously advised him to ask Congress for a declaration of war, and all of the following Sunday, except time taken for attending church services, Polk worked on the address. By noon of Monday, May 11, he had incorporated the suggestions of military, congressional, and cabinet men, and submitted his call for war. The original message had cited "breach of faith" concerning the Slidell mission as the primary cause and mentioned the long-standing boundary and claims grievances, but the dispatch from Taylor had changed the thrust of the argument. Mexico, Polk declared, "has invaded our territory and shed American blood upon the American soil."

The wide support in Congress for war with Mexico gives a misleading view of the popularity of the decision. The legislative scene in no way resembled a healthy debate over the president's message. The Democratic party controlled the House and restricted the time of debate to two hours, despite the Whigs' demand for additional time to study the materials Polk submitted with his paper. The speaker of the House refused to recognize members seeking more information, though two of the opposition managed to secure the floor long enough to denounce Polk's explanation as an "utter falsehood." Young Illinois Congressman Abraham Lincoln later criticized the "war of conquest" and introduced the "spot resolutions," which challenged the president to show the spot where American blood had stained American soil. Others bitterly called it "Mr. Polk's War," and Joshua Giddings of Ohio denounced it as an attempt to spread slavery. "I will not bathe my hands in the blood of the people of Mexico," he declared, "nor will I participate in the guilt of those murders which have been and will hereafter be committed by our army there." Outside Congress, the renowned writer and abolitionist Ralph Waldo Emerson of Massachusetts warned that war with Mexico would raise the issue of slavery and destroy the Union.

Despite the vocal opposition, Congress moved irrevocably toward war. The House voted in favor of the resolution 174 to 14. The next day, May 13, the Senate discussed the measure a little longer than did the House, but the margin for war was also wide—40 to 2. The war bill empowered the president to call out 50,000 volunteers and appropriated $10 million for military and naval needs.

Presidential disclaimers notwithstanding, much of the war's unpopularity was attributable to the issue of whether slavery would extend into territories that the United States might acquire from Mexico. Polk emphasized that the war did not concern slavery. He wrote in his diary that "its introduction in connection with the Mexican War is not only mischievous but wicked." The war nonetheless opened a debate over slavery's expansion that centered on an attempt by antislavery groups in Congress to pass the Wilmot Proviso. House Democrat David Wilmot of Pennsylvania sought to bar slavery from any areas taken from Mexico during the war, and affixed the measure as a rider to the war appropriations bill of August 1846. Northern support was not sufficient to override the opposition of southern Whigs and Polk Democrats; but Wilmot and others repeatedly introduced the proposal over the next few years. The Wilmot Proviso never passed Congress, but it caused heated debates over slavery and the Union.

The Polk administration meanwhile believed that the return of Santa Anna to power would ensure a quick victory. To guarantee peace as quickly as possible following the declaration of war, the American naval commander off Veracruz received a directive to facilitate Santa Anna's return to Mexico at the proper time. Some weeks afterward, Santa Anna assured the president that he intended to "govern in the interest of the masses." In late July Buchanan wrote the Mexican foreign minister that the United States wanted an honorable peace; but before his message arrived in Mexico City, Santa Anna passed through the American blockade at Veracruz in August and during a revolution in Mexico took over the "Liberating Army." When the foreign minister followed Santa Anna's orders and replied that peace considerations would have to await a new Mexican legislature in December, Buchanan irately declared that the United States would "prosecute the war with vigor." In what Polk considered a great betrayal, Santa Anna raised an army and moved north to attack General Taylor.

President Polk's goal in the war became, he said, to "conquer a peace." This would not be easy, for Mexico's standing army was five times larger than that of the United States, and Mexico was confident that the Americans lacked the ability and will to fight. A war on home soil instilled higher morale among Mexico's forces, and many Mexicans believed that America's preoccupation with Britain and the Oregon question would work to their advantage. Taylor received orders to move south from the Rio Grande into "the heart of the enemy's country" to force Santa Anna's surrender, while a second contingent was to leave Fort Leavenworth and pass through Santa Fe. At that point Colonel Alexander W. Doniphan broke off down the Rio Grande to El Paso and by March 1847 had occupied Chihuahua, and Colonel Stephen W. Kearny led a force from Fort Leavenworth toward New Mexico and then ultimately to California.

Meanwhile in May 1846 Californians overthrew Mexican rule in a strange series of events known as the "Bear Flag Revolt," which involved Army Captain John C. Frémont in some shadowy and still undetermined way. Frémont had appeared on the scene during the winter of 1845–46 with an exploratory expedition of sixty-two armed men, ostensibly under orders to determine the best passage to California. The Mexican commander at Monterey ordered him and his armed force to leave the province. After some disagreement the Americans moved up the Sacramento Valley and into Oregon. In May 1846 a marine lieutenant arrived with messages for Consul Larkin and Frémont. The contents of these messages remain unknown, but soon afterward Frémont returned to the San Francisco area and assisted a small group of Californians who led the revolt. In July, after he received unofficial word that the United States and Mexico were at war, he began to work with Commodore Sloat and Captain Robert F. Stockton in occupying California. By the end of the month the United States controlled all regions above Monterey, and soon Stockton, Frémont, and Larkin enlarged the occupation to include San Diego, San Pedro, and Los Angeles. When Washington sent official news of the war,

Stockton announced his country's annexation of California, but a rebellion broke out in Los Angeles in September. Three months later Kearny and a hundred cavalry arrived, and with the help of Stockton and Frémont took back the settlement in early January 1847. California belonged to the United States.

The Polk administration prepared to take the war to the Mexican people by sending a force, under Major General Winfield Scott, by water from New Orleans to Veracruz and then overland to Mexico City. The president had serious misgivings about sending a Whig to do a Democrat's bidding. The two men, in fact, had had troubles before. Polk had been supported for the presidency by Andrew Jackson, who was Scott's longtime enemy; the general, as mentioned, was a Whig. But after Polk searched in vain for a Democratic military leader, he finally gave in and ordered Scott and 10,000 men to finish the war. In March 1847 they left their ships along the shores of Veracruz and on the 29th won the city's surrender. Scott then faced the major arm of Mexican troops under Santa Anna, who had just suffered defeat at the hands of Taylor at Buena Vista and was spoiling for a victory. American forces again won a hard-fought battle at Cerro Gordo. Next the town of Puebla fell, and Scott soon headed toward Mexico City.

In the tradition of the Spanish conquistadors who first invaded Mexico, President Polk sent both an olive branch and a sword to Mexico City in 1847. When Santa Anna called for the Americans to pull out of Mexico as a prerequisite to negotiations, Polk used the victories at Buena Vista and Veracruz to bring Mexico to the peace table through the efforts of a special commissioner, Nicholas Trist. Chief clerk in the State Department, he was the former consul in Havana and had a knowledge of Spanish, but his most important qualification was that he was a loyal Democrat who could report to the president on Scott's political ambitions in the Whig party. Trist received instructions in mid-April to offer as much as $30 million for the Rio Grande boundary, New Mexico, Upper and Lower California, and transit rights across the Isthmus of Tehuantepec. The money would also count toward assuming American damage claims against Mexico to a maximum of $20 million. The least Trist could accept was the Rio Grande border, New Mexico, and Upper California. If this obscure person succeeded in his mission, the Polk administration could take the credit; if he failed, it could disavow him at no cost.

In early May Trist caught up with Scott's forces, but difficulties immediately arose between the men. Scott believed that Polk had intentionally insulted him. Trist's orders to make peace at the earliest possible moment, Scott insisted, interfered with his authority to wage war. The general felt humiliated by Trist's semi-independent status and by a sealed letter he carried to Mexican authorities that Scott was not allowed to see. For almost two months he and Trist refused to talk to each other and though in the same camp communicated only through bitter letters (some thirty pages long). But when Trist became ill in July, the two men reconciled their differences.

Scott and over 10,000 American troops marched out of Puebla toward Mexico City in early August 1847. They had made an effort to end the war short of invading the capital. Trist established communications with Santa Anna through the British minister in Mexico City, and learned that the general would accept peace if he received $10,000 now and an assurance of $1 million when ratification of the treaty took place. Scott agreed and made the initial payment, but like Polk earlier, he too became a victim of Santa Anna's duplicity when the dictator suddenly announced that the Mexican legislature was not amenable to peace talks. The only way to end the war was to take Mexico City. Santa Anna's army was much larger than Scott's, but it was divided by political infighting and demoralized by insufficient food and war matériel. Near the city Scott encountered his first military resistance, but after veering south to avoid the enemy's strongest entrenchments, he won battles at Contreras and Churubusco, and on August 20 he prepared to enter the capital city.

Three days later Santa Anna notified Scott through the British legation that he wanted a cease-fire. The two sides accepted an armistice until the signing of a peace treaty, and barring that success agreed to give forty-eight-hour notice before resuming fire. But Scott's experiences with Santa Anna raised suspicions about whether he was stalling for time, and when the Mexican general refused Trist's conditions for peace, Scott terminated the talks and prepared to storm the city. On September 13 the Americans took the fortress at Chapultepec and the next day seized Mexico City. Two days afterward Santa Anna resigned as president and a new provisional government took over.

President Polk had become increasingly concerned over a growing "All-Mexico movement" in the United States, and before news of the fall of Mexico City reached Washington in early October, he called Trist home and ordered Scott to end the war quickly by taking the capital. Polk realized that the demand for all of Mexico would prolong the war and entail undetermined results, both on the battlefield and in the political wars. He was also apprehensive over the political meaning of better relations between Trist and Scott, and was upset that Trist had forwarded a peace recommendation from Mexico that demanded the Nueces River as the border of Texas. Encouraged by Scott's victories in the field, the president prepared to broaden the war aims to include more but not all of Mexico. He thought the United States should keep New Mexico and California, and that Scott's forces should help install a republican government in Mexico that would favor a just end to the war. Two cabinet members, Buchanan and Secretary of the Treasury Robert Walker, favored American conquest of all of Mexico. The secretary of state recommended that the president announce in his annual message to Congress that the United States "must fulfill that destiny which Providence may have in store for both countries." Polk's words were less prophetic in tone but seemed to be identical in meaning when he declared that the United States should "take the measure of our indemnity into our own hands."

Some contemporaries erroneously believed that southern slaveholders were the major proponents of acquiring all of Mexico. The writer and abolitionist James Russell Lowell, for example, recorded his antiwar, anti-South stance in the *Bigelow Papers* and warned that California would be divided into slave states. Yet most southerners did not want territories from Mexico, where slavery was illegal and the climate and soil were ill suited for its extension. Northerners made known their opposition to the spread of slavery through the Wilmot Proviso. Those who led the movement for all of Mexico were primarily from New York and the West, and nearly all were Democrats who defended their position on the basis of manifest destiny. John L. O'Sullivan's *Democratic Review*, where the term first appeared, called on the United States to take all of North America, while the New York *Herald*, the *Sun*, and the New Orleans *Picayune* agreed that the Mexican people needed American guidance because of their inability to govern themselves. The New York *Evening Post* did not mince words. "The aborigines of this country have not attempted and cannot attempt, to exist *independently* alongside of us. . . . The Mexicans are *aboriginal Indians*, and they must share the destiny of their race." *Niles' Register* of Washington referred to " 'Manifest Destiny' Doctrines" in defending America's treatment of Mexico.

Trist received notice of his recall in mid-November, but he hesitated to leave because the new government in Mexico seemed eager for peace. When he unofficially informed the Mexican leaders that he had to return to Washington, they urged him to complete the negotiations. Scott and a member of the British legation agreed, and Trist decided to remain, on condition that Mexico approved the minimum demands of the United States. He realized that no Mexican government could survive if it sent a delegation to Washington, and he also knew that he had to negotiate a treaty with the Moderate party before it fell from power. Other groups would take over, Trist feared, if suspicions developed that Polk favored the All-Mexico movement. Trist opposed a long guerrilla war that would end with the United States in control of the entire country, but also saddled with costs and responsibilities impossible to meet. He wrote Polk a sixty-five-page letter defending his decision to remain in Mexico despite orders to return home.

The president became irate upon receiving Trist's note on December 6. "I have never in my life felt so indignant," he recorded in his diary. "Mr. Trist, from all I can learn, has lent himself to Gen'l Scott and is his mere tool, and seems to be employed in ministering to his malignant passions." Still fuming in mid-January, Polk bitterly denounced Trist's dispatch as "arrogant, impudent, and very insulting to his Government, and even personally offensive to the President. . . . If there was any legal provision for his punishment he ought to be severely handled. He has acted worse than any man in the public employ whom I have ever known."

THE TREATY OF GUADALUPE HIDALGO

At Guadalupe Hidalgo outside Mexico City, Trist signed a treaty on February 2, 1848, that ended the war with Mexico. The terms comprised the minimum requirements set up in his original directives of April 1847, in that the United States received California, New Mexico (the "Mexican Cession," which constituted the present states of New Mexico, Arizona, Utah, and Nevada), and recognition of America's annexation of Texas with the border at the Rio Grande. In return the United States paid Mexico $15 million and assumed damage claims of $3.25 million. The sum of money awarded Mexico seems large in that Polk considered the territorial gains an indemnity for the war caused by Mexico, but it enabled the Mexican government to tell its people that it had forced the money from the United States as an indemnity. The money might also allow the Polk administration to escape the charges of imperialism already leveled at the United States.

Polk disapproved of the treaty but had to send it to the Senate, both because of mounting opposition to the war and because of the growing All-Mexico movement. Another problem became apparent. "If I were now to reject a treaty," Polk told his cabinet, "made upon my own terms, as authorized in April last, with the unanimous approbation of the Cabinet, the probability is that Congress would not grant either men or money to prosecute the war." The Whigs had captured a majority in the House of Representatives after the election of 1846, and in January of 1848 the Whig-led Senate narrowly passed a resolution denouncing the war as "unnecessarily and unconstitutionally begun by the President of the United States." If he turned down a treaty that met his own instructions, Congress would terminate support for the war, he would have to pull American troops from Mexican territory and lose New Mexico and Upper California, and the Whigs would doubtless win the White House in November. Polk sent the treaty to the Senate on February 22 with a guarded recommendation for approval.

The Treaty of Guadalupe Hidalgo encountered serious obstacles in the Senate. Its passage was uncertain because of that body's divisions over the territorial question. At one time a coalition of fifteen Whigs wanted to return all lands west of the Rio Grande to Mexico, while eleven Democrats (ten from the South and West and one from New York) favored enlarging the conquered territories to include part or all of Chihuahua, Coahuila, Nuevo León, and Tamaulipas. None favored the treaty without amendments. The strange alignment fell apart during the treaty vote, and on March 10 the Senate approved 38 to 14, with 26 Democrats and 12 Whigs comprising the majority and the parties splitting evenly in opposition. On May 30 the two governments exchanged ratifications and President Polk declared the treaty in effect on July 4, 1848.

Polk remained bitter over Trist's behavior. He refused to approve payment for Trist's salary or expenses after the date of his recall, and the emissary disappeared into poverty after losing his job in the State Department. More than two decades afterward, Congress reimbursed him for the salary and expenses incurred after his recall from Mexico, and President Ulysses S. Grant appointed him postmaster in Alexandria, Virginia. This was small recompense for Trist's services in halting the war.

Assessments of the treaty have varied. Whig Philip Hone denounced it as "negotiated by an unauthorized agent, with an unacknowledged government, submitted by an accidental President, to a dissatisfied Senate." This wry comment overlooked the alternative to Trist's treaty, which was protracted guerrilla warfare brought by the swelling push for all of Mexico. The United States had already lost 1,721 men in battle and 11,550 to disease and other factors, while Mexico lost 50,000 men and the chance for empire when it gave up half its land and became locked between the United States and the rest of Latin America. The events of 1846–48 contributed to continued political disorder in Mexico and encouraged a quarter-century of civil war and outside intervention in its affairs.

CONSEQUENCES OF THE MEXICAN WAR

The Mexican War greatly enhanced the power of the United States, and yet paradoxically exposed serious weaknesses in the country's structure. Immense danger came from mixing slavery with expansion, for with the repeated failures of the Wilmot Proviso to pass Congress, the still unanswered question was whether the newly acquired territories would be free or slave. Thus the war raised the issue of race in the acquisition of new lands, and provided a preview of the nation's later problems in the Pacific and Caribbean. The conquest of Mexico opened all areas above the Rio Grande and encouraged American expansion across Indian territories. During the 1820s and 1830s the Americans had moved into areas east of the Mississippi, and those Indians forced to relocate in Missouri and Oklahoma would soon feel the pressure of Americans pushing beyond the mighty river. An American critic of the Mexican War caustically remarked: "If just men should ever again come into power, I believe they ought not to hesitate to retrocede to Mexico the country of which we have most unjustly despoiled her."

If one judges a president strictly on his achievements in office, Polk's administration was a resounding success. He solidified America's security by achieving every territorial objective: the annexation of Texas with the Rio Grande as border, and the acquisition of Oregon, New Mexico, and California. The United States owned the Pacific coast from Puget Sound to San Diego, and had opened the commercial road to Asia. In three years the nation had acquired 1,200,000 square miles of territory and expanded its size by two thirds. Yet misgivings lingered over Polk's methods. Contemporaries called the war with Mexico "Mr. Polk's War," and in 1848 elected a Whig to the presidency, General Zachary Taylor. Congressman

John Quincy Adams of Massachusetts was a life-long continentalist, and yet had been unable to support the president's war message. Adams warned that "it is now established as an irreversible precedent that the President of the United States has but to declare that War exists, with any Nation upon Earth and the War is essentially declared. . . . It is not difficult to foresee what the ultimate issue will be to the people of Mexico," he proclaimed, "but what it will be to the People of the United States is beyond my foresight, and I turn my eyes away from it."

Selected readings

Bauer, Karl Jack, *The Mexican War, 1846–48*. 1974.

Bourne, Kenneth, *Britain and the Balance of Power in North America, 1815–1908*. 1967.

Brack, Gene M., *Mexico Views Manifest Destiny, 1821–1846: An Essay on the Origins of the Mexican War*. 1976.

Campbell, Charles S., *From Revolution to Rapprochement: The United States and Great Britain, 1783–1900*. 1974.

Connor, Seymour V., and Odie B. Faulk, *North America Divided: The Mexican War, 1846–1848*. 1971.

Fuller, John D. P., *The Movement for the Acquisition of All Mexico, 1846–1848*. 1936.

Goetzmann, William H., *When the Eagle Screamed: The Romantic Horizon in American Diplomacy, 1800–1860*. 1966.

Graebner, Norman A., *Empire on the Pacific: A Study in American Continental Expansion*. 1955.

Hietala, Thomas R., *Manifest Design: Anxious Aggrandizement in Late Jacksonian America*. 1985.

Horsman, Reginald, *Race and Manifest Destiny: The Origins of American Racial Anglo-Saxonism*. 1981.

Jones, Wilbur D., *The American Problem in British Diplomacy: 1841–1861*. 1974.

Lander, Jr., Ernest M., *Reluctant Imperialists: Calhoun, the South Carolinians and the Mexican War*. 1980.

Merk, Frederick, *Albert Gallatin and the Oregon Problem*. 1950.

———, *Fruits of Propaganda in the Tyler Administration*. 1971.

———, *Manifest Destiny and Mission in American History*. 1963.

———, *The Monroe Doctrine and American Expansionism, 1843–1849*. 1966.

———, *The Oregon Question: Essays in Anglo-American Diplomacy and Politics*. 1967.

———, *Slavery and the Annexation of Texas*. 1972.

Nevins, Allan, *Frémont: The West's Greatest Adventurer*. 2 vols., 1928.

Perkins, Dexter, *The Monroe Doctrine, 1826–1867*. 1933.

Pletcher, David M., *The Diplomacy of Annexation: Texas, Oregon, and the Mexican War*. 1973.

Price, Glenn W., *Origins of the War with Mexico: The Polk-Stockton Intrigue*. 1967.

Schroeder, John H., *Mr. Polk's War: American Opposition and Dissent, 1846–1848*. 1973.

Sellers, Charles G., *James K. Polk: Continentalist, 1843–1846*. 1966.

Singletary, Otis A., *The Mexican War*. 1960.

Smith, Justin H., *The Annexation of Texas*. 1911.

———, *The War with Mexico*. 2 vols., 1919.

Stenberg, Richard R., "The Failure of Polk's Mexican War Intrigue of 1845," *Pacific Historical Review* 4 (1935): 39–68.

Varg, Paul A., *New England and Foreign Relations, 1789–1850*. 1983.

Weber, David J., *The Mexican Frontier, 1821–1846: The American Southwest under Mexico*. 1982.

Weinberg, Albert K., *Manifest Destiny: A Study of Nationalist Expansion in American History*. 1935.

Chapter Eight

Between the Wars, 1848–1861

YOUNG AMERICA

Manifest destiny in the United States did not run its course with the Mexican War, for expansionist aims continued during the 1850s under the label of *Young America*. The revolutions of 1848 in Europe fired the American imagination and stimulated feelings of nationalism at home, as tens of thousands of immigrants entering the United States tried to arouse interest in intervening against Old World oppression. Americans praised the antimonarchical revolutions in Europe as proof of the virtue of republicanism, and by 1852 this expansionist-interventionist philosophy became the central idea of the Democratic party platform. Before the decade ended in civil war, the United States had celebrated the nationalist efforts of Hungary, Italy, and Ireland; unofficially supported filibusters (private adventurers) in Central America who aimed at annexing Cuba and Nicaragua; revived interest in taking more land from Mexico; and made commercial inroads in both China and Japan. It is true that, despite the excitement over enlarging the American empire, the United States made only one territorial acquisition: the Gadsden Purchase, a narrow strip of land comprising lower Arizona and New Mexico, which was bought for the purpose of constructing a railroad. Americans also came to regard Asia as a special domain for the spread of republican and missionary ideals, along with the interests of business. But the only expansionist effort that approached the pattern of the previous decade—the South's dream of a Caribbean empire—collapsed because of the sectional division over slavery. Altogether it was a swashbuckling, adventuresome time in which Americans, almost like buccaneers, seemed to feel free to grab everything within reach.

Slavery proved a major irritant to expansionism in the 1840s, but it frustrated that spirit in the 1850s. America's acquisitions of Oregon and

California laid the path to Asia. The California gold rush of 1849 stimulated a great new wave of westward migration, which raised interest in constructing a canal or railroad across the isthmus of Central America. Yet the slavery issue impeded any drives into both Canada and Latin America, for southerners realized that Canada would become free states, and northerners recognized that expansion southward would add slave states to the Union. Many Americans lamented slavery's interference in the nation's manifest destiny. Illinois Congressman Abraham Lincoln complained in 1854 that the institution deprived "our republican example of its just influence in the world" and exposed Americans to the charge of being "hypocrites."

Weak national leadership during the 1850s further diffused the country's foreign policy. Presidents and secretaries of state followed whatever expansionist whim seemed popular at the time. Filibusters roamed Latin America, often with the Washington government's tacit blessing; diplomats threatened the use of force to secure Spain's possessions; and Anglophobes worsened relations with Britain regarding Central America. Some leaders sought to involve the United States in the upheavals in Europe, and most welcomed the opportunities for increasing trade with China and opening Japan. Hardly anyone spoke of the responsibilities that came with international involvement. Young America was younger in maturity than in years during the 1850s.

An illustration of the spirit of the times was America's enormous feeling for Hungary. When the Habsburg regime in Austria received Russia's help in putting down the Hungarian revolt in 1849, American sympathy for the rebels was too strong for the new administration to ignore. In June President Zachary Taylor extended recognition to the rebels and drew a vehement protest from the Austrian chargé in Washington, Chevalier Hülsemann. The revolution failed before an American emissary reached Hungary, but Secretary of State Daniel Webster, in that office for the second time, became fearful of the internal division in the United States and tried to use the Hungarian cause to unite Americans. In late 1850 he denounced Austria in the "Hülsemann Note." Events in Hungary, the secretary declared, "appeared to have their origin in those great ideas of responsible and popular governments on which the American constitutions themselves are founded. . . . The power of this republic, at the present moment, is spread over a region, one of the richest and most fertile on the globe, and of an extent in comparison with which the possessions of the House of Habsburg are but as a patch on the earth's surface." Webster's lecture had its desired impact on most Americans; but it infuriated the Austrian monarch.

The exiled leader of the Hungarian rebels, Louis Kossuth, visited the United States in 1851–52, seeking American aid. Support for Kossuth swelled throughout the country upon his arrival in New York in early December 1851, and at a huge bipartisan banquet held in his honor by Congress, Webster rejoiced at the "American model upon the Lower Danube and on the mountains of Hungary." These public pronouncements perhaps enhanced Webster's chances for the presidency, but they helped keep relations strained with the Austrian government until Webster's death in October 1852. In the meantime, the excitement of the parades, speeches, parties, and gifts gave way to the realization that the United States had to stay out of European affairs.

In Mexican affairs, the 1850s took on the character of the previous decade, probably causing Americans to experience a bit of *déjà vu*. The source of trouble was America's old nemesis, Santa Anna. He had again seized power and was again in desperate need of money. Realizing the United States needed land in the Southwest for a railroad to the Pacific, the Mexican minister in Washington let President Franklin Pierce know that a generous monetary offer, accompanied by well-publicized threats to the regime in Mexico City, would bring territorial concessions. America's minister to Mexico, James Gadsden, assured that government that the desired cash outlay was forthcoming for any of five boundaries stipulated by the United States, and the American government made a mock show of force by sending soldiers to the Rio Grande.

At this point similarities with the past came to an end. Santa Anna fulfilled his assurances, even though he agreed to only the minimum boundary that Gadsden had authority to accept. In late December 1853 the two men negotiated an agreement that went through major revision in the United States Senate before meeting approval the following April as the Gadsden Treaty. The United States paid $10 million to Mexico in exchange for a belt of land between the Colorado and Rio Grande rivers and transit rights across the Isthmus of Tehuantepec. In addition, the United States secured a release from the obligations of the Treaty of Guadalupe Hidalgo which had held it responsible for damages in Mexico caused by Indians living on the American side of the border. The two governments exchanged ratifications in Washington in June 1854, and the United States ultimately built the Southern Pacific Railroad.

IMPROVED ANGLO–AMERICAN RELATIONS

For several reasons relations with Britain improved during the late 1850s after serious differences had developed in the first half of the decade. America's acquisition of Oregon and California had underlined the potential of Far Eastern trade, and the United States now sought to link the Atlantic to the Pacific with a canal or railroad. The obvious passageway was either Panama, the narrowest point in the isthmus, or Nicaragua, which was a day closer to the United States and had a series of rivers and lakes that interconnected across most of the country. American hopes for transit rights across the isthmus of Central America ran into difficulties because of competing British interests in the region.

The United States had taken a major step toward gaining access to Central America in 1846, when it negotiated a treaty with New Granada (later Colombia) which allowed American use of Panama. New Granada feared that Britain would seize the isthmus and was willing to exchange transit rights for promises by the United States to safeguard the "perfect neutrality" of the route, maintain "free transit of traffic," and protect New Granada. America's minister to New Granada, Benjamin Bidlack, received this surprising offer from his host government, and without authorization from Washington he signed the treaty. President Polk forwarded it to the Senate where, despite a lengthy discussion caused by fear of foreign entanglement, the agreement met approval in June 1848. The treaty of 1846 ultimately led in 1855 to the completion of the Panama railroad, less than fifty miles in length.

America's success in 1846 caused British concern because of the apparently concerted push toward the Caribbean and Latin America. Britain's economic ties with the United States had grown until by the 1850s it received half of its imports and 80 percent of its cotton from the United States. American merchants in turn imported nearly half of their goods from England, and businessmen welcomed British investments in railroads and other enterprises. Yet these tenuous economic links could snap if American expansion endangered British interests in Latin America. The treaty of 1846 posed a threat to Britain's maritime control in the Caribbean and to its holdings in the southern half of the hemisphere.

In January 1848 the British tried to rectify the situation by seizing the little settlement at San Juan in Nicaragua, renamed Greytown, which sat at the mouth of the San Juan River that cut across the isthmus to the Gulf of Fonseca on the Pacific side. The British had already established a protectorate over the Mosquito Indians along Nicaragua's east coast, and they owned Belize (later British Honduras), the Bay Islands, and a naval center at Jamaica. The occupation of Greytown thus solidified their claims in Central America. In October of the following year a British naval officer acted without orders in seizing Tigre Island near the Pacific terminal point of the projected canal route. The government in London renounced the last act, but Americans were incensed. At almost the same time the British took Greytown, gold was discovered in California and the rush of "forty-niners" necessitated an immediate passageway west through the isthmus of Central America. The United States had to negotiate with Britain.

The culmination of America's effort to set up an Anglo-American arrangement on an isthmian canal was the Clayton-Bulwer Treaty of April 19, 1850. Secretary of State John Clayton won Lord Palmerston's support in opening transit rights to all nations, and signed a pact in Washington to that effect with British Minister Sir Henry Bulwer. The treaty specified that neither nation was to "obtain or maintain for itself any exclusive control" over an isthmian canal, and that "neither will ever erect or maintain any fortifications commanding the same, or in the vicinity thereof, or occupy, or fortify, or colonize, or assume, or exercise any dominion over Nicaragua, Costa Rica, the Mosquito Coast, or any part of Central America." The United States expected the British to withdraw from Greytown

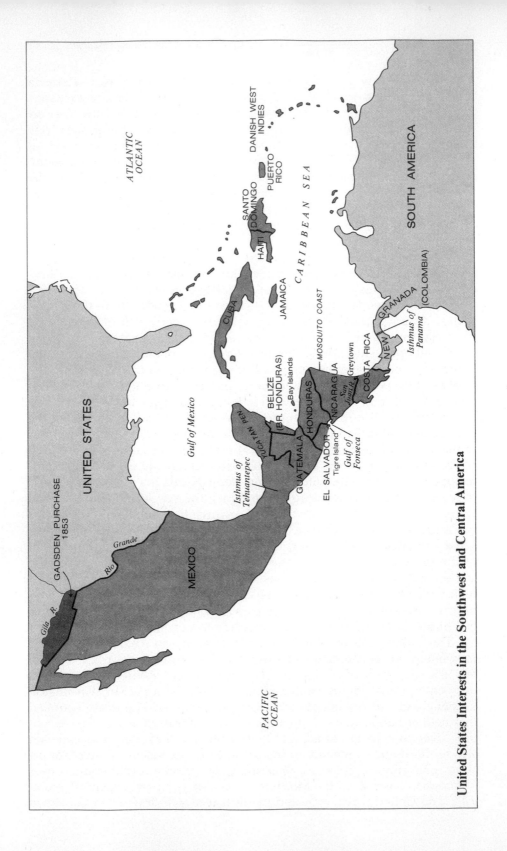

United States Interests in the Southwest and Central America

and the Mosquito Coast, but London refused. Neither side could back down for political reasons, but they managed to conceal their disagreements in a document remarkable for its vagueness. Clayton had kept members of the Senate informed throughout the negotiations, which encouraged quick approval of the treaty.

Despite a wide margin of support in the Senate, the settlement became the object of sharp criticism in the United States. Several members of the opposition Democratic party accused the Taylor administration of caving in to the British, while others complained that the United States had denied its own right to expand south by promising not to take any of Central America. In the clash over the Clayton Bulwer Treaty, Americans for the first time referred to President Monroe's address of 1823 as the Monroe Doctrine. Critics claimed that the United States should have required the British to relinquish areas taken by force; defenders declared the agreement a victory for the Monroe Doctrine because Britain promised not to acquire additional territories in the hemisphere.

Before the president ratified the treaty, the two negotiators exchanged secret notes explaining their understandings of the agreement and virtually altering its meaning. Bulwer claimed it meant no *new* colonization and would not approve withdrawal from present holdings, whereas Clayton asserted that the pact was retroactive in intention and required the British to pull out of the hemisphere. The secretary of state warned that the United States had secured exclusive transit rights in several other Central American countries and that he was prepared to take these treaties to the Senate. Some of the republics, he told Bulwer, sought America's protection against the British. "There is not one of these five Central American states that would not annex themselves to us tomorrow, if they could," Clayton declared, "and if it is any secret worth knowing you are welcome to it—*Some of them have offered and asked to be annexed to the United States already*." These notes remained confidential because their reservations made the treaty almost meaningless. Thus the treaty approved by the Senate differed considerably from the exceptions outlined above. In a strict sense the American secretary of state had violated the Constitution's treaty-making stipulations in arranging the pact with England.

Anglo-American relations in Latin America remained uneasy despite the Clayton-Bulwer Treaty. Within three months the British claimed that in addition to the exemptions of the Bay Islands and Belize, the treaty's provisions had no effect on either Greytown or the Mosquito Coast. In 1852 the British established a colony in the Honduran Bay Islands. Tensions grew in the summer of 1854 after a mob attacked an American diplo-

---

MAP 10

U.S. interests in this part of the hemisphere came into direct conflict with the British.

mat in Greytown. When a United States naval officer failed to win reparations, he proceeded to destroy the town. Though no one died in the bombardment, British and French properties were among the losses. The government in Washington upheld the action despite a heated protest from London, but the crisis blew over when Britain backed off from demanding indemnification and instructed its nationals to present damage claims to Nicaragua on the ground that that government was responsible for events occurring within its territories. Britain had no choice. It had allied with France in the Crimean War that began against Russia that same year, and the Mosquito Coast was not worth war with the United States. In December 1857 Palmerston explained his country's willingness to retreat in Latin America: the Americans "are on the spot, strongly, deeply interested in the matter, totally unscrupulous and dishonest and determined somehow or other to carry their point. We are far away," he continued, "weak from distance, controlled by the indifference of the nation . . . and by its strong commercial interest in maintaining peace."

The obscure language of the Clayton-Bulwer Treaty led to continued minor disagreements over Central America, but the pact relieved tension by discouraging American annexation movements. The treaty was a victory for the Monroe Doctrine and for the United States in that the Americans won the right to build a canal through a British-controlled area. Shortly afterward the American shipper Cornelius Vanderbilt established a steamship and railroad line through Nicaragua, and others constructed a railway across Panama. In 1857 President James Buchanan asked Congress for authorization to send troops to keep both routes open, but the slavery issue again intervened to block such a venture.

Anglo-American relations improved further with the movement toward a reciprocity treaty between the United States and Canada. Near the opening of the decade, American interest in Canada revived when it seemed that British policies might drive the North American provinces from the empire. Repeal of the Corn Laws in 1846 had cost Canada its advantageous position in the grain markets, encouraging political leaders to push for a peaceful break with London and annexation by the United States. England at first responded by removing many commercial restrictions between Canada and other parts of the empire, but America's tariff laws continued to contribute to Canada's difficulties. Canadians meanwhile accused Americans of violating the fishing provisions contained in the Convention of 1818 and tried to stop them from coming closer than three miles off the shore and from buying fishing materials in British ports. Americans retaliated by arming their fishing vessels, while the president dispatched ships to the troubled area with instructions to safeguard the nation's rights at sea. In May 1854, after nearly a year of controversy, Britain accepted an invitation from Washington to discuss these problems.

A number of considerations assured the success of the ensuing negotiations between Secretary of State William Marcy and the governor general of British North America, Lord Elgin. Americans wanted fishing rights, Canadians wanted lower tariffs. Northerners in the United States, it is ironic to note, favored a pact because it pointed to the ultimate annexation of Canada, whereas southerners approved because they believed that an agreement would ease Canada's economic problems and reduce the chances for annexation. Southerners had also recently won a victory for slavery (by the Kansas-Nebraska bill), making some of them amenable to a treaty with Canada that northerners wanted. Finally, the State Department hired a lobbyist, who later said he distributed over $200,000 in American and Canadian funds in Congress and in Canada to further the treaty. Elgin's secretary, Laurence Oliphant, arrogantly claimed that the treaty "floated through on champagne," which was the only way "to deal with hogs."

The Marcy-Elgin Treaty of June 1854 rested on the principle of reciprocity. It removed duties on numerous goods and allowed Americans to fish in areas closed by the Convention of 1818; in return, Canadians secured fishing rights along the Atlantic coast of the United States above the 36th parallel. The United States received free navigation of the St. Lawrence River and its canals in exchange for Britons gaining reciprocal rights to Lake Michigan. The United States withdrew from the pact in 1865, when during the Civil War the Union government accused Canada of pro-Confederate policies and claimed that Canadians had gained more from the treaty than had Americans, a belief encouraged by the Republican party's stand for protective tariffs.

The Crimean War of 1854–56, which found England and France on one side and Russia on the other, provided the backdrop for a sudden but temporary decline in American-British relations. Americans sympathized with Russia because of a past history of stable relations, but also because of recurring Anglophobia. The situation became more confusing when the British minister in Washington, John Crampton, recruited American volunteers for the war, and before long Americans were en route to Halifax and off to the Crimea. Secretary of State Marcy lodged a vigorous protest, and when that brought no results, he sought Crampton's recall. The British Foreign Office refused to comply, but in May 1856 the United States expelled Crampton and three consuls involved in the recruiting. The Pierce administration's decision was partly political, for the Democratic convention met less than a week after the Crampton episode, and the president's anti-British action appealed to a party housing Irish-Americans and Anglophobes.

Anglo-American relations became fairly stable by the latter half of the 1850s. Whereas some Britons objected to Washington's policies in Central America as violations of the Clayton-Bulwer Treaty, others pondered the benefits derived from American control bringing stability to the region and furthering trade. The Atlantic cable laid in 1858 promised closer contact between the nations, as did growing cultural ties. That same year British searches of American ships suspected of engaging in the slave trade caused a brief flareup over an age-old controversy; but when the Buchanan administration sent warships to the Gulf of Mexico to stop such practices, in June 1858 the British renounced the right of search in peace-time. London then eased tension in Central America by signing an agreement in 1859 with Honduras, recognizing that republic's control over the Bay Islands, and the next year it negotiated an arrangement with Nicaragua relinquishing the Mosquito protectorate. Buchanan praised the settlements as triumphs for the Monroe Doctrine.

THE FAR EAST

United States policy in the Far East, directed toward commerce and not territorial acquisition, was the reverse of that pursued in North America. Orientals regarded Westerners as foreign devils and were hesitant to open commercial doors. In the eighteenth century China allowed foreign trading vessels to enter only at Canton and, in an effort to prevent foreign contamination, to conduct business only within "factories" or trading posts that lay outside the city. For years America followed England's lead by seeking most-favored-nation status—the right to the same privileges accorded other countries. As trade avenues were gradually opened, European powers pushed for colonization and spheres of control. The United States, by contrast, encouraged China and Japan to remain open to American merchants. Thus the United States's first policies in Asia were forerunners of the "Open Door" of the late nineteenth century. Most Americans rejected the use of force, as employed by Europeans, and sought to obtain the same economic privileges by other means.

American trade with the Orient had begun shortly after the American Revolution. By the turn of the nineteenth century numerous American ships had followed the lead of the *Empress of China*, which had left New York for Canton in 1784 with furs, cotton, lead, and ginseng (a root believed capable of restoring virility), and returned a year later with a rich cargo of spices, silks, tea, and other Chinese goods. By the 1820s China's interest in cotton seemed to promise a huge Asian market for the American South's chief product.

During the 1830s America's penetration into the Far East deepened. The first American missionaries arrived in China, and merchants from New England and the Middle Atlantic states, along with southern cotton exporters, broadened their contacts in Asia. In 1832 the United States sent a special agent to the Far East, Edmund Roberts, who had instructions to negotiate trade agreements with Cochin China (Indochina), Siam (modern Thailand), Muscat (along the Arabian Sea), and Japan. Few attached importance to the mission; in fact, Roberts had no directives to deal with China for fear of disturbing the existing trade. The following year Roberts signed commercial treaties with Siam and Muscat, but he decided not to talk with Japan until he had a larger delegation and more money for gifts. The Senate approved the two treaties, but Roberts died before he could negotiate a pact with Japan.

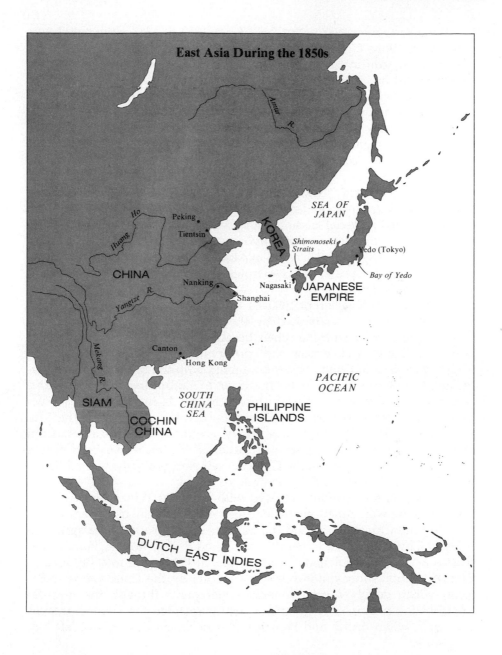

MAP 11

America's involvement in East Asia was restricted primarily to a few contacts with China and Japan.

Britain's Opium War with China from 1839 to 1842 ultimately broke down restrictions on trade. For some time British merchants had sold India-grown opium in China after paying a nominal tax to governing authorities. But in 1839 new leaders in China confiscated a huge supply of the drug from British traders and set off a conflict that lasted three years before the Chinese were defeated. In August 1842 Britain and China signed the Treaty of Nanking, by which Britain won the island of Hong Kong, broader commercial rights, extraterritoriality (right of foreigners to trial in their own courts), and war reparations. China lay open to the West.

The United States took advantage of Britain's commercial gains in China to seek most-favored-nation status. In the summer of 1843 Congress approved a special mission led by Massachusetts Whig Caleb Cushing, who after considerable difficulty negotiated the Treaty of Wanghia in July 1844. The United States could expand its trading privileges in China, establish consular posts, claim extraterritoriality and other rights, and help determine tariff rates.

The Taiping Rebellion of 1850–64 threatened to undo America's relations with China as established by the Cushing Treaty. The American public sympathized with the rebels because their leader was a Christian convert seeking to overthrow the conservative Manchu dynasty in Peking. Americans in China, however, agreed with the British that the government's collapse would open the door to European intervention and upset trade in China. British and Chinese forces clashed at Canton in November 1856, and an American naval launch was fired on from the Chinese forts. The United States Navy, without authorization from Washington, shelled and destroyed the forts. Within a year both Britain and France were fighting in the Chinese civil war, while the United States and Russia maintained official neutrality.

In 1858 all four nations gathered with China at Tientsin to negotiate an end to the war. Americans won lower tariffs and the use of additional ports on the Chinese coast and the Yangtze River, while China agreed to tolerate Christianity and to permit the United States, Britain, France, and Russia to establish diplomatic headquarters at Peking. In 1860 Britain and France secured more commercial concessions by the Convention of Peking, which devolved onto American merchants through the most-favored-nation principle. The emperor finally accepted the Tientsin treaties that year, when British and French forces occupied Peking and left him no choice.

The Treaty of Tientsin of 1858 exemplified the United States's opposition to any nation's establishing permanent control in China. The most-favored-nation approach was America's only instrument for preventing a partition that would end Chinese sovereignty and obstruct trade. Throughout the Taiping Rebellion the American commissioner in Canton worked to safeguard the empire against British and Russian exploitation, and three years later in 1867, the American minister to China, Massachusetts Congressman Anson Burlingame, accepted an invitation from the Chinese government to head a mission to persuade the major powers to limit their demands. He won assurances from Britain, France, and Russia not to seek special advantages during China's period of unrest. The following year he again represented China in securing a treaty in Washington which dealt with travel and commercial rights, consuls, and other matters. The Burlingame Treaty of 1868 also permitted unrestricted Chinese migration into the United States, a provision which reflected America's need for cheap labor to build the nation's first transcontinental railroad.

America's interest in Japan grew more slowly than it did in China, largely because of the island nation's seclusion from the outside world. In the early seventeenth century Japan had come under control of the shoguns (military chieftains) of the Tokugawa family, who barred most outsiders as barbarians. American trade in Shanghai after the Treaty of Wanghia of 1844 made Japan a natural port of call to and from China. Stories circulated about Japan's brutal treatment of shipwrecked American seamen driven into port, and though the allegations were largely untrue, the government in Washington intended to guarantee the safety of the seamen. American steamships also required a coaling station in Asian waters, making the coal in Japan a major attraction. The United States was unsuccessful in opening Japan during the 1840s, but its efforts received renewed impetus in the following decade because of the increased commercial interest in Asia brought on by the recently acquired Pacific coast.

In early 1852 Commodore Matthew C. Perry, veteran of the War of 1812 and younger brother of the hero of Lake Erie, became commander of the East India Squadron and received orders to establish commercial relations with Japan. Perry was to secure trade agreements, a coaling station, and assurances of hospitality for Americans forced into Japanese waters. In July 1853 four American warships under his command entered the Bay of Yedo (later Tokyo). Only two were steamers, but they blew out heavy black smoke and caused one onlooker to remark that Japan was being overrun by "barbarians . . . in floating volcanoes." The "black fleet" waited in the bay for nearly a week with the commodore remaining out of sight to add mystery and importance to the visit. Finally Perry and his entourage came ashore, greeting the Japanese with a thirteen-gun salute and accompanied by 400 armed men and two black bodyguards. A band played "Hail, Columbia" as Perry handed Japanese officials a letter for the emperor calling for a treaty, but the Japanese ordered him to leave. Perry announced that he would return the following year with a larger squadron to pick up the emperor's reply.

Perry's second visit to Japan made a greater show of military force than did the first. In March 1854, after a two-week wait in the harbor with seven warships, he again landed, this time with a seventeen-gun salute followed by three bands playing "The Star-Spangled Banner" while Perry marched in with 500 men, their bayonets and guns on display. The Japanese were more amenable this time. Gifts were exchanged, and Perry's to the Japanese included a model train, a telegraph, and a history of America's war with Mexico that contained drawings of the United States Navy shelling Veracruz. Japan's attitude had softened for several reasons. The country was undergoing great internal change as a new urban-merchant class saw commercial benefits in dealing with the United States. Western weapons were impressive, as a Japanese official would attest after he looked into the mouth of an eight-inch gun and tried to lift a sixty-four-pound cannon ball. The Japanese were also wary of Russian intentions. In August 1853, shortly after Perry's first visit, the Russians inadvertently furthered American interests by coming close to Nagasaki with four ships. Their presence in Japanese waters had become too regular, the Japanese believed, and an understanding with the Americans seemed in order.

Perry negotiated the Treaty of Kanagawa with Japan on March 31, 1854, which was only a limited success because it dealt primarily with the problem of shipwrecked seamen and did not establish broad commercial relations. Signed by the shogun, the treaty opened only two isolated ports for coal and supplies and granted consular privileges in each, but it contained no guarantees of coaling stations or extraterritorial rights. The Japanese promised to assist shipwrecked Americans and to extend most-favored-nation privileges, but they stipulated that business transactions had to take place through Japanese officials, not private merchants.

Americans regarded Perry's venture in the Far East as a major success. Weighed against Japan's past isolation, the pact of 1854 was vital in bringing the country into world affairs and in encouraging America's chances for a general trade agreement. Washington unanimously approved Perry's treaty. Congress voted him a bonus, Boston businessmen awarded him a medal, and the New York Chamber of Commerce gave him silver dinner settings totaling nearly 400 pieces.

The United States attempted to open the door wider to Asia after Perry's treaty with Japan. The following year Dr. Peter Parker, a medical missionary, became American commissioner to China and immediately sought additional concessions in the Far East. The United States sent its first diplomatic representative to Japan in August 1856. Townsend Harris, a New York businessman who had visited Asia on several occasions, became consul general with the responsibility of swinging the door open to Japan. But he lacked military support, and the Japanese refused to welcome him. Harris and his secretary lived in seclusion for over a year until an American vessel arrived, and he heard nothing from the State Department for a year and a half. The Japanese meanwhile blamed him for several natural disasters which they interpreted as divine dissatisfaction with Perry's treaty, and urged him to return home. Yet Harris patiently reminded his hosts that the European nations were more dangerous than the United States, and that it would be more advisable to give America what it wanted than to have the others wrench concessions at the cost of blood.

Harris eventually earned Japan's trust. In June 1857 he secured a convention that broadened America's commercial privileges, and in July of the following year he signed the first major treaty of amity and commerce permitted by Japan with the West. British and French intervention in the ongoing Chinese civil war raised concern about their designs in Asia and probably encouraged the Japanese to come to the negotiating table. The Harris Treaty of 1858 broadened commercial privileges, authorized the establishment of consuls in all ports open for trade, permitted the exchange of diplomatic representatives, drew up fixed tariff schedules, and approved extraterritoriality. The following year Harris became minister to Japan and headed the new American legation in Tokyo.

America's opening of Japan helped stir massive unrest on the island. Japanese isolationists were unhappy with the shogun for dealing with foreigners and rallied around the emperor in resisting outside intervention. By June 1863 the emperor wanted all foreigners out of Japan, and though his wishes were largely unfulfilled, violence ensued and led to the death of the secretary of the American legation. In the Straits of Shimonoseki in 1864 a Japanese officer, without authorization, fired his cannon on foreign vessels and brought retaliatory action through a joint punitive expedition in which the United States took part. By the Convention of 1864 the Japanese made reparations. The American portion of the indemnity was much higher than the costs of the venture, and Congress later reimbursed the full amount to Japan. In 1868 the emperor regained power from the shogunate in the Meiji Restoration, and soon welcomed Western ways and technology. By the turn of the twentieth century America had agreed to grant Japan full control over tariffs and foreigners within its borders.

THE SOUTHERN DREAM OF A CARIBBEAN EMPIRE

Southerners of the 1850s sought an empire in the Caribbean. Much of the area seemed available for the taking, and yet any attempt to accommodate slavery with the spread of the American flag ended in failure. Opposition to the spread of slavery into new territories, embodied in the Wilmot Proviso and growing stronger as the 1850s became turbulent, ensured that expansionist proposals would set off sharp debates because of mutual suspicions between North and South. Both sections had recognized the necessity of solidifying claims to Texas, California, and the Mexican Cession, but trouble erupted over the status of the newly acquired areas: Would they be slave or free? By the 1850s northerners were so concerned about southern motives that they preferred to restrict the size of the Union rather than see it grow to the benefit of the South.

It is doubtful that manifest destiny had ceased to exist among northerners, but the idea's internal contradictions encouraged the two sections to go different ways. Both agreed that its driving spirit was republicanism and the spread of civilized institutions, but they differed on whether slavery was reconcilable with freedom and thus a part of that civilization. Not all Americans looked upon slavery from a moral point of view. Yet even its political aspects became inseparable from moral arguments over whether the institution was right or wrong. When the two sections finally focused on this issue, the possibility of compromise no longer existed.

The only way for the South to build political power was to expand into the Caribbean; the only way for the North to retain it was to block such a move. Senator William H. Seward of New York argued that the prerequisite for America's spread into the Caribbean was the abolition of slavery. But this price was too high for southerners. The Compromise of 1850 encouraged the southern drive toward the Caribbean by requiring California's admission as a free state and by opening the Mexican Cession to "popular sovereignty" in allowing its inhabitants to decide the slavery question. Expansion southward seemed to be the only remedy to the South's continued decline in political power. The Gulf of Mexico, according to expansionist James D. E. B. DeBow of *DeBow's Review*, was the "great *Southern sea*." Slavery would thrive in Cuba, Mexico, Central America, and perhaps in the rest of Latin America. Soon the South's choice became obvious: end slavery, which was out of the question, or leave the Union, which was not.

The first apparent opportunity for southward expansion arose in Yucatán in 1848. The white government of the peninsula, which considered itself independent of Mexico, seemed about to face a revolt by its native Indians. A spokesman for that government notified the administration in Washington that Yucatán would grant the United States "dominion and sovereignty" in exchange for military assistance against the Indians. The Polk administration seemed interested, especially when it appeared that England and Spain might step in. The president told Congress in late April that the United States opposed the transfer in ownership of any area in the hemisphere, even if its residents favored such a change. This was an added twist to the "Polk Corollary" of the Monroe Doctrine, for the original statement had opposed a transfer *without* the approval of people in the area. Further action proved unnecessary when the government of Yucatán managed to settle its problems without a revolution.

Cuba, however, was the prize—the focal point of southern expansionist aims. The United States had a longstanding interest in Cuba. Romanticized as "The Ever Faithful Isle" because it (and Puerto Rico) did not break from Spain when the rest of its Latin American possessions did, Cuba was also known as "The Pearl of the Antilles" and "The World's Sugar Bowl" because of its great production of molasses and sugar. For several decades Cuba had attracted American investment and trade. By mid-century it had become strategically important as well, involving American interests in the Caribbean, the Gulf of Mexico, the Mississippi River, and the isthmus of Central America. The failure in Yucatán, along with the later inability of the Pierce administration to secure rights for a naval base in the Dominican Republic, dramatized Cuba's centrality, and doubly so as the island became a way station to Oregon and California.

President Polk tried to buy Cuba, but Spain had the support of Britain and France in refusing the offer. Four years later the United States turned down an invitation by Britain and France to join them in renouncing plans for acquiring Cuba. No agreement was possible with Europe over an *American* question, Washington declared. Cuba remained a natural object of manifest destiny in the 1850s, furnishing southerners a potential outlet for expanding slavery and gaining political control in Washington.

The North's political predominance in Washington obstructed the formal development of a southern empire in the Caribbean, but that did not rule out measures which operated either just outside the law, or barely within it. A recurring effort at acquiring Cuba was through filibusters. Such private military ventures were well rooted in the American expansionist tradition; West Florida, Texas, and California had been at least partly "liberated" and acquired by that means. Another method was expansionist policies by the Pierce administration that relied upon unorthodox diplomatic procedures or gave unofficial blessing to filibustering. Yet no approach could circumvent the slavery issue. Many followers of filibusters came from the South because of proximity, and more than a few members of the Pierce and Buchanan administrations were southerners or southern sympathizers. The impression was that the South had allied with the expansionist Democratic party to spread slavery.

The first Cuban filibustering expedition of note was led by General Narciso López, an officer in the Spanish military who had been a businessman in Cuba and as a refugee had tried several times to win the island's independence from Spain and permit annexation by the United States. Having married into a slaveholding family in Cuba, López made northerners apprehensive that he was part of a southern conspiracy to extend slavery. He operated out of New York City and New Orleans in attracting volunteers, some of whom were veterans of the war with Mexico and wanted to free Cuba and acquire property on the island. For their services López offered all they could drink and smoke and whatever they pillaged from captured areas—including women. In the event of success, each man would receive a bonus of $1,000 and 160 acres of land on the island. López had several hundred volunteers in his filibustering force on Round Island off Louisiana in September 1849, but the American navy prevented their departure for Cuba. He did not give up. Turning primarily to southerners for assistance, he won the support of John Quitman, successful cotton and sugar grower, former general in the Mexican War, and soon to be governor of Mississippi. López also received help from Laurence Sigur, editor of the New Orleans *Delta*, former Mississippi Senator John Henderson, and the originator of the term manifest destiny, John L. O'Sullivan of New York's *Democratic Review*.

All of López's filibustering attempts were fiascos. In May 1850 he led a force of 700 out of New Orleans for Cuba. Its mission was apparent from the red shirts worn by the men in honor of the European revolutions of 1848. Spanish regulars in Cuba drove them away. Upon their return to the United States, López's followers were arrested by American officials under the Neutrality Act of 1818. All participants went to trial in New Orleans, but after three mistrials for Henderson, the prosecution dropped the cases. In August 1851 López tried again. With a band of 500, he sought to fulfill the promise of a proclamation calling for the acquisition of Cuba according to "inevitable destiny." Once again López ran into trouble. Spanish forces on the island swarmed over the invaders and put them in prison. Authorities kept more than a hundred in jail and executed López and fifty of his cohorts, including Colonel William Crittenden of Kentucky, nephew of the United States attorney general. These actions infuriated the people of New Orleans, for many of the victims came from good southern stock. Unrest spread to Key West and northward to Cincinnati, Pittsburgh, and Philadelphia. A mob stormed the Spanish consulate in New Orleans, and another in Madrid tried to do the same with the American legation. Secretary of State Webster extended apologies to Spain and admitted to America's mistake in not acting forcefully against filibustering. The next year the Spanish queen pardoned the imprisoned members of the López expedition, and Congress appropriated a small reparation for damages to the Spanish consulate in New Orleans.

American interest in Cuba did not end with López's death. For the second time the European powers pushed for a joint self-denying pact regarding Cuba. In April 1852 the governments in London and Paris followed the proddings of Madrid and invited the United States to join them in assuring Spanish control over the island. Though Webster supported the proposal, he died in October and the elections of the following month convinced the new president, Franklin Pierce, that Americans were still expansionists. "The policy of my Administration," Pierce declared in his inaugural address, "will not be controlled by any timid forebodings of evil from expansion. Indeed . . . our attitude as a nation and our position on the globe render the acquisition of . . . [Cuba] eminently important for our protection, if not in the future essential for preservation of the rights of commerce and the peace of the world." Both Secretary of State William Marcy and the minister to England, James Buchanan, were former members of Polk's cabinet and continued to work for the acquisition of Cuba, as did the new minister to Spain, former Senator Pierre Soulé of Louisiana, and the minister to France, John Mason, also a cabinet member under Polk. At first Marcy attempted quietly and unofficially to buy Cuba from Spain, but these efforts soon gave way to Soulé's designs to take the island by force.

If the president's inaugural address was not ample warning of America's intentions regarding Cuba, his appointment of Soulé as minister to Spain certainly was. Soulé was hot-tempered and had been exiled from France for his extreme views on republicanism. His unabashed calls for the acquisition of Cuba made his selection for the post at Madrid an affront to that government. Before departing for Spain, Soulé delivered a fiery speech in New York calling for Cuba's annexation. He did not get along with the other diplomats in Madrid. The French ambassador, the Marquis de Turgot, did not conceal his animosity for Soulé, and eventually the American challenged Turgot to a duel over an alleged insulting remark about Madame Soulé's low-necked dress. Soulé shot him in the leg and crippled him for life. The New York *Herald* moaned, "We wanted an ambassador there, we have sent a matador." Yet the administration in Washington did not recall Soulé, and many Americans praised his conduct.

By late February 1854 a crisis developed with Spain that involved Soulé and American interests in Cuba. Spanish authorities in Havana had clamped down on maritime laws, and on February 28 they seized the cargo of the American merchant steamship *Black Warrior* as it passed between New York and Mobile. The vessel, Havana officials declared, failed to have adequate identification of cargo, an infraction of customs law overlooked numerous times in the past. Many Americans were incensed and Soulé seized the moment to justify a demand for Cuba. He handed a provocative note to Spanish officials in Madrid and followed it with an ultimatum giving Spain forty-eight hours to respond to a demand for $300,000 as reparations to the ship's owners, and the removal of all Spanish officials involved in the seizure. President Pierce meanwhile sharply criticized the Spanish government in a message to Congress. Marcy had instructed his minister to seek only an indemnity, but Soulé had gone beyond.

While Soulé fumed over the *Black Warrior* episode, the Spanish foreign minister in Madrid worked to resolve it peacefully. He thought Soulé had exceeded his orders from Washington and wrote a justification of Spain's behavior that the Pierce administration could not refute. At the same time Spanish officials in Madrid contacted the owners of the American vessel and authorized $53,000 in reparations. The *Black Warrior* returned to its coastal trade, port officials in Havana treated it with deference, and once again the two nations escaped a serious confrontation over Cuba. Soulé continued to believe that the episode had stained America's honor.

In April 1854 The Pierce administration began another effort to buy Cuba that culminated in the Ostend Manifesto. Marcy directed Soulé to offer a maximum of $130 million for the island; the secretary of state included a follow-up instruction, to become operative if the offer were declined, that contained dangerous implications in the hands of a man of Soulé's temperament. Marcy told Soulé that upon refusal "you will then direct your efforts to the next desirable object which is to detach that island from the Spanish dominion and from all dependence on any European power." Marcy later instructed Soulé to meet with Ministers Buchanan in England and Mason in France to "compare opinions as to what may be advisable, and . . . adopt measures for perfect concert of action in aid of [Soulé's] negotiations at Madrid."

After a series of meetings in October at Ostend, Belgium, and at Aix-la-Chapelle in Rhenish Prussia, the three American ministers sent their conclusions to Washington by secret messenger. Though a private report to the secretary of state, portions of it had already appeared in European and American newspapers before Marcy received the packet in November. One writer expressed amazement that the government in Washington had "planned a burglary of great proportions and published a prospectus in advance." The Pierce administration's enemies in the House arranged full publication of the report in March 1855, causing a northern outcry against an alleged southern plot to expand slavery into Cuba.

The so-called Ostend Manifesto set out the importance of Cuba to the United States, explained why Spain should sell, and then declared that "self-preservation is the first law of nature, with states as well as with individuals." After asking the question, "Does Cuba, in the possession of Spain, seriously endanger our internal peace and the existence of our cherished Union?" the diplomats replied that it did. Should Madrid refuse to part with the island for a top offer of $120 million, the United States would be justified "by every law, human and divine," in "wresting it from Spain . . . upon the very same principle that would justify an individual in tearing down the burning house of his neighbor if there were no other means of preventing the flames from destroying his own home." The "flames," the authors of the paper warned, were a black insurrection in Cuba that would cause the island to become "Africanized." Cuba would emerge a "second St. Domingo, with all its attendant horrors to the white race, and suffer the flames to extend to our own neighboring shores, seriously to endanger or actually to consume the fair fabric of our Union." The basis for action would be self-defense if events in Cuba threatened "our internal peace and the existence of our cherished Union." The report bore Soulé's mark, although Buchanan toned it down before writing the final draft.

Several cabinet meetings led to Marcy's decision to reject the idea of taking the island by force. In doing so, he referred to the "robber doctrine," and Soulé, discredited by the Pierce administration, angrily resigned as minister. By the time matters calmed, the administration had lost the November congressional elections, and the Kansas-Nebraska controversy had burst onto the national scene. Democratic leaders blamed part of the election outcome on the expansionist policies toward Cuba and decided to let the matter cool.

The excitement caused by the Ostend Manifesto was attributable to the heated political atmosphere and to the almost fanatical distrust between North and South. Otherwise, the document would probably have received the ridicule it deserved. But the Pierce administration's pro-slavery stance on the Kansas-Nebraska bill had made northerners suspicious of any attempts to annex Cuba. The paper was actually no "manifesto" because no ultimatum was delivered to Spain, but as with other events of the decade, newspapers and politicians preferred exaggeration to truth.

Marcy's April instructions to Soulé were partly responsible for the trouble, even though he must have delighted in seeing his minister in Spain take the abuse, for the secretary had not wanted him there in the first place. Marcy's meaning, as made clear in the rest of the note, was to help Cuba achieve independence through negotiations, making it available for annexation by the United States. He used the word *detach* in his instructions, whereas the manifesto preferred *wrest*. But given Soulé's past performance in Madrid, one has to wonder what Marcy had in mind. Unspoken or unwritten wishes can become inferred policy in the hands of diplomats not known for restraint.

With the expansionist Democrats slowed by the slavery issue, attention again turned to the filibusters. John Quitman, who had supported López's attempts to take Cuba, had meanwhile resigned his position as Mississippi's governor in 1851 because of the controversy over filibustering and had decided to try to seize the island. Should Spain end slavery in Cuba, he feared, the South's institution would be in danger. Besides providing an example of freedom, a new black nation could grow out of Cuba and block the South's spread into the Caribbean. In 1854 Quitman prepared to lead a force of 3,000 to take the island, but he could not overcome the federal government's opposition, the lack of financial support, and failure to arouse help among the Cubans themselves. A year later Quitman gave up on filibustering because of what he called the "humbug administration" in Washington.

The most persistent filibuster was William Walker of Tennessee, who at one time installed himself as head of Nicaragua. Noted for his grayish, steel-like eyes, he tried four times—in 1855, 1857, 1858, and 1860—to invade Latin America. Walker weighed a mere hundred pounds, held a degree in medicine, practiced law in Louisiana, and edited a newspaper before getting involved in filibustering. In 1853 he and a small crew of adventurers seized from Mexico the capital of Lower California at La Paz, but infighting and poor discipline caused them to withdraw. He was tried for violating the Neutrality Act of 1818 but acquitted in San Francisco.

America's interest in building a canal through Nicaragua attracted Walker's attention to Latin America throughout the last half of the 1850s. Hired to keep order in the small country by an American business which transported passengers across Nicaragua to California, Walker was so successful that he finally took control of the republic in 1855 and declared himself president. His government reestablished slavery and intended to resume the slave trade, swore to bind "the Southern states to Nicaragua as if she were one of themselves," and, with the assistance of America's minister in Nicaragua, turned the country's attention to cotton, sugar, rice, and other crops suited to the warm climate and cheap labor. Walker's activities aroused suspicions. Many British thought him the agent of American expansionists who were in violation of the Clayton-Bulwer Treaty, a belief in the United States encouraged by its half-hearted efforts to stop filibustering. Many northerners thought Walker a southern instrument to spread slavery, a belief the Democratic party fostered in 1856 by inserting a statement in its platform praising his desire to "regenerate" Nicaragua. That same year the Pierce administration extended recognition to the Walker government in Nicaragua, partly because it was the only group having authority, but also because the move might be politically beneficial at home.

But Walker's rapid climb to the top in Nicaragua was followed by an even faster fall from power. Shortly after becoming president of Nicaragua, Walker alienated the people by his oppressive rule, and his followers turned on one another or fell victim to liquor and disease. Anglo-French opposition to Walker's regime further undercut his government, and eventually he lost the support of Cornelius Vanderbilt, who had invested in Nicaragua for transit purposes. Vanderbilt's enmity proved costly, for he aided Costa Rica, Guatemala, Honduras, and San Salvador in forcing Walker to flee to the United States in the spring of 1857. Walker still did not give up. By November of that year he was headed back toward Nicaragua, but American naval officers took him into custody near Greytown. He won his release and in 1858 was trying again to reach Nicaragua when his ship hit a reef off British Honduras. In the spring of 1860 he tried a fourth time to regain the presidency of Nicaragua, but in an attack on Honduras he was routed and turned for help to a British official, who handed him over to the Hondurans. In mid-September 1860 Walker died before a firing squad.

The Buchanan administration made a last-ditch effort to acquire Cuba, but it too was stymied by the slavery issue. Immediately after Buchanan's inauguration as president, the United States Supreme Court handed down the Dred Scott decision, which sharpened the animosity over slavery and further reduced chances for taking the island. Republicans sought the Homestead Act to attract Americans westward, while southern Democrats held out for Cuba. Buchanan kept trying. He appointed a wealthy New York banker, August Belmont, to the ministerial post in Madrid, only to have the Senate refuse confirmation because Belmont had earlier suggested that the United States bribe Spain into giving up the island. In December 1858 Buchanan asked Congress to set aside money to buy Cuba lest European powers intervene. The Senate Foreign Relations Committee recommended $30 million for that purpose, but abolitionists in the Republican party blocked a decision until Congress went out of session. Buchanan tried and failed again in 1859 and 1860, and America's efforts at annexing Cuba ended with Abraham Lincoln's election to the presidency, for the Illinois Republican opposed the move.

Buchanan's Caribbean policy was national more than sectional, but it appeared to lean toward the South and slavery. He sought to buy Cuba, place American soldiers in Nicaragua and Panama for safeguarding transportation facilities, and send the army to Mexico to restore domestic order. These measures would have warded off European intervention in the New World and established respect for the Monroe Doctrine. Yet they also would have benefited the South, and that killed the proposals. With neither section willing to compromise, the United States moved into the Civil War, Reconstruction, and rapid domestic developments that changed the nation and turned attention away from Cuba and other expansionist enterprises in Latin America. Slavery ceased to exist in the United States by 1865, and for almost three decades so did active American interest in Cuba and the Caribbean. The principal legacy of the filibustering expeditions was a distrust in Latin America that marred relations with the United States for years.

America's confusing and disjointed foreign policy of the 1850s is understandable only within the context of slavery and the coming of the Civil War. The decade's foreign events lacked cohesion because North and South were divided over several issues, including what each section defined as the national interest, and many Americans from both sections were concerned with whether black slavery was compatible with the republican ideals associated with manifest destiny. Americans agreed that territorial expansion was the means toward empire, but they differed on whether slavery was reconcilable with freedom. Expansion northward was blocked by an alien majority and by a climate unsuited for cotton and slavery; consequently, the South sought an empire in the Caribbean and in Central America. But northerners feared a conspiracy to spread slavery and opposed these expansionist aims. Southerners felt threatened by a growing Republican party that opposed the spread of slavery, and repeatedly exerted pressure on the Democrats to seek the island. Perhaps a number of Americans wanted Cuba in the national interest, but suspicion of the South's motives was so widespread in the North that any expansionist program benefiting the South was subject to attack. Such a chaotic decade was the fitting prelude to the domestic conflict that came in the spring of 1861.

Selected readings

Bourne, Kenneth, *Britain and the Balance of Power in North America, 1815–1908.* 1967.

Brown, Charles H., *Agents of Manifest Destiny: The Lives and Times of the Filibusters.* 1980.

Campbell, Charles S., *From Revolution to Rapprochement: The United States and Great Britain, 1783–1900.* 1974.

Cohen, Warren I., *America's Response to China.* 1971.

Dowty, Alan, *The Limits of American Isolation: The United States and the Crimean War.* 1971.

Fairbank, John K., *Trade and Diplomacy on the China Coast: The Opening of the Treaty Ports, 1842–1854.* 2 vols. 1953.

Fay, Peter W., *The Opium War, 1840–1842.* 1975.

Garber, Paul N., *The Gadsden Treaty*. 1923.

Gulick, Edward V., *Peter Parker and the Opening of China*. 1973.

Johnson, Robert E., *Far China Station: The U.S. Navy in Asian Waters, 1800–1898*. 1979.

Jones, Wilbur D., *The American Problem in British Diplomacy, 1841–1861*. 1974.

May, Robert E., *The Southern Dream of a Caribbean Empire, 1854–1861*. 1973.

Neumann, William L., *America Encounters Japan: From Perry to MacArthur*. 1963.

Perkins, Dexter, *The Monroe Doctrine, 1826–1867*. 1933.

Potter, David, *The Impending Crisis, 1848–1861*. 1976.

Shewmaker, Kenneth E., "Daniel Webster and the Politics of Foreign Policy, 1850–1852," *Journal of American History* 63 (1976):303–315.

———, "Forging the 'Great Chain': Daniel Webster and the Origins of American Foreign Policy toward East Asia and the Pacific, 1841–1852," *American Philosophical Society* 129 (1985):225–59.

Spencer, Donald S., *Louis Kossuth and Young America: A Study of Sectionalism and Foreign Policy, 1848–1852*. 1977.

Treat, Payson, J., *Diplomatic Relations between the United States and Japan: 1853–1895*. 2 vols. 1932.

Van Alstyne, Richard W., *The United States and East Asia*. 1973.

Varg, Paul A., *New England and Foreign Relations, 1789–1850*. 1983.

Walworth, Arthur, *Black Ships Off Japan*. 1946.

Warner, Donald F., *The Idea of Continental Union: Agitation for the Annexation of Canada to the United States, 1849–1893*. 1960.

Williams, Mary W., *Anglo-American Isthmian Diplomacy, 1815–1915*. 1916.

Chapter Nine

The Civil War, 1861–1865

On April 12, 1861, Confederate forces in Charleston opened fire on the federal garrison in Fort Sumter, and the Civil War began. After the election of Abraham Lincoln to the presidency, South Carolina had led seven southern states in announcing secession from the Union, and after the shots at Fort Sumter, four more states joined the Confederate States of America, which had already drawn up a constitution in Montgomery, Alabama. President Lincoln called for 75,000 militiamen to put down what he termed a rebellion. His purpose was to preserve the Union by defeating the South on the battlefield and by preventing European intervention on behalf of the South that could determine the outcome of the war. Should England recognize the Confederacy, Lincoln feared, the Union would have to risk the consequences and declare war on the British.

If the conflict between North and South became sustained, the North's manpower and industrial resources would be the decisive factors. Some 22 million people were above the Mason-Dixon line; only 9 million, including 4 million slaves, were below. Southerners had superior leadership at the outset, and in a short war they would have the advantages of higher morale (a war for southern independence) and of a rich military tradition and frontier existence which better acclimated them to army life. Many southerners were hunters who knew the terrain and could fire rifles, and more than a few were trained officers and soldiers. The image of the northerner, so often accurate, was that of a laborer or mechanic who knew little or nothing about guns, military strategy, and tactics, or of death on the battlefield. The major hope for the Confederacy was to win European recognition of its independence and secure war matériel— and even an ally. It was crucial to the Union to prevent this from happening. The key to both antagonists' policy was England, for as England went, so would go France and perhaps the rest of the Continent.

Abraham Lincoln

Though urged by Republican party members to declare that the Civil War was over slavery, he insisted that his objective was to preserve the Union. (Photo by Lewis E. Walker, ca. 1863; Library of Congress)

1861: UNION DIPLOMACY

Union diplomacy in the Civil War was in the hands of the president and his secretary of state, William H. Seward of New York. Lincoln appeared to be a natural leader of men—perhaps a statesman—who instilled a desire in others to follow him through the perilous times. Lincoln adapted to changing situations and had the wisdom and courage to handle the most strong-willed men of his time. His first challenge came from Seward, a disgruntled, embittered Republican who believed the presidency rightfully belonged to him and made little effort to hide his feelings. Henry Adams, son and secretary of the Union minister in London, Charles Francis Adams, described Seward as a "slouching, slender figure" with a "head like a wise macaw; a beaked nose, shaggy eyebrows, unorderly hair and clothes; hoarse voice; offhand manner; free talk, and perpetual cigar." Seward regarded Lincoln as a clumsy buffoon who had stolen the nomination and eked out the election in a campaign heralded by divisiveness. Seward had been a frontrunner for the presidency until an earlier

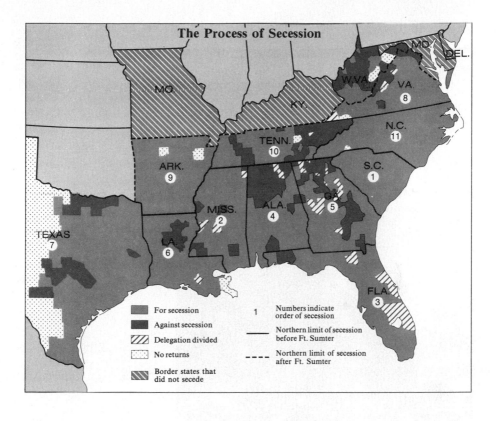

Legend:

- For secession
- Against secession
- Delegation divided
- No returns
- Border states that did not secede
- 1 — Numbers indicate order of secession
- ——— Northern limit of secession before Ft. Sumter
- - - - - Northern limit of secession after Ft. Sumter

MAP 12

One reason why Lincoln refused to declare slavery as the reason for the war was the certainty of driving the border states (slaves states that had not seceded) into the Confederacy.

statement he had made—that the sections were heading for an "irrepressible conflict"—came back to haunt him; but if he could not lead from the highest position in the land, he could occupy the second most important seat as heir apparent to the presidency and act as an English-style prime minister to ensure Americans against Lincoln's shortcomings. The president had breathed new life into Seward's political chances when he appointed him secretary of state, and the New Yorker was not about to let the opportunity pass.

Seward had an anti-British reputation before he joined the president's cabinet. Englishmen remembered his anti-English role in the Alexander McLeod crisis of 1841, and as recently as 1860 he had offended them with derisive remarks to the visiting duke of Newcastle. Seward's first effort to maintain European neutrality was preposterous. In effect he suggested that the administration resolve the sectional crisis at home by involving

William H. Seward

As secretary of state under Lincoln, Seward's major objective was to prevent England from extending recognition to the Confederacy. (Culver Pictures)

the nation in a war abroad. A hard line by the Lincoln administration, he believed, would convince English and other European leaders that intervention on behalf of the Confederacy meant war with the Union. On April 1, 1861, "All Fool's Day," he gave the president a memorandum entitled "Some Thoughts for the President's Consideration," which claimed that Lincoln was "without a policy either domestic or foreign" and suggested that he bring back the secessionists by causing a war with England, France, Russia, or Spain. Though Seward denied interest in leading this policy, he admitted that "I neither seek to evade nor assume responsibility." Lincoln ignored the suggestion. Late in May Seward tried again. He sent a dispatch to London so dangerous that Lincoln found it necessary to make revisions before allowing it to leave the country. Seward's draft warned of war if England recognized Confederate independence, but the president deleted these passages and directed Charles Francis Adams in England to regard the dispatch as only a guide for his behavior. The president's decisions proved wise, for in July Confederate forces in Virginia routed Union troops at Bull Run (Manassas Junction), and made it absurd for the Lincoln administration to threaten England.

Seward's position was based upon a highly questionable assumption. Though it would have been foolish for a *united* America to foment a war with any or all of the European powers, and though it appeared infinitely unwise for a divided nation to risk war, he hoped that the external danger would cause a surge of patriotism that would smooth over internal differences. But, given the intense feeling that had led to secession, Lincoln had no assurance that the South would not simply sign a peace treaty with any European antagonist, thus leaving the North to fend for itself.

With these dangerous flirtations behind him, Seward turned to a more reasoned policy. He advised the president to impose a blockade of the entire southern coast from the Chesapeake Bay to the Rio Grande. On April 19, 1861 Lincoln issued a proclamation to this effect. The Union navy of fewer than a hundred vessels, two-thirds of which were in need of repairs or were outmoded sailing ships, prepared to close about 185 bays or inlets stretching over 3,500 miles of Atlantic and Gulf coastline. It was a "paper blockade," contrary to international law, that nonetheless led to the capture or destruction of more than 1,500 ships and the ultimate control of all major Confederate ports. The British eventually accepted its legality when, as British Foreign Secretary Lord John Russell allowed, the blockade created an "evident danger" to a ship trying to run it.

Lincoln's proclamation of a blockade created a paradox that plagued the administration throughout the war. Lincoln insisted that the South was in rebellion; but under international law, to establish a blockade was automatically to define the antagonists as belligerent, independent nations. The British chose not to exploit this contradiction—partly because of Canada's vulnerability to invasion in case of war with the Union, and also because they worried that the precedent might be used against them in a future war. But they did interpret the blockade as affirming the existence of war and on May 13 declared a neutrality proclamation, which other European governments followed. The declaration of neutrality effectively confirmed the South's status as a belligerent, which meant that Confederate vessels—including privateers that the president of the Confederacy, Jefferson Davis, had offered to commission two days before Lincoln announced the blockade—could plunder Union merchant vessels and secure goods in neutral ports, and that the Confederacy could float loans and purchase war matériel in Europe. In addition, British vessels (as neutrals) could enter blockaded waters with noncontraband goods.

Britain's concern in declaring neutrality was to alert its merchants to the danger of seizure by Union cruisers, but the impression gathered by supporters of the Union was that the government in London was pro-Confederacy. Worse, London's policy seemed to highlight southern sympathies in England, leading observers in both North and South to believe that formal British recognition of Confederate independence would follow. The truth is that British neutrality added credence and authority to the Union blockade. Furthermore, the furor in America over the British stance caused the London government to be more careful in its relations with the Union. But these considerations were not evident at the time. Northerners considered Britain's neutrality proclamation a hostile act.

Seward tried to rectify the dangerous situation. He realized that after the Crimean War the Declaration of Paris of 1856 had, among other things, abolished privateering; he also knew that the United States had turned down an invitation to join the pact with Britain and several Old World nations. Before the Civil War the government in Washington approved privateering because the practice benefited small-navy nations like the United States. The other features of the declaration fitted America's idea of maritime rights advanced since the 1770s—"free ships, free goods," or no confiscation of noncontraband enemy matériel on neutral vessels; neutral noncontraband goods not subject to seizure under an enemy's flag; no "paper blockades"—but these maritime guarantees had not been sufficient to compensate for the provision relating to privateering. Seward recognized that the situation had changed and suggested to the British minister in Washington, Lord Richard Lyons, that he would initial the Declaration of Paris if the United States did not have to accept the sanctity of noncontraband belligerent goods at sea. Lyons allowed this, but inquired about the Washington government's ability to tie the South to the new policy against privateering. Seward responded that southerners would adhere to the Declaration of Paris because they were part of the United States. Lyons looked quizzically at Seward and made a comment that revealed the contradictions in America's maritime policy: "Very well. If they are not independent then the President's proclamation of blockade is not binding. A blockade, according to the convention, applies only to two nations at war."

Had Anglo-American relations been on better terms in 1861, Lyons might have overlooked the inconsistencies in Lincoln's policy. But the British did not realize then what they would realize later—that Anglo-American trade would benefit more from a Union intact than from one divided. Lyons infuriated Seward. "Europe must interpret the law our way or we'll declare war," the secretary of state warned him. We will "commission enough privateers to prey on English commerce on every sea." This was a bluff, and Lyons knew it. The Confederacy could not match the Union's work force and resources, and yet it had a coastline impossible to seal off. The Union navy was under the able leadership of Secretary of the Navy Gideon Welles, but even he was unable to perform miracles with a mere forty-two seaworthy warships—only eight of which were in American waters when the war began. When Seward's request for conditional adherence to the Declaration of Paris arrived in London, Foreign Secretary Russell approved, but with the stipulation that this would not "have any bearing . . . on the internal differences now prevailing in the United States." In other words, the prohibition against privateering would not apply to the present war. As events turned out, privateering did little for the Confederacy because the European governments refused to allow the entry of captured ships and their prizes.

The Union's major means for enforcing the blockade was to invoke the doctrine of "continuous voyage" in determining whether a ship's cargo was subject to seizure. Under this argument, which the British established in the *Essex* case of 1805 and used against the United States in the Napoleonic Wars, the Union could seize vessels entering any neutral port if it decided that the ultimate destination of their cargo was the Confederacy. Thus British ships en route to Nassau, Bermuda, and Havana were open to capture, and, in fact, Union ships captured British ships or confiscated their cargoes in several instances.

The most celebrated case involved the privately owned British steamship *Peterhoff* in 1863. A Union cruiser seized the *Peterhoff* near the Danish West Indies and charged the captain with engaging in a continuous voyage to the Confederacy, even though he had unloaded the cargo at Matamoros on the Mexican side of the Rio Grande, and the goods were to go overland to the Confederacy. The United States Supreme Court eventually ruled in 1866 that only the contraband was subject to capture, for the goods were to have gone from a port not within the blockade limits (Matamoros) and by land to the Confederacy. Yet the court added that if the ship's owners were in collusion with the subterfuge, the *Peterhoff* was also to be a prize. After the war, in the cases of the *Bermuda* in 1865 and the *Springbok* the following year, the court approved confiscation of the vessels because their final destination was a Confederate port. Seward did not disavow capture of the *Peterhoff*, and yet the British did not object even though several prominent European jurists protested America's use of continuous voyage. The London government was satisfied that the United States supported a doctrine important to belligerents seeking control of the seas.

Lincoln knew that the success of the Union depended heavily on the attitude of England: should the English recognize Confederate independence, the French and others would do the same. The responsibility of the president and his secretary of state was to cultivate friendly relations with England. The Atlantic nations had temporarily resolved a major problem in the Western Hemisphere with the Clayton-Bulwer Treaty of 1850, and the warm reception given the visiting prince of Wales in 1860 was suggestive of mutual goodwill. The English press initially supported the Union because the war's purpose seemed to be to stamp out slavery. But no matter what Lincoln's personal feelings were about the institution, he repeatedly insisted that his prime goal was to preserve the Union. He had declared in his inaugural address that "I have no purpose, directly, to interfere with the institution of slavery in the States where it exists"; his central concern was to establish that "no State, upon its own mere motion, can lawfully get out of the Union." He knew that a war to end slavery might cause the secession of the border slave states of Maryland,

Kentucky, Missouri, and Delaware, and that this could give victory to the Confederacy. Yet when Lincoln called only for the preservation of the Union, the British failed to understand his precarious position and soon noted that the South's cry for independence was morally defensible.

The French government under Napoleon III saw many advantages to be gained from an American collapse. The emperor hoped to achieve his ancestors' dream of reestablishing a French empire in the New World, and in October 1861 he proposed joint mediation of the war, motivated by his designs toward tipping the outcome to the Confederacy and implanting French colors in strife-torn Mexico. The French people supported Napoleon's mediation suggestion, although for different reasons. Textile workers needed southern cotton, but not at the cost of conflict. The upper classes detested American democracy and like the English they identified more with southern aristocracy. Although working classes and liberals opposed slavery and favored the Union's republicanism, they had no influence on the French government. Napoleon later welcomed the Confederate minister, but kept the Union representative at a distance. He also permitted French shipbuilding firms to construct and arm vessels for the South, although these efforts did not work out. Mediation seemed acceptable, but Napoleon realized that success depended on London.

1861: CONFEDERATE DIPLOMACY

Britain's inability to comprehend Lincoln's position on slavery led it to accept the South's view of the war: a struggle for independence against northern oppression. Confederate propagandists worked in England to convince the upper classes that the South's only objective was freedom, and that economic ties with the British were vital to both parties. Ironically, Englishmen compared the North to the British empire under King George III, and the South to the American colonies in 1776. The failure of English liberals to understand that a Union victory would necessarily mean the end of slavery perplexed and infuriated American antislavery proponents who wished Lincoln would make plain the inescapable outcome of the conflict. When both the *Times* and *Punch* of London reflected upper-class sentiment and blasted Lincoln and the North, the New York *Herald* led the counterattack in a bitter newspaper exchange that intensified Anglo-American feelings.

British Prime Minister Lord Palmerston and Foreign Secretary Russell exemplified the upper-class viewpoint that the Confederacy would win, and that a lengthy war meant the senseless destruction of life and property. Many of society's leaders found nobility in the southern aristocracy and considered Davis a gentleman and Lincoln the product of a degenerating democratic North. "Wonder to relate," a writer with the London *Times* noted after an interview with Davis; "he does not chew and is neat and clean-looking, with hair trimmed, and boots brushed." But with Lincoln, the predicted results of mob rule in America had reached fulfillment: the experiment in republicanism had sunk into chaos and spewed forth one of its own—a gangly, ax-swinging rube who had risen from the prairies of Illinois to determine the destinies of millions of Americans like him. Englishmen thought the size of America proved its greatest enemy, for they believed that expanding republics faltered in proportion to the amount of freedom citizens gained from governmental control. The prospect of Lincoln's success in the war was unsettling. Many in England were already demanding democratic changes of their own, and Union victory could bring the same anarchy to England.

Government leaders in London also, at first, saw practical advantages in a southern victory that divided the American empire. Russia's ambassador in London explained in 1861: "the English Government, at the bottom of its heart, desires the separation of North America into two republics, which will watch each other jealously and counterbalance one the other. Then England . . . would have nothing to fear from either; for she would dominate them, restraining them by their rival ambitions." Palmerston realized that two Americas would reduce commercial competition, diminish the threat to Canada and other British holdings in the New World, and frustrate manifest destiny. In early 1861 the American Congress had passed the Morrill Tariff, which raised duties and seemed indicative of further moves toward protectionism. British free traders thought that Congress had aimed the bill at them and looked to the advantages of having a southern agricultural nation without tariff walls. They realized that nearly 80 percent of the cotton in their textile mills came from the South. The Civil War provided an opportunity for England to spread its influence in the Americas.

Britain's reaction to the Civil War was thus mixed, but most groups opposed intervention. Conservatives believed that Lincoln was on the side of stability and order and that it was not politic to support a government built on insurrection. Reformers John Bright and Richard Cobden recognized that Union victory would end slavery. Bright declared in Birmingham, England, in December 1862: "I blame men who are eager to admit into the family of nations a State which offers itself to us, based on a principle . . . more odious and more blasphemous than was ever heretofore dreamed of." He continued: "The leaders of this revolt propose this monstrous thing—that, over a territory forty times as large as England, the blight and curse of slavery shall be forever perpetuated." British merchants wanted to stay out of the conflict because northern privateers would raid their ships; they also recognized that a protracted war between North and South would seriously damage Britain's main commercial rival. Finally, they would profit from trading with both sides. Another large group favoring neutrality was the working class. These people were aware of the morbid descriptions of slavery found in Harriet Beecher Stowe's *Uncle Tom's Cabin* and resolved that if the Union freed the slaves, the example would benefit all labor groups. The North took on the image of an egalitarian democracy, whereas the South appeared to be a closed society built on white wealth and black labor.

Confederate diplomats in Europe found that slavery severely hampered their efforts to win recognition. The British had abolished slavery in the empire almost three decades before the Civil War. The South would have been wise to play down the subject of slavery, but it could not hide some of the statements made by its spokesmen. In March 1861 the vice president of the Confederacy, Alexander Stephens, asserted in Savannah that slavery had caused "the late rupture and present revolution." The Confederate government rested "upon the great truth that the Negro is not equal to the white man; that slavery, subordination to the superior race, is his natural and moral condition." When Lincoln declared that the war was to preserve the Union, Englishmen who favored the South could remain in that camp; but if the president changed the war's purpose to destroy slavery, these same people would have to decide whether they could favor a society condoning the institution.

The South pinned its hopes for British recognition on "King Cotton Diplomacy." The Charleston *Mercury* in June 1861 exalted cotton as the key to Confederate victory: "The cards are in our hands! and we intend to play them out to the bankruptcy of every cotton factory in Great Britain and France or the acknowledgment of our independence." In 1858 Senator M. B. Hammond of South Carolina had declared that if England was denied the South's cotton, it "would topple headlong and carry the whole civilized world with her, save the South. No, you dare not make war on cotton. No power on earth dares to make war upon it. Cotton is king!" Nearly a fifth of the English people drew their livelihoods from textile production, and most of the cotton came from the South. By 1860 the British received almost 2 million bales a year. Any obstruction to this flow had the potential of affecting about 5 million British subjects in a business that held up an empire.

The South's reliance on cotton diplomacy set off a flurry of activity abroad. In March 1861 President Davis sent three unofficial agents to Europe to seek recognition, float loans, circulate propaganda, and purchase ships and goods. Their *quid pro quo* was tariff-free trade with the South and the opportunity to broaden European influence in the New World. Britain's reaction was reserved, for it wanted to determine the victor in the war before taking sides. Lyons in Washington advised his London government to grant only an informal audience to the Confederate ministers. "I shall see the Southerners when they come," Russell replied, "but not officially, and keep them at a proper distance."

News of the Confederate commissioners in Europe led Seward to send the Massachusetts lawyer and diplomat Charles Francis Adams as Union minister to London. This was a master stroke, for this descendant of two presidents was gifted in the art of diplomacy. Adams was a cultured gentleman, educated in an English public school, calm in demeanor, and able to mingle socially with Russell and others because he appeared almost British in manner. Adams's appointment served to balance Seward's hot temperament and helped smooth Anglo-American relations.

Adams's work was ready for him when he arrived in London on May 13, 1861. That same day the queen had announced neutrality, which caused him to fear that this move constituted recognition of the South's belligerent status and thus was the prelude to recognizing its independence. The British had not authorized the sale of military goods or the fitting of privateers, but these developments now seemed likely. Russell was evasive when Adams tried to discern how much influence the Confederate emissaries had won in England, but he avoided the temptation to break diplomatic relations. Adams knew that war with England could prove fatal for the Union.

THE *TRENT* AFFAIR

The Confederates' hopes for victory jumped dramatically after they routed Union forces at the Battle of Bull Run. The results made believers of skeptics, allowing the head of President Davis's secret-service operations in Europe, James D. Bulloch, to find a welcome hearing in England when he sought contracts with private firms for building a Confederate navy. Davis acted quickly to take advantage of the Confederacy's favor. To win European recognition, he dispatched James Mason of Virginia to England and John Slidell of Louisiana to France. Mason was colorful and controversial. He had served as senator a decade earlier and had written the Fugitive Slave Law of 1850; while minister to England, however, he would not leave a good impression, often chewing tobacco during the debates in the House of Commons and spitting the juice across the carpet, only some of it reaching the cuspidor. Slidell also had a reputation, for different reasons: he had been Polk's envoy to Mexico during the tumultuous prewar days of 1845. In mid-October 1861 Mason and Slidell slipped through the blockade at Charleston and headed for Havana, where they transferred to the British steamship *Trent*, expecting safe passage to Europe under neutral colors.

Meanwhile, Captain Charles Wilkes of the United States Navy, already well-known for his reports on Oregon, waited aboard his U.S.S. *San Jacinto* outside Cuban waters and without orders stopped the *Trent* in the Bahama channel on November 8, after firing two warning shots across its bow. He sent an officer aboard for Mason and Slidell, who Wilkes claimed were "contraband of war" and traitors to the United States. Mason and Slidell refused to leave the ship, and Wilkes ordered a small detachment of marines to remove them. As they seized Mason in his cabin, Slidell tried to squeeze through a porthole in his quarters and likewise was captured. Wilkes allowed the *Trent* to resume its voyage to England but took the two captives and their two secretaries on board the *San Ja-*

Charles Francis Adams

As Union minister to England during the Civil War, Adams's most difficult tasks were to resolve maritime problems concerning the Trent, Alabama, *and* Laird *rams.* (October 1872 issue of *Vanity Fair;* Library of Congress)

cinto, where he gave them his cabin and welcomed them to his table for meals. A week later the *San Jacinto* arrived at Fortress Monroe in Virginia, and Union forces moved the captives to Fort Warren in Boston.

Northerners rejoiced at the news, feeling that Wilkes had avenged a long succession of British wrongs at sea. To them, it mattered little that Wilkes had violated international law by removing Mason and Slidell. But Wilkes's rash and illegal behavior would soon cause great trouble. Had he based his stand on Mason's attempt to conceal the Confederate mail packet from the *San Jacinto*'s boarding party, the *Trent* would have lost its neutral status and become subject to capture and adjudication before a prize court. Furthermore, "contraband" had no bearing on the *Trent* affair because the vessel's destination was *not* an enemy port and admiralty decisions had never interpreted *persons* as contraband subject to removal. And, despite a later attempt to twist Wilkes's action into "impressment," he had not removed Mason and Slidell as *nationals*, nor had he intended to force them into the Union navy. The entire episode was fraught with legal difficulties, but northerners were frustrated with the war and regarded Wilkes's behavior as a reassertion of American honor. The governor of Massachusetts triumphantly declared that Wilkes had "fired his shot across the bows of the ship that bore the British lion at its head." Banquets were held in his honor, *The New York Times* suggested setting aside another Fourth of July commemoration, the secretary of the navy rewarded him with a promotion and special praise, and the House of Representatives voted him a gold medal.

In Britain the response to the *Trent* affair unleashed a storm of criticism. The stock market plunged as the English accused Seward of trying to instigate a war. "Good God," Henry Adams wrote his brother. "What's got into you all? What do you mean by deserting now the great principles of our fathers, by returning to the vomit of that dog Great Britain?" Palmerston opened an emergency cabinet meeting with a near call to arms: "I don't know whether you are going to stand this, but I'll be damned if I do!" The following day the cabinet recommended that Lyons make three demands: reparations, the immediate release of Mason and Slidell, and a formal apology "for the insult offered to the British flag." In the meantime the government put the navy on alert, readied military supply operations, and sent 11,000 troops to Canada, who left England as a band played "Dixie." Russell prepared to direct Lyons to set a seven-day deadline on the demands; if not met, he was to break relations and return home.

These harsh words might have brought the nations to war had it not been for a timely problem in communications and the intervention of Queen Victoria's consort, Prince Albert. The Atlantic cable that had been laid in the late 1850s was not working, and it took nearly two weeks for news to travel between England and the United States. British officials did not know whether the United States had retreated on the matter and did not want to see war develop if it had. The British note did not arrive in Washington until a month after Americans learned of the *Trent*. Delays on both sides of the Atlantic in receiving news of the *Trent* episode allowed emotions to cool. The chairman of the Senate Foreign Relations Committee, Charles Sumner, recognized the potential disaster awaiting the Union, and called on the Lincoln administration to free the two Confederate ministers. The president was in an unenviable position. If he complied with British demands, he could undermine the already waning support for his government; refusal could bring war with England and the demise of the Union. Seizure of the *Trent* had been a welcome corrective for the despair resulting from Bull Run and, used carefully, it might serve to warn the British that recognition of the Confederacy could mean war with the Union. Lincoln was hesitant to throw away such a potent remedy without examining all factors involved.

In the meantime Prince Albert, who was the queen's private secretary and confidant, searched for an honorable way out of the crisis. Opposing war, he toned down Russell's ultimatum: Lyons was to *ask* about the *Trent* matter and seek reparations. He also told Lyons to accept an explanation rather than demand an apology. The United States should have room to reply that Wilkes had not acted with government orders, "or, if he did, that he misapprehended them." When the revised instructions reached Lyons, he learned that he was "to abstain from anything like menace" when seeking the men's release, and "to be rather easy about the apology." The seven-day deadline remained, and if the United States refused to comply, Lyons was to break diplomatic relations and return home, but *without* warning of war. As fate would have it, Prince Albert was near death and passed away in mid-December 1861, leading to nationwide mourning and allowing further time to defuse the dangerous situation.

On December 19 Seward received the note from Lyons on an informal basis and delivered it to Lincoln for a decision. The first public outcry of satisfaction over Wilkes's actions had toned down, and many influential people were now calling upon the administration to release Mason and Slidell and grant reparations and an apology. In addition, spokesmen from France, Italy, Prussia, Denmark, and Russia condemned the American action as wrong, for they recognized that the *Trent* precedent would endanger all vessels at sea. Adams in London assured his home government that Palmerston's ministry would not retreat from its demands, while the French minister in Washington reiterated his government's position that no break was possible with the long-standing Franco-American respect for neutrality. On Christmas Day Lincoln's cabinet met and was unable to resolve the matter, but the following day it reached a unanimous decision. Lincoln summed up the administration's position when he commented, "One war at a time." Seward was to tell Lyons that Wilkes had the right to search the *Trent* "as a simple, legal and customary belligerent proceeding," but that his failure to take the captured ship as a prize necessitated the prisoners' release.

That same day Seward presented the note to Lyons, and then publicized his reply in the press, explaining to the American people that the United States had won a major diplomatic victory because England had finally recognized the maritime rights that America had fought for during the War of 1812. He declared that Wilkes had acted correctly in searching the *Trent*, but he then added an argument not substantiated in international law: the seizure of Mason and Slidell, Seward asserted, was justified because "persons, as well as property, may become contraband." Though Wilkes failed to take the *Trent* before a prize court for adjudication, he brought attention to a change in British policy that constituted a major advance for free-trade nations like the United States. In a tortured use of international law, Seward asserted that Wilkes had removed two people from a neutral vessel and had committed the act of impressment. If the United States freed the prisoners on these grounds, British approval meant their condemnation of impressment. "If I decide this case in favor of my own government," Seward explained, "I must disavow its most cherished principles, and reverse and forever abandon its essential policy." Yet, he added, "If I maintain those principles, and adhere to that policy, I must surrender the case itself. . . . We are asked to do to the British nation just what we have always insisted all nations ought to do to us." Seward concluded that surrender of the men, who after all were of "comparative unimportance," would have no effect on the "waning proportions of the existing insurrection." The Lincoln administration had escaped a highly dangerous situation and at the same time had left the impression of having gained an American victory by insisting that the *Trent* affair had settled the issue of impressment.

Seward's note on the *Trent* received a favorable reception, except among southerners and their sympathizers. Russell called it a victory for England because Mason and Slidell won their freedom, but cautioned that he did not approve Seward's argument. Spokesmen for the Confederacy recognized that the affair had hurt their cause and now considered Russell "an avowed enemy." Seward's earlier belligerent style of diplomacy had been risky because it convinced Lyons that the United States wanted to instigate a war; in the end it enabled *both* the Union and the government in London to claim victory. A third and critical message became apparent: the outcome of the *Trent* affair signaled a warning that English talk about intervention was just that—talk. The Palmerston ministry knew that war with the Union would open Canada to American invasion, tempt Ireland to cause trouble while England was tied elsewhere, expose British commerce to privateers, and place the antislavery English on the side of the pro-slavery South. No other Anglo-American event had had such potential for war, and yet the trouble had blown over.

1862

On the military front 1862 started well for the Union. General Ulysses S. Grant took Forts Donelson and Henry in Tennessee, and New Orleans fell to Commodore David G. Farragut, thus exposing the Mississippi River to northern control and threatening to separate the West from the rest of the Confederacy. In the East the Union blockade steadily tightened, and a publicized assault on Richmond began under the careful, plodding leadership of General George B. McClellan.

Internationally, developments were mixed. Despite high hopes, "King Cotton Diplomacy" proved to be a failure. Confederate leaders had not taken into account the huge reserves of cotton that Britain had when the war started, thanks to record crops during the three preceding years. Indeed, Britain's overproduction of textiles had resulted in the closing of many factories and the unemployment of thousands of mill workers. In a desperate effort to create a shortage in England, the South destroyed or embargoed two-and-a-half-million bales of cotton. But the Union countered by sending confiscated cotton to Liverpool, and in 1862 British manufacturers bought enough from Egypt and India to tide them through most of the year.

The Confederacy's chances seemed good in another realm of foreign affairs: its agents were successful in contracting for the construction of ships in England that could run the Union blockade and deliver war matériel from Europe. Steamers had repeatedly made it through Union patrols during the first year of the war, but their effectiveness declined with the tightening of the blockade. Besides, those vessels that made it past Union cruisers often carried luxury goods rather than war matériel, which drained money from the South without helping it militarily. But British shipbuilders were favorable to the Confederacy's requests. Though they faced a legal obstacle—the British Foreign Enlistment Act of 1819 made it unlawful to "equip, fit out, or arm in British jurisdiction a ship whose intent is to cruise against the commerce of a friendly power"—they found it easy to circumvent the law by not arming the vessels in England. The shipbuilding firm simply classified vessels under construction as cargo carriers, and upon departure from British waters they entered either the Bahamas or the Azores, where other steamers waited with guns, crews, and officers.

The Lincoln administration regarded the British stance as a violation of neutrality. International law had no provisions affecting a neutral's building of ships and what happened to them, but America's experiences during the Canadian rebellions of the 1830s and with Spain and Mexico during the border problems of the first half of the nineteenth century caused the government in Washington to set high standards for Britain's behavior. In London, Adams vigorously protested the masquerade by which Britain was supplying the South with warships, but Russell replied that he was powerless because the British companies were not breaking the law. Should the government seize the vessels, the courts would uphold the companies.

Confederate agent James G. Bulloch contracted for the building of two ships listed as the *Oreto* and *Enrica*, which later became famous under their Confederate names of *Florida* and *Alabama*. Adams had hotly protested the *Florida*'s departure from Britain, and he was likewise unsuccessful in urging Russell to hold the *Alabama*, then under construction. Adams had gathered testimony that the shipbuilding firm, Laird Brothers of Birkenhead near Liverpool, was working under Confederate contract. No one could doubt the *Alabama*'s destination; work crews had cut placements in the sides for cannon. But by the time Adams convinced Russell that the vessel was to be a Confederate raider, it had slipped out to sea. In late July those involved in the *Alabama*'s construction announced that they were taking the ship with its passengers on a test run down the river. But when the ship reached the Atlantic, the passengers were removed to a tugboat while the *Alabama* went on to Portugal's Azores Islands. There it was fitted with guns and war matériel, and a crew and officers who arrived from England on board two other ships.

These and other vessels built in Britain caused massive destruction of Union ships. The *Florida*, equipped and armed in the Bahamas, took over forty ships before being sunk off the Brazilian coast by a Union warship in October 1864. The *Alabama* began operations in August 1862, and before its sinking two years later by a Union ship-of-war near France, it inflicted more damage on the North than did any other vessel. The *Alabama* sent nineteen Union merchantmen to the bottom within three months, took fifty-seven prizes, and allowed many others to go only on bond. In addition to the work of the *Florida* and the *Alabama*, the *Shenandoah* took forty prizes in the Pacific after its purchase from British owners, and damaged numerous whalers from New England—even after the war was over, for news of the Confederate defeat had not reached the ship's officers. Adams objected to the hospitality shown in British ports toward these vessels, but the *Shenandoah* received repairs, supplies, and crew members in Melbourne, Australia, despite vehement complaints from the American consul. All told, English-built Confederate ships damaged or destroyed nearly 250 Union vessels and were responsible for soaring insurance rates that drove many merchants out of business. Enormous pressure from the Union ultimately caused the Palmerston ministry to change its policy—but not until the spring of 1863. At that time the British government seized the *Alexandra*, another warship headed for the Confederacy. The government failed to prove its case in court and had to pay damages, but the length of the proceedings prevented the South from using the ship to advantage when it did arrive.

Meanwhile, the fighting in America seemed to be tipping in the South's favor. The Union's *Monitor* fought the South's *Merrimack* to a standstill in the "battle of the ironclads" at Hampton Roads, Virginia, but McClellan's drive toward Richmond sputtered to a halt in July. Confederate General Robert E. Lee followed with a second victory at Bull Run and by autumn was prepared to invade the North.

In these circumstances many Englishmen concluded that the war had become a bloody stalemate and that it was time to intervene to stop the fighting and persuade the Union to accept the existence of a southern nation. In mid-September 1862 Palmerston suggested to Russell that England and France offer to mediate "on the basis of a separation." Second Bull Run seemed to indicate the South's ability to stand on its own, and popular pressure grew in England for diplomatic recognition. The London *Times* declared that "the time is approaching when Europe will have to think seriously of its relations to the two belligerents. . . . That North and South must now choose between separation and ruin, material and political, is the opinion of nearly everyone who, looking impartially and from a distance on the conflict, sees what is hidden from the frenzied eyes of the Northern politicians." The British were also beginning to need cotton, and threats of violence by unemployed textile workers in Lancashire drove the ministry into action. Russell agreed with the move for mediation and recommended that "in the case of failure, we ought ourselves to recognize the Southern States as an independent State."

But difficulties developed that eventually blocked the mediation effort. France could not join the venture because of internal problems caused by Napoleon III's recent intervention in Mexico and by his emerging troubles in Italy. Besides, news had arrived that the Russian czar supported the Union as a way to break Britain's hold on the Atlantic. The final consideration was that word had reached London in late September of Lee's invasion of Maryland. Palmerston recommended waiting for the outcome: "It is evident that a great conflict is taking place to the northwest of Washington, and its issue must have a great effect on the state of affairs." He continued that "if the Federals [Unionists] sustain a great defeat, they may be at once ready for mediation, and the iron should be struck while it is hot. If, on the other hand, they should have the best of it, we may wait awhile and see what may follow." Most Englishmen apparently thought the South already "had the best of it." Chancellor of the Exchequer William Gladstone expressed a common English attitude in a stirring speech in behalf of the South. "Jefferson Davis and other leaders of the South," Gladstone said, "have made an army; they are making, it appears, a navy; and they have made what is more than either—they have made a nation."

Palmerston's caution, however, proved well-founded. At Antietam Creek near Sharpsburg, Maryland, Union forces drove back the invaders and the South's stock plummeted. Lee's retreat into Virginia convinced many in England that recognition of the Confederacy would be unwise. Pro-Union groups voiced their usual arguments against recognition, and this time they gained more followers. In November France proposed to join Britain and Russia in arranging a six-month halt in the fighting and an end to the blockade, but the proposal aroused no interest. Three months later, after the Confederacy won the battle of Fredericksburg, Napoleon proposed mediation directly to the Lincoln administration, but again with no success. Congress meanwhile passed a resolution denouncing all attempts at foreign intervention in American affairs. After October 1862 the British never again seriously considered mediation and recognition, and with this the South lost its best hope for victory.

What sealed the issue in Britain was a brilliant stroke by President Lincoln—the issuance of the Emancipation Proclamation. He had been wrestling with the dilemma of how much longer he could ignore the slaves in the border states while fighting the slave-owning Confederacy. In the summer of 1862 word arrived that slaveholders in these states were not favorable to his suggestion of compensated liberation, and he decided to go before his cabinet in July with the draft of a proclamation of emancipation. Most members supported the idea, but Seward, known for his antislavery views before the war, thought that its announcement would have greater impact if the administration awaited a more propitious time. Such a proclamation should be "borne on the bayonets of an advancing army, not dragged in the dust behind a retreating one." Seward did not want to leave the appearance of a cheap effort to stir a slave uprising or to suggest that the Union was frantically searching for a way to win the war. The president agreed to wait for a northern victory.

In September 1862 the outcome at Antietam provided Lincoln with what he labeled a Union triumph. It is debatable whether either side emerged victorious, except that Lee's retreat into Virginia left the Union in control of the field and gave the impression of Confederate defeat. This was enough for the president. Within a week he released a preliminary proclamation which declared that on January 1, 1863, all slaves in areas still in rebellion against the United States were free. Thus he skirted a clash with the border states by exempting them from the proclamation. What is more, the proclamation did not apply to the areas in the Confederacy already brought under Union control.

Initially, the measure satisfied hardly anyone. Southerners denounced it as a desperate effort to foment slave uprisings, and they stiffened their determination to outlast the Union. Abolitionists criticized the proclamation as failing to go far enough, while others decried it as an expedient of war that had no constitutional basis and could not last in the period afterward. Overseas reaction also disappointed Lincoln. Those who favored the Confederacy regarded the proclamation as the Union's last gasp, whereas those who opposed slavery noted the lack of principle in a measure that discriminated among the slaves over which ones would be free.

Those who criticized the Emancipation Proclamation, however, missed one of the president's most crucial intentions—to keep Britain from recognizing the Confederacy. In England reaction to the proclamation ultimately developed into what Lincoln had hoped. At first Palmerston and Russell were skeptical of its real purposes, and the restless, unemployed laborers in the country had no reason to give it much attention. But slowly the realization sank in among antislavery groups that the president had converted the war into a crusade against slavery. The Confederate argument of "independence" against "empire" lost its persuasiveness to the higher purpose of humanitarian reform. John Bright expressed the feelings of England's liberals. "I wish the 1st of January to be here, and the freedom of the Slaves declared from Washington," he asserted to a group at Rochdale. "This will make it impossible for England to interfere for the South, for we are not, I hope, degraded enough to undertake to restore three and one half millions of Negroes to slavery." British recognition of the Confederacy now would have deep symbolic meaning; as one British writer declared, it would be "immoral." If any question remained in the Palmerston ministry about recognizing the South, the surging popular outcry in England in favor of Lincoln and his Emancipation Proclamation helped to remove it.

1863

Events in both Europe and America during the first half of 1863 worked to the Union's advantage. Russia faced a rebellion in Poland that had potential for causing war with Britain and France, and leaving Denmark exposed to Austria and Prussia. Czar Alexander II admired Lincoln, but his primary concern was the British. When the Russian fleet visited New York and San Francisco in the autumn of 1863, Americans mistakenly hailed the events as partial to the Union and a warning to Britain and France not to intervene in the war. They did not understand that the czar feared war with England and France and wanted his ships out of the Baltic and Black seas before enemy vessels hemmed them in. Russia had to establish better relations with the United States because of its need for ice-free ports. However, Alexander did not extend recognition to the Confederacy, and he refused to receive southern diplomats.

In America, important Union military triumphs came in two places almost simultaneously: in the woods near Gettysburg, Pennsylvania, and at Vicksburg on the Mississippi River in northern Mississippi. In July 1863 Union armies under George G. Meade held off Lee's second and last invasion of the North, while Grant won control of the Mississippi River by a successful siege of the Confederate fortress at Vicksburg, which overlooked the great waterway. The battles at Gettysburg and Vicksburg ended the South's hopes for diplomatic recognition. Britain virtually dropped the matter, and Napoleon, who had allowed Confederate agents to contract for the purchase or construction of four war vessels in France, decided by early 1864 to withhold delivery. One of the vessels ultimately made it through Denmark and into Confederate hands, but it arrived too late to have effect.

News of Gettysburg and Vicksburg had not yet reached London when Adams faced another crisis over ships constructed in England for the Confederacy. He exerted pressure on Russell to order the seizure of two five-inch-thick ironclad steamers called *rams*, then under construction by the Laird Company. These fast-moving, highly maneuverable ships were nearly invulnerable to enemy shells, and had four nine-inch guns on revolving turrets; but their most dangerous weapon, many believed, was a seven-foot iron rod resting three feet below water on the foreside, which could sink Union ships blockading the southern coast by piercing their wooden hulls. Adams argued that even though the vessels' papers showed that a private French company had contracted them for Egypt, the rams were for the Confederacy. Yet the British government had no legal justification for confiscating the vessels; they carried no weapons and no evidence proved that they belonged to the Confederacy. Russell offered assurances that his government would not permit the construction of ships for the Confederacy, but Adams was skeptical. He worried that the rams also might escape from England despite the government's best intentions.

Adams's fears seemed substantiated on September 1, when Russell informed him that his government had no legal grounds for detaining the rams. Yet Russell realized the war was turning in the Union's favor and that the American Congress had empowered the president to license privateers that could prey on British shipping. Russell soon notified Palmerston that for the public good he had privately ordered the seizure of the rams. Should there be an effort to seek reparations in the courts, Russell informed Palmerston, "we have satisfied the opinion which prevails here as well as in America that that kind of neutral hostility should not be allowed to go on without some attempt to stop it." The following day, September 4, Russell wrote Adams a second note informing him that the matter was under advisement, but it did not reach the American minister until the afternoon of the next day. In the meantime Adams had only Russell's first note and sent an angry reply on the morning of September 5, which warned that "it would be superfluous in me to point out to your lordship that this is war!" Palmerston bristled at these "insolent threats of war" and suggested that Russell reply "in civil terms, 'You be damned.' " This flareup passed without incident, for three days later Russell notified Adams of his government's decision to seize the rams. In a thinly veiled effort to circumvent the law, the government bought the vessels at a higher price than the private contractors had offered. Britain's decision on the rams calmed Adams, whereas distraught Confederate leaders were angry and disappointed with Britain's failure to extend aid and called their diplomats home.

It is doubtful that the Laird rams could have done much damage, for they became obsolete almost as soon as their purpose was known. The rams were probably unseaworthy and clearly ineffective against a moving ship, and their advent encouraged the faster development of ironclads. The use of the rams also presented practical problems. In March 1862 the Confederate *Virginia* (previously the U.S.S. *Merrimack*) had rammed the *Cumberland* while it sat motionless in Hampton Roads. But when the Confederate captain tried to withdraw the pike from the sinking ship, the force of the engines yanked it off and left it embedded in the wooden hull. Even Adams later had doubts about the rams' effectiveness, but given the emotional atmosphere in the United States during the summer of 1863, no one had time for careful thought.

FRANCE, MEXICO, AND THE END OF THE CIVIL WAR

The Civil War exposed the United States to another danger: it provided France an opportunity to regain a foothold in the New World—this time in Mexico. Political disorder in Mexico furnished an atmosphere conducive to European involvement in 1861. In January a Zapotec Indian, Benito Juárez, became constitutional president of the republic against the wishes of conservative landowners and church groups, and in mid-July he announced a two-year suspension of the country's foreign obligations. That same month Congress in Washington enacted a two-year moratorium on the Mexican government's foreign debt payments. But protests against Juárez's action came from Paris, London, and Madrid, for Mexico was heavily in debt to them. In October Napoleon III of France arranged a cooperative military expedition supported by France, Britain, and Spain, to collect their money.

Lord Russell tried to soften the impact of this interventionist move by asking the Lincoln administration to join the European powers in Mexico. Yet he warned that his invitation did not constitute recognition of the "extravagant pretensions" of the Monroe Doctrine. Seward, faced with the civil war at home, turned down Russell's offer but admitted to these nations' right to use force in collecting debts, as long as they did not engage in territorial or political aggrandizement in Mexico. His suspicions were well founded. Early the following year Palmerston asserted that "the monarchy scheme" would "stop the North Americans . . . in their absorption of Mexico." England was determined to prevent postwar American expansion into Mexico, even to the extent of supporting a monarchical government. The stakes changed when Palmerston and others realized that if Napoleon got deeply involved in Mexico by himself, Britain's chances would increase for establishing a balance of power in Europe.

In December 1861 Spanish soldiers took Veracruz but soon thereafter Spain, along with Britain, decided to drop the costly venture. Napoleon, for his part, had already considered establishing a puppet government in Mexico under the Archduke Ferdinand Maximilian, younger brother of Emperor Francis Joseph of Austria. If Napoleon could save the Catholic Church in Mexico and build a nation strong enough to withstand American expansion, he would regain popularity among French Catholics and revive his country's long-standing dream of a New World empire. A monarchy in Mexico under his direction, he believed, could hold back American expansion south and provide enough commerce and troops to tip the European balance in his favor.

After working out a means for receiving their money, Britain and Spain pulled out of Mexico in April 1862, leaving France on its own. Napoleon's soldiers moved west toward Mexico City, where Juárez's forces held off their advance until 30,000 French reinforcements arrived and took the capital from him in June 1863. While Juárez maintained resistance by guerrilla actions, the thirty-one-year-old Maximilian, accompanied by his youthful wife Carlotta, daughter of the king of Belgium, arrived in Veracruz to head the country in May of 1864. The archduke had agreed, as a condition of French aid, to assume the costs of French intervention as well as the debts Mexico owed France.

The Lincoln administration could do nothing about French involvement in Mexico until the Civil War was over. Seward knew that a prematurely aggressive stand could drive Napoleon into Confederate hands, and he appealed to America's historical claims against foreign intervention in this hemisphere, although never referring to the Monroe Doctrine. He realized the futility in threatening the French while Union forces were locked in combat with southerners. Yet the American public was bitter toward France. In early 1864 the New York *Herald* warned: "As for Mexico, we will, at the close of the rebellion, if the French have not left there before, send 50,000 Northern and 50,000 Southern troops, forming together a grand army to drive the invaders into the Gulf." The House of Representatives unanimously passed a resolution in April, a week before Maximilian took the throne, that condemned France's violation of American policy. Seward meanwhile recalled his minister to Mexico and refused to extend recognition to the new monarch. A sign of the impending Union victory in the war came from the recent nominee for the vice presidency, Andrew Johnson, who in the waning days of the Confederacy declared to a crowd in Nashville that "the day of reckoning is approaching. It will not be long before the Rebellion is put down. . . . And then we will attend to this Mexican affair, and say to Louis Napoleon, 'You cannot found a monarchy on the Continent.' " Johnson boasted that "an expedition into Mexico would be a sort of recreation to the brave soldiers who are now fighting the battles of the Union, and the French concern would be quickly wiped out."

The outcome of the Civil War was also becoming clear to Napoleon. Union forces under General William T. Sherman were cutting a swath of destruction through Georgia and Grant was moving toward Richmond. Napoleon realized he had made a mistake: the venture was enormously expensive. Maximilian was unpopular and inept, the French people opposed involvement in Mexico, and troubles were deepening in Europe. Maximilian's weak government could not survive against a reunited America. Napoleon instructed him not to receive Confederate diplomats and ordered the confiscation of two Confederate rams under construction in France. Finally, he directed a step-by-step withdrawal from Mexico that was under way as the Civil War ended in 1865. Within two years, the French soldiers were gone, but Maximilian stubbornly remained, staunchly asserting his claim to the throne as a Mexican citizen. In June 1867 Juárez's forces, back in control, executed the archduke by a firing squad.

The South's failure to secure British recognition of its independence was crucial to its inability to win the war. Britain's abundant cotton reserves and its capacity to buy elsewhere reduced the South's expected bargaining power. British purchases of northern wheat also gave the Union an advantage, although it is debatable whether this factor was important in maintaining British neutrality. When economic pressure failed, the Confederacy had to secure a decisive victory on the battlefield, but at two critical junctures—Antietam in 1862 and Gettysburg the following year—Lee suffered reverses that had drastic reverberations in London. Lincoln's Emancipation Proclamation further discouraged pro-southern sentiment inside England. Another vital factor was the Confederacy's inability to secure enough armed shipping to break the Union blockade and allow the purchase of war matériel from Europe. In large measure the South's failure to win British recognition helped to determine the outcome of the war.

Selected readings

Adams, Ephraim D., *Great Britain and the American Civil War*. 2 vols., 1925.

Bernath, Stuart L., *Squall Across the Atlantic: American Civil War Prize Cases and Diplomacy*. 1970.

Blumenthal, Henry, *A Reappraisal of Franco-American Relations, 1830–1871*. 1959.

Bourne, Kenneth, *Britain and the Balance of Power in North America, 1815–1908*. 1967.

Campbell, Charles S., *From Revolution to Rapprochement: The United States and Great Britain, 1783–1900*. 1974.

Carroll, Daniel B., *Henri Mercier and the American Civil War*. 1971.

Case, Lynn M., and Warren F. Spencer, *The United States and France: Civil War Diplomacy*. 1970.

Crook, David P., *Diplomacy during the American Civil War*. 1974.

———, *The North, the South, and the Powers, 1861–1865*. 1974.

Cullop, Charles C., *Confederate Propaganda in Europe, 1861–1865*. 1969.

Duberman, Martin, *Charles F. Adams: 1807–1886*. 1961.

Ferris, Norman B., *Desperate Diplomacy: William H. Seward's Foreign Policy*. 1976.

———, *The* Trent *Affair: A Diplomatic Crisis*. 1977.

Graebner, Norman A., "Northern Diplomacy and European Neutrality," in David Donald, ed., *Why the North Won the Civil War*, 55–78. 1960.

Jenkins, Brian, *Britain & the War for the Union*. 2 vols., 1974, 1980.

Jones, Wilbur D., *The Confederate Rams at Birkenhead*. 1961.

Merli, Frank J., *Great Britain and the Confederate Navy: 1861–1865*. 1970.

Monaghan, Jay, *Diplomat in Carpet Slippers: Abraham Lincoln Deals with Foreign Affairs*. 1945.

Niven, John, *Gideon Welles, Lincoln's Secretary of the Navy*. 1973.

Owsley, Frank L. and Harriet Owsley, *King Cotton Diplomacy: Foreign Relations of the Confederate States of America*. Rev. ed. 1959.

Perkins, Dexter, *The Monroe Doctrine, 1826–1867*. 1933.

Spencer, Warren F., *The Confederate Navy in Europe*. 1983.

Warren, Gordon H., *Fountain of Discontent: The* Trent *Affair and Freedom of the Seas*. 1981.

Winks, Robin, *Canada and the United States: The Civil War Years*. 1960.

Chapter Ten

Prelude to American Imperialism, 1865–1897

For three decades following the Civil War, the foreign policy of the United States seemed to lack direction, primarily because of the cataclysmic effects of the war and Reconstruction on the domestic political situation. On the one side the dominant Republican party, concentrated in the Northeast and Midwest, was committed to protectionism at home and to a New England–style of expansionism which was nonimperialist in tone. Rather than seeking empire through territorial gain, one group of Republicans emphasized the missionary role of the United States, another called for foreign markets, and a third, the Liberal wing, was split between imperialists and anti-imperialists. On the other side the Democratic party, based in the South and in the cities with the Irish vote, favored low tariffs on all goods *except* sugar (because of the influence of Louisiana producers), and was anti-imperialist because many of its constituents were anti-black and anti-British. A further obstacle to America's foreign policy was the precarious political balance in Washington: although Republicans had sat in the White House for most of the last half of the century, their presidencies were only one term in length and usually hamstrung by a Congress continually shifting in party control. Thus the United States could not make any firm moves toward world involvement until 1896, when the Republicans won the White House and both houses of Congress, and banded together behind a new kind of foreign expansion built upon a combined missionary and commercial impulse. With the Democrats still floundering, by 1897 the United States was ready to assume a global role under Republican leadership. But first the country had to undergo a time of preparation.

American expansionist interest resumed soon after the Civil War, but in a chaotic and changed fashion. No one had a systematic plan of conquest and the areas sought were seldom part of the continent, in some instances lying outside the hemisphere. Methods of acquisition also changed. The industrial revolution that had become so apparent during the 1850s intensified in the postwar period, and although business and government did not join in a concerted push toward expansion, commercial interests often had Washington's tacit support in searching for investment fields and foreign markets. By the 1890s formal annexation of territory was giving way to "informal empire," or commercial penetration that usually led to the acquisition of colonies with no prospect of gaining statehood. The mood was not national, partly because of the lack of cohesion in the political parties, and partly because of the general fragmentation caused by the Civil War. Anti-imperialist feelings were strong, especially among Americans who recognized their nation's limitations outside the hemisphere, but also among those who feared the incorporation of nonwhite peoples and worried about the negative effects of imperialism on democratic institutions.

The thirty-year period following the Civil War had little pattern or thematic unity in foreign policy, except that the United States sought two basic objectives: to further trade and security through the acquisition of commercial outlets, coaling stations, and naval bases in the Caribbean, Pacific, and Far East; and to construct an isthmian canal that would permit the establishment of a two-ocean navy and assure the safety of the Western Hemisphere. Attention turned from one matter to another, almost haphazardly, and negotiations often failed as domestic politics wheeled presidents in and out with such rapidity that they seldom had time to develop a consistent foreign policy. In fact, the New York *Sun* expressed a widespread feeling that "the diplomatic service has outgrown its usefulness," while Senator Henry Cabot Lodge of Massachusetts, soon to become a leading imperialist, sorrowfully asserted that foreign affairs occupy "but a slight place in American politics, and exert generally only a languid interest." The United States was engaged in a period of transformation from an agricultural to an industrial nation, of education to international needs and interests, and of domestic preparation for a deeper involvement in foreign affairs.

During the last third of the nineteenth century some Americans tried to revive interest in expansionism. Church groups called for increased missionary work among the primitive areas of the world, and soon found themselves with unnatural allies. The English philosopher Herbert Spencer and the Yale sociologist William Graham Sumner, both using Charles Darwin's ideas of evolution, advocated the theories of Social Darwinism and Anglo-Saxon superiority in encouraging Americans to believe that the strong would survive and that the only limitations on growth were self-imposed. Darwin wrote that "there is apparently much truth in the belief that the wonderful progress of the United States as well as the character of the people are the results of natural selection" and that the American nation was "the heir of all ages." Others who popularized these ideas included American historian John Fiske, Reverend Josiah Strong, intellectual Brooks Adams, political scientist John Burgess, and public figures such as William H. Seward, Ulysses S. Grant, James G. Blaine, and the most outspoken of all, Theodore Roosevelt. Brooks Adams and Roosevelt often gathered at Henry Adams's house in Washington, discussing these ideas and developing into a tightly knit group advocating commercial and territorial expansion. The historian Frederick Jackson Turner suggested the imminence of international involvement when in 1893 he declared that the American frontier was closed; the end of free land, he seemed to assert, portended expansion abroad. Philosophers, missionaries, naval officers, business leaders, farmers—all warned that America's hesitation would concede Africa, Asia, and the Pacific to European powers.

America's growing export trade necessitated a larger navy to safeguard projected new sea lanes. During the Civil War, Union naval commanders became aware of the need for coaling stations in the Caribbean and Pacific. Many Americans supported the ideas of Captain Alfred T. Mahan of the navy, who in his central work, *The Influence of Seapower upon*

Alfred T. Mahan

His writings on seapower influenced the thinking of the Germans, Japanese, and Americans—in particular, Theodore Roosevelt. (Contact print from Frances Benjamin Johnson negative; Library of Congress)

History (1890), called for overseas bases, expanded commerce, and an isthmian canal—but only after the United States had built a navy strong enough to protect its possessions. One of the founders of the Naval War College, Admiral Stephen B. Luce, was a major advocate of Mahan's ideas and helped establish the modern American navy. Mahan soon became an instructor at the War College and continued to spread his ideas in the years afterward, with notable impact on Theodore Roosevelt. Congressional and popular support for a navy had been negligible before the mid-1880s, primarily because relative peace in Europe had allowed security in the Western Hemisphere through only minimal effort. Thus while other nations built steel ships, the United States continued to repair sails, replace rotted wooden hulls, and deploy ironclads for inland duties. But growing international rivalries in Europe forced a change in America's world outlook. Interest in steel battleships soon grew so rapidly in the United States that within a decade its fleet ranked seventh in the world.

American expansion encountered many obstacles. Anti-imperialist groups, led by Senator Carl Schurz, writer Mark Twain, and newspaper editor E. L. Godkin, were more interested in bettering America's domestic institutions than in acquiring territories. Despite a growing race for European partition of Africa by the last years of the century, Americans lacked the power to show anything more than mild interest in that continent as a potential trade outlet or source of private adventure. Some Americans simply opposed the addition of dark-skinned peoples to the United States. Godkin fought against the acquisition of Santo Domingo because, he declared, that country had 200,000 "ignorant Catholic Spanish negroes" who might expect American citizenship. Others argued that the establishment of colonies necessarily ruled out self-government and often led to competition that caused wars. The expansionist Democratic party was able to gain control of the presidency on only two occasions between 1865 and well into the new century. Even then, its standard-bearer both times, Grover Cleveland, was not an imperialist. Completion of the transcontinental railroad in 1869 temporarily eased pressure for an isthmian canal, and the danger of European involvement in the Caribbean lessened when Spain pulled out of Santo Domingo in 1865 and France completed its withdrawal from Mexico two years later. America's attention was turned toward Reconstruction and industrial development after the Civil War, causing the expansionist impulse to lie dormant for thirty years.

RENEWED AMERICAN EXPANSIONISM IN THE WESTERN HEMISPHERE

Secretary of State William H. Seward attempted to lead a resurgence of American international concern after the war. A longtime expansionist, he outlined plans for an American empire that would encompass Canada, Latin America, the Pacific, and Asia. To a crowd in Boston in June 1867,

Seward called for "the possession of the American continent and the control of the world." Canada was of prime interest to many Americans. In fact, the Parliament in London, partly because of apprehension over American designs, passed the British North America Act in 1867, which unified the colonies under the Dominion of Canada. Another potential threat to Canada came from the Fenians, a secret Irish Republican Brotherhood established in New York in 1858 to secure the independence of their homeland from Britain. By the end of the American Civil War, this 10,000-member organization planned to embroil Britain and the United States in war and take Canada as hostage in exchange for Ireland's freedom. Meanwhile Seward had other interests in the hemisphere—Caribbean bases in Haiti, Cuba, the Dominican Republic, and the Danish West Indies (Virgin Islands); Tigre Island, which belonged to Honduras; and Alaska, Iceland, and Greenland.

Seward's sole territorial acquisition—that of Alaska in 1867—was the result of several fortuitous circumstances. Seven years earlier, Russia's minister in Washington, Baron Édouard de Stoeckl, had learned of America's interest in establishing telegraph connections across Alaska (then called Russian America) and Siberia to Europe. The Civil War intervened, but when he hinted to Seward in the spring of 1867 that his government was ready to part with Alaska, he found a willing recipient. The acquisition of Alaska would put the United States at the Bering Straits which pointed toward the Aleutian Islands, Asia, and the western Pacific. Russia decided to sell for several reasons: it needed money and Alaska had become a liability; Russia had been unable to colonize the area partly because of its distance; the Russian-American Company was failing as a result of the diminishing number of sea otters; and Alaska's defense costs were prohibitive. Seward could have Alaska; he now must convince Americans that they needed it.

Secret negotiations began with Stoeckl in Washington after Seward persuaded the chairman of the Senate Foreign Relations Committee, Charles Sumner, that Alaska was valuable for trade and natural resources. Late in the evening of March 29, 1867, Stoeckl appeared on Seward's doorstep in Washington and indicated his willingness to sell Alaska. Instead of waiting until morning, Seward surprised Stoeckl by opening the State Department for immediate negotiations, and at 4 A.M. on March 30 the two men signed a treaty. It awarded Alaska to the United States for $7.2 million, considerably more than the $5 million that the Russian government had privately authorized its minister to accept. One of the secretary of state's costliest mistakes was his failure to keep Congress informed. In fact, he did not tell the president and his cabinet of the negotiations until he presented the treaty to Congress.

A stormy political battle began in the United States as soon as the deal became public. On April 8 Sumner defended the treaty in a three-and-one-half-hour speech before the Senate that affixed the name *Alaska* to the area and may have had considerable effect on promoting support for the pact. Initial excitement over renewed expansion encouraged the Senate's approval by an overwhelming margin, but the House stalled over appropriations. Critics expressed concern about the cost of defense, the lack of crop yield, and the likelihood of alienating the British by securing an area locking Canada from the sea. Others simply denounced Alaska as "Seward's Folly," a "Polar Bear Garden," "Frigidia," "Seward's Icebox," "Walrussia," and the land of "walrus-covered icebergs" and of cows that gave ice cream. Seward's treaty constituted "a dark deed done in the night."

House passage of the agreement finally took place on July 14, 1868, over a year later, but the long delay was mainly attributable to an unrelated matter: preoccupation with the impeachment of President Andrew Johnson. In the meantime Stoeckl had considered offering the area as a gift in order to shame the United States into paying for it. But the czar turned down his suggestion for fear that the United States would accept. Rumors circulated that Stoeckl had bribed members of Congress, reporters, and other influential Americans to get the bill through, although Seward told Congress under oath that "I know of no payment to anybody, by him or of any application of the funds which he received." Whatever the truth, Seward was largely responsible for the treaty because of his campaign to educate Americans concerning the value of Alaska. His supporters had another decisive advantage: the United States had already occupied Alaska and raised the flag over the capital at Sitka. With this *fait accompli* in mind, the House approved the treaty, permitting the United States to acquire 591,000 square miles of territory for less than two cents an acre.

The Alaska Treaty contained no assurance of statehood. It stipulated only that civilized peoples of the area would "be admitted to the enjoyment of all the rights, advantages and immunities of citizens of the United States." The principle of citizenship without statehood marked an important alteration in the pattern of American territorial acquisition. Yet as the United States Supreme Court made evident in *Rassmussen* v. *U.S.* in 1905, the treaty and later laws extended American customs and legislation to Alaska, and for practical purposes *did* incorporate the area into the United States.

In the meantime attention had turned to Cuba, where an insurrection that began against Spain in 1868 convinced many Americans of the necessity of intervening in behalf of the islanders. The Cubans seemed to have democratic aspirations, a belief encouraged by exiles in the United States who spread propaganda, bribed reporters and legislators, and organized filibustering expeditions to further their cause. Pressure mounted on the new presidential administration of Ulysses S. Grant to extend recognition to the Cuban rebels. Although Grant appeared interested, his secretary of state, Hamilton Fish, was not. Such action, he warned the president, could provoke a war with Spain that the United States could ill afford and could well lose. Reconstruction at home was the national priority and war would rupture trade. Fish also cited another compelling reason for holding back: the need to resolve the *Alabama* claims issue with Britain and improve relations with that country. His problem was to convince the president that recognition of Cuban belligerency would be a mistake. The task would be difficult. A further complication was Grant's concurrent but abortive interest in annexing the Dominican Republic as a refuge for American blacks.

In August 1869 Fish received a letter from Grant directing him to extend recognition to the Cuban rebels. The secretary ignored the instruction, allowing the president's ardor to cool. But in the summer of the following year Congress called for recognition, and Fish felt so strongly about the matter that he threatened to resign if the president did not ask the legislature to withhold such action. Many newsmen praised Grant's ensuing congressional message as a wise move to keep the United States out of the affair, and popular enthusiasm dissipated enough so that in June 1870 Congress narrowly voted down a resolution of recognition.

As the war in Cuba continued, private American citizens became involved and soon a crisis developed between the United States and Spain. In November 1873 reports reached Washington that a Spanish warship had stopped the *Virginius*, flying American colors, between Cuba and Jamaica. According to the accounts, Spanish officials had escorted the vessel into Santiago harbor, where after a hurried court martial they ordered the execution of fifty-three crew members and passengers as "pirates," including Americans and Englishmen. Had a British warship not prepared to level the Cuban city, more executions could have followed. Americans from the Gulf of Mexico to New England talked of war.

Fish preferred a settlement short of war, but the angry popular mood forced him to react strongly. He gave the Spanish twelve days to apologize and make reparations. In the meantime American military and naval forces prepared for combat. "If Spain cannot redress the outrages perpetrated in her name on Cuba," he asserted, "the United States will." Then news arrived that took some of the fire out of those threats. Fish learned that the *Virginius* was a Cuban gunrunner flying the American flag and carrying fraudulent papers along with munitions and rebels. Spain nonetheless had had no legal grounds for seizing the vessel. No state of war existed, and the Cubans were therefore not belligerents. The government in Madrid apologized for the episode and awarded an indemnity. The United States could doubtless have had war over the *Virginius* affair; but Fish and others chose to follow the thought expressed during the crisis by a former Confederate general: "Surely we have had war enough for one generation."

THE *ALABAMA* CLAIMS DISPUTE WITH BRITAIN

Pressures continued for intervention in Cuba, but Fish managed to turn the administration's attention to the *Alabama* claims controversy with Britain. The British had rejected several American recommendations for arbitration, and even when they finally accepted one proposal, the Johnson-Clarendon Convention of 1869, the American Senate voted against the measure because it contained no apology for the *Alabama* and no provision for indemnifying the indirect costs of the war caused by British policies. Charles Sumner, the leading advocate of British reparations, shocked and infuriated the government in London by demanding both direct and indirect damages that someone later calculated at over $2 billion. Destruction of Union war matériel by the *Alabama* alone amounted to $15 million, he said, but British interference had led to unforeseen costs: soaring insurance rates, American merchants forced to change registry of vessels to neutral nations, and the loss of many more American lives caused by the extended period of war. Fighting went on for two years after Gettysburg, he charged, because of British encouragement to the Confederacy.

Informal negotiations on the claims issue began in Washington during the summer of 1869 but soon grew into proceedings leading to a treaty settlement. With the outbreak of the Franco-Prussian War the following year, London became concerned that the possibility of war with Russia could drive that government into contracting for the building of ships in America. The British were suddenly ready for a general arbitration agreement, and in January 1871 the Foreign Office entrusted a private citizen, Sir John Rose, to begin formal talks with Fish. From February through May, a Joint High Commission of ten members met in Washington to work out a treaty.

The ensuing Treaty of Washington of May 8, 1871 was of major importance in promoting better Anglo-American relations. It provided for arbitration of the *Alabama* issues, resolved British claims of nearly $2 million for property taken during the American Civil War, authorized reciprocal use of canals in the Great Lakes–St. Lawrence River network, and settled numerous long-standing fishing questions recently exacerbated by America's abrogation of the Marcy-Elgin Reciprocity Treaty of the 1850s. The Washington Treaty also called for arbitration to determine the ownership of the San Juan Islands lying between Vancouver Island (British Columbia) and the Territory of Washington in the far northwest, a matter that had grown out of the vague boundary terms of the Oregon Treaty of 1846 and which had received greater attention after the discovery of gold in British Columbia during the late 1850s. The British expressed "regret" on the *Alabama* matter and agreed to a panel of five members to meet in Geneva, Switzerland, to resolve the issue of compensation. The treaty established the principles that a neutral must use "due diligence" in preventing the departure of any ship suspected of engaging in war against a friendly power, and that it could not allow its ports or waterways to become sources of assistance to belligerents. On May 24, 1871, the Senate approved the pact.

The arbitration tribunal established under the Treaty of Washington convened at Lake Geneva in December 1871 and immediately ran into trouble on the indirect claims issue. Charles Francis Adams, Union minister to London during the Civil War, represented the United States, whereas his counterpart was the lord chief justice of England, Sir Alexander Cockburn. Adams almost aborted the talks at the start by introducing Sumner's indirect claims proposal. The matter had not arisen during the Washington negotiations of 1871, and the British did not realize that the Americans had avoided it at that time only because failure to secure that concession would have antagonized the Senate and ended chances for the treaty. The revival of the issue caused a storm of protest in England. The "war prolongation claim" could lead to a British payment of $8 billion, Prime Minister William Gladstone estimated—*eight times* the amount exacted by Germany from France at the end of their war earlier that year.

Fish recognized the danger in calling for indirect claims. To a confidant he wrote that "I never believed that the Tribunal would award a cent for the 'indirect claims.' " It was not in the American interest to hold neutrals "liable for the indirect injuries consequent upon an act of negligence." Recognizing that the United States would be the chief "neutral" in European wars, he declared that "we have too large an extent of coast and too small a police, and too much of the spirit of bold speculation and adventure, to make the doctrine a safe one for our future." Fish, it appears, had raised the issue so that the tribunal might reject it and thus eliminate the possibility of it ever being used against the United States. Adams devised a solution. He convinced the other members of the tribunal to give an "advisory" opinion based on accepted principles of international law. Without the British delegate present, the tribunal ruled in June 1872 against the admission of indirect claims. Both the United States and Britain accepted this decision and the matter was closed.

The arbitration court decided against the British and announced its claims decisions in September 1872. Its members unanimously ruled that the London government had not exercised "due diligence" in its neutrality during the Civil War and was therefore responsible for $15.5 million of destruction caused by the *Alabama*, the *Florida*, and the *Shenandoah*. In the last two cases Cockburn angrily voted against paying the claims and stalked out of the room. The London *Times*, however, approved the court's decision, and British officials eventually attached the canceled draft of the award sum on the Foreign Office wall as a reminder of the danger of indiscreet action.

The remaining issues dealt with under the Treaty of Washington were eventually resolved, with the British winning the larger share. An arbitral commission met for two years in Washington before rejecting all other war claims and awarding Britain nearly $2 million in damages stemming primarily from the illegal American blockade. In the meantime the emperor of Germany, acting as arbiter, awarded the San Juan Islands to the United States. On the fisheries question, an arbitral commission granted $5.5 million to the British as an equivalent for allowing fishing privileges to the Americans during the Washington negotiations of 1871. The American delegate was upset and refused to sign the agreement, but the United States fulfilled its financial obligation.

Overall, the United States fared well from the Treaty of Washington. The monetary awards tipped in America's favor by more than $8 million, and the treaty established a precedent for arbitration and marked a major victory for the principles of neutrality. By resolving the longstanding *Alabama* claims dispute, the settlement prevented a rupture in Anglo-American relations.

LATIN AMERICA

The opening of the Suez Canal in 1869 rekindled American interest in building a canal across the isthmus of Central America. The Clayton-Bulwer Treaty of 1850 remained a major obstacle because it had stipulated joint Anglo-American control over any projected isthmian route. However, in 1869 President Grant took a stance indicative of a changing mood in the country. He became the first executive to insist that the United States should have exclusive control over any canal through the isthmus. In violation of the Clayton-Bulwer Treaty, he established an Interoceanic Canal Commission which authorized surveys of possible canal routes and in 1876 concluded that Nicaragua offered the most feasible site.

In 1879 the architect of the Suez Canal, seventy-five-year-old Ferdinand de Lesseps, aroused American fears of outside interference in the hemisphere when he secured a concession from the government of Colombia and with private support prepared to engineer a canal through its territorial possession of Panama. Early the following year he arrived in the United States to promote the project and to relieve the anxieties of Americans. De Lesseps traveled across the country, hoping his charismatic personality and liberal dispensations of money would befriend Americans. He was not successful. In March of that same year, President Rutherford B. Hayes, Grant's successor, sent a ringing message to the Senate which denounced the de Lesseps project because it proposed a canal on "virtually a part of the coastline of the United States." It was "the right and duty of the United States to assert and maintain such supervision and authority over any interoceanic canal . . . as will protect our national interests." America's objective was "a canal under American control." Hayes was worried that the French government would take over a canal through Panama just as the British had done in acquiring a controlling ownership interest in the Suez Canal in 1875. The House joined the Senate in denouncing the plan. To underline the point, President Hayes ordered two warships to Panama.

Washington's warnings had little effect, and when de Lesseps proceeded with his plans to build the canal, the United States tried to reopen the issue with Britain in 1881. Secretary of State James G. Blaine attempted to persuade the British to accept abrogation or modification of the Clayton-Bulwer Treaty on the ground that his nation could not "perpetuate any treaty that impeaches our right and long-established claim to priority on the American continent." Conditions had changed, he argued; the agreement of 1850 now violated the Monroe Doctrine by challenging America's supremacy in the hemisphere. British Foreign Secretary Lord Granville reminded Blaine of the stipulations in the Clayton-Bulwer Treaty.

That same year of 1881, after de Lesseps's French company had begun work on the canal, the United States again pushed for a route through Nicaragua. Congress permitted the establishment of the Maritime Canal Company to open negotiations, and the Department of State again tried to persuade London to cancel the joint-control provisions of the Clayton-Bulwer Treaty. The United States signed an agreement with Nicaragua in 1884 that secured transit rights, in exchange for a permanent alliance and protection of Nicaragua's possessions. Whereas many Americans worried about allying with a country continually besieged by boundary squabbles, others were more concerned about the effects on Britain. Satisfaction came from flaunting London; so also did danger. The new president after the election of 1884, Democrat Grover Cleveland, asserted that the canal must be for "the world's benefit" and followed the State Department's recommendation to withdraw the treaty from the Senate. Cleveland opposed foreign involvement and warned that the measure violated the Clayton-Bulwer Treaty and would cause problems for the United States in Central America. By the 1890s the canal problem was temporarily quieted when America's Maritime Company failed to raise enough money for a Nicaraguan canal, and de Lesseps's project, with less than half the digging finished, fell victim to bankruptcy, mudslides, corruption, yellow fever, and malaria.

America's interest in a canal was indicative of the growing interest in Latin America, which in turn soon involved the United States in the Pan-American movement. Pan-Americanism was a multilateral doctrine calling for hemispheric cooperation based upon the principle of peace through trade. Blaine was uneasy that the United States had an unfavorable balance of trade with the Latin American republics, and wanted to tighten interhemispheric relations through commercial agreements. He called for an International American Conference to meet in Washington in 1881 to discuss the establishment of close trade relations as a means of "preventing war between the nations of America." But Blaine soon resigned as secretary of state because of political differences within the Republican party, and his successor called off the conference on the ground that Europe might consider it an affront.

In 1889 Blaine returned to the position of secretary of state, and under his leadership the United States sponsored the First International American Conference (or Pan-American Conference) in Washington. The eighteen delegations in attendance rejected his call for lower tariffs and mandatory arbitration of disputes, but they did create the forerunner of the Pan-American Union, the International Bureau of American Repub-

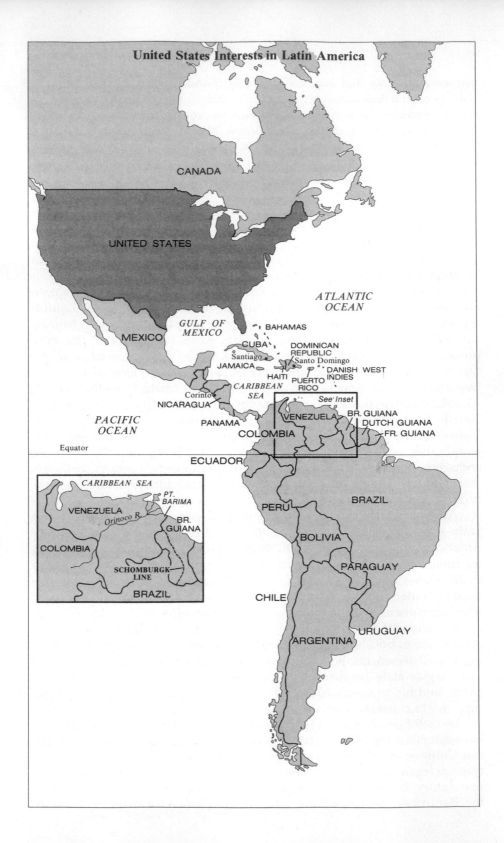

United States Interests in Latin America

lics, which became a central information agency. The conferees also approved individual reciprocity treaties and called for improved communication and transportation facilities throughout the hemisphere. But the Latin Americans voted down arbitration primarily because they distrusted the United States. And, the Republican party refused to support the reciprocity treaties because it favored protectionism. A further blow to Pan-Americanism came in 1891–92, when a crisis developed between Chile and the United States over American interference in that country's civil war. Still, the meeting in Washington set a precedent for other inter-American conferences.

THE PACIFIC AND FAR EAST

For various reasons Americans were receptive to involvement in the Pacific and Far East. Trade was a factor, as were American military and strategic concerns. Perhaps America's attitude was also attributable to the belief that the people of the Far East were backward and thus susceptible to American economic and cultural influences. Whatever the reasons, the United States wanted coaling stations across the Pacific at Midway Island (occupied by the navy in 1867), Samoa, and Hawaii, and sought to broaden its economic penetration of China and Japan. Even Korea seemed to offer commercial possibilities. Completion of the transcontinental railroad in 1869 furthered American interest in the Orient. The main prize was the famed though elusive market of China, and stepping-stones across the Pacific were the vital prerequisites.

Samoa, an archipelago or large group of fourteen islands nearly 4,000 miles from San Francisco and en route to Australia, became a point of contention among the United States, Britain, and Germany by the 1870s. American whaling interests had used the islands in the pre-Civil War period, and afterward the United States competed for the harbors at Apia and Pago Pago. An American steamship company operating out of San Francisco convinced the White House of the value of Pago Pago, and a United States Navy officer soon negotiated a treaty gaining harbor rights in exchange for an American protectorate. The treaty never came to a vote in the Senate, but in 1878 Samoan representatives came to the United States and asked for annexation or the establishment of a protectorate. Washington refused the offer, but negotiated a treaty gaining a coaling station at Pago Pago and the right to use America's "good offices" in settling disputes between Samoa and any government "in amity with the

MAP 13

Despite major domestic problems in the post–Civil War and Reconstruction Era, the United States slowly expanded its involvement in the Caribbean.

United States." The Senate approved, largely because the agreement contained no political pledges to the islands.

In 1879 Britain and Germany likewise secured naval stations in Samoa. Germany had arrived late on the colonial scene, for Britain and France already had claims to Africa and Asia when Prince Otto von Bismarck became interested in colonial expansion during the mid-1880s. The British and Germans tacitly agreed to British control over Egypt in exchange for recognition of German interests in Africa and the South Pacific. By January 1886 Americans felt challenged when Germany raised its flag over Samoa and established virtual control over the government. A confrontation developed in the midst of heightening tension when the American consul, allegedly acting under the "good offices" provision of the 1878 treaty, implanted the Stars and Stripes and tried to restore the Samoan king. The United States called for a conference which met the following year. Though the American delegation insisted on Samoa's integrity, the conference was a failure because Britain's interests elsewhere in the South Pacific compelled it to recognize German priorities in the islands.

Suspicion persisted among the three powers, but they finally achieved a Samoan settlement which was largely attributable to other factors. Late in 1888 Germany declared war on Samoa when a group of rebels tried to overthrow the German puppet government. Both Britain and the United States refused to support Germany, and in view of other growing international troubles Bismarck decided upon a peaceful resolution of the problem. Another factor contributed to an easing of tensions. A tropical storm in 1889 sobered the antagonists by devastating Apia and destroying German and American ships. Bismarck called a conference of all three powers in Berlin, where they drew up a tripartite protectorate over Samoa that restored the monarch and allowed the United States to retain Pago Pago. Ten years later, after a civil war had erupted in Samoa, the three governments again met in Berlin and arranged a partition of the islands between Germany and the United States. Britain gave up its Samoan claims for concessions elsewhere, while America maintained control over several of the islands along with the harbor at Pago Pago.

Much like Samoa, American interest in Hawaii, then called the Sandwich Islands, had deepened since the Civil War. Americans wanted Hawaii as a mission field, a boon to the sugar and whaling industries, and a strategic outpost en route to Asia. The major concern of the United States before the 1890s was not annexation, despite Secretary of State Seward's statement that "a lawful and peaceful annexation of the islands to the United States, with the consent of the people . . . is deemed desirable by this government." He had made the statement to his minister in Hawaii during talks regarding a commercial reciprocity treaty, but the Senate had voted against the treaty in 1870, partly out of fear that such a measure would stir up the anti-imperialists and obstruct eventual annexation. The major concern at this time was to prevent other nations from seizing control. By 1875 Hawaiian sugar plantation owners, dependent upon American markets, warned that unless the United States allowed tariff-free entry of their product, they would establish closer ties with Britain. That year the islands' sugar producers received a tremendous boost by a "reciprocity" treaty allowing their goods to enter the American market duty-free for seven years in exchange for their agreement not to transfer economic or territorial rights to any other country.

The great need for cheap labor in Hawaii unsettled many Americans in the United States because it attracted thousands of Chinese and Japanese workers who might strengthen the islands' ties to the Orient. Of 80,000 inhabitants by the end of the century, only about half were natives. Hawaii was becoming a virtual colony of the United States, and if annexation took place, the racial situation had great potential for trouble. In 1881 the Department of State informed the British that Hawaii was "essentially a part of the American system of states, and a key to the North Pacific trade." Six years later the United States and Hawaii renewed the reciprocity treaty of 1875 and included an amendment granting America naval privileges in Pearl Harbor.

The same year of the renewed reciprocity treaty, 1887, a bloodless coup took place in Hawaii during which the white planters on the islands persuaded the king to approve a new constitution authorizing only property owners to sit in the legislature. Four years later the king died and his sister, Liliuokalani, became monarch. A strong nationalist, she tried to restore the power of the throne and in so doing alarmed white business leaders, causing them to push for annexation of Hawaii by the United States. Business interests on the islands were already hurting from the McKinley Tariff of 1890, which removed Hawaiian sugar from its favored position on the American market and caused economic problems that precipitated a political crisis. Hawaiian sugar planters regarded annexation as the only path to stability, for their product would come under the protection of the high tariff. In the spring of 1892 a spokesman for the islands' sugar interests arrived in Washington for private talks about annexation.

The following January of 1893 Queen Liliuokalani provided the spark that set off a revolution when she called for a new constitution. Less than a week later white planters led an overthrow of the monarchy and nearly all 3,000 Americans on the islands requested annexation by the United States. The American minister to Hawaii, John Stevens, had long favored annexation and immediately secured assistance for the revolution from American marines and sailors on a nearby cruiser. Only one shot was fired and a single person injured in a revolution that brought down a monarchy and pointed toward annexation. Liliuokalani capitulated to what she called "the superior force of the United States of America," but only until Washington could "undo the action of its representative" and restore her "as the constitutional sovereign of the Hawaiian Islands." Stevens meanwhile extended recognition to the new provisional government, raised the American flag, and declared the islands a protectorate of the United States. To the State Department he wrote: "The Hawaiian pear is now fully ripe, and this is the golden hour for the United States to pluck it."

The provisional government in Hawaii sent a commission to Washington to draft an annexation treaty, and in rapid time the document went to the Senate. By the proposed agreement of February, the islands were to become "an integral part of the territory of the United States" in exchange for the award of a lifetime annual pension of $20,000 to the former queen. In the meantime a public debate began over acquiring the islands. Proannexationists cited humanitarian, commercial, and strategic reasons, and warned that if the United States did not take the islands, the British or the Japanese would. Democrats and anti-imperialists charged that the entire affair was ugly and pointed out that imperialist ventures led to colonial burdens. Some declared that the presence of a large nonwhite population in Hawaii raised questions about statehood. Before the Senate could vote, President Cleveland withdrew the treaty from consideration.

The new president thought the Hawaiian affair seemed orchestrated, and he wanted an investigation. Cleveland was also concerned about whether the southern wing of his Democratic party would support the acquisition of a nonwhite population, and whether Americans would allow a noncontiguous territory to become a state. Also, little hope existed that the Hawaiians would subject themselves to the islands' white minority. Finally, with farmers and laborers in the United States currently restless over other matters, the president was hesitant to confront his already troubled administration with another problem. Support for his position came from Secretary of State Walter Gresham, who, although an expansionist, declared that he was "unalterably opposed to stealing territory, or of annexing a people against their consent." A former Democratic congressman, James Blount, meanwhile accepted the president's request to head an inquiry into the Hawaiian situation. The group concluded that Stevens had been integral to the success of the revolution and that the vast majority of islanders favored the queen.

Cleveland faced a nearly impossible situation. He had already outraged expansionists by ordering the lowering of the American flag in Hawaii, and because he had arranged the inquiry into the revolution he now seemed bound to restore the throne to the queen. Yet to do so would require the use of military force against the provisional government—which was comprised of Americans. Such a venture would entail Americans fighting Americans, with the unhappy prospect of the Cleveland administration squelching a republic and restoring a monarchy.

The president made a wise political decision: he turned the matter over to Congress, which did nothing. A heated debate gave the appearance of action and in fact led to two resolutions against interference in Hawaii. In 1894 a convention in Hawaii led to the drafting of a constitution, and on July 4 the "missionary group" in control established the Republic of Hawaii. Cleveland extended recognition and the American Congress eased problems on the islands that same year by passing a new tariff that reestablished Hawaii's favored position in the sugar market.

While the Hawaiian issue simmered, America's interest in the Far East had focused on China and the possibility of expanding commercial and religious influences. America's Far East policy was hesitant more than purposeful, largely because the region's potential was not clear and the United States lacked the power to support an active stance. Yet the idea of a great China market persisted. Interest in cheap labor for building a transcontinental railroad had led to the Burlingame Treaty of 1868, which guaranteed Americans most-favored-nation status in China and facilitated Chinese emigration to the United States. But the need for Chinese labor had dropped with completion of the railroad in 1869, and four years later, when the United States underwent a financial panic that developed into a major depression, the Chinese people's cultural differences and willingness to work for low wages made them a convenient scapegoat for the nation's ills. Violence against the Chinese centered in the Far West, the area of highest Chinese concentration, and by the 1870s many Americans wanted to bar any more from entering the country. The anti-Chinese attitude continued to grow throughout the late nineteenth century as stories came back to the United States of the harsh treatment accorded to its missionaries and other nationals in China. A revision in the Burlingame Treaty seemed essential, and in 1882 Congress responded with the Chinese Exclusion Act, which suspended their entry into the United States for ten years and was renewed periodically up to the 1920s.

Korea also attracted American attention. Called the "hermit nation" because of its isolation, Korea was tied to a China so weak that foreign intervention went virtually uncontrolled. The United States sent an expedition to Korea in 1871 to seek a treaty protecting shipwrecked sailors, but when the Koreans opened fire the American ships destroyed several forts and killed over 300 natives before leaving without a treaty. In 1876 Japan forced Korea to declare independence from China, and four years afterward an American mission arrived to seek the same commercial favors Japan received. Commodore Robert Shufeldt of the United States Navy secured the first agreement by Korea with the West, a treaty of amity and commerce in 1882. It permitted most-favored-nation privileges to Americans, authorized diplomatic and consular representatives, and provided for temporary extraterritorial rights. The Senate approved the treaty the following year. Despite high hopes, American influence in Korea remained negligible during the ensuing period of intense rivalry over the peninsula among Japan, China, and, eventually, Russia.

Increasing competition for Korea led Japan to declare war on China in August 1894. The reverberations of the Sino-Japanese War suggested that the Japanese, Russians, French, Germans, and perhaps the British intended to partition China on a permanent basis. Equality of commercial opportunity, forerunner of the Open Door of the 1890s, was in jeopardy.

The possibility of big power cooperation against American commercial interests convinced the United States that it might soon have to take some action to keep China open.

THE NEED FOR AN ANGLO–AMERICAN RAPPROCHEMENT

One of the most important developments of the late nineteenth century was a rapprochement between Britain and the United States. Four Anglo-American controversies by the 1890s did not offer much hope for improved relations. The fisheries question, a recurring issue since 1783, again caused problems; Americans were upset because of believed British interference in the presidential election of 1888; Canadians and Americans became incensed over seal hunting practices off Alaska; and a boundary dispute between Britain and Venezuela raised questions about the status of the Monroe Doctrine. Yet a major balancing factor was that growing international problems soon made Americans and Englishmen realize that they needed each other.

The fisheries issue threatened Anglo-American relations again when, in the mid-1880s, the United States terminated rights granted Canada by the Treaty of Washington of 1871, and Canadians retaliated by seizing Americans for violating fishing privileges allowed under the Convention of 1818. The House of Representatives in 1887 empowered the president to bar Canadians from American ports. Cleveland signed the measure, but only to place pressure on Canada to change its policy. That November a joint Anglo-American commission met in Washington, and in the following February of 1888 it reached a compromise; but the United States Senate hesitated to approve the pact. Republicans were afraid of a Democratic success so near a presidential election, while Democrats worried that a settlement with Britain would cost them the Irish-American vote. The Senate rejected the treaty.

Cleveland decided to make a bid for popular support by denouncing the British. Two days after the Senate's vote against the treaty, he sent a fiery message to Congress calling on that body to authorize him to cut off all exports to Canada. While Anglophobes and Irish-Americans applauded this jab at Britain, Republican businessmen opposed commercial restrictions and sought to wriggle out of the partisan situation they had helped create. With an election imminent, the verdict rested with the American people.

Anglophobia permeated the campaign of 1888 as Cleveland fell victim to a bizarre episode during his bid for reelection. In an effort to determine the incumbent's real feelings toward England, a Californian wrote a letter of inquiry to the British minister in Washington, Sir Lionel Sackville-West, who violated diplomatic protocol by assuring the correspondent in a letter marked "private" that Cleveland was pro-English. A month later, the reply from Sackville-West appeared in the Republican Los Angeles *Times*.

A New York paper trumpeted headlines that constituted a monument to Sackville-West's indiscretion as well as an epitaph to Cleveland's presidency: "THE BRITISH LION'S PAW THRUST INTO AMERICAN POLITICS TO HELP CLEVELAND."

Reaction was immediate on both sides of the Atlantic. British Foreign Secretary Lord Salisbury sought an investigation, while the president helplessly watched the Irish-American vote slip from his grasp. Cleveland further escalated embittered relations with Britain when he sent Sackville-West home. The British press denounced the president and Salisbury delayed sending a replacement until the following March, when Cleveland surrendered his office to Republican Benjamin Harrison. Domestic political interests in the United States had created the atmosphere for the shoddy affair, but peaceful foreign relations could be the chief casualty.

While this issue smoldered, the new Harrison administration soon became locked in a controversy with Britain over the furbearing seals of the Bering Sea. The Alaska Treaty of 1867 had included United States control over the Pribilof Islands in the Bering Sea, the habitat of nearly 4 million seals. When prices steadily rose for sealskins, thus encouraging mass slaughtering of the animals, Washington restricted the killing to males since females were polygamous and could continue to replenish the supply. But it was virtually impossible to distinguish male from female in the water, and increasing demands for the skins drove hunters into illegal pelagic or open-sea sealing. Since the United States had jurisdiction only over the islands and territorial waters, hunting expeditions led primarily by Canadians stayed outside the three-mile zone and killed the seals, male and female. President Harrison cautioned Canadians that anyone engaged in pelagic sealing was subject to capture, and drew protests from both the English and Canadian governments when he authorized American vessels to patrol the Bering Sea as a *mare clausum* or closed sea—*not* international waters. In early 1890 the Department of State warned the British that pelagic sealing created a state of "lawlessness" on the seas, and that the next step would be an argument for piracy. Russia, the Harrison administration insisted, had long controlled the waters beyond the three-mile limit, and the acquisition of Alaska in 1867 had passed this "prescriptive right" to the United States. In mid-June the London government rejected these arguments and declared the United States "responsible for the consequences."

After another year of disagreement, the United States and Britain submitted the seals dispute to arbitration. In autumn of 1893 a tribunal meeting in Paris ruled against the United States on every count. The Bering Sea was international waters and the Americans had no exclusive property rights over the seals. The United States eventually reimbursed Britain for damages, although by the early 1900s the two nations joined other interested governments in placing regulations on the hunting of seals and ultimately resolved the matter.

The seals controversy was further evidence of the deep distrust between the Anglo-American peoples. If hard feelings developed over such a localized matter, the potential existed for serious trouble should problems arise over vital interests or national honor. Such an event developed in 1895, when Britain became embroiled in a boundary dispute with Venezuela.

The Venezuelan boundary problem had its roots in the early nineteenth century. In 1840 a British explorer and engineer, Robert Schomburgk, drew a border between Venezuela and British Guiana that the former refused to accept. In the meantime the Venezuelans vainly sought assistance from the United States. The region in question affected control of the Orinoco River, which in turn determined the commerce of upper South America. During the 1880s gold was discovered in the disputed area and Venezuela severed relations with Britain. The Venezuelans called for arbitration of the boundary issue, and the British agreed—but only in regions *above* the Schomburgk line and *not* in lands inhabited by Britons. Venezuela turned to Washington for arbitration of the disputed area, but London repeatedly rejected America's proposals. By the 1890s the diplomatic situation had changed enough to foment a crisis over the boundary.

Several reasons explain the stiffening mood in the United States. The depression of the 1890s had encouraged a search for foreign markets, and both President Cleveland and his secretary of state, Richard Olney, were concerned about Europe's deepening commercial penetration of South America. Olney had been a hard-nosed attorney general and now in the State Department was a rigid guardian of America's interests. In 1894 William Scruggs, a former American minister to Venezuela who now worked as special agent for that government, wrote a widely read pamphlet that influenced Olney. Entitled *British Aggressions in Venezuela, or the Monroe Doctrine on Trial*, it warned that British victory in the boundary dispute would give them control over a vital part of South America. Early the following year Congress unanimously approved a joint resolution instructing the president to recommend "most urgently" that Britain and Venezuela submit the matter to arbitration.

But before resolution of the Venezuelan problem, Britain aroused fears about intervention in Nicaragua that in turn cast another shadow over the boundary issue. In April 1895 domestic unrest in that Central American country had led to instances of property damage and expulsion of the British consul, and London retaliated by seizing the port and customs house at Corinto. Though the Nicaraguan government made reparations the following month and British forces withdrew, the Cleveland administration was concerned. It had not initially regarded the seizure of Corinto as a violation of the Monroe Doctrine, but complaints had arisen from the American public over a British admiral's alleged dismissal of the Monroe Doctrine as meaningless. The president was already under attack for his stand on the Hawaiian matter, and the impression seemed to be growing that he was weak on Nicaragua. He *had* to act with resolution on Venezuela. An article by Republican Senator Henry Cabot Lodge had challenged the administration to assert "the supremacy of the Monroe Doctrine . . . peaceably if we can, forcibly if we must," and Olney prepared to do just that. In his proposed note to Britain, he focused on the Monroe Doctrine as his major argument. After Cleveland read the note, he responded that "your deliverance on Venezuelan affairs" was "the best thing of the kind I have ever read and it leads to a conclusion that one cannot escape if he tries—that is, if there's anything in the Monroe Doctrine at all."

Olney's note insisted upon the right of the United States to step into any argument affecting Latin America and the Monroe Doctrine. He referred to the victory of the doctrine in the Maximilian affair of the 1860s, and then quoted passages from it in criticizing Britain's actions in Venezuela. Olney declared that "any permanent political union between a European and an American state" was "unnatural and inexpedient." After claiming the United States's hegemony in North America, he asserted that America's "fiat is law upon the subjects to which it confines its interposition." The United States's "infinite resources combined with its isolated position render it master of the situation and practically invulnerable as against any or all other powers." British use of force in the boundary matter would violate the "noninterference" principle of the Monroe Doctrine and place Venezuela under "virtual duress." Their acquisition of land in Venezuela would encourage other European nations to want to be "permanently encamped on American soil." Olney then gave the note the air of an ultimatum by calling for arbitration and asking for a reply that the president could send Congress when it convened in early December.

Cleveland recognized the political capital to be gained from the note that he referred to as the "twenty-inch gun"; but he also wanted the United States to use the Monroe Doctrine as justification for protecting a small *American* country being bullied by the British. A fellow Democrat assured him, "Turn this Venezuela question up or down, North, South, East or West, and it is a 'winner.' " The European powers, Cleveland believed, had staked out areas in Asia, Africa, and Latin America, and needed a stern warning that the United States's economic and strategic interests in the hemisphere were in danger. Olney had stretched the meaning of Monroe's original declaration to encompass an alleged right of the United States to arbitrate any disagreement in the Western Hemisphere capable of attracting Old World intervention; yet the president complimented him for placing the Monroe Doctrine "on better and more defensible ground than any of your predecessors—*or mine*." Britain's threat to Venezuela seemed providential—if the United States could resolve the issue short of war and with national honor intact.

British Foreign Secretary Salisbury failed to recognize the gravity of the situation and did not send a reply to the United States before Congress assembled in December. Salisbury dismissed Olney's note as an outburst of Anglophobia designed for domestic political consumption.

America's ambassador to England, Thomas Bayard, had been unable to deliver the note to Salisbury until early August, and had then failed to impress upon the foreign secretary the seriousness of the matter. Bayard later recorded that Salisbury "made courteous expression of his thanks, and expressed regret and surprise that it had been considered necessary to present so far-reaching and important a principle and such wide and profound policies of international action in relation to a subject so comparatively small." Salisbury, preoccupied with other pressing issues, finally sent his reply in late November—by mail (not cable), and after going through the American ambassador's office. It arrived in the United States on December 6, with Congress already in session.

Salisbury's note bore a near casual tone, but it left no doubt that he had rejected Olney's argument concerning the Monroe Doctrine. "I must not . . . be understood as expressing any acceptance of [the Monroe Doctrine] on the part of Her Majesty's Government," Salisbury emphasized. "The United States have a right, like any other nation, to interpose in any controversy by which their own interests are affected," he admitted, but "their rights are in no way strengthened or extended by the fact that the controversy affects some territory which is called American." The Monroe Doctrine had no relevance to the Venezuelan boundary matter. "It is not a question of the colonization by a European Power of any portion of America. It is not a question of the imposition upon the communities of South America of any system of government devised in Europe." Without suggesting the possibility of compromise, Salisbury concluded: "It is simply the determination of the frontier of a British possession which belonged to the Throne of England long before the Republic of Venezuela came into existence."

President Cleveland declared that Salisbury's note made him "mad clean through," and prepared to settle the boundary matter by a commission of Americans. In a special congressional message of December 17, 1895, he again highlighted the Monroe Doctrine: "If the balance of power is justly a cause for jealous anxiety among the Governments of the Old World and a subject for our absolute noninterference, none the less is an observance of the Monroe Doctrine of vital concern to our people and their government." Since the British had refused arbitration, he recommended that Congress empower him to appoint a commission to locate the boundary, and that the United States stand ready to enforce that commission's findings. It was, he admitted, "a grievous thing to contemplate the two great English-speaking peoples of the world as being otherwise than friendly competitors in the onward march of civilization." And yet the United States could never submit to "wrong and injustice, and the consequent loss of national self-respect and honor." Though it seemed that Cleveland's anger had taken control of his senses, he had provided an escape from war through a time-consuming boundary commission.

Congress voted $100,000 for the commission amid a wave of acclaim in Venezuela and the United States. The American minister in Venezuela reported that thousands of people had gathered outside the legation to praise President Cleveland, and that parades and demonstrations were widespread. Irish-Americans in the United States prepared for war, while New York City Police Commissioner Theodore Roosevelt proclaimed: "Let the fight come if it must; I don't care whether our sea coast cities are bombarded or not; we would take Canada." The editor of the New York *Tribune*, Whitelaw Reid, exalted the "golden opportunity" for American merchants to expand trade into Central and South America. Though a host of influential Americans denounced the possibility of war over such a small issue, their protests rang hollow before the gathering storm.

What few observers seemed to realize (and what Cleveland and Olney doubtless foresaw) was that the work of a boundary commission would permit the diplomats to take over. European events worked in America's favor. The British had problems in South Africa that would result in the disastrous Boer War, and they faced threats to world peace in Turkey and China. Finally, they were worried about their growing German rival. Salisbury recognized the absurdity in going to war over Venezuela's boundary, and he also understood the need for American friendship. Public figures in Britain further defused the controversy when they joined the press in recalling good relations with the United States. The major concern of both the United States and Britain was to settle the matter by arbitration, but without loss of prestige. Bayard wrote Olney from London in mid-January 1897: "There has been a welcome and unmistakable difference observable, in the manner in which the possibilities of conflict with the United States . . . were discussed and treated in this country."

By early 1897 the two nations were beginning to work their way out of the Venezuelan crisis. The solution did not come easily. They first negotiated the Olney-Pauncefote Treaty in January, which provided for general arbitration of disputes. The Senate, however, added several amendments before narrowly rejecting the package in May. Anglophobia was a factor in its decision, although other considerations were important as well. The senators were concerned that an arbitration panel would take away their control over foreign affairs, whereas Irish-Americans feared that an arbitration treaty could lead to an Anglo-American alliance. The British found a face-saving way out when they proposed that areas occupied by British subjects for fifty years or more could not pass to Venezuela or any other country.

In February 1897 Britain and Venezuela signed a treaty settling the issue, but only after Olney exerted great pressure on the latter to come to the negotiating table. According to the agreement, arbitration would resolve the boundaries of all areas except those inhabited by subjects of either party for fifty years or more. This was a British victory, for the approach removed from consideration the region east of the Schomburgk line of 1840, which British subjects had long inhabited. In October 1899 an arbitral court awarded Britain nearly 90 percent of the disputed territory, leaving Venezuela a small inland strip along the headwaters of the Orinoco River as well as Point Barima, which controlled its mouth. These were the only alterations in the original Schomburgk line. The results did not differ greatly from what Britain had tried to secure from Venezuela numerous times in the past.

The United States embittered many European nations and Latin American republics during the Venezuelan boundary dispute. Several Old World powers—including Germany, France, and Russia—resented the United States's claims of domination in the hemisphere, while in the New World, Argentina, Chile, and Mexico expressed serious misgivings. Three years before the arbitral awards, a group of Latin American states had gathered in Mexico City, where several denounced the expansionist policies of the United States. Venezuelans remained unhappy because they had not participated in all of the negotiations and then had undergone American pressure to sign a pact favorable to the British.

The most far-reaching results of the Venezuelan boundary controversy were its impetus to Anglo-American rapprochement and to American expansionist feeling. The appearance was that the British had retreated and that the Monroe Doctrine stood confirmed, but the truth is that the Cleveland administration had distorted the meaning of the Monroe Doctrine in a matter that the United States considered important to its interests. Both nations, however, had sensed the irrationality of an Anglo-American war and realized their mutual need for friendship. The rapprochement was crucial to England's welfare and to America's rise to world power. The Venezuelan crisis fueled a wave of patriotism in the United States that would emerge in the imperialist and warlike "jingoist" spirit of the late 1890s.

Selected readings

Anderson, David L., *Imperialism and Idealism: American Diplomats in China, 1861–1898*. 1985.

Beisner, Robert L., *From the Old Diplomacy to the New, 1865–1900*. 1975.

Bradford, Richard H., *The Virginius Affair*. 1980.

Campbell, Alexander E., *Great Britain and the United States, 1895–1903*. 1960.

Campbell, Charles S., *From Revolution to Rapprochement: The United States and Great Britain, 1783–1900*. 1974.

———, *The Transformation of American Foreign Relations, 1865–1900*. 1976.

Cook, Adrian, *The Alabama Claims: American Politics and Anglo-American Relations, 1865–1900*. 1975.

Crapol, Edward P., *America for Americans: Economic Nationalism and Anglophobia in the Late Nineteenth Century*. 1973.

Devine, Michael J., *John W. Foster: Politics and Diplomacy in the Imperial Era, 1873– 1917*. 1981.

Dulles, Foster Rhea, *Prelude to World Power: 1860–1900*. 1965.

Eggert, Gerald G., *Richard Olney: Evolution of a Statesman*. 1974.

Faulkner, Harold U., *Politics, Reform and Expansion, 1890–1900*. 1959.

Garraty, John A., *The New Commonwealth, 1877–1890*. 1968.

Goldberg, Joyce S., *The Baltimore Affair*. 1986.

Hagan, Kenneth J., *American Gunboat Diplomacy and the Old Navy, 1877–1889*. 1973.

Harrington, Fred H., *God, Mammon, and the Japanese: Horace N. Allen and Korean-American Relations, 1884–1905*. 1944.

Hofstadter, Richard, *Social Darwinism in American Thought, 1860–1915*. 1944.

Holbo, Paul S., *Tarnished Expansion: The Alaska Scandal, the Press, and Congress, 1867–1871*. 1983.

Jenkins, Brian, *Fenians and Anglo-American Relations during Reconstruction*. 1969.

Jensen, Ronald J., *The Alaska Purchase and Russian-American Relations*. 1975.

Johnson, Robert E., *Far China Station: The U.S. Navy in Asian Waters, 1800–1898*. 1979.

Kennedy, Paul M., *The Samoan Tangle: A Study in Anglo-German-American Relations, 1878–1900*. 1974.

Kushner, Howard I., *Conflict on the Northwest Coast: American-Russian Rivalry in the Pacific Northwest, 1790–1867*. 1975.

LaFeber, Walter, *The New Empire: An Interpretation of American Expansion, 1860– 1898*. 1963.

Langley, Lester D., *The Cuban Policy of the United States: A Brief History*. 1968.

McCabe, James O., *The San Juan Water Boundary Question*. 1965.

Masterman, Sylvia, *The Origins of International Rivalry in Samoa, 1845–1884*. 1934.

May, Ernest R., *Imperial Democracy: The Emergence of America as a Great Power*. 1961.

Morgan, H. Wayne, *From Hayes to McKinley: National Party Politics, 1877–1896*. 1969.

Nevins, Allan, *Hamilton Fish: The Inner History of the Grant Administration*. 1936.

Osborne, Thomas J., *"Empire Can Wait": American Opposition to Hawaiian Annexation, 1893–1898*. 1981.

Paolino, Ernest N., *The Foundations of the American Empire: William Henry Seward and U.S. Foreign Policy*. 1973.

Perkins, Bradford, *The Great Rapprochement: England and the United States, 1895– 1914*. 1968.

Perkins, Dexter, *The Monroe Doctrine, 1867–1907*. 1937.

Plesur, Milton, *America's Outward Thrust: Approaches to Foreign Affairs, 1865–1890*. 1971.

Pletcher, David M., *The Awkward Years: American Foreign Relations under Garfield and Arthur*. 1961.

———, "Rhetoric and Results: A Pragmatic View of American Economic Expansionism, 1865–98," *Diplomatic History* 5 (1981): 93–105.

Ruiz, Ramón, *Cuba: The Making of a Revolution*. 1968.

Russ, W. A., Jr., *The Hawaiian Republic, 1894–98*. 1961.

———, *The Hawaiian Revolution, 1893–94*. 1959.

Seager II, Robert, *Alfred Thayer Mahan*. 1977.

Smith, Goldwin, *The Treaty of Washington, 1871*. 1941.

Sprout, Harold and Margaret, *The Rise of American Naval Power, 1776–1918*. 1944.

Stevens, S. K., *American Expansion in Hawaii, 1842–1898*. 1945.

Tate, Merze, *Hawaii: Reciprocity or Annexation*. 1968.

———, *The United States and the Hawaiian Kingdom: A Political History*. 1965.

Van Deusen, Glyndon G., *William Henry Seward*. 1967.

Walker, Mabel G., *The Fenian Movement*. 1969.

Warner, Donald F., *The Idea of Continental Union: Agitation for the Annexation of Canada to the United States, 1849–1893*. 1960.

Wiebe, Robert H., *The Search for Order, 1877–1920*. 1967.

Williams, William A., *The Roots of the Modern American Empire*, 1969.

———, *The Tragedy of American Diplomacy*. 1959, 1962.

Chapter Eleven

American Imperialism and the New Manifest Destiny, 1897–1900

During the late 1890s the United States increased its involvement in the Caribbean, Pacific, and Orient in a surge of national feeling called the *new manifest destiny*. Whereas the expansionist drive of the 1840s spent itself within the continental United States, the great industrial, technological, and commercial advances of the post–Civil War years turned American interest toward distant shores. Expansion was inevitable and relentless, according to Secretary of State John Hay. "No man, no party, can fight with any chance of final success against a cosmic tendency; no cleverness, no popularity avails against the spirit of the age." One catalyst to America's expansionism was the desire to act before European powers incorporated everything of value. Expansionist Senator Henry Cabot Lodge of Massachusetts declared in 1895: "The great nations are rapidly absorbing for their future expansion and their present defense all the waste places of the earth. It is a movement which makes for civilization and the advancement of the race. As one of the great nations of the world," he warned, "the United States must not fall out of the line of march." Another impetus to American expansion was commercial—encouraged by the Panic of 1893 and the ensuing depression. Perhaps more important, however, some Americans were beginning to believe that their security was not unrelated to events beyond their continental borders. As in the 1840s the ideal converged with the reality: the United States sought to justify realistic expansionist aims with democratic and humanitarian motives. And, as in the earlier period, Americans colored their drive for imperialism—or empire—with labels emphasizing "destiny," "progress," and the

spread of "civilization." Encouraged by the warlike jingoes and the sensa-
tionalist news stories carried by the yellow press, the United States would
enter a war with Spain in 1898 that helped to end the divisive legacy of
the Civil War and furthered the decline of isolationism. At virtually the
same time—and not by sheer coincidence—Americans turned greater attention toward the Far East for both idealistic and realistic reasons. The
overseas expansion of the late 1890s alerted the world that the United
States was about to become a great power.

FINAL OVERTURE TO IMPERIALISM: CUBA AND THE YELLOW PRESS

The renewed insurrection in Cuba in February 1895 led the United States
into the imperialist age. Three years earlier, a Cuban exile in the United
States had established the Cuban Revolutionary Party, which sought to
overthrow Spanish rule on the island. America's official concern over
Cuba had meanwhile declined when Spain abolished slavery and promised other reforms after the Ten Years' War had ended in 1878. In 1890
the American Congress passed the McKinley Tariff, which stimulated the
island's sugar industry, and the following year the United States agreed
to permit tariff-free entry of the Cuban product. But the economic boom
proved temporary, for the Panic of 1893 and Democratic control of Congress led to a new tariff setting high duties and virtually cutting off Cuban
sugar imports. The ensuing depression in Cuba plus accumulated political
and economic grievances set off the insurrection in 1895.

Led by General Máximo Gómez, the Cuban rebels proclaimed a republic on the eastern end of the island and proceeded to extend control
over most of the surrounding region. The war was actually a resumption
of the Ten Years' War, for the Spanish peace had promised much and delivered little. The Cubans had supposedly won amnesty and certain governmental rights, but the problems that had caused the long conflict
persisted. Spain had not fulfilled its assurances of relief, and the bulk of
the island's revenues went either toward paying Cuba's debt or directly
into Spain's coffers. Cuba's complaints went unheeded by Spanish officials on the island, and Gómez, veteran of the Ten Years' War, retaliated
with a "scorched-earth" policy, which entailed dynamiting passenger
trains and destroying the Spanish loyalists' property and sugar plantations—including many owned by Americans. Gómez's intention was to
make the island a liability for the Spanish and force its independence, or
to bring about American intervention in its behalf. By late 1896 the guerrilla forces controlled nearly two-thirds of the island, with the Spanish remaining along the coast and in the cities.

The Cuban war took an uglier twist in February 1896, when Spain's
new captain general on the island, Valeriano Weyler, sought to destroy
the rebels' rural quarters by dividing the island into districts and establishing reconcentration centers. His directives herded all inhabitants of

central and western Cuba into the towns, which Weyler barricaded with trenches rimmed by barbed wire and reinforced by soldiers in guard-houses along the encampments. Nearly half a million Cubans, young and old, male and female, were quartered in hot, unsanitary, and sparsely provisioned barbed-wire enclosures; anyone refusing to go along was shot. By the spring of 1898 the *reconcentrado* policies of "Butcher" Weyler, as he was soon called, led to hunger and disease which took the lives of thousands of the captives (mostly women and children), a large proportion of the Cuban population.

The realities of the reconcentration camps were harsh enough, but the sordid episode soon fell prey to a major development in American news reporting known as *yellow journalism*. William Randolph Hearst had bought the struggling New York *Journal* in late 1895 and prepared to challenge Joseph Pulitzer's New York *World* for top circulation in the country. Dramatic headlines, lurid and exaggerated stories, creative writing, suggestions of sexual misconduct by Spanish officials, graphic detail—all were used to sell newspapers. Hearst hired the famous portrait artist of the Indian and American West, Frederic Remington, to visit Cuba and bring back drawings illustrating the fighting. When Remington notified Hearst of his inability to locate the war, the newspaper owner shot back: "You furnish the pictures and I'll furnish the war." Spain emerged in the yellow press as the sole perpetrator of atrocity in Cuba, and sentiment grew for American intervention to ensure the island's independence.

Day after day the *Journal* and *World* competed with each other for the most dramatic coverage. Hearst's paper described "Weyler the soldier[,] . . . Weyler the brute, the devastator of haciendas, the destroyer of families, and the outrager of women. . . . Pitiless, cold, an exterminator of men." The *Journal* saw no way "to prevent his carnal, animal brain from running riot with itself in inventing tortures and infamies of bloody debauchery." Pulitzer's *World* wrote of "blood on the roadsides, blood in the fields, blood on the doorsteps, blood, blood, blood! The old, the young, the weak, the crippled—all are butchered without mercy." It finally asked, "Is there no nation wise enough, brave enough, and strong enough to restore peace in this bloodsmitten land?"

Hearst's *Journal* exploited sex to sell copy. His press picked up the story of a young Cuban girl named Evangelina Cisneros, who was thrown into prison, allegedly after fending off the advances of her Spanish captors. Thousands of American women responded to Hearst's appeal for help by signing petitions in her behalf, even though the Spanish minister in Washington accused Hearst of fabricating the story. Shortly afterward, a reporter for Hearst's paper made his way to Havana, freed Evangelina by sawing through the jail bars and disguising her as a boy, and brought her to the United States. The *Journal* proudly headlined: "An American Newspaper Accomplishes in a Single Stroke What the Best Efforts of Diplomacy Failed Utterly to Bring about in Many Months." Washington, D.C., and New York City's Madison Square Garden hosted great receptions in her honor, and the governor of Missouri suggested that Hearst send 500 reporters to liberate all of Cuba. Another headline event concerned a group of females removed from an American vessel. Spanish officers had boarded the ship as it prepared to leave Havana, allegedly to search three young Cuban women for rebel mail packets. Highlighting the inflammatory story was Remington's fabricated sketch of a nude female suspect standing before leering Spanish officers. The *Journal* commented that "dishonor" was even more "dreadful" than war. "Does Our Flag Protect Women?"

The yellow press deepened American concern for Cuba. The United States already had economic interests in the outcome of the war. Investors had sunk nearly $50 million into sugar and tobacco production and in iron and manganese mines and other enterprises, and trade between the countries had reached as high as $100 million in an exceptional year. These businesses drastically declined during the revolution. In the meantime the Cuban war became an expense for the American government. Spanish officials on the island arrested Americans who had become naturalized Cubans, and the United States felt bound to secure their freedom. American naval vessels meanwhile patrolled the Atlantic coast to halt illegal arms shipments to the Cuban rebels. In an attempt to end the hostilities, humanitarians, religious leaders, Americans with economic stakes in Cuba, and a large number of daily newspapers from both political camps became allies in denouncing Spanish oppression and urging reform. Few considered annexation of the island as a solution. Interventionists wanted an independent Cuba, not a transfer of title to Washington.

The Cleveland administration resisted the growing popular demand for intervention in Cuba. Yet it could not ignore the pressure from a Republican Congress to recognize Cuban belligerency. The White House had several options. It could recognize the Cuban belligerents, although Secretary of State Richard Olney warned that such a policy would prevent Americans from securing damage claims from Spain after the war. Recognition of Cuban independence was another possibility. Yet both the president and Olney feared that the Cubans were unable to govern themselves and that anarchy would invite Old World intervention. Besides, Spain might declare war and force American involvement on the ground that a Spanish effort to defeat a newly independent Cuba would constitute an infraction of the Monroe Doctrine. The third possibility was the only feasible choice: exert pressure on Madrid to permit the Cubans a degree of autonomy within the empire. In April 1896 Olney sent a note to Spain urging reforms on the island.

But popular sentiment for the rebels continued to grow in the United States, forcing Congress to pass a resolution extending recognition to Cuban belligerency. Anti-American demonstrations in Spain exploded into violence in Barcelona when 15,000 people stoned the American consulate and destroyed the American flag. Despite widespread support for Cuba in the United States, Cleveland warned that should Congress declare war on Spain, he as commander-in-chief of the armed forces would refuse to send Americans to fight. Spain did not implement Washington's reform recommendations, and the administration did not want war. Yet the president had to protect American interests in Cuba. While Congress called for stronger measures, America's consul general in Havana repeatedly urged annexation. With Cleveland's Democratic party disintegrating on the eve of the presidential election of 1896, his administration could do little about the Cuban problem. The situation on the island had to await a new president.

THE CUBAN PROLOGUE TO WAR

In November 1896 the Republican party, led by William McKinley of Ohio, won the White House on a platform stressing expansion. Four years earlier the Republicans had resurrected the term *manifest destiny* and incorporated it into their campaign. Though the race of 1896 had centered on currency and tariff issues, the Republicans called for a "firm, vigorous, and dignified" foreign policy that supported "a naval power commensurate with [America's] position and responsibility." Their platform advocated the acquisition of Hawaii, the construction of a Nicaraguan canal under American ownership and control, and the establishment of a naval base in the West Indies. Though McKinley agreed with Alfred T. Mahan's ideas about the need for a stronger navy, he was not an imperialist. In fact, he assured anti-imperialist Carl Schurz that his administration would permit "no jingo nonsense." McKinley's first secretary of state, John Sherman, declared his opposition "to all acquisitions of territory not on the mainland."

The new administration, however, quickly realized that the Cuban issue was again approaching crisis level and could force American intervention. Spain had not implemented needed reforms, and in June 1897 Washington sent a note to Madrid protesting Weyler's tactics on the island, and the following month instructed the new American minister in Spain, Stewart Woodford, to demand that the Spanish withdraw from Cuba. By the autumn prospects for reform looked better when a liberal government took over in Madrid after the assassination of the prime minister. The new ministry called Weyler home, assured an end to reconcentration policies, and guaranteed more autonomy to the islanders through the election of legislatures. President McKinley told Congress in his annual message in December that the United States should give the reforms a chance. Yet if they yielded no results, he warned, intervention might take place because of "our obligations to ourselves, to civilization and humanity."

By early 1898 Spain's promised political reforms had still not materialized and in January the United States sent the battleship *Maine* to Cuba as a show of force designed to persuade the Spanish to end the war. The Cuban rebels had demanded independence, and the ministry in Madrid soon stood uneasily between them and Spanish loyalists in Cuba who rioted that same month over the question of autonomy. Such a concession, the loyalists feared, would promote the election of a legislature injurious to their interests on the island. Besides, the granting of Cuban independence could bring down the ministry at home. Meanwhile the *Maine*, anchored in Havana harbor, became a symbol of American imperialism and a sign of deepening interventionism by Washington. A close adviser of the president's warned that sending the vessel was like "waving a match in an oil well for fun."

While tensions grew over the *Maine*, a crisis developed when the Department of State in Washington received a copy of a private letter written in late 1897 from the Spanish minister in the United States, Enrique Dupuy deLôme, to a friend in Cuba. DeLôme was frustrated over the events pointing toward war with the United States and described McKinley as "weak and a bidder for the admiration of the crowd, . . . a would-be politician who tries to leave a door open behind himself while keeping on good terms with the jingoes of his party." Worse, to many Americans, deLôme suggested that his government consider economic reprisals, which seemed evidence of Spain's lack of sincerity about peace. By the time the deLôme letter reached Washington, it had become a *cause célèbre* because a rebel partisan had somehow gotten hold of it and shared it with a number of Americans, including William Randolph Hearst. The same day the State Department received the missive, February 9, the letter appeared in the New York *Journal* under the headline, "Worst Insult to the United States in Its History." Madrid's unavoidable decision to recall deLôme, who had already packed his bags, further exacerbated the dangerous situation by removing a man determined for peace. During the next critical weeks Spain had no minister in the United States who could help vent American anger.

Less than a week later, on the night of February 15, the *Maine* blew up in Havana harbor, sending more than 250 American officers and men to their deaths as the 7,000-ton battleship crumpled and sank. Americans charged that Spain was responsible. In their anger, they failed to consider that such an act meant war with the United States—a calamity the Spanish could *not* have wanted. But emotions swept the United States as the New York *Journal* rang out these headlines: "The Warship Maine Was Split In Two By An Enemy's Infernal Machine"; "The Whole Country Thrills With War Fever"; "The Maine Was Destroyed By Treachery." Two days after the incident, the *Journal* included a diagram on the front page allegedly showing the placement of a mine that sank the ship. The paper offered $50,000 for information on the assailants.

President McKinley arranged an immediate inquiry into the explosion. Meanwhile Woodford in Madrid lodged a protest on March 3 over both the deLôme letter and the sinking of the *Maine*. Three days later the president asked Congress for $50 million in arms appropriations, and on March 9 received notice of approval. The government in Madrid, accord-

An explosion sank the Maine *in Havana Harbor on February 15, 1898, making* "Remember the Maine!" *the rallying cry for the Spanish-American War.* (U.S. Navy)

New York *Journal*'s Account of the *Maine* Disaster

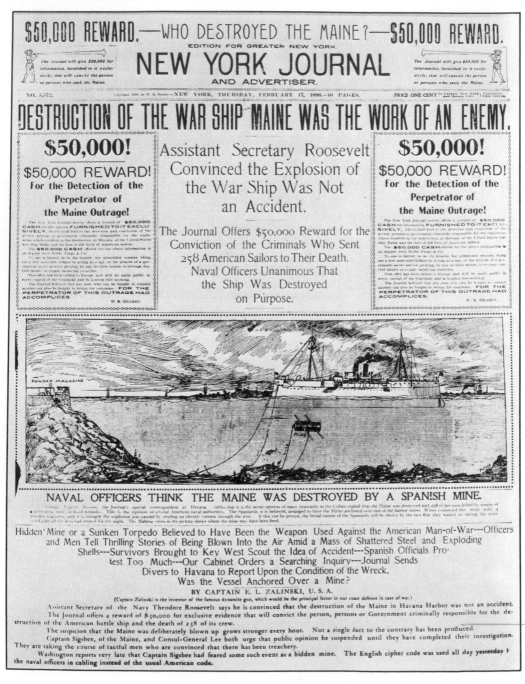

An example of the yellow press. The mystery of the destruction of the Maine *was never solved, and the $50,000 reward remained unclaimed.* (American Heritage Library)

ing to Woodford, found this measure difficult to believe. On March 28 the American court of inquiry, comprised of American naval officers, published its findings on the explosion: although it now seems likely that an overheated boiler blew up the ship, the court in 1898 concluded that an external mine had destroyed the *Maine* but declared that it was unable to determine the 'guilty party. The American people did not need to know any more. Theodore Roosevelt privately wrote that "the *Maine* was sunk by an act of dirty treachery on the part of the Spaniards," while Americans were chanting:

> Remember the *Maine*
> To hell with Spain!

In the midst of the excitement over the *Maine*, a Republican senator, Redfield Proctor of Vermont, reported to his colleagues about his recent private tour of Cuba. With notable absence of passion, which paradoxically made his speech in the Senate more effective, he declared that in the outskirts of Havana, the situation "is not peace nor is it war. It is desolation and distress, misery and starvation." Thousands of Cubans lived in reconcentration camps, and "one-half have died and one-quarter of the living are so diseased that they cannot be saved." Weyler had left the island, but his replacement did not know what to do. Proctor's description of the camps gave credence to the stories in the American press, for he was a known opponent of war. The children wander around with "arms and chest terribly emaciated, eyes swollen, and abdomen bloated to three times the natural size. . . . I was told by one of our consuls," he continued, "that they have been found dead about the markets in the morning, where they had crawled, hoping to get some stray bits of food from the early hucksters." The greatest atrocity was "the entire native population of Cuba, struggling for freedom and deliverance from the worst misgovernment of which I ever had knowledge."

Proctor's account had a major impact on Americans concerned about both humanitarian and property interests on the island. Action in behalf of Cuba's independence seemed justified as a crusade, whereas American businessmen previously opposed to involvement recognized that the United States had to do something before the entire Cuban economy collapsed. *The Wall Street Journal* declared that Proctor's speech had "made the blood boil." Intervention in Cuba, according to *Literary Digest*, was "the plain duty of the United States on the simple ground of humanity."

THE SPANISH–AMERICAN WAR

President McKinley's role in these events is difficult to assess. Despite arguments by some observers that he followed a cold and calculating expansionist policy that included war as a final expedient, other pieces of information suggest that he was a gentle man caught up in uncontrollable forces. By the spring of 1898 he could not sleep without the aid of pow-ders. His mood grew irascible as his invalid wife failed in health, and he continually had to grapple with the jingoes demanding war. A friend claimed that in late March the president broke under the strain and wept over recent events. Congress, McKinley charged, was pushing the nation into war. But this was not entirely true. McKinley's uncertain policies contributed to the confusion. On the one hand, he was a devout Methodist, extremely sensitive to what was going on around him; he was not a single-minded imperialist willing to do anything to expand America's borders. On the other hand, McKinley wanted the spoils but not at the cost of war. Not surprisingly, this attitude seemed weak and indecisive to jingoes such as Theodore Roosevelt.

Political pressures and the desire for reelection in 1900 helped push McKinley toward war. Members of his party demanded war, and rival Democrats led by William Jennings Bryan called for an independent Cuba. The president had little room to maneuver. Spain had moved toward settling the Cuban matter, yet pressure in America for war was enormous. Secretary of War Russell Alger warned that "Congress will declare war in spite of him. He'll get run over and the party with him." A Protestant journal declared that "if it be the will of Almighty God, that by war the last trace of this inhumanity of man to man shall be swept away from this Western Hemisphere, let it come!" When business leaders emphasized recovery from the depression rather than a war that would bring expansion abroad, Roosevelt snorted at Ohio Senator Mark Hanna, one of their biggest spokesmen: "We will have this war for the freedom of Cuba, in spite of the timidity of the commercial interests." Exasperated with the president's indecision, Roosevelt allegedly charged that "McKinley has no more backbone than a chocolate eclair!"

The president emerged with a policy that left room for an eleventh-hour peace. On March 27 the United States notified Spain that it wanted an immediate armistice and peace by October 1, or the president would arbitrate a settlement. McKinley also called for an end to the reconcentration camps and for a program of relief. Though making no demand for the island's independence, Washington sent a telegram to Madrid the next day stipulating Cuba's freedom as the natural outcome of negotiations. The Spanish government was already tottering in early 1898 and could not risk total concession without promoting its downfall. On March 31 Madrid ordered the end of the reconcentration policy, promised immediate reforms in Cuba, agreed to an armistice if the rebels made the request, and offered to submit the *Maine* issue to international arbitration. But the Spanish could not condone McKinley's intervention, and they would not grant Cuban independence.

The same day of the Spanish reply, Woodford notified McKinley that Spain's attitude was changing as fast as was politically possible. "I am told confidentially," he wrote, "that the offer of armistice by the Spanish Government would cause revolution here." Madrid's leaders "are ready to go as far and as fast as they can and still save the dynasty here in

Spain. They know that Cuba is lost." He emphasized that "no Spanish ministry would have dared to do one month ago what this ministry has proposed today." Three days later Woodford informed Washington that the pope had persuaded the government in Madrid to agree to an armistice. "I know that the Queen and her present ministry sincerely desire peace and that the Spanish people desire peace," Woodford wrote. "[I]f you can still give me time and reasonable liberty of action I will get for you the peace you desire so much and for which you have labored so hard."

But the counsels of war in the United States were stronger than the plaintiffs for peace, and Spain's only way out seemed to be to secure European assistance in preventing American intervention in Cuba. Failure to satisfy Washington's expectations would lead to war with the United States; compliance could lead to upheaval at home. All Old World powers except Britain, which needed its American ally to counter the growing influence of Germany, expressed sympathy with Spain and accused America of intending to seize Spanish holdings in the Western Hemisphere. But the German foreign minister offered the Spanish ambassador a realistic appraisal of the situation that precluded European involvement. "You are isolated," he declared, "because everybody wants to be pleasant to the United States, or, at any rate, nobody wants to arouse America's anger; the United States is a rich country, against which you simply cannot sustain a war." Finally, on April 6, the ambassadors of six European governments called on McKinley and urged him to stay out of Cuba. Two days afterward the New York *World* characterized the conversation between the president and his guests in these words: "The six ambassadors remarked: 'We hope for humanity's sake you will not go to war.' McKinley replied: 'We hope if we do go to war, you will understand that it is for humanity's sake.' "

Spain's reply to the president's note of late March was unsatisfactory because it did not concede Cuban independence, and on April 11 McKinley sent Congress a message asking authorization to use force if necessary to stop the war on the island. Two days earlier Madrid had granted a further concession by directing the Spanish troop commander in Cuba to permit a unilateral armistice designed to bring peace. Yet such an armistice seemed hardly enough to the McKinley administration, which now considered Cuba's freedom essential to negotiations. Besides, the armistice was conditional upon a Spanish decision to resume the war, and the Cuban rebels had not complied with the offer because they considered their demand for independence to be nonnegotiable. McKinley emphasized to Congress that "in the name of humanity, in the name of civilization, in behalf of endangered American interests which give us the right and the duty to speak and to act, the war in Cuba must stop." To counteract the "very serious injury to the commerce, trade, and business of our people, and the wanton destruction of property," he asked Congress for authority "to secure a full and final termination of hostilities between the Government of Spain and the people of Cuba." Though he reminded the lawmakers to give "just and careful attention" to Spain's last-hour armistice offer, this came in the message *after* his request for arms. Given the emotional atmosphere in the United States, along with Spain's past performance in failing to deliver promised reforms, most Americans regarded the armistice as another delay tactic. McKinley had *not* asked Congress for a declaration of war; his intention was that the United States should act "as an *impartial neutral*" in ending the war in Cuba.

Congress soon approved a joint resolution in support of McKinley's request, but not until after a floor debate that took on the air of a circus. A resurgent martial spirit became apparent when northern congressmen sang "The Battle Hymn of the Republic" and southerners countered with "Dixie." On April 19 Congress passed a joint resolution (requiring a simple majority in each House) by the margins of 42 to 35 in the Senate and 311 to 6 in the House. The measure *directed* (not authorized) the president to use military force in securing Spain's withdrawal from Cuba and guaranteeing the island's independence, and even though no support was evident for recognition of Cuba as a republic, Congress pledged that the United States would not seek its annexation.

The last part of the joint resolution—the promise against annexing Cuba—was sponsored by Senator Henry Teller of Colorado and seems to have passed unanimously by voice vote. The Teller Amendment proclaimed that "the United States hereby disclaims any disposition or intention to exercise sovereignty, jurisdiction, or control over said Island except for the pacification thereof, and asserts its determination, when that is accomplished, to leave the government and control of the Island to its people." Teller defended his amendment as an effort to ward off expected European charges that the United States had intervened in Cuba "for the purpose of aggrandizement." Yet he carefully added that this restriction relating to Cuba had no bearing on what the United States "may do as to some other islands," which was a veiled reference to Puerto Rico and the Philippines.

Though the Teller Amendment had the appearance of selflessness on the part of the United States, the realization that its sponsor was a well-known expansionist raises questions about motive. Politics was a prime concern, for Teller was a supporter of Bryan, and Bryan's Populist and Democratic followers suspected the McKinley administration of wanting to acquire the island in an effort to protect American investments. For more than a few Americans, the amendment was a transparent effort to salve the consciences of those who did not want the United States to become an imperialist nation. American sugar growers (primarily Louisiana Democrats) were among the strongest advocates of the measure, for they wanted Cuba to remain outside America's tariff walls and thus subject to control. Some legislators worried that if the United States took the island, Americans would become responsible for Cuba's debts. Finally, the promise not to annex Cuba had great appeal to Americans opposed to incorporating nonwhites into their nation. William Graham Sumner of Yale pointed out that "the prospect of adding to the present Senate a number of Cuban senators, either native or carpetbag, is one whose terrors it is not necessary to unfold." The Teller Amendment became a convenient shield for numerous groups who opposed the annexation of Cuba.

The seemingly narrow support for intervention in the upper chamber was misleading. Many of the thirty-five senators voting in opposition actually favored intervention: they did not like the wording of the resolution that supported the independence of Cuba without including recognition of the rebels' republican government. The McKinley administration had insisted, however, that recognition of the rebel regime would severely hamper America's military efforts should war develop with Spain. By 3 A.M. of April 20 (the official date remaining the 19th), Congress sent the joint resolution to the White House for the president's signature.

Events now passed quickly toward a declaration of war with Spain. That same day, April 20, the president approved the congressional resolution and declared that "the people of Cuba are, and of right ought to be, free and independent." He then issued an ultimatum giving Spain three days to "relinquish its authority and government in the Island of Cuba and withdraw its land and naval forces from Cuba and Cuban waters." The following day word reached Washington that Spain had severed diplomatic relations with the United States. On April 23 President McKinley called for 125,000 volunteers and two days later signed the joint resolution. The United States and Spain were at war, effective April 21.

Ideals and reality had again come together in America's decision for war. For many Americans the war with Spain was a crusade to free Cuba from Old World oppression; for others the reasons for war were mixed. More than a few agreed with Senator George Hoar of Massachusetts, who later opposed imperialism but in 1898 wrote that "we cannot look idly on while hundreds of thousands of innocent human beings . . . die of hunger close to our door. If there is ever to be a war it should be to prevent such things as that." Religious leaders prepared to convert more of the island's population to Christianity, imperialists dreamed of empire, politicians looked forward to reelection, business leaders formerly opposed to war now considered the commercial possibilities opened by the imminent end of Spain's colonial system. Whether or not they were for empire, Americans could identify with the prospect of seeing their flag waving over a distant shore. Senator Albert Beveridge of Indiana rejoiced that "at last, God's hour has struck. The American people go forth in a warfare holier than liberty—holy as humanity." The Irish satirist Finley Peter Dunne used his famous fictional news character Mr. Hennessy to beam forth in Irish brogue: "We're a gr-reat people." To which Mr. Dooley agreed: "We ar-re . . . We ar-re that. An' the best iv it is, we know we ar-re."

The Spanish-American War "wasn't much of a war," Roosevelt admitted afterward, "but it was the best war we had." The Spanish were almost as sure they would lose as the Americans were certain they would win. The American author Sherwood Anderson remarked that going to war with Spain was "like robbing an old gypsy woman in a vacant lot at night after a fair." Ambassador to England John Hay, soon to become secretary of state, christened it "a splendid little war." Indeed it was—for the United States. Three months of uninterrupted naval and land victories followed as America's battleships easily outmatched the antiquated vessels that comprised the Spanish navy. Spanish officers and crew were situated far from their home base and were also in a state of declining morale, whereas the American navy was ready and eager, largely due to the efforts of Assistant Secretary of the Navy Theodore Roosevelt. The Spanish army in Cuba was larger than the American force, but was poorly provisioned, exhausted from the long guerrilla war, and cut off from Madrid by America's naval blockade of the island. "We may and must expect a disaster," the Spanish naval commander wrote privately. "But . . . I hold my tongue and go forth resignedly to face the trials which God may be pleased to send me."

The first conflict in the Spanish-American War ironically occurred many miles from Cuba, when Commodore George Dewey engaged a Spanish squadron in the Philippines. The location of the battle was a surprise to many, but it is clear now that the navy had earlier made secret contingency plans that in case of war the United States was first to attack Spain in Manila Bay. The moment arrived when Roosevelt became acting secretary of the navy during the hectic afternoon of February 25, 1898. He instructed Dewey to move the Asiatic Squadron from Hong Kong to Manila Bay and when sure war had begun, the commodore was to "begin offensive operations in the Philippines." Roosevelt immediately resigned his position to accept a commission in the army, leaving the erroneous impression that he had engineered the Manila affair.

Near dawn of May 1, Dewey's cruisers steamed into Manila Bay and prepared for battle. His vessels stayed out of the Spaniards' firing range, methodically and repeatedly circling past the enemy, until by noon they had destroyed the entire squadron. At little cost Dewey held the naval station at Cavite along with Manila Bay, and the War Department prepared to send an occupation force to the city of Manila. Though Dewey would eventually encounter difficulties with German warships in the Philippines, that problem also passed, and he could remark after his triumph in Manila: "If I were a religious man, and I hope I am, I should say that the hand of God was in it."

Dewey's victory at Manila Bay revived the expansionists' arguments for Hawaii, which the Senate had shelved the previous March in light of the approaching war with Spain. On June 16, 1897, President McKinley had agreed to a treaty of annexation, and it went to the Senate that same day. In the meantime the proposal aroused opposition again. Democrats and sugar interests aligned in denouncing the treaty, as did the Japanese

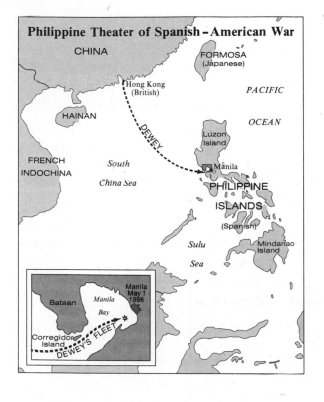

MAP 14

Despite the prevalence of Cuba in America's explanation for war with Spain in 1898, the first battle occurred in the Philippines.

government, which argued that American annexation would endanger the rights of Japan's 25,000 nationals on the islands and disrupt Pacific affairs. Roosevelt would not have hesitated. He told Mahan that "if I had my way we would annex those islands tomorrow [and] . . . hoist our flag over the island leaving all details for after action." The Department of State assured Japan that annexation would not infringe upon its rights, but it also informed the American naval commander in Honolulu that if he detected any evidence of Japanese aggression, he was to raise the American flag and proclaim Hawaii a protectorate. Japan withdrew its protest in December 1897. Troubles with Spain again delayed action, and the Senate adjourned without a decision on the annexation treaty.

Now, in May 1898, the United States seemed determined to hold the Philippines as the gateway to China, and Hawaii suddenly seemed vital as a naval and coaling station en route to the Orient. Hawaii would thus serve as a defensive outpost for America's mainland and as a guardian of its interests in the Pacific and Far East. On May 4, three days after Dewey's triumph, the annexationists introduced a joint resolution in the House that soon received overwhelming approval there and in the Senate. The president signed the bill on July 7 and Hawaii became American territory.

TREATY OF PARIS

After successive American victories at Santiago in Cuba, Guam, the Philippines, and Puerto Rico, the Spanish ambassador in Paris asked the French Foreign Office to intervene for peace. Instructions immediately went to the French ambassador in Washington, who signed an armistice for Spain, effective August 12.

The joy of victory was tempered with the question of what to do with the Philippines. President McKinley recognized Manila's strategic and

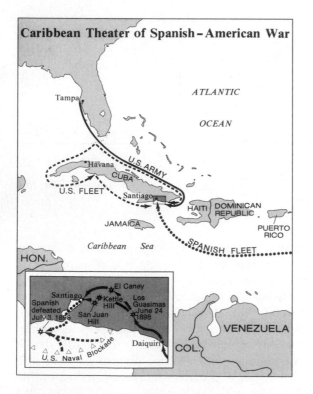

MAP 15

The realities of the war in Cuba were considerably different from the implications contained in Secretary of State Hay's calling it a "splendid little war."

commercial importance and at first had seemed willing to allow Spain to keep all of the Philippines except for the city. But these intentions changed during the war. The acquisitions of Hawaii and Guam provided stepping-stones to China, and the Philippines were the doorway into the Far East. *All* areas seemed vital to the Oriental trade. Assistant Secretary of the Treasury Frank Vanderlip voiced the sentiments of Asia enthusiasts when he called the Philippines the "pickets of the Pacific, standing guard at the entrances to trade with the millions of China and Korea, French Indo-China, the Malay Peninsula, and the islands of Indonesia." American businessmen recognized that the acquisition of colonies might safeguard economic interests in China, continually threatened by foreign powers. The New York *Journal of Commerce* warned that returning the Philippines "would be an act of inconceivable folly in the face of our imperative future necessities for a basis of naval and military force on the Western shores of the Pacific." McKinley feared that the Filipinos were unfit to govern themselves, and that France or Germany would eventually subjugate them. Some time after the war he explained to a group of Methodist clergymen visiting him in the White House that the Philippines were "a gift from the gods" and that "there was nothing left for us to do but to take them all, and to educate the Filipinos, and uplift and civilize and Christianize them."

When America's peace delegation arrived in Paris for the first session at the Quai D'Orsay Palace on September 29, its membership revealed its purpose: four of the five men chosen by McKinley were expansionists,

AFTERMATH: IMPLICATIONS FOR THE FAR EAST

Americans could not enjoy their conquest for long; Filipino rebels and American forces on the islands were soon locked in what developed into three years of combat. The roots of the insurrection traced back to the period before America's war with Spain. By the time the Spanish lost Manila to American soldiers in August 1898, the city was the only major spot in the islands not yet under rebel control. Aguinaldo, who had led an insurrection in 1895 that the Spanish crushed, was under the impression that his homeland would receive freedom upon America's victory over Spain, a belief encouraged by his return from exile on board an American ship, and by Dewey's urgings for him to renew the struggle against the Spanish. Indeed, after the revolution had begun anew in February 1899, Congress in Washington had presented a resolution for independence that failed by only a slender margin. Aguinaldo and his cohorts responded by establishing a government, drawing up a constitution, and proclaiming the Philippine Republic. Washington's decision to retain the islands had strapped them around the American flag. In an effort to put down the Filipinos, the United States dispatched 70,000 troops to the islands, a force four times larger than that used in Cuba.

The end of the guerrilla war in the Philippines came in July 1902, but only after 200,000 Filipinos and 5,000 Americans had died, and the United States had sent 175,000 men to the islands and expended $160 million. More than that, the conflict entailed atrocities committed by both sides, leaving a bitter taste among Americans which doubtless contributed to the rapid demise of the expansionist spirit. The philosopher William and the fifth ultimately became a convert. Three of them were ranking members of the Senate Foreign Relations Committee, which meant that they would also vote on the treaty when it came before the Senate. The delegation was to seek the independence of Cuba, the acquisition of Puerto Rico, and at least the island of Luzon in the Philippines, which was the site of Manila. For almost a month the Spanish and American delegates discussed the fate of Cuba, the Spanish preferring that it come under American ownership. Though the Americans appeared to stand behind the Teller Amendment for selfless reasons, they also realized that the country owning the island would inherit a debt of $400 million that Spanish officials in Cuba had run up in trying to end the rebellion.

By late October the United States had decided to take all of the Philippines. Americans on the islands warned that separating Manila from the Philippines was ill-advised, and that the islands comprised an integrated economic whole. McKinley had recently returned from the Midwest, where he learned of widespread support for holding onto them. Despite demands for independence made by Filipinos under insurgent leader Emilio Aguinaldo, the United States decided that the rebel government near Manila was unstable and that continued disorder could attract German involvement. A protectorate was out of the question in view of the difficulties experienced in Samoa with the islands' regime. The war with Spain, McKinley explained, had thrust upon the United States "new duties and responsibilities," and the Philippines offered a "commercial opportunity to which American statesmanship cannot be indifferent." Through his fictitious Mr. Dooley, Finley Peter Dunne questioned the wisdom of taking the islands, which "not more thin two months since ye learned whether they were islands or canned goods." But Mr. Hennessy expressed American sentiment in declaring: "Hang on to thim. What we've got we must hold." Dooley agreed but remarked prophetically: "We've got the Ph'lippeens, Hinnisy; we've got thim the way Casey got the bulldog—be th' teeth."

After more than two months of negotiations, the United States and Spain emerged with the Treaty of Paris in December 1898. The Spanish agreed to assume Cuba's debt and accepted $20 million from the United States for relinquishing "all claim of sovereignty over and title to Cuba," along with the Philippines, Guam, Puerto Rico, "and other islands now under Spanish sovereignty in the West Indies" (Culebra and a few small islands near Puerto Rico plus the Isle of Pines below Cuba). Inhabitants of the transferred areas were assured religious freedom, but the American Congress was to determine their "civil rights and political status." The

United States had not guaranteed citizenship, nor had it promised statehood. For the first time in America's history, it had acquired colonies.

Arguments against the treaty began early in 1899. Anti-imperialists in the United States were both angered and saddened by what they regarded as a breakdown of American idealism. The Anti-Imperialist League in Boston considered the acquisition of the Philippines a contradiction in policy since the United States had turned down the annexation of Cuba for humanitarian reasons. Hawaii, Puerto Rico, and Guam seemed acceptable additions because white people on the islands formed a potential political base, but the Filipinos were primarily Malays whose incorporation begged trouble. Aguinaldo's demands for independence served notice of bitter resistance to American rule, and a jungle war 6,000 miles from the United States was unthinkable. Many opponents of the treaty asserted that absorption of peoples without their consent was a violation of the Declaration of Independence, the United States Constitution, and other great pronouncements in American history. Senator George Vest of Missouri sponsored a resolution (which never came to a vote) "that under the Constitution of the United States, no power is given to the Federal Government to acquire territory to be held and governed permanently as colonies." Republican Senator Hoar of Massachusetts joined Democrats in proclaiming the unconstitutionality of Old World colonialism "built upon the fundamental idea that the people of immense areas of territory can be held as subjects, never to become citizens." Expansion had turned America into "a cheapjack country, raking after the cart for the leavings of European tyranny." According to another anti-imperialist, "Dewey took Manila with the loss of one man—and all our institutions." And that was not all: American involvement in the Philippines was costly and would lead to international rivalries over the Orient. But despite the support of William Jennings Bryan (who had soured on expansionism, even for humanitarian reasons), Andrew Carnegie, Mark Twain, and other notables, the anti-imperialists were unable to reverse recent events.

The imperialists' counter-arguments in favor of the treaty were difficult to refute. The McKinley administration received valuable assistance from Roosevelt, Lodge, and numerous businessmen in defending the treaty as a boon to trade and the natural outcome of America's superiority. The British poet Rudyard Kipling expressed a strong argument for expansion when he penned these lines for *McClure's Magazine* in February 1899:

> Take up the White Man's burden—
> Ye dare not stoop to less—
> Nor call too loud on Freedom
> To cloke your weariness.

The United States had assumed the responsibility of spreading civilization into backward areas of the world. Social Darwinists hailed the fulfillment of their teachings, commercialists looked forward to the China market, and proponents of a larger navy at last saw their aims become possible. Expansionists also warned that if the United States did not take the areas, Germany, Japan, or some other power would do so. America had to redeem its soldiers by keeping what their blood had bought. As for the danger in acquiring distant areas, expansionist Senator Albert Beveridge of Indiana dramatically declared that "the ocean does not separate us from the lands of our duty and desire—the ocean joins us, a river never to be dredged, a canal never to be repaired." He concluded that "steam joins us, electricity joins us—the very elements are in league with our destiny."

Connecticut Senator Orville Platt advocated a position that later became the essence of Supreme Court decisions on the constitutionality of territorial acquisitions: the United States as a sovereign nation could incorporate territory and institute the type of government it believed best suited for the people involved. Platt insisted that the United States had no duties to assure either citizenship or statehood. Like other nations, it could add dependencies or colonies. The Supreme Court affirmed these principles in the *Insular* cases of 1901, when it declared that the Constitution did not necessarily follow the flag—that American citizenship rights did not automatically extend to territorial inhabitants.

After a bitter fight in the Senate the Treaty of Paris won approval on February 6, 1899, by one vote more than the required two-thirds majority.

Signing the Treaty of Paris of 1899

Secretary of State John Hay signs the ratification of the peace treaty with Spain, while President William McKinley (standing beneath the clock) and others observe. (Library of Congress)

Just two days before the vote, conflict broke out in the Philippines between Aguinaldo's partisans and the American troops, and news of this development probably encouraged support for the treaty as the only alternative to some other power's taking the islands. Several anti-imperialists were won over at the last moment, perhaps in part because of William Jennings Bryan's argument that prolongation of the war with Spain was out of the question and that the United States could grant independence to the Philippines when emotions cooled.

The Spanish-American War, though short and inexpensive compared to other conflicts, had far-reaching consequences. It climaxed the long, steady decline of Spain's empire, and at the same time marked the beginnings of the world's recognition of the power status of the United States. Realities of the war became apparent in proportion to the growing casualty lists. Nearly 5,500 Americans died—less than 400 directly attributable to battle; the bulk were felled by malaria and yellow fever. Yet the war had redeeming features. Some Americans believed the conflict with Spain laid their Civil War to rest. Massachusetts soldiers en route to Cuba met a joyous reception in Baltimore, which was in sharp contrast to that received in 1861 when the state's forces marched through the same city to defend Washington and a mob pelted them with stones. With "Dixie" ringing from the band in 1898, Massachusetts Senator Henry Cabot Lodge tearfully recalled years later that "it was 'roses, roses all the way'—flags, cheers, excited crowds. Tears were in my eyes. I never felt so moved in my life. The war of 1861 was over at last and the great country for which so many died was one again."

Philippine Insurrection

U.S. soldiers occupying native huts during Filipino insurrection of 1899–1902. (Library of Congress)

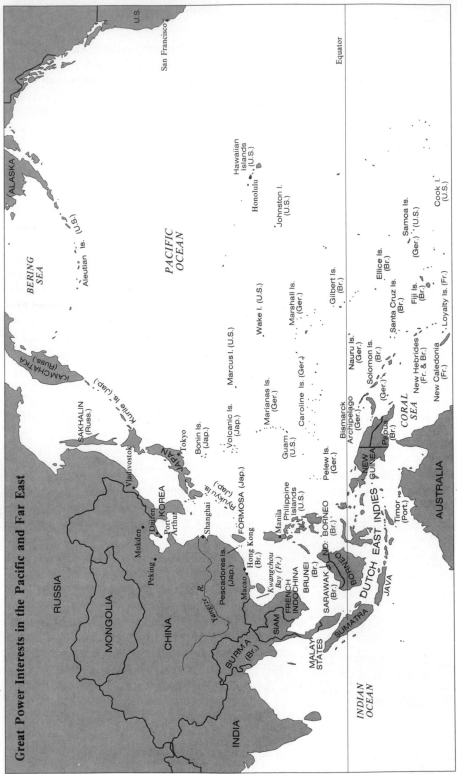

Great Power Interests in the Pacific and Far East

James declared: "Here were the precious beginnings of an indigenous national life, with which . . . it was our first duty to have squared ourselves. . . . We are destroying the lives of these islanders by the thousands, their villages and their cities," he charged. "Could there be a more damning indictment of that whole bloated ideal termed 'modern civilization' than this amounts to?" Mark Twain suggested that the United States paint black over the white stripes in the American flag and replace the stars with a skull and cross bones. Yet the civil governor of the Philippines and later president of the United States, William Howard Taft, declared that America's goal was to "teach those people individual liberty, which shall lift them up to a point of civilization . . . and which shall make them rise to call the name of the United States blessed." Senator Benjamin Tillman, a South Carolina Democrat, delighted in seeing Republicans in the North squirm over the Philippines: "No Republican leader will now dare to wave the bloody shirt and preach a crusade against the South's treatment of the negro. The North has a bloody shirt of its own. Many thousands of them have been made into shrouds for murdered Filipinos, done to death because they were fighting for liberty." The New York *World* moaned over the difficulties in administering "uncivilized" peoples when it addressed these lines to Rudyard Kipling:

> We've taken up the white man's burden
> Of ebony and brown;
> Now will you kindly tell us, Rudyard,
> How we may put it down?

The United States found that the acceptance of international responsibilities made it nearly impossible to lay them aside. During the war it had established control over Hawaii, Guam, the Philippines, and Puerto Rico, and in mid-January of 1899 the American navy occupied Wake Island in the Pacific and proclaimed it American territory. In December of that year Britain and Germany signed a treaty in Washington conceding to the United States the Samoan island of Tutuila, where Pago Pago was located, along with nearby islands known as American Samoa. The following year the native chiefs on Tutuila formally ceded their island to the United States, and four years later, in 1904, the small Manu'a string of islands did the same. Expansion seemed to breed expansion, the anti-imperialists disgustedly declared.

In retrospect most possessions acquired by the United States seemed to form a line pointing to China. Americans had long exaggerated the commercial importance of the Celestial Kingdom, for by the late 1890s the

---

MAP 16

By the end of the nineteenth century, numerous countries (including the United States) had made claims to parts of Asia and the Pacific.

China market consumed only 2 percent of their total exports. But Americans believed the volume would grow in an atmosphere of equal opportunity. Besides, the United States had developed a special paternal interest in the Chinese people. Japan's victory in the Sino-Japanese War of 1894–95 had demonstrated the weakness of China's Manchu dynasty, which in turn led to further outside encroachments upon its sovereignty. Spheres of influence, long-term leases, tariff controls, securing of transportation and communication rights—all were European inroads into the Chinese mainland that caused concern among American commercial and missionary groups. Shortly after the Sino-Japanese War Russia, Germany, Britain, France, and Japan won railroad and commercial concessions in China. Americans worried that their path to the Orient lay cluttered with other countries' entrenched interests.

America's active involvement in China largely originated in Britain's efforts to establish an Open Door policy. Twice in less than a year's time the British had recommended a joint venture to guarantee equal trade opportunities in China, only to have the United States turn down both proposals as a violation of its traditional isolationism. But in 1899 a British visitor to the Orient and member of Parliament, Lord Charles Beresford, aroused great American interest in China through his book *The Breakup of China* and his speeches in the United States calling for the Open Door. In the meantime American merchants and missionaries put pressure on the Department of State to adopt an active China policy. Then, during the summer of that year, a private British citizen working for the Chinese Customs Services in China, Alfred Hippisley, discussed the matter with his longtime friend in the United States, William Rockhill, who was an adviser on Far Eastern affairs to Secretary of State John Hay. Hippisley emphasized the commercial importance of the Open Door to *both* Britain and the United States, and warned that continued outside penetration of the country would worsen conditions—even for the Chinese. He recommended that the United States take the initiative in establishing international respect for the Open Door. Anti-British sentiment in the United States, Hippisley realized, was still too strong to permit London to lead the way.

Hippisley and Rockhill worked with Hay in composing a memorandum that expressed London's wishes and became the basis of America's policy toward China. On September 6, 1899 Hay sent the statement in the form of a diplomatic note to the governments in Berlin, London, and St. Petersburg, and in November to Paris, Rome, and Tokyo. Patterned after the most-favored-nation principles of the earlier part of the century, Hay's circular note called for equal commercial opportunity within the various powers' spheres of influence and took a stand against interference with China's tariff controls. Hay did not condemn spheres of influence, nor did he attempt to safeguard the integrity of China. The success of his Open Door efforts depended on whether the interested powers would either deny imperialist designs in China, or admit to them by remaining silent. All governments sent replies to Washington, but most of them were noncommittal; they conditioned their adherence to the Open Door on the acceptance of its principles by the other parties. When Russia eventually indicated unwillingness to comply, its stand released the others from the pledge. Hay ignored the Russian response and announced in March 1900 that the powers' *unanimous* decision to respect the Open Door had made the policy statement "final and definitive."

One can erroneously dismiss America's Open Door policy as ineffective. The United States lacked the military or naval might to enforce equal commercial opportunity in China, but it also recognized that the balance of power in that section of the world was so tenuous that the involvement of another country in Asian affairs could turn that balance either way. No one wanted war; yet no one could be sure of the other's intentions. As with the most-favored-nation approach, the United States gained equal commercial privileges in China without having to resort to military measures.

Problems in China did not end with Hay's Open Door pronouncements; continued and deepening foreign involvement ultimately led to an outbreak of nationalistic resistance against outsiders, known as the Boxer Rebellion. The Manchu dynasty, which had been in power since the mid-1600s and would collapse in 1911, was incapable of defending its homeland, and in 1900 a secret society known as *I-ho-ch'üan* ("Righteous and Harmonious Fists"), or the Boxers, armed themselves with spears and swords and led an insurrection against foreigners in China. Hundreds of missionaries and Christian converts fell in the bloody rebellion, as the Boxers, allied with imperial soldiers and apparently encouraged by the Manchu government, laid siege on the foreigners isolated in the legation section of Peking.

The United States decided to act when the other powers prepared to send a punitive force that could culminate in the permanent partition of China. In August 1900 the United States contributed 2,500 soldiers from the Philippines to join over 15,000 others from Britain, France, Germany, Japan, and Russia in saving Peking. Meanwhile Hay circulated a second note affirming the Open Door policy, but with a different emphasis. Whereas the first note of September 1899 had advocated only equal commercial opportunity, the one of July 1900 urged respect for that nation's "territorial and administrative entity" and called on the interested powers to "safeguard for the world the principle of equal and impartial trade with all parts of the Chinese Empire." Hay thus broadened the Open Door to include more than trade and more than the areas in China under outside control; his policy now included respect for China's independence. He did not seek a reply this time; this was to be *America's* policy—with or without the other countries' acquiescence. Ironically, each foreign government deepened its involvement in China while affirming agreement with Hay's proclamation—largely to deter the others from expanding their holdings. The Open Door pronouncement of 1900 did not save China:

mutual distrust among the interested powers caused each to claim adherence to the Open Door rather than risk a world war brought on by its rivals' expansionist activities.

America's China policy perhaps lightened the effects of the Boxer Rebellion and the succeeding growth of foreign influence in the country, but questions remain about Hay's claim that the United States sought only an "abstention from plunder" through the Open Door statement. The international expeditionary force put down the insurrection at the cost of numerous lives, and China was assessed a huge reparations bill of about $333 million. But China had been wracked with outside intervention and internal disorder for so long that it could not pay that exorbitant amount. The United States was to receive $25 million, although it kept only $7 million to cover private damage claims and canceled the remainder. This decision bought considerable favor among the Chinese because their government used the huge fund to facilitate the education of their students in the United States. Meanwhile outside intervention continued in China. In fact, in late 1900 Hay gave in to the American navy's wishes and requested a piece of territory and a naval base at Samsah Bay, located within the Japanese sphere of influence. Peking was in no position to refuse, but the Japanese government quietly but firmly called Hay's attention to the Open Door principles. The United States dropped its request.

America's Open Door policy went through several shades of meaning in succeeding years, but it was above all an extension of the most-favored-nation approach of the early 1800s: a guarantee of equal commercial opportunity in China. Despite the apparently selfless aims of the first Open Door declaration of 1899, the truth is that it was an effort to reserve *America's* commercial interests in China. The military weakness of the United States prohibited a stronger stand. The following year Hay's second note announced opposition to violations of China's territorial integrity, but a *statement* of policy was again the most the United States could offer. Unable to enforce the Open Door, America issued pronouncements that nonetheless affirmed its deepening interest in China and the entire Far East.

The United States had become integral to the world scene by the turn of the twentieth century. Though not yet a first-rate power, events of the latter 1890s suggested that it might soon reach that height. The growing rapprochement with Britain; Cuba and the war with Spain; the annexation of Caribbean and Pacific islands; the Open Door in China—all entailed foreign involvements that would no doubt expand in scope because they rested on idealistic as well as realistic considerations. In 1899 the United States took part in the First International Peace Conference at The Hague in the Netherlands. Called by the Russian czar to encourage disarmament, the meeting brought twenty-six nations together to draw up rules of war and devise steps toward peaceful settlement of international disputes through their newly established Permanent Court of Arbitration. European powers meanwhile worried that the United States might ally with Britain. Anglo-American rapprochement had become more of a reality after the Venezuelan episode and the rise of Germany. The British had been partial to the United States during the war with Spain, and the Americans had reciprocated by favoring Britain in its war with the Boers of South Africa. Social, political, and economic similarities underscored the Atlantic understanding, as did personal familial ties between the countries and shared racial views. The London *Times* asserted that "ties of blood" held the nations together, while a leading English journalist declared that his compatriots "should never stand idly by and see a hundred millions of people who speak English trampled on by people who speak Russian or French or German." McKinley's solid reelection victory in 1900, with Theodore Roosevelt at his side as vice president, assured the world that the Americans were beginning to realize that their security rested, at least in part, on international events. The United States would not return to isolationism. Victory in the war with Spain had given Americans the taste of empire. They did not yet fully understand that with power came responsibility.

Selected readings

Beale, Howard K., *Theodore Roosevelt and the Rise of America to World Power.* 1956.

Beisner, Robert L., *From the Old Diplomacy to the New, 1865–1900.* 1975.

————, *Twelve against Empire: The Anti-Imperialists, 1898–1900.* 1968.

Braeman, John, *Albert J. Beveridge: American Nationalist.* 1971.

Campbell, Alexander E., *Great Britain and the United States, 1895–1903.* 1960.

Campbell, Charles S., *From Revolution to Rapprochement: The United States and Great Britain, 1783–1900.* 1974.

————, *Special Business Interests and the Open Door Policy.* 1951.

————, *The Transformation of American Foreign Relations, 1865–1900.* 1976.

Clymer, Kenton J., *Protestant Missionaries in the Philippines, 1898–1916: An Inquiry into the American Colonial Mentality.* 1986.

Cooper, John M., Jr., *The Warrior and the Priest: Woodrow Wilson and Theodore Roosevelt.* 1983.

Cosmas, Graham A., *An Army for Empire: The United States Army in the Spanish-American War.* 1971.

Davis, Calvin D., *The United States and the First Hague Peace Conference.* 1962.

Dulles, Foster Rhea, *Prelude to World Power: 1860–1900.* 1965.

Dunne, Finley Peter, *Mr. Dooley in Peace and War.* 1899.

Faulkner, Harold U., *Politics, Reform and Expansion, 1890–1900.* 1959.

Freidel, Frank, *The Splendid Little War*. 1958.

Gould, Lewis L., *The Spanish-American War and President McKinley*. 1982.

Grenville, John A. S., and George B. Young, *Politics, Strategy, and American Diplomacy*. 1966.

Healy, David, *U.S. Expansionism: The Imperialist Urge in the 1890s*. 1970.

Hofstadter, Richard, "Manifest Destiny and the Philippines," 173–200. In Daniel Aaron, ed., *America in Crisis*. 1952.

Hunt, Michael H., *The Making of a Special Relationship: The U.S. and China to 1914*. 1983.

Johnson, Robert E., *Far China Station: The U.S. Navy in Asian Waters, 1800–1898*. 1979.

Kennan, George F., *American Diplomacy*. Expanded ed., 1984. Originally published as *American Diplomacy, 1900–1950*. 1951.

LaFeber, Walter, *The New Empire: An Interpretation of American Expansion, 1860–1898*. 1963.

Langley, Lester D., *The Cuban Policy of the United States: A Brief History*. 1968.

Leech, Margaret, *In the Days of McKinley*. 1959.

Linderman, Gerald F., *The Mirror of War: American Society and the Spanish-American War*. 1974.

McCormick, Thomas J., *China Market: America's Quest for Informal Empire, 1893–1901*. 1967.

May, Ernest R., *Imperial Democracy: The Emergence of America as a Great Power*. 1961.

Miller, Stuart C., *"Benevolent Assimilation": The American Conquest of the Philippines, 1899–1903*. 1982.

Morgan, H. Wayne, *America's Road to Empire: The War with Spain and Overseas Expansion*. 1965.

———, *From Hayes to McKinley: National Party Politics, 1877–1896*. 1969.

———, *William McKinley and His America*. 1963.

Perkins, Bradford, *The Great Rapprochement: England and the United States, 1895–1914*. 1968.

Perkins, Dexter, *The Monroe Doctrine, 1867–1907*. 1937.

Pratt, Julius W., *Expansionists of 1898*. 1936.

Rickover, Hyman G., *How the Battleship* Maine *Was Destroyed*. 1976.

Ruiz, Ramón, *Cuba: The Making of a Revolution*. 1968.

Schirmer, Daniel B., *Republic or Empire: American Resistance to the Philippine War*. 1972.

Seager II, Robert, *Alfred Thayer Mahan*. 1977.

Smith, Ephraim K., " 'A Question from Which We Could Not Escape': William McKinley and the Decision to Acquire the Philippine Islands," *Diplomatic History* 9 (1985): 363–75.

Spector, Ronald, *Admiral of the New Empire: The Life and Career of George Dewey*. 1974.

Sprout, Harold and Margaret, *The Rise of American Naval Power, 1776–1918*. 1944.

Tompkins, E. Berkeley, *Anti-Imperialism in the United States*. 1970.

Trask, David F., *The War with Spain in 1898*. 1981.

Welch, Richard, *Response to Imperialism: The United States and the Philippine-American War, 1899–1902*. 1979.

Williams, William A., *The Roots of the Modern American Empire*. 1969.

———, *The Tragedy of American Diplomacy*. 1959, 1962.

Young, Marilyn B., *The Rhetoric of Empire*. 1968.

Chapter Twelve

Theodore Roosevelt and the Search for World Order, 1900–1913

The United States and Theodore Roosevelt arrived on the international stage at the same time, a development that was not entirely coincidental. America was not a world power by the opening of the twentieth century, but it soon became the leading determinant in Caribbean matters, a force worth considering in the Far East, and more than an observer of European events. Meanwhile Roosevelt promoted the growing public interest in foreign affairs by dominating the American scene as few leaders have done in the nation's history. A man of forceful personality, with a zest for life and a joy in battle—whether in politics or on the field of war—Roosevelt relished competition that resulted in progress. The reform spirit of the early 1900s—Progressivism—had permeated more than domestic affairs; it offered humanitarian justification for increased involvement in events occurring beyond the continental borders of the United States. Roosevelt saw the need for reforms at home. In foreign policy, he sought world order through the establishment of a balance of power.

Roosevelt's background was rich and cosmopolitan. A graduate of Harvard, he became New York City police commissioner, assistant secretary of the navy, hero of the Spanish-American War, governor of New York, vice president, and, upon the assassination of McKinley in the autumn of 1901, president—an office to which he was elected on his own right three years later. Despite his active public career he found time for world travel, big game hunting in Africa, extensive reading, and writing books. Roosevelt moved easily among wealthy families and intellectuals on both sides of the Atlantic, which facilitated the informal and personal

Theodore Roosevelt

President Theodore Roosevelt on the rostrum in New Castle, Wyoming, in 1903. (Library of Congress)

brand of diplomacy he practiced while in the White House. Roosevelt was "pure act," Henry Adams once remarked. "Teddy," as Ohio Republican Mark Hanna sarcastically called him, tended to pound his fist into his cupped left hand for emphasis and was noted in cartoons and elsewhere for his glasses, mustache, and ever-prominent teeth. When not behind his desk, he could be in the boxing ring, on the tennis court, demonstrating jujitsu, or on his way to Rock Creek Park, followed by uneasy foreign dignitaries whom he had invited for a hike.

Roosevelt urged Americans to support their country's involvement in international affairs. He emphasized to Congress in 1902 that "the increasing interdependence and complexity of international political and economic relations render it incumbent on all civilized and orderly powers to insist on the proper policing of the world." The United States, he declared through a West African proverb, needed to "speak softly and carry a big stick." A follower of Darwinian principles, he adopted a patrician attitude toward the world's unfortunate people and in the spirit of *noblesse oblige* called on Americans to join other Anglo-Saxons in taking up the "white man's burden" and spreading enlightenment, culture, liberty, and order.

The first decade or so of the new century comprised the era of Theodore Roosevelt. His realistic diplomacy was not new to the republic, but rarely has an occupant of the White House displayed such flair and exuberance. At the heart of his showmanship lay a primary concern for American interests. He based his actions upon that consideration and, while president, used almost any method short of war as an instrument of policy.

Roosevelt never pushed beyond his country's limitations. He did not believe in idle threats, for failure to deliver would destroy America's effectiveness abroad. He perceived that the United States had to adopt a foreign policy that would reach only as far as the nation's military capabilities would permit. He wrote William Howard Taft in 1910: "I utterly disbelieve in the policy of bluff, in national and international no less than in private affairs, or in any violation of the old frontier maxim, 'Never draw unless you mean to shoot.' " To implant American power and prestige throughout the world, Roosevelt sought to expand its navy. When he became president, the navy numbered less than twenty major ships, some still under construction. By 1907 it had grown to rank second in the world to Britain, and remained in the top three on the eve of the Great War in 1914, despite Germany's program of rapid naval expansion. Roosevelt also understood the value of keeping other nations uncertain about the course of action the United States might take in a given situation.

The United States was fortunate during the first decade of the twentieth century in that while growing in strength, it was partly isolated and largely unthreatened by outside forces. Both inside and outside the Western Hemisphere, Americans could indulge in an active foreign policy through the show of force rather than the use of force. And Roosevelt could boast afterward that during his administration the United States mediated to end one war and helped to prevent another while itself remaining at peace.

THE PANAMA CANAL

The Spanish-American War had aroused renewed interest in an isthmian canal by dramatizing the difficulty of moving naval vessels between the Atlantic and the Pacific. The American battleship *Oregon*, for example, had left San Francisco for the Caribbean during the first signs of trouble in 1898, but had to steam around South America and through the Strait of Magellan before completing the 14,000-mile, sixty-eight-day voyage. President McKinley reiterated the importance of a canal in his annual message to Congress in December of that year. With the annexation of Hawaii, the "construction of such a maritime highway is now more than ever indispensable," and "our national policy now more imperatively than ever calls for its control by this Government." A French corporation, the New Panama Canal Company, had taken over the bankrupt de Lesseps business along with its equipment and its Panama concessions granted by Colombia, and now sought to sell them to the United States— for the exorbitant sum of $109 million.

Immediately after the negotiations ending the Spanish-American War, McKinley instructed his secretary of state, John Hay, to talk with the British ambassador in Washington, Sir Julian Pauncefote, about revising the joint construction and control provisions of the Clayton-Bulwer Treaty of 1850. The two men reached an agreement in February 1900 which allowed America to build and administer a canal but not to fortify it. The Hay-Pauncefote Treaty then fell into the political swirls of that year's presidential campaign, with Democrats denouncing the pact as capitulation to the British and Irish-Americans opposing it as part of the detested rapprochement with Britain. Roosevelt, at that time governor of New York, emphasized that American control of the canal was vital to the Monroe Doctrine and to the nation's security. He told the well-known naval theorist, Alfred T. Mahan, that "I do not see why we should dig the canal if we are not to fortify it." It was better "to have no canal at all than not give us the power to control it in time of war." Roosevelt urged his friend Senator Henry Cabot Lodge and other Republicans to insist upon full American control.

Shortly after Roosevelt became president in September 1901, he called for new negotiations with Britain on the subject. Hay, invited to remain as secretary of state, worked closely with Lodge, while President Roosevelt publicly emphasized the necessity of America's controlling the canal. In November Hay signed a second agreement with Pauncefote which permitted the United States to build the canal and, by tacit understanding, to fortify it as well. The only stipulation in the second Hay-Pauncefote Treaty was that America had to grant access to any nation's commercial or war vessels "on terms of entire equality." The Senate overwhelmingly approved the pact in December. The second Hay-Pauncefote Treaty released the United States from the Clayton-Bulwer pact and further stimulated the Anglo-American rapprochement.

While Hay and Pauncefote were negotiating their treaty, the Walker Isthmian Canal Commission, established during the McKinley administration, completed its two-year study of the most feasible canal route through Central America and with reservations concluded that it lay through Nicaragua. Engineers on the commission thought Nicaragua's rivers too shallow for a major canal, and yet that route was less expensive than one through Panama, partly because it could be a sea-level canal (whereas Panama's could not), but primarily because the New Panama Canal Company was asking too much money for giving up the transit rights secured from Colombia.

The Walker Commission's findings were sufficient to convince only the House of Representatives. In January of 1902 the House overwhelmingly approved the Hepburn bill, which stipulated that the projected isthmian canal would cut through Nicaragua. Yet final approval depended on the Senate, and there the New Panama Canal Company tried to counter the House decision by lowering its demands to $40 million, the sum that the Walker Commission had estimated the company's holdings to be worth. This change, urged by Philippe Bunau-Varilla, former chief engineer for de Lesseps's operation and now a major stockholder in the New Panama Canal Company, would make the total expenditure for the Panama project considerably less than that required for Nicaragua. The French company had hired the prestigious New York attorney William Nelson Cromwell to begin a lobbying campaign in the Senate for Panama. Meanwhile Bunau-Varilla, who could not get along with Cromwell, worked independently to persuade Roosevelt, members of the Walker Commission, and leading Republican senators to change the route from Nicaragua to Panama.

Factors beyond human control also played a part in the Senate's deliberations. A volcano on the Caribbean island of Martinique had erupted and destroyed a city, killing 30,000 people. Less than two weeks later Mt. Momotombo in Nicaragua threatened to do the same. Bunau-Varilla explained how he seized the moment by hurriedly visiting stamp dealers in Washington:

> I was lucky enough to find there ninety stamps, that is, one for every Senator, showing a beautiful volcano belching forth in magnificent eruption. . . .
> I hastened to paste my precious postage stamps on sheets of paper. . . . Below the stamps were written the following words, which told the whole story: "An official witness of the volcanic activity of Nicaragua."

Bunau-Varilla then placed one stamp showing Mt. Momotombo on each senator's desk in the chamber.

Thus for several reasons Congress switched its favor to Panama. The Senate cast support for Panama in the form of an amendment to the Hepburn bill, and when the lower chamber agreed to accept the change, the bill became law with Roosevelt's signature in June 1902. Under the Spooner Amendment the president was to negotiate with Colombia for transit rights through Panama; if unable to secure an arrangement "within a reasonable time and upon reasonable terms," he could turn to Nicaragua.

Once Panama became the designated route, the last obstacle was Colombia. Hay opened negotiations with the Colombian chargé d'affaires in Washington, Tomás Herrán, who unexpectedly demanded higher yearly lease rates than those offered by the United States. When Hay warned that the United States would deal with Nicaragua, Herrán capitulated. In January 1903 he signed a treaty awarding the United States control of a six-mile-wide strip of land connecting the two oceans, for one hundred years, which actually was in perpetuity (forever), for it was renewable at the "sole and absolute option" of the United States. For these concessions Colombia was to receive $10 million at the outset and annual payments of $250,000 to begin in nine years, the estimated time required to build the canal. Less than a week after Herrán signed the treaty, he received a telegram from Bogotá directing him to delay treaty talks until new instructions arrived. But Herrán made no effort to cancel the treaty he had signed; nor did he inform Hay of the importance of the new instructions. The American Senate acted quickly, approving the Hay-Herrán Treaty in March.

The Colombian government, however, rejected the pact, drawing a furious reaction from Roosevelt. The government in Bogotá, as legal sovereign over Panama, denounced the lease in perpetuity as unconstitutional and disapproved of other provisions affecting the canal zone as a violation of Colombian sovereignty; it also wanted more money to refill a treasury depleted by a lengthy civil war. Colombia sought $10 million from the New Panama Canal Company in exchange for its concessions passing to the United States, and it eventually demanded that the United States raise the initial payment to $15 million. The president would have none of this. He angrily told Hay that "those contemptible little creatures in Bogotá ought to understand how much they are jeopardizing things and imperilling their own future." Negotiating with Colombia was like trying to "nail currant jelly to the wall." Its government was guilty of blackmail and robbery.

And yet, Colombia had a case. Panama was a Colombian colony, and Bogotá's leaders were particularly irritated that the Hay-Herrán Treaty barred them from future negotiations over their own territory. Furthermore, the concession cost could pass to the French firm without Colombia receiving a share. Stall tactics seemed the only way out. The concessions to the French company were due to expire in October 1904, and the government in Bogotá could then sell them directly to the United States—perhaps for $40 million. The congress in Bogotá, called together for the first time in years by a regime that needed popular support, denounced the Hay-Herrán Treaty and in August 1903 the Colombian senate unanimously turned it down.

Leaders in Washington became convinced that the Panamanians might resolve the question by winning their independence. The decision in Bogotá had not surprised Roosevelt; Cromwell had talked with him the previous June and then followed the meeting with an assertion in the New York *World* that if Colombia rejected the pact, Panama would move for independence and grant canal rights to the United States. Roosevelt, the story claimed, supported this approach. Since becoming Colombia's possession, the Panamanians had a history of insurrections—over fifty of them, Roosevelt calculated—about one a year. "You don't have to foment a revolution," he remarked. "All you have to do is take your foot off and one will occur." If questions lingered over the justification for earlier revolts, none could arise now. The Hay-Herrán Treaty had conjured up the economic benefits of a canal through Panama, only to be denied by Colombia's greed. After Colombia voted down the Hay-Herrán Treaty, Panamanian and American inhabitants of the small province gathered privately in August. They must gain independence and negotiate another canal treaty—*before* the United States turned to Nicaragua.

Although many details remain unknown, the ensuing Panama revolution was the result of a conspiracy. Numerous private discussions involving Bunau-Varilla and others took place at the Waldorf-Astoria Hotel in New York City. Bunau-Varilla, in fact, referred to room 1162 as "the cradle of the Panama Republic," for while his wife listened and sewed a flag for the new country, he pledged $100,000 for the revolution and worked with the others in formulating plans for a declaration of independence and a constitution. The conspirators soon organized a small revolutionary force in Panama which included members of the Colombian occupation army. But Colombian loyalists could easily crush the revolt unless the United States acted quickly and favorably toward the rebels. The key to America's policy was the Treaty of 1846 with Colombia (then New Granada), for by it the United States had guaranteed Panama's neutrality. Six times before 1903 American soldiers had entered the isthmian area to restore order during insurrections—four times at Colombia's request. Now the Americans could argue that the threat to Panama came from *Colombia*. No one during the 1840s could have envisioned the United States protecting Panama from its proprietor; but the treaty, strictly speaking, did not prohibit such an act.

Suspicions linger over the question of American complicity in the shadowy events leading to the revolution in early November 1903. Bunau-Varilla, in talking with Roosevelt, Hay, and other notables, could not have expected an *unfavorable* reaction to an insurrection. The Frenchman learned from Hay in October, a week after meeting with the president, that American warships were en route to Central America. Estimating their time of arrival in the city of Colón on the Caribbean side of Panama, he cabled his contacts there that the first ship, the U.S.S. *Nashville*, should be in those waters on November 2. In the early evening of the following day the revolt took place. When the Colombian government sent 400 additional soldiers to Colón, the New Panama Canal Company, which owned the railroad necessary for transporting the men to Panama City, managed not to have any cars available. Commander John Hubbard of the *Nashville* then dispatched American sailors to the scene and the Colombian officer in charge, after being separated from his troops by trickery, accepted a bribe from the rebels' leaders and withdrew from the isthmus. Orders had reached Hubbard that day from the Department of State in Washington: "In the interests of peace, make every effort to prevent [Colombian] Government troops at Colón from proceeding to Panama."

The Panamanian revolution was a huge success. At the cost of only two lives (an innocent bystander and a donkey), the rebels that same day placed the Colombian general under arrest, paid the bribed Colombian officials and soldiers in a formal ceremony in Panama City, and established a provisional government. "Quiet prevails," the American consul assured Washington. One of Bunau-Varilla's cohorts, Dr. Manuel Amador Guerrero, became president of the new republic and in a roaring speech attributed his people's freedom to the United States. "President Roosevelt has made good. . . . Long live the Republic of Panama! Long live President Roosevelt!"

Indeed, it appeared that the role of the United States had been vital to Panama's move for independence. Three days after the revolution Roosevelt extended *de facto* recognition to Panama after learning of the overthrow only an hour before. Washington immediately stationed American soldiers in Panama City to prevent attempts by Colombia to regain control. The Roosevelt administration had doubtless been aware of the imminence of revolution. The president, however, repeatedly denied complicity, and Bunau-Varilla assured suspicious inquirers that through the newspapers he had followed the *Nashville*'s route and correctly predicted its arrival time in Colón. Bunau-Varilla is "a very able fellow," Roosevelt asserted, "and it was his business to find out what he thought our Government would do. I have no doubt that he was able to make a very accurate guess, and to advise his people accordingly. In fact," the president added, "he would have been a very dull man had he been unable to make such a guess."

Questions also remain about events following the revolution. After the new republic received recognition from the United States, it appointed Bunau-Varilla as minister plenipotentiary to Washington to negotiate a treaty granting rights to build, fortify, and operate a transoceanic canal. In less than two weeks, the United States signed a treaty with Bunau-Varilla—a non-Panamanian who had secured the ministerial post as part of a deal whereby he put up money for the revolution, and who ultimately persuaded leaders of the new Panamanian republic to approve the pact sight unseen.

The Hay-Bunau-Varilla Treaty of November 18, 1903 was more generous than the Hay-Herrán pact in that it guaranteed the United States a ten-mile-wide strip of land through Panama, which became the canal zone. In addition, the United States received extremely broad powers in the zone. Though Panama retained civil control over Colón and Panama City, the American government secured in perpetuity "all the rights, power and authority within the Zone. . . which the United States would possess and exercise if it were the sovereign of the territory." As would have been the case with Colombia, Panama was to receive $10 million outright and $250,000 a year beginning nine years after the exchange of ratifications. Article I of the treaty stipulated that "the United States guarantees and will maintain the independence of the Republic of Panama." The United States had established a protectorate over Panama. In the meantime $40 million of American money passed into the treasury of the New Panama Canal Company to be distributed to a list of stockholders never made public.

Hay brought pressure upon the Senate for hurried approval, for he worried that two Panamanian representatives en route to Washington might carry treaty stipulations less favorable than those allowed by Bunau-Varilla. Senate Democrats wanted to know more about suspected White House involvement in the Panamanian uprising, but the president, despite the role of the *Nashville*, proclaimed that "no one connected with this Government had any part in preparing, inciting, or encouraging the late revolution." It was difficult to counter this statement without documentation, and on February 23, 1904, the Senate easily approved the treaty. Six hours after Bunau-Varilla signed it, the Panamanians arrived at the train station in Washington. When he showed them the treaty terms, one nearly fainted.

The United States's behavior during the Panamanian affair drew a mixed public reaction. Democrats and many others in the country de-

Panama Canal

U.S.S. Ohio *passing Cucaracha Slide in 1915, shortly after the opening of the Panama Canal in August 1914.* (Library of Congress)

nounced the president, Europeans complained of America's lack of morality, and in succeeding years Latin Americans intensified their opposition to the Panamanian episode as the United States deepened its Caribbean involvement. If Roosevelt's supporters acted for partisan reasons, they defended their policies on a realistic ground: the United States needed a canal.

Roosevelt never shied away from upholding his actions during the Panama manipulations. To Congress in December 1903, he declared that the United States had a "mandate from civilization" to build an isthmian canal. In his *Autobiography*, he recorded that building the Panama Canal was "by far the most important action I took in foreign affairs." All of his administration's policies, he asserted, had been "carried out in accordance with the highest, finest and nicest standards of public and governmental ethics." Yet skepticism existed even among his cabinet members. In one meeting the president turned to Attorney General Philander C. Knox and declared that "it will be just as well for you to give us a formal legal opinion sustaining my action in this whole matter." Knox shrewdly replied: "No, Mr. President, if I were you I would not have any taint of legality about it." On another occasion Roosevelt went through an elaborate defense of his behavior and turned to Secretary of War Elihu Root for his reaction. The elderly man wryly commented: "You have shown that you were accused of seduction and you have conclusively proved that you were guilty of rape."

The Panama Canal story was still not complete. Several years afterward, as the passageway neared the last stages of construction, Roosevelt told a stadium audience in 1911 at the University of California: "I am interested in the Panama Canal because I started it. If I had followed traditional conservative methods I would have submitted a dignified State paper of probably 200 pages to Congress and the debates on it would have been going on yet; but," he proudly asserted, "I took the Canal Zone and let Congress debate; and while the debate goes on the Canal does also." The engineering feat, led by George Goethals, became possible after Dr. William Gorgas brought under control the two greatest obstacles to de Lesseps's effort: yellow fever and malaria. The Panama Canal, fifty miles in length and consisting of a series of locks, opened for use in August 1914. Seven years later, after Roosevelt had died, the United States, partly out of guilt but also because of the discovery of oil in Colombia, sent that government an additional $25 million ("canalimony," according to one critic) as recompense for its loss of Panama. In the meantime the United States expanded its involvement in Caribbean affairs in an effort to safeguard the canal from foreign encroachments.

THE ROOSEVELT COROLLARY

America's interest in an isthmian canal had underlined the importance of Cuba by the turn of the twentieth century. The Teller Amendment of 1898

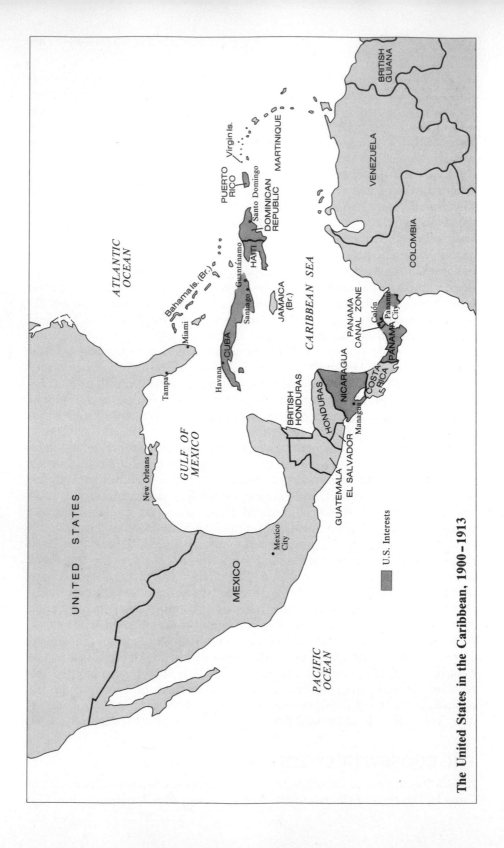

The United States in the Caribbean, 1900–1913

had prohibited its annexation, but the island's location made its independence dangerous because of possible absorption by some other power. President McKinley had warned Congress in December 1899 that Americans had "a grave responsibility for the future good government of Cuba" and that the island had to "be bound to us." The insurrection in the Philippines raised fears in Washington that the same could happen in Cuba. To prevent this, Secretary of War Root appointed General Leonard Wood as military governor of Cuba, charged with the responsibilities of ridding the island of yellow fever, and of instituting an educational program, a public works system, and an orderly government. His efforts were largely unsuccessful, but steps had already been taken toward a more direct American involvement in Cuban affairs.

By early 1901 Root had worked with the chairman of the Senate Foreign Relations Committee, Orville Platt, in drafting a congressional bill establishing an American protectorate over Cuba until that island's government drew up a constitution containing certain stipulations. According to the Platt Amendment, Cuba was nominally free but could not sign a treaty or borrow money without approval from Washington. In the event of internal disorder, the United States could intervene. Finally, Cuba granted the United States "lands necessary for coaling or naval stations." The Platt Amendment became an annex to the new Cuban constitution of 1901 only under Wood's pressure and after Root's assurances that the United States would not intervene unless the Cuban government was in danger. In May 1903 the United States and Cuba formalized the amendment into a treaty, and later that year the American navy built a base at Guantánamo Bay, located near Santiago on the southern side of the island, which the United States was to hold in perpetuity.

The Platt Amendment aroused bitter opposition both inside and outside the United States. While American anti-imperialists revived their arguments against foreign involvement, many Cubans complained that America had merely taken the place of their former Spanish oppressor. President Roosevelt characterized the opposition groups in the United States as "unhung traitors[,] . . . liars, slanderers and scandal mongers," while Root unconvincingly tried to establish a difference between "interventionism" and "interference" with the island's domestic affairs. American intervention, he argued, would occur only to safeguard Cuba's government and preserve the island's independence—*not* to permit interference in internal matters. The United States meanwhile signed the Reciprocity Treaty with Cuba in 1902, which further tied the two peoples together by lowering duties on the island's exports to America.

MAP 17

In the early twentieth century, the United States announced the Roosevelt Corollary of the Monroe Doctrine and sought to "police" Central America and the Caribbean.

In the aftermath of the Platt Amendment the United States repeatedly intervened in Cuba because of the island's internal troubles, and in one period, from 1906 to 1909, it assumed control of the government. Roosevelt opposed annexation but was afraid that continued domestic unrest would force the United States into such a step. He could not understand why the Cubans were unable to "behave themselves." He finally turned to his friend and now secretary of war, William Howard Taft, to resolve the problems on the island. As former civil governor of the Philippines, Taft recognized the importance of settling Cuba's troubles before a full-scale insurrection broke out. He served as provisional governor of Cuba for a month and upon his return home in October 1906, more than 5,000 American soldiers were prepared to implement the reforms called for earlier by General Wood.

The Platt Amendment established a precedent for similar American actions in other parts of the hemisphere and appears to have become the basis of a new Latin American policy by the United States. As early as Roosevelt's first months in office, he seemed to be moving toward a major pronouncement on Latin American affairs that might discourage Old World involvement. Negotiations over Panama and Cuba weighed heavily on his mind when in his first annual message to Congress in December 1901 he asserted that the Monroe Doctrine was "a guarantee of the commercial independence of the Americas." Yet he admitted to limitations on U.S. actions. In a stand similar to that taken by Secretary of State Seward during the European intervention in Mexico during the 1860s, Roosevelt asserted that the United States would "not guarantee any state against punishment if it misconducts itself, provided that punishment does not take the form of the acquisition of territory by any non-American power." Roosevelt appeared to be searching for a middle ground between American interventionism and outright annexation. Like a watchdog, he explained, the United States would oversee Latin America's relations with the Old World.

The first test of Roosevelt's Latin American policy came in Venezuela, where Germany and Britain sought reimbursement of debts long overdue. German intentions in the hemisphere worried Americans more than did those of the British, largely because of the recent rapprochement in Anglo-American relations but also because of recent instances of German expansionism. Kaiser Wilhelm II had tried to improve relations with the United States, but with little success. The Germans called for arbitration of the debt question by the Hague Court, but Venezuelan dictator Cipriano Castro refused. Germany and Britain then notified Washington that they were preparing to use force to collect their money, but at the same time they assured the president that they had no territorial aims. Meeting no opposition from the Roosevelt administration, they issued an ultimatum to Venezuela in December 1902 and proceeded to set up a "pacific blockade" of its main ports. But as tensions mounted, the British shelled two forts and landed troops, and the Germans sank two of Venezuela's gunboats. When American popular reaction stiffened with Germany's additional bombardment of Venezuelan territory, Roosevelt insisted upon arbitration. Germany and Britain agreed to his proposal but maintained the blockade. Castro, called by Roosevelt an "unspeakable villainous little monkey," had deepened European involvement in the hemisphere, endangered the Monroe Doctrine, and forced the United States to intervene.

For reasons not clear in 1902, the Germans had suddenly retreated. Part of the explanation lies in the kaiser's decision to send a new ambassador to Washington, Hermann Speck von Sternburg, who had befriended Roosevelt sometime before and now worked to defuse the dangerous situation. But there is more to the story. In a 1916 reprinting of William R. Thayer's biography of John Hay, the author included a copy of a letter he had recently received from Roosevelt asserting that he had played a major but hidden role in resolving the Venezuelan crisis. As president in 1902, Roosevelt explained in the letter to Thayer, he became alarmed that Germany might establish a base in Venezuela which would endanger an isthmian canal and other American interests. Berlin had at first refused Washington's call for arbitration, according to Roosevelt, and its assurances were not convincing that any seizures of territory would be "temporary." Roosevelt thereupon ordered Admiral George Dewey moved near Puerto Rico and readied for action. If Germany did not agree to arbitration within ten days, Roosevelt told von Sternburg, Dewey would go to Venezuela. The German ambassador expressed "very grave concern," Roosevelt recalled, and warned that such an American action would have "serious consequences." When a week passed with no reply from Berlin, Roosevelt informed the ambassador of a change in plans: Dewey would leave twenty-four hours earlier than previously announced. Germany agreed to arbitration.

Controversy exists over Roosevelt's account of his actions during the Venezuelan crisis of 1902–3. Yet even though critics have argued that he either fabricated or embellished the story, no one can deny that the actions outlined in the letter were well within Roosevelt's character and temperament. Germany did not want a confrontation with the United States and chances are that Roosevelt may have hurried the kaiser into a decision he would have made anyway. The president realized that a German foothold in Venezuela would endanger American interests in the hemisphere; there is little reason to doubt the essence of his testimony.

In February 1903 Germany and Britain lifted the Venezuelan blockade and turned over the claims issue to the Permanent Court of Arbitration at The Hague. The British government had recognized its lack of wisdom in following Germany's lead in Venezuela, and Prime Minister Arthur Balfour had attempted to calm Anglophobes in the United States by renouncing territorial aims in the New World and recognizing the Monroe Doctrine as part of international law. The Hague Court meanwhile decided in favor of Germany and Britain, which drew a concerned reaction in the Western Hemisphere. The Department of State was apprehensive that the decision would encourage the use of force in international disputes and increase the likelihood of European intervention in Latin America. The Argentine minister of foreign affairs, Luis Drago, had opposed the use of force in collecting debts from Venezuela, and in 1902 notified the Roosevelt administration that the loss of investments was a risk business leaders took in any transactions, including those outside their country. The Drago Doctrine, as it became known, was incorporated into international law at the Second Hague Conference of 1907. The United States approved, but added the stipulation that intervention was acceptable only if the debtor nation either refused arbitration or would not abide by its decision.

A second debt problem in the hemisphere, this one in the Dominican Republic, led the Roosevelt administration to issue a formal statement on its Latin American policy. The Dominican government owed nearly $32 million to a host of countries, including Germany and a company in New York holding American and British funds. Over the years the Dominicans had repeatedly assured creditors of remuneration from customs collections, but with no results. Internal disorder had rocked the Dominican Republic since the 1890s, and though some Americans pondered annexation, Roosevelt privately declared, "I have about the same desire to annex it as a gorged boa constrictor might have to swallow a porcupine wrong-end to." Both American and European business leaders exerted pressure on the United States government to act, and though Roosevelt hesitated, he recognized that the Venezuelan arbitration award had established a precedent for the use of force in collecting debts.

Roosevelt prepared to deal with the Dominican situation through a policy later known as the Roosevelt Corollary of the Monroe Doctrine. In May 1904 he indicated the direction of his thinking in a letter to Secretary of War Root, when he pledged American friendship to any nation which acted responsibly in international affairs. He went on to advise Congress in December that the United States had to keep order in the hemisphere. "Chronic wrongdoing may in America, as elsewhere, ultimately require intervention by some civilized nation, and in the Western Hemisphere the adherence of the United States to the Monroe Doctrine may force the United States, however reluctantly, in flagrant cases of such wrongdoing or impotence, to the exercise of an international police power." Later, to the Senate, Roosevelt elaborated on his congressional message. Under the Monroe Doctrine, the United States could not allow any European country to "seize and permanently occupy the territory of one of these republics; and yet such seizure of territory, disguised or undisguised, may eventually offer the only way in which the power in question can collect any debts, unless there is interference on the part of the United States." The president used the situation in the Dominican Republic as the occasion to announce the Roosevelt Corollary, a unilateral statement asserting American police control over the hemisphere.

In December 1904 the United States opened negotiations with the Dominican Republic to resolve the debts controversy. The resulting agreement authorized the New York company to administer the country's customs offices at two ports until the claimants received monetary satisfaction. European creditors immediately objected, causing the Roosevelt administration to worry that its action would set off a race for the remainder of the offices. The Dominican government, as a result of the urgings of the American minister in that country, asked the United States to take over all customs offices and allocate the funds in such a way as to meet the republic's financial obligations at home and abroad. Democrats and others in the United States questioned the constitutionality of such a measure, but Roosevelt sent the proposed agreement to the Senate in January 1905. Under the arrangement, he was to appoint an American to handle receivership duties. Whereas 45 percent of collected funds would go to the Dominicans, most of the remainder would go into a trust fund in a New York bank, reserved for the republic's creditors. Should the Senate oppose the agreement, the balance of the customs revenues would go to the Dominican government as well. The Senate adjourned in March without approving the pact.

Roosevelt was furious and in April 1905 negotiated an executive agreement with the Dominicans which did not require Senate approval and was based upon a *modus vivendi* (temporary arrangement pending final settlement). Though the Democrats called his action unconstitutional, the executive agreement remained in effect until February 1907, when the Senate approved a treaty granting legal standing to the American whom Roosevelt had already sent as customs collector. The Dominicans' creditors scaled down their demands, and the government secured a new bond in the United States to cover the debt and to establish a public works program on the island. Root, by that time secretary of state, defended the pact in the Senate by declaring that the Panama Canal, then under construction, placed Latin American countries "in the front yard of the United States" and forced it "to police the surrounding premises" in the interest of stability and trade.

The Dominican Republic approached economic and political soundness during the following years, but renewed insurrections soon forced the United States to broaden its involvement in the island's affairs. In late 1911 the president of the Dominican Republic was assassinated, and the next year rebels from neighboring Haiti raided and pillaged at will. Customs offices under American control had to shut their doors, and in September 1912 an American commission and several hundred marines arrived to restore order. By December the American force had achieved some stability, but sporadic outbreaks of violence caused Washington to continue military occupation of the island into the early 1920s.

President Taft followed Roosevelt's example in using the Monroe Doctrine as the basis of his Latin American policy, when the United States deepened its influence in Nicaragua through "dollar diplomacy." Defined by Taft as "substituting dollars for bullets," he added that it "appeals alike. . . to idealistic humanitarian sentiments, to the dictates of sound policy and strategy, and to legitimate commercial aims." Under his presidency, American investments and foreign policy became virtually inseparable as the economic and strategic objectives of business and government leaders often ran parallel. When in 1911 the Nicaraguan government threatened to cancel mine concessions to the United States and executed two Americans for aiding an ongoing revolution, the Taft administration sent marines to help bring about a new regime. The Senate in Washington opposed a treaty with Nicaragua that, like a pact negotiated with Honduras that same year (also defeated by the Senate), would have authorized an American loan and placed the United States in charge of customs. But the State Department became party to an agreement involving Nicaragua and various New York banks, which established a receivership similar to that in the Dominican Republic. Another revolution in Nicaragua in late 1912 prompted Washington to send more than 2,000 marines, who put down the insurrection, forced its leaders out of the country, and stationed a small legation guard in the capital of Managua that remained off and on until 1933. Though America's involvement in Nicaragua was primarily to safeguard the areas surrounding the Panama Canal, its policies left a long-standing feeling of distrust in Latin America.

THE ALASKA BOUNDARY

America's diplomatic activities were not confined to the southern half of the hemisphere, for the discovery of gold in the Klondike River area of northwest Canada in 1896 set off a boundary dispute between Alaska and British Columbia that reached dangerous proportions during Roosevelt's presidency. The best route into the area lay through the panhandle of southern Alaska, and the Canadians suddenly argued that the original line in the Anglo-Russian Treaty of 1825, which ran thirty miles inland from the Pacific and became the basis of America's purchase of Alaska over forty years later, did not follow the twisting contours of the coast but moved straight south. If that were correct, the United States would lose commercial control over the Alaskan interior, for Canada would own the headwaters of the larger coves and harbors cutting into North America.

Controversy intensified during the summer of 1898. In June the Canadians claimed the largest bay in the region, the Lynn Canal, which contained three settlements and adjoining harbors (Pyramid, Dyea, and Skagway) providing access to the gold fields as well as connections with the sea. The Canadian government was willing to negotiate, but only if the Americans first accepted its claim to Pyramid Harbor. Secretary of State Hay bitterly condemned the claim: "It is as if a kidnapper, stealing one of your children, should say that his conduct was more than fair, it was even generous, because he left you two."

Hay proposed the establishment of a joint commission to settle the Alaskan boundary dispute, but both nations soon became preoccupied with other more pressing matters. In the meantime the McKinley administration quieted the situation by agreeing to Canada's temporary use of the land at the opening of the Lynn Canal. When Hay recommended the commission approach to Roosevelt shortly after his arrival in the White House, the new president expressed concern that arbitration would lead to a compromise whereby the United States would lose territory that the Canadians had no right to have. In March 1902, however, Roosevelt had to act because rumor was that gold might also be discovered in the disputed territory and force another crisis. To Hay in July, he termed the Canadians' claim "an outrage pure and simple. . . . To pay them anything where they are entitled to nothing would in a case like this come dangerously near blackmail." As tensions mounted in the disputed area, Roosevelt dispatched 800 additional troops to keep order. Late that same year

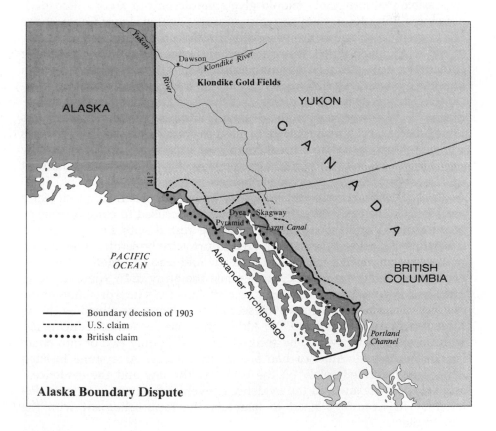

Alaska Boundary Dispute

———— Boundary decision of 1903
----------- U.S. claim
•••••• British claim

MAP 18

President Theodore Roosevelt resorted to a joint commission in settling the dispute, but only after he used various pressures to assure a favorable outcome.

Canada retreated from its demands, indicating that its only concern now was to save face. If the United States agreed to arbitration, the Canadians would accept a decision roughly corresponding with the American position. Canada had no choice. British leaders in London were worried that the Alaskan issue might endanger the Anglo-American rapprochement. British Foreign Secretary Lord Henry Lansdowne expressed the general feeling among his countrymen: "America seems to be our only friend just now, and it would be unfortunate to quarrel with her."

In late January 1903 Britain agreed to Hay's joint-commission proposal. The resulting Convention of 1903 called for "six impartial jurists," three American and three British, to comprise an Alaskan Boundary Tribunal which would gather in London and settle the matter by majority vote. Little imagination was needed to predict the outcome. "In this case," Hay remarked, "it is impossible that we should lose, and not at all impossible that a majority should give a verdict in our favor." Roosevelt appointed Elihu Root, then secretary of war, Senator Henry Cabot Lodge of Massachusetts, and a former senator from Washington, George Turner. None of the men fitted the category of "impartial jurists"; but their choices were politically important because their support for the American boundary claims was well known. The British king appointed a commission consisting of two Canadians and the lord chief justice of England, Richard E. W. Alverstone. Both Alverstone and his Canadian companions understood that the maintenance of good relations with the United States was more important than a breakdown over Alaska's boundary. But they also knew that failure to gain something in the proceedings would pit them against an angry populace at home.

In late 1903 the Alaskan Boundary Tribunal met in London. After weeks of bitter discussions the two Canadians refused to compromise, as did the three Americans, and the outcome rested with England's Lord Alverstone. Roosevelt meanwhile exerted pressure by letting it be known that a decision against the United States would lead to American military occupation of the disputed territory while the army drew the boundary. The London government decided to accept America's interpretation of the line. Despite Canada's threats of secession, Alverstone voted with the three Americans in October 1903. Although he succeeded in reducing the width of the coastal award, he secured for Canada only two of four small islands in dispute. America had a clear-cut victory. Alverstone insisted that he had decided solely on the basis of "the law and the evidence," and yet if so, the law and the evidence conveniently fitted a decision dictated by his country's need to maintain the rapprochement with the United States.

THE FAR EAST

America's attention had in the meantime turned toward the Far East, where growing problems would lead to the Russo-Japanese War of 1904–5. China remained a major concern, for outside powers had expanded their claims in disregard of the Open Door declarations of 1899 and 1900. Russia had joined European powers in obstructing Japan's attempt in 1895 to secure a lease on the Liaotung Peninsula in southern Manchuria, and had refused to withdraw its soldiers from Manchuria after the Boxer Rebellion of 1900. The Russians were now building a railway through northern Manchuria and into Vladivostok, their major port in north Pacific waters, and had won the right to construct and control another railroad connecting Harbin with Port Arthur in the south, where they would soon have a naval base, and at Dairen. These advances into Manchuria threatened Japan's interests both there and in Korea, the latter traditionally regarded as "a dagger pointed at the heart of Japan." The Japanese had extended control over Korea since the end of the Sino-Japanese War in 1895, and they had negotiated an alliance with England in 1902 admitting to each party's special interests in China. What was more important, in exchange for Japan's support of Britain in Europe, the British recognized Japan's political, commercial, and industrial concerns in Korea. The Anglo-Japanese Alliance offered Japan some guarantee that war with Russia would not necessarily lead to France's intervention in behalf of its Russian ally. After Japan failed to negotiate a favorable settlement with Russia over Manchuria and Korea, the Japanese navy launched a surprise attack on Port Arthur in February 1904 which wiped out the Russian fleet. Two days later Japan declared war.

The American people initially joined the Roosevelt administration in praising the Japanese in their war with Russia. "Was not the way the Japs began the fight bully?", remarked Elihu Root. Roosevelt wrote his son less than a week after the Port Arthur attack that "I was thoroughly pleased with the Japanese victory for Japan is playing our game" in trying to halt the Russians. The government in Washington of course maintained official neutrality, but it favored Japan out of expectations that Tokyo would respect the Open Door in China. The president's distaste for Russian leadership and supposed backwardness was as well known as his favor for Japan's industriousness and efficiency. He was determined that France, Russia's ally, and Germany, which supported Russia in the Far East, would not deny Japan the spoils of war. Roosevelt realized that the outcome of the Russo-Japanese War would determine the balance of power in that part of the world and hence affect American interests—particularly in the Philippines and China.

Russia was irate over America's reaction to the war. The Russians were not aware of the change in attitude in the United States brought by their expansionist policies in the Far East, and by their harsh treatment of Jews and political opponents at home. Roosevelt privately considered Czar Nicholas II "a preposterous little creature," yet dangerous because he could close Manchuria to the outside world. Japan, Roosevelt believed, might preserve the Open Door and safeguard American interests. Gradually, however, this hope disappeared as Japan unexpectedly and overwhelmingly won the war by 1905 and soon loomed as a new danger on the Pacific horizon.

The Russo-Japanese War of 1904–5 was expensive, even to the victorious Japanese—so much so that their minister in Washington, Kogoro Takahira, privately asked Roosevelt in the spring of 1905 to intervene and bring the warring powers to the peace table. Russia could not sustain the war because of growing internal problems that would culminate in revolution during the autumn of that same year, and because of pressure from France, which was more concerned about a concurrent crisis with Germany over Morocco than about Russia's plight in the Far East. Roosevelt's condition for intervention was a guarantee for the Open Door policy, which Japan gave but Russia did not. Roosevelt recognized the important role thrust upon him: if he played the balance-of-power game correctly, he might keep the advantage from shifting too far toward Tokyo and thereby preserve America's interests in that part of the world.

Peace talks began on an American naval base in Portsmouth, New Hampshire during August 1905, and only after considerable difficulty did Roosevelt manage a settlement. Japan demanded that Russia give up the Liaotung Peninsula and the South Manchurian Railroad from Harbin to Port Arthur, pull out of Manchuria, recognize Japanese hegemony in Korea and on Sakhalin Island off the north Chinese mainland, and pay $600 million in reparations. The discussions stalemated when Russia refused to relinquish Sakhalin and turned down the reparations demand. Roosevelt feared that Nicholas would rather resume the war than yield to Japan, and sought a compromise calling for Russia to receive the northern half of Sakhalin and Japan the rest, and for the two powers to agree "in principle" to a reparations bill. The czar accepted the first part of the plan, but still refused to pay war damages. Japan eventually complied. Resumption of the war, it realized, would cancel the worth of an indemnity, cause permanent injury at home, and therefore cost more than peace. Japan also discerned a change in American public opinion. Whether due to the demands and seeming arrogance of the Japanese delegates at Portsmouth, or to the Russians' repeated warnings that Japan was the real threat to peace, Americans' ardor for the Japanese had cooled.

The antagonists came to terms with the Treaty of Portsmouth on September 5. Japan regained what it had lost in the war with China in 1894–95: the Liaotung Peninsula, which was the site of Port Arthur, Dairen, and the South Manchurian Railroad. Russia also recognized Japan's special interests in Korea and south Sakhalin. Manchuria returned to China's civil jurisdiction and all Japanese and Russian soldiers were to withdraw except those needed to guard the railroad. Russia remained a prominent force in Asia by retaining the northern half of Sakhalin and the Chinese Eastern Railway in upper Manchuria, but Japan emerged from the Russo-Japanese War as the dominant power in the Far East.

The results of the Portsmouth Conference were mixed. America's relations hardened with both Russia and Japan. Whereas the Russians claimed they could have won the war had America not intervened, the Japanese people, heavily burdened by taxation, blamed their government and that of the United States for failing to win an indemnity and other concessions. Violent anti-government and anti-American demonstrations broke out in Tokyo and other cities. In February 1906 the United States protested commercial discrimination in Japanese-controlled areas in Manchuria; the Japanese, it became clear, had no intentions of respecting the Open Door. While Japanese-American relations deteriorated, Roosevelt accepted the Nobel Peace Prize in 1906 for his efforts at Portsmouth (and for his role in settling the Moroccan dispute, as discussed later).

Another outgrowth of the Russo-Japanese War was the Taft-Katsura "agreed memorandum" of late July 1905. A year earlier Roosevelt had agreed to recognize Japan's special interests in Korea, and in mid-summer of the following year Secretary of War Taft, en route to the Philippines, repeated the assurance in a conversation in Tokyo with Prime Minister Taro Katsura. Japan's ongoing conquests in the war with Russia during the spring of 1905 had caused concern in Washington over the Philippines, and through this informal understanding the United States agreed to drop claims to Korea in exchange for Japan's renunciation of "any aggressive designs whatever" on the islands. Roosevelt approved the memorandum, and within a year the United States closed its legation at Seoul and conducted Korean business through the government in Tokyo.

The Taft-Katsura understanding marked a retreat on the Open Door, but America had no choice. Root explained years afterward that "all we might have done was to make threats which we could not carry out." Such a move would have violated one of Roosevelt's maxims: "I never take a step in foreign policy unless I am assured that I shall be able eventually to carry out my will by force."

Americans were soon to perceive Japan as a threat to their interests at home and abroad. By 1905 about 100,000 Japanese were in the United States, mostly along the west coast, where their presence reminded Californians of recent troubles with the Chinese. Congress had stopped Chinese immigration into the United States during the 1880s, but had not extended the measure to include the Japanese. In 1900 the government in Tokyo had prohibited its laborers from entering the United States, but this ruling was easy to circumvent as Japanese immigrants continued in through Hawaii, Mexico, and Canada. California became the focal point of Japanese immigration, and whether for racial or economic reasons (or both), the state's inhabitants protested that Orientals were undermining the economy by working for lower wages than whites would accept. Japan's recent victory over Russia and the inflammatory articles in the American press stirred a hotbed of emotions over an alleged "yellow peril" that only needed a catalyst to set off trouble.

That catalyst came in October 1906, when the school board in San Francisco restricted the city's ninety-three Japanese children to an Oriental Public School already attended by Chinese and Korean youths. This decision, weakly based on the arguments that the Japanese youths were overaged and were overcrowding the classrooms, drew strong complaints from Tokyo, which felt humiliated by the treatment of its people as racial inferiors.

Roosevelt immediately detected a threat to his foreign policy. Though also concerned about the vast influx of Japanese into the United States, he feared that ill feeling over the school situation might affect relations with Japan and thus endanger America's interests in the Philippines and Hawaii. Roosevelt publicly denounced the school board's decision as a "wicked absurdity" while trying to bring pressure on what he called the "idiots of the California legislature" to halt their racially discriminatory policies. He also recommended that Congress enact laws naturalizing those Japanese who had made America their permanent home. But when he waved the big stick, he drew only the wrath of Californians.

The president lacked the constitutional power to act in this state matter, and he again resorted to personal diplomacy. He arranged for the transportation of San Francisco's mayor and entire school board to Washington, where he discussed the matter with them in the Oval Office. There, in February 1907, the president convinced the school board to withdraw the segregation order in exchange for his promise to halt the flow of Japanese into the United States. Through a series of diplomatic notes in late 1907 and early 1908, he secured an informal "gentlemen's agreement" with Japan whereby its government voluntarily restricted the immigration of laborers into the continental United States, and approved an American policy prohibiting their indirect entrance through Hawaii, Mexico, and Canada. Again, to avoid political wrangling in the Senate, the president implemented the arrangement through executive order.

Roosevelt recognized the possibility of future problems with Japan in the Pacific and decided to send the American fleet on a world cruise to demonstrate its strength, allow crew members to gain firsthand experience at sea, and encourage Congress to appropriate money for a larger navy. In July 1907 the administration announced that the "Great White Fleet"—sixteen battleships and their escorts—would leave the Atlantic for a practice cruise around the world. East Coast Americans complained about being left defenseless, and the chairman of the Senate Committee on Naval Affairs notified Roosevelt that no funds were available. The president crisply replied that he had enough finances on hand to move the navy to the Pacific, and that if Congress wanted to leave the ships there, that was its decision. Congress allotted the money. When European and American newspapers warned of war with Japan, Roosevelt sent Taft to Tokyo, who soon secured that government's assurances of peace. In December the fleet steamed out of Hampton Roads and around Cape Horn, arriving in Lower California and preparing to cross the Pacific and honor invitations from Japan, Australia, and other countries. The Japanese, perhaps wanting a closer view of America's naval power, welcomed the men from the ships with throngs of youths along the roadsides waving small American flags and singing the National Anthem in English. After a three-day visit in Japan, the American fleet departed, making its way through the Suez Canal, European waters, and the Atlantic before returning home safely and without incident in February 1909.

The cruise has drawn a mixed assessment. The president proclaimed it "the most important service that I rendered to peace." And evidence does suggest that the Tokyo visit cleared the air between the nations. Yet a rise in naval armaments programs took place in Japan, Germany, and other countries—perhaps partly in response to the cruise. In the spring of 1908 the U.S. Congress approved the construction of additional battleships. The cruise also demonstrated America's need for Pacific naval bases near Asia, especially to enhance the security of the Philippines.

The visit of the American fleet to Tokyo probably stimulated the Root-Takahira agreement of November 1908. More than a year before, the Japanese ambassador in Washington had on his own initiative recommended that the two countries smooth relations by recognizing both the status quo in the Pacific and the Open Door in China. But the government in Tokyo was not ready for such a pact and called its emissary home for acting without authorization. In 1908, on the day of the American fleet's departure from Japan, Tokyo changed its mind and instructed the new ambassador, Kogoro Takahira, to propose the same sort of arrangement to Secretary of State Root. The Root-Takahira agreement assured the status quo in the Pacific, which was a tacit admission to Japan's dominance in Korea and Manchuria and hence a violation of the Open Door, but at the same time it guaranteed American interests in the Philippines. The agreement also called on each signatory to preserve "by all pacific means" the "independence and integrity of China and the principle of equal opportunity for commerce and industry of all nations in that Empire."

Controversy developed over the measure shortly after Roosevelt likewise enacted it through executive agreement. China was irritated at not having participated in the negotiations. The interested European powers approved the agreement only because the Far East seemed left open for exploitation. Americans praised it for safeguarding the Open Door in China and their own control over the Philippines, whereas the Japanese were pleased because respect for the status quo meant their continued economic control over Manchuria. Yet many Americans were concerned that the agreement only implicitly won Japan's assurances against interfering with America's interests in the Philippines and Hawaii—and at the huge cost of accepting Japan's deepening entrenchment in Manchuria.

If Root left questions about the sanctity of the Open Door, it was because Roosevelt realized that the United States lacked the military strength to stop Japanese expansion in China. He later explained to Taft, then president, that "if the Japanese choose to follow a course of conduct [in Manchuria] to which we are adverse, we cannot stop it unless we are prepared to go to war, and a successful war about Manchuria would require a fleet as good as that of England, plus an army as good as that of Germany." The Open Door "completely disappears as soon as a powerful nation determines to disregard it."

Taft did not fare as well as his predecessor did in Asian affairs. He followed "dollar diplomacy" in China as he had done in Latin America, but before his presidency was over his Asian policies proved disillusioning to the Chinese and threatening to Japan. Whereas Roosevelt had recognized power realities and tried to mollify the Japanese through concessions disguised as treaties, Taft and his secretary of state, Philander C. Knox, attempted to use American investments to undercut outside influence in China. Shortly after Taft's arrival in the White House, he demanded that the Chinese government allow American banking interests to participate in a consortium (international association of banking interests) with England, France, and Germany, which would arrange a loan enabling China either to buy the Manchurian railroads from Russia and Japan, or to build competing railways and drive the others into bankruptcy. Such a so-called neutralization scheme posed a direct challenge to Japan's interests. But continued unrest in China made the Manchurian venture too risky for American bankers. Taft's Asian policies succeeded only in driving Russia and Japan closer together, and by the time he left office four years later, the Open Door in China, both in the commercial and territorial sense, was nearly shut.

THE ALGECIRAS CONFERENCE

One last matter illustrated Roosevelt's belief that America's interests reached beyond the Western Hemisphere: his decision to mediate the Franco-German crisis of 1905 over Morocco. The year before, France had approved British claims in Egypt for reciprocal recognition of its rights in the North African country of Morocco. The Germans decided to test the Anglo-French Entente, or understanding. With France's ally Russia at war with Japan, Kaiser Wilhelm II arrived in the Moroccan capital of Tangier in March 1905 and delivered a belligerent speech praising the sultan as "an absolutely independent sovereign" and demanding German rights in that country. The French turned him down and war seemed imminent. Though the British prepared to support the French, the premier in Paris warned that his country was not prepared for war and could not depend on Russian assistance. The cabinet forced a change in the foreign ministry, and France moved to conciliate the Germans.

The government in Berlin asked Roosevelt to call a meeting of the three interested powers to resolve the Moroccan question. Roosevelt agreed, though reluctantly, because he recognized that a European war would affect everyone, including the United States. The French were also wary about a conference in which they could gain nothing and probably would *lose* territory in a predictable compromise solution. Roosevelt finally convinced them to attend. In the meantime Wilhelm offered assurances that in case of serious disagreements at the conference, he would accept whatever decision Roosevelt considered fair. Roosevelt justified his decision to intervene on the basis of a commercial convention in 1880 that

America signed in Madrid affecting Morocco, and on his desire to prevent the country's partition and preserve the principle of the Open Door. Realizing the opportunity to reset the European balance of power, Roosevelt agreed to send representatives to a conference in the small Spanish coastal town of Algeciras, located near Gibraltar.

The Algeciras Conference opened in January 1906 and closed with a treaty in April. Henry White, ambassador to Italy and ranking member of the American delegation, managed to reconcile the disagreements between the opposing parties without capitulating to Germany's demand for Morocco's partition. By the General Act of Algeciras, Morocco's territorial integrity remained intact, although France and Spain won the right to establish controls over that country's police force. Germany had suffered a severe defeat—and not only at the treaty table. The crisis drove France and England closer together, and convinced many Americans that the government in Berlin wanted war.

Roosevelt later claimed to have been highly instrumental in resolving the crisis. When the Germans opposed French and Spanish control over the Moroccan police force, Wilhelm gave in only after being reminded of his promise to abide by the president's decisions. To soothe the German emperor, Roosevelt asserted that he had flattered him with the "sincerest felicitation" on his policy that had been "masterly from beginning to end." To a friend Roosevelt boasted, "You will notice that while I was most suave and pleasant with the Emperor, yet when it became necessary at the end I stood him on his head with great decision." As mentioned earlier, Roosevelt soon received the Nobel Peace Prize for his roles at Algeciras and Portsmouth.

Americans generally praised Roosevelt's efforts in the success of the Algeciras Conference, although they warned that involvement by the United States did not signal a break with traditional isolationism from European political affairs. The Senate approved the pact in December 1906, but only after attaching an amendment reiterating opposition to Old World entanglements. A number of Americans insisted that their country's security was too much to risk for guaranteeing the sanctity of a North African state neither commercially nor strategically important to the United States. Yet Roosevelt's participation in the Algeciras proceedings was a warning to the Old World that the United States was prepared to make decisions affecting the balance of power outside the Western Hemisphere.

Theodore Roosevelt sought to promote the national interest by introducing the United States to a new and more assertive style of foreign policy. In the Western Hemisphere, he sought to safeguard the American interest by building the Panama Canal and by claiming the right of intervention in Latin American affairs through the Roosevelt Corollary. Outside the hemisphere, his achievements had been less specific. Yet Roosevelt had displayed an understanding of the intricacies of balance-of-power relationships, both on the continent of Europe and in regard to the way European matters affected the Far East and hence the world power system. Two times he mediated international disputes in a manner peculiar for a country built on a tradition of isolationism. Three times he bypassed the Senate in negotiating treaties through executive agreement. The American people remained reluctant to become involved in international politics, but Roosevelt made great advances in shaping a national mood more receptive to big-power status.

Selected Readings

Beale, Howard K., *Theodore Roosevelt and the Rise of America to World Power*. 1956.

Blum, John M., *The Republican Roosevelt*. 1954.

Burton, David H., *Theodore Roosevelt: Confident Imperialist*. 1968.

Campbell, Alexander E., *Great Britain and the United States, 1895–1903*. 1960.

Campbell, Charles S., *Anglo-American Understanding, 1898–1903*. 1957.

Chessman, G. Wallace, *Theodore Roosevelt and the Politics of Power*. 1969.

Coletta, Paolo E., *The Presidency of William Howard Taft*. 1973.

Collin, Richard H., *Theodore Roosevelt, Culture, Diplomacy, and Expansion: A New View of American Imperialism*. 1985.

Cooper, John M., Jr., *The Warrior and the Priest: Woodrow Wilson and Theodore Roosevelt*. 1983.

Daniels, Roger, *The Politics of Prejudice: The Anti-Japanese Movement in California and the Struggle for Japanese Exclusion*. 1962.

Davis, Calvin D., *The United States and the First Hague Peace Conference*. 1962.

——, *The United States and the Second Hague Peace Conference: American Diplomacy and International Organization, 1899–1914*. 1976.

Dennett, Tyler, *John Hay*. 1933.

Esthus, Raymond A., *Theodore Roosevelt and Japan*. 1966.

——, *Theodore Roosevelt and the International Rivalries*. 1970.

Griswold, A. Whitney, *The Far Eastern Policy of the United States*. 1938.

Harbaugh, William H., *The Life and Times of Theodore Roosevelt*. 1975 ed.

Hart, Robert A., *The Great White Fleet: Its Voyage around the World, 1907–1909*. 1965.

Healy, David F., *The United States in Cuba, 1898–1902*. 1963.

Hunt, Michael H., *The Making of a Special Relationship: The United States and China to 1914*. 1983.

Iriye, Akira, *Across the Pacific*. 1967.

——, *Pacific Estrangement: Japanese and American Expansion, 1897–1911*. 1972.

LaFeber, Walter, *The Panama Canal: The Crisis in Historical Perspective*. 1979 ed.

Leopold, Richard W., *Elihu Root and the Conservative Tradition*. 1954.

Marks, Frederick W., *Velvet on Iron: The Diplomacy of Theodore Roosevelt*. 1979.

McCullough, David G., *The Path Between the Seas: The Creation of the Panama Canal, 1870–1914*. 1977.

McKee, Delber L., *Chinese Exclusion versus the Open Door Policy, 1900–1906*. 1976.

Millett, Allan R., *The Politics of Intervention: The Military Occupation of Cuba, 1906–1909*. 1968.

Miner, Dwight C., *The Fight for the Panama Route*. 1940.

Munro, Dana G., *Intervention and Dollar Diplomacy in the Caribbean, 1900–1921*. 1964.

Neu, Charles E., *An Uncertain Friendship: Theodore Roosevelt and Japan, 1906–1909*. 1967.

——, *The Troubled Encounter: The United States and Japan*. 1975.

Ninkovich, Frank, "Theodore Roosevelt: Civilization as Ideology," *Diplomatic History* 10 (1986): 221–45.

Penlington, Norman, *The Alaska Boundary Dispute: A Critical Reappraisal*. 1973.

Perkins, Bradford, *The Great Rapprochement: England and the United States, 1895–1914*. 1968.

Perkins, Dexter, *The Monroe Doctrine, 1867–1907*. 1937.

Pratt, Julius W., *America's Colonial Experiment*. 1950.

——, *America and World Leadership, 1900–1921*. 1967. Originally published as *Challenge and Rejection*. 1967.

Pringle, Henry F., *Theodore Roosevelt*. 1931.

Scholes, Walter V. and Marie V., *The Foreign Policies of the Taft Administration*. 1970.

Tompkins, E. Berkeley, *Anti-Imperialism in the United States: The Great Debate, 1890–1920*. 1970.

Trani, Eugene P., *The Treaty of Portsmouth*. 1969.

Varg, Paul A., *The Making of a Myth: The United States and China, 1897–1912*. 1968.

Vevier, Charles, *The United States and China, 1906–1913*. 1955.

Chapter Thirteen

Woodrow Wilson and the Diplomacy of Idealism: Prologue to Entry into World War I, 1913–1917

The United States took a sharp turn toward the diplomacy of idealism during the two presidential terms of Woodrow Wilson. His administration led America into a world war that Wilson called a crusade for democracy. A military interventionist episode in Russia in 1918–20 assumed political overtones. Problems resulted from the breakup of colonial empires and the place of new nations in the postwar world, and from the search for an effective world peace organization—controversies which were repeated reminders of the constant strain between idealism and realism. At first the president attempted to reconcile the two, but he ultimately became irrevocably committed to idealistic objectives, a path which allowed him no room for compromise.

Critics have found hypocrisy in Wilson's sense of missionary diplomacy; other observers have noted a sincere struggle to impose his ideals onto the realities around him. Wilson was born the son of a Presbyterian minister in Virginia just before the Civil War, and hated war almost to the point of being a pacifist. He earned his Ph.D. in political science at Johns Hopkins University, authored numerous books, and became president of Princeton University and then governor of New Jersey before winning the White House in 1912. Wilson's Democratic administration ended sixteen years of a Republican-controlled presidency, and he looked forward to achieving domestic goals under his New Freedom program; it would be ironic, he asserted, if foreign affairs occupied his time in office. Cold,

Woodrow Wilson and William Howard Taft

At Wilson's inauguration in March 1913. (Library of Congress)

aloof, a moralist, an egotist, and a Calvinist—these qualities combined to persuade Wilson that providence had reserved a place in history for the United States, and that he as president was responsible for ensuring the fulfillment of democratic objectives. Theodore Roosevelt shared similar beliefs in America's superiority, but Wilson went farther than carrying a stick and hoping others would follow; he *wielded* the stick and, like the Spanish conquistadors, he brought both spiritual teachings and a sword. In Latin America and Europe, he believed his mission was to spread democracy—sometimes with the aid of U.S. marines.

RENUNCIATION OF DOLLAR DIPLOMACY IN ASIA AND LATIN AMERICA

Wilson's objective in foreign affairs was to break with his predecessor's policy of "dollar diplomacy." He reflected the Progressive reform spirit of the times when, a week after his inauguration, he publicly expressed opposition to special interest groups. He also criticized upheavals in Latin America as dangerous to the hemisphere. Wilson's statements attracted considerable attention because he released them to the press rather than through the Department of State. His views also won particular repute because of the efforts of his secretary of state, William Jennings Bryan, who had won the position as a political plum for his longtime service to the Democratic party. Bryan was a fundamentalist and a strong advocate of peace whose ideas fitted those of Wilson's during the early days of the administration. He was nonetheless a figurehead in the State Department, for Wilson controlled foreign affairs, even to hammering out dispatches on his own typewriter. But before Bryan resigned after only two years as secretary of state, he worked hard to promote world peace through conciliation or "cooling-off" treaties. Whereas Taft sought to substitute dollars for bullets, Wilson and Bryan intended to replace money with morals.

The Wilson administration wavered in its efforts to end dollar diplomacy in China. The new president again resorted to the newspapers in alleging that American loans violated China's "administrative independence" and encouraged outside interference in its affairs. His refusal to endorse China's financial proposals was welcome news to American investors, for it freed them from a failing enterprise. Yet Wilson was worried that America's economic withdrawal would endanger the Open Door by leaving China for Japan. In 1920 he reversed his stand and placed pressure on mystified American bankers to join a four-power consortium in China, which by that time could do little to slow Japan's economic penetration.

America's relations with Japan were uncertain upon Wilson's ascension to the presidency. Californians feared the "yellow peril" so much that their Republican-dominated legislature had considered prohibiting the Japanese from owning agricultural land. When the Democrats won the White House in 1913, the central obstacle to the measure, party loyalty, was gone, and the Republicans in California prepared such a bill. Wilson urged them to reconsider because of the probable international impact; mass demonstrations against the proposal had already taken place in Japan. But the bill was a concern of the state and he could do no more because of restrictions inherent in the federal system of government. Avoiding a direct reference to the Japanese, California enacted a law barring land ownership by aliens ineligible for citizenship, even though Bryan had visited the state's capital in April 1913 and urged the governor and legislators not to do so. Despite talk of war in both Japan and the United States, the crisis passed when Bryan convinced the Japanese ambassador in Washington that California's actions did not reflect a national policy of discrimination.

The Great War beginning in Europe during August 1914 provided an opportunity for Japan to expand influence in China. During the following January, after Japan had entered the conflict on the side of the Allies and seized German holdings in Asia and the Pacific, the government in Tokyo secretly made "Twenty-one Demands" on China, which if accepted would have converted the country into a Japanese protectorate. The Peking government leaked the demands to Washington, whereupon the United States warned the Japanese of its opposition to the use of force in

China. Tokyo retreated from its most extreme claims, although China soon agreed to most of the others. Two years later, in 1917, America's entry into the war encouraged Japan to seek additional concessions in China. When Britain and France sent missions to the United States in the spring of that year to discuss the war effort, Tokyo ordered a special emissary, Viscount Kikujiro Ishii, to persuade the new secretary of state, Robert Lansing, to recognize Japan's interests in China. In November 1917 Japan and the United States signed the Lansing-Ishii Agreement, which allowed China to retain its "territorial sovereignty" in exchange for America's admission to Japan's "special interests" in China. Lansing interpreted these interests as economic and growing out of geographical contiguity or proximity; the Japanese read them as "paramount" and hence considered themselves under no restrictions as to definition. Though the Chinese protested, the agreement had the important effect of calming relations between Japan and the United States.

The Wilson administration's major efforts toward eliminating dollar diplomacy took place within the Western Hemisphere. America's concern over Latin America had increased with the imminent completion of the Panama Canal. Respect for the Monroe Doctrine was vital, the president emphasized, as was the welfare of Latin American people victimized by oppressive regimes. Before Wilson left the White House, the United States had purchased the Danish West Indies and expanded its involvement in Panama, Nicaragua, Haiti, the Dominican Republic, and Mexico. In numerous instances marines occupied countries, partly to impose democracy through the establishment of "protectorates," but also to promote America's economic and strategic concerns in the Caribbean.

The Taft administration had left its successor a major problem in Central America: the Panama Canal Tolls Act of 1912, which established regulations for the waterway but exempted American intrastate shippers from toll exactions. American businesses dispatching goods between Atlantic and Pacific coastal cities would not have to pay for using the canal. Wilson's antitrust stand might have influenced his initial support for the act, for the huge transcontinental railroads would have to scale down rates to counter the wider competition from smaller shipping lines; but he came to realize that the toll measure threatened the Anglo-American rapprochement by violating the Hay-Pauncefote Treaty with England. That pact of 1901 contained assurances that all nations would pay the same charges. The Taft administration, however, had argued that the treaty meant nations *other* than the United States, and that the tolls clause fitted America's long-standing prohibitions against foreign shippers participating in its coastal trade. Others flatly asserted that the nation building the canal should enjoy special privileges.

The British protested the Tolls Act as a breach of faith. The United States, they asserted, had violated the treaty of 1901 and now expected other nations to make up the financial difference in the amounts not paid by American shippers. Arbitration was the only way out, they insisted.

The Senate in Washington, however, refused to approve the suggestion. America's ambassador to London, Walter Hines Page, warned the White House that the English people considered America's stand "dishonorable" and that he found it difficult to refute the charge. "We made a bargain—a solemn compact—and we have broken it," Page declared. "Whether it were a good bargain or a bad one, a silly one or a wise one; that's far from the point."

Wilson dropped his support for the exemption clause when relations with England seemed endangered and America's honor came into question. In March 1914 he appeared before Congress and called for repeal of the measure. The United States, he declared, was "too big, too powerful, too self-respecting a Nation to interpret with too strained or refined a reading the words of our own promises just because we have power enough to give us leave to read them as we please." Wilson may have hoped that removal of the exemption clause might elevate the United States into a position of moral leadership in the world; the act might also persuade the British to follow his policy in Mexico (discussed later). After heated debates in the Senate, Congress approved his request in June 1914 but reserved the right to restore the exemption clause at any time. The president's action had maintained national honor while encouraging the rapprochement with Britain.

As the Panama Canal approached its opening in August 1914, Americans became increasingly anxious lest another nation build a competing waterway through Nicaragua. A few weeks before Wilson's inauguration, the Taft administration had begun negotiations with that country, intending to gain perpetual and exclusive rights to construct a canal, and a ninety-nine-year lease on two strategic islands for the purpose of building naval bases. For these concessions the United States was to pay $3 million, which Nicaragua would use to reimburse American bankers for past loans. The Senate in Washington, however, refused to approve the pact because it was an overcommitment of American policy. Though the new president was inclined to oppose this agreement as another instance of dollar diplomacy, he could not deny its benefits. Bryan therefore concluded the negotiations and in February 1916 signed the pact with the Nicaraguan minister in Washington, Emiliano Chamorro. The Bryan-Chamorro Treaty bolstered Nicaragua's finances and was expected to help the United States ward off suspected European interests in the isthmus; but it also caused consternation in Costa Rica, El Salvador, and Honduras, whose leaders complained that Nicaragua had permitted concessions belonging to them. The recently established Central American Court of Justice heard their case and decided in their favor, only to have Nicaragua and the United States ignore the ruling. As in the Taft administration, Wilson approved American control over Nicaragua's finances and maintained a small contingent of marines to enforce policy. America's protectorate over Nicaragua lasted until 1933.

Haiti also became a major concern of the United States after the outbreak of war in Europe in 1914. European investments in Haiti were high, causing Americans to fear that domestic trouble in the Caribbean country would lead to foreign intervention. Haiti usually kept up interest payments on debts, but by the early 1900s recurring unrest undercut the already weak financial structure and led to default. Americans were worried that Germany might seize Haiti's harbor of Môle Saint Nicolas and threaten the Panama Canal. When France and Germany sent soldiers to restore order, the Wilson administration became concerned that their stay might become permanent.

The president also feared that continued troubles in Haiti could encourage the ongoing insurrection in its Dominican neighbor, and he prepared to follow Roosevelt's earlier policies in the Caribbean. The United States requested permission from the Haitian government to send an adviser on financial affairs and to establish a customs receivership. It also wanted to oversee elections and to receive assurances that Môle Saint Nicolas would not pass to another government. These moves met such savage opposition from the Haitians that by late July of 1915 the United States had to send more than 2,000 marines to restore order. The State Department meanwhile drew up a treaty virtually assigning Haiti's financial affairs to the United States, and allowing the right of intervention through a general clause guaranteeing "a government adequate for the protection of life, property, and individual liberty." The American military government in Haiti lasted until 1934, although customs controls continued another seven years afterward.

Renewed unrest in the Dominican Republic caused the United States to adopt policies similar to those in Haiti. In 1911 revolutions had broken out again, and the Dominican government had to borrow a huge sum, which caused another debt problem encouraging to foreign intervention. Three years later the Wilson administration authorized Americans to supervise the approaching elections. But when the new Dominican president took office, he rejected an American treaty establishing a financial adviser, broadening receivership powers over domestic and customs revenues, and setting up a constabulary or state police force. In the spring of 1916 the country sank deeper into revolution. The United States sent marines in May, and when another Dominican president refused the American treaty, Wilson ordered the installation of a military government run by the Department of the Navy in Washington. For six years, while the Dominican legislature stood in adjournment, the marines discharged cabinet responsibilities and American engineers improved the country's roads, schools, and sanitation facilities. To the very end, however, the Dominicans bitterly resisted America's intervention.

The war in Europe also caused concern that Germany would defeat Denmark, seize its West Indies possessions (Virgin Islands), and endanger the Panama Canal. To prevent this, the United States negotiated a treaty with Denmark in the summer of 1916 which permitted purchase of the islands. The Wilson administration had already informed the Danish government that if Germany made a move toward the islands, American forces would take them.

The Wilson administration's Caribbean policy was based on concern about safeguarding the hemisphere and the Panama Canal from European intervention. The president first sought treaties, but when necessary resorted to military force in achieving objectives. Critics charged that the White House too readily assumed that domestic unrest was an automatic invitation to Old World involvement. In emphasizing the external dangers caused by revolutions in the Caribbean countries, they asserted, the Wilson administration overlooked genuine internal problems and ignored the people's protests against American policy, while weakly attempting to salve these hard feelings with assurances of economic assistance conducive to democratic reforms. Whatever the truth, the United States sought legitimate security interests in Latin America, but left a legacy of bitter distrust in the southern half of the hemisphere.

MISSIONARY DIPLOMACY IN MEXICO

Wilson's policy in Mexico, though partly determined by concern for the Panama Canal, was more the product of a struggle between the roles of idealism and realism in foreign affairs. Mexico had been unique among Latin American governments in that since 1877 it had remained fairly stable under the iron rule of Porfirio Díaz. But by the turn of the century his dictatorship had begun to weaken. In 1910 a young nationalist visionary, Francisco Madero, led an uprising calling for democratic and economic reforms, and in spring of the following year Díaz was forced into exile. But Madero's reform program endangered foreign holdings in Mexico because it would unseat the conservative landed classes, create massive disorder, and discourage continued investment. By 1913, 50,000 Americans had investments in Mexico valued at $1 billion, more than those of all other countries combined. The revolutionaries blamed the United States for Mexico's ills and for losses of American property and life; but President Taft refused to get involved.

A month before Wilson's inauguration, the American ambassador in Mexico, Henry Lane Wilson (no relation to the president), gave tacit support to an overthrow of the government led by one of Madero's own generals, Victoriano Huerta. Ambassador Wilson regarded Madero as a threat to stability and hence an obstacle to investment; other critics considered him unbalanced because of his spiritual beliefs. Huerta, however, was a favorite of conservative interests and amenable to dollar diplomacy. When he asked the American ambassador for recommendations on what to do with Madero, Henry Lane Wilson advised him to take whatever steps were necessary to bring peace to Mexico. Huerta forced his resignation and, early on a February morning in 1913, Madero and his vice president were shot to death during an alleged escape attempt.

Huerta won recognition from most foreign governments, but Taft held back until the new regime agreed to resolve damage claims questions with the United States. The proposed *quid pro quo* fell through partly because time ran out for Taft's presidential administration and he had to leave office, but also because a former governor of the northern province of Coahuila and follower of Madero, Venustiano Carranza, had stirred a group called the Constitutionalists into a rebellion against Huerta. With American property and lives victimized by both sides in the civil war, Taft turned over the matter to his successor.

President Wilson's Mexican policy marked a new direction in American foreign affairs because it exemplified "missionary diplomacy." Whereas nearly all presidential administrations had extended *de facto* recognition to foreign regimes, Wilson's rejection of Huerta led to the formulation of moral judgments regarding what constituted a "good" government. The president refused to extend recognition to Huerta because he had risen to power over Madero's body and did not advocate reform. In March 1913 Wilson issued a press release declaring that the United States would recognize only those Latin American governments built on "orderly processes of just government based upon law, not upon arbitrary or irregular force." The president aimed his remarks at Nicaragua, but the general nature of the terms meant that Mexico was included. Huerta's regime was oppressive, but it fitted the traditional prerequisite for recognition: it was in control. The British considered Huerta a stabilizing force who would keep Mexico safe for investors. Wilson countered that Huerta headed "a government of butchers," which made it incumbent upon the United States to help the Mexican people. The British should stop allowing oil interests to control their policies and follow the American lead. To a Britisher in the United States, Wilson declared, "I am going to teach the South American republics to elect good men!"

President Wilson had injected a moral dimension into America's Mexican policy when he denounced Huerta as a drunken "brute" and called for his resignation. By late summer of 1913 he had recalled Ambassador Wilson from Mexico City and removed him from the diplomatic service because of his involvement with Huerta and because he had openly opposed the president's policies in Mexico. President Wilson now relied on special agents, who often did not know much about Mexico or the Spanish language, but were his close and trusted acquaintances. Before an audience in Mobile in late October, Wilson insisted that "morality" had to guide American policy, not "material interest." The United States "will never again seek one additonal foot of territory by conquest. She will devote herself to showing that she knows how to make honorable and fruitful use of the territory she has." His rhetoric seemed to signal an end to American territorial imperialism in Latin America; yet it suggested no guarantees against interventionism in the name of righteousness. The irony is that Wilson's diplomacy was potentially more entangling than that of either Roosevelt or Taft. Whereas compromise and retreat can characterize a foreign policy built on realistic interests, they could *not* co-

UNITED STATES

Columbus
Villa's raid, March 1916

Pershing's
expedition,
1916–1917

Parral
Skirmish with
Carranza's troops

MEXICO

Gulf of Mexico

Cuba

Tampico
American sailors arrested
April 1914

1914

PACIFIC
OCEAN

Mexico City
Veracruz
Seized by U.S.
navy, April 1914

BRITISH
HONDURAS

GUATEMALA

HONDURAS

←—— U.S. military expeditions

EL SALVADOR

NICARAGUA

COSTA RICA

America's Intervention in Mexico, 1914–1917

MAP 19

The United States and Mexico almost went to war more than once in this brief period.

exist with absolute standards of right and wrong. A crusade for morality
could lead to a sweeping interventionist policy.

One of Wilson's emissaries, John Lind, reached Mexico's shores on
board an American ship of war and in early August 1913 offered to help
Huerta put down the revolution, on the condition that he then withdraw
from public affairs. This was the first diplomatic effort for Lind, former
governor of Minnesota, but perhaps an even more serious obstacle was
that he was a notorious opponent of Catholicism in an overwhelmingly
Catholic nation. America's conditions for recognition and assistance were
that Huerta had to arrange an immediate cease-fire and sponsor a free
election without participating as a candidate. The Mexican minister of foreign affairs, Federico Gamboa, regarded the choice of Lind and his arrival
by warship as an insult. He then bitterly denounced Lind's proposal as

an attempt to license the president of the United States to "veto" elections in Mexico. Wilson reacted decisively. He cut off arms sales to Mexico, warned Americans to return home, and declared that the United States would follow a policy of "watchful waiting."

The Wilson administration tried to persuade the European governments to join in supporting Carranza, who claimed to favor Madero's program of reform. Huerta did nothing to placate the United States. He arranged a congressional election in October, but on election eve ordered the imprisonment of more than a hundred opposition members of the legislature and seized dictatorial power. When the election confirmed Huerta's control, Wilson countered with another special agent to offer assistance to Carranza in upper Mexico. But Carranza also opposed American intervention. The following month, Wilson informed the other countries having interests in Mexico that he intended to isolate Huerta and force him from office. Should political and economic pressure fail, he declared, the United States's "duty" was to use "less peaceful means to put him out." Wilson's note aroused little support in Europe. The British at first hesitated to alienate Huerta because they ranked second only to the Americans in Mexican investments and were heavily dependent on that country's oil. Yet the imminent threat of Germany and the need for America's friendship gradually forced a change in British policy. They recalled their minister, Sir Lionel Carden, who had opposed America's policy in Mexico, and now likewise encouraged Huerta to resign.

Wilson ignored growing discontent at home with his Mexican policy and with British support prepared to move against Huerta. He made a formal call for Huerta's resignation in November 1913 and the following February lifted the arms embargo to allow sales to Carranza. American criticism persisted. Some warned that Wilson's policy encouraged a climate of unrest ill-suited for investment, while others ridiculed its pious morality and demanded military action. Over seventy Americans had died in the Mexican civil war since 1913, causing more than a few in the United States to demand armed intervention to restore order.

Trouble erupted in the town of Tampico on April 9, 1914, when Huerta's forces arrested seven American sailors and an officer for loading gasoline onto their whaleboat, then docked in a canal running close to Huerta's defense lines against the rebels. Given the tense situation, the arrests were a mistake in judgment, and the Mexican officer in charge realized it immediately. He released the Americans and personally apologized, but this was not enough for the American squadron commander, Rear Admiral Henry Mayo. He demanded a formal, written apology, punishment of the officer responsible, and a twenty-one-gun salute to the American flag—all within twenty-four hours. The Mexican general wrote his regrets for the incident, and Huerta publicly renounced his men's actions, but no salute to the flag would take place unless the United States reciprocated in kind.

The Wilson administration regarded the Tampico incident as an opportunity to facilitate a change of government in Mexico, and on April 20 the president asked Congress for authorization to use military force in taking the port at Veracruz and deposing Huerta by denying him outside help. Bryan supported Mayo because national honor seemed at stake, and just two days later Congress responded favorably to the president's request. In the meantime Wilson had been awakened early in the morning of April 21 to learn that a German steamship was en route to Veracruz carrying weapons and ammunition for Huerta. Rear Admiral Frank Fletcher received telephoned orders to seize the city's port and customs house.

America's military intervention in Veracruz had the potential to cause war. About 800 troops arrived in the city on April 21, where they met unexpected and effective resistance from former prisoners of the town's jails, who had been released and armed by a local officer from Huerta's army. Mexican regulars had pulled out, but the ensuing street fighting before nightfall led to a number of casualties on both sides. The next day 3,000 more marines landed. American and Mexican death tolls climbed as the conflict raged for a few more days. Wilson's policy drew criticism from all sides. Huerta's opponents joined other Latin Americans, investors from the United States, and numerous observers elsewhere in denouncing the Washington administration for using military force over such a small matter. The London *Economist* chided the United States for justifying such rash action "on points of punctilio raised by admirals and generals." If the government in Washington persists in "this return to mediaeval conditions it will be a bad day for civilization." The truth is that the occupation of Veracruz *was* an act of war, despite Wilson's argument that his quarrel was with Huerta, not Mexico. He failed to realize that his interventionist policy made the United States a greater threat to Mexico than did its own internal strife. His efforts, no matter how well-intentioned, could unite the Mexican people against him.

Wilson had created a situation injurious to American prestige no matter what action he took. Withdrawal without reparations would be humiliation, and war with Mexico was aggression; he had no honorable way out. Carranza warned of war with the United States and the American and European press condemned the invasion. Wilson admitted to his personal physician that he was shocked and guilt-ridden by the growing number of American and Mexican casualties in Veracruz. In trying to do what he thought was morally right, he had earned the animosity of nearly everyone.

In late April, with almost 7,000 American forces in Mexico, Wilson turned over the matter to the "ABC Powers" of Argentina, Brazil, and Chile, who had offered to mediate the dispute. The following month the three Latin American nations sponsored a conference in Niagara Falls, Canada, which brought together delegates from Huerta's government and that of the United States. Carranza declined to attend on the ground that outsiders were attempting to determine his country's domestic affairs. The Niagara talks deadlocked when Wilson forbade his representatives to discuss American withdrawal from Mexico, and then declared that Huerta had to renounce his position in favor of a provisional regime under Carranza's Constitutionalist party. The Niagara Conference broke up in July without achieving anything specific, but the United States's decision to attend the meeting provided a way out of war and suggested to Latin Americans that Wilson's earlier goodwill assurances made in Mobile might have substance.

Huerta's regime collapsed soon after the Niagara Conference, leaving the mistaken impression in the United States that the meeting had accomplished its objectives. In mid-July, about two weeks after adjournment, Huerta fled the country, seeking asylum in Spain. Continued upheaval at home, poor finances, and White House pressure had driven him from office. On August 20 Carranza's forces marched into Mexico City.

Yet the civil war in Mexico did not end with Carranza's rise to power, for promised reforms did not materialize, and he soon faced armed resistance from within his own ranks—from Emiliano Zapata in the south and from Pancho Villa in the north. When Villa claimed to support America's policies toward Mexico, Wilson decided to withhold recognition from Carranza's government and give Villa time to broaden his influence. Partly to return Mexico's attention to internal troubles, Wilson ordered American soldiers home from Veracruz in late November 1914. The following month Villa's forces marched into Mexico City, making it appear that Wilson's watching and waiting had brought success. But Carranza's army soon rallied and drove Villa back into the north. In the meantime, however, the nation's capital deteriorated as mass starvation and mob violence prevailed. More than 25,000 foreigners in the city, including 2,500 Americans, suffered along with the Mexican people. American military force in cooperation with that of other hemispheric governments might have saved the city from this plight, but such a consideration was out of the question because of the growing preoccupation with the war in Europe. Carranza, Wilson moaned, "will somehow have to be digested." In October 1915 Secretary of State Robert Lansing called another conference of the ABC Powers and they, along with Bolivia, Guatemala, and Uruguay, proposed that America extend *de facto* recognition to Carranza's government. The United States complied that same month and permitted the sale of arms to Carranza's forces while denying them to his opposition.

American recognition of Carranza did not settle the disorder in Mexico, for Villa resented Wilson's "betrayal" and sought to entangle Carranza and the United States in war. In January 1916 Villa and his followers stopped a train in northern Mexico where they shot sixteen young American engineers on board who had received assurances of safety from Carranza. Three months later Villa crossed the American border before daybreak and raided and burned the town of Columbus, New Mexico, killing seventeen Americans.

News of Villa's attack on American territory brought an immediate response by the United States: Wilson ordered General John J. Pershing to head a "punitive expedition" of 7,000 soldiers to capture Villa. Carranza disapproved but had no choice. He ultimately accepted the "invasion" with the stipulation that in the future, *both* nations had the right to pursue bandits across the border. The American force entered Mexico in mid-March and trudged through 350 miles of desert without catching its prey. Instead of resolving the problem, the expedition created another one, as Carranza complained of the growing size of the force and demanded its immediate withdrawal. The soldiers had nearly doubled in number to 12,000 and trouble had erupted. American and Mexican forces exchanged fire in the town of Parral in April, killing two Americans and forty Mexicans, which soon led Wilson to send 150,000 National Guardsmen to patrol the border. In late June, at Carrizal, the two armies clashed again, with a dozen Americans killed and twenty-three taken captive. War seemed likely.

Despite the failure of the expedition, Wilson at first refused to order Pershing home. The president's hesitancy was partly due to an unwillingness to admit error, but it was also attributable to the effect such a move could have on the elections at home in November. The White House turned down a mediation offer from Latin America, but agreed to Carranza's call for a joint investigatory commission. Though the commission failed to reach a solution, the American representatives recommended that Wilson recall the soldiers (now derisively called the "Perishing Expedition") and leave Mexican concerns to Carranza. America's entry into the European war seemed imminent in early February 1917, and the president ordered Pershing to leave Mexico. As the last of the American soldiers came home, Wilson's Mexican policy lay in shambles. The revolution raged on, Carranza resented the United States and leaned toward Germany in the European war, and Villa still hawked the border, flouting his own country's government as well as that of the United States. In March a new American ambassador arrived in Mexico, assigned the awesome responsibility of repairing relations.

The United States extended *de jure* or lawful recognition to the Carranza regime in late August 1917, although the move came too late to placate most Latin American nations. Wilson remained reluctant until the final moment, but had to relent because the United States had entered the European war the previous April and could not allow troubles with Mexico to continue. The president had averted war with Mexico; he had accepted mediation; he had favored a government in Mexico that claimed interest in reform. Yet his policy in Mexico was paternalistic, which left him open to criticism as the apostle of Americanism who expressed opposition to military force but sent more marines to Latin America than did either Roosevelt or Taft.

MISSIONARY DIPLOMACY IN EUROPE

The Great War of 1914–18 ultimately dominated Americans' attention, convincing them that modern war was worldwide and total, and that only through morality and a reassertion of ideals could the world avoid such a calamity. Roosevelt had foreseen the interrelatedness of global events when he tried to maintain peace through a balance-of-power system. The first sign of changing times came when America found itself unable to remain neutral while trading with both sides during the European conflict. No longer could one distinguish between contraband and noncontraband: in modern warfare, *any* item benefiting the enemy was subject to confiscation. Freedom of the seas thus became one of the first casualties of the Great War. Americans had to take sides in the war. Wilson's moral stance helped to stir an international crusade for the reform of humanity and for the establishment of permanent world peace. Combined with numerous other factors, his idealism helped to promote America's entrance into the war.

An assassin's bullets had shattered the uneasy peace in Europe on June 28, 1914, when a young Serbian nationalist killed the heir to the Austro-Hungarian throne, Archduke Franz Ferdinand, in the streets of Sarajevo in Bosnia. The shots fired in the Balkans echoed throughout the world, tearing down the illusion of security afforded by the system of alliances and armaments and setting off a war between the Allies (England, France, and Russia, later joined by Japan and Italy) and the Central Powers (Germany and Austria-Hungary, later joined by Bulgaria and Turkey) that required four years of fighting to settle. Submarines, tanks, airplanes, poison gas, improved machine guns—all caused mounting casualties among civilians and the military. In the first full year of the war France's casualties numbered 1.3 million, Germany's 848,000, and Britain's 313,000. The German invasion of Belgium seemed particularly atrocious. When Berlin first sought permission to march through that country en route to France, the Belgian king allegedly replied, "Belgium is a nation, not a thoroughfare." Britain's appeal to treaty guarantees of Belgium's neutrality reportedly brought the ill-advised remark from German Chancellor Theobald von Bethmann Hollweg that the British were going to war over a "scrap of paper." In early January 1915 the editor of *Life* magazine declared that for Americans "the great, clear issue of this war is Belgium. If we see anything right at all in this matter," the article continued, "Belgium is a martyr to civilization, sister to all who love liberty or law; assailed, polluted, trampled in the mire, heelmarked in her breast, tattered, homeless."

The reactions of Americans to the outbreak of war were varied, al-

Europe at the Start of World War I

- Allied powers
- Central powers
- Neutral nations

MAP 20

By the summer of 1914, according to Colonel House, Europe was a "powder keg" waiting to explode. In less than three years, the United States was also involved.

though most regarded the conflict as peculiarly European and no concern to them. Wilson later offered the following assessment: "America did not at first see the full meaning of the war. It looked like a natural raking out of the pent-up jealousies and rivalries of the complicated politics of Europe." It was "a war with which we have nothing to do, whose causes cannot touch us." Some American representatives abroad had been unaware of the serious nature of tensions in Europe. The minister to Belgium, Brand Whitlock, had been writing a novel when the assassination took place and later admitted, "I had never heard of Sarajevo. I had not the least idea where it was in this world, if it was in this world." Colonel Edward House, Wilson's closest confidant, had considered the situation in Europe to be a "powder keg" long before the autumn of 1914 and had tried to convince the German ambassador in Washington to join the United States and other world powers in a cooperative program aimed at civilizing backward peoples and assuring investments. America's ambas-

Colonel Edward House

House was President Wilson's closest confidant until their break during the Versailles Treaty proceedings. (National Portrait Gallery)

sador to London, Walter Hines Page, agreed. House sought support for his proposal in Berlin and other European capitals in the spring and early summer of 1914. The assassination ended his hopes.

America's official policy toward the European war was neutrality, but the people were deeply divided in sentiment. In August 1914 Wilson announced a proclamation of neutrality and later that month urged Americans to be "impartial in thought as well as in action." The United States, he asserted, must set an example for peace. But problems were apparent at the outset. Americans were a nation of immigrants with close ties to their homelands. Many Americans felt social, political, economic, and cultural affinities with the British and French; a great number were pro-German, including Americans of German and Irish descent, along with others who for one reason or another were opposed to Russia. The "hyphenates," whether German-Americans, Irish-Americans, or whatever national origin, had pronounced views on the war that were impossible to neutralize.

Although most Americans favored the Allies for practical or personal reasons, Wilson and nearly all members of his administration feared that German victory would set back democracy in favor of world militarism. Wilson's scholarly writings had long reflected his sympathies for Britain's parliamentary form of government, and he would soon join House and Page in believing the war a battle between good and evil. Robert Lansing, then legal counselor in the Department of State, was stronger in opinion: he considered Germany's defeat so important that he wanted the United States to intervene. Page, author and editor, was perfectly acclimated to British life and got along well with Foreign Secretary Sir Edward Grey. In fact, Page did not like the legal pronouncements contained in State Department dispatches and at times toned them down to avoid antagonizing the British.

Americans' longtime distrust of Germany became more widespread after the invasion of Belgium. During the first days of the war, the British had cut the Atlantic cable connecting Germany with the United States, meaning that direct information on the European conflict came only from Allied sources. America's relations with Germany had been uneasy before 1914, encouraging British propagandists to play upon this and early events of the war to foster an unfavorable image of the Germans among influential American newsmen, politicians, ministers, and educators. According to postwar evidence, the British government had engineered a careful propaganda campaign designed to create sympathy for the Allies in the war. Such efforts included letter writing, mailing of books and pamphlets favorable to Britain, and sending speakers to emphasize Anglo-American similarities. The British found a fairly receptive audience in the United States. Americans had long been suspicious of German motives in both hemispheres, and now Kaiser Wilhelm II became the "Beast of Berlin," determined to stamp out democracy everywhere. Cartoonists portrayed the German "Hun" as an animalistic killer of men, women, and children, a despoiler of religion, education, and culture, and a fierce advocate of militarism and barbarism. Always caricatured wearing a mustache, high black boots, and spiked helmet, the Hun leered as he goose-stepped across civilization, bayoneting babies, raping and mutilating women, gathering the helpless for labor gangs, loading corpses for use in soap factories, and executing resisters such as the celebrated British nurse Edith Cavell, who actually was a spy. German armies left behind countless bodies, burned out church buildings and schools, and razed libraries such as the one at the University of Louvain in Belgium. Herbert Hoover, young mining engineer and later president of the United States, headed an American relief group in Belgium that convinced many Americans that German expansion and militarism had interlocked to create a brutal imperialism that used war as its only instrument of policy.

The Wilson administration insisted that the European conflict was subject to the restrictions of international laws guaranteeing the rights of neutrals. The most recent set of codes, the Declaration of London in 1909, should have been the guide to all nations' behavior in the war. But the big powers had not ratified the measure and it had never gone into effect. The British had refused because the Declaration's maritime provisions seemed to favor neutral nations and those with small navies. Hence, the guarantees outlined in the Declaration of Paris of 1856, now outmoded, were the only ones in effect when the war began in 1914. According to this nineteenth-century program, neutral flags bonded the safety of ocean cargoes; contraband was strictly war matériel; neutral vessels could carry noncontraband goods ("free ships, free goods") to and from the ports of belligerents; blockades had to conform to the requirements of "imminent danger." Neutral rights seemed clear in theory, but became muddled in the war. Neither belligerent could permit neutral ships to pass through the war zone without searching them for contraband, and the nature of modern, full-scale war forced a generalized definition of contraband that included all items benefiting the enemy. Britain controlled the seas and without actually proclaiming a blockade succeeded in closing European ports. Their naval commanders followed visit-and-search procedures reminiscent of maritime tactics that a century before had caused war between the English-speaking peoples.

When Germany's invasion of France deadlocked in trench warfare at the Marne River in the autumn of 1914, the central issue in the war was whether Germany could deprive the Allies of access to the sea. The government in London announced in November that in reply to the Germans' decision to mine the open seas, it had decided to lay mines in the North Sea to force Germany into submission. Neutrals wishing to use these waters had to obtain directions from England for safe passage. Despite complaints that the North Sea was not territorial waters, the British declared it a "military area" closed to neutral traffic. Since Germany did not have free use of the Atlantic Ocean, the Central Powers' only recourse was an appeal to international law. The United States found itself between the antagonists, but more immediately affected by the British since their navy controlled the seas. Except for cotton, which for a while remained on the free list because of American pressure, Britain broadened the definition of contraband to include any goods helpful to the enemy. The Royal Navy also searched American mails and interrupted neutrals' use of their own ports and coastlines. In March 1915 the London ministry made it official: its naval commanders would seize all goods "of enemy destination, ownership, or origin." The stalemate at the Marne emphasized the importance of neutral trade, but Britain so narrowed the "rights of neutrals" that the term had lost its meaning.

The strains on Anglo-American relations were serious, but they never broke. Part of the explanation lies in Britain's carefully implemented foreign policy. Foreign Secretary Grey explained after the war that his objective had been "to secure the maximum of blockade that could be enforced without a rupture with the United States." The administration in Washington perhaps left the door open for British maritime infractions when, in December 1914, it admitted that "imperative necessity to protect their [the Allies'] national safety" might justify actions that in other contexts were illegal. As Lansing conceded, his country's diplomatic notes were often designed to leave the impression of protest without reaching the level of an ultimatum; chances were, he believed, that America might join the Allies and be expected to use tactics it now condemned. After the war Lansing explained in his memoirs that the notes sent to England were "long and exhaustive treatises which opened up new subjects of discussion rather than closing those in controversy. Short and emphatic notes were dangerous. Everything was submerged in verbosity. It was done with deliberate purpose." Such an approach "insured continuance of the controversies and left the questions unsettled, which was necessary in order to leave this country free to act and even to act illegally when it entered the war."

To finance the war effort the Allies initially hoped to draw upon monetary accounts owed by the United States in Europe, but these were quickly exhausted and Britain and France had to seek direct American loans. When J. P. Morgan and Company in New York asked the State Department its position on the matter in August 1914, Bryan frowned upon loans to belligerents as a violation of neutrality. "Money," he wrote the president, was the "worst of all contrabands because it commands all other things." Yet Bryan failed to recognize that both precedent and law stood on the side of the Allies' request. Belligerents in the past, including the Union and Confederate governments during the American Civil War, had financed their efforts through money borrowed from neutral nations. American bankers had loaned money to Japan during its war with Russia in 1904–5. Bryan finally realized that his policy was legally unsound and that the munitions traffic was mutually beneficial to the United States and the Allies. A spokesman for the State Department had also convincingly argued that whereas loans by neutral governments were a violation of neutrality, loans by private individuals were not. Bryan relented in October 1914, but stipulated that the administration would approve "credits," not loans, thus maintaining the fiction of avoiding financial involvement in the war.

THE *LUSITANIA*

The government in Berlin had meanwhile adopted new tactics designed to break the deadlock in the trenches. On February 4, 1915, it announced that in two weeks it would begin a policy of "unrestricted submarine warfare" on enemy ships (firing without warning) within a "war zone" surrounding the British Isles. This decision was of questionable wisdom. Britain and France combined had nearly five times more submarines than Germany. At the time of the announcement the Germans had 21 U-boats, only 4 of which were usable, and even though that number grew to over 125 within three years, logistical difficulties made it impossible to send more than a third to sea at one time. Germany nonetheless ordered submarine commanders to sink all intruders on sight and warned neutrals to stay out of the war zone for fear of being mistaken as an enemy. Citizens from neutral nations, Germany warned, should not book passage on lin-

German U-Boat

A crowd inspects a German U-boat stranded on the south coast of England during the Great War. (Library of Congress)

ers belonging to belligerents. Within a week Wilson warned that the United States would hold Germany to "strict accountability" for any harm to Americans. Washington would adopt all measures needed "to safeguard American lives and property and to secure to American citizens the full enjoyment of their acknowledged rights on the high seas."

Germany's use of the submarine reinforced the growing conviction that maritime codes of international law were outdated by the time of the Great War. Traditional practice called for belligerent vessels to patrol ports just beyond the three-mile zone. But Britain soon argued that because of long-range guns and German submarines, it must station its vessels on the high seas. The British then used the doctrine of "continuous voyage" (defining a cargo's status by determining the ship's *ultimate* destination, a policy used by the British during the War of 1812 and by the Union in the Civil War) to justify seizures of American commercial vessels en route to other neutral nations, who in turn might allow cargoes to enter Germany in their own ships. Past practice also permitted a belligerent to search a neutral's cargo at sea; if suspected of carrying contraband, the ship went to a prize court for adjudication. But modern merchant vessels were larger and more time was required for inspecting cargo and papers. The submarine forced a change in this procedure. Nothing was more inviting to the enemy than to find its opponent motionless at sea; the British decided that a careful and safe examination of cargo could take place only within their harbors. Such a policy caused resentment, for it meant delay, broken contracts, and financial losses. Though some American merchants suspected their British competitors of pressing the London government into this policy, the crucial factor was the submarine.

German maritime policies likewise upset Americans, but much more so because use of the submarine increased the chances for loss of life. The fragile submarine was incapable of meeting the requirements of international law without risking destruction. It had to rely on the element of surprise. Slow to surface, slow to move, and even slower to submerge, the U-boat could not adhere to maritime rules by its commander warning a vessel before attack; British naval and merchant marine commanders were under orders to ram or shell enemy submarines because of their known vulnerability. The submarine's small size also forbade taking on passengers from a ship about to be destroyed. The German U-boat raised the image of barbarism. Wilson later drew a clear distinction between German and British policy when he declared that "property rights can be vindicated by claims for damages when the war is over, and no modern nation can decline to arbitrate such claims; but the fundamental rights of humanity cannot be. The loss of life," he emphasized, "is irreparable."

During the first two months of unrestricted submarine warfare, the Germans sank about ninety vessels in the war zone, including the British *Falaba*, with the loss of one American, and torpedoed (without sinking) an American oil tanker, the *Gulflight*, with several casualties; but no attack aroused as much furor as that caused by the sinking of the British luxury liner *Lusitania* on May 7, 1915. Experts considered the vessel unsinkable because it had 175 watertight compartments, could outrun any submarine, and was so huge (a seventh of a mile long, the largest passenger liner afloat) that its sinking was inconceivable. For eight years it had crossed the Atlantic with record speed. Its owner, the Cunard Line, had used government funds in building this model vessel, and in return the *Lusitania* was readily adaptable to gun fittings in war, and half its crew were members of the naval reserve. On the outside the *Lusitania* was a lavish showcase of wealth and splendor; with its four smokestacks silhouetted against the sky it suggested a portrait in motion. But on the inside the reality of war rested below its decks. As 1,257 passengers and 702 crew members moved from stem to stern during the Atlantic voyage, they crossed over a cargo below of foodstuffs and contraband, including more than a thousand cases of empty shrapnel shells, nearly twenty cases of nonexplosive fuses, and over 4 million rounds of rifle ammunition. As the *Lusitania* prepared to depart from New York harbor it carried both "babies and bullets," according to a member of the State Department.

The Imperial German Embassy in Washington had on the morning of May 1 warned Americans through fifty newspapers not to travel on the *Lusitania*, about to depart from New York. Next to the advertisement for the Cunard Line, it ran a "Notice" reminding readers that ships entering the war zone around the British Isles were subject to attack. Instead of frightening passengers, the announcement seems to have spurred excitement about seeing a submarine on the trip overseas. Captain William Turner of the *Lusitania* scoffed at the danger. "Do you think all these people would be booking passage on board the *Lusitania*," the veteran seaman asked newspapermen, "if they thought she could be caught by a German submarine? Why it's the best joke I've heard in many days, this talk of torpedoing!" Nearly 200 Americans joined the other passengers boarding the ship. No word of caution came from the government in Washington. Such a warning would violate freedom of the seas, Wilson reminded Bryan, who had expressed fear that American travel on belligerent ships would cause trouble. The agent for the Cunard Line in the United States dismissed the German warning as a cheap scare tactic. "The truth is that the *Lusitania* is the safest boat on the sea. She is too fast for any submarine. No German war vessel can get her or near her."

The *Lusitania* left New York for Liverpool just past noon on May 1, its crew not at maximum capacity and not of top caliber because the more experienced men had been assigned to the Royal Navy. Five days later the *Lusitania* was near Ireland when Turner received a message out of Queenstown (present-day Cobh): "Submarines active off south coast of Ireland." U-boats had sunk two vessels in those waters earlier that day, but Turner failed to follow standing orders in such conditions. He did not avoid headlands, nor did he move into the middle of the channel and maintain maximum speed and a zigzag course.

The British warning had been accurate: Lieutenant Walter Schwieger commanded a U-boat in the waters off the Irish coast. He had remained below during the following morning of May 7 because of fog and the presence of British patrol ships, but he surfaced before 2 P.M. and saw a large ship with four smokestacks on the distant horizon. He headed toward the vessel, submerged to the side, and fired a single torpedo. The watch on the *Lusitania*'s starboard sounded a warning as he saw the projectile cutting a trail of foam and bubbles in the water. But despite a full minute's notice, his warning went unheeded because Turner was not on deck as he should have been in those waters. Thirty seconds before impact, another lookout shouted the warning and Turner got to the bridge just before the torpedo struck. Schwieger's log recorded the drama:

> . . . four funnels and two masts of a steamer . . . . Ship is made out to be large passenger steamer. . . . Clean bow shot at a distance of 700 meters. . . . Torpedo hits starboard side right behind the bridge. An unusually heavy explosion takes place with a very strong explosion cloud (cloud reaches far beyond front funnel). The explosion of the torpedo must have been followed by a second one (boiler or coal or powder?). . . . The ship stops immediately and heels over to starboard very quickly, immersing simultaneously at the bow. . . . [T]he name *Lusitania* becomes visible in gold letters.

In eighteen minutes a single torpedo had driven the *Lusitania* from serenity to confusion and into the deep. Passengers frantically tried to board lifeboats, only to find that the rapid and extreme list to starboard swung some of the craft helplessly away from deck, while those lifeboats on the opposite side of the ship were bounced to bits against the hull. The torpedo revealed that the boasted engineering genius of the *Lusitania*'s construction —the watertight compartments—proved to be its major flaw. The sealed off damaged section confined the sea water to starboard, as the system was supposed to do; but by not permitting the tremendous volume of inrushing water to disperse evenly throughout the hull the enormous concentration of weight helped drag the vessel to its side and to the bottom. Nearly 1,200 perished, including 128 Americans, as the *Lusitania* briefly stood on its bow on the ocean floor, and with rudders jutting above the shallow waters seemed to heave and sigh before disappearing beneath the surface.

Reaction in the United States to the sinking of the *Lusitania* was a mixture of stunned disbelief and revulsion. Many Americans considered it an atrocity. The New York *Nation* proclaimed it "a deed for which a Hun would blush, a Turk be ashamed, and a Barbary pirate apologize. To speak of technicalities and the rules of war, in the face of such wholesale murder on the high seas, is a waste of time." The *Nation* asserted that the "law of nations and the law of God have been alike trampled upon. . . . The torpedo that sank the *Lusitania* also sank Germany in the opinion of mankind." Germany, the magazine continued, "has affronted the moral sense of the world and sacrificed her standing among the nations." Evangelist Billy Sunday called it "Damnable! Damnable! Absolutely hellish!"

A cabinet meeting had just broken up when Wilson received the news; though shocked and indignant, he did not want to respond publicly until he had had time to consider his stance and to determine that of fellow Americans. On May 10 in Philadelphia, after allowing his compatriots' emotions to simmer for three days, he delivered an address that he thought was a reflection of the popular mood. "There is such a thing as a man being too proud to fight. There is such a thing as a nation being so right that it does not need to convince others by force that it is right." The following morning he informed his cabinet that he would send a note to Berlin demanding recognition of Americans' rights to cross the sea and a renunciation of further sinkings of unarmed vessels. Bryan only reluctantly supported the idea because he believed that in the interests of neutrality, a similar note should go to Britain warning against its violations of America's maritime rights. Wilson rejected Bryan's proposal. On May 12 the government in London tried to assure America's entry into the war by releasing the Bryce Report, a document supposedly given the stamp of veracity by having the name of the respected writer and diplomat Viscount James Bryce affixed to it. The report graphically depicted the German atrocities allegedly committed in Belgium and France. But the

The *New York Times* Headlines the *Lusitania* Disaster of May 7, 1915

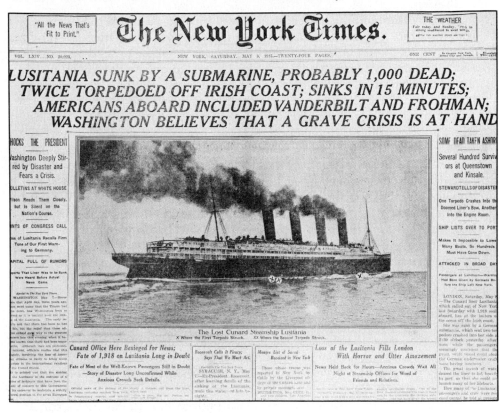

Though the Germans' sinking of the Lusitania *was not an immediate cause of U.S. entry into World War I, it remains one of the worst maritime tragedies of all time.* (New York Public Library)

decision for war did not come. The following day, the United States informed Germany that it expected indemnities for the *Lusitania*'s victims. Roosevelt was livid with the Wilson administration's seeming inaction; but he was one of only a few Americans who demanded war. Most were appalled by the disaster, but admitted that passengers on the *Lusitania* had traveled at their own risk.

The government in Berlin was divided in reaction to the *Lusitania* incident, but it soon termed the sinking an act of self-defense. Chancellor Bethmann Hollweg had long dreaded the possibility of a submarine forcing war onto the United States and attempted to defuse this dangerous situation by avoiding a direct reply to Wilson's note. Yet he posed questions that the United States had to confront. The *Lusitania*, according to the German note, was a virtual ship of war because it was fitted for arms, carried munitions and other war matériel, and was under orders to ram submarines. The sinking was "self-defense" and Germany recommended arbitration.

The Wilson administration at first was incredulous with the German response, but soon it too became deeply divided over the matter. On June 1 the president met with his cabinet to discuss whether to send a second and more sternly worded note to Berlin. A heated debate developed over Bryan's proposal to send a note to London as well. When his colleagues voted down the idea, Bryan accused them of favoring the Allies. This was an "unfair and unjust" remark, the president shot back in the greatly intensified atmosphere. Bryan soon resigned his cabinet post. The second *Lusitania* note, he explained, criticized Germany too sharply; the administration sent no equivalent warning to England; Wilson refused to warn Americans against traveling on belligerent ships; and the president continually ignored him in formulating policy. Bryan privately told Wilson that "Colonel House has been Secretary of State, not I, and I have never had your full confidence." The president replaced Bryan with Robert Lansing who was openly pro-Ally in sympathy.

By late summer of 1915, changed conditions in the United States led Washington to authorize loans to the Allies. Bryan was gone, Lansing favored loans, and the country was in severe economic straits. War loans would stimulate the economy and prevent a depression, Lansing argued along with Secretary of the Treasury William McAdoo. Wilson was convinced. He permitted the Morgan company to underwrite a huge loan to the Allies, and soon American merchants were providing munitions as well. By the end of the year the United States had experienced considerable economic recovery.

Britain's control of the seas caused a built-in bias in America's commercial activity that further endangered relations with Germany. As munitions sales climbed, German complaints became louder. *The Fatherland,* the major German-American propaganda organ in the United States, remarked that "we [Americans] prattle about humanity, while we manufacture poisoned shrapnel and picric acid for profit. Ten thousand German widows, ten thousand orphans, ten thousand graves bear the legend 'Made in America.'" Lansing denied that the administration was pro-Ally. If one belligerent has geographical, military, or naval advantages, "the rules of neutral conduct cannot be varied so as to favor the less fortunate combatant." His analysis revealed the danger inherent in a neutral's wish to trade with both belligerents. By the spring of 1917 the United States had loaned the Allies $2.3 billion, the Germans only $27 million. The advantage belonged to the maritime power, and that was Britain.

Germany had reason to complain about America's wartime commercial policies. Britain's decision to arm its merchant ships raised legitimate questions about whether these vessels should enter neutral ports; yet the government in Washington merely labeled these measures "defensive" and permitted their entry. Regarding the sale of munitions, the Wilson administration explained that no law prevented private Americans from selling war matériel to belligerents. In fact, the Department of State argued, a ban on such sales would help the Germans, since they had more munitions plants than did the Allies, and would thus constitute a violation of neutrality. If Germany wanted to buy these same goods, this was lawful; but it had to come to the United States to get them. Surely it was not America's fault that Britain controlled the seas. An American embargo on the munitions trade would aid Germany whereas the continuation of sales helped the Allies. No middle ground was possible. Profits dictated the sale of these goods, and Congress refused to alienate its constituency by ending the lucrative business. The safest stance for the Wilson administration was to ignore Germany's complaints and thereby tacitly approve the arms traffic.

Germany had meanwhile undergone a silent retreat on its maritime policies, but America did not know that and relations continued to deteriorate. A month after the *Lusitania* sinking, Berlin secretly directed U-boat commanders to refrain from attacking passenger liners without warning. The ensuing calm at sea did not stop Americans from exerting pressure on the Wilson administration to exact reparations for past damages. Roosevelt ridiculed "Professor Wilson," while one American newspaper played upon John Paul Jones's famous words by facetiously declaring that "we have not yet begun to write." Despite Berlin's secret orders, in August 1915 a submarine commander torpedoed the *Arabic*, a British passenger vessel en route to New York, and two more Americans died. The following month Lansing ordered the expulsion of the Austro-Hungarian ambassador for possessing materials (which the British secret service intercepted and turned over to the Americans) revealing attempts to instigate strikes in munitions plants. Washington also published documents confiscated from a German spy in the United States that showed Germany's intentions to sabotage munitions industries. In December Lansing secured the recall of the German military and naval attachés. When in 1916 the Black Tom munitions factory in New Jersey exploded with a loss of over $20 million, Americans blamed German conspirators.

Emotions in the United States over the *Arabic* episode seemed dangerous enough to cause the German ambassador in Washington, Count Johann von Bernstorff, to take unauthorized action in an attempt to halt his country's perilous submarine policy. On September 1, without first securing approval from his home government, he released a statement later known as the "*Arabic* pledge": "Liners will not be sunk by our submarines without warning and without safety of the lives of noncombatants, provided that the liners do not try to escape or offer resistance." The note did not mention merchant ships, and America's continued protests led representatives in Berlin to announce in early October that orders to U-boat commanders "have been made so stringent that a recurrence of incidents similar to the *Arabic* case is considered out of the question."

On February 4, 1916, almost nine months after the sinking of the *Lusitania*, the German government expressed regret and agreed to make reparations, which it did during the early 1920s. Germany never admitted wrongdoing, did not offer an apology, and continued its calls for arbitration. Yet no popular clamor for war developed in the United States, and the drawn-out exchanges of notes allowed emotions to calm while leaving the impression that Wilsonian diplomacy had achieved a victory. The administration in Washington chose to regard the promise of indemnification as satisfactory, and dropped the matter.

THE DECISION TO INTERVENE

The United States made several attempts in early 1916 to mediate an end to the war. House spent two weeks in London trying to determine acceptable conditions for peace, but left for Berlin with nothing substantial to offer. The German response was the same. Moving to Paris, House later recorded in his diary that he went beyond his instructions in assuring the French that *"in the event the Allies are successful during the next few months I promised that the President would not intervene. In the event that they were losing ground, I promised the President would intervene."* House did not tell Wilson that he had made these assurances to France. He then returned to London and met again with Grey. The president had authorized House to guarantee America's "moral force" against the Central Powers if they rejected peace talks, but when Grey recorded his conversation with House, the moral assurances seemed to include physical force as well. According to the House-Grey memorandum of February 22, "President Wilson was ready, on hearing from France and England that the moment was opportune, to propose that a conference should be summoned to put an end to the war. Should the Allies accept this proposal, and should Germany refuse it, the United States would [probably] enter the war against Germany." Wilson approved the essentials of the House-Grey memorandum, but had carefully injected the word "probably" (in brackets) in the sentence, thereby nearly assuring America's entry into the war. The Allies, however, turned down Wilson's proposal, perhaps because the insertion of "probably" as a qualifier made it appear indecisive, but undoubtedly more because they hoped to win the war without being bound to the president. Yet the Allies had secured moral support. The British interpreted the message as a sign that America's objections to their maritime actions were more form than substance.

Some congressional members were growing suspicious that Wilson sought America's entry into the war, and tried to enact legislation that would bar citizens from traveling on armed belligerent ships. They were particularly concerned about a new twist in Germany's submarine policies. In February Berlin announced that its U-boats had orders to sink armed merchant vessels without warning. Texas Representative Jeff McLemore sponsored a bill warning Americans not to travel on such ships, and about a month afterward Oklahoma Senator Thomas Gore did the same. The Gore-McLemore resolution attracted widespread interest in

Congress, although Wilson indignantly regarded it as an infringement of the executive's authority over foreign policy, a slur on America's honor, and a violation of international law. He sent an emotionally charged letter to the chairman of the Senate Foreign Relations Committee on February 24, asserting that he could not "consent to any abridgement of the rights of American citizens in any respect. . . . Once accept a single abatement of right," he warned, "and many other humiliations would certainly follow, and the whole fine fabric of international law might crumble under our hands piece by piece." White House pressure paid off. Congress tabled the Gore-McLemore resolution.

On March 24 the crisis pitch built again as a German submarine torpedoed and severely disabled the *Sussex,* an unarmed French passenger ship passing through the English Channel. No Americans were among the near eighty who lost their lives in the attack, but four were injured. The German commander evidently thought the vessel a British minelayer, for in outline and from a distance the *Sussex* looked like one. In fact, his belief that he had hit a warship led Berlin to deny that a submarine had attacked an unarmed vessel. This seemingly flagrant lie infuriated the Wilson administration and the American people, causing many, including Lansing and House, to push for a break in diplomatic relations.

Americans regarded the *Sussex* incident as an infraction of the German promises given after both the *Lusitania* and *Arabic* sinkings. The president faced enormous pressure to break relations with Germany, but he knew that his country was currently in trouble with Mexico and that his people were not united on maritime issues. On April 18 Wilson sent an ultimatum to Berlin warning that if it did not halt "submarine warfare against passenger and freight-carrying vessels," the United States would "sever diplomatic relations with the German Empire altogether."

Germany's reply to Wilson's note came on May 4 in the form of the so-called "*Sussex* pledge," which only seemed encouraging. Germany guaranteed that merchant ships would "not be sunk without warning and without saving human lives, unless these ships attempt to escape or offer resistance." But it conditioned this promise upon the United States's success in convincing Britain to lift its blockade. Should this fail, "the German Government would then be facing a new situation, in which it must reserve itself complete liberty of action." The war, of course, had dictated this German response. On the one hand, Germany could not be too rigid because its military offensive in Europe was grinding down into heavy losses at Verdun; on the other, Germany could not forgo using its most effective weapon—the submarine. The United States had little chance of persuading the British to drop the blockade, but the general impression among Americans was that Wilson had forced Berlin to call off the submarines. The truth was that his ultimatum surrendered the diplomatic initiative to Germany. Should its submarine policies continue, the United States would face the choice of submission or war.

Like a seesaw, America's relations with Britain deteriorated in almost direct proportion to their improvement with Germany after the *Sussex* case. The United States again considered mediation in the summer of 1916, but the time was not auspicious because Britain was preparing to open an offensive in the west, while France was engaged in the mighty defensive at Verdun. Both Allied belligerents hoped to gain a stronger military position before agreeing to peace negotiations. Even when the French lines held against the Germans and the British met defeat on the Somme River, neither government was interested in ending the war. America's relations with Britain had meanwhile hardened as London brutally put down an Irish rebellion in April and soon imposed greater restrictions on neutrals' trade with the Central Powers.

In July 1916 the British infuriated Americans by releasing a "blacklist" of more than eighty business leaders or companies in the United States that traded with the enemy. The president, Page, *The New York Times,* and other Americans considered the blacklist a monumental mistake. Wilson told House: "I am, I must admit, about at the end of my patience with Great Britain and the Allies. This blacklist business is the last straw." Congress tried to counter the blacklist by authorizing the president to close American ports to British subjects adhering to Britain's policy. It also passed the Naval Act of 1916 in response to Wilson's challenge to build a navy larger than Britain's that would allow Americans to "do what we please." The president reacted furiously to the blacklist, for such a measure compromised the principle of freedom of the seas, infringed upon the rights of citizens, was economically harmful to the United States, and, during the tight presidential campaign of 1916, would probably affect the vote of the Irish and German constituency. His protests were somewhat effective. The British soon shortened their blacklist.

After Wilson narrowly won reelection on a platform of "He Kept Us Out of War," he tried again to intervene for peace. Notes would go to both belligerents, asking their objectives in the war and urging negotiations. But before he could act, on December 12 Berlin announced interest in a peace conference. Germany had recently improved its military position by defeating Russia on the eastern front, crushing Rumania, winning control of the Balkans, and holding back French and Belgian forces in the west. If Wilson at this point showed interest in the German offer, the impression would be that he and the Germans had acted in collusion against the Allies; yet if he refused, an opportunity for peace might escape. The president went ahead with his notes on December 18. London and Paris were not interested. They were particularly offended by Wilson's assertion that "the objects which the statesmen of the belligerents on both sides have in mind in this war are virtually the same." The Allies found it difficult to believe that the United States did not consider their cause just. One British spokesman called Wilson an "ass," while another declared that everyone was "mad as hell." The king, nerves shattered by the war, wept over Wilson's inability to understand that democracy was at stake.

On January 22, 1917 Wilson appeared before the Senate to push his mediation efforts and to call for "peace without victory" and the establishment of a world organization to maintain that peace. The previous May he had recommended such an organization in a speech before the League to Enforce Peace. The United States should be a member, but only if peace terms were reconcilable with America's postwar aims of peace without victory, freedom of the seas, reductions in arms, and self-government for all peoples. But the belligerents had come too far to accept a stalemate. Wilson nonetheless insisted on "equality of nations" as the avenue to lasting peace. For a third time he offered American mediation; and for a third time both sides refused.

Germany had already decided to resume unrestricted submarine warfare on February 1, 1917, thus removing the likelihood of America's securing the peace without entering the war. German-American relations had improved during the months since the *Sussex* incident and the announcement of the British blacklist; Bethmann Hollweg and other moderates in Berlin urged great care in matters affecting American neutrality. Only America could save the Allies, they declared, and the German high command should gear its policy toward preventing America's involvement in the war. But the moderates lost the initiative to Admiral Alfred von Tirpitz and other military and naval leaders who were unwilling to compromise on war issues. The submarine, they argued, would force British capitulation before the United States could mobilize for war.

Ambassador Bernstorff in Washington likewise tried to convince his superiors in Berlin that unrestricted submarine warfare would force American entry into the war and perhaps ensure Allied victory. The *Sussex* pledge, he insisted, should determine his nation's maritime policies; in time Wilson would persuade the Allies to retreat from their extreme conditions for peace. But Bernstorff was unsuccessful and on January 31 notified Lansing that Britain's naval actions had forced his home government to resume unrestricted submarine warfare the following day. Several members of Berlin's high command recognized that the decision was a gamble, for they feared that American entry could come before Britain's defeat. But the German admiralty discounted the threat of American intervention. The United States's munitions trade with the Allies, one admiral underlined, would not affect the course of the war since Britain controlled the seas, and America's ships as belligerents could carry no more goods than they did as neutrals. Proponents of the new policy considered it the only way to end Britain's blockade and bring victory. Besides, German naval officers believed that their U-boats could cut off America's shipments of war matériel and break British resistance in six months. Matters could not be worse with the United States in the war, German Field Marshal Paul von Hindenburg remarked to Bethmann Hollweg, as they surveyed mounting casualty lists from trench warfare.

Wilson's previous pronouncements against Germany's use of the submarine necessitated a strong response to the new policy, and on February

3 the United States took a step closer to war: it broke diplomatic relations with Germany. Evidence indicates that Wilson still had hopes for peace. Should the United States enter the conflict, he feared, no disinterested civilized nation would be left to construct a lasting peace. Yet he also realized that the new German policy would confine American ships to port, hurting the economy and endangering the national interest by giving the appearance of capitulation. Had the Germans refrained from any maritime act against American vessels after the new policy of February 1, the Wilson administration might have stayed out of the war. As the final seconds ticked away, Wilson perhaps hoped that the implications of ruptured relations would awaken Germany to the folly of antagonizing the United States. But both the Germans and the Americans had been moving into positions which allowed no honorable retreat. Berlin's decision to use the submarine without restrictions virtually assured America's participation in the war. Neither *wanted* to fight the other, but both became locked into policies that permitted only a step backward into dishonor, or a plunge forward into war.

While Washington anxiously awaited news from the Atlantic, another crisis developed when British Naval Intelligence handed Page in London a secret telegram sent from German Foreign Minister Arthur Zimmermann in Berlin to his emissary in Mexico City. The so-called Zimmermann Telegram of February 24, 1917, which the British intercepted from two German transmissions, suggested the possibility of Germany negotiating a military alliance with Carranza's government in Mexico, should the United States enter the war; in exchange, Germany would aid Mexico in regaining Arizona, California, and New Mexico, lands lost in the war with the United States in 1848. The telegram also hinted at persuading Japan, one of the Allies, into joining the German-Mexican pact against the United States. Such an arrangement, if consummated, posed a direct threat to America's security—especially in the Southwest and Far West, areas previously untouched by Germany's war policies but traditionally concerned about Mexican and Japanese infiltration. The telegram was particularly exasperating to Wilson because in the interest of neutrality he had allowed both sets of belligerents to send communications through State Department wires and the American embassy in Berlin. He was furious and believed himself duped and American honor betrayed. After the American press published the telegram on March 1, Roosevelt, still fuming over the *Lusitania* and succeeding crises, warned that if the president did not ask Congress for war, he would "skin him alive."

The Zimmermann Telegram had deep implications for America's diplomacy. Perhaps the German foreign minister intended only to stir trouble between Mexico and the United States and thus weaken America's effectiveness should it enter the war with Germany. But the telegram was a blunder that unleashed a popular storm which Zimmermann could hardly have expected. Its contents were no different in tone and objective than other secret treaties made in Europe that had helped bring on the war. But Zimmermann's proposals struck America directly. One can understand their impact on the United States only within the context of the "Age of Innocence" that still colored America's outlook toward the world. The wars of the Old World had always been "over there"; yet for the first time they threatened to intrude "over here." This startling revelation rudely introduced many Americans to the nature of world politics. Roosevelt, while president, had urged his countrymen to recognize that the growing interrelatedness of world affairs made a balance of power on the international scale vital to peace. The Zimmermann Telegram posed a threat to America's security, substantiated the image of the Hun that British propagandists had long portrayed, involved Americans heretofore insulated from the European conflict, and removed Wilson's waning hope for uncovering some form of decency among German leaders. The telegram helped push the United States closer to war because it substantiated charges from Atlantic coast Americans that unrestricted submarine warfare was only one of several German threats to the nation's honor and security.

Events on the Atlantic forced the United States into action. A German submarine sank the British merchant vessel *Laconia* in late February, taking two Americans down with it. On March 1, the same day the Zimmermann Telegram appeared in the newspapers, Wilson asked Congress for authorization to arm the country's merchant vessels and to use "any other instrumentalities or methods" to safeguard American property and lives. But he encountered strong opposition from Senators Robert LaFollette of Wisconsin and George Norris of Nebraska, who led a filibuster against the bill until Congress went out of session. The "little group of willful men," as Wilson bitterly called them, only temporarily blocked the measure, for Lansing presented a convincing legal argument for Wilson to arm the ships on his own authority as president and commander-in-chief of the armed forces. On March 12 Wilson announced that he was doing so. Within a few days news arrived that justified his decision. A German submarine had sunk an unarmed American merchant ship on March 12, the same day of his announcement, and even though there was no loss of life, in a three-day span from March 16 to 18 the U-boats sank three other unarmed freighters, killing many aboard. American ships had become prey to German submarine commanders, leaving the president no choice but to seek war.

On April 2 Wilson went before a special joint session of Congress and asked for a declaration of war on Germany. The government in Berlin had forced the United States into this position, he explained, for German submarines had waged a "war against all nations"—a "warfare against mankind." Americans must preserve honor and safeguard civilization. He added that events in Russia during the previous month had signaled an important change in the tenor of the war. A revolution had brought down the czar and removed a barrier to fighting a war for democracy. Thus the idealists, Jewish-Americans, and others who had opposed Russia could now join the Allies in their struggle against "Prussian autocracy" and militarism. The United States, Wilson proclaimed, had "to vindicate the principles of peace and justice." It "shall fight for the things which we have always carried nearest our hearts,—for democracy, for the right of those who submit to authority to have a voice in their own government, for the rights and liberties of small nations, for a universal dominion of right by such a concert of free peoples as shall bring peace and safety to all nations and make the world itself at last free." In a moving statement, he declared that "the world must be made safe for democracy." Oratory was one of Wilson's fortes, and he used it to advantage that day. Congress greeted his message with a moment of silence, followed by ringing applause.

On April 6, with overwhelming congressional approval, Wilson announced that the United States was at war with Germany. Idealism and realism had merged into the joint aim of fulfilling the tenets of missionary diplomacy and at the same time safeguarding the national interest. Wilson had ingeniously touched American emotions by calling for a "war to end all wars" and to "make the world safe for democracy." The probability is that he believed what he said; chances are that many Americans also did. It was the only type of war a peace-loving president and nation could wage: one for world reform designed to bring permanent peace.

Selected readings

Bailey, Thomas A., and Paul B. Ryan, *The* Lusitania *Disaster.* 1975.

Buehrig, Edward H., *Woodrow Wilson and the Balance of Power.* 1955.

Clements, Kendrick A., *William Jennings Bryan, Missionary Isolationist.* 1983.

———, "Woodrow Wilson's Mexican Policy, 1913–1915," *Diplomatic History* 4 (1980): 113–36.

Clendenen, Clarence C., *The United States and Pancho Villa.* 1961.

Cohen, Warren I., *The American Revisionists: The Lessons of Intervention in World War I.* 1967.

Coogan, John W., *The End of Neutrality: The U.S., Britain, and Maritime Rights, 1899–1915.* 1981.

Cooper, John M., Jr., *The Vanity of Power: American Isolationism and World War I, 1914–1917.* 1969.

———, *The Warrior and the Priest: Woodrow Wilson and Theodore Roosevelt.* 1983.

Curry, Roy W., *Woodrow Wilson and Far Eastern Policy, 1913–1921.* 1957.

Devlin, Patrick, *Too Proud to Fight: Woodrow Wilson's Neutrality.* 1974.

Gardner, Lloyd C., *Safe for Democracy: The Anglo-American Response to Revolution, 1913-1923.* 1984.

Gilderhus, Mark T., *Diplomacy and Revolution: U.S.–Mexican Relations under Wilson and Carranza.* 1977.

Gregory, Ross, *The Origins of American Intervention in the First World War.* 1971.

Grieb, Kenneth J., *The United States and Huerta*. 1969.

Haley, P. Edward, *Revolution and Intervention: The Diplomacy of Taft and Wilson with Mexico, 1910–1917*. 1970.

Healy, David F., *Gunboat Diplomacy in the Wilson Era: The U.S. Navy in Haiti, 1915–1916*. 1976.

Hill, L.D., *Emissaries to a Revolution: Woodrow Wilson's Executive Agents in Mexico*. 1973.

Joseph, Gilbert M., *Revolution from Without: Yucatán, Mexico, and the United States, 1880–1924*. 1982.

Kennan, George F., *American Diplomacy*. Expanded ed. 1984. Originally published as *American Diplomacy, 1900–1950*. 1951.

Langley, Lester D., *The Banana Wars: An Inner History of American Empire, 1900–1934*. 1983.

Levin, N. Gordon, Jr., *Woodrow Wilson and World Politics: America's Response to War and Revolution*. 1968.

Link, Arthur S., *Wilson: Campaigns for Progressivism and Peace*. 1965.

———, *Wilson: Confusions and Crises, 1915–1916*. 1964.

———, *Wilson: The New Freedom*. 1956.

———, *Wilson: The Struggle for Neutrality, 1914–1915*. 1960.

———, *Woodrow Wilson and the Progressive Era, 1910–1917*. 1954.

———, *Woodrow Wilson: Revolution, War, and Peace*, 1979. Rev. ed. of *Wilson the Diplomatist: A Look at His Major Foreign Policies*. 1957.

———, ed., *Woodrow Wilson and a Revolutionary World, 1913–1921*. 1982.

May, Ernest R., *The World War and American Isolation, 1914–1917*. 1959.

Millis, Walter, *Road to War: America, 1914–1917*. 1935.

Munro, Dana G., *Intervention and Dollar Diplomacy in the Caribbean, 1900–1921*. 1964.

Quirk, Robert E., *An Affair of Honor: Woodrow Wilson and the Occupation of Veracruz*. 1962.

Reed, James, *The Missionary Mind and American East Asia Policy, 1911–1915*. 1983.

Safford, Jeffrey J., *Wilsonian Maritime Diplomacy, 1913–1921*. 1978.

Schmidt, Hans, *The United States Occupation of Haiti, 1915–1934*. 1971.

Seymour, Charles, *American Diplomacy during the World War*. 1934.

Smith, Daniel M., *The Great Departure: The United States and World War I, 1914–1920*. 1965.

———, *Robert Lansing and American Neutrality, 1914–1917*. 1958.

Smith, R. F., *The United States and Revolutionary Nationalism in Mexico, 1916–1932*. 1972.

Tansill, Charles C., *America Goes to War*. 1942.

Tien-yi Li, *Woodrow Wilson's China Policy, 1913–1917*. 1952.

Tuchman, Barbara W., *The Guns of August*. 1962.

———, *The Zimmermann Telegram*. 1958.

Chapter Fourteen

World War I and the League of Nations, 1917–1921

AMERICA AT WAR

The pace of events picked up quickly after America declared war on Germany in April 1917. Austria-Hungary and Turkey broke relations with the United States, and even though Congress never declared war on Germany's allies Bulgaria or Turkey, it did so on Austria-Hungary in December. The governments of Britain, France, Italy, and Belgium sent missions to Washington to discuss the military role of their new ally, but were surprised to learn that the United States did not want its soldiers to fill the frontal ranks on the battle scene. The head of the American Expeditionary Force (AEF), General John J. Pershing, staunchly opposed the use of his men within foreign units under foreign command. Americans would maintain their national identity and their longtime opposition to entangling alliances by entering the war as an "associated power." Though not technically an "ally," the United States did as much for its "associates" in the war as if a formal alignment existed. It continued loans to the Allies, set up a War Industries Board to supervise the production of war materials, and ordered the navy to shift construction emphasis from battleships to destroyers and submarine chasers. The navy also cooperated with the British in using the convoy system and in laying mines along the narrow entrances to the North Sea, closing it to German submarines.

The speed with which the United States sent soldiers to Europe suggested that unrestricted submarine warfare was the Germans' biggest mistake of the war. At the time of America's declaration of war, its army numbered 130,000, with 180,000 National Guardsmen in reserve. Some of the men had had military experience in Cuba, the Philippines, or Mexico, but most were hardly ready for combat on the Western Front. The Ameri-

The British Commander in France, Sir Douglas Haig, and General John J. Pershing

At Chaumont, France, during World War I. (Library of Congress)

can navy, the Germans thought, would be of little value in the war, and the American "air service" was an adjunct of the army and had no planes fitted with machine guns capable of challenging those of the enemy. But the United States surprised the Germans with its mobilization program. The Allies requested a million American troops by the close of 1918, and the United States not only had that many men in Europe more than six months before the target date, but it doubled the number by the following October.

The United States was not as ill-prepared for war in 1917 as the Germans had calculated. Theodore Roosevelt and activist organizations had been exerting pressure on Congress for military expansion since 1914. President Wilson had not ignored the need for military readiness. He had tried to persuade Congress in December 1915 to expand the army and navy, but peace groups fought the measure as an unwelcome boon to big business and as a threat to civil liberties and social reform programs. Early the following year Wilson took his case to the American people, and with the continual news of submarine warfare as background, he convinced

Congress in May 1916 to approve the National Defense Act. It enlarged the army and the National Guard and established summer training camps to build a manpower reserve. By the following autumn Congress had also expanded the navy and merchant marine.

In Wilson's war message of April 1917 he had asked for 500,000 additional soldiers, and Congress responded the following month with the Selective Service Act. It required the registration of all males between eighteen and forty-five years of age, and by war's end the measure had created a fighting force of nearly 5 million men. They went through six months of training with a seventeen-hour day, usually using broom handles, shovels, and sticks as substitutes for rifles. Some men never held a rifle until they arrived in France, and officers most often came from upper-class families and learned their responsibilities in ninety-day training sessions. When the war came to a close, American deaths totaled 112,000, over half of them attributable to a massive flu epidemic in 1918 and the remainder to combat.

The first American troops reached France in early July 1917. But before General Pershing would send the "Doughboys" to battle, as they were called, he insisted upon a change in Allied strategy and objectives. Trench warfare had caused too many deaths, he argued; open-field combat was essential to victory. Pershing wanted two additional months of training time to introduce his men to trench warfare and the uses of gas. In October 1917 the first Americans died in combat. The following spring the AEF fought alongside the command on the Western Front under Marshal Ferdinand Foch of France.

America's wartime diplomacy included an effort to isolate Germany by persuading Austria-Hungary to drop out of the conflict. The only weak spot in the Central Powers seemed to be Austria-Hungary. Almost as soon as it had declared war on Serbia in 1914, Austria-Hungary wanted to withdraw. In late 1916 Emperor Francis Joseph died and his successor wanted a face-saving peace. The Dual Monarchy was quickly eroding as numerous minority groups became more restless and soldiers increasingly deserted the ranks. Wilson sought to exploit these openings by arranging Austria-Hungary's withdrawal from the war before it collapsed from within. His strategy was not successful, for the presence nearby of German soldiers made it dangerous to consider giving in to the Allies, whereas the continuation of war encouraged the drive for independence among various nationalities who took advantage of the monarchy's vulnerability. By the summer of 1918 the Austro-Hungarian empire lay in pieces.

Wilson announced his goals for the postwar world on January 8, 1918, when he delivered his Fourteen Points address before Congress. Certain guarantees, he insisted, were essential to a peace settlement: freedom of the seas, arms limitations programs, economic interdependence promoted by the removal of barriers to trade, fair settlement of colonial claims and the restoration of Belgium, and the right of the Russian people to self-determination. The president argued that to avert war through secret alliances, the nations must agree to "open covenants, openly arrived at." Many assumed that this phrase meant an end to secret negotiations, but this was not so: Wilson recognized the necessity of private discussions but opposed private agreements that went into effect without appearing before the world in final, published treaty forms. The fourteenth point was indispensable: the establishment of a "general association of nations" to guarantee "political independence and territorial integrity to great and small states alike."

Wilson had several reasons for this address. His peace program greatly differed from that of the Allies, as made clear by the Russian revolutionists' recent publication of the Allies' secret London agreements with the czar in 1915. Under these, France was to receive Alsace-Lorraine and the Saar Valley, whereas the German area west of the Rhine River, containing nearly 5 million people, was to become an independent buffer zone. Italy won guarantees to the Brenner Pass in the Tyrol, which necessitated Austria's giving up Trieste and Trentino (or South Tyrol) and other lands along the top of the Adriatic Sea. Japan was assured of Germany's possessions in the North Pacific and its economic rights in the Shantung Peninsula in China. Russia was to have Constantinople and other parts of the Turkish Empire in Asia Minor. The remainder of Turkey would go to Britain, France, Italy, and Greece. In the Fourteen Points address, Wilson sought to boost Allied morale, arouse popular support for just war aims, and undermine the will of the enemy by offering a humane peace. He was also concerned about Russia, where a provisional government had replaced Czar Nicholas II after his fall in March 1917. Despite Allied hopes that the Russians would continue their war against Germany, they had lost the will to fight. Vladimir Lenin, exiled by the czar, had returned to Russia in early 1917 declaring that his people needed "peace, bread, and land." In November he and Leon Trotsky led the Bolsheviks (or Communists) in establishing a new regime of Soviets (working-class committees). Wilson and the Allies feared that the Bolsheviks would lead the Russians out of the war.

Wilson hoped that a liberal program for peace would appeal to the Bolsheviks, who had called for self-determination and no exchange of territories or payments of indemnities. The Allies feared that the new Russian leaders might sign a separate peace with Germany, for after the Bolsheviks' call for an end to the war, only the Central Powers had expressed interest in the terms. Colonel House was in Europe in late 1917 and urged the Allied governments to counter the Bolshevik offer with one designed to keep Russia in the war, but neither France nor Italy would retreat on territorial or other claims. Allied leaders had already lost a large number of men and could not return from the battlefront empty-handed. The United States had to take the initiative, and Wilson was not disposed to ignore the opportunity. He praised the Bolsheviks' suggestions for peace and declared America's wish to help the Russian people reach "liberty and ordered peace." Point 6 urged the withdrawal of occupation armies from Russia followed by that country's entrance "into the society of free nations under institutions of her own choosing." The world's treatment of the Russians, Wilson warned, would be the "acid test" of its "good will."

Wilson's peace program became effective wartime propaganda through the efforts of the American Committee on Public Information, headed by George Creel. The committee circulated more than 60 million copies of the president's Fourteen Points throughout the world, while the Allies dropped 100,000 pamphlets a day into Germany and Austria-Hungary. Translations of the peace offer called for fair and honorable terms and no "unconditional surrender." They emphasized that America's conflict was with the "military masters" in Berlin, not the German people with whom the United States felt only "sympathy and friendship." America was certain that the German people's interests lay in accepting Wilson's generous peace rather than in following their government's disastrous war. Wilson's Fourteen Points intended to weaken resistance to the Allies by assuring a new world after the war.

The Allies faced many dark moments in the war by the spring of 1918 as they repeatedly failed to break the back of the German armies. Wilson tried two more times in February and March of 1918 to discourage the possibility of peace negotiations between Germany and Russia, when he approved the Bolsheviks' opposition to exactions based on the war, and reiterated his call for self-determination. But the Bolsheviks had signed an armistice with Germany in mid-December 1917, and on March 3 of the following year they negotiated the Treaty of Brest-Litovsk. The Russians made peace at the cost of transferring to German control almost a third of their population and over a million square miles of territory between the Baltic and Black seas. More important, the end of the war in the east freed forty German divisions for the Western Front. In a major offensive launched that same month of March, the Germans by late May had pushed the Allies back to the Marne River, not fifty miles from Paris, destroying Wilson's hopes for peace without victory. To a crowd in Baltimore, he declared that "Germany has once more said that force, and force alone, shall decide whether Justice and Peace shall reign. . . . There is, therefore, but one response possible from us: Force, Force to the utmost." On July 4 he asserted that "the Past and Present are in deadly grapple, and the peoples of the world are being done to death between them. . . . There can be no compromise." The small number of American Doughboys already in France helped resist this onslaught at Saint-Mihiel and Belleau Wood, until at Château-Thierry in June the Allied and Associated Powers blunted the enemy drive.

Meanwhile, concern had grown over events in Russia. Britain and France had already convinced the United States to join them in an international military expedition in Russia, which aimed at diverting German troops back to the Eastern Front and protecting Russian military goods

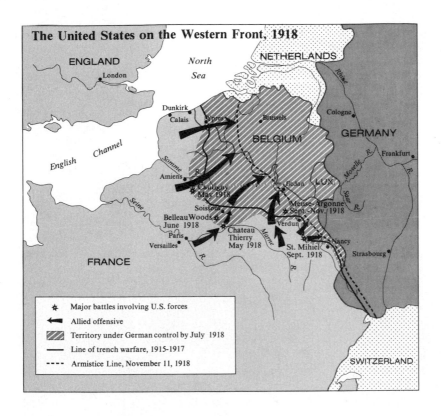

MAP 21

The arrival of the American Expeditionary Force (or "doughboys") broke the stalemate along the Western Front and ultimately led to Allied victory.

and railroads from German takeover. Wilson declared that the American forces also had orders to assist the return to the Western Front of a legion of soldiers from Czechoslovakia who had joined the Russian army in an effort to secure a homeland in Austria-Hungary. The plan called for sending 9,000 American members of the armed forces to Vladivostok in Siberia to help the Czechs back to Europe via the Pacific Ocean, transcontinental United States, and Atlantic. Another objective became apparent: American intervention might slow the advances of Japan, which in subsequent months would send an unusually large contingent of nearly 73,000 men to Siberia for the ostensible reason of protecting Allied war matériel from both the Germans and the Bolsheviks. Wilson also sent about 5,000 troops to Murmansk and Archangel in northern Russia to aid British soldiers trying to safeguard military goods from the Germans.

But as the international force moved into Russia, the issue of inter-

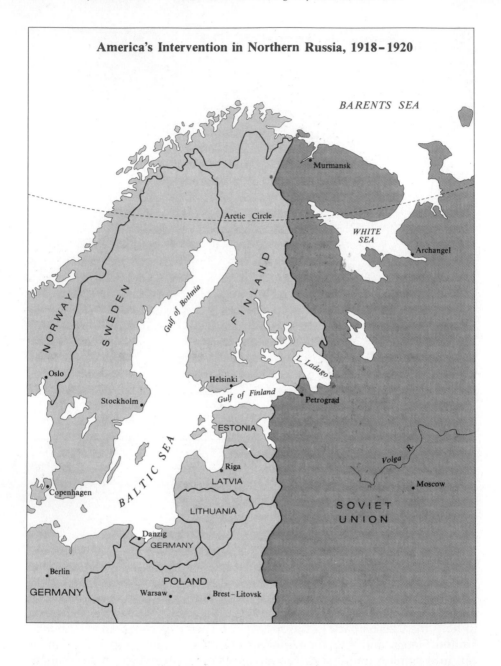

America's Intervention in Northern Russia, 1918–1920

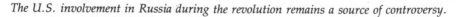

MAP 22

The U.S. involvement in Russia during the revolution remains a source of controversy.

vention became enormously complicated. By mid-1918 the Czechs were fighting the Bolsheviks over control of the Trans-Siberian Railroad, which meant that Allied assistance to the Czechs now implied opposition to the Bolshevik Reds in their civil war against the Whites. Wilson had stipulated no intervention in Russia's internal affairs, but for unexplained reasons his orders arrived late and a few Americans had already joined British and French soldiers in fighting the Bolsheviks over the railroad. An interventionist effort initially designed for military purposes had taken on a political appearance: the United States, critics would later allege, had sought to steer the Russian Revolution into democratic channels. American forces did not return home until early 1920, whereas Japan's remained until late 1922. In the meantime a "Red Scare" broke out in the United States in 1919–20, doubtless reinforcing a decision in Washington to refuse recognition to the Bolshevik regime. Questions remained about the motives for America's intervention, but it is certain that the episode left a legacy of distrust in Russia.

In July 1918 the war along the Western Front turned against the Germans. The Allies and more than a million American soldiers rebuffed the German assault at Château-Thierry, and in the Meuse-Argonne offensive of late September split the Hindenburg Line and approached the borders of Belgium and Germany. The head of the German army, General Erich Ludendorff, urged his government to ask for peace. On October 4, while Americans were fighting in the Argonne Forest, the German chancellor appealed to Wilson for an armistice based on the Fourteen Points. The president, however, proved more difficult to deal with than the Germans had expected. He first wanted them to admit defeat and accept a cease-fire that would not allow them to begin the war anew. The Germans should not totally disarm, Wilson told House, for if the balance tipped too far toward the Allies, real peace would become almost impossible. Finally, the government in Berlin would have to change hands before the United States could consider an armistice.

Ensuing pressure on Kaiser Wilhelm II forced his abdication in early November, and on the day he fled the country a provisional government took over in Germany. With mutinies spreading among German soldiers and violence rocking the nation's cities, the German high command recognized that morale was shattered and the war was over. The kaiser's armies were in a fairly sound military position along the Western Front, but an attempt to continue the war, combined with Germany cracking from within, could lead to an Allied invasion and a vindictive peace. Bulgaria had quit the war in late September, Turkey did the same a month afterward, and Austria-Hungary followed suit in early November. Germany had no alternative but to sue for peace. When the Germans laid down their arms, the AEF held over a fifth of the Western Front. American military forces and matériel had turned the long stalemate into an Allied victory.

But problems suddenly developed among the victorious powers: the Allies opposed a peace based on Wilson's Fourteen Points. The British adamantly opposed freedom of the seas; the French wanted heavy war reparations that would crush Germany. American pressure convinced both Allies to compromise, but at the price of considerable ill will. House, still in Europe, warned that the United States would sign a separate peace with Germany and cut back postwar economic assistance to Britain and France. He also discussed the effects of the president's publicizing the Allies' war aims. Britain and France reluctantly accepted Wilson's conditions but inserted two qualifications: the *Allies* were to define "freedom of the seas," and Germany had to make indemnities "for all damage done to the civilian population of the Allies and their property." On these unhappy notes, the antagonists took the first major steps toward ending the war. Wilson, however, had emerged as the architect of peace.

On November 9 the Germans received notification through the prearmistice agreement that the Fourteen Points would be the basis for peace. Marshal Foch would meanwhile determine the military terms of the cease-fire. He and Pershing set severe military and naval conditions that denied Germany any possibility of rejecting treaty terms. The French were to occupy all territories west of the Rhine River, and Germany was to relinquish its fleet, its largest weapons, and a huge number of locomotives and box cars. At 5 A.M. on November 11, 1918 German representatives signed armistice papers in Foch's headquarters in a railway car in the Compiègne Forest.

THE PARIS PEACE CONFERENCE

The end of the war left considerable apprehension about the kind of peace lying ahead. Roosevelt and many other Americans were dissatisfied because the Allied and Associated Powers had not invaded Berlin and executed the kaiser. But whatever complaints might arise, Wilson had won the opportunity for achieving his central objective in entering the war: to sit at the peace table and draft a peace treaty preventing future wars. The United States would participate in the talks scheduled to begin in Paris in 1919, Wilson's Fourteen Points to be the basis of those discussions.

The previous October Wilson had called on Americans to elect a Democratic Congress that would allow him, he declared, to "continue to be your unembarrassed spokesman in affairs at home and abroad." Republicans denounced this move as demagoguery because it implied that only the Democrats were patriots. The Republicans were furious because they had rallied around Wilson's plea for a political truce during the war, only to have Wilson break it. For whatever reasons, the voters returned a Republican majority in both chambers (the Senate by only two seats). The results would compromise Wilson's position at Paris by suggesting to his European counterparts that he did not represent the majority of his own people and was certainly not an emissary for the world. Roosevelt put it bluntly: "Mr. Wilson has no authority whatever to speak for the American people at this time. His leadership has just been emphatically repudiated by them."

Wilson compounded his first political error by announcing a week after the armistice that he personally would lead the American peace delegation to Paris. Some immediately questioned the legality of a president leaving the country while in office; but they were never able to cite a law upholding their point. Confidants warned that Wilson would become involved in heated debates over details, and that his idealistic aims would suffer if he failed to win on all points. Secretary of State Lansing added that Wilson's image as the world's moral leader could remain intact only if he stayed above such matters. If he operated out of the White House, he could avoid petty, selfish quarrels and make decisions without coming under the pressure of negotiators in Paris. Many in Congress argued that domestic matters demanded his attention and that he should send a delegation, not lead it. Most of all, if he stayed home he could maintain contact with national opinion. Wilson countered that he could not entrust the issues to someone else. The meeting was among heads of state, he declared. "I must go."

Wilson's selection of members of the American Peace Commission also hurt his program. No Republican of political weight sat on it; no senator received an invitation. The president headed a delegation of loyalists: House; Lansing; General Tasker Bliss, America's representative on the Supreme War Council in Paris that had coordinated the Allied effort; and Republican Henry White, a career diplomat with no party influence. Wilson did not confer with members of the Senate Foreign Relations Committee before choosing the delegation, and he did not consult them before leaving for Paris. Had he done so, he might have made room for one of the following: Senator Henry Cabot Lodge, an archenemy of the president who was to become chairman of the powerful Foreign Relations Committee on March 4, 1919; Elihu Root, elder statesman with considerable diplomatic experience; William Howard Taft, former president; and Charles Evans Hughes, loser of the close presidential contest of 1916 and a respected member of the Republican party. All but Lodge had indicated interest in Wilson's peace program and his call for a league of nations. The president, however, insisted on managing the commission his own way. He had lost touch with political reality, for even if successful in Paris, he still had to guide the treaty through the Senate in Washington. Many in the United States recognized the approaching trouble. An American editor described the commission in this manner:

Name	Occupation	Representing
Woodrow Wilson	President	Himself
Robert Lansing	Secretary of state	The executive
Henry White	None	Nobody
Edward M. House	Scout	The executive
Tasker H. Bliss	Soldier	The commander-in-chief

Humorist Will Rogers wryly commented that Wilson had told the Republicans: "I tell you what, we will split 50-50—I will go and you fellows can stay."

The American Peace Commission, along with numerous advisers and a cargo of books, reports, maps, and other scholarly materials, pulled out of New York harbor on board the *George Washington* on December 4, 1918. The group seemed prepared for anything. At Wilson's urgings, House had earlier established "The Inquiry," a team of historians, economists, bankers, and other specialists, who spent more than a year in New York City formulating recommendations on the issues that probably would dominate the negotiations. They compiled nearly 2,000 reports for the American delegates to study, and later drafted parts of the treaty with Germany.

After a nine-day voyage the Americans arrived in France, where they received an enthusiastic welcome that only temporarily hid the troubles lying ahead. Wilson toured the continent for a month, examining the war's destruction and learning that he had become the Messiah to the people of Europe. In Paris a woman wrote: "Wilson, you have given back the father to his home, the ploughman to his field. . . . You have saved our fiancés; love blooms again. Wilson, you have saved our children. Through you evil is punished. Wilson! Wilson! Glory to you, who, like Jesus, have said: Peace on Earth and Good Will to Men!" Wilson believed his mission just: he had a universal mandate from the people to override the selfish ambitions of Allied leaders and achieve lasting peace. He still did not understand that the peace desired by the victors was not based on the precepts of the Sermon on the Mount, but on the wrath God promised to wrongdoers. Germany was not to receive forgiveness; Germany was to be destroyed.

The proceedings in Paris were chaotic from beginning to end. Angry crowds hovered around the scene of the meetings—the French Foreign Office—shouting at the peacemakers, peering through keyholes, banging on the doors and windows, throwing rocks on the roof, demanding revenge. Inside the high-ceilinged halls, poor acoustics, continual loud talk, and wandering delegates prevented speakers from being heard more than a few rows from the front. Most of the thirty-two Allied and Associated Powers, including Britain's four dominions and India, sought security and expansion—not the moralization of the world. The several hundred delegates held ten plenary or general sessions from January through June of 1919, but found that the size of the gathering made it difficult to conduct business. At first the "Supreme Council" or "Council of Ten," comprised of two members each from Britain, France, Italy, Japan, and the United States, handled the major issues in secret and then sent reports to the plenary sessions for final decisions. But this procedure proved cumbersome. By March the "Big Four" or "Council of Four" (Britain, France, Italy, and the United States) took care of important business, many times without the presence of secretaries, whereas fifty-two commissions handled the detailed work of meetings and drafted most of the treaty. All the while, hundreds of reporters swarmed outside the palace, anxiously seeking any news. In a surprise ruling on the opening day of the conference, they had been denied entrance. Rather than gathering firsthand information, the reporters had to depend on a messenger who came out and read a terse and uninformative summary of each day's proceedings. The results were bitter competition for scraps of news, rumors converted into fact by the printed page, and dark suspicions of the actual proceedings inside the chambers.

The general feeling at first was that the work of the conference was preliminary to a final round of negotiations between the victors and the defeated. As in many instances of opening bargaining talks, demands were extreme but open to modification and alteration. Sometime in the course of the meetings, however, these assumptions fell aside, the harsh preliminary terms remained, and German representatives had only the choice of accepting them or renewing the war. The Treaty of Versailles, as German leaders would proclaim afterward, was a *Diktat*, a dictated peace warranting revenge. Whereas Wilson fought for national self-determination and a league of nations built upon the Fourteen Points, the French were interested only in security and vengeance, and that meant harsh conditions for Germany. The severe terms contained in the preliminary peace eventually became the Treaty of Versailles.

One of the most serious obstacles to Wilson's program was the Allies' secret territorial arrangements made in London in 1915. The European powers involved were infuriated when the Bolsheviks published copies of the secret treaties, and yet, except for the Japanese claim to Shantung, Wilson had been aware of these agreements shortly after the United States entered the war. He never discussed them, however, probably to avoid any American commitments while hoping to use his nation's vast economic strength to win a fair peace. The French had even recommended the suspension of all secret agreements, but Wilson chose not to accept this offer and ultimately hurt his cause of self-determination.

But the central problem in Paris was the Allies' vengeful spirit. The other members of the Big Four—Premier Georges Clemenceau of France, Prime Minister David Lloyd George of Britain, and Vittorio Orlando of Italy—had promised their people that they would avenge German wrongs. Clemenceau, seventy-eight years of age, heavily mustached, and called "The Tiger," made no effort to conceal his animosity for the Germans. During the Franco-Prussian War of 1870–71 he had watched the enemy invade Paris, and had seen his people barely survive. In the Great War French casualty lists numbered nearly 4 million, including half of the country's males between the ages of twenty and thirty-two, while the physical destruction was awesome because much of the fighting had taken place in France. Clemenceau, presiding officer of the conference,

The Big Four in Paris, 1919

From left to right: George (England), Orlando (Italy), Clemenceau (France), and Wilson (United States). (National Archives)

had no stomach for Wilson's idealisms. "God gave us the Ten Commandments, and we broke them," he declared. "Wilson gives us the Fourteen Points. We shall see." Lloyd George, a consummate politician, wanted to maintain Germany's capacity to buy British goods without allowing it to threaten the balance of power that he hoped to bring about through the reconstruction of France. Like Clemenceau, he became exasperated with Wilson, declaring him "the most extraordinary compound I have ever encountered of the noble visionary, the implacable and unscrupulous partisan, the exalted idealist and the man of rather petty personal rancour." Orlando's concern was to secure the regions just above Italy. Recent congressional elections did not allow Wilson to claim popular leverage at home; the Big Three refused to give him the lead in Paris.

The first formal meeting in Paris took place on January 12, with Russia noticeably absent. None of the countries represented in Paris had extended recognition to the Bolshevik government, and they now refused to invite Russia to the proceedings. France charged that the Russians' withdrawal from the war and their separate peace with Germany cost them any right to participate in peace talks. Wilson and Lloyd George thought it unwise to draw new boundaries in Europe without Russia's participation, but they finally retreated, justifying their decision on the basis of the civil war still going on over whether the "Reds" or the "Whites" were the voice of Russia. In January Wilson urged those in Paris to call upon the Russian antagonists to accept a cease-fire and meet with the Allies and the United States to work out a peace agreement. Though the Reds showed interest, the Whites, encouraged by the French, refused to attend. Wilson did not give up. With Lloyd George's approval, he directed William Bullitt, a twenty-eight-year-old attaché from the American Peace Commission, to accompany the well-known journalist Lincoln Steffens on a secret mission to Russia in February to discuss armistice terms. Bullitt was inexperienced, liberal in view, and so anxious to please that he exceeded his instructions. He authorized the withdrawal of Allied forces from Russia if the Bolsheviks would assure their enemies sufficient territory to allow the war to wind down. Lenin offered favorable conditions, but before Bullitt could return to Paris the newspapers learned of his mission. The resulting cry of protest caused Lloyd George to disavow the mission, while Wilson pleaded a headache (which probably was true, for he experienced a physical and nervous collapse a day or so later), and sent Bullitt to talk with House. Bullitt was bitterly disillusioned by this treatment and by news of the harsh peace conditions the Allies were considering for Germany. He resigned his commission and went home. The Russians were not in Paris, but the specter of Bolshevism clouded all discussions.

Wilson recognized that the hatred evident in Paris made the establishment of a league of nations *within* the treaty text vital to peace. His counterparts insisted upon drawing the peace treaty first, but he was worried that if things were done in that order, the delegates would dismiss the league in their haste to divide the spoils of war. After considerable debate he won his way. Wilson's struggle for the league took place concurrently with his attempt to establish the principle of self-determination during the discussions over colonies and the birth of new nations. The Allies' commitments to Japan and Britain's promises to its dominions proved the primary barrier to Wilson's call for an "absolutely impartial adjustment of all colonial claims." The most he could get was the "mandate system," whereby former German and Turkish possessions would come under the trusteeship of league members until the freed territories were capable of governing themselves. Wilson had intended that small neutral nations such as Switzerland should administer the mandates, but the former colonies instead went to the victorious powers. He had been unable to budge the Allies from their territorial commitments, and that made a league of nations even more essential.

Wilson had to compromise on territorial questions to save the league. Over a million square miles of territory changed hands, which in itself was a violation of self-determination. The mandate system and the establishment of new states left the erroneous impression that Wilson's assurances of self-determination had prevailed. Yet under the mandates, the Allied powers won most of their territorial demands, while the fledgling independent states were weak and susceptible to outside influence. A saving factor was that in the end most European peoples were aligned with those of similar nationalities. Adoption of the league, Wilson hoped, would remedy the remaining ills.

The president won a big victory when the Paris delegates agreed in late January to incorporate the league covenant into the text of the treaty. He chaired the League of Nations Commission that wrote the covenant, and along with House, who composed its draft, completed the document in ten days of enormous pressure. The central governing body within the League was to be a Council of five permanent members from the major powers (the Big Four and Japan), along with representatives elected from other member states on a rotating basis. There would also be an Assembly comprised of all League members. Article 10 of the covenant, the president proclaimed, was the major safeguard against war because it established the principle of collective security. According to its terms, League members would "respect and preserve as against external aggression the territorial integrity and existing political independence of all Members of the League." In instances of aggression the Council would "advise upon the means by which this obligation shall be fulfilled." While the delegates in Paris studied the draft set before them on February 14, the president prepared to return home to take care of executive responsibilities and to outline the contents of the League covenant to his people.

Opposition to the negotiations in Paris greeted Wilson upon his arrival in the United States in late February. Before leaving Europe he had had cables sent to members of the Senate Foreign Relations and House Foreign Affairs committees, asking them to refrain from making public comments about the matter until he could discuss the peace program with them. But isolationists led by Senator William Borah of Idaho had already begun criticizing Wilson's work in Paris. Weeks before the president sent the treaty to the Senate, Borah had secured a copy and read the entire text into the *Congressional Record*. When Wilson arrived in Boston, he attacked those who failed to recognize that America had a mission to guarantee freedom to humankind. By the time the congressional committees met with him at a White House dinner on February 26, the atmosphere was tense. Not all members were present, the most conspicuous absentee being Borah, who turned down the invitation. Wilson was aware of the congressmen's concern that the League requirement to defend all members' integrity would endanger America's independence of action, and he defended the covenant in a lengthy, acrimonious session. Supporters thought he had fared well; anti-League congressmen came away unconvinced. Republican Senator Frank Brandegee of Connecticut remarked, "I feel as if I had been wandering with Alice in Wonderland and had tea with the Mad Hatter."

By early March the battle lines were becoming clear. League skeptics were beginning to gather around Senator Lodge of Massachusetts, close friend of Roosevelt's and new chairman of the Foreign Relations Committee. The impending struggle over the League seemed to draw out the antagonists by design. Wilson and Lodge were bitter personal and political enemies; each held high academic degrees that perhaps encouraged a sense of jealousy. Whereas the president held a Ph.D. in political science from Princeton and supported American involvement in an organization based on collective security, Lodge had a Ph.D. in history from Harvard and saw little in the past to justify a departure from independent American action in foreign affairs. Wilson's enemies regarded him as straitlaced and stubborn; Lodge's enemies compared his mind to the New England farmland: "Naturally barren, but highly cultivated."

The day before Congress closed its session on March 4, Lodge persuaded thirty-nine Republican senators (more than the third necessary to defeat a treaty) to sign a Round Robin statement declaring that "the constitution of the League of Nations in the form now proposed . . . should not be accepted by the United States." Once the United States signed a peace treaty with Germany, "the proposal for a League of Nations to insure the permanent peace of the world should then be taken up for careful and serious consideration." The warning was clear: the Senate would not approve a treaty that included the League covenant in its text. Yet the Senate had never before refused a peace treaty. That same evening Wilson assured an assembly in New York's Metropolitan Opera House that the Senate would approve the League. The covenant, he declared, would be so tightly woven into the treaty text that a vote against the League would defeat the entire treaty. Even the senators, he felt confident, would not tear down the structure of peace to get at the League.

Wilson returned to Paris in mid-March, indignant over what he considered to be the petty behavior of Lodge and his colleagues; yet he realized that they were a formidable political bloc that could wreck the League. A bipartisan group of League supporters, including former President Taft, had talked with Wilson about making changes in the covenant to assure Senate approval, and upon his return to Paris, he called a meeting of the League of Nations Commissions to suggest four revisions: League members could pull out after two years' notice; domestic matters, including tariffs and immigration, would not come under League jurisdiction; no member could be required to assume mandate responsibilities; the League had no power that could endanger the Monroe Doctrine. But Wilson opposed any alterations in Article 10; to change it, he believed, would destroy the League. Wilson was irritated that during his time home, the conferees in Paris had set the League aside for other matters and that House and Lansing had given in to some of the other delegates' demands. He was determined to carry the fight to the end.

Wilson's biggest battle in Paris was with the French. Clemenceau had demanded the Saar Basin and its coal deposits, German reparations for *all* costs of the war (not merely damages), and, to achieve security against future German invasion, French occupation of German lands west of the

Henry Cabot Lodge in 1910

As a Massachusetts Republican and chairman of the Senate Foreign Relations Committee, Lodge was President Wilson's chief antagonist during the battle in the United States over the League of Nations. (American Heritage Library)

Rhine River as a buffer state. Wilson argued that the French demands violated self-determination because the areas in question were Germanic. Clemenceau objected. To House he impatiently declared, "I can get on with you. You are practical. I understand you, but talking to Wilson is something like talking to Jesus Christ!" During the most heated arguments over France's demands in early April, Wilson became ill with influenza. But despite fits of coughing and a temperature soaring to 103°, he rose from his bed to shout "no" to demands made by Clemenceau, Orlando, and Lloyd George as they sat in the study adjoining his bedroom.

Perhaps Wilson's warning on April 7 that he would return home was decisive, for shortly afterward Clemenceau agreed to a compromise. France got Alsace-Lorraine, but the Rhineland, along with a belt of territory about thirty miles wide on the eastern side of the river, was to be permanently demilitarized and occupied by Allied forces for fifteen years, thereby creating the buffer zone that the French wanted on both sides of the Rhine. France also won the coal mines of the Saar, although the basin would come under League supervision for fifteen years. Afterward a plebiscite would determine whether the Saar would become French or German or remain under international direction. For these terms, Wilson and Lloyd George agreed to a joint security pact guaranteeing their military aid if Germany attacked France. But the Senate in Washington later refused to vote for it, thus releasing the British from any obligation. France received neither the Rhineland nor the security guarantees.

Italy's demands similarly challenged the principle of self-determination. Under the secret London agreements of 1915 Italy was to receive areas in the Alps containing more than 200,000 Germans of Austrian descent. Italy also wanted the city of Fiume, which now constituted a vital outlet to the Adriatic Sea for the new state of Yugoslavia. Whereas most residents of the city were Italian, the majority of those in its outlying districts were Slavs. These demands had not been part of the secret pact of 1915, and Wilson fought them as violations of self-determination. He had earlier approved Italy's claim to the South Tyrol up to the Brenner Pass as important to security, and he later accepted the argument for Trieste. But Wilson refused to consider Italy's demand for Fiume. When he appealed directly to the Italian people, he infuriated Orlando and his colleague. They stalked out of the hall and returned home, where their people and parliament praised them and attacked the American president. The Fiume question remained unsettled at Paris.

Japan also presented serious problems. It sought the Germans' holdings in the North Pacific as well as their economic concessions in China's Shantung Peninsula, and it also hoped to persuade the Allied powers to include in the League covenant a declaration of racial equality. The British dominions, however, led the opposition to such a statement; Australia and others had passed discriminatory legislation against Asians and did not want such a precedent set in Paris. But since Wilson chaired the committee that voted down the Japanese request, the United States drew the blame. The Japanese therefore became adamant about securing Germany's rights in Shantung. They argued that a secret treaty with Britain in 1917 guaranteed them the peninsula and Germany's Pacific islands, in exchange for their support of Britain's claim to Germany's islands in the South Pacific. In the Twenty-one Demands of 1915, the Japanese noted, China had ceded all rights that Japan secured from Germany in the war, and Britain and France had secretly assured Japan that they would support that claim. The Chinese were furious, for they argued that the concessions to Japan had come only under duress and that Shantung housed 30 million Chinese people and was the birthplace of Confucius. Wilson was concerned about self-determination and did not want China to lose what the Germans had originally taken by force, but he was also worried that Japan might join Italy in leaving the conference and thereby abort the League of Nations.

The delegates attempted to draw a compromise on the Japanese demands. Japan received the mandate over Germany's islands in the North Pacific—the Marshalls, Carolines, and Marianas—and it won Germany's economic rights in Shantung, in exchange for a promise (honored in 1923) that Japan would "hand back the Shantung Peninsula in full sovereignty to China retaining only the economic privileges granted to Germany." China later refused to sign the treaty. Indeed, its terms hurt Wilson's image as defender of self-determination. The American press criticized the president's treatment of China, even though he considered the concession another part of the price necessary to win the League. The Shantung settlement, Wilson later remarked, "was the best that could be had out of a dirty past."

On the German question Wilson sought a fair settlement that would not contain the seeds of another war; but he likewise had to give in to the Allies' demands that Germany accept full blame for the war and agree to pay reparations for *all* damages. "If we humiliate the German people and drive them too far," he warned, "we shall destroy all form of government, and Bolshevism will take its place." His counterparts at the conference believed differently. France and Britain wanted Germany to sign a statement assuming total responsibility for the war and its aftermath. The "war guilt" clause, Article 231 of the treaty, was an admission that Germany and its cohorts had caused "all the loss and damages" incurred by the Allies "as a consequence of the war imposed upon them by the aggression of Germany and her allies." The facts do not support this allegation, but the Germans were forced to sign; they had laid down their arms in accordance with the armistice and the Allies had not. Wilson went along with the Allies because he believed the League of Nations could override these problems later on.

The reparations demands caused deep German resentment, toward both the Allies and Wilson. Besides believing the terms excessive, the Germans had trusted Wilson, who in February 1918 had promised "no punitive damages." Germany's agreement to the armistice had rested on this assurance, although the Allies asserted that their conditions for the restoration of German-occupied territories included reparations "for all damages done to the civilian population of the Allies and their property by the aggression of Germany." One could interpret this statement as a pledge against assessing Germany for all costs of the war, but the Allies had not made this clear. In fact, British leaders promised in the parliamentary election campaign of December 1918 that they would charge Germany for *all* expenses related to the war. At first Wilson refused to consider the proposition, but Lloyd George argued that the Germans should assume responsibility for pensions and other payments to Allied soldiers and their families as "damages done to the civilian population." This interpretation greatly increased the amount Britain and its allies would receive, but Wilson acquiesced—perhaps with the understanding that this would not raise the *total* assessment on Germany but would increase the percentage *within* the sum awarded to the British. In actuality, the Allies elevated the overall damage claim by tacking on pensions and similar allotments to other charges that they set.

The delegates in Paris could not agree on a reparations figure and turned over the matter to a Reparations Commission. Two years later, in 1921, the commission set the figure at $33 billion—thirty-three times the amount levied on France in 1871 after its war with Prussia.

One cannot evaluate the impact on Germany of the reparations charge without considering the other parts of the treaty that obstructed its ability to pay. Germany was to give up all colonies, most of its merchant vessels, a great part of its industrial and agricultural resources, and its coal in the Saar and iron ore in Lorraine. East Prussia was separated from Germany by the Polish Corridor, which granted Poland passage to the sea through an area that had belonged to Germany for hundreds of years. Furthermore, the German port of Danzig in the Corridor was to become a free city under League supervision. Finally, about 7 million German-speaking Austrians were denied unification with Germany because of French opposition. Thus Germany was to surrender more than 6 million people (a tenth of its total) and one-eighth of its territory.

The Germans were allowed into the treaty proceedings—*after* the delegates had negotiated the terms—and at Versailles were given the document to sign, not to discuss. In an extremely tense plenary session in the Trianon Palace on May 17, 1919, Clemenceau handed the treaty to Count Brockdorff-Rantzau, head of the German delegation. As he did so, the French leader declared in cold, biting language that "it is neither the time nor the place for superfluous words. . . . The time has come when we must settle our accounts. You have asked for peace," Clemenceau concluded. "We are ready to give you peace." The Germans did not stand to receive the document from the already standing Clemenceau, nor did they assume the appearance of a defeated people. Numerous members of the Allied delegations, particularly the British, were displeased with the treaty and even the slightest show of conciliation by the Germans at this crucial juncture might have led to an easing of terms. Those who drafted the document had done so in independent groups, many under the assumption that their requirements were for bargaining purposes and subject to revision as the negotiations progressed. But when drafted articles came together in treaty form, many delegates realized that the severity of the total package prevented an equitable adjustment of claims in line with the Fourteen Points.

On May 29 the Germans delivered their response to the Versailles Treaty. They bitterly denounced the entire document instead of specific sections and put the delegates on the defensive by suggesting that they were evil and vindictive. Most of the negotiators rallied around Clemenceau, and nearly all terms remained unchanged. The Germans had the choice of signing the treaty or resuming the war. The latter was unthinkable: their will was broken, they had disarmed while the Allies had not, and Foch had promised to carry renewed fighting into Berlin. On June 23, less than two hours before the armistice was to expire, Germany agreed to the terms. Five days later the signing ceremony took place in the Palace of Versailles's Hall of Mirrors, the same place where the Prussians had announced the creation of the German Empire after their conquest of France in 1871. Germany had lost the war and now had lost the peace. Most of its people directed their bitterness toward France and Britain, but many regarded Wilson as central to the humiliation.

THE TREATY FIGHT IN THE UNITED STATES

When Wilson made his second and final return to the United States in July he found that opposition to the League was growing. On July 10 he turned over the treaty package to the Senate with assurances that "the hand of God" had shaped the peace. He later told the French ambassador in Washington that he would reject any amendments to the treaty. "I shall consent to nothing. The Senate must take its medicine." To a journalist he emphasized that *the Senate is going to ratify the treaty.*

Opposition to the League in the United States came from varied sources. Politics was important, for Republicans did not want Democrats to enter the campaign of 1920 with the League of Nations as an asset and Wilson as standard-bearer a third time. Numerous ethnic groups criticized the treaty. German-Americans denounced the terms, Italian-Americans insisted upon Fiume, Irish-Americans wanted freedom from Britain, and other minorities wondered what had happened to self-determination. Racist fears also shaped reactions to the League. Missouri Senator James Reed remarked: "Think of submitting questions involving the very life of the United States to a tribunal on which a nigger from Liberia, a nigger from Honduras, a nigger from India . . . each have votes equal to that of the great United States."

The spirit of Progressive reform also permeated the arguments of those who fought the League. Nebraska Senator George Norris believed that the proposed organization lacked the means for preventing war and claimed it would further big power interests. Senator Robert LaFollette of Wisconsin warned that the League's authority to halt aggression could be used to put down colonial rebellions against repressive governments. Article 10 of the covenant, Borah declared, would send "our boys to fight throughout the world by order of the League." It also set back self-determination by authorizing the use of military force in protecting the interests of imperial powers. Big business would combine with bankers to run the organization. "If the Savior of men would revisit the earth and declare for a League of Nations," Borah proclaimed, "I would be opposed to it."

The emotions of war had raised hopes for a better world, and, as is often the case, the post-crusade attitude had turned from idealism toward reality, leaving bitter disillusionment. The interventionists had only temporarily shelved isolationism, for the Fourteen Points had not changed the world. Renewed war in Europe seemed likely, and Americans had had enough of the Old World to seek the sanctity afforded by two oceans. Article 10, they feared, required the United States to forgo sovereignty in the interests of internationalism. The sacrifices Wilson sought had not made the world safe for democracy, nor had they ended the threat of war. The intriguing question is whether many Americans might have accepted a compromise between the programs advocated by Wilson and Lodge; but neither man seemed willing to consider limited international involvement.

The Senate was divided over the League. The Republican party held the majority by only a two-vote margin. Sixteen of the forty-nine Republicans opposed the League with or without changes, and were called the "irreconcilables." Led by Borah, Norris, and LaFollette, they were referred to as "bitter-enders" or the "Battalion of Death." The remainder of the party broke into roughly three degrees of reaction: perhaps as many as ten favored moderate revisions but would support the League; nearly eighteen aligned with Lodge, chairman of the Foreign Relations Committee and recently chosen majority leader, in wanting major alterations as a condition for joining the organization; the rest fell somewhere between the two groups. Lodge recognized that the Senate Democrats had mixed feelings and would give varying levels of support to amendments he might propose. Should the treaty pass, he wanted enough changes to protect the United States from outside interference in its affairs.

Lodge's motives for opposing the League are uncertain. One might attribute them to his loyalty to Roosevelt, who consistently opposed Wilson, or to Lodge's animosity toward the president. Yet more was probably involved. Lodge had always been an ardent nationalist and imperialist who would have predictable doubts about American participation in an international organization built upon collective security. It is not clear whether he intended to destroy Wilson's League of Nations from the first or merely to insert revisions making it safe for American membership. He proposed a series of "reservations" that he claimed would safeguard the constitutional role of Congress in foreign policy. Amendments, he realized, would necessitate new negotiations with the European powers for acceptance, whereas reservations would go into effect with or without their approval. Article 10 was the central threat. If Congress specifically retained the power to approve any American action, Lodge seemed amenable to the League. As chairman of the Senate Foreign Relations Committee, he helped pack it with members unfriendly to the League. Ten of the seventeen members were Republicans, including Borah and five other irreconcilables, and only one of the remaining four Republicans favored the treaty without change. Among the seven Democrats, one had a record in foreign policy of supporting Lodge more than Wilson.

Perhaps at first Lodge saw little chance of defeating the League, but hoped that its support would diminish with the passage of time. He realized that the introduction of amendments would lead to lengthy hearings and tie up the League proposal in committee. In the meantime, opponents of the treaty could remind Americans of Old World dangers. When the treaty came before the Foreign Relations Committee, Lodge read all 264 pages of the text into the official record, a stall tactic that required two weeks and did not permit the hearings to begin until July 31. Six more weeks would pass as sixty witnesses gave testimony that filled 1,200 pages of the record. Some people, such as Secretary of State Lansing, were informative; others spoke for minority groups and merely aired grievances about the treaty. The most damaging testimony came from William Bullitt, who had resigned the Paris peace commission when Wilson ignored his negotiations with Lenin. Bullitt caused a sensation when he told the Senate committee that Lansing had privately described the League as "entirely useless" and that if the Senate understood the treaty's implications, it would vote down Wilson's program. If Lodge's methods were transparent in motive, they were working. By the autumn of 1919 the treaty seemed to be losing popularity.

The culmination came with a three-hour public meeting in the White House on August 19 between the president and Lodge's Foreign Relations Committee. Wilson told the senators that he was agreeable to incorporating explanatory sections into the general peace pact, but he would not accept them as formal terms. Such a measure, he asserted, would alter the proposal and necessitate another series of negotiations with the Allies to secure their approval. Yet it was unclear where to insert these interpretive provisions, and when Wilson refused to attach them to the ratification resolution, the Senate considered this unreasonable.

Wilson refused to compromise on Article 10. The deals he had accepted in Paris had sapped his reservoir of concessions, and he was in no mood to grant more in the United States. Should Congress specifically assert the right to determine whether to defend another country, he believed, the core of the League would cease to exist. Yet he doubtless understood that the war had greatly damaged the military capacity of the Allied governments and that if the United States decided against intervening in a given situation, the other four members would hesitate to act. If Wilson thought this privately, he could not express it publicly. He came close to an admission during his speeches on behalf of the League in the autumn of 1919. Article 10, he explained, bound the United States morally but not legally to use military means in enforcing League decisions. But this statement impressed many as a confusing attempt to use expediency in achieving his goals. He could not explicitly guarantee American protection from the decisions of the League Council.

Wilson was a political warrior and would not submit to the Senate's wishes: he would take his case to the American people. Though sixty-three years of age, in failing health, and exhausted by his long fight for domestic reform, the war effort, and the ordeal in Paris, he set out in September on an 8,000-mile speaking tour through the Old Northwest, Upper Mississippi Valley, and Far West. In these centers of isolationist sentiment he delivered over thirty major speeches, as well as numerous short addresses along the way (from the rear of the train), all warning that the Senate's failure to approve the pact would betray the millions of boys who died in the war, encourage a resurgence of aggression, and require another intervention in European affairs. Those who opposed the treaty, he charged, were traitors to humanity. Isolationist senators such as Borah and California's Hiram Johnson became alarmed over the crowds gathering to hear the president, and began speaking in the same places a day or so later in an attempt to dismantle his progress. Wilson appeared to win converts among the people, but his derogatory remarks about League opponents in the Senate only hardened their positions and ensured a more difficult time for acceptance of his position in that body—the only battleground that could ultimately decide the issue.

Wilson's health broke under the excessive heat and pressure of countless speeches, press conferences, and interviews. Blinding headaches hit him as in Paris, and he experienced a noticeable trembling of the body and severe loss of emotional control. Yet he seemed willing to sacrifice himself for the treaty. In Pueblo, Colorado, on September 25, a crowd greeted him with a ten-minute standing ovation. He tearfully urged support for the League as humanity's last hope for peace, but at the close was so mentally and physically drained that he turned ashen on the platform and later collapsed on the train. Rushed back to Washington, he suffered a massive stroke a few days afterward that paralyzed the left side of his body and made him a virtual invalid.

Wilson's stroke isolated him and seemed to harden his resistance to compromise. For nearly eight months he did not see his cabinet, and during the first few weeks of his convalescence no one except his doctor and his wife were able to talk with him. Mrs. Wilson, the former Edith Bolling, had sole access to the president and decided which papers and eventually which people got into his room. By early 1920 House and Lansing had suggested compromises to save the League, and for that they completed the fall from grace that had begun in Paris. Everyone had betrayed him, Wilson seemed to believe, but he would not forsake the cause. When rumors spread about whether the "sick man" in the White House was steering the ship of state, Senate Republicans sent a committee to inquire about his health. Senator Albert Fall headed it and declared, "Well, Mr. President, we have all been praying for you." Wilson snapped back, "Which way, Senator?"

After considerable wrangling in the Senate, Lodge emerged in November with fourteen reservations (coincidental with Wilson's Fourteen Points?) that would have to precede passage of the treaty. More discussions and changes followed before the Republicans, supported by more than a few Democrats, indicated approval. Before Wilson left Washington for the speaking tour west, he had offered terms of a compromise through Senate Minority Leader Gilbert Hitchcock, who then proceeded to add one provision that dealt with Britain's right to more than one vote because of its dominions. Yet even though Wilson's attempts were similar to those offered by Lodge, they failed to resolve objections over Article

10, the Monroe Doctrine, the League's relation to domestic matters, and withdrawal of membership. All five issues had come before the Senate in November. By this time, however, even the moderates had promised to support Lodge's program. His second reservation related to Article 10 and guaranteed no American action without the consent of Congress. His fifth reservation protected the Monroe Doctrine from any arbitral or investigatory procedure under the League. The sixth refused the United States's approval of Japan's rights in Shantung, and the last, the fourteenth, renounced American subjection to a League decision in which "any member of the league and its self-governing dominions, colonies, or parts of empire, in the aggregate have cast more than one vote." Lodge had inserted another safeguard in the introduction to the Senate resolution. Ratification of the treaty was to require approval of *all* fourteen reservations by three of the four "principal allied and associated powers" (Britain, France, Italy, and Japan). It seemed unlikely that either Britain or Japan would accept Lodge's reservations explained above.

That same month of November Wilson informed members of his party that a vote for the Lodge reservations was a vote against the League. Still bedridden, he wrote Hitchcock that the Democrats must defeat the treaty containing the reservations. Hitchcock warned that fellow party members would not do this unless Wilson permitted some changes in his treaty proposal. "Let Lodge compromise!" Wilson snorted. "Well, of course, he must compromise also," Hitchcock declared, "but we might well hold out the olive branch." The president quickly replied, "Let Lodge hold out the olive branch." On November 19 the Senate voted against two versions of the League covenant. The first bill contained Lodge's reservations, and all Democrats save four followed the president's bidding and banded with the irreconcilables to defeat it in two roll calls. After considerable discussion the Senate decided not to vote on Hitchcock's suggested changes, and the second bill, that without reservations, likewise failed to pass. Perhaps a few of those who supported the League but voted against it hoped their move might lead to a coalition of moderates that could pass a compromise treaty. Others were doubtless afraid of the president's wrath should they break party ranks. Enormous pressure from the White House had maintained party unity against amendments to the treaty, but with the bizarre result that Democrats joined Republicans (including the irreconcilables) in ensuring its defeat. Republicans noted that Wilson had blocked America's membership in the League, not they. Brandegee, an irreconcilable, turned to Lodge and remarked, "We can always depend on Mr. Wilson. He never has failed us."

By early 1920 supporters of the treaty believed it wise to accept the Lodge reservations and save the League. Colonel House, Herbert Hoover, William Jennings Bryan, and William Howard Taft called for compromise, while Britain and France gave indications that they would accept a treaty with or without reservations. Wilson still opposed changes. He wrote a letter to those at the Jackson Day dinner on January 8 stating that Lodge's reservations would kill the treaty and that the presidential election later that year should be "a great and solemn referendum" on the people's will. He had earlier considered a proposal that senators opposed to the treaty should resign and run for reelection in 1920 on the League issue. If most of them won, he and his vice president would resign after he took steps to assure that a Republican completed his term in the White House. The bulk of Americans, Wilson believed, supported the treaty.

The negative votes on the treaty in November did not kill the issue. The great majority of senators claimed to favor a League with reservations, and they faced pressure from numerous Americans interested in the treaty. Nearly thirty national organizations, boasting 20 million members, sent delegates to Lodge to demand acceptance of the treaty. But when he considered a compromise, Borah and other irreconcilables abruptly ended that thought by warning that they would unseat him as party majority leader. The treaty came before the Senate for the last time on March 19, 1920. Now laden with fifteen reservations (the new one calling for Ireland's independence), it failed again, this time by a close margin of 49 to 35. Despite pressure from Wilson's cabinet members, twenty-one Democrats broke with the president to support this proposal; had seven more done so, the treaty would have passed. Yet even then, Wilson would have refused to ratify the resolution.

THE LEAGUE AND THE PRESIDENTIAL ELECTION OF 1920

Despite Wilson's claim that the presidential election of 1920 was a referendum on the treaty, the issues were too muddled to draw conclusions. The Democrats, led by Governor James Cox of Ohio, called for "immediate ratification of the treaty without reservations," although their candidate left the door open for compromise. The Republican platform supported "agreement among the nations to preserve the peace of the world" but not at the cost of "national independence." Party nominee Warren G. Harding, who as a senator had favored the League with reservations, became increasingly vague on the matter and prevented the race from focusing on the League. The Republicans could not express interest in the League without driving out the irreconcilables, and yet their candidate had supported the treaty with the Lodge reservations. Harding declared in the campaign that he favored an "association of nations" but fuzzily suggested one greatly improved over Wilson's proposal. As the contest wore on he became more outspoken against the United States's membership in the League. A month before election day Harding told a crowd in Des Moines, Iowa that Cox "favors going into the Paris League and I favor staying out."

If Harding did not confuse voters, a public declaration by thirty-one well-known Republicans in behalf of both the League *and* Harding surely did. A week after the candidate's renunciation of American membership in the organization, these Republicans (including Hoover, Charles Evans Hughes, Elihu Root, and Henry Stimson) explained that if Harding won the election, he should persuade other nations to strike Article 10 from the League covenant as a condition to America's membership.

There is no way to determine the meaning of the election. A vote for Cox could have meant support for the League, whereas one for Harding could have indicated either favor for Root and the others who were for the League, or one for Borah and the irreconcilables who opposed it. Harding won by a landslide, and even while the irreconcilables proclaimed the treaty issue dead, the thirty-one Republicans who signed the public statement looked forward to dropping Article 10 and joining the League. Two of them became members of the new president's cabinet (Hughes as secretary of state and Hoover as secretary of commerce), but when the administration later seemed to move toward League membership, the isolationists in the Senate warned that if the president did not back off they would fight every part of his administration's program. In April 1921 Harding announced to Congress that he would not support American membership in *any* organization of nations. Such a move would betray "the deliberate expression of the American people in the recent election." Congress officially ended the war in July and the following month concluded a treaty with Germany that tied the United States to all parts of the Versailles Treaty *except* the League. Despite Harding's assurances about a popular mandate against the League, the vote in 1920 was more for a return to "normalcy" than a verdict on the League. Americans were tired of crusades. Wilsonian reformism at home and abroad lost the election and took the League down with it.

Selected readings

Bailey, Thomas A., *Woodrow Wilson and the Great Betrayal.* 1945.

———, *Woodrow Wilson and the Lost Peace.* 1944.

Coffman, Edward M., *The War to End All Wars: The American Military Experience in World War I.* 1968.

Cooper, John M., Jr., *The Warrior and the Priest: Woodrow Wilson and Theodore Roosevelt.* 1983.

Ferrell, Robert H., *Woodrow Wilson and World War I, 1917–1921.* 1985.

Fleming, Denna F., *The United States and the League of Nations, 1918–1920.* 1932.

Gelfand, Lawrence E., *The Inquiry: American Preparations for Peace, 1917–1919.* 1963.

George, Alexander L., and Juliette L. George, *Woodrow Wilson and Colonel House: A Personality Study.* 1956.

Goldhurst, Richard, *The Midnight War: The American Intervention in Russia, 1918–1920.* 1978.

Hawley, Elis W., *The Great War and the Search for a Modern Order: A History of the American People and Their Institutions, 1917–1933.* 1979.

Kennan, George F., *American Diplomacy.* Expanded ed. 1984. Originally published as *American Diplomacy, 1900–1950.* 1951.

————, *The Decision to Intervene.* 1958.

————, *Russia Leaves the War.* 1956.

Kuehl, Warren F., *Seeking World Order: The United States and International Organization to 1920.* 1969.

Levin, N. Gordon, Jr., *Woodrow Wilson and World Politics: America's Response to War and Revolution.* 1968.

Link, Arthur S., *Woodrow Wilson: Revolution, War, and Peace.* 1979. Rev. ed. of *Wilson the Diplomatist: A Look at His Major Foreign Policies.* 1957.

————, ed., *Woodrow Wilson and a Revolutionary World, 1913–1921.* 1982.

Livermore, Seward W., *Politics Is Adjourned: Woodrow Wilson and the War Congress, 1916–1918.* 1966.

Maddox, Robert J., *William E. Borah and American Foreign Policy.* 1969.

Mayer, Arno J., *Political Origins of the New Diplomacy, 1917–1918.* 1959.

————. *Peacemaking: Containment and Counterrevolution at Versailles.* 1967.

Mee, Charles L., Jr., *The End of Order: Versailles, 1919.* 1980.

Osgood, Robert, *Ideals and Self-Interest in America's Foreign Relations: The Great Transformation.* 1953.

Peterson, H. C., and Gilbert C. Fite, *Opponents of War, 1917–1918.* 1968.

Pratt, Julius W., *America and World Leadership, 1900–1921.* 1967. Originally published as *Challenge and Rejection.* 1967.

Schwabe, Klaus, *Woodrow Wilson, Revolutionary Germany, and Peacemaking, 1918–1919: Missionary Diplomacy and the Realities of Power.* 1985.

Stallings, Laurence, *The Doughboys: The Story of the AEF, 1917–1918.* 1963.

Stone, Ralph, *The Irreconcilables: The Fight against the League of Nations.* 1970.

Thompson, John M., *Russia, Bolshevism, and the Versailles Peace.* 1966.

Unterberger, Betty M., *America's Siberian Expedition.* 1956.

Walworth, Arthur, *America's Moment, 1918: American Diplomacy at the End of World War I.* 1977.

Weinstein, Edwin A., *Woodrow Wilson: A Medical and Psychological Biography.* 1981.

Widenor, William C., *Henry Cabot Lodge and the Search for an American Foreign Policy.* 1980.

Chapter Fifteen

The Movement toward Internationalism, 1921–1933

Of all nations in the Western world, only the United States emerged from World War I stronger than when the war began. Germany was devastated and humiliated; the Austro-Hungarian empire had been dismembered. The Russian empire, upon the triumph of the Bolsheviks, had seen czarist tyranny replaced by civil war, economic chaos, and communist government by terror. The "victors" in Europe—Britain, France, and Italy—had suffered awesome destruction of property and had accumulated public debts of unprecedented and unmanageable proportions. Both sides had lost the cream of their young manhood: more than 8 million killed, another 21 million wounded, and countless more demoralized and disillusioned. The United States, by contrast, lost nearly 50,000 soldiers in combat and another 200,000 were wounded; for most of the 4.8 million Americans who volunteered or were drafted for military service, the war was at worst a nuisance and at best an exhilarating experience. Economically the war brought not destruction but a huge increase in productive capacity, together with profits in the form of many billions of dollars owed by the Allies for war matériel America had supplied them. Indeed, America's economic expansion was so great relative to other nations that, during the postwar decade, it was producing 70 percent of the world's petroleum, 40 percent of the world's coal, and nearly half of the world's industrial output.

In these circumstances the United States found itself thrust into a role it was not entirely willing and altogether unable to play: that of world leader. In this role the Americans failed, but not (as historical myth would have it) for want of trying. Despite the emphasis upon domestic and hemispheric affairs, the refusal to join the League of Nations and the

World Court, the influence of vociferous isolationist and pacifist groups, and the bungling of financiers, the United States took the initiative in trying to establish international peace and order through nonmilitary means. Though moderately successful in the hemisphere, it failed outside the Americas partly because of naiveté and inexperience, and partly because of forces unleashed by the Great War that were beyond the capacity of any nation to manage. Only upon the collapse of the world economy between 1929 and 1933 did the United States retreat into a shell of irresponsibility.

ATTEMPTS AT DISARMAMENT

Superficially, it does seem that the United States embraced isolationism in 1921. When a reporter asked President Warren G. Harding about European affairs, Harding is said to have replied, "I don't know anything about this European stuff." Republican presidents Calvin Coolidge and Herbert Hoover followed the same pattern and devoted their attention principally to domestic matters, leaving foreign affairs mainly to their able secretaries of state.

With Europe in shambles after the war, the United States sought to secure the Western Hemisphere by working toward better relations with the Latin American states, long in disarray after the interventionist policies of Presidents Roosevelt, Taft, and Wilson. The defeat of Germany had alleviated fears of outside control of the Panama Canal, allowing the United States to reconsider its relationship with Latin America. In addition, many Americans regarded trade as fundamental to world peace, whereas others were opposed to their government's interventionist policies in the Caribbean. During the decade the United States signed a treaty with Colombia compensating that country for America's earlier acquisition of canal rights in Panama, offered assurances in Rio de Janeiro that it sought no territory in Latin America, withdrew its forces from the Dominican Republic, and settled long-standing problems with Mexico relating to land reforms and government expropriations of oil and minerals belonging to Americans. Relations with Latin America hardened again, however, when in 1928 at the Sixth Inter-American Conference in Havana, Secretary of State Frank B. Kellogg refused to issue a pledge against intervention because at some time the United States might need to protect its citizens' lives and property. Still, by the end of the 1920s the United States was preparing to embark upon a course in hemispheric affairs that would focus on allaying the ill feelings caused by the Monroe Doctrine, Roosevelt Corollary, and Wilson's missionary diplomacy.

By the time Hoover became president in 1929, considerable pressure had built for the renunciation of American interventionism in Latin America and the conversion of the Monroe Doctrine into a multilateral instrument of policy. The president-elect had just returned from a lengthy goodwill tour of Latin America in November 1928 that set the tone for what would later be called the Good Neighbor policy, and in his inaugural address he furthered this feeling by indicating interest in ending the presence of U.S. marines in the Caribbean. Indeed, in 1930 the government published a 236-page document written by Undersecretary of State J. Reuben Clark, entitled a *Memorandum on the Monroe Doctrine,* which was ambiguous in wording but repudiated the Roosevelt Corollary and seemed to assure an end to military intervention in Latin America. In reality the Clark memorandum only renounced intervention based on the Monroe Doctrine, retaining by implication the right to intervene on the basis of America's national interest. The memorandum was also an expression of long-standing State Department sentiments. Yet the United States appeared to have reversed past policies, even while continuing to spread influence in the hemisphere by indirect means. When the Great Depression deepened unrest in Latin America and helped set off numerous revolutions, Hoover dropped Wilson's moral approach to recognition and returned to the principles of *de facto* recognition. By the early 1930s American marines had pulled out of Nicaragua and Haiti, and the United States had ended its protectorate over Cuba by abrogating the Platt Amendment. The result was improved relations with Latin America.

In matters outside the hemisphere the United States avoided anything that suggested an official connection with the League of Nations, including participation in the so-called World Court. The United States had initially proposed that kind of institution—a court of international law, not of arbitration—at the First Hague Conference in 1899 and again in the Second Hague Conference in 1907. But the tribunal established at The Hague was built on arbitration. The covenant of the League had authorized its council to create a court of international law, separate and apart from the League, and in May 1922 the Permanent Court of International Justice, or World Court, was established. Soon afterward Secretary of State Charles Evans Hughes persuaded President Harding to ask the Senate to approve American membership, but the chairman of the Foreign Relations Committee after Lodge's death, the irreconcilable isolationist William Borah, led a successful fight against the proposal. Membership in the Court, he warned, would lead the United States into the League. Similarly, the Senate blocked various other State Department efforts that might promote American participation in League affairs.

Despite the Harding administration's initial efforts to ignore the League, Hughes sent observers to its meetings in Geneva, and the United States took part in its business related to social work, drug control activities, efforts to halt the white slave traffic, and arms limitations talks. Moreover, Hughes, later Secretary of State Kellogg, and other Americans served on the Court over the years. In addition, the Republican secretaries of state worked diligently to negotiate bilateral and multilateral arbitration and conciliation treaties outside the framework of the League of Nations, all with a view toward establishing world order through law.

But the most important American initiatives aimed toward disarmament. Conventional wisdom of the time held that the Great War had resulted from the armaments race in Europe during the decade or so before 1914. It followed logically from that premise that if the major powers reduced their military establishments, international tensions would decline and international trust would increase accordingly, and the prospects for a lasting peace would be immeasurably enhanced. So thinking, the United States initiated and participated in half a dozen international disarmament conferences during the 1920s and early 1930s.

The first of these conferences arose from the threat of a postwar naval armaments race among the United States, Britain, and Japan. The United States Navy was second in the world to Britain and posed a threat to Japan by expanding its fleet in the Pacific and building a base at Pearl Harbor. Japan ranked third in the world in naval power after the war, and by 1921 a third of its budget was devoted to expanding its fleet. This program bolstered rumors that the Japanese intended to fortify mandated German islands in the Pacific, and probably contributed to the call by the Department of the Navy in Washington to build a larger fleet. Meanwhile the British had alienated Americans by their recent renewal of the Anglo-Japanese Alliance of 1902, and by their attempts to establish oil rights in the Middle East. Yet both the United States and Britain were reluctant to enter an expensive naval race.

Japan was in a precarious position after the Great War. France had joined the United States and Britain in assigning more vessels to the Far East, and should the three nations reach an understanding in Asia, Japan would stand alone. Problems had already developed over China, Shantung, Siberia, and the Japanese mandates in the Pacific. But the British also had troubles with the United States, and they were under pressure from Canada to terminate the alliance with Japan. To be relieved of that obligation, British Prime Minister David Lloyd George would have to give Japan something in return—perhaps American concessions in Asia and the Pacific Ocean. The time was right for arms limitations talks.

In late 1920 Borah introduced a resolution calling for a disarmament conference involving the United States, Britain, and Japan. Such a move, he argued, would reduce arms expenditures and promote peace. Though Harding favored naval expansion, he changed his stand after Congress overwhelmingly approved the Borah resolution. He announced a meeting on naval disarmament to convene in Washington in November 1921. France and Italy were also to receive invitations, and when the British recommended that the delegates focus on the Pacific and Far East, it became necessary to include China, Belgium, Portugal, and the Netherlands.

On November 12, 1921, Hughes opened the first session of the Washington Naval Conference and stunned everyone by proposing specific arms limitations and cutbacks. Declaring that "the way to disarm is to disarm," he called for a ten-year holiday on the construction of capital ships, which were battleships or battle cruisers of more than 10,000 tons and fitted with a minimum of eight-inch guns. To fulfill these requirements, he explained, the United States would have to scrap thirty such vessels, Britain nineteen, and Japan seventeen. In half an hour Hughes had called for junking nearly 2 million tons of ships, a figure that a British journalist declared to be more "than all the admirals of the world have sunk in a cycle of centuries." An American journalist wrote that Hughes's recommendations had caused one British admiral to come "forward in his chair with the manner of a bulldog, sleeping on a sunny doorstep, who had been poked in the stomach by the impudent foot of an itinerant soapcanvasser."

Hughes's speech drew thunderous applause and even tears from observers who sensed an end to war. A British newsman wrote: "It is an audacious and astonishing scheme, and took us off our feet. The few men to whom I spoke babbled incoherently. What will they say in London? To see a British First Lord of the Admiralty, and another late First Lord, sitting at a table with the American Secretary of State telling them how many ships they might keep and how many they should scrap, struck me as a delightfully fantastic idea."

The first major settlement at the Washington Conference was the Four-Power Treaty among the United States, Britain, Japan, and France. Signed on December 13, 1921, it achieved one of the United States's major objectives by terminating the Anglo-Japanese Alliance of 1902, and won Japan's assent to later disarmament terms by assuring the status quo in the Pacific. Hughes had made clear that the Anglo-Japanese pact seemed directed at the United States, and argued that Japan could give it up because Germany and Russia were no longer threats in the Far East. The Four-Power Treaty left the implication of armed cooperation when the signatories promised to "communicate with one another fully and frankly in order to arrive at an understanding as to the most efficient measures to be taken, jointly or separately, to meet the exigencies of the particular situation." Since each nation guaranteed respect for the other's Pacific holdings, the advantage went to Japan—the power with the largest possessions in the Pacific. The Senate later hesitated to approve the pact out of fear that a deeper commitment could violate isolationism, but it finally did so after attaching an amendment that the United States would make "no commitment to armed force, no alliance, no obligation to join in any defense."

On the day the Washington Naval Conference adjourned, February 6, 1922, the delegates agreed to their second important pact—disarmament conditions contained in the Five-Power Treaty. The United States, Britain, Japan, France, and Italy approved a ten-year moratorium on the building of capital ships and set a maximum tonnage on aircraft carriers. Hughes worked out a ratio plan on battleships and battle cruisers with the number "1" as the base and equivalent to about 100,000 tons. He called for a relationship of 5:5:3:1.75:1.75, with the United States and Britain occupying the two top positions in capital ships and aircraft carriers, and with Japan second, followed by France and Italy. After the ten years the signatories could replace the older vessels but only to a maximum size of 35,000 tons and with guns no larger than sixteen-inch bores. The plan worked to the advantage of the United States, because the provision included ships already completed plus those under construction. Had the plan applied only to those already built, Britain would have led the way; had it included those completed, under construction, and planned, Japan would have approached the strength of the United States.

Neither Japan nor France favored the Five-Power Treaty. The Japanese ambassador to the United States bitterly labeled it "Rolls-Royce-Rolls-Royce-Ford," but American Military Intelligence had earlier learned through breaking Tokyo's secret diplomatic codes that the Japanese would accept the ratio plan if the British and Americans promised no new fortifications or reinforcements in their Pacific holdings. The Anglo-Americans had done so under the Four-Power Treaty. France was also displeased with the ratio plan. It wanted a navy large enough to protect its coastal areas and overseas possessions, but another consideration was important: Germany. France sought to base disarmament figures on its security needs against Germany, which would have meant doubling its allotment of capital tonnage. The French were still upset over the failure of the United States and Britain to ratify the Security Pact negotiated at Versailles in 1919, and remained determined to build a defense system in Europe strong enough to contain the Germans. Britain, however, forced the French into accepting the treaty terms by leaking their demands and thus earning worldwide condemnation. The French relented, but with the stipulation that the ratio plan would have no bearing on lesser craft. The Five-Power Treaty therefore carried a near fatal weakness in that it set no maximum tonnage on vessels outside the "warship" catgeory—submarines, destroyers, and small cruisers. Within a year the naval race resumed as nations sought to acquire smaller vessels not included in the Five-Power Treaty.

On February 6, 1922, the delegates in Washington signed their third agreement—the Nine-Power Treaty, which affirmed the Open Door in China. All signatory powers promised to "respect the sovereignty, the independence, and the territorial integrity of China," which could "develop and maintain . . . an effective and stable government." These assurances included equal commercial opportunity, for Hughes inserted the words of the secret protocol attached to the Lansing-Ishii Agreement of 1917. The protocol guaranteed against any power "taking advantage of conditions in China in order to seek special rights or privileges which would abridge the rights of subjects or citizens of the friendly States, and from countenancing action inimical to the security of such States." Yet the Nine-Power Treaty did not seek to correct past violations of China's sovereignty, and with no provision for enforcement its success depended solely upon the signatories honoring their pledges.

The Washington Conference led to other agreements which did not become part of the treaties. Japan consented to end its military occupation of Shantung and allowed Chinese control over the major railroad through the peninsula. Thus Japan fulfilled assurances given at Versailles in 1919, even though it maintained political and economic influence on the Chinese mainland. More than a year after the Washington Conference Japan annulled the Lansing-Ishii Agreement, which had approved its "special interests" in China. Japan also granted the United States cable, missionary, and property rights on the Pacific island of Yap, in exchange for America's recognition of Japan's mandates over Germany's former Pacific possessions—the Carolines, Marianas, and Marshalls. Finally, Hughes had informed the Japanese that the United States refused to accept any arrangement that "might impair existing treaty rights or the political or territorial integrity of Russia." Japan thus agreed to withdraw from Russian Siberia and the northern half of Sakhalin Island, which it did in 1922 and 1925, respectively.

The Washington Conference of 1921–22 consisted of a series of compromises, even though the agreements were a tacit recognition of Japan's leadership in the Pacific and Asia. The United States and Britain could not change the situation without a costly arms program, and even then Japan's geographical location gave it an advantage in the Orient. Japan had mandates over the surrounding Pacific islands, but the United States's abrogation of the Anglo-Japanese Alliance diminished the threat to the Open Door in China, and momentarily assured its hold on the Philippines. If relations with Japan improved because of the conference, they veered downward in 1924, when the U.S. Congress capitulated to racial pressures and passed the Johnson Immigration Act barring "aliens ineligible to citizenship" (the Japanese and other Asians) from entering the country. When the act went into effect the Japanese declared it "National Humiliation Day" at home.

Subsequent efforts at disarmament failed to match even the limited success of the 1921–22 conference. President Coolidge invited Britain, France, Italy, and Japan to gather with the United States in Geneva during the summer of 1927. But France and Italy declined to attend, and Britain and the United States soon engaged in such intense disagreements over their needs for "domestic safety" and the definition of large and small vessels that Japan tried to mediate between them. After six weeks of heated discussions the Geneva Conference broke up, leaving hardened Anglo-American relations and a dying faith in disarmament as a means toward peace. The following year, in Coolidge's Armistice Day address, he chastised those nations that "made agreements limiting that class of combat vessels in which we were superior, but refused limitation in the class in which they were superior."

Renewed disarmament efforts at the London Naval Conference of 1930 affirmed that trying to control the amount of arms was an attack on only the symptoms of trouble, not the disease: the real problem was the distrust and insecurity caused by competing national ambitions. In April, after three months of discussions, the United States, Britain, France, Italy, and Japan reached agreements which again offered only the illusion of peace. First, the United States won parity or equality with Britain on all vessels, even though this entailed the *addition* of American armaments rather than disarmament. Second, the powers saved a considerable amount of money by agreeing to a five-year extension of the ten-year moratorium on the replacement of capital ships, which by the Five-Power Treaty of 1922 was to begin in 1931. Third, Japan received parity with Britain and the United States in submarines and made substantial gains on them in cruisers and destroyers. Fourth, the powers passed the so-called escalator clause which provided that, should any of the three signatories be threatened by any nation not party to this treaty, it could expand its fleet larger than the terms drawn in London. Ill feelings were evident at the London Conference. The United States rejected French demands for guarantees of military security prior to participating in disarmament agreements, and both France and Italy refused to approve the final cruiser arrangements. Nonetheless, the Senate in Washington overwhelmingly approved the pact in July 1930, although it also passed a resolution freeing the United States from any secret arrangements.

The powers attempted disarmament two more times. Nearly sixty nations assembled at the World Disarmament Conference in Geneva in 1932, only to adjourn without results two years later in the face of growing troubles in Europe and the Far East. As stipulated at the London Conference of 1930, the nations met again in London in 1935, but when Japan failed to win full naval parity with the United States and Britain, its delegates walked out of the proceedings. Insecurity and distrust in both Europe and Asia continued to obstruct the hopes for disarmament.

OUTLAWING WAR

As the tough-minded approach to a peace based in power politics was running its futile course, a soft approach, based upon goodwill, was taking its place. This was the movement to prevent war by universal renunciation, by "outlawing" war. Naive as the notion may appear in retrospect—and as it appeared to realists at the time—it had one strong argument in its favor: realpolitik had been tried and led to the catastrophe of world war. It is not certain whose brainchild the movement was. Besides its support from an assortment of intellectuals, socialists, and pacifists, the leading exponent of outlawing war was a Chicago lawyer, Salmon Levinson, who backed the idea financially and won the endorsement of Senator Borah. Other leaders in the movement included Nicholas M. Butler, the president of Columbia University, and one of its faculty members, James T. Shotwell, noted professor of international relations and trustee of the Carnegie Endowment for International Peace. Shotwell won the attention of French Foreign Minister Aristide Briand and induced him to make such a proposal in the spring of 1927. In early April Briand extended a public invitation to the United States, through the Associated

Press, to join France in renouncing war. His letter to the American people declared that France was "ready publicly to subscribe, with the United States, to any mutual engagement tending, as between those two countries, to 'outlaw war,' to use an American phrase."

Briand's seemingly idealistic gesture had a basis in realpolitik: he hoped to pull the United States into France's defense system against Germany, which already included Belgium, Czechoslovakia, Poland, Rumania, and Yugoslavia. His proposal would not bind the United States to intervene in a Franco-German war. Rather, a joint renunciation of war would prohibit the United States from retaliating against France should it violate neutral rights in a war with Germany. Briand declared that America's cooperation with France "would greatly contribute in the eyes of the world to broaden and strengthen the foundation upon which the international policy of peace is being raised."

Secretary of State Kellogg was furious with Briand's tactics. The French foreign minister had already won the support of American peace groups, which now urged Kellogg to accept the French offer. But the secretary of state opposed any arrangement hinting at a European alliance. He initially ignored Briand's plea, but came under pressure to accept it from the *The New York Times* and numerous public figures and organizations. Then the image of Franco-American friendship received a boost when Charles Lindbergh made a solo flight across the Atlantic and landed in Paris in May 1927. Petitions containing 2 million signatures rolled into Washington. Kellogg had no choice but to agree to talk about the invitation. In June the French foreign minister handed America's ambassador in Paris a draft of the proposed treaty, which he called a "Pact of Perpetual Friendship."

In late December 1927 Kellogg found a way out of the imbroglio. The Senate Foreign Relations Committee informed him that it would approve a general treaty renouncing war, but not one with France alone. Kellogg's resulting counterproposal illustrated the diplomatic principle that the more parties to a treaty, the less binding it becomes. Briand's proposal was so good, Kellogg indicated, that France and the United States should invite *all* nations to join. Kellogg's arrangement removed all dangers of European entanglements. America retained the right to defend itself and the Monroe Doctrine, and it accepted no responsibility for enforcing the pact against any signatory who violated it. To eliminate doubt, the Senate Foreign Relations Committee emphasized that "the treaty does not provide sanctions, express or implied."

The idea of such a multilateral pact won immediate support in Washington, and after Kellogg sent the proposal to Briand in late December, the two nations made arrangements for a conference in Paris to outlaw war. The French foreign minister was displeased with Kellogg's maneuverings, but had no choice. He had won the Nobel Peace Prize earlier in the 1920s for the Treaty of Locarno and could not publicly refuse a general settlement renouncing war. After three months of delay Briand agreed to the proposal, but with reservations designed to safeguard what he called his country's right of "legitimate self-defense." On August 27, 1928, the representatives of fifteen nations gathered in Paris and in an elaborate ceremony signed the Kellogg-Briand Pact, or Pact of Paris, which renounced war as "an instrument of national policy" and supported "pacific means" in resolving "international controversies." Afterward the signatories invited other nations to join the pact, and sixty-two governments did—including Germany, Italy, Japan, and the Soviet Union. The American Senate approved the treaty almost unanimously. Yet the results were misleading. Missouri Senator James Reed called the pact an "international kiss," while Senator Carter Glass of Virginia offered the most truthful assessment even as he voted for it. "I am not willing that anybody in Virginia shall think that I am simple enough to suppose that it is worth a postage stamp in the direction of accomplishing permanent peace." He warned that "it is going to confuse the minds of many good and pious people who think that peace may be secured by polite professions of neighborly and brotherly love." The Senate was not naive. Nor was President Coolidge, who signed a naval appropriations bill for the construction of fifteen large cruisers less than a month after he ratified the pact outlawing war. Kellogg, for his part in the Pact of Paris, received the Nobel Peace Prize.

THE WAR DEBTS AND REPARATIONS PROBLEM

As indicated, the efforts of both kinds of peace seekers, realists and idealists alike, ignored the fundamental causes of tensions and wars among nations. The proposed peace plans also disregarded the gravest international problem of the period—the financial dislocations that were impelling the world toward another calamity, the collapse of the international economic order. Leaders in every nation failed to perceive this danger, partly because the forces behind it were so large as to be invisible, partly because the leaders were shortsighted.

The international economic disorders of the postwar period were extremely complex. Wartime destruction of physical property in Europe was so great that, under the best of circumstances, only with great difficulty could its economies have regained their capacity to feed, clothe, and house their citizens; and circumstances were hardly the best. The major obstacle to recovery was the burden of debts owed by governments to their own citizens, to other governments, and to private creditors in other countries. Britain, France, and Italy owed large sums to their citizens who had bought government bonds, and in addition they owed nearly $10 billion to the U.S. government and several billion more to New York banks. The debts of the former Allies to their own citizens might have been scaled down in both interest and principle, or the debts might have been effectively repudiated by inflating them out of existence, had their citizens been willing to tolerate such courses. The debts due the United States were another matter. Had American markets been open to the Allies' manufactured goods and farm products, international obligations might conceivably have been met by exports to the United States. But American producers, not wishing to be run out of business by cheap foreign goods, demanded an increased protective tariff, and got it in the Fordney-McCumber Act of 1922. Its high tariff schedules precluded the possibility of Europe's paying its American debts by normal means.

But the former Allies had an abnormal means at their disposal, and they seized upon it. The French, bitter over the destruction of lives and property inflicted by the Germans, remembered that Germany had extracted a huge reparations settlement from them after the Franco-Prussian War. Forgetting that the result had been an international economic depression, they demanded that Germany pay for all damages it had caused during the Great War. The delegates at Versailles had agreed to reparations in principle, and in April 1921 the Allied Reparations Commission fixed Germany's obligation at about $33 billion. If Germany met its reparations payment on schedule, France, Britain, and Italy could meet their obligations to the United States on schedule.

The flaw in this arrangement was that Germany was unable to pay, on schedule or otherwise. Like the victorious powers in the war, its productive capacity had been devastated, and its economy was weakened further by the course its postwar Weimar Republic government followed in trying to cope with internal financial obligations. In a word, that course was to inflate its currency by printing unsecured paper money at an ever increasing rate. International depreciation of German currency inevitably followed. The German mark, which before the war had been at 4.2 to the American dollar, fell to 162 to the dollar at the end of 1921, and to 7,000 at the end of 1922. A year later it took 4 trillion marks to make a dollar, and Germany's traditional frugal middle class had been wiped out.

Belatedly, the United States acted to reduce the burden of both debts and reparations, though as a matter of principle it refused to agree to a total cancellation. "They hired the money, didn't they?" Coolidge allegedly remarked. During the Paris peace talks of 1919 President Wilson had rejected suggestions to cancel war debts, despite arguments by some members of Congress that such a move would add to America's contribution to victory, ensure better international relations, and avert Allied bankruptcy. He and others realized that to cancel the European debt would in effect mean that the American taxpayer would be assuming the Allied debt by having to meet the Treasury's bond obligations. Two times in 1920 the British opposed cancellation in the interest of European recovery. The Allies, unhappy over America's late entry into the war, believed that the credits advanced by the United States should be its shared costs in victory. If the United States canceled British obligations, London would do the same for France, and Paris might lower its reparations demands of Germany. The United States, however, refused to link war debts with German reparations. Debt cancellation was out of the question.

In the summer of 1921 President Harding recommended that the United States attempt to ease the obligations of the war debts, and the following February Congress established the World War Foreign Debt Commission to work out details. Congress stipulated no debt cancellations but agreed to a lowered interest rate and to an extended maturity date. Yet the debtor nations still could not meet these terms. In early 1923 the United States again agreed with Britain to lower the interest rate and not to exact full return for sixty-two years. The other chief debtors—France, Italy, and Belgium—refused the arrangement because they first wanted reparations from Germany, which had defaulted on its payments in 1922. The international financial situation grew worse, and by 1925 the commission was willing to go much farther. In the spring of the following year it scaled down the debts by drastic margins. The commission canceled four-fifths of the Italian debt and nearly two-thirds of the French, and reduced interest to a nominal rate. Even then the French called the United States "Uncle Shylock" and cartoonists changed the stars on Uncle Sam's hat to dollar signs. The debts remained beyond the Allies' ability to pay unless they received reparations payments from Germany.

In 1924 the United States tried to solve the German problem with the Dawes Plan. The occasion for the American intervention in the matter was that, when Germany first defaulted on reparations payments, France and Belgium retaliated by occupying the industrialized Ruhr Valley in January 1923. Secretary of State Hughes had already suggested that an investigatory team scale down the reparations bill according to Germany's capacity to pay. His recommendation now won approval and the Reparations Commission established two committees, with Chicago banker Charles G. Dawes to act as a private citizen in heading one of them. Dawes's plan of September 1924 permitted private American investments in Germany of $200 million, and established a system of yearly reparations payments without setting a deadline for the fulfillment of obligations. The purpose of the plan was to save the German economy by tying reparations to the nation's financial recovery.

The Dawes Plan worked fairly well, but the European economy still threatened to collapse under the burdens of debts and reparations, and in 1929 Germany's creditors sought a final resolution of the question through the Young Plan. Owen D. Young, chairman of General Electric Company, also acted in a private capacity in heading a committee which lowered the reparations bill to $9 billion plus interest, and gave Germany fifty-nine years to make payments at a lowered interest. The Young Plan also provided (without official American concurrence) that reductions in war debts would have a proportional effect on reparations. Europe had linked debts with reparations despite America's efforts to keep them separate. The number of annual reparations payments as well as the total amount to be paid were about equal to that owed the United States in European wartime credits.

The Dawes and Young Plans created a shaky, circular financial system whereby the United States furnished much of the money Germany used for reparations payments to the Allies, who in turn used the money to meet war debt obligations to Americans. From 1924 to 1931 Germany received $2.25 billion in American loans; Germany paid the Allies $2.75 billion in reparations; and the Allies paid the United States $2 billion for war debts. The system worked as long as foreign recipients of American loans and investments could meet interest payments and return some of the principal. But ultimately America's debtors could satisfy their obligations only by selling goods and services in the foreign markets, especially in the United States.

The onset of the Great Depression forced a reconsideration of the reparations and debts issues. After the crash of 1929 President Hoover tried to protect American businesses through a higher tariff, arguing that there was no connection between tariff duties and the European debtors' capacity to pay. Over the objections of more than a thousand economists, he signed the Hawley-Smoot Act into law in June 1930. The highest tariff in the country's history, it further damaged the international financial situation and alienated European nations opposed to America's isolationism and nationalistic economic policies. Hoover then believed it wise to temporarily suspend the collection of both war debts and reparations, which in itself was a tacit admission that the European governments would not give up reparations demands without an accompanying release from debt collections. All governments concerned immediately approved, and in December 1931 Congress implemented a one-year moratorium with the understanding that payments would resume when the moratorium expired the following December. Hoover also recommended that the World War Foreign Debt Commission reexamine the problem. But Congress would not approve a new investigation because such a procedure might lead to either cancellation or reduction of debts. Had the United States opposed the moratorium, the results would have been German default on private American loans, the destruction of American bankers' collateral in Germany, and widespread bank closings in the United States. Still, the plan was only temporarily effective, for it could not protect America's investments from the effects of the depression.

The European nations finally acted on their own. The debtor governments came to believe that the United States would cut the debts figure if they reduced the German reparations bill. With this hope in mind, they gathered in Lausanne, Switzerland, in the summer of 1932 and authorized Germany to cancel 90 percent of its bill, but with the stipulation that the United States reciprocate with equivalent reductions in war debts. This caused a furor in Washington. Despite Hoover's warnings that America's failure to comply would end all payments, Congress insisted on the original reparations figure. He then appealed to President-elect Franklin D. Roosevelt to ask Congress to revive the War Debt Commission and scale down debts. This move also failed.

On December 15, 1932, the moratorium expired and the United States notified the European debtors that payments were due. Most governments met their obligations for a short while, but then sent token sums. Finally, even these stopped. By mid-1934 all debtor nations except Finland had defaulted.

CRISIS IN MANCHURIA

Total economic collapse had taken place in every industrialized nation by the early 1930s. Unemployment ranged from 25 percent in the United States to perhaps 80 percent in Germany; probably half the industrial workers of the world were out of work, and farmers were no better off. In short, the banking and monetary systems of every nation lay in ruins. All this was calamitous enough in its own right. What was more, it was a threat to world peace, for in Japan, Germany, and Italy powerful groups came to believe that the solution to economic problems was foreign conquest.

Japan was the first to succumb to this illusion. Japan wanted China's northern province of Manchuria, for it could absorb Japan's overflow population, provide markets for cotton and silk, furnish mineral resources, and aid the defense against the Russians. The Japanese army had become more democratized after the Great War and thus had turned into a haven for young, spirited peasants who had moved into officer positions, and who now emerged as super-patriots determined to make Japan a world power. Their initial objective was to bring about a "Showa restoration," or a moral rebirth of the nation built upon returning power to the Showa, the reigning name for Emperor Hirohito. Though the emperors in Japan had never held the power that this new group attributed to them, the belief, however mythical, was strong enough to instill a deep sense of loyalty to one another. But the younger officers had been unable to wrest control from the civilian moderates, who had insisted upon abiding by the agreements reached at the London Naval Conference of 1930. Politicians had hurt the nation, the militarists believed; they would restore the nation's world prominence by first establishing hegemony in Manchuria.

Civil war in China during the 1920s again invited outside intervention. Americans had initially sympathized with the nationalist uprising against the Manchu dynasty that began in 1911. Under the leadership of Sun Yat-sen, the Kuomintang or Nationalist People's Party promised modernization through extensive reforms. Yet when Americans joined other Western nations in refusing to aid the rebels, Sun turned to Russia. The Bolsheviks, hoping to hold back Japan and the West, sent advisers to instruct the Chinese on how to strengthen their Nationalist party. But Sun Yat-sen died in 1925, before he could unite the country with the aid of Chinese communists allowed into the party. The Nationalists in Shanghai, however, rebelled and attacked foreign holdings and foreigners— including Americans and Christian missionaries. The new leader of the Kuomintang armies, General Chiang Kai-shek, then turned northward,

Japanese Expansion to 1941

MAP 23

Japan's invasion of Manchuria in 1931–1932 was the high point of its expansionist activities before December 1941.

seizing nearly half of China from the independent war lords. The government in Washington became so alarmed that it sent soldiers and warships to protect its holdings and citizens. In 1926–27 Chiang ordered the Russian advisers out of the country and prepared to purge the Nationalist party of the communists, whose leader, Mao Tse-tung, managed to establish a rebel government in the south.

Japan could not allow the Chinese Nationalists to regain control in Manchuria. Though Russia's sphere of interest in the north had diminished after the Bolshevik Revolution, the Japanese meanwhile had pulled out of Shantung, Russian Siberia, and northern Sakhalin, and had annulled the Lansing-Ishii Agreement of 1917. Chiang's forces continued their move northward and in the Yangtze Valley established a new government at Nanking. Two years later, in 1928, they took over the ancient imperial capital at Peking and changed its name to Peiping (to mean "Northern Peace" rather than "Northern Capital"). That same year the United States signed a treaty acknowledging China's control over tariffs and securing most-favored-nation treatment. Though the treaty did not renounce extraterritoriality, its signing was a major concession because it constituted American recognition of the Nationalist government. The Japanese were worried about America's growing influence in China, even though the image was larger than the reality. By 1930 only 1 percent of American investment overseas was in China, and during the previous seven years the United States only exported 3 percent of its goods to China. Trade with Japan was twice as large. Still, the myth persisted of a boundless "China market." America's longtime sentiment toward the Chinese helped to override the inadequacies of the trade, while Chiang won favor because he opposed communism and was a Christian. Another attraction was that he had married a Chinese businessman's daughter, who had an American education and strong links with influential Americans having interests in China. The dangers of Russian and American growth in China unsettled the Japanese. When a change in government in Manchuria implanted a ruler favorable to the Nationalists, the Open Door seemed shut.

By the summer of 1929 China's relations with the Soviet Union had deteriorated so badly that war broke out when the Nationalists tried to gain control of the Chinese Eastern Railway and to reestablish their country's authority in upper Manchuria. The Japanese feared that the Chinese might do the same with the South Manchurian Railway and other Japanese holdings in Manchuria. Worse, the Russians might win the war and take everything. Secretary of State Henry L. Stimson, the former secretary of war under Taft, had reminded both antagonists of the Kellogg-Briand Pact against war, but the Russians claimed self-defense as they invaded Manchuria in August. In November Stimson sent a circular letter urging the two nations to end the conflict. Through the combined efforts of the League of Nations and the United States, a cease-fire resulted in Shanghai in May 1931. But the Russians had won the war.

The end of the Russo-Chinese War did not resolve the tensions in China, for a number of incidents occurred as Japan's militarists sought to expand into Manchuria. In the summer of 1931 the Japanese press accused the Chinese of executing one of Japan's undercover army officers in Manchuria. Japanese moderates tried to resolve the matter peaceably, despite the army's call to take Manchuria. But shortly before midnight on September 18, 1931, an explosion tore apart a small section of the South Manchurian Railway outside the capital at Mukden. The Japanese accused the Chinese of sabotage, although it is likely that young Japanese officers of the Kwantung or Manchurian Army fabricated the story to justify occupation of the entire province. Japanese forces, without orders from either the premier or Foreign Office, quickly seized the Chinese barracks in Mukden along with other important positions near the railroad.

Chiang's government in China appealed to the United States and the League of Nations. The Japanese had violated League responsibilities, the Nine-Power Treaty of 1922 guaranteeing the Open Door in China, and the Kellogg-Briand Pact—even though they dismissed the events in Manchuria as "incidents" and not war. The Mukden incident, it appeared, was a dangerous example of unchecked aggression. Stimson realized that Japan was dependent on American oil and other goods, and he argued for an economic boycott. But his suggestion was opposed by President Hoover, who considered economic pressure by the United States to be a violation of the tenets of isolationism and feared that such a move would lead to war. Yet the chief executive did not seem to oppose sanctions by the League. Stimson, however, knew the League would not act. Britain and France hesitated to cut off trade in depression times, and both preferred giving in to Japan rather than risking their holdings in the Far East. Stimson also realized that a hardline policy toward Japan could strengthen the militarists in that country at the expense of the moderates. His only recourse was to notify the Japanese of his government's disapproval of their actions. Stimson urged the two nations to stop fighting, and sent an observer to the League when it discussed the matter. But this symbolic move had little impact because the American representative was under orders to participate only when the Council discussed the relationship of the Kellogg-Briand Pact to the crisis. When the Council proposed sending an investigatory commission to Manchuria, Japan protested. Moderates in Tokyo assured both the United States and the League that the Japanese government would restrain its army. The Council nonetheless set a deadline of November 16 for Japan's withdrawal from the railroad area.

But the Japanese military seemed ready to take northern Manchuria. By the winter of 1931–32 Japanese forces threatened to expand along the South Manchurian Railway and into Russia's sphere—that part of upper Manchuria adjoining the Russian section of the Chinese Eastern Railway. The League Council meanwhile reconvened on November 16, the date set for Japan's departure from Manchuria. Two days later the Japanese seized an area above the Chinese Eastern Railway, apparently in preparation for a sweep across Manchuria.

The United States responded to Japan's thrust into Manchuria on January 7, 1932, by announcing the Stimson Doctrine of nonrecognition. When the Japanese won Chinchow in southern Manchuria, they broke the Chinese army's last point of resistance. The secretary of state accused the Japanese of violating their nonaggression pledges and, probably under Hoover's prodding, declared that America refused to recognize governments established by force. In a stance consistent with that of the Wilson administration, the United States again departed from the princi-

William Borah and Henry L. Stimson in 1929

Borah was an "irreconcilable" who bitterly opposed Wilson's League of Nations and later disagreed with the Franklin D. Roosevelt administration's warnings of the German threat during the 1930s. Stimson advocated nonrecognition of Japan's holdings in Manchuria in the early 1930s, later called for an oil embargo on Japan, and then served in Roosevelt's cabinet as secretary of war. (Library of Congress)

ples of *de facto* recognition. Stimson, who undoubtedly would have preferred the use of force, realized that such a response was out of the question because of the isolationist mood in the United States, the absence of American military leverage in that part of the world, the refusal of either Britain or France to join the nonrecognition stand, and Hoover's aversion to war. The president, a Quaker, saw no alternative to nonrecognition despite his fears that the Japanese had begun a concerted drive to take all of China.

As in the Wilson presidency, moral pressure failed because the Hoover administration lacked the will and the means for enforcement. In late January Japan retaliated against a Chinese boycott on its goods by bombarding Shanghai, which led the United States to send additional military forces to join the small number already in the city. Yet American soldiers were not under orders to fight the Japanese. Stimson later explained that his hope had been to remind them of America's "great size and military strength." Japan "was afraid of that, and I was willing to let her be afraid of that without telling her that we were not going to use it against her." The tactic did not work. It seems clear that Japan had no pattern for conquest and that its officers merely reacted to situations as they developed. But the newsreels, pictures, and firsthand accounts of the bombings in Shanghai caused worldwide revulsion. Japan's attack on the city posed a threat to British interests in the Yangtze Valley and raised demands for Japanese-Chinese negotiations.

As Japan's forces continued to spread into Manchuria, it became increasingly evident that America's nonrecognition policy had proved ineffectual. Ignoring an aggressor seldom reforms him, American diplomat Hugh Wilson noted almost a decade after the Stimson Doctrine. "If the nations of the world feel strongly enough to condemn," he asserted, "they should feel strongly enough to use force. . . . To condemn only merely intensifies the heat. . . . Condemnation creates a community of the damned who are forced outside the pale, who have nothing to lose by the violation of all laws of order and international good faith." Indeed, nonrecognition was an admission to Japan's upper hand in Asia, for Washington could not enforce its appeals. Events in Manchuria exposed the fatal flaw in the treaties of the 1920s: the West lacked the will to enforce them. America's isolationist impulse, its lack of military power in Asia, and the Great Depression dictated a policy of inaction.

The Japanese restructured Manchuria into the puppet regime of Manchukuo ("country of the Manchus") in mid-February 1932, and drew another restrained response from the United States. Within a week Stimson sent a public letter to Borah, chairman of the Senate Foreign Relations Committee, which called on other nations to join America's nonrecognition policy and strongly implied that if Japan continued its aggressions in China, the United States might terminate the Five-Power Treaty of 1922, fortify Guam and the Philippines, and strengthen its naval forces in the Pacific. Japan, Stimson wrote, had violated "the principles of fair play, patience, and mutual goodwill." Stimson's letter had some effect. In March the League of Nations announced support for nonrecognition and assured opposition to any matter "brought about by means contrary to the Covenant of the League of Nations or to the Pact of Paris." But the Great Depression prevented economic or military sanctions. Japan's assault eased, however, largely because of the costs of the expedition and the continued resistance by the Chinese. Japan withdrew from Shanghai in May 1932, but only after driving out Chinese forces and saving face.

Meanwhile the League of Nations had appointed a commission headed by England's Earl of Lytton to investigate the crisis in the Far East. In September 1932 the Lytton Commission reported to the League that Japan was primarily responsible for the Manchurian crisis. The report admitted that China had failed to protect Japan's legitimate rights in Manchuria; but it also suggested that Japan was guilty of aggression in the Mukden incident. Manchukuo, the findings showed, was not an outgrowth of the popular will; the Japanese had stirred resentment among dissatisfied groups in China and fomented a drive for independence. The Lytton Commission recommended that Manchuria receive autonomy but remain under Chinese political control, and called on the withdrawal of Japanese and Chinese soldiers and the establishment of a gendarmerie or local police force to restore order in the province. The two governments would then sign a treaty guaranteeing Japanese interests and peaceful settlement of disputes. Thus the commission sought to maintain Chinese authority in Manchuria without endangering Japan's legitimate economic concerns. Two weeks after Lytton submitted his findings to the League, Japan extended formal recognition to Manchukuo.

On February 24, 1933 the League of Nations adopted the Lytton Report. The leader of the Japanese delegation, Yosuke Matsuoka, left no doubt about his feelings when he emotionally declared to the Assembly that his country's position was similar to that faced by Christ as he went to the cross. Japan served the stipulated two-year notice of withdrawal from the League.

Stimson was pleased that the League's adoption of the Lytton Report virtually meant acceptance of the doctrine of nonrecognition, and yet this so-called triumph for American policy left a dangerous legacy. Stimson's appeals to morality had heightened Japan's animosity toward the United States, deepened its already embittered reaction to the Open Door, and made America its central obstacle to expansion in the Far East. Furthermore, nonrecognition had underlined America's reluctance to break with its rigid isolationist tradition. By announcing a stand of opposition and then doing nothing to enforce it, the United States had inadvertently encouraged Japan to take actions that set an example of aggression unchallenged by the West.

Selected readings

Adler, Selig, *The Isolationist Impulse: Its Twentieth Century Reaction.* 1957.

——, *The Uncertain Giant: American Foreign Policy between the Wars, 1921–1941.* 1965.

Buckingham, Peter H., *The Open Door Peace with the Former Central Powers, 1921–1929.* 1983.

Buckley, Thomas H., *The United States and the Washington Conference, 1921–1922.* 1970.

Costigliola, Frank, *Awkward Dominion: American Political, Economic, and Cultural Relations with Europe, 1919–1933.* 1984.

DeConde, Alexander, *Herbert Hoover's Latin American Policy.* 1951.

Dingman, Roger, *Power in the Pacific: The Origins of Naval Arms Limitation, 1914–1922.* 1976.

Doenecke, Justus D., *When the Wicked Rise: American Opinion-Makers and the Manchurian Crisis of 1931–1933.* 1984.

Ellis, L. Ethan, *Republican Foreign Policy, 1921–1933.* 1968.

Ferrell, Robert H., *Frank B. Kellogg and Henry L. Stimson*. 1963.

———, *Peace in Their Time: The Origins of the Kellogg-Briand Pact*. 1952.

Filene, Peter, *Americans and the Soviet Experiment, 1917–1933*. 1967.

Fleming, Denna F., *The United States and World Organization, 1920–1933*. 1938.

Glad, Betty, *Charles Evans Hughes and the Illusions of Innocence: A Study of American Diplomacy*. 1966.

Grieb, Kenneth J., *The Latin American Policy of Warren J. Harding*. 1976.

Hogan, Michael J., *Informal Entente: The Private Structure of Cooperation in Anglo-American Economic Diplomacy, 1918–1928*. 1977.

Josephson, Harold, "Outlawing War: Internationalism and the Pact of Paris," *Diplomatic History* 3 (1979): 377–90.

Kamman, William, *A Search for Stability: United States Diplomacy toward Nicaragua, 1925–1933*. 1968.

Leffler, Melvyn P., *The Elusive Quest: America's Pursuit of European Stability and French Security, 1919–1933*. 1979.

Maddox, Robert J., *William E. Borah and American Foreign Policy*. 1969.

Munro, Dana G., *The United States and the Caribbean Republics, 1921–1933*. 1974.

Pelz, Stephen E., *Road to Pearl Harbor: The Failure of the Second London Naval Conference and the Onset of World War II*. 1974.

Shewmaker, Kenneth E., *Americans and Chinese Communists, 1927–1945: A Persuading Encounter*. 1971.

Steward, Dick, *Trade and Hemisphere: The Good Neighbor Policy and Reciprocal Trade*. 1975.

Thorne, Chistopher, *The Limits of Foreign Policy: The West, the League and the Far Eastern Crisis of 1931–1933*. 1973.

Vinson, J. Chalmers, *The Parchment Peace*. 1956.

Wheeler, Gerald E., *Prelude to Pearl Harbor: The United States Navy and the Far East, 1921–1931*. 1963.

Wilson, Joan Hoff, *American Business and Foreign Policy, 1920–1933*. 1971.

———, *Ideology and Economics: U.S. Relations with the Soviet Union, 1918–1933*. 1974.

Wood, Bryce, *The Making of the Good Neighbor Policy*. 1961.

Chapter Sixteen

The Coming of World War II, 1933–1939

On March 4, 1933 Franklin D. Roosevelt took the oath as president of the United States and almost immediately began an active, personal form of diplomacy that was to be the hallmark of his administration's foreign policy. He had been assistant secretary of the navy under President Wilson, and as vice presidential candidate in 1920 had supported both the Versailles Treaty and the League of Nations. But early in his 1932 campaign for the presidential nomination he had won the backing of newspaper publisher William Randolph Hearst, an influential isolationist and Democrat, by renouncing support of the League. Roosevelt, a New York patrician and Harvard graduate, was, in a sense, a combination of his distant cousin Theodore Roosevelt and former President Wilson in that he would eventually seek world order through a "policeman" approach led by the United States. Pragmatic, charismatic, and even enigmatic, Roosevelt was an unusual mixture of straightforwardness and cunning, of realist and idealist, who defied his enemies with his political ability. He implanted his personality, as both the "lion" and the "fox," onto his twelve years in the White House, years that were to become known as the Roosevelt Era.

Roosevelt, who aroused either love or hate and rarely a lukewarm feeling, would become one of the most dominant personalities on the world scene in a time characterized by forceful international leaders. Stricken with infantile paralysis in 1921 at the age of thirty-nine, he had surprised many by overcoming his inability to walk and pursuing a political career. During the first years of his presidency, however, he had to be extremely cautious in following an internationalist course in foreign affairs because of the prevailing isolationist feeling in the country. Though he usually took the lead in making policy, the realities of politics and public

Franklin D. Roosevelt and Harry S. Truman at Roosevelt's Fourth Inaugural in 1945

Roosevelt died in April 1945, leaving the presidency to Truman. (Library of Congress)

opinion kept him from venturing too far ahead of his constituents. Even so, he often ignored his secretary of state, Cordell Hull, forcing Hull to learn secondhand what the administration's policy was toward Europe. Except in matters affecting Latin America and the Far East, Roosevelt sought advice primarily from Henry Morgenthau, Jr., secretary of the treasury, Harry Hopkins, confidant after the outbreak of war in Europe, Sumner Welles, ambassador to Cuba and later undersecretary of state, and William Bullitt, Wilson's peace emissary during the Russian civil war and America's first ambassador to the Soviet Union. Through force of character and personality, Roosevelt relegated others in his administration to live and work in his shadow.

GREAT DEPRESSION DIPLOMACY

Problems stemming from the Great Depression dominated Roosevelt's first two terms in office, although his reform efforts inside the country were integrally related to foreign affairs. In the early 1930s the German Nazi party leader Adolf Hitler used the Depression, hatred for the Versailles Treaty, and anti-Semitic feeling to achieve dictatorial powers as the

Cordell Hull

As secretary of state for over a decade, he dealt primarily with Latin American and Asian affairs, while President Roosevelt focused on Europe and the Atlantic. (Library of Congress)

Führer or leader. Similar developments in Italy had already given rise to the dictatorship of Fascist Benito Mussolini, who had led his army of Black Shirts into power by clamping down on communism and socialism and ending strikes and other internal disorders. But Roosevelt's concern was domestic reform; even in foreign policy he sought to build sufficient international trade to promote America's internal recovery. Consequently, his administration's initial priority was to establish a network of reciprocal trade treaties designed to benefit the United States. The focus of attention became Latin America, and the leader in formulating such a policy was Hull.

The Roosevelt administration's first attempt to enhance trade with Latin America was through broadening his predecessor's Good Neighbor policy. Though Roosevelt did not refer to any particular area of the world, he declared in his inaugural address that "in the field of world policy I would dedicate this Nation to the policy of the good neighbor—the neighbor who resolutely respects himself and, because he does so, respects the rights of others." Such a move was easier for the government in Washington after World War I because the German threat to Latin America had

ended and the United States Navy was supreme in the hemisphere. Yet
Roosevelt's good neighbor assurances did not fundamentally change
American interests and attitudes in the hemisphere. The president found
it more advantageous to his country to emphasize a multilateral relationship with Latin America rather than the long-standing unilateral interventionist policy of the Monroe Doctrine. Examples of the new direction in
policy came in the early 1930s with the withdrawal of American marines
from Haiti and Nicaragua, and with Ambassador Welles's work in terminating the Platt Amendment in Cuba, with the exception that the United
States would maintain the naval base at Guantánamo until both parties
agreed to end it.

To increase trade throughout the hemisphere, the United States tried
to win the trust of Latin Americans at the Seventh International Conference of American States in Montevideo, Uruguay, in December 1933. Hull
had called for reciprocal trade agreements to erase the effects of the high
Hawley-Smoot Tariff of 1930, but as he arrived to chair the U.S. delegation in Montevideo, there were signs in the streets reading "Down with
Hull." After delivering a strong statement against foreign intervention, he
signed a convention declaring that "no state has the right to intervene in
the internal or external affairs of another." Yet Hull asserted his nation's
right to self-defense by stipulating that the United States could intervene
"by the law of nations as generally recognized and accepted." Two days
after the conference Roosevelt publicly declared that "the definite policy
of the United States from now on is one opposed to armed intervention."
The American Senate overwhelmingly approved the Montevideo convention, offering hope for improved relations with Latin America.

A second broad attempt by the new president to deal with the depression resulted from his predecessor's promise that the United States would
attend a forthcoming World Economic Conference in London, designed
to stabilize the international currency situation. Numerous studies had
tied the seriousness of the depression to high tariffs, war debts, the termination of foreign loans, and the decision by Britain and other nations to
leave the gold standard. The last measure had posed serious obstacles to
the convertibility of paper money. Without a common medium of exchange, the world's trade virtually ceased. From the international point of
view it seemed economically sound to return to the gold standard in an
effort to stabilize the currency and stimulate trade. Roosevelt appeared to
agree on this point, although he refused to permit the negotiation of war
debts: "That stays with Poppa—right here," he declared.

In the spring of 1933 the representatives of eleven nations met with
the president in Washington, and departed with the impression that they
had secured his assurance that international monetary stabilization was
to be the priority of the upcoming conference. The gathering in London,
Roosevelt had asserted, would "establish order by stabilization of currencies. It must supplement individual domestic programs for economic recovery by wise-considered international action."

But soon after the Washington meeting, additional economic reversals in the United States forced it off the gold standard as well. Roosevelt feared that if the dollar was tied to gold and hence to the fluctuations of international trade, he would lose control over his domestic recovery program. Furthermore, the purchasing power of the dollar had risen with the depression, forcing debtors into the undesirable position of having to pay back loans incurred when the dollar was not worth as much. Thus, Roosevelt sought to devalue or drive down the dollar to the level of the previous decade, but he could not do this if American currency was dependent upon the prevailing rate of international exchange. Roosevelt had to be free to manipulate the currency within the United States. But he did not decide to adopt this policy until *after* the American delegation, led by Hull, had left for England.

In mid-June the delegates from the United States assembled in London with those of sixty-three other nations, to remove barriers to international trade; but trouble immediately developed when the Roosevelt administration announced its change in policy. Hull was as surprised as the others attending the conference. He was ready to present a proposal for lowered tariffs through reciprocity arrangements, but while he was en route to London, the president, as noted, had scrapped the program. In a note to the American delegation, Roosevelt expressed opposition to international currency stabilization and emphasized domestic recovery. "The sound internal economic system of a nation," he asserted, "is a greater factor in its well-being than the price of its currency in changing terms of the currencies of other nations." The United States would not become a party to reciprocal tariff agreements, nor would it return to the gold standard. If the dollar were convertible into other currency, he reasoned, the nation's domestic purchasing power would be at the mercy of the irregularities of world trade.

The London Conference had little chance for success primarily because of competing national interests, but also because Roosevelt's actions had encouraged a sharp rise in the costs of foreign goods. France, Italy, Belgium, and other nations demanded stabilization through a return to the gold standard, accused the United States of subverting the conference, and called for adjournment. Hull managed to keep them there for three more weeks, until late July, when the meeting broke up in failure. The outcome incidentally helped to end the war debt issue, for afterward only Finland made its payment in December, and in the following year, 1934, Congress passed the Johnson Act prohibiting loans to nations already in default. America's strongly nationalistic stance on these monetary matters deepened European hostility.

A third administration program designed to alleviate the economic situation, but also carrying political objectives, was the decision to extend recognition to Russia. Many in the Western world disliked the methods used by the Bolsheviks in their rise to power in 1917, and the United States and other nations refused to grant recognition when the new Russian regime called for world revolution, opposed capitalism, expropriated private properties, and repudiated the debts of the czar and of the provisional government. But nonrecognition throughout the 1920s had not forced changes in the Soviet government, and pressure for American recognition developed among business leaders interested in the Soviet market and among liberals who thought it no concern of the United States what kind of regime the Russians had. During the 1920s General Electric, DuPont, Ford, and other American companies signed commercial agreements with the Soviet Union which dramatically increased trade. But after the crash of 1929, exchanges dropped and spokesmen for business urged diplomatic recognition to stimulate a revival in commerce. As with the near mythical "China market," American business leaders spoke of great commercial gains in the Soviet Union without explaining how the Russians would pay for American goods.

Other proponents of recognition of the Soviet Union were fearful of German and Japanese expansion and hoped that a revitalized Russia could restore a power balance to the world. After supporting the decision not to invite Russia to either Versailles in 1919 or the Washington Conference of 1921–22, many Americans now understood the impossibility of ignoring a nation that could have great impact on both Europe and Asia. The United States's official reason for nonrecognition was the more than $600 million owed Americans and their government, but Americans linked their distrust of the Bolsheviks with the Red Scare of 1919–20 in the United States. The radical, atheist, and anticapitalist nature of this revolutionary system caused suspicions in America. Nonetheless, it now seemed prudent to use any means available for slowing the spread of Germany and Japan.

Some Americans were concerned about the welfare of the Russian people after the Great War and sought to extend economic aid. Famine had devastated the huge country in 1921, and Russian author Maxim Gorky led others in seeking help from the United States. Herbert Hoover, secretary of commerce in the Harding administration, signed an agreement with Russia in 1921 that authorized relief assistance. Hoover had long argued that such an approach would undercut revolutionary forces and enhance America's influence in Russia. Within three years the American Relief Administration raised $50 million from American citizens and the government in Washington to help the Russian people. The head of the relief program in Russia, Colonel William Haskell, boasted in 1923 that America's efforts had destroyed communism in that country.

In a move indicative of Roosevelt's approach to foreign affairs, he insisted that he could establish formal relations with Russia if he could meet with a representative of that country. In October 1933 Roosevelt arranged a secret meeting between his personal emissary and special assistant to the secretary of state, William Bullitt, and the head of the Soviet Information Bureau in Washington. Bullitt, the reader will recall, had attempted a settlement with Lenin in 1919 and now had a second chance to establish relations. A few days afterward the White House received a favorable response to its overtures, and Roosevelt publicized the recent correspondence with Russia's figurehead president, Mikhail Kalinin. Roosevelt called for personal discussions with the Russians, and Kalinin accepted with the statement that the establishment of relations would promote peace. Russia's motives were partly commercial, but it was also concerned about halting Japan's spread into China. Any Russo-American settlement would rest solely on mutual need.

Negotiations were stiff and uncertain when they began in Washington in November 1933. The Soviet commissar for foreign affairs, Maxim Litvinov, arrived in the United States on November 7. Roosevelt dominated the American side of the negotiations, especially after Hull left for the Montevideo Conference. The president's introduction to Litvinov took place in the White House Blue Room, though Roosevelt lightheartedly remarked that the most appropriate meeting place might have been the Red Room. Despite the attempt at humor, the talks did not go well until the two men moved from specifics to generalities. Litvinov stipulated the granting of recognition prior to the discussions, but Roosevelt realized that to do so would give away his major bargaining card. As the tension mounted, the president recommended that the two men meet privately so "they could, if need be, insult each other with impunity." Yet they could not resolve the issues arising from the war debts and the confiscation of American properties by the Bolsheviks. Litvinov denied responsibility for the money sought by the United States and argued that the czar and provisional government should have paid off the debts before their fall to the Bolsheviks. The two men rid themselves of the matter by agreeing to turn to it at another time.

During the evening of November 16, Roosevelt and Litvinov reached an agreement that gave only the appearance of success. The United States extended recognition to Russia in return for its promise to halt subversion and propaganda against the United States, guarantee civil and religious liberties to Americans in Russia, and resolve the debts and claims questions at a later time. The United States refused to authorize a loan, despite talk about it during the negotiations. American business leaders, Roosevelt realized, were reluctant to lend money to a country that had repudiated prerevolutionary debts. In Moscow, Soviet Premier Joseph Stalin was restrained but pleased with the discussions, and the Department of State was guardedly optimistic. Yet despite commercial treaties with Russia in 1935 and 1937, trade declined because the Russians lacked the means to buy American goods and in turn did not have items attractive to American consumers.

The United States sent Bullitt as its first ambassador to Russia, but within two years he had resigned in disgust. His initial optimism had quickly vanished because of ill treatment characterized by continuous insults, the oppressive policies of the Soviet government, and a general atmosphere of suspicion and secrecy. Despite Russia's pledge against anti-

American propaganda, American communists criticized the United States during the Comintern (Communist International) Congress in Moscow in 1935. Bullitt's hopes for socialist reform in Russia disappeared as the political assassinations intensified into the purges of the mid-1930s. He returned home in 1936, a bitterly disillusioned man, before going to France as ambassador.

Meanwhile, in early 1934 Hull moved toward the establishment of reciprocal trade agreements while in Montevideo. Advocates pointed out that during the nineteenth century, tariffs were lower than at any time in history and so was the number of wars. Skeptics countered that low tariffs and world peace were coincidental and that the absence of a major war was attributable to the dominance of the British navy and to the world's preoccupation with industrial expansion. Still, a program of economic interdependence seemed worth the effort, and Hull won executive approval. As a southerner he favored low tariffs, but more was at stake than regional loyalty. Hull noted in his memoirs that "it seemed virtually impossible to develop friendly relations with other nations in the political sphere so long as we provoked their animosity in the economic sphere. How could we promote peace with them while waging war on them commercially?" The major obstacle in 1933 was that Roosevelt's New Deal program necessitated a high tariff to protect the nation's economy. One factor changing the president's stance was the conference in Montevideo, for those in attendance demonstrated widespread favor for lower tariffs on a reciprocal basis. Another was the secretary's persistent arguments for the interlocked nature of trade and peace. Protracted world economic disorder, Hull warned, would encourage dictatorships and make people susceptible to Bolshevism. As he told a congressional committee, world trade "is not only calculated to aid materially in the restoration of prosperity everywhere, but it is the greatest civilizer and peacemaker in the experience of the human race."

Congress responded with the Reciprocal Trade Agreements Act of June 1934, which sought to stimulate foreign purchases of American goods. To remove the issue from politics, the act authorized the president to lower tariffs on a reciprocal basis up to 50 percent through bilateral executive agreements based on the most-favored-nation principle. Thus the agreements went into effect without Senate approval, and each party automatically received the lowest tariff rates awarded anyone else. By 1940 the Executive Office had negotiated bilateral treaties on a reciprocal basis with over twenty nations. The treaties drove down duties and encouraged international trade, but they did not prevent war.

RISE OF THE DICTATORS

The rise of the dictators by the mid-1930s eventually forced a change in America's foreign policy, although the nation's isolationist impulse at first deterred any action stronger than economic or moral pressures. Besides

Japan's growing influence in the Far East, Germany's interests in Europe had expanded under the lead of Hitler. While in prison during the early 1920s, he had written *Mein Kampf (My Struggle)*, which set out his aims for Germany under the banner of the National Socialists, or Nazi party. He became chancellor in January 1933 and the following year took on full dictatorial powers. Determined to achieve *Lebensraum* ("living space") for his people, he called for a Pan-German movement to regain territories lost at Versailles in 1919. He quickly established one-party rule, stripped Jews of citizenship, installed a central state, and called for immediate arms equality. Roosevelt became alarmed by the threat of Germany's expansionism, and tried to arrange a compromise disarmament program and a general nonaggression agreement. He proposed consultation with other powers if a crisis ensued and agreed not to interfere with the League of Nations if it placed sanctions on an aggressor. Thus Roosevelt made cooperation with the League conditional upon a general disarmament plan. But Hitler announced that Germany would not agree to a smaller armaments program than that of other nations, and in October 1933 withdrew Germany from both the League of Nations and the Geneva Disarmament Conference. American representatives in Europe soon warned that Germany intended to dominate the world. Ambassador William Dodd wrote from Berlin that the Germans were confident that the United States would not intervene if Germany sought to surround Russia by taking the Polish Corridor, Lithuania, Latvia, and Estonia. Most German people, Dodd declared, would support Hitler even in "outright conquest."

Hitler disregarded the Versailles Treaty when he announced in March 1935 that Germany planned a rearmament program that entailed compulsory military training aimed at creating an army of 500,000, five times greater than that allowed by the treaty. This move was justified, he declared, because the other powers had not fulfilled their pledges on general disarmament. Britain, France, and Italy protested, although in June Britain approved Germany's decision to build a navy more than a third the size of its own—much larger than permitted under the Versailles Treaty.

Americans did not approve Germany's military and naval buildup, but believed that Britain and France should deal with the problem, while the United States should remain isolated from Europe. Disillusionment with the Great War had set in, causing American hostility to new entanglements. Revisionist historians had meanwhile absolved Germany of total responsibility for the war and argued that President Wilson's pro-Ally policies had resulted from the work of propagandists and business interests. America's isolationist attitude was also attributable to domestic reformers who feared that involvement in another war would end the New Deal and squelch civil liberties at home. Those who condemned America's entry into the Great War as a mistake included the scientist Albert Einstein, the airplane pilot and folk hero Charles Lindbergh, the historian Charles A. Beard, Senators William Borah and George Norris, and a number of groups on the college campuses. At Princeton University students founded an organization called the Veterans of Future Wars and declared that since most soldiers would die in the next conflict, each participant should receive a $1,000 bonus as a prerequisite for going to war. Other antiwar groups circulated posters displaying the horrors of war under the label, "Hello Sucker."

Bitterness over the Great War remained a major force in America's foreign policy for some time. By 1934 the focus of isolationist discontent was on munitions makers who had profited from the war. A best-selling Book-of-the-Month Club selection was *Merchants of Death* by Helmuth Engelbrecht and Frank Hanighen, which argued that arms makers had exploited American neutrality through war profiteering, and then pushed the United States into the war to protect their investments abroad. The following year another Book-of-the-Month Club selection, Walter Millis's *Road to War: America, 1914–1917*, made virtually the same argument. From the autumn of 1934 through 1936 isolationist Senator Gerald P. Nye of North Dakota headed a committee investigating arms and munitions makers. Public hearings, punctuated by dramatic revelations of huge profits from America's entry, suggested but never proved the widespread belief that the United States had entered the war to protect its loans to the Allies.

The Ethiopian crisis of 1935 led the United States to extend its stance of neutrality toward the Italian aggressions. Fascist leader Benito Mussolini had earlier established control over the East African states of Somaliland and Eritrea, and now he sought oil concessions from neighboring Ethiopia. After fighting erupted in December 1934 near the common border of Ethiopia and Italian Somaliland, Mussolini prepared to use full military force. By the summer of 1935 the Roosevelt administration wanted authority to determine the aggressor in a conflict and to send aid to the victim. But Congress refused this suggestion as interventionist in nature and passed instead the Neutrality Act of August, which barred America's arms trade with all belligerents and authorized the president to warn Americans against traveling on belligerent ships. The overall effect of the measure was to assure Mussolini that the United States would not extend aid to Ethiopia. The president signed the bill, but warned that it would "drag us into war instead of keeping us out."

In October 1935 Italian forces rolled into Ethiopia and drew a restrained reaction from Washington. Roosevelt declared a state of war between the antagonists and cut off trade to both by invoking the Neutrality Act, but he did have the consolation of knowing that Ethiopia's isolation would have prevented it from receiving American goods in large quantity anyway. Another aspect of the administration's neutrality stand offered no consolation, however: the United States could not halt the sale of oil to Italy because that product was not on the arms or munitions list. American oil was fueling the aggression. Roosevelt could only announce a "moral embargo" on oil and other goods, hoping that American business leaders would voluntarily restrict the flow. The appeal had little impact; America's trade with Italy, especially in oil, actually increased during the African crisis.

The reaction in Europe to events in Ethiopia only appeared to be stronger than that of the United States, for the continental nations likewise refused to restrain Italy. The League of Nations labeled Italy the aggressor and imposed economic sanctions on war matériel, loans, and purchases of certain Italian goods, but the list did not include oil, steel, iron, coal, and coke. Even though the French had interests in Africa and the British were concerned about the Mediterranean, neither government wanted to adopt economic policies detrimental to their people in depression times. The Royal Navy made a show of force by moving its Mediterranean fleet to the Suez Canal and another naval contingent to Gibraltar. But the British made no effort to obstruct the movement of Italy's troops or warships. Both Britain and France were primarily concerned with Germany and seemed to consider Ethiopia a small price for keeping Italy out of the German camp and preventing a larger war. Indeed, in December 1935 the British and French governments recommended that Italy receive nearly all of its demands in Ethiopia. The English people so roundly criticized this proposal that the British foreign secretary who helped sponsor it, Sir Samuel Hoare, resigned under pressure.

In late February 1936 Congress passed another, more broadly based Neutrality Act. Whereas the earlier one had empowered the president to widen the embargo to include any new belligerents in a conflict, the second one *required* him to do so. It also prohibited loans to belligerents, but added that any American republic victimized by a non-American state would receive assistance—including war matériel. Both Neutrality Acts would expire on May 1, 1937.

The divided and weak European response to the Italian invasion of Ethiopia doubtless encouraged Hitler to believe that he would encounter no resistance to future actions. Both the British and the French had considered imposing an oil embargo on Italy, but Hitler's repudiation of the Treaty of Versailles and other actions caused France to shy away from such a measure. In March 1936 the German armies reoccupied the Rhineland bordering France and Belgium, thus ignoring the Treaty of Versailles's declaration that the area was to be permanently demilitarized, and the Locarno Pact of 1925, which had guaranteed the borders of countries to Germany's west. The move severed the French connection with Czechoslovakia, and it threatened the Maginot Line, a military defense network stretching along the Franco-German border, built by France following the Great War. With no French support forthcoming, Britain refused to close the Suez Canal and thus ensured Italy's victory over Ethiopia. Mussolini's armies took the Ethiopian capital of Addis Ababa in early May 1936 and shortly afterward annexed the entire country. The League's sanctions expired in June and were lifted the following month. When the League refused to cancel Ethiopia's membership, Italy withdrew from the organization in July, following actions already taken by Japan and Germany.

The scene then shifted to Spain, where the Nationalists, under General Francisco Franco, rebelled against the Republican and secular government in Madrid and set off a three-year civil war that invited foreign intervention. France tried to persuade the European powers to stay out of Spanish affairs for fear of causing a full-scale war, but it was clear that the French, British, and Russians favored the Republicans or Loyalists, whereas the Germans and Italians wanted Franco to win because his regime would be alien to France. Little time passed before Germany and Italy sent military assistance to Franco and the Soviet Union extended aid to the communists, who were among the Republican forces. Britain and France countered with the International Nonintervention Committee, whose membership included Germany and Italy. Though the organization guaranteed formal nonintervention in Spain, Hitler and Mussolini continued to send aid privately, while the Soviet Union, Mexico, and a number of Americans (who considered the war a battle for democracy) helped the Republicans. Britain and France could do nothing because they had tied their hands by establishing the Nonintervention Committee.

The United States followed the European lead and urged nonintervention in the Spanish Civil War. Though the Neutrality Acts applied only to wars between foreign nations and not to domestic conflicts, Roosevelt wanted Congress to institute an arms embargo against Spain. In early January 1937 Congress overwhelmingly passed a joint resolution to that effect, but the embargo did not achieve the desired results. America's decision to stay out of the civil war hurt the Loyalists and encouraged German and Italian efforts to establish a fascist regime in Spain. The Spanish government ultimately collapsed, allowing Franco's forces to take over in 1939.

By November 1936 the dictatorships in Germany, Italy, and Japan had moved closer together. The Germans and Italians had differed with each other on only a single issue. When the Nazi party in Austria made an abortive attempt to seize the government in 1936, Mussolini sent troops to the Austrian border because he did not want a strong Germany at the Brenner Pass. But Hitler offered assurances that Austria would remain independent and did not express opposition to Italy's invasion of Ethiopia; in addition, both leaders favored Franco in the Spanish Civil War. Consequently, in October 1936, Hitler and Mussolini signed a pact guaranteeing cooperation toward Spain, opposition to communism, and recognition of Italy's control of Ethiopia. One month afterward, Germany and Japan allied in the Anti-Comintern Pact, which reflected Japan's extensive thrust into China and both signatories' hatred for Russia. When Italy joined the pact a year later, it became the Rome-Berlin-Tokyo Axis.

War clouds over Europe plus the growing influence of Germany and Italy in Latin America caused the Roosevelt administration to tighten its hemispheric policies. In March 1936, at the height of the German and Italian crises, the United States signed a pact with Panama (not approved by the Senate until 1939), which terminated the original treaty of 1903 establishing an American protectorate over Panama, and disclaimed any right of intervention. The United States also renounced the right to add new territory that might become necessary to running the canal, though retaining the right to defend the waterway in the event of a crisis.

In December 1936 the Inter-American Conference for the Maintenance of Peace assembled in Buenos Aires, Argentina, where Hull chaired the American delegation and Roosevelt traveled 7,000 miles to address the opening session on the importance of hemispheric unity. The conferees agreed to consultation should there be a threat to peace, the United States joined others in a Declaration of Solidarity, and Hull assured nonintervention by approving the following statement: "The High Contracting Parties declare inadmissible the intervention of any one of them, directly or indirectly, and for whatever reason, in the internal or external affairs of any other of the Parties." Though the United States had taken a stand against only military intervention, numerous Latin American states thought the policy included economic involvement. The agreement to consult did not specify procedural steps, but it encouraged hopes of American nonintervention by helping to convert the Monroe Doctrine from unilateral to multilateral status. The pacts signed by the United States at Panama and Buenos Aires reinforced the Good Neighbor policy and strengthened relations with Latin America.

THE CHINA INCIDENT

Meanwhile, in the Far East the calm in Japanese-Chinese relations continued uneasily throughout the first four years of Roosevelt's presidency. The new administration in Washington had supported the Stimson policy of nonrecognition of Manchukuo largely because isolationist sentiment permitted no choice, but also because America's lack of military preparedness prevented anything other than veiled threats. The Roosevelt administration had extended recognition to Russia partly to instill concern in Japan about the possible Russo-American alliance. The administration also ordered the fleet to remain in the Pacific and urged Congress to build a larger navy. Growing apprehension over the insecurity of the Philippines and other Pacific possessions guided America's Asian policy. But there seemed little else the White House could do except follow a policy of nonconfrontation. Indeed, in May 1933 the Japanese and Chinese agreed to a cease-fire, which established a neutral zone south of the Great Wall of China.

The Manchurian question remained unsettled, however, for at a press conference in the spring of 1934 the Foreign Office in Tokyo announced that Japan's "position and mission" gave it sole responsibility for maintaining "peace and order in East Asia." A short time later its ambassador in Washington proposed a joint settlement of the Far Eastern matter which called for the establishment of American and Japanese spheres of interest in the Pacific, and cooperation in erecting "a reign of law and order in the regions geographically adjacent to their respective countries." Japan's own "Monroe Doctrine" for Asia, as its proponents sometimes called it, would have established Japanese control over China, with nothing of equal value going to the United States. It also would have violated the moral obligations of the Open Door. Hull turned down the proposal. Japan meanwhile gave the necessary two-year notice of abrogation of the Washington and London treaties of the 1920s and 1930s, relieving itself of restrictions on naval construction. In April 1935 Japanese Foreign Minister Koki Hirota informed the American and British Ambassadors in Tokyo that his government had made the Open Door guarantees conditional upon other nations' diplomatic recognition of Manchukuo; until that took place, "no dispute whatever could be entertained with regard to that country."

Tokyo's interest in northern China soon led to the outbreak of the Sino-Japanese War in 1937, a conflict that lasted until the close of World War II in 1945. Japan had called for the independence of upper China, repeatedly urging the government in Nanking to extend *de facto* recognition to Manchukuo and to help stamp out communism in Asia. Though the Roosevelt administration knew that these stipulations would have facilitated Japan's control over China, it still sought to avert a collision with the Japanese and apparently would have accepted such an agreement. In mid-1937, however, Chinese and Japanese soldiers clashed at the Marco Polo Bridge outside Peiping in what became known as the China Incident. As Japanese forces swept into China afterward, stories spread of government by intimidation and assassination. American newsreel cameras recorded the conflict for theaters back home, as the bombings, lootings, and burnings spread into Peiping and Shanghai. The Japanese offensive in northern China soon became locked in conflict with the forces of Nationalist Chiang Kai-shek and Communist Mao Tse-tung, now temporarily in league against the common enemy.

The United States followed a mixed policy during the war in China. Its ambassador in Tokyo, Joseph Grew, considered Japan the aggressor, but warned that intervention might strengthen the militarists in that country. He urged America only to safeguard its 10,000 nationals and their property in China. Washington sent more marines to Shanghai and suggested that Americans evacuate the country. It also warned both antagonists that America expected reparations for damages.

Congress was more cautious than the president. The Neutrality Acts of 1935 and 1936 had expired on May 1, 1937, but that same day Congress renewed them indefinitely. It also authorized the president to invoke neutrality in a foreign civil war if the sale of war matériel to either side could endanger American interests. Thus the Neutrality Act of 1937 again prohibited Americans from traveling on belligerent ships, and it repeated the ban on loans and munitions sales. But it also exempted Latin America from the law and permitted Britain and other maritime nations to pick up nonmilitary goods through a cash-and-carry provision to expire on May 1, 1939. Such an allowance would prevent belligerent destruction of American ships and property, and would avoid the granting of credits that could again drag the United States into war.

Roosevelt decided against invoking the Neutrality Act of 1937 because his refusal to do so tacitly allowed the Chinese to buy American arms and supplies. The act had permitted some maneuverability by the administration. It declared that "whenever the President shall find that there exists a state of war between, or among, two or more foreign states, the President shall proclaim such fact." As China and Japan resumed their conflict the following July, Roosevelt did not invoke neutrality on the basis that he did not "find" a war. The Japanese had not declared war, and the "incident" in China had not technically violated the Kellogg-Briand Pact. Thus the president could arrange aid to the Chinese. He meanwhile ordered that no government vessels should carry war matériel to either side in the conflict, and cautioned private citizens against looking to Washington for protection should they violate his directives. The irony is that America's efforts to maintain neutrality constituted a message to aggressors that the United States would not aid victims. In Congress's determination to adhere to isolationism, it enacted a law that encouraged a widening of the war.

On October 5, 1937, in Chicago, the isolationist center of the Midwest, Roosevelt made a public statement on the China crisis when he suggested the need for a worldwide "quarantine" on aggressors. The "epidemic" of "international lawlessness," he warned, could lead to American involvement in a world war. Though not referring to Japan or any other nation, he was considering some form of pressure on treaty violators. "The peace, the freedom, and the security of 90 percent of the population of the world," he declared, "is being jeopardized by the remaining 10 percent, who are threatening a breakdown of all international order and law. Surely the 90 percent who want to live in peace under law and in accordance with moral standards . . . can and must find some way to make their will prevail. . . . There must be positive endeavors to preserve peace." The "Quarantine Speech" aroused such virulent opposition among isolationists that the president retreated into ambiguity. He explained afterward that he had had no specific program in mind to counteract Japan's aggressions in China, although later documentation shows that he privately considered economic reprisals.

The crisis deepened as the Japanese seized Shanghai and then took the capital of Nanking at the cost of 100,000 Chinese lives. Americans in China complained of brutal treatment by Japanese soldiers, and sent reports of bombs hitting American schools and hospitals, despite the Stars and Stripes painted on their roofs. A United Press International photograph captured the horror of the war by showing a crying baby sitting alone among the bombed-out remnants of a railroad yard in Shanghai. In the meantime the League Assembly recommended that the signatories to the Nine-Power Treaty try to resolve the problem. The United States joined eighteen other nations in Brussels, Belgium, to discuss the Far Eastern situation. Japan refused to attend but declared its actions defensive, the Nine-Power Treaty dated, and the Kellogg-Briand Pact irrelevant. At the end of three weeks of meetings, the participants went home after making a plea for the Open Door in China.

The United States seemed to be drawn more into the Asian conflict when in the daytime of December 12, 1937, Japanese pilots bombed and sank the American gunboat *Panay* on the Yangtze River in China as the sailors helped Americans evacuate the embassy in Nanking. In the fray three Standard Oil tankers under the *Panay*'s escort were also sunk, and two Americans died and thirty were wounded, including those machine-gunned as they swam for safety. The Roosevelt administration demanded an apology and reparations, and the government in Japan immediately complied. The foreign minister personally apologized to Grew in Tokyo, the Japanese government paid over $2 million in reparations, and its citizens contributed to a fund for the victims. Once again it appeared that Japanese militarists had only temporarily gotten out of hand, and within weeks the crisis passed.

American isolationist feeling necessitated administration policies that were indirect in nature, for despite the *Panay* incident the public remained opposed to intervention in China. Two days afterward, isolationists in Congress supported an amendment sponsored by Indiana Congressman Louis Ludlow, which provided that except for invasion, the United States could not go to war without the majority approval of Americans as expressed in a national referendum. The president warned that such a law would strip the Executive Office of authority in foreign affairs, and even Michigan's isolationist Senator Arthur Vandenberg proclaimed that it "would be as sensible to require a town meeting before permitting the fire department to put out the blaze." Yet support for the measure seemed formidable, and only great pressure from the White House defeated it in the House of Representatives by a slender margin. Faced with such strong isolationist sentiment, the Roosevelt administration in July 1938 resorted to a "moral embargo," which involved Hull sending a letter informing American manufacturers that the government "strongly opposed" the sale of planes to nations that bombed civilians. Most business leaders complied. The United States also helped China expand its transportation network, and it bought silver from China, which allowed the Chinese to acquire weapons and war matériel from Americans. In the meantime Congress appropriated funds to naval construction, and the United States took over a few Pacific islands as potential bases. By October, however, the Chinese government had withdrawn to Chungking on the upper Yangtze River, leaving Japan in control of the major ports, coastal cities, and railroads.

Japan responded to America's implicit warnings on November 3, 1938, when Prime Minister Fumimaro Konoye, a popular but weak figure, announced the formation of a "New Order" in East Asia revolving around Japan, Manchukuo, and China. America's appeals to the Open Door and to treaties involving China had no effect, although Japan conceded that American recognition of the New Order would lead to increased trade. Perhaps the economic enticement was worth pursuing. The fact was that America's commerce with China was still not large. From 1931 to 1935 about a fifth of the foreign trade of the United States was with the Far East, and Japan's share was three times that of China's. Yet many Americans either felt a moral commitment to the Chinese, or they believed in the mythical "China market." For whatever reason or combination of reasons, Washington reaffirmed support for the Open Door and subsequent treaty rights, and negotiated a loan for China through the Export-Import Bank. By the end of 1938 the lines of division were clear between the United States and Japan: the Open Door in China was incompatible with the New Order.

CRISIS IN EUROPE

In early 1938 Hitler turned toward Austria in beginning his expansionist drive to the east. He called Austrian Chancellor Kurt von Schuschnigg to his Bavarian refuge at Berchtesgaden and demanded that he award positions in the government's cabinet to members of the Austrian Nazi party. Schuschnigg did so, but called for a plebiscite which he thought would rally his people against imminent German annexation. Hitler demanded Schuschnigg's resignation and stationed troops along the Austrian border, raising the possibility of invasion and forcing the chancellor's compliance on March 11. The following day the new head of Austria, Arthur Seyss-Inquart of the Nazi party, invited German soldiers into the country, ostensibly to keep order. Over protests from London and Paris, Germany announced the *Anschluss* (annexation) of Austria on March 14.

Hitler's push eastward then focused on the Germans in Czechoslovakia, who he claimed were in need of liberation from oppressive rule. Nearly a fourth of Czechoslovakia's 14 million inhabitants were Germans, most of whom lived in the Sudeten (south) region lining the western side of the republic. Like a letter "v" laid on its side, the Sudetenland pierced Germany to the north, west, and south. Since 1932 the Nazi party had been working for Sudeten autonomy within Czechoslovakia, preparatory for annexation by Germany. But when Germany prepared to annex the Sudetenland, the Czechs, bolstered by a capable army and military pacts with Russia and France, indicated their willingness to fight. The British intervened in September 1938.

British Prime Minister Neville Chamberlain feared a full-scale European war. His election in mid-1937 had affirmed the popularity of his "appeasement" policy, for in the campaign he had attributed Germany's

actions to the unfair provisions of the Versailles Treaty and seemed willing to concede its control over German-speaking peoples in Austria,
Czechoslovakia, and Poland. Once Germany got what it deserved, Chamberlain hoped that nation would join the West in halting the communists
in Russia. The priority now was to prevent Czech resistance to Germany's
demands.

In mid-September Chamberlain visited Hitler twice to persuade him
to approve a compromise proposal that the British and French had persuaded the Czechs to accept. Every region in Czechoslovakia in which
more than half of its inhabitants were German would go to Germany; an
international commission would draw a new border; the remainder of
Czechoslovakia would become independent. But Hitler rejected the proposal and demanded all of the Sudetenland. He expected a prompt withdrawal of Czech officials, and he wanted plebiscites held in areas with
questionable German constituencies. Furthermore, he asserted, German
military occupation would begin on October 1. Hitler's ultimatum caused
the Czechs to mobilize. While Paris and London assured them assistance
if attacked, Mussolini promised aid to Hitler.

Under Western pressure, Hitler agreed to meet at Munich in late September with Mussolini, Chamberlain, and French Premier Édouard Daladier to deal with the question of Czechoslovakia. Isolationist feeling in the
United States precluded direct involvement in European affairs, although
Roosevelt supported Chamberlain and Daladier in asking Mussolini to
persuade Hitler to accept a peaceful resolution of the Czech issue. Roosevelt wrote Hitler: "Should you agree to a solution in this peaceful manner
I am convinced that hundreds of millions throughout the world would
recognize your action as an outstanding historic service to humanity."
Presumably the president hoped that discussions would buy time and
permit a resolution of the problem.

At the Munich Conference of September 29 and 30, 1938, Britain,
France, and Italy approved the transfer of the Sudetenland to Germany.
The outcome was virtually identical to the demands contained in Hitler's
ultimatum of a few days earlier. Chamberlain returned to London and
proclaimed "peace with honour" and "peace for our time," while Roosevelt sent him a letter of praise. Hitler offered assurances at Munich that
the Sudetenland was "the last territorial claim which I have to make in
Europe."

But trouble continued to spread despite the Munich settlement. The
Soviet Union had again not received an invitation to a conference that involved its interests. In fact, the French and British decision to meet without the Soviets perhaps pushed Stalin closer to Hitler; the Red Armies
were not prepared to resist an expected Nazi invasion and the only alternative was negotiation. The West's decision to meet Hitler's demands was
also an effort to buy time. A generation that had seen millions of its youth
die in one world war considered any chance for peace worth a try. But
even while Chamberlain attempted to appease Hitler, the British govern-

ment stepped up its armaments program. The Munich agreements turned Germany toward the east, whether or not by French and British design as Stalin believed, and they proved to be the last step before the collapse of Czechoslovakia.

While Americans deluded themselves into believing that the Munich Conference had averted war, the Roosevelt administration adopted measures suggesting its awareness of danger. A month before the conference, the president met with Canadian Prime Minister Mackenzie King to arrange mutual assurances of help, and in October he asked Congress to bolster the national defense. The United States began a program of airplane manufacturing, and in December it sent delegates to the Eighth International Conference of American States in Lima, Peru, which focused on hemispheric cooperation against European dangers. The ensuing Declaration of Lima proclaimed that upon the request of any foreign minister, the others would consult about countering a threat. The United States meanwhile agreed to sell bombers to France, and the Roosevelt administration pushed for revisions in the neutrality laws that would permit aid to victims of aggression. In the president's annual message to Congress of January 1939, he asserted that there were "many methods short of war" capable of demonstrating America's sentiment, and complained that present neutrality legislation "may actually give aid to an aggressor and deny it to the victim." Changes had to take place. Despite problems in Asia, Washington's primary concern was Europe. Its policy toward the Sino-Japanese War was to employ any measure short of war with Japan; its stance toward Europe was to pursue the most stringent program acceptable to isolationists.

In the spring of 1939 war seemed closer in Europe as Hitler and Mussolini resumed expansion. Nazi armies absorbed Czechoslovakia in March—breaking Hitler's assurances at Munich—and that same month Hitler intensified pressure on Poland for the port city of Danzig and a strip of land through the Polish Corridor which would connect Germany with East Prussia. The Polish government turned down his demands, and Britain and France pledged support. The German leader privately remarked that "England may talk big," but "she is sure not to resort to armed intervention in the conflict." In April Italian troops occupied Albania, and Britain and France offered assurances to Rumania and Greece, seemingly next in Mussolini's path. Roosevelt urged Germany and Italy to join a ten-year guarantee of nonaggression against the thirty-one governments in Europe and the Near East. If successful, the United States would encourage negotiations toward scaling down armaments and reestablishing world trade. No answer came from Italy, and two weeks later Hitler sarcastically announced that all thirty-one governments had assured him they trusted Germany and did not need America's guarantees.

The German and Italian refusals to pledge nonaggression pushed the Roosevelt administration into seeking repeal of the arms embargo. The cash-and-carry provision on nonmilitary goods would expire on May 1,

1939, and Hitler could interpret a failure to lift the arms embargo as America's refusal to assist Britain and France. The president and Hull met with the Senate leaders in July to warn of war in Europe and to advocate American help to the British and French. But isolationist William Borah replied that his sources were more reliable than those of the State Department, and they told him war was unlikely. Opposition to repeal of the Neutrality Act was too strong, and Congress adjourned in August without passing a new bill. Failure to reenact neutrality legislation carried another dangerous implication: should war break out in Europe, American cargo vessels were under no prohibitions against entering the combat zone.

Fear of German assault drove the Soviet Union into negotiations, first with neighboring states, then with Britain and France, and when unsuccessful in both instances, with Germany. Despite bitterness with the West over Munich, Soviet leaders tried from April through August of 1939 to secure a defensive pact with any government willing to take a stand against Germany. But Poland, Rumania, and the Baltic States feared that Soviet territorial guarantees meant Soviet occupation. Stalin's overtures to Britain and France had likewise failed; to buy time he negotiated with Hitler. On August 20 Germany and the Soviet Union announced a commercial pact. Three days later German Foreign Minister Joachim von Ribbentrop signed a nonaggression agreement in Moscow with Soviet Foreign Commissar Vyacheslav M. Molotov that guaranteed Soviet neutrality if Germany invaded Poland. The pact also contained secret assurances of a Nazi-Soviet partition of Poland, as well as clarification of areas sought by each in the Baltic region. Stalin's approach was identical to that used by the West at Munich: give in to Hitler's demands and turn Germany in another direction. A member of the Department of State in Washington, Jay Pierrepont Moffat, recorded in his diary just after receiving news of the Nonaggression Pact that "these last two days have given me the feeling of sitting in a house where somebody is dying upstairs. There is relatively little to do and yet the suspense continues unabated."

While America's attention was on the growing crisis in Europe, Japan had alarmed the West by establishing control over the islands that lay in the French and British sea lanes of East Asia. Such a move endangered French Indochina, British and Dutch possessions in Southeast Asia, and American interests in the Philippines. Grew in Tokyo was concerned that Washington might enact measures against Japan that would drive it into war against the United States. The former secretary of state, Henry L. Stimson, headed the American Committee for Nonparticipation in Japanese Aggression, which called for an embargo on oil and scrap iron. According to a poll taken that summer of 1939, 82 percent of the American public wanted to end the sale of war matériel to Japan. Yet the Roosevelt administration hesitated because an embargo might force Tokyo into a war that the United States was not militarily prepared to fight. On July 26, 1939 the State Department left the impression that economic sanctions were imminent when it gave Japan the required six months' notice for ending the long-standing Treaty of Commerce and Navigation of 1911.

The threatened cutoff of American trade caused leaders of the Japanese army to push for an alliance with Germany that would assure Soviet neutrality while they secured control over the oil, rice, rubber, and tin of Southeast Asia. They argued this policy with cabinet, naval, and business figures, who feared that expansion south would lead to economic pressures and possibly war with the United States. The hardliners had to back off in August 1939, however, when Germany violated the Anti-Comintern Pact with Japan and joined the Soviet Union in the Nonaggression Pact. Whereas Hitler was under fewer controls in Europe, Stalin was free to move in the Far East. The threatened abrogation of the commercial treaty with the United States and the implications of the Nazi-Soviet Pact temporarily eased relations between Tokyo and Washington.

The autumn of 1939 seemed an opportune time to reconstruct relations with Japan. Threatened economic sanctions and the negotiation of the Nonaggression Pact restrained the warlords in Tokyo and renewed the moderates' hopes for reconciliation with the United States. But internal discussions in Tokyo were, of course, secret and no one in Washington seemed to sense the moment. Grew urged his home government to drop the Open Door pledges and recognize Japan's control over China. His proposal encountered stringent opposition from Hull, who was outraged by Japan's actions in the Far East and believed the United States morally bound to China. Before long the secretary of state's pronouncements helped to elevate the principles of the Open Door to the status of official policy. Grew's call for accommodation on realistic terms might not have changed the course of events, but it would have provided time for the United States to prepare for war in the Pacific. The twin fears of economic sanctions and the Nazi-Soviet Pact isolated Japan, restrained the militarists, and suggested the need for a compromise on China that might have bolstered the moderates in Japan.

This opportunity passed when on September 1, 1939, World War II began in Europe.

Selected readings

Ambrose, Stephen E., *Rise to Globalism: American Foreign Policy since 1938*. 4th ed. 1985.

Anderson, Irvine H., *The Standard-Vacuum Oil Company and United States East Asian Policy, 1933–1941*. 1975.

Bailey, Thomas A., *America Faces Russia*. 1950.

Bemis, Samuel F., *The Latin-American Policy of the United States*. 1943.

Bennett, Edward M., *Franklin D. Roosevelt and the Search for Security: American-Soviet Relations, 1933–1939*. 1985.

————, *Recognition of Russia: An American Foreign Policy Dilemma.* 1970.

Bishop, Donald G., *The Roosevelt-Litvinov Agreements: The American View.* 1965.

Borg, Dorothy, *The United States and the Far Eastern Crisis of 1933–1938.* 1964.

Browder, Robert P., *The Origins of Soviet-American Diplomacy.* 1953.

Cohen, Warren I., *The American Revisionists: The Lessons of Intervention in World War I.* 1967.

Cole, Wayne S., *Charles A. Lindbergh and the Battle against American Intervention in World War II.* 1974.

————, *Roosevelt and the Isolationists, 1932–45.* 1983.

————, *Senator Gerald P. Nye and American Foreign Relations.* 1962.

Compton, James V., *The Swastika and the Eagle: Hitler, the United States and the Origins of World War II.* 1967.

Crowley, James B., *Japan's Quest for Autonomy: National Security and Foreign Policy, 1930–1938.* 1966.

Dallek, Robert, *Franklin D. Roosevelt and American Foreign Policy, 1932–1945.* 1979.

Divine, Robert A., *The Illusion of Neutrality.* 1962.

————, *The Reluctant Belligerent: American Entry into World War II.* Rev. ed. 1979.

Ferrell, Robert H., *American Diplomacy in the Great Depression.* 1957.

Gardner, Lloyd C., *Economic Aspects of New Deal Diplomacy.* 1964.

Gellman, Irwin, *Good Neighbor Diplomacy.* 1979.

Griswold, A. Whitney, *The Far Eastern Policy of the United States.* 1938.

Jablon, Howard, *Crossroads of Decision: The State Department and Foreign Policy, 1933–1937.* 1983.

Jonas, Manfred, *Isolationism in America, 1935–1941.* 1966.

————, *The United States and Germany: A Diplomatic History.* 1984.

Kennan, George F., *American Diplomacy.* Expanded ed. 1984. Originally published as *American Diplomacy, 1900–1950.* 1951.

Langer, William, and S. E. Gleason, *The Challenge to Isolation, 1937–1940.* 1952.

Little, Douglas, *Malevolent Neutrality: The United States, Great Britain, and the Origins of the Spanish Civil War.* 1985.

Offner, Arnold A., *American Appeasement: United States Foreign Policy and Germany, 1933–1938.* 1969.

Steward, Dick, *Trade and Hemisphere: The Good Neighbor Policy and Reciprocal Trade.* 1975.

Williams, William A., *American-Russian Relations, 1781–1947.* 1952.

Wiltz, John E., *In Search of Peace: The Senate Munitions Inquiry, 1934–1936.* 1963.

Wood, Bryce, *The Making of the Good Neighbor Policy.* 1961.

Chapter Seventeen

To Pearl Harbor, 1939–1941

WAR IN EUROPE

On September 1, 1939, Hitler's military machine rolled over Poland, and two days later Britain and France honored their pledges to that country and declared war on Germany. The Second World War had begun. British Prime Minister Chamberlain lamented that "everything that I have worked for has crashed into ruins." In a fireside chat over the radio, President Roosevelt asked Americans to be neutral in action, but admitted that he did not expect them to be neutral in thought. That same month the foreign ministers of the American republics approved the Declaration of Panama, which warned the belligerent powers to stay out of a "safety belt" reaching 300 miles out to sea around North and South America below Canada. The American nations were to patrol these waters and report violations, although their means of enforcement remained unclear. In mid-September Poland collapsed and, in line with the secret provisions of the Nazi-Soviet Pact of 1939, the Germans and Russians divided the country between them.

After the fall of Poland the conflict in Europe surprisingly settled into the *Sitzkrieg* or "phony war" of the winter of 1939–40. Attention turned to the far north, where the Russians sought to subjugate Finland in the "Winter War" as part of an effort to secure their northern borders against German attack. Roosevelt countered by urging American business leaders to cut off war matériel to Russia, and Congress suspended Finland's World War I debt obligations and approved a huge loan. But the credits were limited to *non*military goods, and had little effect on stopping the Soviet assault. Finland capitulated under severe terms in March 1940, and shortly afterward Russia seized the Baltic States of Estonia, Latvia, and Lithuania. Meanwhile in the Atlantic the Germans began using magnetic mines outside British harbors—a new weapon in violation of maritime law—and the Allies retaliated with an illegal blockade of Germany's exports. As in 1916, the United States protested violations of freedom of the seas when Britain opened America's mail, searched its cargo, and caused delayed shipments. But Americans in 1939–40 were more willing to overlook British infractions because the aggressors were more clearly defined than in the First World War.

The Roosevelt administration quickened its efforts to repeal the arms embargo and allow Britain and France to buy war matériel on a cash-and-carry basis. Such a step, the president assured the American people, would help keep the United States out of the war. Isolationists again charged that financial entanglements had pulled the country into war in 1917, and they bitterly fought any changes in neutrality legislation. To win his program, Roosevelt persuaded a Republican journalist from Kansas, William Allen White, to head a "Nonpartisan Committee for Peace through Revision of the Neutrality Act." After an appeal from the White House, Congress began a debate that lasted six weeks and culminated in November 1939 with a revised Neutrality Act. It repealed the arms embargo and allowed purchases on a cash-and-carry basis; to satisfy opponents of the bill, Americans were prohibited from entering combat areas designated by the president. The United States had taken a major step away from isolationism: Britain and France could buy war goods for cash if they came and got them.

In the spring of 1940 the phony war abruptly came to an end when the Germans opened an offensive in Europe called the *Blitzkrieg*, or "lightning war." Hitler's panzer (armor) divisions overran Denmark, Norway, Belgium, the Netherlands, and Luxembourg, en route to the English Channel to cut off the British expeditionary force before turning toward France. Britain's abortive attempt in May to drive the Germans out of Norway led to Chamberlain's fall from power, and in early June nearly 350,000 soldiers, mostly British, barely managed to evacuate Europe at Dunkirk. But they had suffered a devastating defeat and left heavy war machinery on the beaches. With Hitler's forces preparing to destroy France, the new prime minister of Britain, Winston Churchill, went before Parliament on the day Dunkirk fell to exhort his countrymen:

> [W]e shall not flag or fail. We shall go on to the end, we shall fight in France, we shall fight in the seas and oceans, we shall fight with growing confidence and growing strength in the air, we shall defend our island, whatever the cost may be, we shall fight on the beaches, we shall fight on the landing-grounds, we shall fight in the fields and in the streets, we shall fight in the hills; we shall never surrender, and even if, which I do not for a moment believe, this island or a large part of it were subjugated and starving, then our Empire beyond the seas, armed and guarded by the British Fleet, would carry on the struggle, until, in God's good time, the New World, with all its power and might, steps forth to the rescue and the liberation of the Old.

The German Assault, 1939–1941

Germany and axis powers

German occupied countries, 1941

Allied countries

Neutral countries

German advances

MAP 24

Except for the failure to defeat Britain, the German Blitzkrieg achieved a series of almost unbroken victories in the period before 1941.

The imminent fall of France stirred the Roosevelt administration into stronger action. After Germany attacked Denmark and Norway, the United States froze those two countries' assets in America to prevent Hitler from getting them. Concern had also grown among Americans that French and Dutch possessions in the Western Hemisphere could fall to Germany and thereby endanger the Panama Canal and the United States. Congress therefore passed a resolution in June expressing opposition to the transfer of territory in the Americas "from one non-American power to another non-American power." That same month Mussolini declared war on France and drew a bitter retort from the president. Speaking before the graduating class of the University of Virginia in Charlottesville, Roosevelt declared that "the hand that held the dagger has struck it into the back of its neighbor." The United States, he promised, would help those people resisting aggression while itself preparing for "any emergency and every defense." On June 22 Americans were stunned when France collapsed before the Nazi war machine. More shocks were to come as French Marshal Henri Philippe Pétain established a government at Vichy, in the southeastern part of the country, that collaborated with the Germans and avoided a total German takeover. The following month the United States became a party to the Act of Havana, which authorized the American republics to occupy any European possession in the hemisphere threatened by an outside power, thereby making the Monroe Doctrine a multilateral pact. Americans realized that only Britain stood between them and Germany.

The Roosevelt administration began preparations toward helping the English survive the German air assault that became known as the Battle of Britain during the summer of 1940. America increased the production of war goods, enlarged its air corps, and took steps toward creating a two-ocean navy. In August Roosevelt met with Canadian Prime Minister Mackenzie King to establish a Permanent Joint Board on Defense. When Franco of Spain seemed on the verge of joining the Axis in the war, Roosevelt worked with the British in exerting economic pressure on Spain and allowing the Royal Navy to maintain its hold on Gibraltar and hence the entrance into the Mediterranean. The president also won congressional approval to move the National Guard into the service of the federal government, and he sent American military officers to London to discuss closer cooperation against the German navy. To win public support, William Allen White, instrumental in bringing about revision of the Neutrality Act, established the Committee to Defend America by Aiding the Allies. Polls substantiated this approach: whereas 80 percent of Americans opposed going to war, nearly the same number favored helping England.

Some administration measures were of questionable legality. The White House turned over planes to American manufacturers who built aircraft for the government, with the understanding that the older models would go to the British. It also sold outdated military goods to private business leaders, who then dealt them to the British. For a time American pilots flew to a point just south of Canada and left their craft for the Canadians to haul across the border. British pilots were trained in Florida, rather than having to undergo the harsh weather of Canada. During June alone, more than $43 million worth of cannons, machine guns, rifles, mortars, and ammunition went to Britain—without technically violating neutrality legislation. Perhaps to mute criticism of his policies, Roosevelt had appointed two leading Republicans to his cabinet, Henry L. Stimson as secretary of war and Frank Knox as secretary of the navy. Both men opposed isolationism.

The successes of the German *Blitzkrieg* in Europe changed the tone of America's relations with Japan. Americans realized that Hitler's advances had tied up the West and exposed its possessions in the Pacific and Southeast Asia to Japan. Should the Japanese seize the area's oil, rice, rubber, and tin, the long stalemate in China would end with their victory. After the fall of the Netherlands and France, Tokyo demanded that England and Vichy France halt the flow of goods to China from Burma and Indochina, and pushed for oil concessions from the Dutch East Indies. With Britain's fall seemingly imminent, the Japanese could move into Malaya, leaving the United States as their only barrier to control of Asia. The United States's commercial treaty of 1911 with Japan had expired in late January 1940, and the Department of State had attempted to force concessions by maintaining trade on a day-to-day basis. The Roosevelt administration also ordered the Pacific fleet to remain at Pearl Harbor until further notice. The United States was attempting to steer a dangerous course between honoring its Open Door pledges to China and avoiding policies that might lead to war with Japan.

Since Japan's war machine was heavily dependent on American oil, demands for an embargo came from numerous officials in Washington, including Stimson, Knox, and Secretary of the Treasury Henry Morgenthau, Jr. Roosevelt and Hull remained opposed for more than one reason. They still tried to treat events in Asia separately from those in Europe, declaring that the preservation of England and the defeat of Germany were priorities. Though this argument seemed narrow in perception, another part of their stand had more validity. Whereas the *threat* of an oil embargo might discourage Japanese expansion, its *implementation* might push Japan into the Axis alliance, drive the Japanese deeper into Southeast Asia for oil, and cause war with the United States. Hull wrote in his memoirs that "our best tactic was to keep them guessing." Roosevelt's military advisers added weight to his position. They warned that Congress had not authorized a two-ocean navy until that year, and that the United States was not prepared for war in the Pacific. Chief of Naval Operations Harold Stark stressed the need for time and warned against any action provoking Japan. In July, however, Stimson and Morgenthau convinced the president to tighten economic pressures by forbidding the export without a license of quality scrap metal, petroleum, and other products, and by stopping the sale of aviation fuel outside the Western

Hemisphere except to Britain. After a bitter cabinet fight over the new measure, the president gave in to Undersecretary of State Sumner Welles, who wanted to restrict the embargo to aviation gasoline and to the best quality scrap iron and steel. But Japan's continued encroachments in Indochina and America's growing fear of a Japanese military alliance with Germany soon forced another change in administration policy. In September the White House added all scrap metals and steel to the list of embargoed goods, although it still refrained from stopping the flow of oil.

The desperate situation in Britain caused Roosevelt to take a bold step without first securing congressional approval: he expanded American assistance through the destroyers-bases deal of early September 1940. According to its terms, the United States traded fifty overage destroyers for ninety-nine-year leases on eight British bases in the New World, extending from Newfoundland south to British Guiana. To assure Americans that the destroyers would not be used against them, the British publicly promised never to surrender their fleet to Germany. The arrangement, critics exclaimed, violated international law and raised serious questions in the United States about the legality of selling military items to other nations. Though the attorney general in Washington defended the deal as a retaliatory measure against Germany's illegal actions, the president decided to sidestep a lengthy congressional inquiry and the necessity of Senate approval by concluding the arrangement through executive agreement. His method infuriated Congress, but that body eventually confirmed the deal by appropriating funds for provisioning the naval bases. Churchill privately called the deal a "decidedly unneutral act" that was essential to British security, and Roosevelt told Congress that it was "the most important action in the reinforcement of our national defense . . . since the Louisiana Purchase." Both men were correct. In practical terms, the United States ended neutrality with the destroyers-bases deal and became a nonbelligerent actively aiding the British in the war against Germany.

As the presidential election of 1940 loomed near, isolationists became deeply concerned that the Roosevelt administration intended to take the United States into the war. The destroyers-bases deal seemed to confirm their fears, and later in September, the White House put pressure on Congress to approve the Selective Training and Service Act, which established America's first peacetime military draft. To secure its passage the president relied on the public support of Stimson, a Republican, and the Army chief of staff, General George C. Marshall. They faced formidable opposition from folk-hero Charles Lindbergh, who joined the isolationists in fighting intervention through the America First Committee, established the day following the destroyers-bases deal. The Democrats meanwhile broke precedent by nominating Roosevelt for a third term, while the Republicans countered with Indiana's Wendell Willkie, a wealthy businessman and liberal who approved helping the British and agreed with Roosevelt not to use either the destroyers-bases deal or the Selective Service Act as issues in the campaign. Both parties renounced American participation in "any foreign war," although the Democrats added the qualifying phrase, "except in case of attack."

Neither candidate intended to emphasize foreign policy, but as the campaign wore on, those plans changed. At one point Willkie accused his opponent of secretly wanting war, and declared that "if you elect me president I will never send an American boy to fight in any European war." Roosevelt retaliated in Boston with the assurance that "I have said this before, but I shall say it again and again and again: Your boys are not going to be sent into any foreign wars." His statement, however, did not rule out war in the event of attack. "Of course we'll fight if we're attacked," Roosevelt later admitted. "If somebody attacks us, then it isn't a foreign war, is it?" The blunt nature of his remark in Boston would later open him to charges of deception, and at the time it drew a bitter reaction from Willkie. Roosevelt easily won reelection, although with a smaller margin than the landslide of 1936.

Soon afterward Roosevelt embarked on an even more controversial course in foreign affairs when he sought to lend or lease Britain any goods necessary to win the war. In a fireside chat of late December 1940, he again assured Americans nationwide that his pro-Allied policies were designed to keep the United States out of the war. Conceding that shipments of war matériel enhanced the possibility of America's involvement, he quickly added that "our national policy is not directed toward war. Its sole purpose is to keep war away from our country and our people." The United States had to become "the great arsenal of democracy." In his annual message to Congress of January 1941, Roosevelt emphasized the necessity of protecting the Four Freedoms of life—freedom of speech and worship, and freedom from want and fear. The United States had to lend or lease any materials needed by the British. "I am trying to . . . eliminate the silly, foolish old dollar sign," he explained. If a neighbor's house is burning, we surely would allow him to use our garden hose. Once the fire is quenched, "he gives it back to me and thanks me very much for the use of it." Should there be damage to it, he replaces it with another of equivalent value.

The bitterness of the debate surfaced when the president angrily denounced isolationist Senator Burton K. Wheeler's assessment of the lend-lease proposal. The Montana Democrat had declared that "the lend-lease-give program is the New Deal's triple A foreign policy; it will plow under every fourth American boy." Roosevelt sharply rebuked him. At a press conference he asserted that Wheeler's comment was "the most untruthful[,] . . . the most dastardly, unpatriotic thing that has ever been said. Quote me on that. That really is the rottenest thing that has been said in public life in my generation."

Thus the battle lines were drawn for a fight in Congress. The White House engineer for the lend-lease bill was Democratic Representative John McCormack of Massachusetts, who was concerned that his Irish constituency in Boston would oppose a bill with his name on it that was intended to help the British. He finally managed to have the measure designated as Lend-Lease Bill H.R. 1776, which added a patriotic ring and averted his own political knell. Mothers marched in Washington with signs declaring "Kill Bill 1776 Not Our Boys," and Robert Taft, isolationist Republican senator from Ohio, asserted that "lending war equipment is a good deal like lending chewing gum. You don't want it back." The historian Charles A. Beard begged the United States to "preserve one stronghold of order and sanity even against the gates of hell." Yet the isolationists could not deny Britain's desperate plight.

Roosevelt's Lend-Lease measure passed Congress by vote of 260 to 161 in the House and 60 to 31 in the Senate, and on March 11 he signed it into law. "An Act to Promote the Defense of the United States" permitted the United States to "sell, transfer title to, exchange, lease, lend, or otherwise dispose of" any "defense article" or "defense information" to "any country whose defense the President deems vital to the defense of the United States." Congress initially appropriated $7 billion for the program, but eventually approved more than $50 billion in Lend-Lease funds by the time the war was over. Of the total, Britain received $31.6 billion of goods, including nearly a million feet of fire hose in the first package alone. Isolationist Senator Arthur Vandenberg, Republican from Michigan, charged that "we have torn up 150 years of traditional American foreign policy. We have tossed Washington's Farewell Address in the discard." Roosevelt called it a measure for peace. But even while Congress had debated the bill from January through March of 1941, American and British military and naval staff officers were meeting privately in Washington to formulate a joint strategy in the event of America's entry into the war against Germany. The so-called ABC-1 staff agreements provided that if the United States joined Britain in the war, the newly allied forces would first concentrate on the Germans in the Atlantic while fighting a defensive war against Japan in the Pacific. The Lend-Lease Act was monumental in putting a stamp on the end of neutrality. More than that, it was an unofficial U.S. declaration of war on the Axis powers.

Soon after passage of the act, another heated argument erupted as administration supporters called for convoys to protect ships carrying Lend-Lease materials, while opponents in Congress tried to pass a joint resolution against them. Roosevelt recognized that the United States could not escort such vessels without raising questions about the nation's nonbelligerent status. The Lend-Lease Act posed seemingly insurmountable obstacles to convoys. It declared that "nothing in this Act shall be construed to authorize or to permit the authorization of convoying by naval vessels of the United States . . . or . . . the entry of any American vessel into a combat area." Several members of Roosevelt's cabinet—including Stimson, Knox, Morgenthau, and Secretary of the Interior Harold Ickes—wanted the president to authorize American convoys to protect British ships, but Stimson recognized that Roosevelt had created his own dilemma by his earlier assurances against any action conducive to war. Roosevelt therefore hesitated to use American convoys because he feared public disfavor. But he found an opening in the Declaration of Panama of 1939, for it had proclaimed a wide security zone in the Atlantic that the American states had to protect. In April the president authorized a "neutrality patrol" that could go beyond that zone in the Atlantic to provide information helpful to the security of the United States and to notify the British of the presence of enemy ships or planes. Though the patrols did not safeguard all Lend-Lease shipments, their use provided some assurance and eased the outcry over convoys.

By May 1941 the United States had become an active participant in the Atlantic theater of the European war. Its navy cooperated with Britain in locating German submarines and other vessels, and in April dropped its first depth charges on a U-boat. That same month the United States secured approval from Denmark's government-in-exile to occupy Greenland. Roosevelt also removed the Red Sea from the "combat zone," enabling American ships to transport goods to the British fighting in North Africa. In the meantime German maritime warfare became more effective as U-boats began operating in groups called wolf packs. On May 21, 1941, the Germans sank their first American vessel, the freighter *Robin Moor*. Though no loss of life resulted, the Germans refused Roosevelt's call for reparations. In retaliation, the United States froze German and Italian assets and closed their consulates, moves which drew similar responses against Americans in those countries.

GROWING GLOBAL CHARACTER OF THE WAR

Germany's military successes in the Balkans and North Africa had meanwhile turned attention from America's steadily deteriorating relations with Japan. In August 1940 Prime Minister Konoye had reflected the growing influence of the hardliners in his new cabinet when he expanded the objectives of the New Order into those of the Greater East Asia Co-Prosperity Sphere. The new foreign minister was Yosuke Matsuoka, who had led the walkout from the League of Nations in 1933 and whom Hull considered "as crooked as a basket of fishhooks." The minister of war was General Hideki Tojo who, like Matsuoka, advocated military expansion. As with the New Order, Greater East Asia would have Japan, Manchuria, and China at its center, but Matsuoka explained that the new program would be wider in scope. It would encompass German islands mandated to Japan in 1920 (the Carolines, Marianas, and Marshalls), French possessions in the Pacific and in Indochina, British Malaya and Borneo, the Dutch East Indies, Burma, Thailand (or Siam), India, New Zealand, and Australia. The foreign minister did not mention the Philippines, but he inserted an "etc." at the end of the list and remarked that "this sphere could be automatically broadened in the course of time." Japan began its push toward isolating China when in September it pressed

Vichy France for concessions in northern Indochina. When the United States protested, Matsuoka remarked that "the Western Powers taught Japan the game of poker but after acquiring most of the chips they pronounced the game immoral and took up contract bridge."

Less than a week after Japan's gains in Indochina, delegates from Germany, Italy, and Japan gathered in Berlin and signed the Tripartite Pact of September 27, 1940, which in large part was aimed at the United States. The three signatories guaranteed each other's spheres of influence in Europe and Asia and promised to "assist one another with all political, economic and military means when one of the three contracting Parties is attacked by a power at present not involved in the European War or in the Sino-Japanese Conflict." Since another article in the pact exempted the Soviet Union from the warning, the United States remained the only power "not involved" in either conflict.

The three-power agreement instilled new hope in Japan's expansionist aims. Whereas Germany sought to prevent America's entry into the European war, Japan counted upon the Rome-Berlin-Tokyo Axis to keep the United States out of the Pacific. In the meantime the Japanese could encourage good relations with the Soviet Union and close the ring around China. Militarists in Tokyo were elated because the Tripartite Pact made the Nazi-Soviet Nonaggression Pact a dead letter. The new power alignment would force Chiang into an agreement, enabling Japan to reassign its troops elsewhere. Japan would be free to take British, French, and Dutch possessions in East Asia without interference from the United States.

The Tripartite Pact showed that it was impossible to separate events in the Far East from those in Europe. Roosevelt and Hull had been correct in their arguments against the embargo on scrap iron. The embargo encouraged Japan to ally with Germany and Italy, and the Axis now posed a threat to American interests in the Pacific. The new alliance had the potential of cutting off Britain's supplies from East Asia and forcing the ill-prepared United States into the war. The Roosevelt administration was beginning to realize that support for Britain in the Atlantic necessitated protection of British and American interests in Asia. The Department of State warned Americans to leave the Far East, and in November the White House approved a loan to China. America's policies bought time by temporarily slowing Japan's advances and helping to keep China in the war.

American leaders increasingly understood how the war in Europe had automatic repercussions in Asia and the Pacific. Roosevelt wrote Grew in Tokyo in January 1941 that "we must recognize that the hostilities in Europe, in Africa, and in Asia are all parts of a single world conflict. We must, consequently, recognize that our interests are menaced both in Europe and in the Far East. . . . Our strategy of self-defense," he asserted, "must be a global strategy which takes account of every front and takes advantage of every opportunity to contribute to our total security." The

British had to have the resources of the Far East to keep their war effort alive in the Middle East, the Mediterranean, and Europe. The United States had to keep communication and supply lines open throughout the world.

America's broadly scoped policy carried dangerous implications for its relations with Japan. Less than a week after receiving Roosevelt's message, Grew noted in his diary that "there is a lot of talk around town to the effect that the Japanese, in case of a break with the United States, are planning to go all out in a surprise mass attack at Pearl Harbor." Though in his report he dismissed this as one of many rumors then circulating in Tokyo, Grew had earlier begun to retreat from his hopes for accommodation with the Japanese. The previous September of 1940, he had cabled Washington the famous Green Light message. Japan, he declared, was "one of the predatory powers; she has submerged all moral and ethical sense and has become unashamedly and frankly opportunist, seeking at every turn to profit by the weakness of others. Her policy of southward expansion definitely threatens American interests in the Pacific." America could have no distinct policy for either Europe or Asia, the Roosevelt administration had come to realize; every action in one region of the world profoundly affected the situation in the other.

Fear of an oil embargo caused the government in Tokyo to try to negotiate its differences with America. Retired Admiral Kichisaburo Nomura, known friend of the Western powers and of Roosevelt, arrived in Washington in February as ambassador. Though he met with Hull forty times in the next nine months, they could not resolve the impasse between the New Order and the Open Door. Other problems became apparent. Communication difficulties developed in the discussions because Nomura could not understand English very well and attempted to work without a translator, and also because of the unauthorized intervention of a group of private American citizens called the John Doe Associates. Their leaders, two Catholic missionaries, had earlier returned from Japan with a liberal peace offer, allegedly from Konoye, which they were to present to Roosevelt. It pledged Japan's withdrawal from China and the Tripartite Pact in exchange for restored trading rights with the United States. But the initial hopes in Washington quickly disappeared. After the missionaries talked with a high Japanese official sent from the War Ministry in Tokyo, they returned to Hull on April 9 with a Draft Understanding that reflected the hardline views of Matsuoka. There was no longer any assurance of Japan's withdrawal from either China or the Tripartite Pact, although Japan did agree to meet its obligations under the pact only if the United States attacked Germany. Furthermore, Japan would ease its pressure on Southeast Asia only if Washington lifted commercial restrictions and helped Japan secure raw materials in the South Pacific. Thus the Japanese expected the United States to cut off aid to China and persuade Chiang Kai-shek to accept their conditions for peace. The long-standing internal conflict between moderates and hardliners in Japan had now emerged as two diametrically opposed policy statements, which further damaged relations with the United States.

Hull was unhappy with Japan's proposals, but decided against an outright rejection in hopes of reaching a better settlement. The secretary agreed to use the terms as a *modus vivendi* or temporary basis for settlement, but told Nomura that in return the Japanese had to accept four principles of conduct in foreign affairs: respect for the sovereignty of all nations, noninterference in their domestic concerns, recognition of equal trade opportunity, and acceptance of the status quo in the Pacific. The two sets of demands were mutually exclusive. Nomura, however, mistakenly thought that Hull had accepted the Draft Understanding, and failed to mention the four principles when he passed the information to his government. Matsuoka and others in Tokyo therefore regarded Hull's reply as an American proposal and worked out a counterplan with conditions more favorable to Japan. Hull was incredulous when he read this in May. Japanese leaders finally came to understand that Hull's four principles were vital, but now interpreted them as a change in position since talking with Nomura. Each side was disenchanted with the apparent lack of good faith shown by the other. In reality, neither Washington nor Tokyo had changed its stand. The Doe group's involvement had combined with Nomura's inept diplomacy to leave mutual and erroneous impressions of duplicity.

Failure of the Hull-Nomura talks led Japan to prepare for its thrust southward by signing a nonaggression pact with the Soviet Union in April. Foreign Ministers Matsuoka and Molotov negotiated a five-year agreement in Moscow guaranteeing neutrality if either party went to war. Mutual self-interests, of course, had led to such an arrangement between these longtime bitter enemies. Stalin expected a German assault and sought the agreement to free him from having to protect his country's eastern frontier from the Japanese. Tokyo had secured its northern holdings from Soviet attack and now could move south.

On June 22, 1941, Hitler's armies shocked the world by invading the Soviet Union and radically changing the complexion of the war. Democratic Senator Harry S. Truman of Missouri perhaps expressed the initial reaction of more than a few Americans when *The New York Times* quoted him as saying: "If we see that Germany is winning the war we ought to help Russia and if Russia is winning we ought to help Germany, and . . . let them kill as many as possible." But Churchill recognized the opportunity afforded by the invasion and declared that "if Hitler invaded Hell I would make at least a favorable reference to the Devil in the House of Commons." The British soon sent aid to the Soviet Union by sea around the northern tip of Norway and into Murmansk, and they made it clear that American assistance was required in protecting Lend-Lease imports if the program was to continue. In July 4,000 U.S. marines occupied Iceland, enabling the American navy to escort American, Icelandic, and other vessels moving between the United States and Iceland. Thus the

United States joined Canada in protecting Lend-Lease carriers en route to Iceland, where British convoys accompanied them to the British Isles.

Though the British immediately sent aid to the Soviet Union, the Roosevelt administration was hesitant about extending Lend-Lease assistance because of fear that the Soviets could not withstand the German assault. Two days following the German invasion the president assured reporters that the United States would "give all aid we possibly can to Russia." But he was evasive on whether that included Lend-Lease. That same day the United States released $40 million in recently frozen Soviet assets, and a day later permitted American ships to carry goods to Russia's Pacific port of Vladivostok. Finally, Roosevelt ignored the objections of military advisers and decided to take a chance on the Soviets' ability to survive. After declaring that he had no intention of invoking the Neutrality Act in the Russo-German conflict, he extended Lend-Lease to the Soviet Union. Most Americans regarded his decision as another step toward securing their own country without having to go to war.

Germany's invasion of the Soviet Union also had a major impact on Far Eastern affairs, for Japan seized the advantage and began its drive south. The Japanese had failed to persuade the government of the Netherlands, then in exile in London, to turn over the East Indies. An Imperial Conference in Tokyo led to the decision to expand into southern Indochina and Thailand, as steps toward occupying British Singapore and the Netherlands East Indies. The record of the July meeting indicated the resolve of those present: "[W]e will not be deterred by the possibility of being involved in a war with England and America." Japan then turned back to Vichy France to demand bases in southern Indochina. Whereas the earlier agreement granted Japan access to Saigon's airfields and harbor and placed Singapore within bombing range, the new arrangement in July established a joint protectorate over all of Indochina, thereby endangering American interests in the Philippines. Roosevelt believed that until the recent events in the Soviet Union, the Japanese were unsure of their policy. In July he wrote in a letter that the Japanese were having "a real drag-down and knockout fight among themselves" over whether to "attack Russia, attack the South Seas . . . or . . . sit on the fence and be more friendly with us. No one knows what the decision will be but . . . it is terribly important for the control of the Atlantic for us to help to keep peace in the Pacific. I simply have not got enough Navy to go around."

On July 25 Roosevelt reacted to Japan's thrust into southern Indochina with an executive order freezing Japanese assets in the United States. Britain and the Netherlands did the same, and Japan faced an embargo on all war matériel—including oil. These developments narrowed Japan's options: either cancel plans for Greater East Asia, or seize the oil of the Dutch East Indies as a step toward achieving the program. The basic facts were that 80 percent of Japan's oil came from American producers, and that its reserve would last no longer than eighteen months. Roosevelt knew the freeze would force Japan's hand. He nationalized

American forces in the Philippines and called former Army Chief of Staff Douglas MacArthur out of retirement, promoting him to commanding general of the army in the Far East. *The New York Times* called the freeze "the most drastic blow short of actual war." Grew wrote in his diary: "The obvious conclusion is eventual war."

Japan's decision to move south did not surprise the United States, for in August 1940 the Office of Naval Intelligence had cracked the highest Japanese secret diplomatic code—the Purple Cipher—and soon had a collection of information that was code-named Magic. Churchill urged Roosevelt to warn Tokyo that attacks on British or Dutch holdings in the Far East could mean war, and even though the State Department convinced the president to tone down his message, his meaning was clear. On August 17 Roosevelt warned Nomura that if Japan took "any further steps in pursuance of a policy or program of military domination by force or threat of force on neighboring countries," the United States would "take immediately any and all steps which it may deem necessary toward safeguarding the legitimate rights and interest of the United States and American nationals and toward insuring the safety and security of the United States."

Negotiations in Washington during the summer of 1941 only hardened each side's demands. Hull refused to retreat from America's pledges to China, and Nomura, unaware of the military's preparations in Tokyo, repeatedly sought recognition of his nation's gains in China. The Japanese ambassador impressed Americans with his sincerity and integrity, and Konoye in Tokyo had a reputation for moderation. But the militarists under General Tojo were gaining control.

THE ATLANTIC CHARTER

From August 9–12, 1941, Roosevelt and Churchill secretly met to discuss the coordination of policy in case the United States entered the war. On a British battleship in Placentia Bay off Newfoundland, they formulated a joint statement that would ultimately guide the nations' policies through the end of the war. Roosevelt, with the help of a cane and his son Elliott, joined the British prime minister after walking the length of the vessel before 1,500 men standing at attention. Sunday church services on August 10 highlighted the singing of "Onward Christian Soldiers," which brought tears to the president's eyes and led him to remark to his son that "if nothing else had happened, that would have cemented us. 'Onward Christian Soldiers.' We *are*, and we *will*, go on, with God's help." Churchill saw deep meaning in the day's events. In his memoirs of the war, he noted

> . . . the symbolism of the Union Jack and the Stars and Stripes draped side by side on the pulpit; . . . the highest naval, military, and air officers of Britain and the United States grouped in one body behind the President and me;

the close-packed ranks of British and American sailors, completely intermingled, sharing the same books and joining fervently together in the prayers and hymns familiar to both. . . . Every word seemed to stir the heart. It was a great hour to live.

In a press release after the conference, Britain and the United States stated their common objectives in what became known as the Atlantic Charter. These included a nonaggression pledge, formation of a collective

Franklin D. Roosevelt and Winston Churchill

Aboard H.M.S. Prince of Wales *off Newfoundland in August 1941 as they formulate the Atlantic Charter. Left to right: Admiral Ernest J. King, General George C. Marshall, General Sir John Dill, Admiral Harold A. Stark, and Admiral Sir Dudley Pound.* (National Archives)

security system, self-determination of peoples, no territorial aggrandizement, freedom of the seas, and a reduction in commercial restrictions. The affirmation of such principles helped to alleviate America's fears that Britain and the Soviet Union might reject democracy and partition postwar Europe between them. The Americans' call for commercial freedom had met expected resistance from the British, who wanted to maintain their system of imperial preferences. The public declaration, however, allowed the British to hold onto what they had. It called for equal commercial access to the world's markets and raw materials, but promised "due respect for their existing obligations." Roosevelt would make no commitment to Churchill's proposal for a new League of Nations, but agreed to "the establishment of a wider and permanent system of general security." This broad statement would perhaps avert a confrontation with America's isolationists.

The Atlantic Charter was a virtual Anglo-American alliance against the Axis. The Soviet Union was not present, but two weeks before the meeting at Placentia, Roosevelt's confidant, Harry Hopkins, had traveled to Moscow and returned with an optimistic report that the Soviets would not collapse before the Germans. Churchill and Roosevelt sent a communiqué to Stalin, praising his "splendid defense" against Hitler and guaranteeing their assistance. When Churchill returned to England, he assured the House of Commons that the Atlantic Charter posed no threat to his country's colonial possessions; it applied only to "nations of Europe now under the Nazi yoke." Despite hopes of American involvement in the conflict, a British observer noted that "there isn't the slightest chance of the U.S. entering the war until compelled to do so by a direct attack on its own territory." Yet the prime minister was optimistic. He wrote afterward that "the fact alone of the United States, still technically neutral, joining with a belligerent Power in making such a declaration was astonishing. The inclusion in it of a reference to 'the final destruction of the Nazi tyranny' . . . amounted to a challenge which in ordinary times would have implied warlike action." In September those present at an Inter-Allied Meeting in London announced formal approval of the Atlantic Charter, and the Soviets agreed to a limited acceptance of its principles.

An incident involving the American destroyer *Greer* soon caused events in the Atlantic to take on the character of an undeclared war between the United States and Germany. On September 4, a German submarine fired on the *Greer* off Iceland and drew a heated reaction from Roosevelt. Before gathering the full story, he took advantage of the incident to justify stretching the naval patrol system to Iceland. The Germans, he declared over nationwide radio, were guilty of "piracy." If the "rattlesnakes of the Atlantic" entered American waters, they did so at their own risk. The *Greer* "was carrying American mail to Iceland. . . . She was then and there attacked by a submarine. . . . I tell you the blunt fact that the German submarine fired first upon this American destroyer without warning, and with deliberate design to sink her." This incident was "one determined step toward creating a permanent world system based on force, terror, and murder." The navy now had orders to "shoot-on-sight," a decision resulting from "months and months of constant thought and anxiety and prayer." From now on, the United States would protect any ship in "our defensive waters."

But Roosevelt had not revealed all of the truth. A British patrol plane had notified the *Greer* that a German submarine lay ten miles ahead in its path, and the destroyer pursued it for over three hours while the British plane dropped depth charges. Finally, the submarine commander turned in desperation and fired a torpedo at the *Greer,* missing it by 300 feet. The *Greer* dropped depth charges and drew another torpedo that missed again. After more pursuit the *Greer* quit the chase and resumed its voyage to Iceland.

Roosevelt was correct in believing that Hitler sought to avert a confrontation with the United States until after the collapse of Britain and the Soviet Union. Whereas isolationists claimed the president was purposely stirring trouble with his destroyers-bases deal, Lend-Lease, sea patrols, public condemnations of the Nazis, and shoot-on-sight orders, Hitler ordered his naval commanders to avoid combat with the United States unless the U-boats were in danger. In early October the *Führer* declared that "when I see the enemy leveling his rifle at me, I am not going to wait till he presses the trigger. I would rather be the first to press the trigger." Hitler considered Americans too weak to go to war. The United States was a "Jewish rubbish heap," hopelessly divided by economic depression and racial impurities. America's haven for immigrants and oppressed peoples had become "half Judaized, half negrified." He considered the United States no threat to Germany.

The undeclared naval war continued in the Atlantic. In mid-October 1941 a German submarine torpedoed the American destroyer *Kearney* southwest of Iceland, killing eleven men. Ten days later Roosevelt declared that "we have wished to avoid shooting. But the shooting has started. And history has recorded who fired the first shot." The *Kearney* "is not just a Navy ship. She belongs to every man, woman, and child in this Nation. Hitler's torpedo was directed at every American, whether he lives on our sea coasts or in the innermost part of the country." Roosevelt did not mention that the *Kearney,* like the *Greer,* had been in pursuit of German submarines at the time of attack. Repeal of the Neutrality Act of 1939, he insisted, was imperative to permit the arming of merchant ships and to allow their entry into the combat zones. The day following the attack the House voted by a wide margin to arm merchant ships, throwing the matter before the Senate. By the end of the month the Germans had sunk an American tanker, and during the night of October 31 they sent down the first naval vessel, the destroyer *Reuben James,* with the loss of more than a hundred men. Despite these events, the America First Committee claimed that the president's request for repeal of the Neutrality Act was tantamount to "asking Congress to issue an engraved drowning license to American seamen."

By November 1941 war with Germany was a matter of time. The American navy was shooting on sight, dropping depth charges on U-boats, and dodging torpedoes in the North Atlantic. That same month Congress authorized the first Lend-Lease shipments to the Soviet Union, which ultimately received $11 billion in assistance under the program. Less than two weeks later Congress narrowly approved a revised Neutrality Act, which permitted American merchant vessels to arm themselves and to enter the combat zones when carrying war matériel to Britain. With attention almost wholly on Europe and the Atlantic, war came suddenly for the United States—thousands of miles away at Pearl Harbor, Hawaii.

PEARL HARBOR

Seen in retrospect, the United States's decision in July 1941 to freeze Japanese assets had set the events in motion that led to war with Japan. On September 6 an Imperial Conference in Tokyo resulted in the decision that if negotiations in Washington did not take a favorable turn by early October, Japan would declare war on the United States, Britain, and the Netherlands. Emperor Hirohito and several in the army and navy were not enthusiastic about the decision, but they followed the Supreme Command of both services. Prime Minister Konoye had six weeks to secure American concessions regarding China.

That autumn, Konoye proposed a personal meeting with Roosevelt in the Pacific to resolve their nations' problems. The idea attracted Grew's support, for he thought that the war in China, the American embargo, and deepening suspicions of Hitler had convinced the Japanese of the foolhardiness of going to war with America. Roosevelt favored the suggestion until he talked with Hull. The secretary of state did not believe that Konoye spoke for militarists, and warned that since the Japanese had called the meeting, a failure to reach a settlement would place the onus on the United States. He insisted that Japan give a "clear-cut manifestation," *before* the conference, of its intention to withdraw from China and Indochina. Grew learned that Konoye was interested in accepting Hull's four principles of international conduct, but that he could not make specific assurances. The ambassador believed that Konoye was afraid that someone in the Foreign Office would reveal the concessions to Matsuoka and other hardliners and thus provoke an internal crisis. Roosevelt declined to meet with Konoye without a preliminary agreement. There is little reason to believe that such a meeting could have been successful, for in truth no honorable compromise was possible between the Open Door and the Greater East Asia Co-Prosperity Sphere. Yet such a meeting might have led to a temporary understanding, which would have given the United States more time to bolster its Pacific holdings. When Konoye's gamble failed, hardliners in Tokyo forced his resignation on October 16, and two days later their spokesman, General Tojo, became premier.

On November 5 another Imperial Conference led to the decision to complete preparations for war by early December, but to continue the negotiations by sending another emissary, Saburo Kurusu, to join Ambassador Nomura in Washington. Magic intercepts revealed that the men had two proposals—Plan A and Plan B—the second containing more concessions than the first, but not to be presented unless Plan A was rejected. The decoders also learned that the deadline for the talks was November 29. "After that," the message declared, "things are automatically going to happen."

No surprises were contained in either plan presented by the Japanese envoys. On November 7 Hull immediately rejected Plan A because it again sought America's acquiescence to Japan's domination of Asia. Ten days later Kurusu tried to encourage a settlement when, in reference to the Tripartite Pact, he assured the president that Japan "had no intention of becoming a tool of Germany nor did she mean to wait until the United States became deeply involved in the battle of the Atlantic and then stab her in the back." Nomura and Kurusu presented their final offer on November 20. Plan B called for both governments to refrain from sending troops into Southeast Asia or the South Pacific, except for Indochina; to help one another acquire goods from the Dutch East Indies; and to reestablish trade relations as they were before Roosevelt froze Japanese assets—including Japan's receiving the "required quantity of oil." Plan B also stipulated that if America stayed out of China, Japan would evacuate Indochina when there was either peace in China or an "equitable peace" in the Pacific. Hull rejected Plan B as "virtually a surrender."

Late in November Hull tried to gain time for the American army and navy by advocating a truce of three months accompanied by a *modus vivendi*. According to his proposal, the United States would grant oil concessions if Tokyo disavowed force, evacuated southern Indochina, and reduced its forces in northern Indochina. Hull sent the paper to the diplomatic representatives in Washington of Britain, China, Australia, and the Netherlands. The proposal drew no support. Chiang Kai-shek complained of the lack of guarantees for China, whereas the others warned that China might pull out of the war, releasing Japanese forces for use elsewhere and taking away the major point for launching an invasion of Japan if war developed. The White House dropped Hull's *modus vivendi* without forwarding it to Japan.

On November 26 Hull presented to Japan a ten-point program that comprised America's final proposal. It provided for Japan to withdraw from China and Indochina, virtually disavow the Tripartite Pact, recognize the Chinese Nationalist government, and join a multilateral nonaggression pact in East Asia. In return, Washington would restore trade, remove the freeze on Japanese assets, assist Tokyo in stabilizing its currency, and try to end extraterritoriality in China. Hull's proposal was not an ultimatum, but it was an admission to the likelihood of war. Japan could not pull out of China.

Hull realized that the outcome of his counteroffer to Japan would be rejection and probably war. The following day he told Stimson: "I have washed my hands of it, and it is now in the hands of you and Knox, the army and navy." Yet the army and navy were not ready for a Pacific war. Stimson warned that among other preparations the United States needed at least three months to assemble enough B-17 bombers (Flying Fortresses) to safeguard the Philippines. Hull meanwhile warned the British ambassador to expect a Japanese move "suddenly and with every element of surprise."

Magic intercepts of November 27 established that Japan had decided on war, although they did not reveal where. One Far Eastern specialist in the State Department remained unconvinced. Stanley Hornbeck, who probably had not seen the decoded messages, believed the Japanese were not prepared to go to war with the United States before mid-December. No one goes to war "out of desperation," he assured anxious colleagues in Washington. Japanese forces nonetheless seemed to be gathering in Indochina for an attack on Singapore, Thailand, Borneo, the Dutch East Indies, or perhaps the Philippines. Roosevelt's major concern was that a Japanese attack in Southeast Asia might avoid hitting American possessions and make it difficult to secure a congressional decision for war.

Confusion took over at this crucial juncture. On November 28 General George C. Marshall sent an alert to Pearl Harbor. But in Hawaii Lieutenant General Walter Short had recently worked out a new warning system that was different from that used by both the Pentagon in Washington and the navy in the islands under Admiral Husband Kimmel. Whereas stage 1 had previously signaled full alert for attack and 3 for sabotage, he reversed the numbers. Consequently, when Marshall's stage 1 warning arrived, the army mistakenly prepared for sabotage.

Roosevelt tried several last-second measures to prevent war. He prepared a congressional message showing that a Japanese assault in Southeast Asia would endanger American interests and warrant retaliation. He considered an appeal to Emperor Hirohito, which proposed assurances that no country would take Indochina if Japan agreed to withdraw. A week of debate passed before the message went to Tokyo on the evening of December 6. For the first time the United States had made a proposal to Japan that did not mention China. It came too late.

Japan's decision to attack Pearl Harbor was the product of desperation and illusion. General Tojo and his supporters regarded the United States as the aggressor because the freeze of July 1941 had left Japan only two choices—war, or retreat from China. The latter was unthinkable, for no government could survive if it gave up the territorial gains of the last decade. Japan's military machine consumed 12,000 tons of oil a day, making the American embargo an act of provocation and dictating the push south for the oil of the Dutch East Indies. Japan realized that the United States had ten times the industrial might and twice the population. Yet a string of quick conquests in the Pacific might force a favorable settlement in China and Southeast Asia.

The minister who planned the attack on Pearl Harbor was Admiral Isoroku Yamamoto, who once remarked that he enlisted in the navy "so I could return Admiral Perry's visit." Now, as commander-in-chief of the Combined Fleet, he told General Tojo that he could assure six months of resistance but no guarantees afterward. America's military and industrial capabilities, he warned, were too extensive for Japan to wage a prolonged war. It had to disable America's Pacific Fleet at Pearl Harbor to facilitate the southward thrust. Such an attack would furnish time for the Japanese to seize much of the Far East before the United States could recover. By then, Tokyo's leaders believed, America would be in the European war and could not fight on two fronts at the same time. The Washington government would have to negotiate a treaty recognizing Greater East Asia. On December 1, 1941, the cabinet met with the emperor and approved Tojo's call for war on the United States, Britain, and the Netherlands.

During the November negotiations in Washington, a large Japanese carrier task force of thirty-three vessels, under command of Vice-Admiral Chuichi Nagumo, gathered in the Kurile Islands awaiting orders from Tokyo. High above the flagship *Akagi* waved the same flag that had flown over one of the battleships that had surprised the Russians in Tsushima Straits in 1905. To conceal the fleet's location in the Kuriles, Japan ordered its radio operators in port to send out false messages, and arranged to have large groups of sailors sent to Tokyo during their leaves. In the early morning of November 25, six carriers with bombers and fighter escorts, two battleships, and accompanying cruisers, destroyers, tankers, and submarines broke eastward into the icy North Pacific for a radio-silent, 3,000-mile journey toward Hawaii, subject to recall in the event of a breakthrough in the negotiations in Washington. To avoid leaving a trail, Nagumo forbade the dumping of garbage and oil drums into the ocean. He decreed a total blackout at night and used the highest quality fuel to reduce smoke. On December 2 the final orders came to "climb Mount Niitaka." The next day captains announced to crews that the force was to attack Pearl Harbor at dawn on December 8 Tokyo time (December 7 in Hawaii).

Americans had lost radio contact with the Japanese fleet in the North Pacific in mid-November. Their patrols also were no help. They operated only 500 miles below the Aleutians and 500 miles above Hawaii, leaving a large void between. In fact, on December 7 aircraft from the U.S. Navy were not on patrol north of the islands. Nagumo's fleet moved due east to a spot 800 miles above Hawaii, refueled, and veered southward. At 6:00 A.M., just before daylight, 353 planes began taking off for the final 230 miles of their destination.

In Pearl Harbor on Sunday morning, December 7, 1941, two young

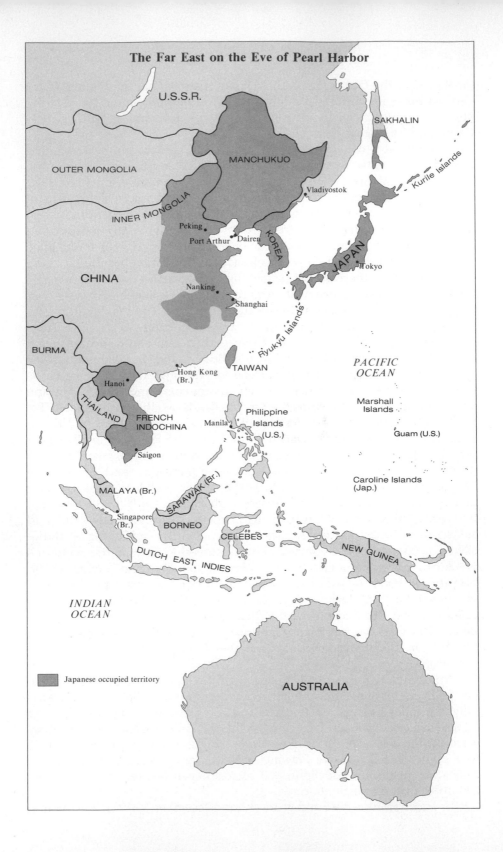

The Far East on the Eve of Pearl Harbor

U.S.S.R.

SAKHALIN

OUTER MONGOLIA

MANCHUKUO

Kurile Islands

INNER MONGOLIA

Vladivostok

Peking

Port Arthur Dairen

KOREA

JAPAN

Tokyo

CHINA

Nanking

Shanghai

Ryukyu Islands

BURMA

Hong Kong
(Br.)

TAIWAN

PACIFIC
OCEAN

Hanoi

THAILAND

FRENCH
INDOCHINA

Manila

Philippine
Islands
(U.S.)

Marshall
Islands

Guam (U.S.)

Saigon

Caroline Islands
(Jap.)

MALAYA (Br.)

SARAWAK (Br.)

Singapore
(Br.)

BORNEO

CELEBES

NEW GUINEA

DUTCH EAST INDIES

INDIAN
OCEAN

Japanese occupied territory

AUSTRALIA

radar operators on duty noted "something completely out of the ordinary" on the screen. An unusually large number of blips suggested that many planes were about 137 miles north of Oahu and rapidly approaching the islands. No warning went out. Their superiors at first did not believe the blips were planes, and later dismissed them as American B-17s due to arrive that morning. Suddenly the skies were filled with planes bearing the emblem of the Rising Sun. At 7:55 A.M., Hawaiian time, the pursuit officer at Oahu saw the first bombs fall as he went outside to watch what he presumed to be the "Navy bombers in bombing practice over Pearl Harbor." Shortly afterward Washington received the message: "AIR RAID PEARL HARBOR. THIS IS NO DRILL."

Japan's attack on Pearl Harbor was devastating. In two hours its forces sank or disabled eight American battleships, damaged several cruisers and destroyers, and wrecked nearly all 347 American planes as they sat wing-tip to wing-tip on the runways for better surveillance because of the fear of sabotage. The Japanese inflicted 3,435 casualties, including more than 2,400 dead. American commanders had believed that aerial torpedoes could not be effective in the shallow forty-five-foot-deep channels of Pearl Harbor. But a few days before the attack, the Japanese had discovered that the attachment of wooden stabilizers to the torpedoes' fins kept them from touching the bottom and allowed them to hit their targets. There were saving factors on the American side. Admiral William F. Halsey and his carrier striking force were in the Pacific on special assignment at the time of attack. The map used by the Japanese pilots was outdated, which explains their failure to hit the fuel tanks and installations; otherwise, the United States might have had to withdraw the remainder of the fleet to the west coast of America. Japan lost twenty-nine planes, fifty-five men, and six submarines.

Though Roosevelt's critics would later read conspiracy into the attack at Pearl Harbor, they have not found proof for the charge. The Japanese success was more likely attributable to audacity and illogic, rather than to a claimed presidential design to take the United States into the war through the "back door." According to this argument, Roosevelt was unable to convince Americans that Hitler was a threat to their interests (the "front door" to war), and therefore enticed a Japanese attack at Pearl Harbor by stationing the Pacific Fleet in those waters, not imagining the possibility of such destruction. Yet the critics, after years of searching the historical records, have failed to uncover the evidence, if indeed it ever existed. It seems safe to conclude that the American tragedy of December 7, 1941, resulted from a faulty intelligence network, erroneous assump-

---

MAP 25

The Japanese were able to take advantage of the war in Europe to expand their interests in Asia.

Bombing of Pearl Harbor

"Day of Infamy," December 7, 1941. (National Archives)

tions about Japan's intentions and capacities, and numerous other errors in judgment and procedure.

Meanwhile in Washington, Nomura and Kurusu were unaware of their government's decision to attack Pearl Harbor, and prepared to follow Tojo's directive to deliver his official rejection of Hull's ten-point proposal at precisely 1:00 P.M., twenty minutes before the scheduled time of attack. The evening before, Magic had intercepted the first thirteen parts of the Japanese message. After denouncing America's policy in the Far East, the message claimed that Hull's proposal "ignores Japan's sacrifices in the four years in China, menaces the Empire's existence itself, and disparages its honor and prestige." The president read the note before a pacing Harry Hopkins and declared that "this means war." Shortly after breakfast on December 7, the fourteenth and final section of the message was in Roosevelt's hands. Its last paragraph was chilling: "The Japanese Government regrets to have to notify hereby the American government that in view of the attitude of the American government it cannot but consider that it is impossible to reach an agreement through further negotiations." Word immediately went to Marshall at the Pentagon, who sent an alert to both the Philippines and Hawaii—not by his scrambler telephone, which he regarded as insecure, but by the army's message center to avoid suggesting to Japan that the United States had broken the Purple Cipher. When transmitting problems developed, the signal officer, unaware of the importance of the message, sent it by Western Union, which caused a lengthy delay.

Typing difficulties in the Japanese Embassy in Washington held off delivery of the note by Nomura and Kurusu until 2:20 P.M., Washington time—*after* the first bombs had hit Pearl Harbor. Hull had learned of the attack a half hour earlier. When the envoys arrived in his office he did not offer them a seat, and they sensed the tension while settling uncomfortably in the soft leather chairs. Hull went through the motions of reading the note that Magic had provided some four hours before, and then glared coldly at Nomura. "I must say in all my fifty years of public service I have never seen a document that was more crowded with infamous falsehoods and distortions—on a scale so huge that I never imagined until today that any government on this planet was capable of uttering them." He showed the stunned envoys to the door.

The aftermath was anticlimactic. About two hours following the attack on Pearl Harbor, the Japanese government declared war on the United States. A little after 3:00 P.M., Hawaiian time, over seven hours after the first wave of bombers, Marshall's warning message reached the desk of General Short, who sent a copy to Admiral Kimmel. The message informed the American commanders at Pearl Harbor that the Japanese were delivering an ultimatum to Washington at 1:00 P.M. (8:00 A.M. in Hawaii). "Just what significance the hour set may have we do not know, but be on the alert accordingly." Kimmel threw the paper into the waste basket. Washington learned later that afternoon that Japan had gone on to attack the Philippines, Thailand, Malaya, and other places in the Pacific.

Roosevelt appeared before Congress at 12:29 P.M. the day following the Pearl Harbor attack. Democrats and Republicans applauded before he began speaking from his notes in the black notebook before him. Among the dignitaries in the huge chamber was Mrs. Woodrow Wilson, who had attended a similar congressional session twenty-five years before. The president began: "Yesterday, December 7, 1941—a date which will live in infamy—the United States of America was suddenly and deliberately attacked by naval and air forces of the Empire of Japan." He now sought recognition of the "state of war" which Japan had "thrust upon the United States." In six minutes he had finished. Before the attack, isolationists and pacifists in the country resisted the possibility of war; anger over Pearl Harbor quieted them as no other single event could have done. In less than an hour on December 8, the Senate voted unanimously for war, and the House followed with only one dissent. America's decision for war came after that of the British a few hours earlier.

Three days later, on December 11, Germany and Italy declared war on the United States, resolving the dilemma of whether to declare war on Japan's Axis partners. Both houses of Congress reacted that same day by unanimously voting for war with Germany and Italy. Hitler's decision freed Roosevelt from enormous public pressure to concentrate solely on Japan, and greatly relieved Churchill, who wanted full-scale assistance against the Nazis. In line with the ABC-1 staff agreements of early 1941, the Roosevelt administration prepared to focus first on the Axis in Europe.

Selected readings

Ambrose, Stephen E., *Rise to Globalism: American Foreign Policy since 1938*. 4th ed. 1985.

Bailey, Thomas A., and Paul B. Ryan, *Hitler vs. Roosevelt: The Undeclared Naval War*. 1979.

Beard, Charles A., *President Roosevelt and the Coming of the War*. 1948.

Butow, Robert J. C., *Tojo and the Coming of the War*. 1961.

Churchill, Winston S., *The Second World War*. 6 vols. 1948–1953.

Clifford, J. Garry, and Samuel R. Spencer, Jr., *The First Peacetime Draft*. 1986.

Cole, Wayne S., *America First: The Battle against Intervention, 1940–1941*. 1953.

———, *Roosevelt and the Isolationists, 1932–1945*. 1983.

Dallek, Robert, *Franklin D. Roosevelt and American Foreign Policy, 1932–1945*. 1979.

Divine, Robert A., *The Illusion of Neutrality*. 1962.

———, *The Reluctant Belligerent: American Entry into World War II*. Rev. ed. 1979.

Farago, Ladislas, *The Broken Seal: The Story of "Operation Magic" and the Pearl Harbor Disaster*. 1967.

Feis, Herbert, *The Road to Pearl Harbor*. 1950.

Friedländer, Saul, *Prelude to Downfall: Hitler and the United States, 1939–1941*. 1967.

Heinrichs, Waldo, "President Franklin D. Roosevelt's Intervention in the Battle of the Atlantic, 1941," *Diplomatic History* 10 (1986): 311–32.

Kimball, Warren F., *The Most Unsordid Act: Lend-Lease, 1939–1941*. 1969.

Langer, William L., and S. Everett Gleason, *The Challenge to Isolation, 1937–1940*. 1952.

———, *The Undeclared War, 1940–1941*. 1953.

Melosi, Martin, *The Shadow of Pearl Harbor*. 1977.

Neu, Charles E., *The Troubled Encounter: The United States and Japan*. 1975.

Offner, Arnold A., *The Origins of the Second World War*. 1975.

Prange, Gordon W., *At Dawn We Slept: The Untold Story of Pearl Harbor*. 1981.

Reynolds, David, *The Creation of the Anglo-American Alliance, 1937–1941*. 1982.

Schroeder, Paul W., *The Axis Alliance and Japanese-American Relations, 1941*. 1958.

Tansill, Charles C., *Back Door to War: The Roosevelt Foreign Policy, 1933-1941*. 1952.

Toland, John, *Infamy: Pearl Harbor and Its Aftermath*. 1982.

———, *The Rising Sun: The Decline and Fall of the Japanese Empire, 1936-1945*. 2 vols. 1970.

Utley, Jonathan G., *Going to War with Japan, 1937–1941.* 1985.

Wilson, Theodore A., *The First Summit: Roosevelt and Churchill at Placentia Bay, 1941.* 1969.

Wiltz, John E., *From Isolation to War, 1931–1941.* 1968.

Wohlstetter, Roberta, *Pearl Harbor: Warning and Decision.* 1962.

Chapter Eighteen

Wartime Diplomacy and the Origins of the Cold War, 1941–1945

THE STRANGE ALLIANCE

The central thread holding together the Strange Alliance of World War II was the common need to defeat Hitler. Once the Nazis were destroyed, the Big Three—Great Britain, the Soviet Union, and the United States—would revert to their individual interests and drift apart. The wartime unity of two alien ways of life could not permanently dispel their fundamental differences. The democracies still felt revulsion at Marxist ideology, the bloody purges of the 1930s, the Soviet attack on Finland in 1939 and occupation of the Baltic States the following year, and the Nazi-Soviet Nonaggression Pact; the Soviets distrusted capitalism and became immediately suspicious of their Anglo-American partners in the war. Some Americans, to be sure, believed that wartime cooperation would smooth doubts in the period afterward; indeed, the war did temporarily set aside ideological differences, leaving the impression that the problems straining the alliance were of no major consequence. Yet beneath the surface, these difficulties and others remained hidden only until the tide of war turned in favor of the Allies and attention began to focus on postwar matters.

These harsh undertones were especially evident in the disagreements over the "second front." From the time of the United States's entry into the war until the Allied invasion of Normandy on June 6, 1944, the Soviets bore the brunt of the fighting against the Nazis and continually urged the Americans and British to relieve them by opening an assault on Germany's western side. But for military and political reasons Churchill overcame Roosevelt's hesitancy and won the argument for a landing in North

Africa, followed by an invasion of Italy through the "soft underbelly" of Europe. American military leaders questioned the strategic wisdom of the North African campaign, but when British efforts in Egypt faltered in early 1942, Roosevelt gave in to Churchill's wishes and postponed a cross-channel invasion. The second front became feasible only in mid-1943, when the United States achieved military superiority and thus became the leader of the Allied war effort.

Other wartime difficulties revealed the lack of trust between the Americans and British on the one side and the Soviets on the other. They rarely shared military strategies, did not agree on reciprocal use of airstrips, refused to cooperate in accepting the surrenders of Axis powers, and worried that their partners might sign a separate peace with the Germans. They also disagreed over the makeup and procedure of the projected United Nations Organization, the position Nationalist China would occupy in the postwar world, and the amounts of Lend-Lease war matériel that should go to the Soviet Union. And, the United States and Britain did not share with Russia their research into atomic weaponry. Despite the grand aims proclaimed in the Atlantic Charter, only the United States and Britain pledged themselves to its support, and in the end both of them twisted its pronouncements to satisfy their national interests. The Soviet Union indicated approval of the Charter with the exception "that the practical application of these principles will necessarily adapt itself to the circumstances, needs, and historic peculiarities of particular countries." Stalin could not reconcile the Charter's democratic objectives with his overarching concern for security along the Soviet Union's western border; he insisted upon having "friendly" neighboring states.

The Soviet quest for security required expansion along its western borders, and this forecasted a clash with the defenders of the Atlantic Charter. In late 1941 Stalin demanded that Britain recognize Soviet annexation of the Baltic States and part of Finland. When London passed this to Washington for consideration, the United States turned it down as a violation of the Atlantic Charter. Yet when Soviet Foreign Commissar Vyacheslav M. Molotov later demanded a piece of Rumania and recognition of Soviet control over eastern Poland, the British agreed to a twenty-year pact by which both nations promised to "act in accordance with the two principles of not seeking territorial aggrandizement for themselves and of noninterference in the internal affairs of other States." The British were determined to maintain their empire, which meant turning away from self-determination. Americans, too, understood the importance of national security. They could not grant independence to the strategically important Pacific islands and expect to remain secure.

Thus, ironically, the Strange Alliance began to disintegrate in proportion to the successes of its war effort. National and ideological differences began to surface again among the Big Three, and despite the apparent early 1945 achievements of the wartime conferences, the alliance would continue its collapse into Cold War.

BEGINNINGS OF THE ALLIANCE

Shortly after Pearl Harbor the United States moved rapidly toward closer relations with the British against the Axis, and in late December Churchill crossed the Atlantic to discuss strategy with Roosevelt. The visit, code-named Arcadia, led to the establishment in January 1942 of the Combined Chiefs of Staff (CCS), which was comprised of America's Joint Chiefs of Staff and representatives of the British Chiefs, who together set up quarters in the Pentagon. Under the direction of the president and prime minister, the CCS formulated and implemented a strategy (that deeply satisfied Churchill) calling for Germany's defeat before turning to Japan. The Americans and British did not enter a formal alliance, but the United States drafted the "Declaration by United Nations" on January 1, which established what Churchill termed the Grand Alliance of the United Kingdom, Soviet Union, United States, Nationalist China, and all others opposing the Axis and endorsing the Atlantic Charter. Ultimately signed by forty-seven nations, the Declaration provided unity in wartime, prohibited a separate peace, and encouraged the creation of a postwar peace organization.

The United States also sought greater unity within the hemisphere. It formalized by treaty the Act of Havana of July 1940, by which representatives from each American republic could temporarily install a provisional government in any European possession in the New World that was in danger of enemy takeover. In mid-January 1942 the American republics gathered in Rio de Janeiro and proclaimed that a violation of one nation's sovereignty was a threat to all. America's Good Neighbor policy perhaps paid dividends, for every Latin American republic except Chile and Argentina immediately broke diplomatic relations with the Axis. The former did a year later, and the latter declared war on the Axis in late March 1945.

The United States talked about raising Nationalist China to major power status, despite opposition from Churchill. Though Roosevelt agreed to concentrate America's resources in Europe and Russia, he was fearful of a separate Sino-Japanese peace, and he intended to establish a postwar balance of power in the Far East that included China as the dominant force. But the United States based its hopes on an exaggerated estimate of China that resulted from decades of self-delusion and paternal sentiment. America's long-standing commitment to the Open Door, combined with its determination to fit Chiang Kai-shek into the mold of a capable, Christian, democratic leader, convinced Americans that China could become a postwar pillar of peace. Yet by the time the United States entered the war, China had already undergone four difficult years of conflict with the Japanese which forced Chiang to retreat inland to Chungking. Churchill was incredulous that the United States "rated the Chinese armies as a factor to be mentioned in the same breath as the armies of

Russia." The hope of making China into a major power, he privately remarked during the war, was "an absolute farce." In reality, however, Roosevelt's China policy was primarily a matter of rhetoric, for neither American military nor economic aid matched his promises. Germany was the priority in the war; until its defeat the United States hoped to keep China in the war to occupy Japan.

Until mid-1943 Churchill's argument against a second front in Western Europe prevailed, largely because the British had more men and matériel in the war than did the United States. Stalin repeatedly demanded an immediate cross-channel invasion of Europe to draw the Germans out of Russia, but even though General Dwight D. Eisenhower warned that a postponed second front could drive the Soviet Union out of the war and bring the "blackest day in history," Churchill won the argument for an assault through southern Europe. The United States suspected that Britain emphasized the Mediterranean to preserve its imperial controls in the postwar period, whereas the British insisted that their strategy was vital to softening Germany *before* an invasion through France. The truth doubtless encompasses both arguments. Churchill was legitimately concerned about postwar arrangements in Central Europe should the Soviet armies get there first. But he also had practical wartime considerations. The deaths of thousands of British soldiers in the trenches of World War I convinced him not to be hasty about a channel assault. The lessons of Dunkirk also bore heavily on his mind. Before sending forces into France, Churchill wanted Germany reeling from a blockade, aerial bombardments, and simultaneous attacks from the south and east. The problem was that Roosevelt had told Molotov in Washington in May 1942 that he thought a second front possible that year. The president perhaps hoped that such a statement would postpone the determination of boundaries until after the war, but his assurances deepened Stalin's suspicions that his allies sought to prolong the Russo-German war to drain both countries and benefit the West.

Britain's success in engineering Operation TORCH in November 1942 demonstrated how the exigencies of war often overcame the incompatibilities of ideologies. Rather than a cross-channel attack, this strategy entailed an Allied invasion of French North Africa, followed by assaults on Sicily and Italy in the summer of 1943. To achieve success, Anglo-American forces made an arrangement with Franco in Spain that facilitated the Allied landing in North Africa. In the spirit of Churchill's earlier remark about helping the Russians against Hitler, Roosevelt cited a Bulgarian proverb: "In time of great peril, my son, you may walk with the Devil until you have crossed the bridge." The United States and Britain were aware of Franco's fascist and pro-Axis neutrality, but they also recognized that should Spain seize Gibraltar, it could cut off the Allies from the Mediterranean and severely hamper the North African campaign. After assuring Franco that they had no interest in his African possessions, Britain and the United States furnished Spain enough raw materials (including oil) for daily consumption, and bought Spanish ore at a higher price than market value, thereby tying the country to the Allies without giving it enough to cause trouble. For added assurance, they sent a huge military contingent to prevent an assault from Franco's 150,000 men in Spanish Morocco. After the landing in Africa, the United States stopped the oil shipments. The strategy was successful. Franco did not interfere with the North African campaign and with each Axis defeat his neutrality shifted more in favor of the Allies.

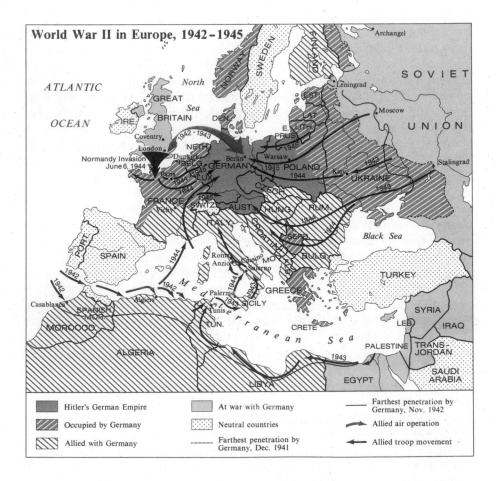

MAP 26

After Germany reached its peak in territorial control in 1942, the Allies slowly turned the tide with their victory in North Africa and invasion of Europe.

The United States also maintained relations with Vichy France, which had averted occupation by collaborating with the Nazis. At the same time, although it sent Lend-Lease matériel to areas under Free French control, America refused to recognize the government of "Free France," then in exile in London and led by General Charles de Gaulle. The American ambassador to Vichy France, Admiral William Leahy, authorized shipments of coal, sugar, and cotton to persuade the French to withhold naval assistance from the Axis. Help from Vichy France also proved critical to the Allied invasion of North Africa, for American agents in Algiers and French Morocco had made secret agreements with the French to facilitate the landing. During the expedition, in fact, the commander of Vichy forces in Algiers, Admiral Jean François Darlan, ordered his men to cease firing on the Allies as they approached the shore. Two days earlier General Eisenhower had reached an agreement with Darlan recognizing him as French leader in North Africa in exchange for his assistance in the Allied invasion. Shortly thereafter Darlan was assassinated. In October 1944 the Big Three recognized de Gaulle as head of the provisional government of France.

After the successful North African landing, Roosevelt and Churchill met at Casablanca in French Morocco in mid-January 1943 to discuss future military campaigns and to reassure the Soviets of continued Allied unity. Stalin had declined an invitation to the conference because of his preoccupation with the war in Russia. Roosevelt, however, took this to mean that the Soviets were concerned over the delayed second front and the Anglo-American success in North Africa. He had to convince Stalin that neither the United States nor Britain would sign separate peace treaties with Hitler's allies—a goal not easy to achieve in view of the recent Anglo-American dealings with Spain and Vichy France.

At Casablanca Roosevelt and Churchill first decided to go ahead with the invasion of Sicily and Italy, and then turned to their major concern of assuring the Soviets that they would sign no early peace with the Axis. Consequently, near the close of the conference, Roosevelt told reporters that "the democracies' war plans were to compel the 'unconditional surrender' of the Axis." In contrast with the outcome of World War I, the victors in this war intended to leave no doubts about which side had lost. Unconditional surrender, Roosevelt added, did not mean "the destruction of the population of Germany, Italy, or Japan," but it did mean "the destruction of the philosophies in those countries which are based on conquest and the subjugation of other people." The declaration possibly hardened Axis resistance and lengthened the war. It perhaps also helped to set the pattern for the postwar era by guaranteeing a power imbalance which the Soviet armies quickly exploited. But the immediate aims of the Casablanca Declaration were to encourage continued wartime cooperation among the Allies, and postpone arguments over postwar matters. The British and Americans were too dependent on the Red Army to fall **out** over postwar boundaries in Eastern Europe. A breakdown in the alliance could have promoted independent action by Soviet forces in the Balkans and Central Europe. Worse, a race between the Russians and the Anglo-Americans for military control in Europe could have caused war between members of the alliance. The Casablanca Declaration helped to hold the Big Three together.

TOWARD POSTWAR ARRANGEMENTS

The Allies' successful North African campaign helped to turn the war in their favor by mid-1943 and encouraged all three powers to look toward postwar arrangements. German forces had surrendered at Stalingrad in early February, and in mid-May both the Germans and the Italians laid down their arms in North Africa. Another development encouraged Americans: the Soviet Union dissolved the Comintern in May. The U.S. Navy had meanwhile pushed back the Japanese at Midway and was on the offensive in the Pacific. In the summer of 1943 the German offensive in Russia failed, while the Allied assault on Sicily led to Mussolini's fall and the surrender of Italy in early September, followed by its turnaround declaration of war on Germany the next month.

The successes in the war, however, increasingly exposed the sore spots in the alliance. By the summer of 1943 the Soviets were upset because the emphasis in Lend-Lease shipments had shifted to the Mediterranean and Pacific rather than to their own country. Stalin was also displeased at first with the Anglo-American attempt to negotiate a separate peace with Italy. But he did not push the issue, probably because he realized that his two wartime partners had set a valuable precedent: the armies which liberated a country from the Germans would determine its postwar status. Finally, the Allies had still not agreed upon a second front. Roosevelt had argued for a cross-channel invasion during the spring, but again Churchill refused. Though the Germans failed to take either Moscow or Stalingrad, they had overrun the oil fields of the Caucasus, killing millions of Soviet soldiers and civilians. Stalin had received assurances of the opening of a second front in the spring of 1943, but learned of another postponement. Then he got word that Roosevelt and Churchill had decided in Quebec in August 1943 that the invasion would not take place until May of the following year. Stalin had meanwhile written Roosevelt: "Need I speak of the dishearteningly negative impression that this fresh postponement of the second front . . . will produce in the Soviet Union?" Again, he complained to the president: "To date it has been like this, the U.S.A. and Britain reached agreement between themselves while the U.S.S.R. [Union of Soviet Socialist Republics] is informed . . . as a third party looking passively on. I must say that this situation cannot be tolerated any longer."

In view of the strained relations within the alliance, the United States and Britain decided to meet with the Soviet Union in Moscow at a Council

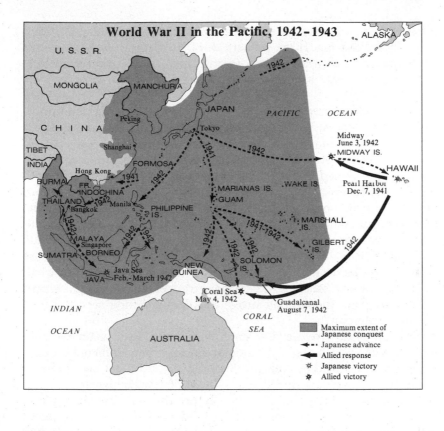

MAP 27

The Japanese reached the height of their power in Asia in 1943.

of Foreign Ministers conference in October 1943. Hull was elderly, in poor health, and afraid of flying, but he insisted on making the long trip to meet with British Foreign Secretary Anthony Eden and Soviet Foreign Commissar Molotov. Postwar questions dominated the discussions, for Stalin was concerned that the Italian surrender would allow American and British armies to reach Central Europe before the Russians. With his armies 600 miles away, he would find it difficult to restore boundaries to their 1941 status.

The Moscow Conference had several notable results. It led to the establishment of an Advisory Council on Italy, which promoted Allied cooperation and guaranteed a government "made more democratic by the introduction of representatives of those sections of the Italian people who have always opposed Fascism." The foreign ministers agreed to establish a European Advisory Commission in London to make proposals on wartime issues and work out peace arrangements. They issued a declaration calling for "a free and independent Austria," and they agreed to partition Germany among the Big Three powers until they could decide its fate. Stalin again received assurances of a second front, and he promised Russia's entry into the war against Japan after the conflict in Europe was over.

The meeting in Moscow also led, in October, to the Declaration of Four Nations on General Security, the first Allied guarantee of a postwar world peace organization. Congress in Washington had recently passed resolutions of overwhelming support for such a move, and, at Hull's urgings, Molotov agreed to allow the Chinese ambassador in Moscow to join the Big Three in calling for "a general international organization, based on the principle of the sovereign equality of all peace-loving states, and open to membership by all such states, large and small, for the maintenance of international peace and security." Later, before Congress, Hull asserted optimistically that the Moscow Conference showed that there would "no longer be need for spheres of influence, for alliances, for a balance of power, or any other of the special arrangements through which, in the unhappy past, the nations strove to safeguard their security or to promote their interests."

The Big Three also released a statement from Moscow on German wartime atrocities, which assured punishment for crimes inflicted on peoples in countries occupied by Nazi armies— but not for those acts committed against their own Jewish citizens. News of Jewish persecutions in Germany had reached the United States before the war, but throughout the Great Depression Americans had opposed the entrance of refugees seeking asylum while millions of Americans were unemployed. During the war the immigration restrictions remained in effect, as the Department of State feared that German or Soviet spies might easily be hidden among refugees. By August 1942 the United States had received reports of the Nazis' mass extermination of Jews, but neither the State Department nor the White House had an official reaction. Research later established that in Poland, at Auschwitz-Birkenau, about a million Jews perished in specially constructed gas chambers, and that by the autumn of 1942 the Germans had killed all but 70,000 of the 380,000 Jewish residents of Warsaw. In January 1944 Secretary of the Treasury Henry Morgenthau, Jr., persuaded the president to establish a War Refugee Board authorized to set up refugee centers in the countries bordering Germany. And Roosevelt later called the Nazis' mass murders "one of the blackest crimes of all history." But despite pressure on Americans to bomb railways leading to the extermination camps, the War Department countered that this would divert the military effort and delay victory—the only sensible way to save the Jews. By the end of the war the Nazis had executed 6 million Jews, about 60 percent of the total of those Jews living in the European areas seized by Germany.

Meanwhile Roosevelt, wanting to inject more life into the wartime role of China, invited Chiang Kai-shek to meet with himself and Churchill in Cairo, Egypt, in November 1943. The three leaders issued the Cairo Declaration, which called for the unconditional surrender of Japan and proclaimed that "Japan shall be stripped of all the islands in the Pacific" acquired since 1914. Manchuria, Formosa, and the Pescadores would be returned to China, whereas Korea was to be "free and independent" in "due course." The president had earlier secured an end to extraterritoriality and other special privileges in China, and now, in December, the U.S. Congress repealed exclusion laws, authorized immigration on the same quota system long applicable to Europeans, and permitted naturalization. The Cairo Declaration of unconditional surrender perhaps made the Japanese fight harder, but it also raised Chinese and Korean morale, and it assured the Soviets of no separate peace with Japan.

After the Cairo Conference, Roosevelt, Churchill, and Stalin met, for the first time, in the Iranian capital of Teheran in late November 1943. Both military and political matters were on the agenda, but the three leaders were as interested in examining each other as in dealing with the issues. Roosevelt considered Stalin "very confident, very sure of himself[,] . . . altogether quite impressive." The president seems to have decided to develop a close relationship with Stalin—even at Churchill's expense. Roosevelt refused to meet privately with the prime minister for fear that Stalin would suspect them of working together; yet he talked with the Soviet premier three times without Churchill being present. Stalin was not averse to playing a macabre game. At a dinner party he infuriated Churchill by lightheartedly suggesting that the Allies exterminate 50,000 to 100,000 German officers. When the prime minister indignantly retorted that his people could not condone "mass executions," Roosevelt remarked that surely a more acceptable figure would be 49,000. Churchill stalked from the room, later consoled by Roosevelt's assurance that he had been joking.

A number of exploratory discussions helped to establish each nation's position. Roosevelt and Churchill realized that Stalin would not sacrifice Soviet security for the Atlantic Charter. When Roosevelt declared that numerous Americans of Baltic stock sought self-determination for Lithuania, Latvia, and Estonia, Stalin refused to negotiate over these people because, he asserted, they had already voted to become part of the Soviet Union. But Americans "neither knew nor understood this," the president explained. Then the American government had "some propaganda work" ahead of it, Stalin replied. On Poland, Stalin cited security reasons for wanting its borders moved farther west to include parts of Germany to the Oder River; in the meantime the Soviet Union would incorporate Poland's eastern territory to the Curzon Line, which included regions in White Russia and the Ukraine. Roosevelt agreed with Stalin's objectives, but warned that for political reasons he could not "publicly take part in any such arrangement at the present time." The presidential election of

1944 lay ahead, he privately told the Soviet premier, and 6 million Polish-American voters could determine the outcome. Stalin affirmed his understanding of the president's position.

The German question also caused disagreements at Teheran. Stalin wanted Germany's total dismemberment. Roosevelt recommended dividing the country into five autonomous districts and setting up international supervision of the Kiel Canal and Ruhr and Saar valleys. Churchill sought to strip power from Prussia and tie the remainder of Germany to Austria and Hungary in a Danubian confederation. The three leaders decided to postpone the issue for future consideration. Though Stalin's expectations violated the Atlantic Charter's pledge against territorial changes without "the freely expressed wishes of the peoples concerned," the West needed Soviet help in the war. A key consideration was that the Red Armies were already in or close to the areas in question.

Before the conference adjourned on December 1, the president called for a world peace organization led by the "Four Policemen," which implied the creation of balance-of-power relationships based on spheres of influence. Stalin shared Churchill's doubts about China's potential, but agreed that any peace organization had to be "world-wide and not regional." The Soviet premier raised the possibility of establishing two regional organizations: in Europe, the Big Three plus one other nation; in Asia, the Big Three and China. Churchill was pleased with the proposed arrangements. A major threat to world peace, he believed, was "hungry" and "ambitious" nations, and he wanted "the leading nations of the world in the position of rich, happy men." Upon the president's return home, he told Americans that he "got along fine" with Stalin and that the United States would "get along very well with him and the Russian people—very well indeed."

The major decision reached at Teheran was that Operation OVERLORD, the long-debated cross-channel assault on Europe, would begin in the spring of 1944, and that it would occur simultaneously with an Allied drive through southern France and a Soviet offensive from the east. Accordingly, on the morning of June 6, 1944, Allied forces launched an invasion at Normandy Beach in France. In the east, Soviet armies began a major drive through Poland and the Balkans that forced the surrender of Germany's partner nations. As Allied forces liberated Nazi-held territories in their push toward Berlin, the imminent defeat of Germany further eroded the wartime alliance.

In late August 1944, after the Allied success at Normandy, the United States gathered with Britain, the Soviet Union, and China at an estate in Washington, D.C. called Dumbarton Oaks, to make plans for a postwar United Nations Organization. Their draft charter called for a Security Council of the big powers, a General Assembly of all member nations, a Secretariat, an Economic and Social Council, and an International Court of Justice. Disagreements immediately arose over several matters. The United States wanted China to become a permanent member of the Security Council, whereas Britain wanted France. The Soviet Union finally agreed to allow both China and France into the Council, provided that each power had a veto over Council proceedings. But the discussions broke down over voting arrangements in the Council and membership in the Assembly. The Soviets wanted Council members to have the veto power on all issues, whether substantive (legal rights and principles) or procedural (rules of form), which included the right to veto a discussion, an inquiry into, or proposals about resolving a dispute short of war. The Americans would approve the suspension of a member's veto on only those matters in which that member was a party. On the second issue involving the Assembly, the Soviets wanted equal representation for all of their sixteen republics. This would counter Britain's ''bloc'' of voters from the Commonwealth and the United States's ''bloc'' of Latin American states. The conference adjourned in October without a resolution of these issues. But it had emerged with a working draft of a UN charter.

The Allied military advance into Europe also raised the issue of postwar Germany, which the Americans initially tried to resolve in the autumn of 1944 by the Morgenthau Plan. The central debate among the Allies was whether to rebuild Germany and integrate it into the European economy, or punish and reform the country with economic reprisals, high reparations, and the establishment of a decentralized system of government. Morgenthau presented a plan to the president calling for the dismemberment of Germany and the elimination of its war potential. Hull and Stimson warned that harsh treatment of Germany would prolong disorder in Europe, but in a memorandum to Stimson the president explained his position. "It is of the utmost importance that every person in Germany should realize that this time Germany is a defeated nation." He added that "I do not want them to starve to death but . . . if they need food to keep body and soul together beyond what we have, they should be fed three times a day with soup from Army group kitchens. . . . They will remember that experience all their lives."

At the Quebec Conference of mid-September Roosevelt and Churchill temporarily seemed to support Morgenthau's recommendations for Germany when they initialed a memorandum containing the essence of his plan: "This programme for eliminating the war-making industries in the Ruhr and in the Saar is looking forward to converting Germany into a country primarily agricultural and pastoral in its character." Perhaps to avoid division on the eve of a presidential election, Roosevelt later retreated on his stand. He told Stimson that he had approved the plan "without much thought," but that he hoped the British "might inherit Germany's Ruhr business" to help their economic recovery. Churchill likewise changed his stance. He later claimed that he had "violently opposed the idea" at first, but had relented to the "insistent" demands of Roosevelt and Morgenthau. Though no deal was consummated at Quebec, the prime minister perhaps was amenable to the plan to ensure the approval of nearly $7 billion of postwar aid tentatively offered by the

United States. In any case, the Morgenthau Plan served as propaganda for the Nazis, who called it a "satanic plan of annihilation" inspired by the Jews, and urged the Germans to resist it to the death.

In October 1944 Churchill and Stalin met in Moscow and negotiated the controversial "percentages agreement," a clear example of power politics based on spheres of influence. Churchill had warned Roosevelt that they were nearing a "showdown with the Russians" over the Balkans, and in early 1944 had urged a settlement. The president, however, was unable to attend the conference but arranged for his ambassador to Russia, W. Averell Harriman, to sit in as observer. Roosevelt was uneasy about the postwar objectives of both Churchill and Stalin. He did not favor permanent spheres of influence, but would accept a temporary wartime division of authority. The problem was that as Churchill and Stalin came together that autumn, the military advantages belonged to the Soviet Union. The Red Army controlled Rumania; the communist partisan leader Josip Broz Tito was gaining hold in Yugoslavia (with Allied promises of support); the Soviets were assisting the communists' spread into Bulgaria; and Greece threatened to break down in a civil war that could result in a communist takeover. The previous June of 1944, Roosevelt had gone against State Department advice in agreeing to Soviet control over Rumania and British hegemony in Greece, each for three months. He then notified Stalin that the United States would not be bound by any agreements reached in Moscow.

During the Moscow meeting Churchill made a proposal that caused controversy for many years. He scratched a series of percentage figures onto a scrap of paper and shoved it across the table to Stalin. The prime minister recommended that the Soviet Union receive 90 percent control in Rumania in exchange for Britain's receiving the same in Greece; that there be a 50–50 split in Yugoslavia and Hungary; and that the Soviets get 75 percent control in Bulgaria, the remainder going to the "others." Stalin read the proposal, Churchill recalled, and "took his blue pencil and made a large tick upon it." Perhaps the paper should be burned, Churchill noted. "No, you keep it," Stalin replied. Churchill's proposal left the impression that his imperial interests had not changed, and that the Soviet Union had secured British approval of its spheres of influence in Eastern Europe.

In the meantime the dismal performance of Chiang's Nationalist Army had proved Churchill correct: China was not ready to become one of the world's Four Policemen. In July 1944 Roosevelt turned over the Chinese command to General Joseph Stilwell, who had been chief of staff to the Nationalist Army for over two years but failed to get along with Chiang. The following November, after continued lack of success led to the replacement of Stilwell with General Albert C. Wedemeyer, Roosevelt appointed General Patrick Hurley as ambassador to Chungking. Like his predecessor, Hurley opposed communism, but at first favored a coalition government comprised of Chiang's Nationalists and Mao's Communists.

Then he underwent a change of heart. Against all advice and without orders, Hurley shifted the goal of his mission from mediating the dispute in China to saving the Nationalist government. The previous August Hurley had talked with Molotov in Moscow and felt confident that the Soviets intended to help Chiang, and that Mao's forces were no threat because they "had no relation whatever to Communism." Yet those around Hurley argued that Mao's form of communism was tied to the peasants and the land, and warned that refusal to help his forces would push them into the arms of the Soviet Union. Some of the so-called "China hands" had already talked with Mao, and in January 1945 informed Washington that he was willing to meet with Roosevelt. Hurley suspected his staff of being pro-communist and blocked the meeting. He accused his embassy assistant, John Paton Davies, of trying to subvert Chiang and later arranged to have Davies and a career diplomat, John Service, transferred from China. In February Hurley arrived in Washington, where he convinced Roosevelt to continue supporting Chiang.

YALTA

By the beginning of 1945, amid an air of impending Allied victory, the Big Three prepared to deal with postwar problems at a summit conference in Yalta on the Black Sea. Anglo-American forces had been fighting the Germans in the Battle of the Bulge in Belgium since the middle of December and were beginning to make their way toward the Rhine, while the Red Armies had pierced the German front en route to Berlin and were in control of Rumania, Poland, Czechoslovakia, Bulgaria, Hungary, and Yugoslavia. In the Far East, Japan was a long way from surrender. It remained strong in the Philippines and the Marianas, its soldiers numbered 2 million on the Chinese mainland and another 2 million at home, and it had over 5,000 kamikaze (suicide) planes ready for action and another 7,000 in reserve. The West was in no position to make demands in either Europe or Asia. The Soviet Union dominated the field in the West, and the Japanese were entrenched in the East. The Americans and British believed that Stalin's forces were vital to ending the war in Europe and would be critical to the effort in Asia. The United States had perfected no new weapons by early 1945, and its military experts anticipated a siege of the Japanese islands which, without Soviet assistance, could last until December 1946 and cost a million American lives. In early January 1945 Churchill warned Roosevelt that "this may well be a fateful Conference, coming at a moment when the Great Allies are so divided and the shadow of the war lengthens out before us. At the present time, the end of this war may well prove to be more disappointing than was the last."

From February 4 through 11, 1945, the Big Three met at a Crimean resort close to Yalta. The time had come to formulate postwar policy toward Eastern Europe, lay plans for Germany's partitioning, occupation, and meeting of war reparations, determine voting and membership regu-

Churchill, Roosevelt, and Stalin at Yalta

The Big Three meet in the Crimea in February 1945 to make postwar global arrangements. (Franklin D. Roosevelt Library, Hyde Park, New York)

lations for the United Nations Organization, and finalize Soviet entry into the war in Asia. These would be difficult tasks. The idealism of the Atlantic Charter stood in stark contrast with the realities of the world situation. The Americans sought a United Nations, Soviet entry into the war against Japan, diminished communist influence in Poland, and major power status for Nationalist China. The Soviets wanted a central voice in Poland, favorable boundaries in Eastern Europe, a flattened Germany burdened with large-scale reparations, and major concessions in the Far East. Churchill wanted a French zone in Germany, the safeguarding of Poland from the Soviet Union, and, most of all, preservation of the British Empire. The three sets of demands were incompatible.

The Yalta proceedings would cause controversy for years after the war. Critics would accuse Roosevelt of giving away huge portions of Europe and Asia to the Russians in an unnecessary effort to persuade them to enter the war against Japan. Actually, the Big Three had reached most of the settlements on an informal basis earlier at Teheran. The powers made secret agreements at Yalta that were deemed essential to the war effort, but in the years afterward these same agreements took on the appearance of Anglo-American capitulation to the Soviet Union. Most settlements were purposely vague in wording but loud in rhetoric, open to interpretations that benefited each party—and, for that reason, detrimental to peace. And finally, the Soviets refused to abide by those stipulations that were not subject to flexible readings. With their armies in control of many of the disputed areas, the West could do little short of war. Perhaps, Roosevelt hoped, the Big Three powers could reconcile their differences through a United Nations Organization.

The most exasperating problem at Yalta was Poland; of eight plenary sessions at the conference, seven dealt with that question. Churchill called it "the most urgent reason for the Yalta Conference," for he realized that the Soviets regarded favorable boundaries and a strong position within the Polish government as essential to their security. Two German invasions of Russia in the twentieth century had taken place through Poland. As Stalin explained at Yalta, "the question of Poland is not only a question of honor but also a question of security. Throughout history, Poland has been the corridor through which the enemy has passed into Russia." Poland was a matter "of life and death for the Soviet Union." No success could take place at Yalta without concessions to the Soviets regarding Poland. The problem there exemplified those that would disrupt other countries after the war: two governments claiming legitimacy, one recognized by the Soviets, the other by the West. The United States and Britain considered the London-based government-in-exile to be Poland's legitimate ruling authority, whereas the Soviet Union supported the Lublin provisional government led by the communists. Stalin demanded Anglo-American support for boundaries that would award Poland a section of eastern Germany along the Oder-Neisse line, which would be compensation for Russia's receiving a large part of east Poland as a buffer along the Curzon Line of 1919. If granted, Poland would lose 40 percent of its territory and five million of its people. These expectations were in violation of the Atlantic Charter, but such an argument rang hollow since Poland was already under Red Army control.

The Yalta agreements on Poland are comprehensible only in relation to Soviet security demands and the military advantages held by its armies. Favorable boundaries and a "friendly" regime, in the eyes of the Kremlin, were vital interests. Yet the United States and Britain salvaged something. They won the establishment of the Polish Provisional Government of National Unity, which was to be a coalition of communists from the Lublin group along with "democratic leaders from Poland itself and from Poles abroad." The Lublin government, the starting point for postwar rule, was "pledged to the holding of free and unfettered elections as soon as possible." Thus, Poland's government was to be "more broadly based" through the reorganization of the provisional government along democratic guidelines. On the boundary issue, Poland's temporary eastern border was to be the Curzon Line, but its western boundary remained uncertain. Even though Roosevelt and Churchill were receptive to the Oder River, they were unwilling to drop the line to the Western Neisse.

Yalta and Poland

YALTA TREATY AGREEMENT

▨ Polish territory lost to the Soviet Union

▨ Polish territory gained from Germany

━━ Polish boundary established at Yalta

── Pre–World War II boundaries

SWEDEN

DENMARK

ESTONIA

LATVIA

BALTIC SEA

LITHUANIA

GERMANY

Danzig

Polish Corridor

EAST PRUSSIA

Oder R.

Berlin •

Oder–Neisse Line

Neisse R.

POLAND

• Warsaw

Lublin •

Curzon Line

SOVIET UNION

CZECHOSLOVAKIA

AUSTRIA

HUNGARY

Dnieper R.

RUMANIA

YUGOSLAVIA

ADRIATIC SEA

BULGARIA

BLACK SEA

Yalta •

ITALY

ALBANIA

GREECE

AEGEAN SEA

TURKEY

MEDITERRANEAN SEA

The conferees decided that "the final delimitation of the Western frontier of Poland should thereafter await the Peace Conference." Yet the Big Three never convened talks on Poland. Americans interpreted the Yalta accords to mean that a new government would emerge, but many considered this wishful thinking. Admiral Leahy warned, "Mr. President, this is so elastic that the Russians can stretch it all the way from Yalta to Washington without technically breaking it." Roosevelt replied, "I know, Bill—I know it. But it's the best I can do for Poland at this time."

One of the chief reasons for the optimism that pervaded the Yalta Conference and afterward was Stalin's agreement to the Declaration on Liberated Europe. Sponsored by the United States, it promised Big Three cooperation in forming "interim governmental authorities broadly representative of all democratic elements in the population and pledged to the earliest possible establishment through free elections of governments responsive to the will of the people." Stalin thus consented to "free" and "democratic" governments in Eastern Europe. Hope was not unwarranted, for up to this point he had seemed to keep his promises. He had honored the "percentages agreement" by not interfering with Britain's military actions in Greece during the civil war of December 1944, and his troops were marching toward Berlin to wind down the European war. Weeks after Yalta, when his lack of good faith became evident in Rumania, Poland, and other places in Eastern Europe, the United States and Britain could at least point to the Yalta Declaration in casting moral condemnation on Soviet behavior.

The second major subject discussed at Yalta was Germany. The Big Three did not settle Germany's postwar status, but they were in no mood for conciliation and agreed to "take such steps, including the complete disarmament, demilitarization and the dismemberment of Germany as they deem requisite for future peace and security." The negotiators decided to partition Germany into four military zones, the fourth a French sector created from "within the British and American zones." Eastern Germany and eastern Berlin fell under Soviet occupation, western Germany and western Berlin went to the other three powers, and all four received seats on the Allied Control Commission for Germany. Stalin had opposed French participation because of their quick collapse in the war, followed by the Vichy government's collaboration with the Germans. Roosevelt had earlier agreed with this view but now changed his position in hope of winning the support of the Free French leader, General Charles de Gaulle, on other postwar issues. Churchill argued that because of expected American troop withdrawals after the war, a strong France was needed to balance off Germany. He also made reference to the Sovi-

---

MAP 28

Stalin considered a "friendly" Poland to be vital to Soviet security.

ets' alignment with the Germans before the June 1941 Nazi invasion, when he pointedly remarked that "every nation had had their difficulties in the beginning of the war and had made mistakes."

German reparations were also a vital subject of the discussions. Stalin demanded extensive reparations "for the purpose of military and economic disarmament of Germany," whereas Churchill insisted upon sufficient reparations "to destroy the German war potential." Roosevelt and Churchill vaguely conceded to reparations "in kind," but declined to specify an amount until they could assess Germany's economic potential after the war. Roosevelt was particularly concerned about avoiding another war debts–reparations imbroglio in which, as after World War I, the United States paid much of the bill. The Big Three called for the establishment of a reparations commission; the Soviet Union and United States believed that such a commission should use as "a basis of discussion the figure of reparations as $20 billion and 50 percent of these should go to the Soviet Union." The Soviets had made this proposal sometime before the conference, and even though the Yalta agreement postponed final settlements until after future talks, Stalin probably thought he had secured his counterparts' approval of the Soviet Union receiving $10 billion. The Big Three agreed to secrecy on all arrangements affecting Germany out of fear that the news would help Nazi propagandists and prolong the war.

The third matter discussed at Yalta was the projected United Nations Organization. The Big Three had worked out the draft for a charter at Dumbarton Oaks, even though voting and membership questions remained unsettled. Roosevelt thought the UN so vital that he would make concessions on other matters. But Stalin's position on unrestricted use of the veto was unacceptable to Roosevelt and Churchill, for they wanted the UN to become a forum for discussion of all matters brought before the Council. Stalin finally agreed to suspension of the veto in procedural matters, thereby guaranteeing freedom of discussion, but retained the right of veto in substantive issues. After Stalin's concession, the United States was not in a good position to deny his request for two additional seats in the General Assembly, one for the Ukraine and the other for White Russia. To prevent political problems at home, Roosevelt secured the consent of Churchill and Stalin to two additional seats for the United States—a right it never exercised. These voting arrangements remained secret. Finally, the Big Three set the date and place for the meeting of the UN Conference on World Organization: April 25, 1945, in the United States—later designated to be in San Francisco.

Questions over Nazi-liberated territories also caused division during the Yalta discussions of the UN. Since it seemed undesirable either to annex the areas or to grant their freedom, the Big Three emerged with a solution similar to the mandate system established under League of Nations supervision: territorial trusteeships. But this agreement concerned the British delegates, who felt their empire threatened. Churchill had told Foreign Secretary Anthony Eden that "if the Americans want to take Jap-

anese islands which they have conquered, let them do so with our blessing and any form of words that may be agreeable to them. But 'Hands
Off the British Empire' is our maxim."

The United States's opposition to colonial rule had become increasingly evident. Roosevelt had made clear that British and French colonial
rule violated the principle of self-determination, and Hull had earlier
warned that Britain's system of "imperial preference" endangered the
open world market he sought to create through reciprocal trade agreements. As early as November 1942—just after Operation TORCH had begun—Churchill declared before the House of Commons: "I have not
become the King's First Minister in order to preside over the liquidation
of the British Empire." The United States knew that the UN trusteeships
posed a potential danger to Britain's colonial concerns in the Mediterranean, Persian Gulf, and Far East. In fact, some of Churchill's wartime actions now seemed to fit a pattern designed to defend his colonial interests
and the Mediterranean "lifeline": repeated delays on the second front, insistence on an invasion through North Africa and Italy, and his call for
the Anglo-Americans to get into Central Europe before the Russians.
Churchill regarded the trusteeships as a means by which the United
States intended to break up the British Empire. At one point during the
Yalta proceedings he stormed: "I will not have one scrap of British Territory flung into that area. . . . I will have no suggestion that the British
Empire is to be put into the dock and examined by everybody to see
whether it is up to their standard." Stalin "beamed" at this tirade, Eden
later recalled. The Soviet premier stood and paced the room, stopping to
applaud at times. The British had cause for concern. Roosevelt had secretly told Stalin of his desire to dismantle the British Empire, which included granting sovereignty over Hong Kong to China.

The fourth set of discussions at Yalta related to the Far East and
proved the most controversial of all because, for military reasons, the arrangements were secret. Roosevelt had come prepared to deal with Stalin's demands regarding the Far East. Ambassador Harriman had talked
with the premier in Moscow the previous December and realized that Stalin had raised territorial expectations to the level of demands. On December 15 Harriman forwarded them by telegraph to the White House.
Consequently, Roosevelt's Yalta agreements on the Far East were the result of six weeks of studied preparation.

At Yalta Stalin secured a favored position in the Far East in exchange
for his pledge to enter the war against Japan "in two or three months"
following the defeat of Germany, which was the time required to relocate
soldiers to the Far East. For Stalin's promise to enter the war, the Soviet
Union was to regain several possessions lost in the war against Japan in
1904–5. Although the United States did not consult the Chinese before
making these agreements, Roosevelt promised to secure Chiang's approval. To salve the Chinese, Stalin agreed to recognize their sovereignty
over Manchuria and to negotiate a treaty of aid with the Nationalist gov-

ernment. Chiang read the terms in June and considered them "generally OK." The Big Three guaranteed that all conditions would be "unquestionably . . . fulfilled" after Japan's surrender, but also agreed to keep them secret because news of Soviet entry into the war might stiffen Japan's resistance. Roosevelt had assured Churchill and Stalin that any matter discussed with the Chinese became "known to the whole world in twenty-four hours."

Public reaction to the Yalta agreements was instantaneous and overwhelmingly favorable. *Time* magazine hailed the peace conference as the "New Dawn" of civilization. The Declaration on Liberated Europe, the promise of a United Nations, the general atmosphere of goodwill—all made Yalta the grand climax to the greatest war ever fought. On March 1 Roosevelt, weak and drawn, appeared before Congress to report on the conference. Forced to sit in a chair for the first time during an address because of his frail health and the weight of his steel leg braces, he declared that the discussions on the UN pointed to "the end of the system of unilateral action and exclusive alliances and spheres of influence and balances of power." Former President Hoover called Yalta a "great hope to the world," writer William L. Shirer labeled it a "landmark in human history," and even the hard-nosed Churchill assured the House of Commons that "I know of no government which stands to its obligations . . . more solidly than the Russian government."

Indeed, it appeared that a new age had arrived, for the divisive Yalta discussions relating to Germany, much of Poland, and the Far East would remain secret for about a year. Roosevelt's confidant, Harry Hopkins, gave the most realistic analysis of the American delegation's feelings at the time of the conference: "We really believed in our hearts that this was the dawn of the new day we had all been praying for and talking about for so many years. We were absolutely certain that we had won the first great victory of the peace—and, by 'we,' I mean *all* of us, the whole civilized human race." The Russians had proved "reasonable and farseeing and there wasn't any doubt in the minds of the President or any of us that we could live with them and get along with them peacefully for as far into the future as any of us could imagine. But," Hopkins cautioned, "I have to make one amendment to that—I think we all had in our minds the reservation that we could not foretell what the results would be if anything should happen to Stalin. We felt sure that we could count on him to be reasonable and sensible and understanding—but we never could be sure who or what might be in back of him there in the Kremlin."

TRUMAN AND THE END OF WORLD WAR II

On April 12, 1945, Roosevelt suddenly died of a cerebral hemorrhage in Warm Springs, Georgia, leaving the Executive Office to Harry S. Truman. As vice president for less than four months, the former bank clerk, farmer, merchant, captain in World War I, and senator from Missouri was unaware of the vast complexities of the war, largely because Roosevelt had kept him uninformed. Truman was a relative unknown, except that he had headed a wartime Senate committee charged with the responsibility of investigating the national defense program. Brash, assertive, outspoken, unreflective, hot-tempered, lacking vision—these descriptions and more would follow him during his tenure as president. Truman was willing to learn, however, and what was just as important, he was capable of making hard decisions.

The abrupt change in government leadership would eventually cause a long debate over whether ensuing events in foreign affairs might have been much different had Roosevelt lived. Some observers have noted a sharp turn toward a hardline policy that worsened relations with the Soviet Union and helped bring on the heightened international tensions referred to as the "Cold War." Less than two weeks after becoming chief executive, Truman so severely chastised Molotov for the Soviets' infractions of the Yalta accords on Poland that the foreign minister declared, "I have never been talked to like that in my life." "Carry out your agreements," the new president shot back, "and you won't get talked to like that." Proponents of this argument also point out that those who surrounded Truman were deeply suspicious of the Soviets, including Leahy, who considered Stalin "a liar and a crook," and Harriman in Moscow, who regarded the Russians as "barbarians" not yet housebroken. Since many of these men had also served the previous administration, it seems that Roosevelt indeed was in firm control of foreign policy. Yet had he survived into the postwar period, the Soviet violations of treaty agreements and other understandings would have become obvious to him as well. Since considerable evidence has appeared that he had already become disenchanted with the Soviets shortly before his death, it seems unlikely that anything but a Cold War could have developed after the end of World War II.

In one important sense, however, a change had occurred in April 1945: Roosevelt's successor listened more to his advisers, especially those in the State and War (later Defense) Departments. If there was consistency in America's outlook toward foreign affairs, it emanated from those members of the diplomatic corps and military service who had long questioned Soviet motives and continually called for a policy based on realistic self-interest. With Roosevelt at the helm, their warnings had little effect; with Truman in office, they were able to act upon the dual premises that Stalin was not trustworthy and not interested in the ideals of the Atlantic Charter. The Soviets' primary concern, Truman's advisers argued, was security, and this necessitated Soviet control over the neighboring states of Eastern Europe, either through communist infiltration of the governments, or, as a last resort, through the use of military force. Thus, upon Truman's elevation to the presidency, the primary change in foreign policy direction rested on the growing reliance of the White House on State and War Department advisers, both of which groups called for a stronger stance against Soviet aggression.

The new president's first big decision was to proceed with plans for the United Nations Conference on International Organization, to be held in San Francisco in April 1945. Unlike the Paris deliberations of 1919, this time the drafting of the charter for the world organization was kept separate from the peacemaking process. In this manner, the outcome of one set of agreements would not automatically determine the fate of the other. Secretary of State Edward R. Stettinius, Jr., who had succeeded Hull the previous year, headed an eight-member bipartisan delegation to San Francisco, which included the heads of the Senate Foreign Relations Committee and the House Committee on Foreign Affairs. In all, nearly 300 delegates from fifty nations attended; but in fact the Big Four of Stettinius, British Foreign Secretary Eden, Soviet Foreign Commissar Molotov, and Chinese Foreign Minister T. V. Soong made the key decisions during the evenings spent in the Stettinius penthouse apartment atop the Fairmont Hotel. Instructions from the new president to Stettinius were to "write a document that would pass the U.S. Senate and that would not arouse such opposition as confronted Woodrow Wilson."

The resultant UN Charter formalized the various compartments within the organization called for at Dumbarton Oaks and Yalta. The Security Council, comprised of the Big Five as permanent members along with six others chosen by the General Assembly for two-year terms, was to be the police force of the UN. The Council could render decisions binding on all members, which included making recommendations for breaking diplomatic relations and exerting economic pressure. The intention was to establish an armed force furnished by member states and under the direction of a Military Staff Committee, but this force never materialized because the committee failed to agree on its makeup. The charter prohibited the suspension of the veto on procedural matters, which meant that small countries could take problems before the Security Council if the majority of its members agreed to hear them. The General Assembly also became an international forum. Its members could engage in almost unlimited debate, and they could make proposals on any international issue falling within the scope of the charter.

The UN Charter also provided for numerous other organizations. The Economic and Social Council was to work under the Assembly and coordinate the work of "specialized agencies." It could "make recommendations for the purpose of promoting respect for, and observance of, human rights and fundamental freedoms for all." The Trusteeship Council, also emerging from the San Francisco meeting, aimed at the ultimate independence of colonial peoples, but its responsibilities were so vaguely worded that Britain and France managed to hold onto their empires, and the United States was able to assume control over Japan's Pacific possessions. According to the charter, any area in a territory under trust could be des-

ignated a "strategic area" and placed under the auspices of the Security
Council. Thus Council members could use the veto to maintain exclusive
control over any trusteed area. Article 51 of the charter approved the formation of regional pacts and declared that members had "the inherent
right of individual or collective self-defense" in the event of attack, until
the Security Council could take "measures necessary to maintain international peace and security." Finally, the charter created the International
Court of Justice, the Secretariat for dispensing administrative duties, and
many other special agencies.

On June 26 the delegates signed the UN Charter. About a month afterward, the U.S. Senate approved American membership by the margin
of 89 to 2.

While the UN Conference moved toward conclusion, Allied forces
completed the military operations that led to the collapse of Germany and
the declaration of "V-E Day" on May 8, 1945. The combined armies had
entered Germany from the east and west, and on May 1 reports came that
the Soviets had entered Berlin and that Hitler and his bride had committed suicide in their bunker beneath the city. Six days later the German
army agreed to surrender terms. In early June the Allied Control Commission began work in Berlin. The war in Europe was over.

On V-E Day President Truman called for the "unconditional surrender" of Japan, which he insisted did not mean "the extermination or en-
slavement of the Japanese people." Peace groups in Japan had gained
leverage with every Allied victory, but the army and others held on partly
because the Allies' call for unconditional surrender did not guarantee
maintenance of the emperor. Japanese peace advocates tried in June to
persuade Russia to mediate an end to the war, but they were refused. It
thus appeared that an American invasion of Japan, supported by Soviet
entry into the war, would be necessary. Indeed, the War Department had
plans under way for an invasion of Japan to begin on November 1.

But in the meantime Soviet-American relations threatened to come
apart over the Lend-Lease program and recent events in Poland. Shortly
after Germany's defeat, the Truman administration abruptly terminated
Lend-Lease aid to the Soviet Union, a decision the president partly reversed when the Kremlin interpreted the move as White House pressure
aimed at postwar concessions. The administration saw little use in trying
to convince the Soviets that the sudden cutoff was attributable to the end
of the war in Europe. Stalin called the cessation of Lend-Lease "brutal"
and warned that "if the refusal to continue Lend-Lease was designed as
pressure on the Russians in order to soften them up, then it was a fundamental mistake." In view of growing suspicions of Soviet motives in Poland, Truman persuaded the ailing Harry Hopkins to make the arduous
trip to Moscow to smooth over differences that might obstruct the war
effort in the Far East.

Hopkins's mission to Moscow was a mild success. He assured Stalin
that the cancellation of Lend-Lease was not an attempt to exert pressure

on the Soviet Union, yet he warned that the government in Washington was losing patience over Moscow's laxity in implementing the Yalta agreements in Poland. Stalin replied that free elections in Poland would lead to the installation of the London government-in-exile, a group opposed to the Soviet Union. "In the course of twenty-five years," he emphasized in an argument he had made earlier at Yalta, "the Germans had twice invaded Russia via Poland. Neither the British nor American people had experienced such German invasions which were a horrible thing to endure and the results of which were not easily forgotten. . . . Poland has served as a corridor for the German attacks on Russia. . . . It is therefore in Russia's vital interest that Poland should be both strong and friendly." Harriman raised a point vital to understanding Stalin's views on America's relation to the Polish question, and therefore essential to comprehending the mutual misunderstanding crucial to the origins of the Cold War. The Soviet premier, Harriman explained, could not "understand why we should want to interfere with Soviet policy in a country like Poland, which he considers so important to Russia's security, unless we have some ulterior motive." Nonetheless, Stalin assured Hopkins that those Polish not associated with the Lublin regime could have a few ministries in the government, and he repeated his promises to enter the war against Japan and to respect the Chinese Nationalist government. Before returning home, Hopkins made final arrangements for another Big Three conference, this one to be at Potsdam, outside Berlin. Hopkins's mission to Moscow temporarily eased difficulties with the Soviet Union and allowed the Allies to concentrate on Japan.

From mid-July through early August 1945, the Big Three gathered in Potsdam to finalize plans for postwar Germany and for ending the war in the Far East. After Truman's first encounter with Stalin, he wrote his family that the Russians were "pig-headed" and allegedly said about the Soviet premier that "I thought he was an S.O.B. But, of course, I guess he thinks I'm one, too." Churchill was in Potsdam until mid-conference, when his Conservative party lost the elections to the Labour party and Clement Attlee replaced him as prime minister, and Ernest Bevin succeeded Eden as foreign secretary. Before Churchill departed, he had gained a favorable impression of the new president: Truman had "exceptional character and ability with . . . simple and direct methods of speech, and a great deal of self-confidence and resolution."

On the first day of the Potsdam Conference, July 17, Truman received word that American scientists in New Mexico had successfully exploded an atomic device the previous day. The secret "Manhattan Project" had been under way since August 1942, and would so profoundly change the course of history that no one in 1945 could have guessed its impact. Problems remained in adapting the mechanism for use in a bomb, and in getting the heavy apparatus airborne. There also was no guarantee that another detonating device would work, and if so, how soon it could be developed. But the researchers had proved the feasibility of nuclear fis-

Churchill, Truman, and Stalin at Potsdam

The Big Three meet in Germany in July-August 1945 to discuss postwar arrangements and to call for the unconditional surrender of Japan. (Imperial War Museum, London)

sion, and its conceivable use as a weapon raised hopes for ending the war without a costly invasion of Japan. On the same day that Truman learned the news he informed Stalin that the United States had developed "a new weapon of unusual destructive force." Stalin's only reply was that he hoped the United States would use it on the Japanese. His spy network had probably already uncovered the atomic project, but like the Americans he could not have known its potential. After the Americans at Potsdam informed Churchill of the successful test, he declared the following day that "now I know what happened to Truman yesterday. . . . When he got to the meeting after having read this report he was a changed man. He told the Russians just where they got on and off and generally bossed the whole meeting."

The development of the potential for an atomic bomb did not mean that the United States was able to achieve all of its objectives at Potsdam. Soviet armies were in control of Eastern Europe, and local Communist parties sat in key government positions in nearly all countries involved. The Soviets meanwhile made a secret arrangement with Poland's Provisional Government, which temporarily drew its western boundary at the Oder and Western Neisse rivers to compensate for Poland's territorial losses in the east resulting from the adjusted border at the Curzon Line. In regard to Germany, the Big Three followed the Yalta agreements by dividing the country into four zones with a military governor in each, but with Germany remaining "a single economic unity." The United States did not agree to any reparations figure until the Allies could ascertain how much the Germans could pay, and it denied Stalin access to Germany's industrial wealth (located in Western zones) by authorizing each nation to exact reparations from its zone of occupation only. Truman realized that Germany was important to Europe's economic rehabilitation and he shied away from the proposals contained in the Morgenthau Plan; in fact, he had arranged Morgenthau's removal from the Treasury office. The Big Three would equally divide Germany's commercial and naval vessels among themselves, remove all vestiges of Nazism, and sponsor war crimes trials. Finally, they agreed to establish a Council of Foreign Ministers of the United States, Britain, the Soviet Union, and France, which would deal with matters not settled at Potsdam.

On July 26 the United States, Britain, and China signed the Potsdam Declaration, which repeated the Casablanca call of January 1943 for Japan's unconditional surrender. Such terms entailed disarmament, the loss of possessions acquired during the last half-century, an end to militarism, and the removal of any other obstacles to the planting of democracy. Allied occupation would last until there was "established in accordance with the freely expressed will of the Japanese people a peacefully inclined and responsible government." Though the Allies dropped thousands of leaflets over Japan warning that the alternative to surrender was destruction, Japan at first wanted to await word from the Soviet Union of possible mediation. Besides, since the Japanese had undergone bombing attacks before that were terrifying in their consequences, surely they could withstand more. Finally, the Japanese cabinet yielded to the military's pressure and informed reporters that it was adopting the posture of *mokusatsu*, a term unfortunately open to two meanings. Whereas the Tokyo government intended merely to "withhold comment" on the Potsdam Declaration, Japanese newspapers read the term as a decision to ignore the warning.

Japan's apparent rejection of unconditional surrender presented the United States with a choice: either begin a long and costly invasion of the Japanese islands, or use the newly developed atomic weapon and possibly end the war quickly and with minimal loss of American lives. Truman chose the latter course. His decision was no doubt partly attributable to the momentum resulting from the creation of the Manhattan Project and its successful culmination—a weapon designed to bring the war to a rapid close. It seemed inconceivable not to use the bomb after all the time and expense put into the program. If the bomb proved successful, the United States would also gain a stronger negotiating position in the postwar world if it could demonstrate its power, gain sole control over Japan, and end the war in Asia before Soviet entry. The president probably consid-

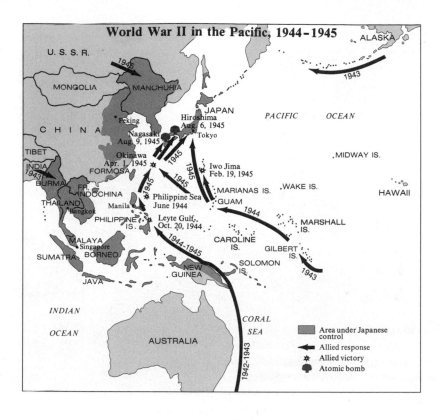

MAP 29

*After the Japanese were halted in the Battle of the Coral Sea, the Allies began a
counterattack in mid-1942 that eventually led to the dropping of atomic bombs on
Hiroshima and Nagasaki and the Japanese surrender in August 1945.*

ered these factors; certainly he recalled the bombing of Pearl Harbor. But
he insisted that his central motive in using the new weapon was to save
lives by ending the war quickly.

On August 6, four days after the close of the Potsdam Conference,
from Tinian Island in the Marianas, an American B-29 struggled into the
air shortly before 3:00 A.M. carrying a 10,000-pound bomb labeled the
"Little Boy." The commander of the *Enola Gay*, Colonel Paul Tibbets, had
as his destination the islands of Japan; on the six-hour flight, two observer planes with cameras and scientists aboard followed closely behind.
Tibbets learned from a weather plane, sent a little over an hour ahead,
that the skies were clear over Hiroshima, a city of 250,000 that was a center of war production and one of Japan's regional military headquarters.
Just above the city the *Enola Gay* released its cargo, which fell for nearly

Hiroshima, Japan

After the explosion of the atomic bomb, August 6, 1945. (U.S. Air Force)

a minute before exploding less than half a mile above the ground. At 8:15 A.M. a flash of light streaked across the sky, followed by an enormous boom and burst of heat which scattered debris nearly eight miles into the atmosphere. By the time the world's first atomic bomb had achieved full impact, over 80 percent of Hiroshima's buildings in a four-square-mile area were leveled, 80,000 lay dead, and that many more were injured. Three days later, August 9, the United States dropped a second atomic bomb on Nagasaki, virtually destroying the city and killing another 35,000.

News of the atomic destruction drew mixed reactions in Washington. Truman called it "the greatest thing in history," but Leahy was not so sure. "[I]n being the first to use it," he believed, "we had adopted the ethical standard common to the barbarians of the Dark Ages. I was not taught to make war in that fashion, and wars cannot be won by destroying women and children." Then and later, critics have argued that the administration should first have pursued peace talks; used conventional bombings and a blockade; awaited the outcome of a Soviet declaration of war on Japan; invaded Japan through the island of Kyushu; described the new bomb to Japan and offered a chance to surrender; set off a bomb in some deserted spot before an international team of observers that included Japanese representatives. Japan was so close to defeat, they asserted, that the bomb was not necessary. Defenders of the administration have countered every argument with the most telling one: America's military experts guaranteed a long war with heavy loss of life in the event of invasion. They also noted that Soviet entry would have stiffened Japan's resistance, not broken it; that there was no assurance that the explosion of a bomb in a deserted place would have had the impact of one used in a city; that it might not have detonated.

Japan had to surrender. On August 10, the day after the destruction in Nagasaki, the Japanese government agreed to the terms announced at Potsdam, but with the stipulation that the declaration "does not comprise any demand which prejudices the prerogatives of His Majesty as a Sovereign Ruler." The Allies allowed the emperor to retain his throne, but made him subject to the control of the Allied Supreme Commander. Two days earlier the Soviet Union entered the war and ordered its armies into Manchuria, Korea, and southern Sakhalin, exactly three months after the surrender of Germany and almost a week before the Kremlin signed a treaty of assistance with Nationalist China in line with the Yalta agreements. For railway and port rights in Manchuria and the maintenance of the status quo in Outer Mongolia, the Soviets agreed to help the Nationalists, promised to stay out of China's domestic affairs, and recognized China's sovereignty in Manchuria. The same day as the Russo-Chinese treaty, August 14, the Allies agreed to accept Japan's surrender. On September 2, 1945 ("V-J Day"), aboard the American battleship *Missouri* in Tokyo Bay, the Japanese formally surrendered to the Allies, under the command of General Douglas MacArthur. World War II was over.

BASES OF THE COLD WAR

One of the most far-reaching effects of the Second World War was the bipolar division between two ideologically and culturally different systems: the United States and the Soviet Union. Hitler's "greatest crime," according to Harriman, was that his collapse exposed Europe to the Russians. The Soviet Union had paid dearly in population and resources and now expected generous indemnities, full equality in international affairs, and absolute security along all borders. The war had devastated Europe and Asia, killing 35 million in Europe alone and creating millions of refugees or "displaced persons." But the most profound fact was that of those who died in Europe, 20 million were Russians.

The victors were better prepared for postwar reconstruction than they had been in 1918. The United Nations Relief and Rehabilitation Administration (UNRRA) had come into being in Washington, D.C. in November 1943, to assist the war's victims and to prevent them from turning in desperation toward totalitarian political systems such as communism. Headed by and mostly financed by the United States, UNRRA lasted until the middle of 1947 and helped more than a million displaced persons in

Europe and Asia, including those in the Soviet Union. In July 1944, 1,300 delegates from forty-four nations had attended the United Nations Monetary and Financial Conference at a mountain resort in New Hampshire called Bretton Woods, where they established the International Monetary Fund and the International Bank for Reconstruction and Development, or World Bank. Dominated by Americans, the organizations were designed to loan money for reconstruction and economic recovery that would reestablish financial stability and international trade. The United States had political objectives in these and other relief programs: economic rehabilitation was the prerequisite to promoting the stability and order vital to preventing Europe and Asia from becoming breeding grounds for communism and Soviet control. The ideal of helping those ravaged by the war was compatible with the reality of stopping the postwar spread of communism.

The two most controversial aspects of World War II were the Yalta Conference and the atomic bomb, for both were integral to the Soviet-American tensions that soon became known as Cold War. Few wartime conferences have drawn as much praise followed by such bitter condemnation as did Yalta. Critics of the conference have overlooked the unbroken antipathy between Russia and the United States that had existed since the Bolshevik Revolution of 1917, and have argued that Roosevelt's personal diplomacy instilled hope at Yalta for the postwar world that Truman destroyed by his unbending stance and unnecessary use of the bomb. Yet the truth is that hatred of Hitler was the central bond of the wartime alliance, and that the Nazis' demise in 1945 again exposed the incompatibility of capitalism and communism, of American and Soviet cultures, of the Atlantic Charter and Soviet security. Evidence lay in the mutual wartime suspicions concerning the second front and other matters; further proof rested in the unfulfilled assurances of free and democratic elections in Poland and Eastern Europe, and in the bitter disagreements over Germany. The role of diplomacy would become even more vital as the mutual needs of the war only temporarily overrode these divisive feelings.

After Yalta and before the bomb, America believed it needed Soviet entry into the Asian war and therefore approved the so-called concessions that it could not have prevented anyway. Roosevelt could not have given away either Europe or Asia because they never belonged to him. Besides, one wonders what military action the United States would have been willing and able to carry out to remove Soviet forces already in Europe, and to stop them from advancing into the Far East. The United States was not in the position to dictate terms. Churchill gave the most realistic rebuttal to critics of Yalta: "What would have happened if we had quarreled with Russia while the Germans still had three or four hundred divisions on the fighting front?" Some critics have blamed Roosevelt for calling off the American drive into Berlin for political reasons; yet it was General Eisenhower who for military reasons held back his forces at the Elbe River.

Though certainly aware of the political ramifications of such a decision, he considered it more important to bring a rapid end to the war. Eisenhower later explained that his men were in a state of exhaustion, dangerously separated from their supply line, farther from the city than were the Russians, and facing a more difficult terrain. Besides, a siege of Berlin would have taken thousands of American lives and yielded the same results as if they had not participated. Eisenhower was correct. The Soviet march into Berlin cost over 100,000 men, and afterward the United States still shared in occupying the city and country. Some observers have argued that Roosevelt should have used economic aid as a club to force political concessions; others have countered that Stalin could just as easily have made threats based on a takeover of Berlin during the Yalta proceedings. Yet the Soviet premier directed his armies to stop the thrust into the city. It is questionable why, but some believe that a major victory at this time would have raised Western fears of the Soviet Union and upset his objectives at Yalta. Britain's Sir Alexander Cadogan thought that Stalin downplayed his military successes because they "seemed to have given him the added assurance enabling him to take broad views and to be unafraid of making concessions."

Arguments also developed over the Yalta agreements relating to the Far East. It is doubtful that the Soviet Union was entitled to areas in Asia on the basis of the war with Japan in 1904–5. The Russians had been the aggressors in the period covering 1894 to 1904, and did not have a strong argument for areas belonging to China. Recognition of the Soviet Union's "preeminent interests" condoned aggression and violated America's Open Door pledges to China. Yet China did not lose territories at Yalta; *Japan* did. China actually regained sovereignty in Manchuria, whereas Outer Mongolia had been estranged from China and tipped toward Soviet hegemony for some time. Soviet assistance against Japan seemed vital in February 1945, and Americans realized there was no way short of war to dislodge the Red Armies from Europe and keep them out of Asia. Admittedly, the United States Strategic Bombing Survey declared after the war that Japan would have surrendered no later than December 31, 1945, even without Soviet entry, an invasion of Japan, and use of the atomic bomb. But Roosevelt did not know this at Yalta. Events afterward substantiated the military's fears about an invasion of Japan: Americans sustained heavy losses in taking Iwo Jima and Okinawa, islands not integrally connected with the Japanese homeland.

In 1970 Harriman offered the most incisive comment about the Yalta Conference: "If we hadn't had the Yalta agreements *we* would have been blamed for all the postwar tensions." Many arrangements of February 1945 were products of previous understandings, but so much attention had been focused on Yalta that the meeting offered impossible hopes while at the same time turning attention to the issues of war that became the bases of the Cold War. Had the Soviets adhered to the terms at Yalta, the Anglo-Americans would have limited Soviet expansion into Europe and Asia; but the Soviets realized that these conditions endangered their security. The principle of self-determination contained in the Atlantic Charter was irreconcilable with the Soviets' drive for national safety. The only resort for the United States was to make sure that the world recognized the Soviet Union as the aggressor in the postwar period. The Yalta agreements accomplished this objective. The irony is that the United States then developed a weapon of such massive force that it won the war, but drove the Soviet Union into a more aggressive drive for security through expansion. The bomb that ended World War II necessitated a United Nations organization to maintain world peace; at the same time the bomb left a legacy of Cold War.

Selected readings

Abzug, Robert H., *Inside the Vicious Heart: Americans and the Liberation of Nazi Concentration Camps.* 1985.

Alperovitz, Gar, *Atomic Diplomacy: Hiroshima and Potsdam.* 1965.

Ambrose, Stephen E., *Eisenhower.* Vol. 1, *Soldier, General of the Army, President-Elect, 1890–1952.* 1983.

———, *Rise to Globalism: American Foreign Policy Since 1938.* 4th ed. 1985.

Beaulac, Willard L., *Franco: Silent Ally in World War II.* 1986.

Beitzell, Robert, *The Uneasy Alliance: America, Britain, and Russia, 1941–1943.* 1972.

Blumenthal, Henry, *Illusion and Reality in Franco-American Diplomacy, 1914–1945.* 1986.

Buchanan, A. Russell, *The United States and World War II.* 2 vols. 1964.

Buhite, Russell D., *Decisions at Yalta: An Appraisal of Summit Diplomacy.* 1986.

———, *Patrick J. Hurley and American Foreign Policy.* 1973.

Burns, James M., *Roosevelt: The Soldier of Freedom.* 1970.

Butow, Robert J. C., *Japan's Decision to Surrender.* 1954.

———, *The John Doe Associates: Backdoor Diplomacy for Peace, 1941.* 1974.

Campbell, Thomas M., *Masquerade Peace: America's UN Policy, 1944–1945.* 1973.

Churchill, Winston S., *The Second World War.* 6 vols. 1948–1953.

Clemens, Diane S., *Yalta.* 1970.

Cohen, Warren I., *America's Response to China: An Interpretive History of Sino-American Relations.* 1971.

Cole, Wayne S., *Roosevelt and the Isolationists, 1932–1945.* 1983.

Dallek, Robert, *Franklin D. Roosevelt and American Foreign Policy, 1932–1945.* 1979.

Davis, Lynn E., *The Cold War Begins: Soviet-American Conflict over Eastern Europe.* 1974.

DeSantis, Hugh, *The Diplomacy of Silence: The American Foreign Service, the Soviet Union, and the Cold War, 1933–1947.* 1980.

Divine, Robert A., *Roosevelt and World War II.* 1969.

————, *Second Chance: The Triumph of Internationalism in America during World War II.* 1967.

Dower, John W., *War without Mercy: Race and Power in the Pacific War.* 1986.

Feingold, Henry L., *Politics of Rescue: The Roosevelt Administration and the Holocaust, 1938–1945.* 1970.

Feis, Herbert, *The Atomic Bomb and the End of World War II.* 1966. Originally published as *Japan Subdued: The Atomic Bomb and the End of the War in the Pacific.* 1961.

————, *Between War and Peace: The Potsdam Conference.* 1960.

————, *The China Tangle: The American Effort in China from Pearl Hurbor to the Marshall Mission.* 1953.

————, *Churchill, Roosevelt, Stalin.* 1957.

Ferrell, Robert H., *Harry S. Truman and the Modern American Presidency.* 1983.

Friedman, Saul S., *No Haven for the Oppressed: United States Policy toward Jewish Refugees, 1938–1945.* 1973.

Gaddis, John L., *The United States and the Origins of the Cold War, 1941–1947.* 1972.

Hathaway, Robert M., *Ambiguous Partnership: Britain and America, 1944–1947.* 1981.

Helmreich, Jonathan E., *Gathering Rare Ores: The Diplomacy of Uranium Acquisition, 1943–1954.* 1986.

Herring, George C., Jr., *Aid to Russia, 1941–1946: Strategy, Diplomacy, and the Origins of the Cold War.* 1973.

Hoyt, Edwin P., *Japan's War: The Great Pacific Conflict, 1853 to 1952.* 1986.

Hurstfield, Julian G., *America and the French Nation, 1939–1945.* 1986.

Iriye, Akira, *Power and Culture: The Japanese-American War, 1941–1945.* 1981.

Kolko, Gabriel, *The Politics of War: The World and United States Foreign Policy, 1943–1945.* 1968.

Kurzman, Dan, *Day of the Bomb: Countdown to Hiroshima.* 1986.

Langer, William L., *Our Vichy Gamble.* 1947.

Levering, Ralph B., *American Opinion and the Russian Alliance.* 1976.

Lukas, Richard C., *The Strange Allies: The United States and Poland, 1941–1945.* 1978.

Lundestad, Geir, *The American Non-Policy towards Eastern Europe, 1943–1947.* 1975.

McCann, Frank D., Jr., *The Brazilian-American Alliance, 1937–1945.* 1973.

McNeill, William H., *America, Britain, & Russia: Their Co-operation and Conflict, 1941–1946.* 1953.

Mastny, Vojtech, *Russia's Road to the Cold War: Diplomacy, Strategy, and the Politics of Communism, 1941–1945.* 1979.

Mee, Charles L., Jr., *Meeting at Potsdam.* 1975.

O'Connor, Raymond G., *Diplomacy for Victory: FDR and Unconditional Surrender.* 1971.

Sainsbury, Keith, *The Turning Point: Roosevelt, Stalin, Churchill, and Chiang-Kai-shek, 1943: The Moscow, Cairo, and Teheran Conferences.* 1985.

Schaffer, Ronald, *Wings of Judgment: American Bombing in World War II.* 1985.

Schaller, Michael, *The U.S. Crusade in China, 1938–1945.* 1979.

Sherwin, Martin J., *A World Destroyed: The Atomic Bomb and the Grand Alliance.* 1975.

Smith, Bradley F., *The Shadow Warriors: O.S.S. and the Origins of the C.I.A.* 1983.

Smith, Gaddis, *American Diplomacy during the Second World War, 1941–1945.* 2nd ed. 1985.

Snell, John L., *Illusion and Necessity: The Diplomacy of Global War, 1939–1945.* 1963.

———, ed., *The Meaning of Yalta.* 1956.

Spector, Ronald H., *Eagle against the Sun: The American War with Japan.* 1985.

Stoler, Mark A., *The Politics of the Second Front: American Military Planning and Diplomacy in Coalition Warfare, 1941–1943.* 1977.

Thorne, Christopher, *Allies of a Kind: The United States, Britain, and the War against Japan, 1941–1945.* 1978.

Tuchman, Barbara W., *Stilwell and the American Experience in China, 1911–1945.* 1970.

Wood, Bryce, *The Dismantling of the Good Neighbor Policy.* 1985.

Woods, Randall B., *The Roosevelt Foreign Policy Establishment and the Good Neighbor: The United States and Argentina, 1941–1945.* 1979.

Wyman, David S., *The Abandonment of the Jews: America and the Holocaust, 1941–1945.* 1984.

Chapter Nineteen

Cold War and Containment in Europe and the Near East, 1945–1950

The bipolar power structure of the postwar world soon contributed to the American belief that nearly every international problem emanated from the Soviet Union. Distrust between the superpowers received impetus from the clashing ideologies of capitalism and communism. Each nation constructed exaggerated images of the other's military strength until each rival perceived the other as omnipotent (especially when both nations had the bomb) and omnipresent. Their opposing ideologies took on spiritual overtones, leaving no room for compromise and apparently driving them into missions to spread their orthodoxies throughout the world. The times called for extraordinary leaders of state who could convince their counterparts that a push for security did not necessarily entail imperialist aggression. Some members of the Truman administration were aware of the Soviets' traditional drive westward and admitted to their postwar need for security along borders fronting Poland and Eastern Europe; but few were willing to retreat on the idealistic promises of the Atlantic Charter and Yalta Declaration. At the same time Stalin, a realist and nationalist rather than an ideologue committed to worldwide communist revolution, refused to endanger his people in the name of Eastern European self-determination. The Soviet Union had undergone invasion along its western frontier numerous times. Since "friendly neighbors" were unlikely to emerge from democratic elections, he was willing to use local communist movements when to his advantage. If the battle lines between East and West were not clear in the autumn of 1945, discerning observers could have predicted trouble as each power tried to satisfy its

Harry S. Truman

Among the foreign policy decisions of his administration were the Truman Doctrine, Marshall Plan, Berlin airlift, NATO, Point Four, and Korean War. (Library of Congress)

aims. By 1947 the intensification of these conflicting interests had taken the appellation of Cold War.

Fear of Soviet communist aggression stimulated American political and military intervention in postwar Europe and the Near East. By 1950 the United States had proclaimed the Truman Doctrine and Marshall Plan and joined the North Atlantic Treaty Organization. It had also approved a peacetime draft and called for an expanded military budget based on the possibility of war with the Soviet Union. The success of the atomic bomb had created a paradox: America possessed the most powerful weapon in the world, and yet the sheer destructive power of the bomb prohibited its use except in matters directly threatening the United States.

The Soviets were not equipped for full-scale aggression in the immediate postwar period. Though they had extensive ground forces in Eastern Europe and Germany, they lacked a strong navy and air force, did not have atomic weapons, and had sustained crippling economic and population losses in the war. The Soviets, therefore, resorted to means short of total war in achieving postwar objectives. Infiltration of a country through subversive methods and the use of its people as proxies —these became the hallmarks of Soviet expansion, whether for security or aggression. The primary goal was national security, which led to a series of efforts to safeguard Soviet borders that the West interpreted as territorial aggressions similar to those of the 1930s. The Soviets, hurt so badly by the war, undoubtedly had no pattern for conquest, even though Americans believed that Stalin's support of the Lublin government in Poland was the first step in a well-organized plan. The communists sought expansion, according to Americans long reared in anti-Soviet feeling and fearful of the conspiratorial and revolutionary nature of communist ideology. President Truman noted in 1947 that "there isn't any difference in totalitarian states. I don't care what you call them, Nazi, Communist, or Fascist." Tension mounted most immediately in Eastern Europe, but the center point of East-West rivalry was always Germany.

The rapid postwar demobilization of America's military forces was a vital determinant in the nation's foreign policy. Overseas troops received orders to return home soon after the fighting ended in Europe, leaving a vacuum which Washington policymakers feared the Soviets intended to fill. Americans believed that wars ended when the firing ceased, forgetting that power balances can shift as the victors tie up the loose ends of a conflict. But Americans were in no mood for further commitments. Depression followed by war had sapped their willingness to sacrifice, and foreign affairs no longer had priority. The nation sought demobilization and reconversion of the economy to peacetime production. The military was severely weakened by a policy that granted the hurried discharge of soldiers through a point system based on length of service, for it meant that battle-seasoned veterans went home first. In an address at the Pentagon in 1950, General George C. Marshall recalled the military problems facing the nation during the Cold War of the 1940s:

> I remember, when I was Secretary of State, I was being pressed constantly, particularly when in Moscow, by radio message after radio message to give the Russians hell. . . . When I got back, I was getting the same appeal in relation to the Far East and China. At that time, my facilities for giving them hell—and I am a soldier and know something about the ability to give hell—was 1⅓ divisions over the entire United States. That is quite a proposition when you deal with somebody with over 260.

For several reasons the Truman administration feared that American citizens, as during the late 1920s, would want to turn from international affairs after World War II. Such a policy at first appeared feasible. President Roosevelt had left the foundations of a United Nations organization to keep the peace, the United States held military predominance in the world primarily because of the bomb, prosperity born in war would combine with superior economic resources to enable the country to surge far ahead of others, and the Russians seemed to have changed. General Eisenhower had noted after visiting Moscow that "nothing guides Russian policy so much as a desire for friendship with the United States." Yet, ironically, diplomats had little leverage because of the destructive magni-

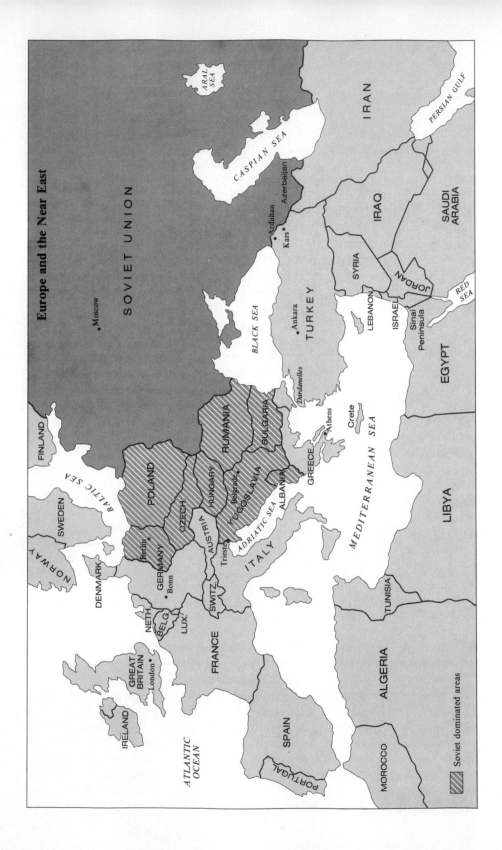

Europe and the Near East

tude of the bomb. What events could be so profoundly and directly threatening to America's security that they would justify use of the bomb? Soviet-American tension was unavoidable because of differing ideologies, cultures, and definitions of security. But, leaders of both nations realized, that tension must never lead to war. A fine line ran between toughness and aggression, between security and expansion; the times demanded careful leadership because the climate of distrust made any words susceptible to misinterpretation.

The postwar world situation almost inevitably led the United States into adopting a form of economic diplomacy that gradually became military in thrust. As in the 1930s, America's leaders argued that international trade was vital to world peace, the spread of democratic institutions, and the prevention of another postwar depression. Truman made his position clear when he declared that "the three—peace, freedom, and world trade—are inseparable." Americans would prosper, of course, from an economically open world, but most believed that such a system would benefit everyone else too. Yet war-devastated Europeans could not buy American goods. The path to peace therefore seemed to lie in an ambitious foreign aid program. By 1950, however, America's involvement in European and Near Eastern affairs had become so military in nature that almost every action taken had the potential of widening the division between East and West and intensifying the Cold War.

ONSET OF THE COLD WAR

The first Soviet-American postwar difficulties arose at a series of Council of Foreign Ministers meetings in late 1945. From September through October the ministers met in London to draw peace treaties with Italy and the other Axis states—Rumania, Bulgaria, Hungary, and Finland. Despite an agenda that related only to European matters, Soviet Foreign Commissar Molotov repeatedly raised protests against the United States's independent actions in Japan. He also wanted Italy to award the Soviet Union some territory in the Mediterranean and $100 million in reparations. America's secretary of state, James F. Byrnes, joined the British in opposing Soviet advances into the Mediterranean and in arguing that Italy's war-ravaged economy could not permit huge reparations. He also rejected any peace terms with Rumania and Bulgaria that did not require the establishment of democratic governments. Molotov refused to give assurances in the matter, defending his stance by pointing to Britain's control in Greece and to America's occupation of Japan. At one point during the proceedings, Molotov asked Byrnes if he had "an atomic bomb in his

MAP 30

These areas, and in particular the "northern tier" of Greece, Turkey, and Iran, became the focal points of the Cold War in the early part of the Truman administration.

side pocket." The South Carolinian replied, "You don't know Southerners. We carry our artillery in our hip pocket. If you don't cut out all this stalling and let us get down to work, I am going to pull an atomic bomb out of my hip pocket and let you have it." Molotov and the interpreter laughed, although Byrnes's remark suggested that Washington's policymakers were aware of the diplomatic advantages afforded by the bomb. After several attempts to deal with the German and Austrian questions, the conference ended in a deadlock.

The following December, at the Moscow Conference of Foreign Ministers, Soviet attitudes appeared to have softened. In return for Byrnes's agreement to recognize the Soviet-controlled Rumanian and Bulgarian governments and for recommending an Allied control council for Japan, Stalin accepted a more broadly based representation in Rumania and Bulgaria, promised to attend a peace conference in Paris in 1946, and consented to cooperate in the establishment of a program of international atomic supervision. The atmosphere in Moscow was less tense than in London, but Soviet behavior had made an impression on Truman. He sharply rebuked Byrnes's "appeasement policy" and claimed he had "lost his nerve in Moscow." In January 1946 Truman wrote Byrnes that he was "tired of babying the Soviets."

By early 1946 the United States's attitude toward the Soviet Union had become more rigid. Secretary of the Navy James V. Forrestal opposed any attempt to "buy understanding and sympathy" from the Russians. "We tried that once with Hitler," he remarked. Republican Senator Arthur Vandenberg of Michigan encouraged the United States to adopt a harder line toward the Soviets and recalled what happened when the West gave in to aggressors during the 1930s. In February Americans learned that a ring of spies in Canada had relayed information on atomic research to the Soviet Union.

Problems in Iran emerged as the first major issue for the newly established United Nations Organization. An Anglo-Soviet agreement in 1942 had approved the wartime occupation of Iran, with the stipulation that each force would withdraw six months after the fighting ended. In the meantime the British retained a virtual monopoly on Iranian oil production and marketing that they had held since the beginning of the century, whereas an American firm secured a small concession in 1944, prompting the Soviets to seek the same. When a communist-inspired revolution broke out in the northern province of Azerbaijan in late 1945, Moscow sent arms and troops to aid the rebels. The Iranian government worked with the United States in bringing the matter before the UN, then meeting in London. The Security Council investigated the matter and turned it over to the Soviets and Iranians to negotiate. Moscow demanded the permanent installation of its troops in Iran, control of a proposed oil company, and autonomy for Azerbaijan. Iran refused. When the deadline for the Soviets' withdrawal came and passed in March 1946, the West became alarmed that they had both increased their armies and brought in additional heavy military goods. Yet no attempt was made to overthrow the Iranian government, probably because of the opposition of the United States and the worldwide hostility toward the Soviets' actions. The Soviets pulled out of Iran in May, after securing autonomy for Azerbaijan and the assurance of oil concessions (which never materialized). The following December the United States sent aid to Iran that helped to put down unrest in Azerbaijan. Though the Soviets did not intervene, the Truman administration recognized that East-West rivalries in the Near East, as well as in Eastern Europe, could result in dangerously escalated tensions.

In the midst of the Iranian troubles, rhetorical exchanges highlighted the differences between East and West. Stalin delivered a spirited speech praising Leninist doctrine and denouncing the West, in which he argued that an inevitable clash between communism and capitalism necessitated a massive Soviet military buildup. Though he probably intended this speech for domestic consumption, Americans considered it a prelude to new Soviet aggression. Moscow began to tighten controls in Eastern Europe and at home, and launched a propaganda campaign against the United States and the West. Less than two weeks later, on February 22, the American chargé in Moscow, George F. Kennan, sent his home office

George F. Kennan

As chargé in Moscow in 1946, he wrote the "long telegram," and as a member of the State Department's Policy Planning Staff, he wrote an article entitled, "The Sources of Soviet Conduct"—both of which helped to establish him as the chief architect of America's containment policy. (Wide World)

the famous "long telegram," a sixteen-page warning that the Soviets had a "neurotic" view of the world and were "committed fanatically to the belief that with [the] US there can be no permanent modus vivendi." Their fear of "capitalist encirclement," Kennan continued, has now reasserted "the traditional and instinctive Russian sense of insecurity." Americans had to prepare a counterforce short of war to discourage Soviet expansion. The president read the telegram as did many officials in the State Department.

In March 1946 Churchill affirmed a seemingly certain East-West confrontation when he delivered a blunt warning of Soviet intentions. Before a Westminster College crowd in Fulton, Missouri, and with Truman on the dais, the British statesman dramatically proclaimed that "from Stettin in the Baltic to Trieste in the Adriatic, an iron curtain has descended across the continent." The Soviets do not want war; they seek "the fruits of war and the indefinite expansion of their power and doctrines." The only recourse was a "fraternal association of English-speaking peoples." A *Pravda* interview with Stalin soon appeared in *The New York Times*, which carried the Soviet premier's assertion that Churchill's appeal for an Anglo-American alliance was a "call to war" as dangerous in its racial implications as those of Hitler's. Surely the European nations did not want to replace the "lordship of Hitler" with the "lordship of Churchill."

Other developments pointed to worsening Soviet-American relations during the spring of 1946. The Soviets had wanted a huge loan from the United States for reconstruction purposes, but even though Secretary of Commerce Henry Wallace and Secretary of the Treasury Henry Morgenthau, Jr., favored it as a stimulus to trade and better relations, Truman opposed the measure without some reciprocal gain. The former American ambassador to the Soviet Union, W. Averell Harriman, had apparently won Truman's support by advocating foreign aid as "one of the most effective weapons at our disposal." The president later asserted that the Soviets would have to come to the United States because "we held all the cards" and should "play them as American cards." The United States had proposed new negotiations regarding Eastern Europe, along with the possibility of Soviet involvement in the World Bank, but the Soviets did not favor either idea. The first could lead to concessions to the West, and the second would entail subordination to an organization controlled by the United States. But in May the Soviets suddenly reversed their position and expressed interest in talking about Eastern Europe. Their message aroused considerable uncertainty within the Truman administration, for its advisers did not believe that Moscow was ready to retreat in Eastern Europe, and they realized that funds in the World Bank were too low to permit a major loan. The Department of State therefore turned down the Soviet proposal and promptly ended discussions of a loan. That same month the military governor of the American zone in Germany, General Lucius Clay, cut off reparations from that zone to the Soviet Union until it cooperated in furthering German economic unity. The Soviets doubtless interpreted America's rejection of the loan and the termination of German reparations as an economic offensive by the United States.

Another major contention between the United States and the Soviet Union was the proposal for international control of atomic weaponry through the Baruch Plan. The United States, Britain, and Canada had called for an international organization to regulate atomic energy, and in January 1946 the UN General Assembly responded with the formation of the Atomic Energy Commission. Less than six months later, on June 14, the American representative on the AEC, financier Bernard Baruch, proposed a series of measures that became known as the Baruch Plan. An International Atomic Development Authority was to regulate "all atomic energy activities potentially dangerous to world security" through a system of licensing and on-site inspections. Once this agency established controls, the United States would dispose of its atomic stockpile and halt further production. The United States would give up its monopoly on the atomic bomb—*after* the Soviets stopped their research and permitted on-the-spot verification. To allow the program to work, Baruch insisted on suspension of the veto in the Security Council. The choice was "World Peace or World Destruction."

Not surprisingly, the Soviet Union rejected the Baruch Plan. The Kremlin could not approve a program of international atomic control dominated by the United States, nor could it allow inspection and forgo use of the veto in such a substantive matter. The Americans, Moscow counterproposed, should destroy their atomic stockpile, agree to outlaw atomic weapons without setting up international controls, and allow the veto to apply to atomic energy matters. After months of wrangling, the Soviet delegate in the Security Council, Andrei Gromyko, declared that suspension of the veto would lead to "unlimited interference" in "the economic life of the countries on whose territories this control would be carried out, and . . . in their internal affairs." Proponents of the Baruch Plan "completely ignore national interests of other countries and proceed from . . . the interests actually of one country; that is, the United States of America."

There was little hope for international atomic energy controls. The United States could not surrender its monopoly on atomic weapons because of the strength of the Red Army; the Soviets refused to cut back on ground forces because of America's possession of the bomb. One way out of this dilemma was for the West to build up its land armies; the other was for the Soviets to develop their own atomic bomb. As for the Baruch Plan, it was dead.

By autumn of 1946 the Truman administration's growing hardline approach to Soviet affairs became increasingly evident during the controversy over Germany. The only part of the matter that East and West agreed upon was that Germany should continue to exist as a nation; beyond that, they fell out over whether its government should be democratic or communist. After the war, and consistent with the Yalta agreements, the Soviets confiscated huge amounts of foodstuffs, gathered large numbers of Germans for forced labor, and dismantled and took home entire industrial plants and other materials from their eastern zone. The Soviets failed to fulfill the Potsdam reparations agreements requiring the occupation forces to send food and supplies to the other zones, but in doing so they forced Germans outside the eastern sector to become dependent on the United States for assistance.

At Stuttgart in September, Secretary of State Byrnes repeated an earlier proposal for the economic unity of Germany, but this time he added the idea of political reunification based on a federal system of government. Thus the Germans could achieve industrial recovery, meet reparations demands, and contribute to rebuilding the European economy. After the purging of Nazism from Germany and the sentencing of war criminals at the Nuremberg trials, Americans believed that they had accomplished their objective of punishing Germany without destroying it. In line with the Potsdam accords, Germany was now to resume its place in Europe—as a democratic nation. Yet France quickly joined the Soviets in objecting to a revived Germany. Byrnes tried to allay these fears by countering that the United States would enter a four-power alliance requiring the maintenance of American troops in Germany for forty years. The Soviet Union turned down Byrnes's offer. In January 1947 the West took a step toward German unification when the United States and Britain combined their occupied areas into "Bizonia." Moscow rejected an invitation to merge its zone with theirs because, it asserted, such a move would promote the permanent partition of Germany. France likewise held back.

The Truman administration had meanwhile asked for an in-house study of the motives behind Soviet behavior and the recommended actions by the United States. The result was a report in September 1946, prepared by presidential counsel Clark Clifford, that the president considered so explosive that he gathered all copies and kept them locked away. The Clifford memorandum, drawing heavily from Kennan's ideas, advised the United States to prepare for atomic and biological warfare because of Soviet aggressions encouraged by fear of capitalist encirclement. Moreover, these Soviet aggressions would stop only if met by American counterpressure, both military and economic.

Secretary of Commerce Wallace was worried that the Truman administration's militant Soviet policies would lead to war. A former member of Roosevelt's cabinet and his vice president until January 1945, Wallace remained an ardent New Deal liberal and a strong advocate of getting along with the Soviets. In a September 1946 speech at Madison Square Garden in New York, he declared that " 'getting tough' never brought anything real and lasting—whether for schoolyard bullies or businessmen or world powers. The tougher we get, the tougher the Russians will get." The only recourse was for Americans to "get out of eastern Europe" and allow the Soviets to arrange their own security. Wallace had repeatedly criticized the new president's domestic and foreign policies, and after some confusion over whether the secretary had had prior approval to deliver the address, Truman secured his resignation. "The Reds, phonies and 'parlor pinks,'" the president recorded in his diary, "seem to be banded together and are becoming a national danger. I am afraid they are a sabotage front for Uncle Joe Stalin."

The Wallace episode suggested deep division within the administration over the direction of foreign policy, but this quickly changed in the spring of 1947 when a sharp deterioration in American-Soviet relations prompted the United States to draw the line against Soviet expansion. After another unsuccessful Council of Foreign Ministers meeting in Moscow, the focus of trouble abruptly shifted from Western and Eastern Europe to the fringe area along the top of the Mediterranean—the "northern tier" of Greece, Turkey, and Iran. Rebuffed in Iran a year earlier, the Soviets now seemed determined to stage a communist takeover in Greece and to wrest the straits from Turkey. Success in these two ventures would permit Soviet access to the Persian Gulf, the Mediterranean, and, ultimately, the entire Middle East. The alarming prospect was that Soviet hegemony in this oil-rich region would promote the collapse of Western Europe without the firing of a single shot. Greece and Turkey suddenly became the last barrier to a break in Britain's Mediterranean lifeline. The controlling power in the eastern Mediterranean would determine the fate of the World Island—that huge area adjoining the Mediterranean, the Near and Middle East, and North Africa.

FORMATION OF THE TRUMAN DOCTRINE

The Truman administration's immediate concern was Greece. That small country had been under Nazi occupation until October 1944, and then had experienced sporadic outbreaks of civil war that took on the bitterness of a vendetta. The central issue was whether Greece would remain monarchical or turn toward a democratic system of government. King George II had fled the country during the war and established a government-in-exile, first in London and then in Cairo. The British promised support in his bid to return to power after the German withdrawal, but opposition came from a communist-led guerrilla resistance group called the National Popular Liberation Army, or ELAS, and its political counterpart, the National Liberation Front, or EAM. In the period after Germany pulled out of the country, the Greek Communist party, the KKE, spoke of building a Greater Greece. But the new state meant different things to different people. To Greek nationalists, it meant territorial expansion northward and the enhancement of Greece as a nation; to hard-core communists it entailed meshing the Greeks into a Balkan federation or Macedonian free state led by Slavs. EAM/ELAS had considerable popular support as long as it sustained an image of promoting Greek interests.

Germany's withdrawal from Greece set off major fighting in the streets of Athens by December of 1944, leading the British to send troops to aid Greek national forces in putting down the communist-led rebellion and arranging an uneasy truce at Varkiza in February. Widespread apprehension had developed over whether the Soviets would help the KKE, but they did not for several reasons. As pointed out earlier, during the previous October of 1944 Stalin and Churchill had negotiated the percentages agreement in Moscow, which recognized a British sphere of interest in Greece in exchange for Soviet hegemony in Rumania. According to a contemporary, the Soviet premier opposed spontaneous, indigenous revolutions not susceptible to Moscow's control. It also seems likely that Stalin realized that Soviet interference in Greece on the eve of the Yalta Conference could have hurt his chances for achieving favorable postwar adjustments in Europe and Asia. For whatever reason or combination of reasons, he did not order the Red Army to intervene in the December uprising in Greece.

The Varkiza agreement called for a plebiscite to determine the people's will concerning the form of government, followed by the election of a constituent assembly. But during succeeding months the Athens government heated the political atmosphere by repressing opposition to the monarchy. By March 1946, when the plebiscite was scheduled to take place, the British and Americans had reversed the political procedure stipulated at Varkiza. Over KKE protests and its eventual abstention, the general elections took place first, which brought in a constituent assembly favorable to the monarchy, and in the following September a plebiscite indicated great popular support for the king's return. Americans were part of an international observer team that attested to the fairness of the elections, although the Soviet press joined the KKE and others in criticizing the outcome and labeling the British-supported government in Athens as "monarcho-fascist."

Most of the problems in Greece were of domestic origin, but the outcome of the March elections set off the civil war of 1946–49 that many Americans automatically assumed was Soviet-inspired. In August 1946 the guerrillas resumed raids on villages and towns, receiving assistance from the communist regimes in Yugoslavia, Albania, and Bulgaria. For territorial ambitions rather than ideological ties, the communist leader in Yugoslavia, Josip Broz Tito, soon furnished the bulk of the aid by providing sanctuary, material goods, and training and hospital facilities. Tito hoped to build a Balkan federation by acquiring Trieste at the top of the Adriatic Sea, and annexing part of Greece to permit access to the Mediterranean. The British, however, became convinced that aid to the guerrillas came indirectly from Moscow, and they warned Americans of the imminent collapse of Greece to communism. Though most rebels were probably Greek nationalists and not communists interested in world revolution, the West believed that communist leadership in the uprising necessarily meant links to the Kremlin. America's ambassador to Greece, Lincoln MacVeagh, warned that Yugoslavia, Albania, and Bulgaria were

Moscow's puppets and that the fall of Greece would open the Mediterranean to the Soviets. By the spring of 1947 the United States regarded Greece as the supreme test of the Free World's will.

Turkey was also part of the West's concern. Located along the Soviet border, Turkey controlled the straits connecting the Black Sea with the Mediterranean and was vital to Moscow's push for a warm water link to the Middle East. For two hundred years the Russians had wanted the straits. In the post-World War II period they sought a revision of the Montreux Convention of 1936, which had recognized Turkish control of the straits. The Soviets wanted the Dardanelles, along with Kars and Ardahan on the east side of the Black Sea, the last two of which they had lost after World War I. They were especially bitter that during World War II the Turks had allowed Germany to use the straits to enter the Black Sea and attack the Soviet Union. At Yalta Stalin declared that he could not allow Turkey to have "a hand on Russia's throat," and at Potsdam he sought to salvage the straits by opposing the United States's call for internationalization of all inland waterways. Turkey was anti-Soviet, Stalin told the American ambassador in Moscow, and control of the straits was "a matter of our security." Soon after the war Moscow launched a propaganda campaign against the Turks, and by early 1947 Soviet troops had amassed along the common border, causing a "war of nerves" and forcing the government in Ankara to appropriate sparse funds for military preparations.

The Turkish crisis of late 1946 did not surprise the United States. In the autumn of that year it had sent an aircraft carrier into the area to demonstrate support for Turkey, and had warned Moscow that any move toward the straits would cause the United States to take the issue before the UN Security Council. Truman had agreed with Undersecretary of State Dean Acheson to stand firm. "We might as well find out whether the Russians were bent on world conquest now," the president declared. The Soviets relaxed their demands, although Washington believed this only a reprieve and would not relax its vigilance. A State Department study had earlier asserted that Turkish control of the straits "constitutes the stopper in the neck of the bottle through which Soviet political and military influence could most effectively flow into the eastern Mediterranean and Middle East."

The twin crises along the northern rim of the Mediterranean merged into an American problem in February 1947, when the British government informed the United States that it was no longer financially able to maintain commitments in Greece and Turkey. On February 21 the Department of State received two notes from the British announcing an end to economic assistance in Greece and Turkey on March 31, and warning that if aid were to continue the United States would have to assume the responsibility. George C. Marshall, who had replaced Byrnes as secretary of state in January, was out of the office that Friday afternoon. The task of formulating an official reaction to the notes fell to Acheson, who recognized the

Dean Acheson

President Truman's secretary of state who became a Pulitzer-Prize winning author in 1969 for his book Present at the Creation. (National Portrait Gallery)

need to intervene in Greece and Turkey and immediately authorized a State Department policy planning group to draft a favorable response to London.

Events moved quickly in Washington. The director of the newly organized Near Eastern Affairs Division, Loy Henderson, worked with others in the State Department in writing a plan outlining American economic assistance to Greece and Turkey. From Acheson's desk the draft went before the State-War-Navy Coordinating Committee (SWNCC), which believed that economic rehabilitation in Greece could not succeed until the Athens government wound down the civil war. SWNCC therefore called for a shift in emphasis to military aid. In the meantime the Greek government followed the State Department's recommendation to make a formal request for help, and Acheson easily secured Truman's support by warning that the collapse of Greece and Turkey would open the Mediterranean to the Soviet Union. Members of Congress from both parties received invitations to the White House to join the administration in forming a bipartisan foreign policy aimed at halting a communist drive engineered by the

Army Chief of Staff General George C. Marshall Near Reggio, Italy, in February 1945

He eventually became President Truman's secretary of state and a proponent of the Marshall Plan in Europe. (U.S. Army)

Kremlin. Though the oil of the Middle East was a crucial factor in America's thinking, the administration presumed that everyone understood this and emphasized the battle with communism. Senator Arthur Vandenberg, chairman of the Foreign Relations Committee, supported the approach and warned that success in implementing such a proposal would come only if the administration engaged in a major campaign to scare the American people about the dangers of a communist takeover.

This whirlwind of activity in Washington culminated in the Truman Doctrine. Before a joint session of Congress on March 12, 1947, the president outlined the dangers in Greece and Turkey and then pointed to the bipolarity of interests in the world. He did not specify the Soviet Union as the cause of unrest in the Mediterranean world, although the allusions were unmistakable. One set of ideas was totalitarian and repressive, Truman asserted, the other democratic and supportive of freedom. Should Greece and Turkey fall to communism, the forces of oppression could stamp out freedom in the Near and Middle East. "I believe," he emphasized in the main thrust of the Truman Doctrine, "that it must be the policy of the United States to support free peoples who are resisting attempted subjugation by armed minorities or by outside pressures." To save Greece and Turkey, he called on Congress to support a military and economic aid program of $400 million, most of which would be military and would go to Greece. He also sought authorization for sending military and civilian advisers to administer the aid programs.

Considerable resistance immediately arose against what appeared to be a drastic shift in the direction of the nation's foreign policy. Marshall and George F. Kennan, recently recalled from Moscow to serve in the State Department office, later thought the anti-communist tone of the message was too severe, but the president had followed the advice of special counsel Clark Clifford in delivering a "blunt" statement of America's position on recent events along the Mediterranean. Kennan argued that there was no military threat in either Greece or Turkey, and that the Soviet challenge was primarily political; economic assistance was the main remedy. Truman's language was "grandiose" and "sweeping," and would lead to a worldwide crusade that the United States was not prepared to support. When critics inquired why the United States did not act through the United Nations, Acheson explained that the situation was an emergency, that the UN had no funds except what the United States provided, and that once the crisis had passed, the UN could assume responsibility. Vandenberg helped to ward off this criticism. He first warned Congress that failure to act would encourage a "Communist chain reaction from the Dardanelles to the China Sea and westward to the rim of the Atlantic." He then sponsored an amendment assuring Americans that the United States would retreat from its commitments to the Truman Doctrine when the UN was able to assume them. Others complained that the United States had made a blanket commitment to worldwide foreign aid which would bankrupt the country. Acheson countered that the Truman Doctrine applied specifically to Greece and Turkey, and that the administration would consider aid to other countries on their "individual merits." To other skeptics the administration admitted that neither Greece nor Turkey was democratic, but noted that those situations might change if the United States could safeguard both nations' right to choose a government. Isolationist Republican Robert Taft insisted that the United States was pulling Britain's chestnuts out of the fire; Acheson responded that whatever happened in Greece and Turkey affected America's interests.

The arguments continued for weeks, but in May 1947 Congress approved the Greek-Turkish Aid bills, and by that autumn American aid was en route to both countries.

By the summer of 1947 the United States had moved toward a more cohesive foreign policy that gradually became known as containment, and that was based in part on Kennan's theories of attempting to thwart Soviet expansion through any means short of war. In July he expanded his ideas in an anonymously written article for *Foreign Affairs* magazine which he entitled, "The Sources of Soviet Conduct." Signing it "X," Kennan warned that the basis of Stalin's behavior was Marxist-Leninist ideology combined with his exploitation of the Soviets' fear of "capitalist encirclement" in mobilizing the people behind his policies. The Kremlin was in no hurry to achieve world conquest. Its "political action is a fluid stream which moves constantly, wherever it is permitted to move, toward a given goal." The only solution was "a long-term, patient but firm and vigilant containment." The United States had to counter the Soviets "at a series of constantly shifting geographical and political points, corresponding to the shifts and maneuvers of Soviet policy." Such an American policy might lead to "either the breakup or the gradual mellowing of Soviet power." Kennan did not clarify whether he meant containment through military or economic means. The result was that policymakers would interpret his writings as a warning that all over the world the Soviets intended to instigate crises designed to enhance the spread of communist ideology, and that the United States had to be militarily ready to halt this new form of aggression wherever it occurred.

The same month that Kennan's article appeared, Congress left little doubt about the direction of America's foreign policy when it passed the National Security Act. It gave statutory sanction to the Joint Chiefs of Staff, and established a National Security Council to advise the president, a secretary of defense to replace the secretary of war and to coordinate control over the nation's armed forces, and a Central Intelligence Agency to gather and analyze intelligence at home. An amendment to the act in 1949 created the Department of Defense, and the CIA's activities were later expanded to include covert operations outside the country. Containment, whether by military or economic means, or both, became the guiding principle of the administration's foreign policy.

Columnist Walter Lippmann was among more than a few Americans who were not pleased with the doctrine of containment. He warned that it would lead to a worldwide ideological crusade because it failed to delineate which areas sought by the Soviets were of vital importance to the United States. In addition, Lippmann believed, Stalin was motivated more by historic Soviet expansionist aims than by communist ideology. The real issue was a balance of power. The United States should confront the Soviets with naval bases in the eastern Mediterranean, along with other visible signs of American strength. There was danger in attempting to stop Soviet expansion with "dispersed American power in the service of a heterogeneous collection of unstable governments and of contending parties and factions which happen to be opposed to the Soviet Union." Such a policy would harden the Soviet military presence in Europe while draining America's resources and will. It presumed Soviet involvement in all of Europe and Asia, which in turn was dependent upon the questionable premises that Moscow had the ability to coordinate its own foreign policy as well as to mold that of its allies. The solution was for Washington and Moscow to arrange a mutual withdrawal of military forces from Central Europe and thus defuse the dangerous situation. Containment, Lippmann concluded, was a "strategic monstrosity."

The Truman Doctrine meanwhile stabilized Greece and Turkey, appearing to establish the credibility of America's containment policy. Nearly 300 American military and civilian advisers and a host of support personnel offered advisory assistance to the Greek National Army in its war against the guerrillas. American advice and firepower were essential, although Tito's independent posture in the communist world caused a rift between Yugoslavia and the Soviet Union that was also important in winding down the civil war in Greece. A year after Tito defected from the Communist Information Bureau (Cominform) in July 1948, he closed the border to Greek guerrillas and cut off assistance. The guerrillas had to raid and pillage the Greek countryside for provisions and to seize hostages as military inductees. Popular resistance to their methods grew, leading to increased support for the king. Though the war had at first gone so badly for the Greek government that some officials in Washington considered sending American troops, in October 1949 the royalist forces finally scattered the guerrillas into the northern mountains of Greece or into Albania, and the fighting came to an end. The crisis likewise passed in Turkey as America's military assistance bolstered the country against Soviet pressure. Both successes were fortuitous, for in May 1948 the United States had extended recognition to the new Jewish state of Israel (discussed in a later chapter), whose creation set off the first of many crises in the Middle East. For the time being, however, containment seemed to have yielded a monumental success in the Near East, and hence in the Cold War. At the same time, the results encouraged Americans to attribute problems in other countries to a huge monolithic or singularly directed form of communism emanating from the Kremlin, and not to difficulties arising from within the countries. The forecast was deepening American involvement in foreign affairs.

HEIGHTENING OF THE COLD WAR

While the Truman Doctrine was under way, the administration turned toward resolving the economic problems in Europe left by the war. Europe, Churchill lamented, was "a rubble heap, a charnel house, a breeding ground of pestilence and hate." Despite billions of dollars of American assistance through the United Nations Relief and Rehabilitation Administration (UNRRA) and other organizations by mid-1947, Europe lay open to despair, revolution, and totalitarian exploitation, particularly in France and Italy where local Communist parties were strong. Furthermore, the

United States had withdrawn from UNRRA in 1946 because of charges that communist Eastern European nations were distributing food only to political allies. The last American aid installments arrived the following year, forcing an end to UNRRA and highlighting the desire of Americans, in Acheson's words, to extend relief "in accordance with our judgment and supervised with American personnel." The central dilemma was that no recovery could take place in Europe without Germany being an integral part of that recovery. And that entailed further alienation of the Soviet Union.

In the spring of 1947, after a frustrating Council of Foreign Ministers' conference in Moscow, Secretary of State Marshall visited Western Europe and was visibly shaken by the devastation. Europeans were unable to buy American products, the drought of 1946 had almost wiped out the grain crop, and the winter of 1946–47 had brought heavy snowstorms followed by spring floods, threatening the next year's yield and raising the possibility of famine across the continent. Coal was reserved for emergency use only in England, where officials had ordered brief daily shutdowns of electricity to save the diminishing supply. Communist party victories in the elections in France and Italy would mean that for a second time within the decade, Britain would stand alone. In exchange for Britain's relaxation of commercial restrictions, the United States had approved a loan of $4.4 billion in July 1946, but even this was not enough to stave off impending disaster. Upon Marshall's return to Washington he instructed Kennan, now head of the State Department's new Policy Planning Staff, to prepare a study of the European situation and recommend a policy promoting relief and recovery.

At Harvard University's commencement ceremony on June 5, 1947, the secretary of state delivered an address on European affairs that became the essence of the Marshall Plan. Partly basing his remarks on Kennan's report, Marshall lamented the "economic, social, and political deterioration" of Europe and warned that the situation was conducive to political instability and the obstruction of peace. Kennan had earlier argued that "world communism is like a malignant parasite which feeds only on diseased tissue." Marshall now expressed this thought, which had become the prevailing view in the State Department. Following the stand advocated by Undersecretary of State for Economic Affairs William L. Clayton, Marshall called upon all of the European governments—East and West—to draw up a mutual aid program and inform the United States how it could contribute to their recovery. "The initiative," he emphasized, "must come from Europe."

To avoid antagonizing the Soviets, Marshall later insisted, the United States could not distinguish between the forms of government receiving assistance. "Our policy is directed not against any country or doctrine but against hunger, poverty, desperation, and chaos." As Acheson noted in an earlier speech in Mississippi, the problems were common to all Europeans. Such a stance, however, raised fears that American money might go to communist Eastern Europe and even to the Soviet Union. This was unlikely, according to Kennan and Charles E. Bohlen, principal writer of Marshall's Harvard address and later ambassador to Moscow. The Soviets, Kennan believed, could not accept America's help, especially when the stipulation for receiving aid included participation by the United States in planning the recipient's economy, and full disclosure of that government's files to verify need. However, everyone realized that if Moscow accepted the American invitation and Congress refused to approve an aid bill, the United States would suffer a serious propaganda defeat.

Marshall's offer of economic assistance caused a flurry of activity in Europe. In late June British Foreign Secretary Ernest Bevin met in Paris with French Foreign Minister Georges Bidault, and after considerable discussion they decided to invite Soviet Foreign Commissar Molotov to join them. Molotov hesitated to attend, even though he doubtless realized that failure to do so would increase the chances of a Western alliance; yet if the Soviet Union became part of that bloc, its allied states would be susceptible to Western penetration. American money, Molotov feared, might draw Eastern Europe toward the West, revive Germany, and endanger Soviet military security. Although disgruntled by the situation, he finally accepted the invitation. Accompanied by eighty-nine economic advisers and clerks, Molotov attended the meeting in Paris, where he soon termed the aid proposal a "new venture in American imperialism" and objected to nearly every aspect of the program. He opposed American control over reconstruction and wanted a decentralized approach to preserve the integrity of each participant. He did not want a combined list of goods needed; each government should compile its own list and send it to the United States. Bevin and Bidault disagreed. The following day Molotov warned them not to act without Soviet approval. His arguments had little effect. Bevin and Bidault would not accept these stipulations and Molotov stalked out of the conference.

After Molotov's departure, France and Britain invited over twenty European governments to Paris to draft a proposal for aid from the United States. Those governments under Soviet influence—Yugoslavia, Albania, Bulgaria, Poland, Rumania, Czechoslovakia, Hungary, and Finland—either did not attend, or turned down assistance on the basis that the aid program constituted an "imperialist" conspiracy. There is reason to believe that Poland and Czechoslovakia rejected American aid with great reluctance. Both had shown interest in participating but changed their minds because, they declared, acceptance "might be construed as an action against the Soviet Union." By September, sixteen Western European governments requested a four-year allotment of $22 billion of assistance aimed at bringing economic stability to the continent by 1951.

The Soviet Union tried several tactics to lessen the impact of the proposed Marshall Plan. It negotiated defense pacts with Finland, Bulgaria, Hungary, and Rumania, which were additions to those already signed with Poland, Czechoslovakia, and Yugoslavia. It rigged elections in Hungary to assure communist victory. In early October 1947 Molotov arranged the establishment of the Cominform in Belgrade, a nine-member organization which succeeded the Comintern dissolved four years earlier, and now attempted to disrupt American influence in Europe. Moscow also announced the Molotov Plan, a series of bilateral treaties promising Soviet economic assistance to communist governments in Europe. Strikes broke out in Italy and France, which apparently were communist efforts to destroy faith in those governments and prevent them from becoming recipients of Marshall Plan aid.

In January 1948, shortly after another abortive Council of Foreign Ministers meeting in London, Truman sparked a lively debate over the European aid bill when he asked Congress to appropriate $6.8 billion for fifteen months, followed by over $10 billion during the next three years. The purpose, he stated, was to "contribute to world peace and to its own security by assisting in the recovery of sixteen countries which, like the United States, are devoted to the preservation of the free institutions and enduring peace among nations." Economic and political stability in Europe meant trade for the United States and a halt to the spread of communism. Wallace, already ousted from the administration over a policy dispute, called it a "Martial Plan," and Senator Taft denounced the program as a "European T.V.A." Too much money had already gone overseas, many charged, and such a program might worsen American-Soviet relations and further divide Europe into hostile camps.

It quickly became evident that Congress would approve the aid program. Among its supporters were farmers, laborers, manufacturers, and the press. The situation in Czechoslovakia promoted the bill's passage when, in an action reminiscent of the Munich crisis of 1938–39, the communists overthrew the republic in February and installed a regime tied to the Kremlin. The death of Czech Foreign Minister Jan Masaryk, reported as suicide though attributed by Truman to "foul play," especially appalled the West. Other inducements to congressional support of the Marshall Plan were the forced Russo-Finnish alliance, the expected communist victory in the impending elections in Italy, and rising tensions in Germany. General Clay in Berlin noted a "new tenseness in every Soviet individual with whom we have official relations." War "may come with dramatic suddenness." The Senate approved the aid bill by a wide margin, and as it went to the House, Truman delivered a speech to Congress calling for a universal military training program and resumption of the selective service.

In March 1948 the House of Representatives overwhelmingly approved the Economic Cooperation Act (ECA), or Marshall Plan, which became a prime example of the administration's containment policy. The act established the European Recovery Program, which eventually provided over $12 billion of assistance by its termination date of 1952. Congress also restored selective service, and even though it rejected universal military training, it strengthened the air force. In the meantime the European governments, as members of the Organization of European Economic Cooperation (OEEC), prepared to receive American aid.

The Marshall Plan, which the president signed into law on April 3, was a combination of ideal and reality. While attempting to help Europe for humanitarian reasons, it sought to halt the spread of communism. By extending credits to Europeans to purchase American goods, the United States hoped to restore order to the continent, prevent communist takeover, enhance American prestige, and promote economic growth. The program was primarily a success. It perhaps affected the elections in Italy, which the communists lost. Europe moved toward economic recovery, although it did not become commercially interdependent; cartels and other obstacles to trade remained. In addition, the Marshall Plan, like the Truman Doctrine, became heavily military in character. When it ended in 1952, 80 percent of its assistance had become military, partly stemming from the fears caused by the Korean War beginning in 1950, and partly from the decision of 1951 to merge the ECA with the Military Defense Aid Program, which became the Mutual Security Program in 1952 and continued to distribute funds to Europe. The successes of the Marshall Plan bore mixed results, however: the aid program drove the wedge deeper between East and West by helping to reconstruct Germany and encouraging Moscow to clamp down on Eastern Europe.

The Marshall Plan contributed to the Soviets' fear of a reunified Germany and helped bring on a crisis in Berlin during the summer of 1948. The city lay less than a hundred miles within the Soviet zone of occupation, landlocked from the West though guaranteed access by air. France had recently joined its occupation forces with those of the United States and Britain in creating "Trizonia," which they believed might save the country's economy, but which the Soviets feared would lead to the West's ultimate absorption of their eastern zone. The German economy was in dire shape. The reichsmark was so inflated that American cigarettes had become a medium of exchange. Food supplies and steel production were down, relief costs were rising, and the Communist party was becoming stronger. The Western governments had met in London that spring and recommended that the Germans elect a constitutional convention to establish a government for the western section of Germany. They had also instituted changes in the currency system designed to ease the inflationary spiral and promote economic reunification.

In early June the West established the West German Republic, while the Joint Chiefs of Staff in the United States urged the Truman administration to seek a military alliance with Western European countries that would include the use of German troops. Though the Council of Foreign Ministers had repeatedly failed to resolve the German unification question, the growing economic unity of the West's three zones increased the likelihood of a self-governing West Germany. In the spring of 1948 representatives of the United States, Britain, France, Belgium, Luxembourg, and the Netherlands gathered in London to establish a government in West Germany. The Ruhr industries would still be under their supervision, in cooperation with the West Germans. Residents of West Germany would elect a parliament, which would draft a constitution for a federal government inviting East German membership. To alleviate fears of a re-armed Germany, the United States and others would maintain restrictions on West Germany's foreign activities, prevent rearmament, and terminate foreign occupation only when calm returned to Europe. The wisest approach for the time being was to secure a defense alignment with Western Europe that did not include Germany, while working toward the independence of that country's western zones.

There were precedents in the Western Hemisphere for collective defense arrangements. In August 1947 representatives of the United States had attended a conference in Rio de Janeiro which established a regional defense agreement, encouraged multilateral status for the Monroe Doctrine, and assured help to any American republic under armed assault until the UN Security Council could act. The Inter-American Treaty of Mutual Assistance of September, or Rio Pact, fulfilled the intentions of Article 51 of the UN Charter by providing collective security in the hemisphere. In early 1948 Marshall sought a treaty against communism when he led an American delegation to the Ninth International Conference of American States at Bogotá, Colombia. Street riots, rumored to be communist-inspired, temporarily disrupted the conference and underscored the need for an agreement. After a temporary adjournment necessitated by the violence, the Latin American republics returned to ally against communism in another regional defense pact—the Organization of American States (OAS), which went into effect in 1951.

The United States meanwhile continued to work toward a military pact in Europe. In March 1948 Britain, France, Belgium, Luxembourg, and the Netherlands signed the Brussels Treaty, which established a fifty-year collective defense system known as Western Union, and shortly afterward Truman called on Congress to support the pact. In June the U.S. Senate overwhelmingly approved the Vandenberg resolution, which called for America's cooperation "with such regional and other collective arrangements as are based on continuous and effective self-help and mutual aid, and as affect its national security." The United States, the resolution continued, should make known "its determination to exercise the right of individual or collective self-defense under article 51 [of the UN Charter] should any armed attack occur affecting its national security."

By the summer of 1948 the West's new measures seemed to threaten Moscow, driving Soviet foreign policy into disarray. Western European nations were banding together under the Marshall Plan and had moved closer to a military alliance with the United States. An independent West Germany necessarily meant its eventual incorporation into a military organization opposed to the Soviets. American economic assistance had already gone to Yugoslavia, whose communist regime under Tito had left the communist bloc and revealed a crack in the assumed monolith. With Germany revived, Western Europe strengthened and unified, and Eastern Europe perhaps loosening its loyalties to Moscow, the security of the Soviet Union came into question.

That same June of 1948 the United States faced another major test of containment—the Soviets blockaded Berlin in an effort to force Allied evacuation of the city and dangerously reduce America's influence in Europe. With no pact guaranteeing land or water connections, it seemed that the West either had to pull out of Berlin, or use force to open the surface routes. The American military governor, General Clay, had warned the Pentagon in early April that "when Berlin falls, Western Germany will be next. If we mean . . . to hold Europe against communism, we must not budge. . . . If we withdraw, our position in Europe is threatened. If America does not understand this now, then it never will and communism will run rampant. I believe the future of democracy requires us to stay." The Soviet action was a bluff, Clay believed; the United States should test the blockade by ordering an armed convoy into Berlin.

But Truman, realizing that the Red Army held a ten-to-one advantage in Europe, rejected the use of force and instead decided upon a massive airlift, carried out in conjunction with the British and designed to deliver supplies into the western part of the city. No questions could arise about its legality, for the Allied Control Council had earlier authorized the establishment of three air lanes connecting West Germany with Berlin. By the spring of 1949 the Anglo-American airlift, occasionally harassed but never attacked by Soviet planes, had provided over 13,000 tons of goods per day, enough to meet the needs of Americans plus the city's other 2,500,000 residents. From the beginning of the airlift in late June 1948, each citizen in West Berlin received more than half a ton of supplies from planes arriving daily at three-minute intervals.

THE NORTH ATLANTIC TREATY ORGANIZATION AND NSC-68

The ongoing Berlin crisis was an important stimulus to the formation of a European defense pact, and on April 4, 1949, twelve nations assembled in Washington, D.C. to sign the North Atlantic Treaty. The United States, Britain, Canada, France, Italy, Belgium, Luxembourg, Norway, Denmark, Iceland, Portugal, and the Netherlands became charter members of the North Atlantic Treaty Organization (NATO), whose membership grew to fifteen by the mid-1950s with the additions of Greece, Turkey, and West Germany. Unlike the Rio Pact of 1947, NATO was a military alliance of permanent duration, combining signatories "by means of continuous and effective self-help and mutual aid." Article 5 of the treaty of 1949 declared that "an armed attack against one or more [signatory nations] . . . shall be considered an attack against them all," and promised "such action as it deems necessary, including the use of armed force." The United States alone possessed atomic weapons, and NATO had the Strategic Air Command (SAC) with its long-range bombers. Direction of the new organization would come through the North Atlantic Council, comprised of the foreign, defense, and finance ministers of member nations.

The ensuing debate over America's membership in NATO raised familiar arguments. Critics warned against involvement in European wars and impending bankruptcy caused by foreign commitments. Taft claimed that NATO would cause an arms race and, in an argument remindful of the Lodge-Wilson fight over the League of Nations, he declared that the pact would tie American soldiers to Europe without constitutional sanction. Advocates of NATO countered that the pact contained no provisions for mandatory military action, that America had vital interests in Europe's security, and that Soviet attack was unlikely, largely because only the United States had the bomb. Acheson, now secretary of state after Marshall's resignation in January 1949, assured the Senate that membership in NATO did not require America to commit more ground forces to Europe; the new system constituted a warning to the Soviets that NATO and the American presence would have a "tripwire" effect which would generate a nuclear response in an extremity.

The success of the Berlin airlift and the establishment of NATO forced the Soviets to call off the blockade in May 1949, giving the West a major victory in the Cold War and at the same time catalyzing the movement for a collective security system in Europe. Anxious moments had not led to a military confrontation; the United States had acted calmly, legally, and with resolution; and world public opinion had meanwhile judged the Soviet Union to be in the wrong. In exchange for the Soviet retreat, the United States agreed to attend another Council of Foreign Ministers meeting in Paris later that month. Though the conference led to no agreements on Germany, Soviet actions in Berlin had solidified the West German Republic and encouraged America to join the European defense system.

The U.S. Senate approved America's membership in NATO by a wide margin on July 21, 1949, and two days later the president signed the agreement. That same day he sent Congress the Mutual Defense Assistance Bill, which sought a one-year appropriation of $1.5 billion to revamp and expand Europe's military strength. Thus NATO provided an alternative to America's use of the bomb in deterring Soviet aggression. At the same time America's pledge to use the bomb secured its much-needed European bases for B-29 bombers. Vandenberg considered NATO "the most important step in American foreign policy since the promulgation of the Monroe Doctrine." Indeed, the United States had joined its first entangling alliance in Europe since the treaty with France in 1778, and its first formal military alliance in peacetime. It had also become part of a military organization which hardened the divisions of the Cold War.

Another objective of the Truman administration's European policy was to win Allied support for rearming West Germany and making it part of NATO's military force. The organization needed Germany's industrial resources and manpower, although France and the Benelux nations remained concerned about their longtime enemy. West Germany had 50 million people and had begun economic and political recovery. It now seemed on the verge of a military buildup. In September 1949 Trizonia became West Germany, or the German Federal Republic, with its capital at Bonn and under the chancellorship of Konrad Adenauer. The government was civilian in orientation, although Allied military occupation continued under a High Commission of three members, one each from the Western occupying powers. As noted earlier, the United States approved Marshall Plan assistance for the new republic and agreed to participate in the international administration of the Ruhr Valley.

The movement for West German military integration into NATO received a sudden boost in late September 1949, when Truman stunned the American people by announcing that the Soviet Union had exploded an atomic bomb—ten years earlier than some experts had predicted. While this development unsettled Americans at home, it also severely weakened the central bond of NATO: America's atomic monopoly. The following month the Soviets announced the formation of the German Democratic Republic of East Germany. Two Germanies and two Berlins—each trying to absorb the other—became symbols of the East-West struggle for Europe. Western Europe's hatred for Germany, the Truman administration was convinced, would have to give way to the immediate need of halting further Soviet advances across the continent. NATO required the integration of West German soldiers to balance the strength of the Red Army.

Prevailing thought in Washington dictated that with the East and West in atomic deadlock, the United States would have to contain Soviet infiltration and control of potential new nations and their resources. In the president's inaugural address of January 1949, he had outlined his foreign policy objectives: support for the UN, the Marshall Plan, "freedom-loving nations," and, the fourth point, "a bold new program for making the benefits of our scientific advances and industrial progress available for the improvement and growth of underdeveloped areas." The last, a Technical Assistance Program for Latin America, Asia, and Africa, became known as Point Four. It aimed at combating "hunger, misery, and despair," and thus preventing the spread of communism into the southern half of the globe. Congress implemented Point Four in 1950 by allocating the modest sum of $35 million for technical aid and placing the program under the Technical Cooperation Administration. Despite the dearth of funds, the United States soon negotiated agreements with more than thirty countries and helped fight disease and famine while raising living standards through the building of facilities for hydroelectric power and irrigation. Less than a week after the president called for Point Four, the Soviets established a Council for Mutual Economic Assistance, designed to help their fellow communist states.

By 1950 the United States's emphasis in foreign aid had shifted dramatically from economic to military assistance. The Truman Doctrine had proved SWNCC to be correct: crushing the rebellion in Greece *was* the necessary prerequisite to the economic rehabilitation of the country. Marshall Plan aid gradually became more military in orientation. The Soviets' explosion of an atomic device, and the victory of the communist forces in China shortly afterward, seemed too close in time to be coincidental. In January 1950 the president ordered the development of a hydrogen bomb that would be hundreds of times more powerful than either bomb used on Japan. Whereas the atomic bomb resulted from splitting uranium and plutonium, the hydrogen bomb (or "Super") was derived from the formation of helium by fusing light elements of hydrogen and thereby releasing tremendous explosive energy. America's priorities had become unmistakably military with the establishment of NATO, for that organization's stated purpose was to maintain a ground force large enough to hold off Soviet attack until the United States could engage the Strategic Air Command. Yet NATO's conventional land forces never became as large as hoped, for America's European allies seemed satisfied to remain under free nuclear protection while continuing to block the use of West German troops.

In late January 1950 Truman directed the Departments of State and Defense "to make an overall review and reassessment of American foreign and defense policy in the light of the loss of China, the Soviet mastery of atomic energy and the prospect of the fusion bomb." There was no foreseeable end to the communist threat, according to the resulting National Security Council Study #68 which the president signed in April. As Acheson later noted, the top secret document "combined the ideology of communist doctrine and the power of the Russian state into an aggressive expansionist drive, which found its chief opponent, and, therefore, target in the antithetical ideas and power of our own country." The Free World faced danger from a "combination of ideological zeal and fighting power."

NSC-68 urged the United States to "strike out on a bold and massive program of rebuilding the West's defensive potential to surpass that of the Soviet world, and of meeting each fresh challenge promptly and unequivocally." Americans were to defend the noncommunists from Soviet encroachments through a military-oriented, activist policy of containment. Such an objective necessitated expenditures almost four times what they were to be in 1950. NSC-68, not declassified until the mid-1970s (and even then by accident), had defined the world's problems in the broad terms of communism versus democracy, and had called on the United States to take the lead in restoring world stability and halting communism. No longer was there a distinction between the security of the United States and that of the world; they had meshed. But before the Truman administration could decide how to implement these recommendations, justification for a military buildup suddenly appeared in June 1950, when war broke out in Korea.

Selected readings

Acheson, Dean, *Present at the Creation: My Years in the State Department*. 1969.

Alexander, G.M., *The Prelude to the Truman Doctrine: British Policy in Greece, 1944–1947*. 1982.

Ambrose, Stephen E., *Rise to Globalism: American Foreign Policy since 1938*. 4th ed. 1985.

Anderson, Irvine H., *Aramco, The United States, and Saudi Arabia: A Study of the Dynamics of Foreign Oil Policy, 1933–1950*. 1981.

Anderson, Terry H., *The United States, Great Britain, and the Cold War, 1944–1947*. 1981.

Boll, Michael M., *Cold War in the Balkans: American Foreign Policy and the Emergence of Communist Bulgaria, 1943–1947*. 1984.

Browder, Robert P., and Thomas G. Smith, *Independent: A Biography of Lewis W. Douglas*. 1986.

Byrnes, James F., *All in One Lifetime*. 1958.

———, *Speaking Frankly*. 1947.

Campbell, Thomas M., *Masquerade Peace: America's UN Policy*. 1973.

DeSantis, Hugh, *The Diplomacy of Silence: The American Foreign Service, the Soviet Union, and the Cold War, 1933–1947*. 1980.

Doenecke, Justus D., *Not to the Swift: The Old Isolationists in the Cold War Era*. 1979.

Donovan, John C., *The Cold Warriors*. 1974.

Donovan, Robert J., *Conflict and Crisis: The Presidency of Harry S Truman, 1945–1948*. 1977.

———, *Tumultuous Years: The Presidency of Harry S Truman, 1949–1953*. 1982.

Dozer, Donald, *Are We Good Neighbors?* 1961.

Feis, Herbert, *From Trust to Terror: The Onset of the Cold War, 1945–1950*. 1970.

Ferrell, Robert H., *Harry S. Truman and the Modern American Presidency*. 1983.

Freeland, Richard, *The Truman Doctrine and the Origins of McCarthyism*. 1971.

Gaddis, John L., *Strategies of Containment: A Critical Appraisal of Postwar American National Security Policy*. 1982.

————, *The United States and the Origins of the Cold War, 1941–1947*. 1972.

Gardner, Lloyd C., *Architects of Illusion: Men and Ideas in American Foreign Policy, 1941–1949*. 1970.

Gimbel, John, *The American Occupation of Germany*. 1968.

————, *The Origins of the Marshall Plan*. 1976.

Goldman, Eric F., *The Crucial Decade and After*. 1960.

Green, David, *The Containment of Latin America: A History of the Myths and Realities of the Good Neighbor Policy*. 1971.

Harbutt, Fraser J., *The Iron Curtain: Churchill, America, and the Origins of the Cold War*. 1986.

Hathaway, Robert M., *Ambiguous Partnership: Britain and America, 1944–1947*. 1981.

Haynes, Richard F., *The Awesome Power: Harry S. Truman as Commander-in-Chief*. 1983.

Herken, Gregg, *Counsels of War*. 1985.

————, *The Winning Weapon: The Atomic Bomb in the Cold War, 1945–1950*. 1980.

Hogan, Michael J., *The Marshall Plan: America, Britain, and the Reconstruction of Western Europe*. 1987.

Iatrides, John O., *Revolt in Athens: The Greek Communist "Second Round," 1944–1945*. 1972.

Ireland, Timothy P., *Creating the Entangling Alliance: The Origins of NATO*. 1981.

Jenkins, Roy, *Truman*. 1986.

Jones, Joseph, *The Fifteen Weeks*. 1955.

Kaplan, Lawrence S., *A Community of Interests: NATO and the Military Assistance Program, 1948–1951*. 1980.

————, *The United States and NATO: The Formative Years*. 1984.

Kennan, George F., *American Diplomacy*. Expanded ed. 1984. Originally published as *American Diplomacy, 1900–1950*. 1951.

Kolko, Joyce, and Gabriel Kolko, *The Limits of Power: The World and United States Foreign Policy, 1945–1954*. 1972.

Kuklick, Bruce, *American Policy and the Division of Germany: The Clash with Russia over Reparations*. 1972.

Kuniholm, Bruce R., *The Origins of the Cold War in the Near East: Great Power Conflict and Diplomacy in Iran, Turkey, and Greece*. 1980.

LaFeber, Walter, *America, Russia, and the Cold War, 1945–1984*. 5th ed. 1985.

Larson, Deborah W., *Origins of Containment: A Psychological Explanation*. 1985.

Lees, Lorraine M., "The American Decision to Assist Tito, 1948–1949," *Diplomatic History* 2 (1978): 407–22.

Leffler, Melvyn P., "The American Conception of National Security and the Beginnings of the Cold War, 1945–48," *American Historical Review* 89 (1984): 346–81.

————, "Strategy, Diplomacy, and the Cold War: The United States, Turkey, and NATO, 1945–1952," *Journal of American History* 71 (1985): 807–25.

Leonard, Thomas M., *The United States and Central America, 1944–1949: Perceptions of Political Dynamics*. 1984.

Loescher, Gil, and John A. Scanlan, *Calculated Kindness: Refugees and America's Half-Open Door, 1945 to the Present*. 1986.

Lukas, Richard C., *Bitter Legacy: Polish-American Relations in the Wake of World War II*. 1982.

Lundestad, Geir, *The American Non-Policy towards Eastern Europe, 1943–1947*. 1975.

McFarland, Stephen L., "A Peripheral View of the Origins of the Cold War: The Crises in Iran, 1941–47," *Diplomatic History* 4 (1980): 333–51.

Mastny, Vojtech, *Russia's Road to the Cold War: Diplomacy, Strategy, and the Politics of Communism, 1941–1945*. 1979.

Mayers, David A., *Cracking the Monolith: U.S. Policy Against the Sino-Soviet Alliance, 1949–1955*. 1986.

Mazuzan, George T., *Warren R. Austin at the U.N., 1946–1953*. 1977.

Robert L. Messer, *The End of an Alliance: James F. Byrnes, Roosevelt, Truman, and the Origins of the Cold War*. 1982.

Miller, Aaron D., *Search for Security: Saudi Arabian Oil and American Foreign Policy, 1939–1949*. 1980.

Miller, James E., *The United States and Italy, 1940–1950: The Politics and Diplomacy of Stabilization*. 1986.

Nelson, Anna K., "President Truman and the Evolution of the National Security Council," *Journal of American History* 72 (1985): 360–78.

Osgood, Robert E., *NATO: The Entangling Alliance*. 1962.

Patterson, Thomas G., *On Every Front: The Making of the Cold War*. 1979.

———, *Soviet-American Confrontation: Postwar Reconstruction and the Origins of the Cold War*. 1973.

Patterson, James T., *Mr. Republican: A Biography of Robert Taft*. 1972.

Pfau, Richard, "Containment in Iran, 1946: The Shift to an Active Policy," *Diplomatic History* 1 (1977): 359–72.

Pollard, Robert A., *Economic Security and the Origins of the Cold War, 1945–1950*. 1985.

Randall, Stephen J., *United States Foreign Oil Policy, 1919–1948: For Profits and Security*. 1985.

Ranelagh, John, *The Agency: The Rise and Fall of the CIA*. 1986.

Raucher, Alan R., *Paul G. Hoffman: Architect of Foreign Aid*. 1986.

Rearden, Steven L., *History of the Office of the Secretary of Defense*. Vol. 1, *The Formative Years, 1947–1950*. 1984.

Reid, Escott, *Time of Fear and Hope: The Making of the North Atlantic Treaty, 1947–1949*. 1977.

Rose, Lisle A., *After Yalta*. 1973.

Schlaim, Avi, *The United States and the Berlin Blockade, 1948–1949: A Study in Crisis Decision-Making*. 1983.

Snetsinger, John, *Truman, the Jewish Vote, and the Creation of Israel*. 1974.

Spanier, John W., *American Foreign Policy since World War II*. 9th ed. 1983.

Spector, Ronald H., *Advice and Support: The Early Years of the U.S. Army in Vietnam: 1941–1960*. 1983.

Steel, Ronald, *Walter Lippmann and the American Century*. 1980.

Stoff, Michael B., *Oil, War, and American Security: The Search for a National Policy on Foreign Oil, 1941–1947*. 1980.

Thomas, Hugh, *Armed Truce: The Beginnings of the Cold War, 1945–46*. 1987.

Truman, Harry S., *Memoirs*. 2 vols. 1956.

Ulam, Adam B., *The Rivals: America and Russia since World War II*. 1971.

Wala, Michael, "Selling the Marshall Plan at Home: The Committee for the Marshall Plan to Aid European Recovery," *Diplomatic History* 10 (1986): 247–65.

Ward, Patricia D., *The Threat of Peace: James F. Byrnes and the Council of Foreign Ministers, 1945–1946*. 1979.

Whitnah, Donald R., and Edgar L. Erickson, *The American Occupation of Austria: Planning and Early Years*. 1985.

Wittner, Lawrence S., *American Intervention in Greece, 1943–1949*. 1982.

Yergin, Daniel, *Shattered Peace: The Origins of the Cold War and the National Security State*. 1978.

Chapter Twenty

Cold War and Containment in the Far East, 1950–1953

On June 25, 1950, 75,000 North Korean troops, using Soviet-made tanks and artillery, invaded the Republic of Korea along a 150-mile front and set off the first major military conflict of the Cold War. Succeeding events in Asia became symbolic of the new tactics necessitated by the dangers of atomic warfare, for the sudden and dramatic return to conventional conflict highlighted the irony of possessing the bomb but not being able to use it. Americans believed they were fighting the communists by proxy—that Moscow had manipulated the North Koreans into the attack and that the United States had to deal with this new threat by any method short of all-out war. Kennan's theories seemed correct: the Soviets were determined to test the American will by probing soft spots throughout the world. The United States had shored up Europe and the Near East by the Truman Doctrine, Marshall Plan, and NATO; proponents of containment were convinced that the Soviets had now turned to the Far East.

Recent events in Asia reinforced that belief. America's postwar occupation of Japan under General Douglas MacArthur had implanted democratic reforms that underlay a model of Western ideals in the Far East. But then, in late 1949, Chiang Kai-shek's Chinese Nationalist forces had collapsed before Mao Tse-tung's Communists and retreated to the island of Formosa. The appearance was that a monolithic communism operating out of the Kremlin had brought the "fall" of China and now sought to counter America's successes in Japan as a threat to Soviet influence in Asia. Washington perceived the invasion of Korea as being, for practical purposes, a Soviet invasion, and sought to resist it by working through a United Nations force dominated by American soldiers, money, and war matériel. To avoid the label of war, the conflict was officially called a police action.

American policy in regard to the Far East was based upon three assumptions, all of them unsound. The first was that communism in Korea, China, and every place else in Asia was a single movement directed by Moscow. In fact, there were many communist movements, some more or less controlled by the Kremlin and others not; and thus the United States failed to exploit these differences to its own strategic advantage. The second assumption was that every revolutionary movement in the Orient was communist-inspired or had communism as its goal. The fact was that the most powerful impelling force for revolutionary change in Asia was not ideology but nationalism; and thus, despite an official (and usually sincere) American policy of anticolonialism, discontented Orientals perceived America's continued presence and intervention in the Far East as the same style of colonialism practiced by France, Britain, and the Netherlands. The third assumption was that "limited war" was a viable method for deterring the spread of communism. The fact was that the American people, accustomed to fighting through to victory, were unwilling to endure the frustrations that limited war entails; and thus, in 1952 they voted the Democrats out of power for the first time in twenty years.

JAPAN

America's occupation of Japan lasted from 1945 through 1952. In December 1945 the United States, Britain, and China gathered with the Soviet Union in Moscow and established an advisory group in Tokyo known as the Four-Power Allied Council for Japan. The United States rejected the Soviets' call for a share in the occupation of Japan and agreed to their participation only in an advisory capacity. Authority rested in the Supreme Commander for the Allied Powers (SCAP) in Japan, General Douglas MacArthur. He worked under the supervision of the Far Eastern Advisory Commission in Washington, D.C., which was comprised of the eleven nations (later expanded to thirteen) that had fought Japan in the war. By character and personality, MacArthur dominated policy in Japan. His stern, authoritarian, and military manner appealed to people accustomed to worshipping an emperor. The war's devastation left the Japanese no choice.

America's initial aims were to reduce Japan to lesser power status and to institute an ambitious democratic reform program; the first intention was gradually changed as Asia became the scene of Cold War rivalry and the grand hopes for making China into a major power sputtered and failed. The second goal remained constant and soon became integral to restoring Japan to a position strong enough to balance off Soviet influence in the Far East. MacArthur drew up a constitution for Japan in May 1947, patterned after that of the United States. Under it, Japan "forever renounced war as a sovereign right of the nation and the threat or use of

Douglas MacArthur at Japanese Surrender Ceremonies in 1945

He later headed the American occupation of Japan before becoming commander of UN forces during the Korean War. (National Archives)

force as a means of settling international disputes." Japan also agreed to discard "land, sea, and air forces, as well as other war potential." Americans reformed the education system, barred warmakers from official positions in the country, sponsored war crimes trials, stripped Japan of overseas possessions, and allowed it to retain only the four islands comprising the homeland. The monarchy remained only in form, for final power rested in delegates chosen by the people—including females (a revolution in itself). The United States also encouraged economic opportunity by breaking up industrial monopolies and dividing huge land tracts among the peasants. As the Cold War intensified in Asia by 1950, America's occupation forces relaxed restrictions on industrial production and encouraged former Japanese leaders to reassume official responsibilities. Japan became a model of democratic reform in the Far East and a source of embarrassment to the Soviet Union.

CHINA

The resumption of civil war in China after the end of World War II had threatened to cause the government's collapse under communist attack. America's paternal policy toward China had expressed itself in missionary and humanitarian interests, in the Open Door with its drive for the fabled "China market," and in Franklin D. Roosevelt's objective of establishing the country as a postwar world power. Yet trade expectations never materialized and China did not become the reformed mammoth capable of bringing a balance of power to Asia. In August 1945 the Soviets signed a treaty with the Nationalists which was a signal to the communists that they were on their own. Chiang's forces meanwhile received American assistance in regaining control over the cities and the China coast, while communist forces held onto the upper interior and moved toward Manchuria, where they confiscated war matériel from the Japanese and accepted secret aid from the Soviets, despite Stalin's treaty with Chiang. Mao refused subordination to Moscow, which led Stalin to remark that the Chinese communists were "not real communists" but " 'margarine' communists." Despite the crack in the alleged communist monolith, Americans continued to believe that the movement, whether inspired by Stalin or Mao, could cause the collapse of Nationalist China and constitute a defeat in the Cold War.

America's ambassador to Nationalist China, General Patrick Hurley, thought that Moscow's decision in August 1945 to help Chiang provided an opportunity to defeat Mao's Communist forces. Hurley first tried to persuade Chiang and Mao to settle their differences, but after six weeks

Chiang Kai-shek and Wife

He headed the Chinese Nationalists (Kuomintang) until defeated in the civil war with Mao Tse-tung's Communists and driven off the mainland to Formosa in October 1949.
(Roger Viollet)

Mao Tse-tung and U.S. Ambassador Patrick Hurley

Arriving at Chungking airport from Yenan for conference with chiefs of Central Chinese government in August 1945. (National Archives)

of negotiations in Chungking he failed, largely because Chiang demanded too much. Hurley resigned his post in November and accused the Foreign Service of supporting Mao (whom he called "Mouse Dung"). Hurley's rebuke left an erroneous impression of the Foreign Service officers, for they had for sometime emphasized that Mao would win the civil war because of the Nationalists' weaknesses and Chiang's failure to arouse popular support. But their assessment questioned America's traditional support for China and for that they appeared to be communist sympathizers.

After Hurley's resignation, President Truman appointed General George C. Marshall, retired Army chief of staff, to head a special mission to resolve the problems in China. Like Stilwell and Hurley before him, Marshall was to arrange a cease-fire and build a coalition government, but with Chiang's regime as "the only legal government" and "foundation of the new political structure." Marshall tried to bring the opposing groups together, but this objective showed that Washington had failed to recognize Mao's strength. Marshall did secure a truce in January 1946, and the communists seemed interested in a coalition government—perhaps as a less costly route to victory. Under terms of the truce, each side was to scale down its armies before combining them into a single force, to be trained by a thousand Americans in a Joint United States Military Advisory Group situated in Nanking. Both antagonists would then write a new constitution for China. But the Marshall mission failed because neither the new government nor army came into being.

Stilwell and the Foreign Service officers in China had been correct; Chiang's army was incapable of uniting the country. Peace lasted fitfully through 1946, but in the meantime the communists established control over nearly all of Manchuria. Marshall realized that war was imminent and returned to the United States. The following month he submitted a report attributing the dire situation in China to "extremist elements on both sides." Compromise between Chiang's conservative supporters and Mao's self-proclaimed "Marxists" was out of the question. That same month, January 1947, Marshall became secretary of state.

Fear of a communist takeover in China and pressure from the Republicans to save the huge country led Truman to send another mission during the summer of 1947. General Albert C. Wedemeyer, the new appointee, recommended UN supervision of Manchuria, massive "moral, advisory, and material support" to the Nationalists, and a wide range of reforms in the army requiring the help of 10,000 American military advisers. His proposals won no support from the Truman administration. In fact, Marshall prevented their release to the public. Given the magnitude of American commitments in Europe, the secretary of state opposed further involvement in China and warned that UN intervention in Manchuria could cause Moscow to call for a reciprocal arrangement in Greece. Past experience, he warned, suggested the futility in attempting to reform the Nationalist Army. The secretary was amenable to limited military and economic aid to the Nationalists, and he authorized a few advisers to upgrade Chiang's army. But this was as far as he would go. America's postwar priorities had become strikingly similar to those before 1941: an emphasis on Europe and a hope that problems in Asia would take care of themselves.

Marshall's recommendations for China were not sufficient to prevent a communist victory. In May 1948 Congress appropriated $400 million of military and economic aid under the Foreign Assistance Act. Whereas critics warned that this was not enough, Senator Vandenberg contended that no amount was enough: "China aid is like sticking your finger in the lake and looking for the hole." On August 5, 1949 the State Department issued a White Paper containing over a thousand pages of text and documents attributing China's impending collapse to the ineptitude of Chiang's Nationalists. In covering remarks, Dean Acheson, who had become secretary of state in January 1949, offered what was undoubtedly the correct assessment of the situation. "Nothing that this country did or could have done within the reasonable limits of its capabilities could have changed that result," he wrote; "nothing that was left undone by this country has contributed to it. It was the product of internal Chinese forces." Acheson concluded that "a decision was arrived at within China, if only a decision by default." The first loyalty of the Chinese communists, according to the White Paper, was to the Soviet Union.

Events in China took on momentum as the communists tightened their hold on the country. At a September conference in Peking (formerly Peiping but now changed back to the title of ancient days), they drew up a constitution for the "People's Republic of China," which had the outward markings of democracy. Mao declared the regime in effect on October 1, with Mao as head and Chou En-lai as premier and foreign minister. The Soviet Union extended recognition the next day, leading Chiang's Nationalists to break relations with Moscow on October 3. Despite eventual recognition of Communist China by Britain and other noncommunist countries, the United States again departed from *de facto* recognition policy and on October 4 affirmed support for the Nationalists as China's legitimate government. After a series of retreats from Nanking, then from Canton, and finally Chungking, the Nationalists withdrew from the mainland for the island of Formosa (also known as Taiwan) and in December resumed governmental functions in the capital city of Taipei.

Several factors contributed to Chiang's failure, none of which the United States could have controlled. Americans did not lose China to communism; they never owned or controlled the country. Despite the unfortunate comparison of China to Greece, a proportionate economic and military aid program in China would have required much more money and many more military advisers. Ambassador John L. Stuart, born in China and president of Yenching University in Peiping, probably offered the best explanation of China's collapse. In his memoirs, *Fifty Years in China*, he attributed the outcome to "a gigantic struggle between two political ideologies with the overtones of democratic idealism perverted by bureaucratic incompetence on the one side, succumbing to a dynamic socialized reform vitiated by Communist dogma, intolerance and ruthlessness on the other. And the great mass of suffering inarticulate victims cared for neither but were powerless to do anything about it." Avid party members were few on either side. The Chinese people were "merely Chinese" who wanted " to live their own lives with a minimum of government interference or oppression."

The fall of China to communism was attributable to a long history of internal troubles, to repeated instances of outside intervention, to World War II, and to Chiang's disastrous rule. Group after group had vied for control in Peiping, while in the provinces numerous independent warlords competed for power. Chiang's early military successes had come to an abrupt end during the Sino-Japanese War of the 1930s, which itself meshed into the events of World War II. Billions of dollars of American aid to Chiang disappeared in inflation, bureaucratic inefficiency, nepotism, and corruption. He failed to win popular support because of the lack of land reforms, the constant instability of the country, his own ineptitude, and the devastation of the world war. Chiang's strength rested on the landlords, who opposed land reform, whereas the communists gained widespread peasant support by promising agrarian reforms. The revolution swept the countryside while Chiang's forces remained in the cities, insulated from the need for change.

The decision in Washington to withhold recognition of Communist China did not necessarily imply protection to Formosa, but Americans soon found that refusal to help the Nationalists left the appearance of tacit favor for the Communists. In January 1950 Truman informed Chiang's advocates in the United States that he had no plans for furnishing "military aid or advice" to the Nationalists. But that stance quickly changed. Members of the Republican party were already claiming that communists in Washington had betrayed Nationalist China. Alger Hiss, an official in the State Department who had been in Yalta during the alleged "giveaways" in Europe and Asia, won acquittal from espionage charges in a sensational trial, although in January 1950 a jury convicted him of perjury. The following month Republican Senator Joe McCarthy of Wisconsin charged the State Department with housing communists, and shortly afterward British physicist Klaus Fuchs was convicted of turning over atomic secrets to the Soviet Union. The resulting wave of fear and suspicion aroused by "McCarthyism" discredited Acheson, who had remained loyal to his friend Hiss, and whose mustache and Ivy League clothing gave him the image of a dangerous intellectual—more European than American. The fallout did not stop with him. The national hysteria hurt the Foreign Service, converted judgmental errors into a believed communist conspiracy, and made the administration wary of admitting to any mistakes or failures in diplomatic policy which critics could label as treason, or at least as being "soft on communism."

In February 1950 the Soviet Union and Communist China alarmed Americans by signing a thirty-year mutual defense pact. The treaty added to the impression in the United States that one brand of communism, guided by the Kremlin, was spreading throughout the world. Americans became convinced that Red China had come under the Soviet heel. Few realized that the agreement of 1950 resulted from mutual need and not from ideological ties. Mao wanted to stem the United States's deepening influence in Asia, whereas Stalin sought assurances for the Yalta guarantees and was leery of a strong and independent Communist China. The Soviets demanded that Mao's China replace Chiang's Nationalists in the United Nations Security Council. When this effort failed, the Soviet delegate walked out, signifying his government's boycott of that organization.

THE KOREAN WAR

Japan and China constituted an important and related background to the conflict in Korea, for that peninsula had become the hot spot of the Cold War by mid-1950 and the ensuing problems quickly raised questions about America's resolve in Japan and the effectiveness of its policies in China. Korea became symbolic of the East-West struggle.

The Soviet Union and the United States had temporarily divided the country at the 38th parallel in 1945, with the understanding that the Soviets would wind down the war against Japanese invasion forces in the north and the United States would do the same in the south. Afterward full withdrawal would take place, in line with wartime agreements that Korea was to be "free and independent." The partition at the 38th parallel was a military decision, even though it cut off the industrialized north from the agricultural south and left the north larger in area though smaller in population. It was a sound decision from Washington's view because the United States was unable to transport soldiers there immediately, and the Soviet agreement to remain above the 38th parallel perhaps would prevent it from occupying all of Korea.

Problems developed over the implementation of the agreement. In December 1945 and again in March 1947, the Soviet and American foreign ministers agreed in Moscow that the military commands in Korea should discuss the procedure for installing a government favorable to reuniting the north and south. But the talks each time failed to resolve the composition of that government. The United States referred the Korean issue to the UN General Assembly, which in November 1947 established a Temporary Commission on Korea to sponsor nationwide elections. But the Soviets refused to allow the commissioners above the 38th parallel. Elections took place in May 1948—only in the south. Syngman Rhee, seventy-three years old and a longtime resident of the United States with a doctorate degree in international law from Princeton, emerged as president of the Republic of Korea in Seoul, whereas in September Kim Il-sung became president of a Soviet puppet regime in Pyongyang, capital of the Democratic People's Republic of Korea. The following December Rhee signed an economic and military aid pact with the United States. When the question of South Korea's admission to the United Nations came before the Security Council, the Soviet delegate vetoed the measure. As in Germany, two Koreas became symbolic of the Cold War rivalry.

Meanwhile the government in North Korea had become militarily superior to that in the south. Both had armies, but whereas the Soviets had provided heavy artillery and tanks to North Korea, the Americans were fearful of Rhee's dictatorial rule and of his undisguised intention to reunite the Koreas, and refused to grant anything more than light defensive weaponry. Only after great pressure from Washington did Rhee hold long-promised general elections, and when they did take place the results exposed his shaky control in South Korea. Yet the United States had no feasible alternative to Rhee except withdrawal. The Soviet Union withdrew its troops from Korea in December 1948 and the United States did the same in June 1949, but neither power's commitment had ceased. The Soviets left behind heavy artillery and tanks, whereas Washington maintained a considerable amount of light military equipment and 400 technical and military advisers.

South Korean President Syngman Rhee

Delivering address to Republic of Korea troops in November 1956. (U.S. Army)

By early 1950 the United States appeared to have left the South Koreans on their own. The military withdrawal reinforced that impression. In Japan MacArthur announced opposition to a land war in Asia. The American army had ten poorly equipped and inadequately manned divisions, and the Joint Chiefs of Staff considered South Korea of secondary importance. On January 12, 1950, Acheson seemed to affirm his nation's retreat from the Far East. Before the National Press Club in Washington, D.C., he defined the "defense perimeter" of the United States in Asia as a line running through the Aleutians, Japan, the Ryukyus, and the Philippines, which implied that America had made no assurances relating to either Formosa or the Chinese mainland. Should aggression occur, Acheson emphasized, "the initial reliance must be on the people attacked to resist it and then upon the commitments of the entire civilized world under the Charter of the United Nations which so far has not proved a weak reed to lean on by any people who are determined to protect their independence against outside aggression." The secretary was perhaps attempting to give subtle notification to the Red Chinese that the United States wished to withdraw support from the Nationalists. Not inconsistent with this supposition, he wished to place emphasis on economic and administrative assistance to Korea rather than military, exemplifying the belief in Washington that sound economies and democratic governments were the best insurance against communism. Whatever his intentions, the effect was not what he had anticipated. Observers were convinced that Acheson had removed both South Korea and Formosa from the American defense system.

When in the summer of 1950 the North Korean forces launched their invasion of South Korea, they met little resistance. News of the attack reached Washington, which was thirteen hours behind Korean time, late in the evening of June 24. Acheson met with other State Department officers and decided that America's reaction would be through the UN Security Council. Truman was at home in Independence, Missouri, and returned to Washington the following day. Meanwhile the Department of State worked all night drafting a resolution condemning the North Korean aggression, which the American delegation would present to the Se-

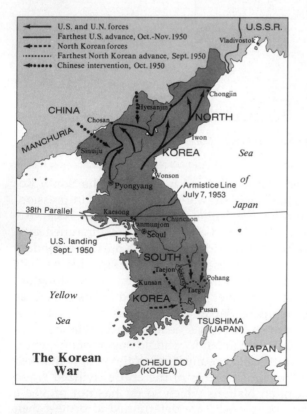

MAP 31

Over three years of war resulted in a stalemate as the fighting came to a close in almost exactly the same area it began.

curity Council. The Truman administration ordered Americans in Seoul to evacuate at once.

No debate took place in Washington about whether the Soviet Union had engineered the attack; the assumption was that Moscow was responsible and the United States had to act. Officials in Washington agreed that the Soviets had begun probing for weak areas susceptible to communist takeover. Korea was a test of America's will in the Far East. The Department of State alerted its foreign offices to this danger: "Possible that Korea is only the first of series of coordinated actions on part of Soviets. Maintain utmost vigilance."

Without Soviet, Chinese, and North Korean documentation, it is impossible to know whether North Korea had carried out an invasion that surprised the Soviets as much as it did the West. The ideas underlying the containment theory held that the Soviets preferred what Acheson called "subversion and penetration" to military force. Before the Senate, he later explained that "the view was generally held that since the Communists had far from exhausted the potentialities for obtaining their objectives through guerrilla and psychological warfare, political pressure and intimidation, such means would probably continue to be used rather than overt military aggression." Yet several considerations raised questions about this stance. Kim Il-sung and Syngman Rhee were bitter rivals. Border incidents had dramatically increased before June; the same morning of the attack, South Korean forces had raided a town above the 38th parallel. Had Moscow known of the impending North Korean attack, its delegate would surely have returned to the Security Council, where he could have vetoed UN military action and bought time for the North Koreans before the General Assembly could act. But once America's policymakers assumed Soviet complicity in the attack, they became locked in a test of their commitment to Asia. North Korea's effort to reunify the country by force caused the Truman administration to alter its Korean policy and adopt stronger measures than merely extending economic aid and military advice. State Department official John Foster Dulles publicly expressed the common belief that the North Koreans "did not do this purely on their own but as part of the world strategy of international communism." The successes of America's containment policy in Europe and the Near East had seemingly evoked this new Soviet response.

Questions remain about the Kremlin's assumed role in these events. An interesting theory is that the Soviets were unaware of the impending North Korean attack, perhaps at first even wanting to call it off, but that its surprising success offered the opportunity of accomplishing everything they sought in the Far East. Indeed, the Soviets could cite the progress of the attack as further evidence of America's military weakness, already exemplified in China. Moreover, the North Koreans' actions threatened to diminish America's credibility in Japan. If America's prestige fell in Asia, only the Soviet Union would gain—as long as it quietly furnished military assistance to the North Koreans while labeling the United States, the region's unmistakable outsider, as the interventionist aggressor. Whatever the background of the attack, the Soviet Union had at the least fallen into a seemingly no-lose situation.

Truman never doubted the need to take strong action. Here was opportunity to regain flagging popular support, largely resulting from the Republicans' charges that the administration was "soft on communism"; but Truman regarded the North Korean attack as another test of the Free World's commitment to liberty. "Communism," he wrote in his *Memoirs*, "was acting in Korea just as Hitler, Mussolini, and the Japanese had acted ten, fifteen, and twenty years earlier." He assured a senator that his administration would not give in to the Soviet Union and told reporters that Korea was "the Greece of the Far East." Acheson explained years afterward that "to back away from this challenge, in view of our capacity for meeting it, would be highly destructive of the power and prestige of the United States."

The believed Soviet threat in Asia caused both the United States and its NATO allies to move with resolution. By the afternoon following the attack, the Security Council had overwhelmingly approved (9 to 0, the Soviets absent and Yugoslavia abstaining) the American resolution labeling the attack a "breach of the peace" and calling on the North Koreans to withdraw above the 38th parallel. The Council then approved a second resolution urging member nations to "furnish such assistance to the Republic of Korea as may be necessary to repel the armed attack and to restore international peace and security." Truman warned the Red Chinese not to exploit the Korean situation by attacking the Nationalists on Formosa. To emphasize the point he approved military assistance to the Philippines and Indochina. Communism, the president explained, "has passed beyond the use of subversion to conquer independent nations and will now use armed invasion and war." In a single day he had committed the United States to Nationalist China, the Philippines (just granted independence by the United States in July 1946), and Indochina, all of which were undergoing severe internal problems believed to be communist-inspired.

On June 27 Truman ordered the Seventh Fleet to the Chinese coast to "prevent any attack on Formosa"—as the president declared, to deter a resurgence of civil war. Whether to "leash" Chiang or to protect Formosa, Truman's actions angered Red China because they constituted interference in its domestic affairs. They also upset members of the UN who had extended recognition to the communist regime and believed it justified in wanting to absorb Formosa. But with the Republicans charging the administration with already having "lost" China, the White House had little choice but to adopt strong policies to prevent the loss of South Korea. To keep the war limited in nature, Truman emphasized that the United States sought only "to restore peace and. . . the border."

When Seoul fell to the North Koreans on June 28, the weaknesses in

America's containment effort became increasingly evident and led to the decision to send American troops to save South Korea. On June 29 Truman approved American air strikes above the 38th parallel, and the following day in Tokyo MacArthur recommended that the United States send soldiers, blockade the coast, and bomb areas in North Korea "wherever militarily necessary." In a decision Truman later termed "the most important" of his presidency, he ordered American combat forces into Korea. Only sixteen of the sixty UN members eventually did the same. While South Korea furnished considerable military forces, the United States provided over a million members of the armed forces and the great bulk of planes, ships, goods, and money. The president did not ask Congress for a declaration of war because, he explained, it was a "police action." The situation was desperate. The North Koreans had driven the South Koreans into Pusan at the bottom of the peninsula and were on the verge of forcing them into the sea. MacArthur received orders on June 30 to use military forces "to insure the retention of a port and air base in the general area of Pusan." Acheson later explained with some satisfaction that the decision to send soldiers to Korea "removed the recommendations of NSC-68 from the realm of theory and made them immediate budget issues." According to that document, the Soviet Union sought "domination of the Eurasian land mass," leaving the United States no alternative to a global military policy.

Great symbolic importance rested in America's decision to commit troops to Korea. Bases in the peninsula were not vital. Soviet control of Korea could not have posed a greater threat to Japan than did Soviet bases in Manchuria or China. The limited size of America's military force in 1950 meant that the relocation of ground forces in Asia would seriously weaken Europe. Yet the symbolism of the commitment was fast approaching the level of the American national interest: the United States had found it necessary to demonstrate assurances to the South Koreans, Japanese, and other peoples subject to aggression—especially the Europeans. Failure to do so would have constituted a major defeat in the propaganda war with the communists and perhaps have sacrificed all hopes of winning the allegiance of the emerging postwar nations. Furthermore, a weak will would raise doubts among America's NATO allies.

Truman repeatedly emphasized the global context of the war. The decision to use combat troops escalated Korean events into a conflict having international ramifications. On July 8 the Security Council chose MacArthur to head the UN forces in Korea, and on August 1 the Soviet representative to the Council, Yakov Malik, returned to his seat. To soothe anxious Europeans who were worried that America's priorities had shifted toward Asia, Truman launched a military buildup on the continent. Acheson horrified the British and French by proposing that Germany contribute ten divisions to the European defense system. He overcame vehement protests by assuring them that the United States would send four additional divisions to the continent. Finally, the president announced that General Eisenhower had agreed to go on leave from the presidency of Columbia University and become NATO's Supreme Commander.

The UN forces now prepared to take the offensive. While South Korean units and a small number of American forces were backed to the water's edge at Pusan, on September 15 MacArthur launched a daring amphibious landing at Inchon on the western side of the peninsula, hundreds of miles behind the North Korean front. Most military experts had declared that such a landing could not work because of enormous tides and rocky cliffs; MacArthur promised that "we shall land at Inchon, and I shall crush them." He succeeded magnificently and soon freed Seoul from the communists. The counter-invasion broke the North Koreans' advance and drove them back above the 38th parallel. Meanwhile, South Korean and American forces gained the initiative in Pusan and severed the enemies' supply line. And despite these successes, Americans noted one telling fact: neither the Soviet Union nor Red China had intervened.

MacArthur's landing at Inchon had an exhilarating effect in the United States, and soon highlighted a major policy decision in Washington already made in early August. The Truman administration had decided to convert the policy of containment into a liberating force through what became known as rollback, and the new military situation afforded by MacArthur's successes provided an excellent opportunity for its implementation. In late September State Department official H. Freeman Matthews wrote the Joint Chiefs of Staff that if the United States could reunify Korea, "the resultant defeat to the Soviet Union and to the Communist world" would be of "momentous significance." Korea would join Japan as models of national self-determination in Asia, and at the same time mark the successful culmination of America's Korean policy established during the Second World War. Over protests from Kennan, who warned that the Russians would never allow MacArthur near the "gates of Vladivostok," the administration approved the advance across the 38th parallel that would set an example for the world by liberating all of Korea from communist control.

The Red Chinese meanwhile assured India's delegate to the UN, who informed the Assembly, that they, the Chinese, would not "sit back with folded hands and let the Americans come to the border." Washington ignored the warning. MacArthur was confident that the Chinese would stay out of the conflict and had earlier given the president personal assurances at Wake Island. "We are no longer fearful of their [Chinese] intervention," the general told Truman. "They have no air force . . . [and] if the Chinese tried to get down to Pyongyang there would be the greatest slaughter." To other members of the administration, MacArthur asserted that "the Oriental follows a winner. If we win, the Chinese will not follow the USSR [Union of Soviet Socialist Republics]." With the support of the State and Defense Departments and the Joint Chiefs of Staff, the United States took its case for an expanded military effort to the UN. On

October 9, the same day that American jets strafed a Soviet airstrip near Vladivostok, the General Assembly resolved that MacArthur should push for "a unified, independent and democratic Korea."

The UN's action in reality was pro forma. On September 29 MacArthur had learned that the administration in Washington was displeased with his apparent decision to stop at the 38th parallel and await UN approval before moving northward. George C. Marshall, now secretary of defense, cabled MacArthur: "We want you to feel unhampered tactically and strategically to proceed north of 38th parallel. Announcement above referred to may precipitate embarrassment in the UN where evident desire is not to be confronted with necessity of a vote on passage, rather to find you have found it militarily necessary to do so." MacArthur replied that he had not declared any intention of halting his advance, and that the parallel was "not a factor in the mil[itary] employment of our forces." He added that "unless and until the enemy capitulates, I regard all of Korea open for our mil[itary] operations." MacArthur promised reporters that "the war very definitely is coming to an end shortly." The UN decision to cross the 38th parallel elevated the Cold War to a level just short of full conflict. Before the end of October, UN forces were bombing the bridges connecting the Chinese banks of the Yalu River with those of North Korea.

The Truman administration seems not to have recognized that the UN invasion of North Korea was tantamount to a thrust toward China. Mao had not been on good terms with the North Koreans and had not expected the original attack on South Korea. He could not have wanted to enter the Korean conflict after his own recent long and costly civil war. His philosophy of survival argued against military confrontation with a superior military force. But Mao recognized that failure to halt the UN drive toward the Yalu River would discredit his regime's claim to the mainland and endanger his own leadership. Furthermore, here was opportunity, perhaps too soon presented, for the Peking government to come of age. Should it establish hegemony over that area, Mao would gain a stature in the Far East approaching that of the Soviets. Pushed into action by the UN decision to move toward the Yalu, Red China prepared to protect its vital interests in Asia.

The manner of Red China's intervention in the Korean War suggested that Mao was reluctant to act. On October 26 "Chinese volunteers" attacked the UN forces, halting their advance and driving them back. A week later the Chinese disappeared from the field. The message should have been clear: Mao had warned the UN to confine the fighting to South Korea. His priority, it seemed, was still Formosa, as evidenced by his agreement to send representatives to the UN to discuss the situation in Formosa. MacArthur did not see it that way. He called for an all-out attack and on November 24, the day of the Chinese delegates' arrival at the UN, declared that his men would be "home by Christmas," after they saw the Yalu. This news infuriated the Red Chinese and the Europeans, who accused MacArthur of trying to "wreck the negotiations" over Formosa. Two days later, as UN soldiers again fought their way northward, the first of thousands of Red Chinese soldiers suddenly swarmed into the seventy-five-mile-wide gap between MacArthur's two advancing flanks, driving his troops below the 38th parallel within two weeks.

Red China's second entry into the fighting drastically changed the tenor of the Korean conflict. MacArthur called it "an entirely new war" and sought an air bombardment of China, and the UN General Assembly overwhelmingly condemned China for aggression. When Truman left the impression with reporters that use of the atomic bomb was under consideration, British Prime Minister Clement Attlee rushed to Washington to urge a negotiated settlement of the conflict in Korea. Meanwhile, the president secured additional military appropriations from Congress to bolster Europe and other parts of the world. In a few weeks the Chinese again pushed the UN forces below the 38th parallel and took Seoul. The UN sought a cease-fire, but China refused until the following conditions were met: withdrawal of "foreign troops" from Korea, cessation of U.S. support to Formosa, and admission of Red China to the UN Security Council as the legitimate Chinese government. The United States rejected all three demands.

The Chinese intervention sparked a major debate within the Truman administration over whether to return to the original objectives of containment. After a massive countereffort, MacArthur's forces stopped the Chinese assault and began another offensive that took them back to the 38th parallel in March 1951. Truman called for a negotiated settlement, while MacArthur destroyed chances for a cease-fire by crossing the border again and demanding that the Chinese surrender unconditionally. The United States, he asserted, should blockade the Chinese coast, bomb the enemies' "privileged sanctuary" in Manchuria and the major Chinese industrial centers, permit the Nationalists to attack the mainland, and, as he later noted in his *Reminiscences*, "sever Korea from Manchuria by laying a field of radioactive wastes—the byproducts of atomic manufacture—across all the major lines of enemy supply." Truman objected. Supported by the Joint Chiefs of Staff, he argued that MacArthur's strategy was militarily unsound: a blockade and bombings could cause Soviet intervention in accordance with its defensive pact with Red China; these tactics would not affect inland communication and supply lines; Chiang had proved his ineptitude on the battlefield; use of atomic materials could bring on World War III; America's European allies were not supportive.

MacArthur opposed restrictions on his military actions. Insisting that Asia would be the major battleground between communism and the Free World, he argued that the United States should "go it alone if necessary." He publicly implied that Truman was guilty of appeasement, and in a move raising questions about the constitutionality of civilian authority over military authority, he wrote a letter to the leading Republican in the House of Representatives, Joseph Martin, in which he asserted : "There is no substitute for victory." In Asia, MacArthur wrote, "the communist conspirators have elected to make their play for global conquest. Here we fight Europe's war with arms while the diplomats there still fight it with words." Martin dramatically read the letter before the House on April 5, 1951. MacArthur had earlier ignored the president's directive against issuing public statements concerning foreign policy without prior approval from the State Department. Publication of the letter now challenged the president either to remove MacArthur from his Far Eastern duties on grounds of insubordination, or to change policy to suit the commander in the field. Truman, with full support from the Joint Chiefs of Staff, chose to relieve MacArthur of his Far Eastern command.

The announcement on April 11 of the so-called firing of MacArthur set off an immediate storm of protest in the United States that even led some Americans to demand the impeachment of Truman. The furor was attributable to several factors. Frustrations over the no-win nature of containment ("police actions" or "limited wars") headed the list, for this approach violated both the American military tradition of total victory and the related illusion that the United States had "won" all of its wars. The rage over the treatment of MacArthur also provided an outlet for isolationist discontent with America's recent foreign policy and for Republican desperation over losing the White House in 1948. Suspicion of communist infiltration of the government also bothered Americans, who regarded the Hiss case and the sensational charges by McCarthy as only the surface of a dark conspiracy. Many events since the Democrats' victory in 1932 had suggested a pattern of un-Americanism: the socialistic nature of the New Deal; recognition of Russia; Roosevelt's alleged "maneuverings" of the United States into World War II; the Yalta "betrayals"; the "fall" of China to communism; and now the Truman administration's decision to fire the only person brave enough to assert that there was "no substitute for victory." McCarthy's accusations took on greater credibility with the removal of MacArthur. "How can we account for our present situation," asked the senator, "unless we believe that men high in this government are concerting to deliver us to disaster? This must be the product of a great conspiracy on a scale so immense as to dwarf any previous venture in the history of man."

Another reason for the public's wrath was the impression that all MacArthur wanted was a UN assault on the Chinese mainland. But in 1964, a few days after his death, the general's earlier private conversations with two reporters became public. MacArthur in 1951 had wanted to drop atomic bombs on North Korea, followed by a land assault comprised of Americans and Nationalist Chinese. These forces would have invaded North Korea from the west and east, exerting a stranglehold on the Korean peninsula that would have led to total victory in less than two weeks. No reinforcements could have arrived from the north because in the meantime the UN would have laid a five-mile-wide strip of cobalt along the Chinese-Korean border. For the lifetime of the cobalt—over half a century— no one could have entered the zone. MacArthur had no fear of Soviet intervention. "It makes me laugh," he declared, "that Russia would commit its armies to a war in China's behalf at the end of an endless one-track railroad to a peninsular battleground that led only to the sea. Russia could not have engaged us," he continued. "She would not have fought for China. She is already unhappy and uncertain over the colossus she has encouraged." He concluded that "it was in our power to destroy the Red Chinese army and Chinese military power. And probably for all time. My plan was a cinch."

MacArthur's popularity in the United States remained high for about six weeks before beginning to recede—in line with the president's prediction. In April the general received a tremendous public welcome upon his return to the United States for the first time since 1937. Congress invited him to speak before a joint session, which was covered by radio and television. In his address he called for a stepped-up war in Asia and ended with a moving peroration that "old soldiers never die; they just fade away." But in subsequent Senate inquiries, General Omar Bradley, chairman of the Joint Chiefs of Staff, gave a persuasive defense of the administration. "Taking on Red China" would have created "a larger deadlock at greater expense" and without the support of America's allies. The Soviet Union was the "main antagonist" and Western Europe the "main prize." An assault on China would have involved the United States "in the wrong war at the wrong place at the wrong time and with the wrong enemy." Bradley's argument was calm, reasoned, and based on military and political realities, not on emotional charges of communist subterfuge and American cowardice and stupidity. But perhaps just as important to the argument, Truman repeatedly reminded Americans that their European allies opposed MacArthur's attempt to widen the conflict, and that civilian authority outranked the military in the United States. MacArthur's actions, the president insisted, were a violation of the Constitution.

Meanwhile, hopes for an end to the Korean conflict arose when the communists agreed to engage in truce talks in the summer of 1951. On June 23 the Soviet delegate to the Security Council called for a cease-fire. The Chinese Communists approved, but with the stipulation that foreign soldiers had to pull out of Korea. Armistice discussions began in early July at Kaesong near the 38th parallel, although they were eventually moved to Panmunjom. In November the antagonists tentatively accepted an armistice line at the point where the fighting ended, but the United States refused to approve UN withdrawal from South Korea. The communists then heightened their demands and accused the United States of using germ warfare, and violence broke out among the prisoners of war in UN camps. The talks stalemated. Over the next year and a half the antagonists argued about the location of the cease-fire line, the steps necessary to implement an armistice agreement, and the repatriation of prisoners. By the spring of 1952 only the last question remained an issue. Whereas the communists wanted all prisoners returned, the UN refused to repatriate those who did not want to go home. This was no small problem; nearly half of the UN's 170,000 POWs opposed repatriation.

While the fighting continued under the leadership of MacArthur's replacement, General Matthew Ridgway, the United States moved toward establishing a tighter alliance with countries in the Far East. On August 30, 1951, it signed a security pact with the Philippines, and two days later it became party to the Tripartite Security Treaty (ANZUS) with Australia and New Zealand. Both pacts were intended to allay those countries' anxieties over Washington's real objective: to rebuild Japan as a counterweight to Soviet influence in the Far East. Thus the Korean War catalyzed a move already under way in Tokyo to conclude a peace treaty with Japan and make it an ally against communism. More than fifty nations gathered in San Francisco in early September to begin negotiations under the leadership of John Foster Dulles, adviser to the secretary of state. Four days later the United States secured the Peace of Reconciliation, which recognized Japan's sovereignty but only over its home islands, awarded the United States a base on Okinawa, and referred reparations problems to individual negotiations between Japan and concerned countries. There were no prohibitions against Japanese rearmaments, and the United States would continue to occupy the Ryukyu and Bonin islands. That same day, September 8, the United States and Japan signed a Security Treaty permitting American soldiers to remain in Japan as long as necessary "to contribute to the maintenance of international peace and security in the Far East and to the security of Japan." On April 28, 1952, the two treaties with Japan went into effect, marking the close of America's administration of the Tokyo government, and officially ending World War II in the Pacific.

The fighting continued in Korea, however, arousing deeper concern within the United States that it would widen into a global conflict. American planes bombed hydroelectric plants on the Yalu River in June 1952, and in early October Truman declared that "we are fighting in Korea so we won't have to fight in Wichita, or in Chicago, or in New Orleans, or in San Francisco Bay." Later that same year in November, American scientists developed the hydrogen bomb, a thermonuclear device of a thousand times more destructive capacity than the atomic bombs dropped over Hiroshima and Nagasaki. Instead of comforting Americans, this news added to their uneasiness over the military escalation in Korea and intensified demands for an immediate end to the conflict.

ARMISTICE IN KOREA

As the presidential election of 1952 approached, Americans became increasingly suspicious that communist sympathizers in Washington were obstructing the war effort. The campaign tied these issues together when the Republicans used the symbol "K_1C_2" to refer to Korea, communism, and the several instances of corruption recently uncovered among administration officials. The party's candidate, Dwight D. Eisenhower, aroused enormous support by promising that if victorious, "I shall go to Korea." His unquestioned honesty, disarmingly homespun personality, and numerous military successes in World War II won him the confidence of voters. Eisenhower rolled over Adlai Stevenson of Illinois with 55 percent of the popular vote, and in December went to Korea for three days. There he mingled with the soldiers on the front and announced support for the UN decision not to return POWs who refused to go home.

Shortly after his inauguration in January 1953, President Eisenhower moved toward ending the Korean conflict. His administration took on the image of boldness and resolution, partly because of the outspoken nature of his secretary of state, Wall Street attorney John Foster Dulles. Almost bred as a diplomat, from a long line of familial experience in the State Department, this son of a Presbyterian minister viewed the Cold War as a near-religious conflict between the forces of good and evil. He promised an aggressive foreign policy and soon became identified with the terms massive retaliation, brinkmanship, liberation, and the New Look in suggesting that the United States was willing to use military force and even atomic weaponry in freeing people from communism. The Eisenhower-Dulles team left the implication that the United States was at last turning from containment. The president had earlier notified the North Koreans and Red Chinese through private channels that he wanted an immediate cease-fire; should they fail to comply, he warned, the United States might retaliate "under circumstances of our choosing." In his first State of the Union Message, he announced that the Seventh Fleet would "no longer be employed to shield Communist China," implying that he had "unleashed" Chiang Kai-shek to attack the mainland. Eisenhower's resort to the "MacArthur strategy" sounded convincing—so much so that Dulles had to make a sudden trip to London and Paris to calm America's worried allies. Another factor also encouraged the prospects for peace: Stalin died in March 1953, opening the possibility of a softer line from Moscow. His successor, Georgi Malenkov, seemed moderate in tone and more interested in focusing on his country's internal problems.

In July 1953 armistice talks began in earnest at Panmunjom, and by the end of the month the negotiators had reached an agreement. The previous month Syngman Rhee threatened to break up the talks when he suddenly freed 27,000 North Korean POWs who opposed communism, in an effort to abort a settlement that he knew would not unify the Koreas under his rule. Rhee was a "zealous, irrational, and illogical fanatic," according to a presidential envoy sent from Washington. But the communists did not break off talks, which suggested that they, too, wanted to end the war. The antagonists finally agreed to the establishment of a neutral commission to deal with prisoner exchanges. The armistice line was to be the present battle front, which meant that although the North Koreans lost some territory, the war would end at approximately the same place it had begun—the 38th parallel. A demilitarized zone would exist between the Koreas. The United States won Rhee's acquiescence by assuring military and economic aid.

The Korean War had an enormous and yet mixed effect on international affairs. Unrest remained between the Koreas, which outside nations continued to exploit. If the conflict did little for Soviet prestige in Asia, it greatly enhanced that of the Red Chinese. Their intervention in behalf of the North Koreans had a powerful impact on nations growing increasingly neutralist in the world's power struggles. The war also postponed any chance there might have been of the United States's extending recognition to Red China; America's support for Nationalist China was stronger than ever. The war stimulated the American economy, although at great expense. The United States furnished half of the ground forces, more than 80 percent of the naval assistance, and over 90 percent of the air power. It expended over $15 billion and incurred 138,000 casualties (four-fifths attributable to the fighting above the parallel), including 34,000 dead. South Korea suffered more than a million casualties, whereas the Chinese and North Koreans counted over a million dead.

The establishment of a truce meant that no one had won the conflict: Korea remained divided and in an uneasy stalemate. World affairs became more tense in August 1953 when the Soviet Union likewise exploded a hydrogen bomb. According to the physicist Robert Oppenheimer, the two superpowers were like "two scorpions in a bottle, each capable of killing the other, but only at the risk of his own life." Yet the UN had gained in stature in containing communist aggression, and in October 1953 the United States and South Korea signed a mutual defense pact, which the Senate overwhelmingly approved the following year. The most important legacy of the Korean conflict, however, was its impetus to containment. Despite the new foreign policy labels associated with the Eisenhower administration, the United States had solidified its acceptance of the containment doctrine, which meant continued military buildups, repeated refusals to compromise with the communists, and a virtual guarantee to the endlessness of the Cold War. President Eisenhower offered the bluntest appraisal: "We have won an armistice on a single battleground, not peace in the world. We may not now relax our guard nor cease our quest."

Selected readings

Acheson, Dean, *Present at the Creation: My Years in the State Department.* 1969.

Ambrose, Stephen E., *Rise to Globalism: American Foreign Policy since 1938.* 4th ed. 1985.

Blum, Robert M., *Drawing the Line: The Origins of the American Containment Policy in East Asia.* 1982.

Borden, William S., *The Pacific Alliance: United States Foreign Economic Policy and Japanese Trade Recovery, 1947–1955.* 1984.

Buhite, Russell D., *Soviet-American Relations in Asia, 1945–1954.* 1982.

Caridi, Ronald J., *The Korean War and American Politics: The Republican Party as a Case Study.* 1968.

Cumings, Bruce, *The Origins of the Korean War: Liberation and the Emergence of Separate Regimes, 1945–1947.* 1981.

Dobbs, Charles M., *The Unwanted Symbol: American Foreign Policy, the Cold War, and Korea, 1945–1950.* 1981.

Donovan, Robert J., *Tumultuous Years: The Presidency of Harry S Truman, 1949–1953.* 1982.

Feis, Herbert, *The China Tangle.* 1953.

Ferrell, Robert H., *Harry S. Truman and the Modern American Presidency.* 1983.

Foot, Rosemary, *The Wrong War: American Policy and the Dimensions of the Korean Conflict, 1950–1953.* 1985.

Gaddis, John L., *Strategies of Containment: A Critical Appraisal of Postwar American National Security Policy.* 1982.

George, Alexander L., *The Chinese Communist Army in Action: The Korean War and Its Aftermath.* 1967.

Goulden, Joseph C., *Korea: The Untold Story of War.* 1982.

Hart, Robert A., *The Eccentric Tradition: American Diplomacy in the Far East.* 1976.

Herring, George C., Jr., *America's Longest War: The United States and Vietnam, 1950–1975.* 2d ed. 1986.

Hess, Gary R., *The United States' Emergence as a Southeast Asian Power, 1940–1950.* 1987.

Higgins, Trumbull, *Korea and the Fall of MacArthur.* 1960.

Iriye, Akira, *The Cold War in Asia: A Historical Introduction.* 1974.

James, D. Clayton, *The Years of MacArthur.* Vol. 3, *Triumph and Disaster, 1945–1964.* 1985.

Kaufman, Burton I., *The Korean War: Challenges in Crisis, Credibility, and Command.* 1986.

Keefer, Edward C., "President Dwight D. Eisenhower and the End of the Korean War," *Diplomatic History* 10 (1986): 267–89.

LaFeber, Walter, *America, Russia, and the Cold War, 1945–1984.* 5th ed. 1985.

Leckie, Robert, *Conflict: The History of the Korean War, 1950–1953.* 1962.

Levine, Steven I., "A New Look at American Mediation in the Chinese Civil War: The Marshall Mission and Manchuria," *Diplomatic History* 3 (1979): 349–75.

McLean, David, "American Nationalism, the China Myth, and the Truman Doctrine: The Question of Accommodation with Peking, 1949–50," *Diplomatic History* 10 (1986): 25–42.

McMahon, Robert J., *Colonialism and Cold War: The United States and the Struggle for Indonesian Independence, 1945–1949.* 1982.

Matray, James I., *The Reluctant Crusade: American Foreign Policy in Korea, 1941–1950.* 1985.

————, "Truman's Plan for Victory: National Self-Determination and the Thirty-Eighth Parallel Decision in Korea," *Journal of American History* 66 (Sept. 1979): 314–33.

May, Ernest R., *The Truman Administration and China, 1945–1949.* 1975.

Paige, Glenn D., *The Korean Decision, June 24–30, 1950.* 1968.

Purifoy, Lewis M., *Truman's China Policy: McCarthyism and the Diplomacy of Hysteria.* 1976.

Rees, David, *Korea: The Limited War.* 1964.

Rose, Lisle A., *Roots of Tragedy: The United States and the Struggle for Asia, 1945–1953.* 1976.

Rovere, Richard H., and Arthur M. Schlesinger, Jr., *The MacArthur Controversy and American Foreign Policy.* 1965. Revised and expanded version of the authors' *The General and the President.* 1951.

Schaller, Michael, *The American Occupation of Japan: The Origins of the Cold War in Asia.* 1985.

Spanier, John W., *American Foreign Policy Since World War II.* 9th ed. 1983.

————, *The Truman-MacArthur Controversy and the Korean War.* 1959.

Spector, Ronald H., *Advice and Support: The Early Years of the U.S. Army in Vietnam: 1941–1960.* 1983.

Stueck, William W., "The Korean War as International History," *Diplomatic History* 10 (1986): 291–309.

Stueck, William W., Jr., *The Road to Confrontation: American Policy toward China and Korea, 1947–1950.* 1981.

————, *The Wedemeyer Mission: American Politics and Foreign Policy during the Cold War.* 1984

Theoharis, Athan G., *Seeds of Repression: Harry S. Truman and the Origins of McCarthyism.* 1971.

————, *The Yalta Myths: An Issue in U.S. Politics, 1945–1955.* 1970.

Truman, Harry S., *Memoirs.* 2 vols. 1956.

Tsou, Tang, *America's Failure in China, 1941–1950.* 1963.

Tucker, Nancy B., *Patterns in the Dust: Chinese-American Relations and the Recognition Controversy, 1949–1950.* 1983.

Ulam, Adam B., *The Rivals: America and Russia since World War II.* 1971.

Whiting, Allen S., *China Crosses the Yalu: The Decision to Enter the Korean War.* 1960.

Chapter Twenty-One

Containment Continued: The Eisenhower Years, 1953–1961

Despite the Cold War rhetoric of the Eisenhower presidency, America's foreign policy remained essentially that of containment. Secretary of State John Foster Dulles, stern and self-righteous in manner, suggested that the administration had discarded containment for "liberation" when he called for a cutback in conventional forces and a heavy reliance upon nuclear weapons. America's containment policy, Dulles warned in *Life* magazine, endangered civil liberties by necessitating excessive taxes and a refusal to seek victory. The United States needed "a policy of boldness" which would enable Americans "to retaliate instantly against open aggression by Red armies, so that if it occurred anywhere, we could and would strike back where it hurts, by means of our own choosing." Four years later he elaborated on these ideas in another article in *Life*. "The ability to get to the verge without getting into the war is the necessary art," he asserted. "If you cannot master it, you inevitably get into war. If you try to run away from it, if you are scared to go to the brink, you are lost." Yet the events of the 1950s showed that President Eisenhower recognized the realities of the nuclear standoff and often restrained his secretary of state by implementing a cautious foreign policy that avoided challenges to Soviet spheres of influence. Nikita Khrushchev, who became premier in 1958, later reminisced that Dulles "knew how far he could push us, and he never pushed us too far."

THE 1950s: AN AGE OF INTERNATIONAL TURMOIL

Several crises during the decade highlighted the growing Cold War and tested the capacity of the Eisenhower-Dulles foreign policy team to contain the spread of Soviet communism. Korea (see previous chapter), the

Secretary of State John Foster Dulles

Holding press conference upon his arrival in Taipei, Taiwan, in October 1958, just before conferring with Generalissimo Chiang Kai-shek, president of Nationalist China. (U.S. Army)

Third World, Iran, Latin America, Indochina, Poland, Hungary, Suez, China, Berlin, the U-2 incident—all problems appeared to be communist in origin. Eisenhower recognized that a balance of nuclear terror had developed that rested precariously upon mutual Soviet-American distrust, and that the only way to maintain peace lay in diplomacy based upon nuclear strength as leverage. While Dulles publicly advocated massive retaliation, Eisenhower quietly exercised restraints. Yet America's driving force throughout the decade was a Cold War perception of the world that interpreted nearly every event as part of the struggle with the Soviet Union.

The rising postwar Third World nations played a vital role in the Cold War. By 1960 thirty-seven nations had emerged in Asia, Africa, and the Middle East, many rich in natural resources and increasingly important as Americans and Soviets searched out strategic bases. The largely uncontrollable factor was the growing number of nationalist revolutions that erupted from the anticolonial sentiment of World War II. Leaders were often leftist, Marxist, and only ostensibly democratic, building a following among peoples who were economically and politically desperate and hence subject to Moscow's assumed proxies all over the world. One could never be sure which direction a social revolution would take, and rather than risk a communist takeover, the simplest approach was to support those leaders who were anticommunist and promised stability, even at the cost of personal freedoms. A further complication was that as these peoples were accorded national status, they often adopted neutralist postures, preferring to play one superpower against the other rather than taking sides and becoming the scene of nuclear war.

Policymakers in Washington found themselves in an unenviable position in relation to the Third World. They considered the stakes too high to allow a revolution to run its course, and for that reason the Eisenhower administration continued and even broadened the Truman policy of interventionism. Arguing that the Soviet Union was meddling in nearly every hot spot in the world, the United States extended military, economic, and political assistance, manipulated governments by virtually establishing surrogates in positions of power, participated in coups through the CIA, and demanded loyalty in the UN and in other ways. Thus the United States adopted many of the same measures that it criticized the Soviet Union for using. Rather than regarding Third World unrest as local in origin, the Eisenhower administration established a precedent for equating nationalism and neutralism with communism and assuming that the party line emanated solely from the Kremlin.

Eisenhower's foreign policy, like that of Truman's, sought to achieve order and stability in the Third World through economic and military measures. Some of the methods changed. His administration considered reciprocal trade agreements (even with Eastern Europe) to be more important than foreign aid programs in curbing communism, and it depended more on the Export-Import Bank in combating economic problems overseas. American exports doubled from 1952 to 1960, although military aid under the Mutual Security Program averaged more than $3 billion a year in expenditures abroad. Conservative Republicans fought both reciprocal trade pacts and the use of executive agreements in foreign affairs. Allied with conservative Democrats, they came within a single vote of passing the Bricker amendment, which would have changed the Constitution to allow congressional regulation of executive agreements with foreign countries. The White House maintained control over foreign policy, although it continued to operate within the limitations imposed by domestic politics.

The political atmosphere resulting from McCarthyism obstructed the formulation of a realistic policy in dealing with another major development of the period: the growing diversity in the communist world. Moscow's hold had begun to loosen as local communist parties preferred national objectives to ideology and threatened to diffuse the bipolar nature of the international power structure. The first signal came in mid-1948, when Yugoslavia and the Soviet Union broke relations. A more profound change occurred during the 1950s, when the Red Chinese intervened in the Korean War, gaining them prestige in Asia at Soviet expense. An American foreign policy built on caution and restraint seemed wise, and yet internal politics put pressure on Washington to pursue an activist policy braced with rhetoric and warning. Furthermore, the policy's anticommunist thrust led America to support reactionary, repressive regimes, often putting it on the side of those opposing domestic reforms.

America's racial policies at home also hurt its international standing and helped communist propaganda. In December 1952 the United States attorney general urged the Supreme Court to rule against school segregation on the ground that "it is in the context of the present world struggle between freedom and tyranny that the problem of racial discrimination must be viewed." Two years later the Supreme Court struck down segregation in the case of *Brown* v. *Board of Education*, although its implementation was delayed by ensuing events of the decade. In perhaps the most publicized incident, in 1957 Eisenhower had to send federal troops to protect black school children in Little Rock, Arkansas. The state, according to the president, had performed a "tremendous disservice . . . to the nation in the eyes of the world." While the Department of State and Voice of America tried to fend off Soviet propaganda, the United States competed for Third World support and tried to hold together a Western alliance comprised of Britain, France, and other former colonial powers.

More so than the preceding administration, Eisenhower called for negotiations with the Soviet Union. In April 1953, before the resolution of the Korean War, he had delivered a speech entitled "The Chance for Peace" which pushed for improved relations with Stalin's more moderate successor, Georgi Malenkov. Eisenhower's subsequent proposals for disarmament had no immediate effect, for in June workers in East Berlin set off a crisis in Germany by walking off their jobs in demonstration against increased work loads. When their action grew into protests against the Soviet Union, Red troops and tanks crushed the upheaval in less than twenty-four hours. The lesson seemed clear: disharmony in the communist world had left the door ajar for an easing of East-West relations. By the end of the year the Korean War had wound down, and Moscow had established diplomatic relations with Yugoslavia and Greece, dropped territorial demands on Turkey, relaxed denunciations of the United States, and liberated the captives in Stalin's labor camps. Eisenhower went before the UN General Assembly in early December 1953 to recommend a slowdown in the nuclear arms race and to advocate international cooperation in industrial development.

THE CIA IN IRAN AND GUATEMALA

But before talks could begin, the Eisenhower administration had to deal with problems in Iran that many in Washington attributed to communist infiltration. In 1953 it appeared that Premier Mohammed Mossadegh had moved too close to the Soviet Union through the Tudeh, the Communist party in Iran. Two years earlier Mossadegh had nationalized the Anglo-Iranian Oil Company, and in 1953 had seized control over the government, forcing Shah (King) Mohammed Riza Pahlavi into exile. Though Mossadegh's nationalism was probably his greatest liability to the West, the United States cut off aid in the autumn of that year and worked through the CIA, Iranian royalists, and British officials in organizing demonstrations in Teheran which embarrassed his government and led to his overthrow and imprisonment. American military aid helped to restore the young shah to the throne in August. In return he agreed to a consortium awarding Iran's oil production rights primarily to Britain (40 percent) and to the United States (five American companies receiving 40 percent), with the remainder split between a French and a Dutch firm. Iran and the consortium would divide the profits evenly. In 1957 the CIA assisted the shah, who was anticommunist and pro-American, in establishing a secret police network called SAVAK, which used torture, arbitrary imprisonment, and other repressive measures in guaranteeing loyalty to the throne. The Eisenhower administration proclaimed that Iran was no longer in danger of a communist takeover.

Growing unrest in Latin America also seemed to be communist-inspired. Latin Americans had long needed economic assistance, but their pleas for help had seldom attracted attention in Washington. While the United States extended aid to Europe, the Near East, and the Far East by the end of the 1940s, trouble had continued to fester in Latin America as prices declined on the world market, poverty, illiteracy, and disease became more widespread, and as long-standing overpopulation and production problems further complicated the situation. Latin Americans wanted low-term government loans or outright grants, and they needed help in stabilizing prices. Reaction in the United States was not enthusiastic. Leaders in Washington favored industrial growth through private funds, and tied these to Latin American guarantees against nationalization of foreign holdings. Many Latin American leaders considered private investment akin to imperialist exploitation, for American businesses had traditionally drained the region of natural resources.

The Eisenhower administration instituted changes in Latin American policy that only gave the appearance of humanitarian concern, for in reality they reflected an emphasis upon ridding the hemisphere of communism. The president's brother Milton, who was president of Johns Hopkins University, headed a mission in 1953 that visited ten South American states and proposed price stabilization, public loans, stimulation of private investment, and increased technical assistance under the Point Four program. But these measures were insufficient to meet the need. By the early 1950s mounting economic and political unrest in Latin America had combined with growing nationalist fervor to create an explosive situation.

Problems in Guatemala became the focal point of Washington's concern over Latin America, for the republic, led by leftist president Jacobo Arbenz Guzmán, was infiltrated by communists. Arbenz had aroused massive unrest by calling for land reforms in a country where 2 percent of its people owned 70 percent of the land. The largest landholder in Guatemala was an American firm, United Fruit Company, some of whose land the Arbenz regime expropriated in 1953 without offering what the company considered to be adequate compensation. To regain its holdings, United Fruit warned the State Department in Washington that if Arbenz was successful, communism would spread into all of Latin America. Guatemala lay within air striking distance of the Panama Canal, the company's representatives reminded Washington, and Arbenz was moving close to the Soviet Union in the United Nations. American Ambassador John Peurifoy, who had been in Greece during the civil war of the 1940s, assured Washington that Arbenz "thought like a Communist and talked like a Communist, and if not actually one, would do until one came along."

The Eisenhower administration at first adopted diplomatic measures designed to bring about the fall of Arbenz. In March 1954, at the Tenth International Conference of American States in Caracas, Venezuela, the United States secured a near unanimous vote (Guatemala the lone dissenter) condemning "the domination or control of the political institutions of any American state by the international Communist movement." The statement was milder than Dulles wanted, and even then, several of those voting for the resolution complained that they had done so only under pressure from the United States. Over the protests of Guatemala's foreign minister that the declaration meant "the internationalization of McCarthyism," the United States cut off aid to his country.

After diplomatic efforts had failed to undercut the Arbenz regime, Washington participated in its overthrow. The CIA cooperated with an exiled Guatemalan army colonel, Carlos Castillo Armas, in building a mercenary army in Honduras and on an island off Nicaragua. Arbenz appealed to the UN Security Council for help, but the United States blocked substantive consideration. In May a Swedish vessel arrived in Guatemala carrying machine guns and rifles produced in Czechoslovakia. The United States did not interfere with the unloading of the weapons, but the CIA airlifted arms and other materials near United Fruit possessions in Guatemala.

The coup was swift and effective. In June of 1954 Castillo began the assault while CIA pilots in American planes bombed Guatemala City. Arbenz's army deserted, forcing him to flee the country. Castillo took power, United Fruit got back its land, and the new regime moved close to the United States. The Eisenhower administration hailed the fall of Arbenz as a victory for democracy over communism. Yet the social, economic, and political situation in Guatemala did not improve, and the ill feeling resulting from the intervention hurt Latin American-U. S. relations for years.

SOUTHEAST ASIA

Meanwhile the Eisenhower administration faced another Third World problem: the ongoing rebellion in Indochina against the French. During the 1860s France had instituted colonial rule over the small S-shaped province, and in the early 1880s it established protectorates over Laos and Cambodia, soon incorporating them—with Vietnam's three colonies of Annam, Tonkin, and Cochin China—into Indochina. The French extracted vast quantities of rice, rubber, tin, oil, and tungsten from the area, but did little to help its people, the great majority of whom were poverty-stricken country peasants. Ho Chi Minh appeared as a self-appointed representative for Indochina at the Paris Peace Conference ending World War I, where he won no support for democratic reforms at home. Disillusioned, he joined the French Communist party and throughout the 1920s and 1930s lived and campaigned in China, Russia, Thailand, and Vietnam. During that time he established the Indochinese Communist party, which unsuccessfully tried to overthrow French rule.

The onset of World War II had a profound effect on Indochina. After Japan seized the area in 1941, Indochinese nationalists formed an underground resistance organization called the Vietminh, which combined the various nationalist groups under Ho's Communist leadership and used China as its base of operations. Toward the end of the war the Vietminh cooperated with America's Office of Strategic Services against the Japanese, and Ho spoke of support from Washington in implanting American ideals in an independent Indochina during the postwar period. In late August 1945 the Vietminh established the Democratic Republic of Vietnam (DRV), with its capital in Hanoi. After the war, Ho reiterated his call for Indochinese independence.

But America was not favorable to Ho Chi Minh's Vietminh forces. Washington had priorities elsewhere until, in the autumn of 1944, the Department of State recognized the growing importance of Southeast Asia to America's interest in the Philippines. President Roosevelt opposed colonialism and instead tried to establish an international trusteeship over Indochina; but he encountered vehement opposition from the British, who feared that such an example would endanger their colonial interests. When Roosevelt died, the State Department convinced President Truman that the restoration of French hegemony in Southeast Asia was necessary to win their support in Europe. Consequently, after the war wound down in Asia, Indochina returned to French control in 1946.

MAP 32

When Ho Chi Minh's Vietminh forces defeated the French at Dienbienphu in 1954, they had won their independence only in the north. After the Geneva Conference of that same year, the United States engaged in a policy of "nationbuilding" that was supportive of Diem's government in the south.

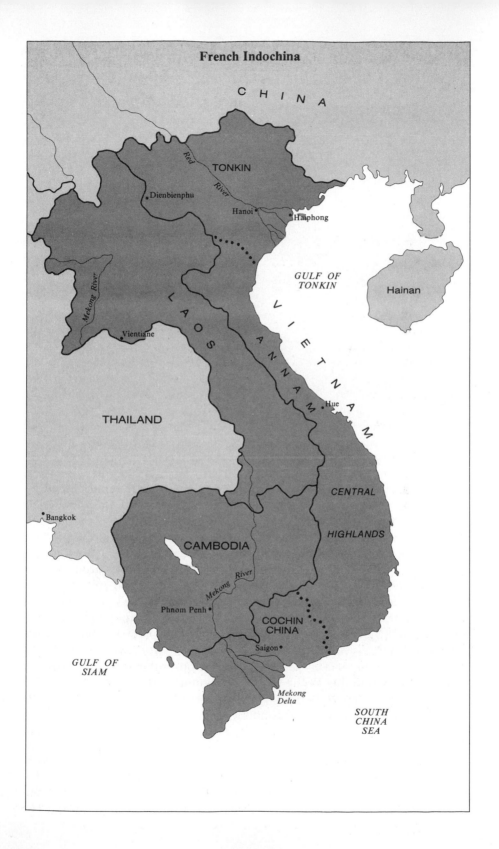

French Indochina

Ho Chi Minh

*Leader of the Vietminh during World War II, who later fought for Vietnam's
independence and re-unification until his death in September 1969.* (National Archives)

Vietminh resistance immediately formed against the French, leading
to the First Indochinese War. In March 1946 Ho Chi Minh and the French
attempted to resolve their differences. Vietnam was to become a "free
state" within the French Union, in return for joining Laos and Cambodia
under a French protectorate called the "Associated States." But conflict
broke out in November when the French did not follow through on a
promised plebiscite. The French bombarded Haiphong and seized the cities, while Vietminh guerrillas solidified control over the countryside. In
1949 the French installed the emperor of Annam, Bao Dai, as ruler of Vietnam and widened his domain to include Cochin China. Though concerned about his people, Bao Dai did not push for reforms primarily
because he was too closely tied to his sponsors in Paris and to wealthy
landholders within his regime. The Vietminh meanwhile drew widespread popular support as the representatives of nationalism. They were
also the "rebels," and the war continued.

American interest in Indochina jumped dramatically during the early
1950s because of the fall of China to communism and the outbreak of the
Korean War. The Truman administration also realized that to win French
support for its European policies, it had to back French interests in Indochina; although Secretary of State Acheson termed this "blackmail," the
payments came easier because the Department of State believed that Ho

Chi Minh was Moscow's communist agent. Acheson, in fact, told the Senate in 1949 that Ho was an "outright Commie." In February 1950 the United States joined Britain in extending recognition to the government of Bao Dai. Indochina, according to Assistant Secretary of State Dean Rusk, had become "the most strategically important area of Southeast Asia."

As Southeast Asia became increasingly important in the Cold War, the Truman administration stepped up military aid to the French. By 1954 the United States had sent more than 300 military advisers and great amounts of aid that constituted 80 percent of France's war expenditures. Red China and the Soviet Union countered by recognizing the Democratic Republic of Vietnam and extending military aid. The French commander in Indochina, General Henri Navarre, meanwhile called for a massive military buildup of the Vietnamese National Army and enough additional French soldiers to launch a major offensive against the Vietminh stronghold in the Red River Delta. Though Dulles was confident that the Navarre Plan would "break the organized body of Communist aggression by the end of the 1955 fighting season," the general was not that sure. The best result, he told leaders in Paris, was a stalemate that might lead to a peace treaty with the Vietminh. Even as the United States began its aid program in 1950, the Vietminh controlled two-thirds of the countryside, counted hundreds of thousands within its ranks, and had taken the offensive in the war.

The showdown in the First Indochinese War came in March 1954 when the Vietminh, armed with Chinese artillery, surrounded a combined French and Vietnamese army of 20,000 in the village of Dienbienphu, a remote valley fortress encircled by hills a thousand feet high and located in northwest Vietnam. Navarre had intended to lure the Vietminh into an open engagement that would allow his superior weapons to take their toll. But the guerrillas surprised the French by laboriously transporting heavy artillery to the high areas ringing the garrison. The French were isolated. The government in Paris appealed to the United States for an air strike and full-scale military intervention. The alternative, warned the French, would be the fall of Indochina and the rest of Southeast Asia to communism.

The Eisenhower administration was divided in reaction to the French plea, but appeared to lean toward intervention. Vice President Richard M. Nixon aroused stiff public opposition in April when he declared in an unauthorized remark that "if to avoid further Communist expansion in Asia and Indochina, we must take the risk now by putting our boys in, I think the Executive has to take the politically unpopular decision and do it." Dulles also wanted to send American soldiers and bomb the area, but Army Chief of Staff Matthew Ridgway staunchly opposed direct involvement because it would lead to heavy American casualties and seriously undermine America's commitment to Europe. At a press conference, Eisenhower spoke of the "domino theory," by which he seemed to imply that American military intervention was necessary to prevent the fall of Indochina and a chain reaction that would cause the collapse of the entire region. Yet he questioned the value of an air strike in guerrilla warfare and in densely forested topography. He also opposed the argument of Air Force Chief of Staff Nathan Twining, who wanted to drop three atomic bombs on the Vietminh forces at Dienbienphu to "clean those Commies out of there."

In the end Eisenhower refused to intervene at Dienbienphu. An air strike, he asserted, was "just silly." Years later in a television interview with Walter Cronkite, Eisenhower explained that "I couldn't think of anything probably less effective . . . unless you were willing to use weapons that could have destroyed the jungles all around the area for miles and that would have probably destroyed Dienbienphu itself." There was no such thing as "partial involvement," Admiral A. C. Davis warned. "One cannot go over Niagara Falls in a barrel only slightly." Eisenhower refused to act unilaterally and without both popular support at home and a French pledge of independence to Indochina. He had none of these. America's allies were not interested in Dulles's call for "United Action," the British in particular refusing to believe that the fall of Indochina would bring down all of Southeast Asia. A recent Gallup poll in the United States had shown ten to one opposition to the use of American combat troops. Finally, the French refused to guarantee independence to Indochina. Eisenhower criticized them for using "weasel words in promising independence," and refused to allow American forces to become "junior partners" to the French. Congress agreed with the president's reasoning.

On May 7, after a fifty-five-day siege, the French and Vietnamese forces surrendered at Dienbienphu. A guerrilla army had proved the feasibility of defeating the superior conventional force of a major power.

There is an ominous note about the situation in Indochina: had the Red Chinese threatened to intervene, Eisenhower was prepared to use nuclear weapons as deterrence. Red China, he explained, was "the head instead of the tail of the snake," and its involvement would have necessitated an American military response. In June Dulles warned Peking that its entry in the war "would be a deliberate threat to the United States itself." The publication in the 1970s of *The Pentagon Papers*, a huge collection of top secret Defense Department documents, shows that the president and his secretary of state were prepared to take these actions. In late May 1954 Eisenhower approved proposals by the Joint Chiefs of Staff for "employing atomic weapons" in the event of China's involvement in Indochina. He added, however, that such a move would have come only after congressional approval and with the help of America's allies. "Unilateral action by the United States in cases of this kind would destroy us," he told an aide. "If we intervened alone in this case we would be expected to intervene alone in other parts of the world."

A conference had meanwhile convened in Geneva to discuss Korea and Indochina, and by July the nineteen delegations present, including the Soviet Union, North Korea, Red China, and the United States, had reached a series of agreements on Southeast Asia. The Geneva Accords arranged an armistice in Indochina, recognized the independence of Laos and Cambodia, and constructed a "provisional military demarcation line" at the 17th parallel in Vietnam, placing 13 million Vietnamese above the division and 10 million below it. The agreements emphasized that this was a temporary partition, not "a political or territorial boundary." The delegates recognized Vietminh control over Hanoi and Haiphong in the north, and agreed that Bao Dai should remain emperor of the south. This arrangement seemed palatable to some members of the Eisenhower administration because of the recently installed premier in the south, Ngo Dinh Diem. Even though a Catholic in a country overwhelmingly non-Catholic, Diem was a nationalist, he opposed the French and the communists, and he had lived in exile in the United States for years. The Geneva agreements stipulated that free elections would take place in 1956 to unite the Vietnams, followed by elections in Laos and Cambodia. Neither region of Vietnam was to enter into military pacts or permit foreign occupation.

The United States, however, refused to sign the Geneva agreements.

President Ngo Dinh Diem of South Vietnam

Arriving for beginning of the National Day parade in Saigon on October 26, 1962. A little over a year later, he would be dead, assassinated during a coup by generals of the South Vietnamese Army. (U.S. Army)

The administration did not recognize Red China, detested negotiations with communists, and recognized the political unpopularity of a pact awarding territory to the Vietminh at the expense of the Associated States. The Eisenhower administration also disliked the prohibitions against the introduction of new military forces and weaponry, and against a move by either part of Vietnam to join a military pact. Eisenhower realized, however, that the communists had won the war, and he agreed with the National Security Council's warnings that Red China would now encourage the spread of communism into all of Southeast Asia. A two-year delay in elections was advantageous, the president believed, for he was certain that Ho Chi Minh would easily win if elections took place immediately. Thus the United States pledged not to interfere with fulfillment of the accords—but did not guarantee to act against any threat to them by others. It declared that it would not participate in any "threat of the use of force to disturb" the Geneva terms, and promised to support "free elections supervised by the United Nations." To ensure against communist takeover, the Eisenhower administration prepared to aid the noncommunists in the south. The State of Vietnam (South) joined the United States in refusing to sign the Accords.

To protect Western interests, the United States took the lead in establishing the Southeast Asia Treaty Organization (SEATO) to safeguard South Vietnam, Laos, and Cambodia from communism. Toward that objective Dulles called a conference at Manila in September, which was attended by the United States, Britain, France, Australia, New Zealand, the Philippines, Thailand, and Pakistan. Other leading governments of that region—India, Indonesia, Burma, and Ceylon—did not attend because they preferred neutralism to antagonizing the Red Chinese, whereas Britain's refusal to recognize the Nationalists on Formosa barred that government from the proceedings. On September 6 the delegates approved a recommendation by President Ramón Magsaysay of the Philippines, which established a Pacific Charter assuring support for "equal rights and self-determination of peoples." Fear of an imminent Red Chinese invasion of Formosa hurried the proceedings. Two days after approval of the Pacific Charter, the delegates signed the Southeast Asia Collective Defense Treaty, which asserted that in the event of attack, each signatory would "consult immediately" according to each member's "constitutional processes." Unlike NATO, there was no central armed force; the new organization depended on America's military support. Headquartered in Bangkok, SEATO went into effect in 1955.

By 1955 the United States was firmly committed to Diem. The organization of SEATO raised questions about the sanctity of the Geneva Accords because it implied that South Vietnam was a separate country. The United States also violated the Accords by stipulating that in exchange for Diem's assurances to institute social and economic reforms, it would send military and economic aid. But had Diem wanted to do so, he could not have implemented sweeping changes because his regime was elitist and his major support came from the landlords. In fact, given Vietnam's devastation from the war, it is doubtful that the United States could have found a less likely place to engage in nationbuilding. While American military advisers worked to improve Diem's army, the French pulled out of Vietnam in the summer of 1955, upset that the United States was using Diem to gain a foothold in Indochina. Diem faced the monumental task of trying to shore up a fragmented society, increasingly staggered by vast influxes of northern refugees who were mostly Catholic and had different traditions and cultures from those already in the south. The south, in fact, was becoming a haven for a variety of independent sects, each with its own beliefs and its own warlords and armies. Dulles had already begun hedging on the likelihood of an election in South Vietnam in 1956. He told reporters that the United States would recognize a government opposed to Diem only if "it seems to be expressive of the real will of the people and if it is truly representative." Dulles further expressed fear that the South Vietnamese did not understand that Ho Chi Minh was an advocate of international communism. In a statement that raised more questions than it answered, he emphasized that until the South Vietnamese recognized Diem's attractions, there could be no valid electoral process.

America's fear of communism in Southeast Asia led it to overlook many faults in Diem's regime. In October 1955 he held a plebiscite in South Vietnam, overwhelmingly winning the presidency over Bao Dai in an obviously fixed election. A young senator from Massachusetts, John F. Kennedy, nonetheless called Diem's Republic of Vietnam the "cornerstone of the Free World in Southeast Asia, the keystone in the arch, the finger in the dike." He continued: "It is our offspring, we cannot abandon it, we cannot ignore its needs." While Diem solidified his control through increasingly repressive measures, the Vietminh in South Vietnam established the National Liberation Front in December 1960, an organization dominated by communists and called the Vietcong or Vietnamese communists.

RED CHINA

In a move doubtless related to America's deepening involvement in Asia, in the autumn of 1954 the Red Chinese began a bombardment of the offshore Nationalist-controlled islands of Quemoy, Matsu, and the Tachens, in apparent preparation for an invasion of Formosa. They did not need an impetus. The Nationalists had bombed the mainland, and had long harassed the communists by firing on their ships and launching commando expeditions ashore. In August Premier Chou En-lai called for the liberation of Formosa because, he asserted, it had become an American military base. But Eisenhower warned that "any invasion of Formosa would have to run over the Seventh Fleet." In early September the Red Chinese seemed ready to seize the islands as a first step to invading Formosa. Chiang had heavily fortified Quemoy, and the Red Chinese began shelling it on September 3, killing two American military advisers during the bombardment.

Some members of the Eisenhower administration reacted strongly to these events, insisting that even though the islands were not vital to American interests, they were symbolic of Free World resistance to communism. The Joint Chiefs of Staff recommended that the president instruct the Nationalists to bomb the Chinese mainland; should this lead to a communist attack on Quemoy, they continued, the United States should aid its defense. Nixon declared that "we should stand ready to call international Communism's bluff on any pot, large or small. If we let them know that we will defend freedom when the stakes are small, the Soviets are not encouraged to threaten freedom where the stakes are higher." Quemoy and Matsu were important in "the poker game of world politics."

The president, however, agreed with General Ridgway, who warned that such a policy would cause war with China. "We're not talking now about a limited, brush-fire war," Eisenhower asserted to the National Security Council. "We're talking about going to the threshold of World War III. . . . Moreover, if we get into a general war, the logical enemy will be Russia, not China, and we'll have to strike there." Dulles had initially supported the Joint Chiefs' call for action but now had to change course. The president had already ordered him to Formosa to negotiate a treaty promising America's protection to Formosa, but leaving the welfare of the offshore islands in an ambiguous position. Dulles had wanted to specify them in the pact, but Eisenhower insisted upon a vague authorization of America's commitment to "such other territories as may be determined by mutual agreement." In December the United States and Formosa signed a mutual defense pact assuring against unilateral military action in exchange for America's guarantee to keep forces "in and about" the island. The following month, after the Red Chinese seized one of the Tachens, Dulles warned the president of "at least an even chance that the United States will have to go to war."

But Eisenhower had laid the basis for a peaceful resolution of the crisis. The defense treaty had allowed him to satisfy Chiang's supporters within the Republican party and yet at the same time to place restraints on the Nationalists. In January 1955 Congress overwhelmingly approved the "Formosa Resolution," authorizing the president to use military force in defending Formosa and "such related positions and territories" as he considered necessary. Thus, Eisenhower's options remained open, leaving the Chinese uncertain about whether he would protect Quemoy, Matsu, and the Tachens. In a letter to Winston Churchill, the president expressed concern about being able to distinguish "between an attack that has only as its objective the capture of an off-shore island and one that is primarily a preliminary movement to an all-out attack on Formosa." America's policy depended on "circumstances as they might arise."

The artillery barrage continued, however, leading the Eisenhower administration to issue a public warning that it was considering the use of nuclear weapons. In March Dulles asserted in a speech that to stop the "aggressive fanaticism" of the Chinese, the United States was willing to use "new and powerful weapons of precision which can utterly destroy military targets without endangering unrelated civilian centers." Though the CIA argued that a "clean" nuclear assault was an impossibility—that it would kill up to 14 million Chinese civilians—Eisenhower assured reporters that Dulles was correct. He later wrote in his memoirs that his intention had been to convince the Chinese communists that he would defend Formosa. If so, it worked: the shelling stopped in April. Eisenhower's implied use of massive retaliation had proved effective; Red China had no nuclear weapons and could not depend on Soviet assistance. The war scare encouraged Washington to push for peace through summit negotiations.

THE SPIRIT OF GENEVA AND EUROPE

By early 1955 the situation had also stabilized in Europe, allowing the Eisenhower administration to resume negotiation attempts with the Soviet Union. The United States had earlier failed to persuade the French to accept the integration of West German soldiers into an organization known as the European Defense Community, but in 1954 the European states had agreed to place West German forces under the control of a Western European Union. France accepted, but at the price of a British commitment of four divisions to Europe and a pledge by the United States to retain its troops already there since 1951. In turn, West German Chancellor Konrad Adenauer pledged not to produce long-range missiles and atomic, chemical, or bacteriological weapons without the consent of NATO's commander and two-thirds approval of the WEU Council. The other members guaranteed that West Germany would not "have recourse to force to achieve the reunification of Germany or the modification of the present boundaries" of Germany. This plan resulted in an alliance of individual nations that went into effect in May 1955. West Germany also became part of NATO that year. A European standoff developed when the Soviets countered with the Warsaw Pact, a military organization of themselves, East Germany, and loyal Eastern European communist states.

The time for a Soviet-American agreement seemed auspicious. Premier Malenkov had resigned in February 1955 and his successor was Nikolai Bulganin, although the real power was Nikita Khrushchev, first secretary of the Communist party. The new Soviet regime seemed amenable to East-West cooperation. It approved a small number of visits by American tourists, and the United States allowed the entry of Soviet agriculturalists and journalists. In May the Soviet Union joined the United States, Britain, and France in signing the Austrian State Treaty, ending ten years of joint occupation and establishing that country's independence and neutrality. The day of the treaty-signing ceremony, the Soviets agreed to meet with the United States, Britain, and France in Geneva in July.

The Geneva Conference of 1955 convened amid an air of optimism tempered by caution and uncertainty. The United States was confident both in its strength and in the Soviet Union's economic weaknesses. America's European allies were more concerned about stopping the race to war; NATO war games had recently indicated that if fighting broke out on the continent, over 170 atomic bombs would hit Western Europe.

Despite the widely heralded "spirit of Geneva," the Big Four reached no important agreements at the week-long conference. Both sides presented proposals virtually assured of failures. The Soviets called for an end to NATO, the withdrawal of American soldiers from the continent, and a ban on the production and use of atomic weapons; the West pressed for the unification of Germany through democratic elections. On arms control, Eisenhower made an "open skies" proposal, by which the United States and the Soviet Union would furnish maps of each other's military complexes to allow each to conduct aerial surveillance of the other's territory. The president was not naive. He used this piece of drama to counter the Soviets' earlier call for disarmament. "We knew the Soviets wouldn't accept it," he later recalled. Yet the president hoped that the proposal might ease international tension by opening the way to less comprehensive arms control measures. In a letter to General Alfred Gruenther, Eisenhower explained that his intention had been to secure "an immense gain in mutual confidence and trust." At Geneva the United States and the Soviet Union agreed only to encourage cultural exchanges; the other issues they forwarded to a meeting of the Big Four's foreign ministers.

The Geneva Conference nonetheless left the impression that a thaw had developed in the Cold War. Eisenhower spoke of the "new spirit of conciliation and cooperation," and the Soviets' decision to recognize West Germany that same year seemed to be an outgrowth of the new atmosphere. Yet it soon became evident that the conference was a show in which photographers took many pictures that created the illusion of Soviet-American friendship. Khrushchev boasted that "we had established ourselves as able to hold our own in the international arena." Dulles warned against expecting an "era of good feelings," while W. Averell Harriman, former ambassador to Moscow, expressed concern that the "free world was psychologically disarmed" by the "spirit of Geneva" and warned that it was a "smoke screen" for Soviet expansion. Khrushchev emphasized that no change had taken place in Soviet attitude. "[I]f anybody thinks that for this reason we shall forget about Marx, Engels, and Lenin, he is mistaken. This will happen when shrimps learn to whistle."

In February 1956 Khrushchev shocked friends and foes alike by calling for peaceful coexistence and the de-Stalinization of Eastern Europe. Before the Twentieth Congress of the Communist party in Moscow, the first secretary delivered a speech in which he turned from Lenin's assertion of the inevitability of war between communists and capitalists, and called for a communist victory through peaceful means. He then denounced Stalin's domestic crimes and urged party members to accept diversity in the communist world. Khrushchev had several objectives, including an expansion of his power at home, a loosening of restraints on the country's economy to promote production, and a maintenance of domestic control short of outright repression. Eastern European nations were bewildered and yet guardedly encouraged. There was little justification for the latter. Khrushchev had called for a new approach to the same goal: a communist triumph by Soviet exploitation of the uncommitted nations of the world, whether or not they were communist. The CIA soon secured a copy of his address and circulated copies in Eastern Europe and elsewhere. The Department of State published the speech in April.

The erosion of communist unity had not gone unnoticed by the Eisenhower administration. Tito's defection, the growing division between the Soviets and the Red Chinese, and now an admission to "national Communism"—all suggested that America needed to examine recent instances of unrest throughout the world to determine whether the Soviets were losing their grip on the communist movement. Khrushchev's recognition of "Titoism" in 1955 was an important sign of change, as were the Soviets' decisions to disband the Cominform, to arrange an exchange of visits between Tito and Khrushchev, and to negotiate a pact with Yugoslavia which contained the surprising assertion that there were "different roads to socialism."

But before the United States could assess the potential impact of this new Soviet policy, thousands of dissidents in Poland and Hungary seized upon Khrushchev's speech as an invitation to self-determination and rose in revolt against Stalinist leaders in their countries. Americans interpreted the upheavals as fulfillments of Dulles's goal of "liberation" and supported the Voice of America and Radio Free Europe in encouraging further resistance in Eastern Europe. The dangerous implication was that the United States would assist anyone taking the first step toward breaking Soviet ties.

In June 1956 riotous demonstrations among workers in Poland soon developed into a widespread revolt against Soviet dominance in the country. The Soviets threatened to use force to put down the uprising, but in October Polish communists, led by Wladyslaw Gomulka, met with Khrushchev and warned of full-scale armed resistance if the Soviets tried a coup. Khrushchev accepted Gomulka (earlier rejected by Stalin as "Titoist") as chairman of the Polish Communist party. Poland remained communist and within the Warsaw Pact, even though its relationship with the Soviet Union was uneasy. Poland appeared to have won autonomy in October, when it elected Gomulka chairman of the Communist party. As was the case with Yugoslavia in 1948, the United States extended economic aid to Poland.

The successes in Poland probably had a direct effect on Hungary, for in late October 1956 demonstrations in Budapest against Stalinism grew into violence aimed at the communist government and at the Soviet Union. The leader of the insurrection, Imre Nagy, feared Soviet military intervention and tried to restrain the extremism of his followers, but matters got out of hand as the rebels demanded freedom, toppled the huge statue of Stalin in the city, and killed several Stalinist communists. Nagy soon emerged as head of a new regime that included noncommunist members. It broke with the Warsaw Pact, demanded the withdrawal of Soviet troops, and announced a neutralist position in international affairs. The new government then turned to the United States for aid based on the assurances of Eisenhower-Dulles "liberation."

The Eisenhower administration found itself in the uncomfortable position of wanting to see the Hungarians succeed but unable to do anything in an area vital to Soviet interests. Dulles praised the revolution as proof of the "weakness of Soviet imperialism" and noted that these "captive peoples should never have reason to doubt that they have in us a sincere and dedicated friend who shares their aspirations." The secretary, however, was in ill health and would soon undergo surgery for cancer; but even if Dulles had been healthy, the administration would not have intervened in Hungary. It is impossible to determine whether Eisenhower's foreign policy pronouncements influenced the outbreak of the Hungarian revolution, but they doubtless led the rebels to believe that American aid would arrive after they took the initial step toward independence. The United States publicly expressed sympathy, introduced UN resolutions condemning Soviet actions and calling for withdrawal, and opened its door to thousands of Hungarian refugees. But that was the extent of American involvement. The administration in Washington recognized that intervention could have led to war with the Soviet Union. Besides, troubles had meanwhile erupted in the Middle East, an area regarded as crucial to America's interests.

Events in Hungary threatened to establish a precedent for other communist states, and for that reason the Soviet Union had to act. It first installed a communist regime, which immediately requested Moscow's help in restoring order. On November 4, at the height of the concurrent crisis in the Middle East, Red tanks and troops stormed into Budapest to put down the revolution. Nagy sought refuge in the Yugoslav embassy, but came out after allegedly receiving assurances of a seat in the new government. (The Soviets later executed him.) After weeks of street fighting, the Soviets squelched the rebellion at the cost of 30,000 Hungarian lives. "Poor fellows, poor fellows," Eisenhower lamented to a reporter. "I think about them all the time. I wish there were some way of helping them."

Several revealing aspects about American and Soviet behavior emerged from the Hungarian crisis. Eisenhower "liberation" offered false hopes in areas vital to the Soviet Union. Moscow permitted nationalist uprisings only if they did not damage Soviet prestige or set precedents dangerous to international communism. The Soviets lost respect among communists in other countries, for their troops had not performed well, their allies' military forces had often defected, and Hungarian youths had not been converted to communism. The revolution was a severe propaganda defeat for Moscow, but Hungary remained within the Soviet bloc.

SUEZ

Toward the last stages of the Hungarian revolution, attention suddenly shifted to the Middle East, where a major power confrontation threatened to develop during the Suez crisis of 1956. Ancient issues in this region, combined with its growing military and strategic importance in the postwar era, created a situation conducive to war. The ingredients were there: Arab-Israeli conflict, Anglo-Egyptian rivalry, emerging nationalisms after World War II, big power interests in oil, suspicions between East and West, and divisiveness among the Western powers. The Eisenhower administration feared that continued disorder in the Middle East would invite Soviet involvement.

British policy lay at the root of many problems in the Middle East. During the First World War Britain had issued the Balfour Declaration, which offered hope to the Zionist movement by guaranteeing "the establishment in Palestine of a National Home for the Jewish people." The year before, however, the British had assured the Arabs an independent state out of the remains of the Ottoman Empire—including Palestine. The two promises were irreconcilable. At Versailles in 1919 Britain was assigned the League of Nations mandate over Palestine, and for years afterward attempted to resolve these conflicting policies. In more than one instance it turned away ships bearing Jewish refugees as they approached Palestine. Meanwhile, in September 1922, the American Congress approved a joint resolution endorsing the Balfour Declaration. Two years later the United States negotiated a treaty recognizing the British mandate over Palestine, and thereby set the direction of its own Palestinian policy.

Hitler's persecutions of the Jews during World War II revived Zionism and drove many European Jews toward their "homeland" in the postwar period. In 1947 Britain announced an end to its Palestinian mandate the following year, leaving the question for the United Nations. The General Assembly in late November 1947 decided to partition Palestine into Arab and Jewish states and to establish international supervision of the ancient city of Jerusalem. But this plan aroused bitter Arab opposition. The Arabs had twice as many people in Palestine as did the Jews, and they had resided there for centuries. The partition also awarded the Jews the largest section of Palestine's farmland, along with most of its urban and railroad areas. The Arab delegation in the General Assembly stalked out in protest. On May 14, 1948, the day before Britain's mandate came to an end, the Jews proclaimed the state of Israel. Less than fifteen minutes later, President Truman rejected the advice of his diplomatic and military coun-

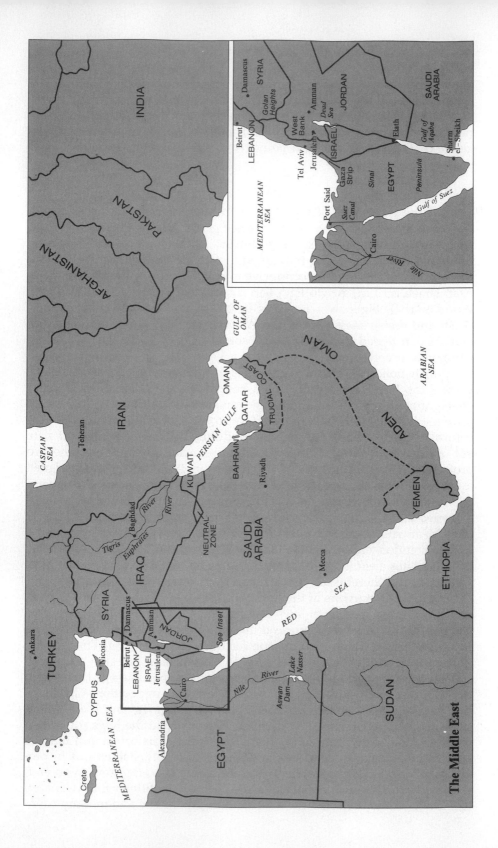

The Middle East

selors and extended *de facto* recognition. Three days afterward the Soviet Union did the same.

In explaining America's rapid recognition of Israel, Truman emphasized humanitarian concern for the Jews, but he could not have been oblivious to domestic political considerations. He had earlier called on Britain to permit 100,000 Jews to enter Palestine. A few days afterward his probable Republican opponent in the presidential election of 1948, New York Governor Thomas Dewey, recommended raising the number to several hundred thousand. The election of 1948, everyone knew, would be close, and the Jewish vote in New York could award the White House to the Republicans for the first time since 1933. The Department of State had joined military advisers in opposing the UN partition plan because it would alienate the Arabs. The president supported the partition for humanitarian and political reasons.

Conflict erupted as the neighboring Arab states invaded Palestine, only to be driven back by the smaller yet better equipped Israeli forces—most of whose heavy weaponry was from communist Czechoslovakia. Sentiment for Hitler's wartime victims and the need for the Jewish-American vote at home had led to a pro-Israel feeling in Washington; and yet the realization that two-thirds of the world's oil reserves were in the Middle East, whose borders touched 3,000 miles of the Soviet Union, caused a serious dilemma. Americans had more than enough oil for the present, but this could change with time. The United States had numerous ties with the Jews, but it also wanted to outmaneuver the Soviets for the Middle East's oil and sites for military bases. Washington had to devise a policy satisfactory to Jewish-Americans without driving the Arabs into the Soviet camp.

An armistice in July 1949 only temporarily wound down Arab-Israeli hostilities. Through UN mediation Israel received more land than the partition award had allowed, whereas Egypt and Jordan assumed control over the Arab section of Palestine. International supervision of Jerusalem never materialized, leaving the city divided between Israel and Jordan. The Arab states meanwhile boycotted Israel and cut off its land access to the outside, while Egypt closed the Suez Canal to its use. Another problem had appeared. The creation of Israel had led to the displacement of nearly 800,000 Palestinian Arabs, who now lived in poverty just outside the new state and were not welcomed by any of the Arab states. The UN Relief and Works Agency for Palestine Refugees tried to ease the situation, but some of the homeless Arabs had already organized terrorist bands to raid Israel.

MAP 33

The Suez crisis of 1956 almost shattered the Western alliance, raised the stature of the Russians in the Middle East, and forced the United States to take a more active part in that region's affairs.

America's Middle East policy remained uncertain because of its conflicting Jewish and Arab interests. Indeed, the United States was soon caught in a dilemma between the Zionists at home and in Israel, and America's oil interests in that part of the world. To prevent further troubles believed conducive to Soviet intervention, the United States worked with the UN Palestine Conciliation Commission, and in May 1950 joined Britain and France in the Tripartite Declaration, which assured that should either the Israelis or Arabs violate the armistice in Palestine, the three powers would "immediately take action, both within and outside the United Nations." Finally, the State Department devised a complicated financial arrangement with Saudi Arabia by which the United States acquired Arabian oil for a generous secret subsidy, while allowing the Truman administration to remain officially and publicly on the side of the Israelis. The United States meanwhile extended economic and technical aid to most governments of the Middle East, called for land and resettlement programs in Egypt and Iraq, and helped Saudi Arabia reform its tariff and customs laws. The problems persisted.

In 1952 dissidents in the Egyptian army rose in rebellion against the corrupt regime of King Farouk, forcing him out of the country and within two years installing their leader, Colonel Gamal Abdel Nasser, as premier. Nasser gained widespread popular support by instituting a program of land reform and promising to end Britain's control of the Suez Canal. That same year, 1954, the United States helped secure two agreements between Britain and Egypt, by which the British would gradually withdraw their military forces from the Suez Canal over the next twenty months. Britain's longtime involvement in Egypt would come to a close in 1956.

To preserve stability and Western influence in the Middle East, the United States supported but did not join the Baghdad Pact of 1955. Iraq had earlier that year pulled away from the Arab states in signing a Pact of Mutual Assistance with Turkey. Iran, Pakistan, and Britain later joined the agreement and set up headquarters in Baghdad (capital of Iraq) for the Middle East Treaty Organization (METO). The United States occasionally took part in the proceedings and extended military assistance on an individual basis. But it would go no further for fear of deepening Nasser's animosity toward the West, antagonizing Israel, or alienating the rising numbers in Asia and Africa who opposed the organization. The Baghdad Pact was part of Dulles's attempt to establish a defense line between Turkey and Pakistan and connect it with that already constructed around the Soviet Union by NATO and SEATO. The effects were not all the secretary intended. METO united the Arabs against the West and invited the Soviet Union to exploit Arab hostility toward the Jews. A decline in Western influence became plain by the autumn of 1955. The French were deeply involved in putting down an uprising in Algeria encouraged by Egypt, and British efforts to persuade Jordan to join the Baghdad Pact led to violent demonstrations in its capital of Amman.

In the meantime the situation worsened in the Suez area. The Israelis had retaliated for repeated border troubles by raiding Egypt's Gaza Strip along their common frontier in February 1955, and in late September Nasser mortgaged his country's entire year's cotton crop for an arms deal with Czechoslovakia, which was acting as a front for the Soviet Union. The following December the United States attempted to pull Nasser toward the West by agreeing to help finance the construction of the Aswan Dam, on the Nile River, to promote electricity and irrigation. Over a billion dollars was to come from the World Bank plus American and British funds. Jewish-Americans put pressure on the Eisenhower administration to cancel the deal, while southern members of Congress warned that such a dam would hurt their own cotton manufacturers.

The Eisenhower administration failed to undercut the Soviets and win Egypt's support. The president and his secretary of state were already upset with a recent decision by Nasser to recognize Red China, and they now feared that the arms deal was proof of a shift from neutralism to a pro-Soviet allegiance. Dulles put it simply: "Do nations which play both sides get better treatment than nations which are stalwart and work with us?" The administration's answer to Nasser's blackmail tactics came in July 1956, when it suddenly and dramatically retracted the loan offer for the Aswan Dam. Dulles had not consulted the British, who had agreed to share the financial burden, and he had chosen to make the announcement on the day Nasser's foreign minister arrived in Washington to discuss the arrangement. Dulles was confident that the move would call the Soviet bluff and set an example for neutralists.

But the Soviets did not have time to act: Nasser nationalized the canal by taking over the British- and French-controlled Universal Suez Canal Company, and announced that he would use the canal tolls to build the dam. The move was legal, for he promised to compensate the stockholders and pledged to keep the passage open. But Nasser's action humiliated the British and infuriated the French. Dulles immediately flew to London to confer with British Prime Minister Anthony Eden and French Premier Guy Mollet, both of whom had discussed the use of force in regaining control over the canal. At a meeting of the twenty-four nations chiefly dependent on the canal, the vast majority supported the establishment of an international organization to administer the waterway. Nasser, however, rejected the plan because the organization would be under British and French control. Dulles recommended forming a Suez Canal Users Association (SCUA) to collect the tolls and divide the funds between canal maintenance and payments to owners. Nasser likewise turned down this plan. In October the UN Security Council responded to the Anglo-French request for assistance by establishing guidelines for the canal's administration that included assurances of Egyptian sovereignty, no outside interference with the canal's operation, and "free and open transit through the Canal." Egypt accepted these terms, although Britain and France doubted that Nasser would abide by them. Eden and Mollet decided to act on their own.

By late October 1956, simultaneously with the upheavals in Poland and Hungary the crisis building in the Middle East threatened to cause an East-West confrontation. France, England, and Israel secretly collaborated to invade Egypt and bring about Nasser's collapse. Israel moved first. Its forces overran the Egyptian forces in the Gaza Strip and Sinai Peninsula, seizing nearly all of the Czech arms along with 6,000 Egyptian soldiers, and then headed toward the Suez Canal. The day following the invasion, Britain and France feigned surprise at Israel's actions and called for a cease-fire which stipulated that both Egypt and Israel were to withdraw ten miles from the canal, giving Israel a hundred miles of Egyptian territory. Thus the British and French had violated the Tripartite Declaration of May 1950 that, with the United States, had guaranteed no border violations of either Israel or the Arab states. Nasser rejected the Anglo-French proposal and closed the canal by sinking ships in its passageway. Arab militants meanwhile sabotaged pumphouses that sent oil from the Persian Gulf to the Mediterranean, causing a shortage in Western Europe that necessitated a severe rationing program and underlined the importance of the Middle East. On the same day that Nasser turned down the Anglo-French demand, October 30, the United States and the Soviet Union sponsored cease-fire resolutions in the UN Security Council. Both Britain and France vetoed the measures. The next day, according to plan, their combined forces began an offensive that culminated in the bombing of Egyptian air strips, in preparation for seizing Port Said at the north end of the canal. The timing was not opportune, for the Anglo-French military action blunted America's concurrent protests against Soviet actions in Budapest.

Eisenhower, in the heat of a reelection campaign, became livid with the British and French when he learned of their actions in the Middle East. With Dulles hospitalized for cancer treatment, Eisenhower took the lead. He called Eden on the phone and gave his wartime friend a verbal lashing that brought the prime minister to tears. Eisenhower then blasted the British and French over radio and television on October 31 for actions that endangered peace in the Middle East by pulling in the Soviet Union, and for turning the world's attention from Moscow's brutal suppression of Hungary. In early November the UN General Assembly overwhelmingly approved an American resolution for cutting back Latin American oil to Britain and France, as leverage to force them into a cease-fire and to withdraw to the previous armistice line. Bulganin and Khrushchev meanwhile sought to exploit the rift in the Western alliance by suggesting a plan for joint military action with the United States. The Soviets were prepared to fire rockets onto London and Paris to halt the invasion and to send "volunteers" to evict the "aggressors." Eisenhower dismissed the Soviets' proposal as "unthinkable," but became increasingly disturbed about the possibility of a nuclear confrontation. The president assured the head of the CIA, Allen Dulles, that "if the Soviets should attack Britain and France directly, we would of course be in a major war." The Hungarian and Suez crises rallied the American people around the president and helped sweep him to reelection that week.

The results were not surprising: Britain and France relented to the combined pressure of the United States, the UN, and the Soviet Union. On November 5 the General Assembly proposed the establishment of an Emergency Force for Palestine, and the next day Britain, France, and Israel agreed to a cease-fire. By Christmas, UNEF forces occupied the Gaza Strip and the Gulf of Aqaba, providing the Israelis with both protection from Egypt and a water link to the Red Sea through the port of Elath. But the Israelis had not secured use of the canal. In March 1957, under American pressure, they withdrew behind the original armistice lines.

The Suez crisis furthered Soviet influence in the Middle East. The United States had helped to save Nasser, but at the cost of British and French prestige, which put a severe strain on the Western alliance. Though suffering a humiliating defeat by the Israelis, Nasser held the canal and enjoyed great respect throughout the Arab world. America's retraction of money for the Aswan Dam drove Nasser closer to the Soviets, who had acquired stature in the Middle East and who now gave him arms and finances for construction of the dam. The United States, however, had protected its oil interests and now saw no choice but to assume the responsibilities for maintaining order in the Middle East, formerly undertaken by the British and the French.

America's concern over Soviet penetration into the Middle East led to the announcement of the Eisenhower Doctrine in the spring of 1957. Moscow had negotiated economic and military agreements with Egypt and Syria, and Washington feared that with Syria's help Nasser might emerge as leader of the Arab world, but under Soviet influence. In January the president asked Congress for approval to issue a warning that the United States was prepared to defend the Middle East from outside encroachments. After lengthy debates, in March Congress approved a joint resolution that became known as the Eisenhower Doctrine. It empowered the president to use military force if any government of the Middle East requested protection against "overt armed aggression from any nation controlled by International Communism." Congress also guaranteed economic and military aid for the Middle East. Dulles noted with satisfaction that "gradually, one part of the world after another is being brought into it [America's defense system] and perhaps we may end up with a, what you might call, universal doctrine reflected by multilateral treaties or multilateral worldwide authority from Congress." Though critics complained that communist subversion was a greater danger than armed attack, the Eisenhower administration had dramatically assumed the Anglo-French peacekeeping role in the Middle East. Furthermore, its policy marked a commitment to containment, though under a different name.

The Eisenhower Doctrine underwent immediate tests in Jordan and Lebanon, although in both cases Arab nationalism was probably a greater threat to Middle East stability than Soviet communism. When a leftist coup supported by Egypt and Syria threatened to overthrow Jordan's pro-Western King Saddam Hussein in the spring of 1957, the United States sent economic and military aid and moved the Sixth Fleet to the eastern Mediterranean. The situation eased. Early the following year Egypt, Syria, and Yemen established the United Arab Republic (U.A.R.), with Nasser as president. Jordan and Iraq countered with the Arab Union. In mid-July a military coup in Iraq led to the installation of a "republican" regime that moved close to the Soviet Union. The West erroneously assumed that Nasser was behind the revolution in Iraq and feared the same in Lebanon, located along the eastern Mediterranean. Its pro-Western president, Camille Chamoun, believed that the U.A.R. was aiding a Muslim armed insurrection, and joined Jordan in asking the United States and Britain for protection. Eisenhower responded by dispatching 14,000 marines to Lebanon in July 1958, and Britain sent 3,000 paratroopers to bolster Jordan's Hussein, again in danger of overthrow.

By the autumn of 1958 both the Jordanian and Lebanese crises had passed without incident. With the UN Security Council stymied and the Soviets accusing the West of imperialism and calling for its withdrawal, Arab leaders in the General Assembly took the lead toward peace. They proposed a resolution pledging mutual nonintervention in each other's domestic affairs, and asked the UN secretary-general to guarantee its implementation in Jordan and Lebanon. The resolution prepared the way for military withdrawal, while American diplomat Robert Murphy helped mediate an end to Lebanon's internal troubles. The United States pulled out of Lebanon in October, and Britain left Jordan the following month. In March 1959 Eisenhower negotiated separate executive agreements with Turkey, Iran, and Pakistan, which guaranteed American military assistance should they come under attack. Iraq withdrew from the Baghdad Pact that same month in favor of a neutralist position, and the organization moved its headquarters to Ankara, Turkey, where it became known as the Central Treaty Organization (CENTO), comprised of Turkey, Britain, Iran, and Pakistan.

BERLIN AND THE SPIRIT OF CAMP DAVID

Despite Eisenhower's easy reelection, Americans were still uneasy about the Democrats' charges that the Soviet Union had surged ahead in the Cold War. Indeed, the United States faced a paradoxical situation: any move toward peace through disarmament could imply weakness, invite Soviet expansion, and lead to war. Early in 1957 Polish Foreign Minister Adam Rapacki recommended the establishment of a denuclearized zone in Central and Eastern Europe; the Soviets endorsed the plan but the Eisenhower administration showed no interest. In June the Senate approved the Atoms-for-Peace Treaty, which Eisenhower had proposed four years earlier. Similar to the abortive Baruch Plan of 1946, it called for the major powers to share atomic materials through an International Atomic Energy Agency. But the safeguards did not work, and the joint contributions of fissionable materials to the agency promoted nuclear proliferation. In late 1957 Moscow shocked Americans twice: first in late August by announcing the development of an intercontinental ballistic missile (ICBM), and then on October 4 by launching the Sputnik, the first space satellite of human origin. The irony is that the Eisenhower administration knew from secret U-2 reconnaissance planes flying high over the Soviet Union that Sputnik posed no threat to the United States, but the president could not say anything for fear of revealing the aerial operations. A second irony is that Khrushchev was aware of the reconnaissance flights but also could say nothing; the U-2s flew above Soviet firing range and a protest would have constituted an admission to his nation's incapability of defending itself against espionage. The British ambassador in Washington noted that "the Russian success in launching the satellite has been something equivalent to Pearl Harbor. The American cocksureness is shaken." The following month the Soviets sent Sputnik II into orbit—carrying a canine passenger. Someone remarked that the Soviets would probably send cows on the next flight, thus constituting "the herd shot 'round the world."

The Eisenhower administration moved to regain the lead in the Cold War. The Gaither Report, a top-secret study by the Ford Foundation Commission which the American press uncovered and published, had enormous public impact because of its call for a huge armaments program to counter the Soviets' growing military and economic power. While researchers stepped up work on ballistic missiles, the president hesitated to turn the nation into what he termed a "garrison state," but dispatched SAC bombers to bolster the NATO alliance, agreed to furnish intermediate range ballistic missiles to NATO allies, and approved the continuation of U-2 flights. In January 1958 the United States launched Explorer I, America's first space satellite, and by July had established the National Aeronautics and Space Administration (NASA) to further aerospace research. Congress passed the National Defense Education Act (NDEA) in September to provide federal aid for education in science, mathematics, and foreign languages.

As the military and missile buildup threatened to race out of control by late 1957, Soviet specialist George F. Kennan, longtime advocate of the containment theory, now called for the "disengagement" of foreign military forces from Germany and Eastern Europe. In the Reith Lectures in London, he urged the major powers to construct a unified, neutral Germany built around the "free city" of Berlin. Kennan argued that if the United States could separate the German issue from NATO and the rivalries of the Cold War, the Soviets might withdraw their armies from Eastern Europe. Should the Eisenhower administration de-emphasize NATO and turn to diplomacy, the Soviets might reciprocate by dismantling the

Warsaw Pact. Then the European Common Market would have a chance to promote the economic integration of the continent through the elimination of tariffs and other obstacles to unity.

But Washington was not interested in disengagement. Former Secretary of State Dean Acheson regarded the idea as isolationist and warned that it would undercut the Western alliance by encouraging the Red Army to take Europe and negotiate a military agreement with an independent Germany. "Mr. Kennan has never, in my judgment," Acheson remarked, "grasped the realities of power relationships, but takes a rather mystical attitude toward them. To Mr. Kennan there is no Soviet military threat in Europe."

As the Western allies increasingly disagreed over European policy, the Soviets seized the moment in an attempt to win concessions in Berlin. The western sector of the city had become a dangerous example for unhappy East Germans. While they suffered severe economic and political hardships, West Berlin was prospering, and serving as an espionage and propaganda center for the West. Nearly 3 million East German defectors had gone there since 1949. The glaring contrasts in life-styles between the two Germanies tended to emphasize the superiority of capitalism over communism. Though the United States refused to recognize East Germany, it openly praised the courage of the East German people, sent armaments to West Germany to bolster the 11,000 American, British, and French soldiers occupying West Berlin, and repeatedly called for democratic elections to unite the Germans into one state. West Berlin was a "bone in the throat," admitted Khrushchev, now Soviet premier. The arming of West Germany, he complained, was a violation of wartime pledges to prevent the country from again becoming a military power. The imminent move by the West German government to join France, Italy, Belgium, Luxembourg, and the Netherlands in the European Common Market finally pushed Khrushchev into action. Germany, he feared, was about to become irrevocably tied to the West.

In November 1958 Khrushchev delivered a blustery speech announcing abrogation of the wartime agreements relating to Germany and demanding an end to Western occupation of West Berlin. Unless negotiations began in six months, he warned, the Soviet Union would sign a separate peace treaty with the East Germans terminating occupation and isolating West Berlin about a hundred miles inside a communist nation. The Allies would then have to work out passage rights into Berlin through the East German government which, he reminded them, they did not recognize. Should they use force, the signatories of the Warsaw Pact stood ready to help East Germany. Berlin should be a "free city" within a confederation of East and West Germany, Khrushchev stated in notes to Washington, London, and Paris.

Khrushchev's ultimatum placed the United States in a bind. Recognition of East Germany would virtually turn it over to the Soviets and permanently divide the country. Kennan's plea for disengagement was out of the question. Furthermore, should the United States pull out of West Berlin, the Adenauer government's faith in NATO and the Common Market would diminish, laying the groundwork for another Soviet-German arrangement only slightly less dangerous than the pact they negotiated in 1939. Some Americans, including Acheson and Army Chief of Staff Maxwell Taylor, recommended that the United States determine whether this was a Soviet bluff by sending more soldiers to West Berlin. Dulles told the press that "we are most solemnly committed to hold West Berlin, if need be by military force." General Nathan Twining, chairman of the Joint Chiefs of Staff, assured the president that he was ready "to fight a general nuclear war." But Eisenhower was not. "[D]estruction is not a good police force," he declared. "You don't throw hand grenades around streets to police the streets so that people won't be molested by thugs." The outcome largely depended upon the attitude of the Western allies, who had recently drifted apart.

The West surprised Khrushchev by uniting against his demands. At first the NATO allies had disagreed over what action to take. President Charles de Gaulle of France did not favor German reunification, but he refused to retreat on Berlin. British Prime Minister Harold Macmillan, realizing that a Soviet nuclear attack would focus on England, seemed to support the conversion of West Berlin into a free city in line with Khrushchev's ultimatum. Eisenhower, however, refused to budge. "Any sign of Western weakness at this forward position," he warned, "could be misinterpreted with grievous consequences." Though he first wanted to "give peace forces a chance," he made clear that if the East Germans stopped any American vehicle after the six-month deadline, the United States would order a small armed convoy to Berlin. Should that convoy encounter interference, Eisenhower emphasized, he would institute an airlift, sever relations with Moscow, take the matter before the UN, and prepare for war. The president privately remarked that "in this gamble, we are not going to be betting white chips, building up the pot gradually and fearfully. Khrushchev should know that when we decide to act, our whole stack will be in the pot."

After many anxious moments the Berlin crisis faded without incident. In December 1958 the foreign ministers of the United States, Britain, France, and West Germany met in Paris and decided not to capitulate, and two days later the NATO Council pledged support. The wartime victory over Germany had been a cooperative Allied effort, the West argued, and the Soviet Union had no right to alter the situation without common consent. Seeing the West unified, Khrushchev backed off from his ultimatum with the lame explanation that he had not meant six months in a literal sense. He agreed that the Big Four's foreign ministers should meet in Geneva to discuss Germany, Europe, and disarmament.

Perhaps because of America's preoccupation with the Lebanon and Berlin crises, problems had again flared in the Formosa Straits, where in the autumn of 1958 the Red Chinese resumed their bombardment of Quemoy, now fortified with 100,000 Nationalists, or a third of Chiang's army. Mao perhaps had no serious thoughts about an invasion of Formosa, but he might have intended either to force the surrender of Quemoy or to cause a strong American action that would gain him Soviet support. Indeed, such a strategy, if it existed, appeared to be working. Peking radio threatened to "smash the American paper tiger and liberate Taiwan [Formosa]," and Khrushchev warned that "an attack on the Chinese People's Republic is an attack on the Soviet Union." Dulles recommended small atomic bombs—"air bursts, so that there would be no appreciable fallout or large civilian casualties." Eisenhower instead approved airlifts of Chiang's troops, authorized the Seventh Fleet to convoy the nationalists' supply ships, and, most ominous, dispatched marines into Quemoy bearing howitzers capable of delivering atomic shells. In September he asserted over television that the desertion of Quemoy would be a "Western Pacific Munich." Americans would not engage in "appeasement."

As in 1954 the Formosa crisis again quickly dissipated. Should the Red Chinese agree to a cease-fire, Dulles proposed, the United States would seek a reduction of the Nationalist forces on Quemoy. He sweetened the offer by publicly declaring that the United States had "no commitment" to support Chiang's return to the mainland. The Red Chinese responded by calling off the firing for a week; in return, Eisenhower ordered the Seventh Fleet to stop convoying Chiang's supply ships. Dulles traveled to Formosa in October and convinced Chiang to cut back on the number of soldiers on the islands and renounce forceful attempts to take the mainland. Peking nonetheless announced its intention to shell Quemoy on alternate days, a ploy that permitted Chiang to supply his troops on Quemoy and yet allowed the Red Chinese to maintain a formal protest against the Nationalists' presence on the island. Eisenhower expressed bewilderment over this "Gilbert and Sullivan war." Mao later declared with wonder, "Who would have thought when we fired a few shots at Quemoy and Matsu that it would stir up such an earth-shattering storm?"

After Dulles's departure from the State Department in the spring of 1959, Eisenhower played a more visible role in relations with Moscow. An encouraging sign was Vice President Nixon's visit to the Soviet Union in July, followed by Khrushchev's tour of the United States in September. Not all was harmonious. Nixon, who once characterized Khrushchev as a "bare knuckle slugger who had gouged, kneed, and kicked" his way to the top, took advantage of television cameras to score a Cold War victory in the famous "kitchen debate." Before a model kitchen at the American National Exhibition in Moscow, he and Khrushchev engaged in an animated discussion of capitalism and socialism in which Nixon shook his finger at Khrushchev, much to the delight of Americans. Eisenhower later welcomed Khrushchev to the United States, hoping to "soften up the Soviet leader even a little bit." Khrushchev was short-tempered and unpolished in manner and speech, yet Eisenhower considered him a "powerful, skillful, ruthless, and highly ambitious politician" who was "blinded by his dedication to the Marxist theory of world revolution and Communist domination." Khrushchev admitted that Eisenhower was "a good man, but he wasn't very tough."

Khrushchev's visit to the United States suggested that an improvement had occurred in Soviet-American relations. But there were touchy moments. After touring an IBM plant, the premier concluded that the scant dress of actresses on a Hollywood set was proof of capitalism's decay; and he became upset that in the interest of security he was unable to see Disneyland. Yet Khrushchev toned down his belligerence by promising "peaceful coexistence" and explaining that his promise to "bury capitalism" did not constitute a military threat. "I say it again—I've almost worn my tongue thin repeating it—you may live under capitalism and we will live under socialism and build communism. The one whose system proves better will win. We will not bury you, nor will you bury us." Khrushchev called for total disarmament in a speech before the UN General Assembly in New York, but would permit no inspection of Soviet arms.

After less than two weeks inside the United States, the Soviet premier accepted Eisenhower's invitation to his Camp David mountain retreat in Maryland to discuss Berlin. Though the two heads of state reached no settlement, they clarified their stands on major issues, expressed interest in negotiating on Berlin, renounced the use of force, and indicated support for disarmament. The "spirit of Camp David" seemed genuine when Eisenhower announced his intention to visit the Soviet Union in the spring of 1960.

THE U–2 INCIDENT

After the Camp David meeting Britain and France joined the United States in calling for a summit conference; but before it could take place Soviet-American relations suddenly plummeted. On May 1, 1960, an American U-2 reconnaissance plane was over a thousand miles inside Soviet air space when a Soviet surface-to-air missile (SAM) brought it down. The U-2's pilot, Francis Gary Powers, parachuted safely from the plane. Soviet authorities seized both him and the wreckage.

The Soviets' heated protests over this intrusion of air space drew a confused and bungled reaction from the United States. On May 3 NASA announced that a weather "research airplane" operating over Turkey had apparently gone down; two days later Khrushchev coldly declared that Soviet missiles had shot down an American plane over Soviet territory. To this charge, the State Department supported the NASA cover by admitting that a "civilian" piloting a weather plane had mistakenly flown over Soviet air space. A spokesman for the agency declared on May 6 that "there was absolutely no—N-O—no—deliberate attempt to violate Soviet air space, and there never has been."

That same day Khrushchev exhibited photographs of Powers, the

Eisenhower and Khrushchev

Shortly after the Soviet leader arrived in the United States in 1959. (UPI)

The U-2 Crisis

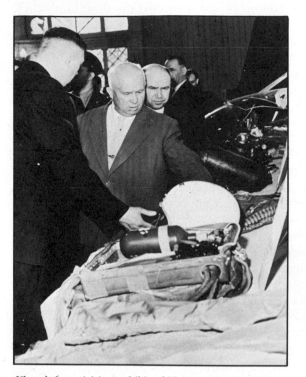

Khrushchev visiting exhibit of U-2 remains in 1960. (Library of Congress)

downed plane, and its reconnaissance instruments, and followed these dramatic revelations with pictures of Soviet military plants taken by U-2 cameras. The State Department then conceded that the U-2 had "probably" been on an intelligence mission, but on May 9 the new secretary of state, Christian Herter, admitted to full knowledge of the flights. When Khrushchev left Eisenhower a face-saving way out by expressing doubt that he was involved, the president infuriated him and shocked everyone else by accepting responsibility for the missions and defending them on the basis of national security. Soviet secrecy, Eisenhower declared in his weekly press conference, had necessitated such measures to prevent "another Pearl Harbor."

The summit conference opened in Paris on May 16 in the midst of intense animosity over the U-2 episode. Khrushchev's furious reaction far outweighed the magnitude of the incident, and undoubtedly was attributable to his desires to quiet critics at home who were starving for a Cold War victory, and to subvert a conference in which his demands on Germany had no chance for success. While in Paris he bitterly attacked the United States and refused to discuss anything until Eisenhower apologized for the flight, punished those involved, and announced an end to U-2 activities over the Soviet Union. He also canceled the president's invitation to the Soviet Union. Eisenhower guaranteed only that no more U-2 flights would occur during his presidency. When de Gaulle and Macmillan tried to mediate, Khrushchev stormed out, ending the summit conference one day after it began.

The United States's actions during the U-2 affair had helped to intensify the Cold War during the summer of 1960. Washington's clumsy handling of the incident invited attack. Whereas Eisenhower's restraint enhanced his popularity at home, his apparent ineptitude damaged America's image abroad. Furthermore, the episode forced accommodations in policy. After Khrushchev warned of a nuclear assault on those neutralist nations permitting U-2 bases, protesters in Japan demonstrated against the presence of three U-2s and opposed a mutual defense pact with the United States. Washington removed the planes before the treaty went into effect in June 1960, but Eisenhower had to cancel a visit to Japan because of security risks. In September Khrushchev arrived at the UN in New York and spent almost a month inside the United States without receiving an invitation from Eisenhower to meet with him. The Soviet premier bragged about his country's missile production, tried to shout down British Prime Minister Macmillan, called the UN a "spitoon," and at one point took off his shoe, shook it at the speaker, and pounded it on the table. Khrushchev's angry outbursts deepened the division between East and West and made a Berlin settlement more remote.

LATIN AMERICA

Meanwhile problems in Latin America had heated again. Over two years earlier Vice President Nixon had made a goodwill visit to eight countries in South America, attempting to assure Latin Americans, he asserted, that they were "not only our neighbors but our best friends." But he encountered angry crowds at every stop, including students at the University of the Republic in Montevideo, Uruguay, and at San Marcos University in Lima, Peru. Confronting what Nixon later called a "bunch of Communist thugs," he barely escaped rocks and eggs thrown by protesters yelling "Nixon get out." In Caracas, Venezuela, a mob shouting "Death to Nixon" surrounded his limousine, rocked it, kicked in its sides, and broke the windows before the driver could speed away. Eisenhower dispatched a thousand marines to American bases in the Caribbean to prevent further incidents.

Nixon attributed these ill feelings primarily to communists, an argument perhaps bolstered by the realization that by the mid-1950s nearly twenty Latin American republics had signed commercial agreements with either the Soviet Union or its allied states. The former president of Costa

Rica, however, explained that Latin Americans hated the United States for backing dictators. In Venezuela, for example, the United States had long supported dictator Marcos Pérez Jiménez; even after his overthrow by a military junta in 1958 it awarded asylum to him and his police chief.

The Eisenhower administration encouraged reforms in Latin America, largely because it believed that the region's economic problems could lead to a communist takeover. In 1958 a Brazilian diplomat in Washington complained that since 1946 the State Department had followed "two patterns of action: the Marshall Plan dedicated to Europe and the John Foster Dulles Plan dedicated to Asia and the Middle East." To remedy the situation, the president's brother Milton made a second fact-finding visit to Latin America. The following year, 1959, the United States adopted several measures to cure what the president called "the festering sore of underdevelopment." It established the Inter-American Development Bank to float loans, tried to stabilize coffee prices by restricting America's exports, and worked toward ending tariffs and establishing a common market among the Americans. In early 1960 the president visited South America, but the following August received only lukewarm support from Congress after requesting $500 million in economic aid for the region. In September twenty-one American states approved the Act of Bogotá, designed to implement the economic and social reform program.

The heightened Cold War tensions carried over into the presidential election of 1960. Nixon, vice president for eight years, easily won the Republican nomination, while Senator John F. Kennedy of Massachusetts emerged as the Democrats' candidate. Both men tried to portray youth and strength of leadership against communism. Nixon suggested longtime experience in the office closest to the presidency, and courage in standing up to Khrushchev in Moscow and to the alleged communists in Latin America. Kennedy, naval war hero, member of the Senate Foreign Relations Committee, and author of *Why England Slept* and of the Pulitzer Prize winning *Profiles in Courage*, called for a hardline approach to Soviet affairs and promised support to anyone willing to fight communism. While Nixon defended Eisenhower's policies, Kennedy accused the Republicans of permitting the United States to fall behind the Soviet Union in economic development and in the missile race. "I think it's time America started moving again," Kennedy declared at the close of his first television debate with Nixon. Promising victory in the Cold War, Kennedy and the Democratic party won the election by a narrow margin.

President Kennedy inherited a world pulsating with Cold War tension. Berlin, Southeast Asia, Red China, the Third World—all areas suggested the need for careful diplomacy rather than angry rhetoric. Yet in a chilling reminder of the Republicans' tactics in 1952, the Democrats had guaranteed victory in the Cold War. In his inaugural address Kennedy assured Americans that his administration would not shrink from communism anywhere in the world.

Selected readings

Adams, Sherman, *Firsthand Report: The Story of the Eisenhower Administration*. 1961.

Alexander, Charles C., *Holding the Line: The Eisenhower Era, 1952–1961*. 1975.

Ambrose, Stephen E., *Eisenhower*. Vol. 2, *The President*. 1984.

———, *Ike's Spies: Eisenhower and the Espionage Establishment*. 1981.

———, *Rise to Globalism: American Foreign Policy Since 1938*. 4th ed. 1985.

Beschloss, Michael R., *Mayday: Eisenhower, Khrushchev and the U-2 Affair*. 1986.

Cook, Blanche W., *The Declassified Eisenhower: A Divided Legacy*. 1981.

Cooper, Chester L., *The Lion's Last Roar: Suez, 1956*. 1978.

Divine, Robert A., *Blowing on the Wind: The Nuclear Test Ban Debate, 1954–1960*. 1978.

———, *Eisenhower and the Cold War*. 1981.

Donovan, Robert J., *Eisenhower: The Inside Story*. 1956

Eisenhower, Dwight D., *The White House Years: Mandate for Change, 1953–1956*. 1963.

———, *The White House Years: Waging Peace, 1956–1961*. 1965.

Finer, Herman, *Dulles over Suez: The Theory and Practice of His Diplomacy*. 1964.

Gaddis, John L., *Strategies of Containment: A Critical Appraisal of Postwar American National Security Policy*. 1982.

Gerson, Louis, *John Foster Dulles*. 1968.

Gordon, Leonard H. D., "United States Opposition to Use of Force in the Taiwan Strait, 1954–1962," *Journal of American History* 72 (1985): 637–60.

Graebner, Norman A., *The New Isolationism: A Study in Politics and Foreign Policy since 1950*. 1956.

Gurtov, Melvin, *The First Vietnam Crisis: Chinese Communist Strategy and United States Involvement, 1953–1954*. 1967.

Herring, George C., Jr., *America's Longest War: The United States and Vietnam, 1950–1975*. 2d ed. 1986.

———, and Richard H. Immerman, "Eisenhower, Dulles, and Dienbienphu: 'The Day We Didn't Go to War' Revisited," *Journal of American History* 71 (1984): 343–68.

Hess, Gary R., "The First American Commitment in Indochina: The Acceptance of the 'Bao Dai Solution,' 1950," *Diplomatic History* 2 (1978): 331–50.

Hoopes, Townsend, *The Devil and John Foster Dulles*. 1973.

Hughes, Emmet J., *The Ordeal of Power: A Political Memoir of the Eisenhower Years*. 1963.

Immerman, Richard, *The CIA in Guatemala: The Foreign Policy of Intervention*. 1982.

Kahin, George M., *Intervention: How America Became Involved in Vietnam*. 1986.

Karnow, Stanley, *Vietnam: A History*. 1983.

Kattenburg, Paul, *The Vietnam Trauma in American Foreign Policy, 1945–1975*. 1982.

Kaufman, Burton I., *Trade and Aid: Eisenhower's Foreign Economic Policy, 1953–1961*. 1982.

Killian, James R., *Sputnik, Scientists and Eisenhower*. 1978.

Kolko, Gabriel, *Anatomy of War: Vietnam, the United States, and the Modern Historical Experience*. 1986.

LaFeber, Walter, *America, Russia, and the Cold War, 1945–1984*. 5th ed., 1985.

Latham, Earl, *The Communist Controversy in Washington*. 1969.

Lloyd, Selwyn, *Suez, 1956*. 1978.

Melanson, Richard A., and David Mayers, eds., *Reevaluating Eisenhower: American Foreign Policy in the Fifties*. 1987.

Neff, Donald, *Warriors at Suez: Eisenhower Takes America into the Middle East*. 1981.

Parmet, Herbert S., *Eisenhower and the American Crusades*. 1972.

Patterson, James T., *Mr. Republican: A Biography of Robert A. Taft*. 1972.

Pruessen, Ronald W., *John Foster Dulles: The Road to Power*. 1982.

Randle, Robert R., *Geneva 1954: The Settlement of the Indochina War*. 1969.

Richardson, Elmo, *The Presidency of Dwight D. Eisenhower*. 1979.

Rubin, Barry, *The Arab States and the Palestine Conflict*. 1981.

Schick, Jack M., *The Berlin Crisis, 1958–1962*. 1971.

Schlesinger, Stephen, and Stephen Kinzer, *Bitter Fruit: The Untold Story of the American Coup in Guatemala*. 1982.

Sheehan, Michael K., *Iran: The Impact of U. S. Interests and Policies, 1941–1954*. 1968.

Smith, R. B., *An International History of the Vietnam War*. Vol. 1, *Revolution versus Containment, 1955–1961*. 1983.

Snetsinger, John, *Truman, the Jewish Vote, and the Creation of Israel*. 1979.

Spanier, John W., *American Foreign Policy since World War II*. 9th ed., 1983.

Spector, Ronald H., *Advice and Support: The Early Years of the U. S. Army in Vietnam: 1941–1960*. 1983.

Spiegel, Steven L., *The Other Arab-Israeli Conflict: Making America's Middle East Policy, from Truman to Reagan*. 1985.

Stevenson, Richard W., *The Rise and Fall of Détente: Relaxations of Tensions in US–Soviet Relations, 1953–1984*. 1985.

Stookey, Robert W., *America and the Arab States: An Uneasy Encounter*. 1975.

Thomas, Hugh, *Suez*. 1967.

Ulam, Adam B., *The Rivals: America and Russia since World War II*. 1971.

Welch, Richard E., Jr., *Response to Revolution: The United States and the Cuban Revolution, 1959–1961*. 1985.

Wise, David, and Thomas B. Ross, *The U-2 Affair*. 1962.

Chapter Twenty-Two

Containment at the Brink: Kennedy and Cuba, 1961–1963

When sworn in on January 20, 1961, President John F. Kennedy called for a deep commitment from Americans to resolve the world's problems. "Let every nation know that we shall pay any price, bear any burden, meet any hardship, support any friend or oppose any foe in order to assure the survival and success of liberty." Containment to its fullest extent was the promise of the new administration, for Kennedy intended the doctrine to encompass the globe with military and/or economic force. Staunchly anticommunist, he was a product of the eras of appeasement and McCarthyism. Kennedy also symbolized a changing of the order, much as Franklin D. Roosevelt did to many Americans almost three decades before. As the youngest elected president—forty-three years of age—Kennedy had replaced the oldest ever to occupy that office—Eisenhower at seventy. Kennedy's campaign program likewise suggested an abrupt change from that of the previous administration: the "New Frontier" assured a return to government activism in both domestic and foreign affairs. Though a bipartisan "conservative coalition" in Congress blocked much of the new president's domestic program, his foreign policy aroused considerable support because it coincided with the basic premise of Americans: that a monolithic communism emanating from the Kremlin threatened to absorb the nations of the world. Kennedy's concern was more sophisticated, however, in that he recognized the fragmentation among the communists and regarded Red China to be as dangerous as the Soviet Union. Yet he believed it the responsibility of the United States to guarantee each people's right to choose their form of government. The forecast was confrontation with the Soviet Union.

KENNEDY'S FOREIGN POLICY

Never was image more important than reality than during Kennedy's brief tenure in the White House. Both abruptly ended for him in November 1963 with an assassin's bullet in Dallas, but even before these tragic events emblazoned the ideal, Americans spoke of the "Kennedy style," his grace under pressure, the youthful and athletic family in the Executive Mansion, the revival of intellectual leadership in the country, and the wit and humor shown by the president, especially during his numerous press conferences. But even as these adjectives suggested advantages in leadership, ironically they carried with them disadvantages in international relations when the president faced Soviet Premier Khrushchev. In promising to close the alleged "missile gap," Kennedy exemplified his belief that only through a display of superior strength could he discard his image of youthful immaturity and inexperience in office and earn the respect of Moscow's leader. At one point during a discussion of a summit meeting with Khrushchev, Kennedy declared: "I have to show him that we can be as tough as he is. . . . I'll have to sit down with him, and let him see who he's dealing with."

Supported by a "brain trust" of advisers, Kennedy appeared capable of turning the irrationality of the Cold War into paths based on reason. Secretary of Defense Robert McNamara, for whom Kennedy had the greatest admiration, was a fast-rising business executive from Ford Motor Company. Secretary of State Dean Rusk, who held that position for eight years, was a Rhodes Scholar, career officer in the State Department, and former president of the Rockefeller Foundation. Intensely loyal, he obeyed orders in a quiet, unassuming manner. McGeorge Bundy and Walt Rostow, college professors turned presidential advisers, were hard-line anticommunists. Kennedy also relied heavily on his brother, Attorney General Robert F. Kennedy, and on his chief speechwriter Theodore Sorensen, although in the opening days of the administration he more closely adhered to diplomatic, military, and intelligence experts. The president's promise to close the missile gap encouraged an arms buildup, although U-2 flights soon substantiated America's military superiority and confirmed that the Soviets were not engaged in a large missile expansion program.

The Kennedy administration advocated a program of "flexible response," which permitted America to defend itself against all types of war. From 1961 to 1963 the defense budget increased dramatically, allowing American ICBMs (Intercontinental Ballistic Missiles) to grow almost sevenfold in number and giving the United States a three-to-one advantage over the Soviet Union. A group of special forces in the army, known as the Green Berets, would concentrate on counterinsurgency measures against guerrilla uprisings believed to be communist-inspired. The United States would maintain sufficient conventional strength to deal with limited conflicts, while building its nuclear stockpile as a deterrent of all-

White House Meeting

Left to right: Secretary of State Dean Rusk, Vice President Lyndon B. Johnson, Attorney General Robert F. Kennedy, and President John F. Kennedy. (White House)

out-war. In the meantime, civil defense programs provided protection against radioactive fallout in the unlikely event of nuclear war. Finally, the administration worked closely with the United Nations in keeping peace through collective security. The United States was seemingly prepared for any military threat.

In a special address to Congress in May 1961, the president declared that "the great battleground for the defense and expansion of freedom today is . . . Asia, Latin America, Africa and the Middle East, the lands of the rising peoples." To prevent the spread of communism into the Third World, the administration's foreign aid program encouraged the development of democratic nations. Like his predecessor in the White House, Kennedy intended to channel the nationalist fervor of emerging nations into orderly societies capable of resisting leftist revolutions inspired by communists. Modernization through American aid became the means for converting potential revolutionary situations into evolutionary developments that would bring the domestic stability vital to elections and economic advance. Mao Tse-tung's explanation of his success in China struck

Kennedy as correct: "[G]uerrillas are like fish, and the people are the water in which fish swim. If the temperature of the water is right, the fish will thrive and multiply."

The 1960s were a turbulent era at home and abroad, and more so because events were intricately intertwined. Kennedy's activist foreign policy and his concern for halting communism carried his administration into an ill-fated venture in Cuba that colored his remaining days in office. The president tended to base his assessment of nearly every hot spot in the Cold War—Berlin, the Third World, and Southeast Asia, particularly Vietnam—upon his bitter experiences with Fidel Castro's Cuba beginning in early 1961.

CUBA

Kennedy's problems with Cuba were under way before he became president. During the 1950s the United States, interested in stability and security in the Caribbean, sold arms to Cuba's dictatorial ruler Fulgencio Batista, and furnished military advisers through the Mutual Security Program. But whereas the image of Cuba was that of gambling casinos, tourism, and a nightclub atmosphere, the reality was that the overwhelming majority of islanders were poverty-stricken, the best lands belonged to American businesses, and the government in Havana ignored the need for reform. Cuba was ready for revolution. Fidel Castro, a young middle-class law school graduate, called for far-reaching reforms and with eighty cohorts began guerrilla operations against the government in 1956. Within two years his following had grown in number and strength, with weapons provided by Cubans in the United States. A coup seemed imminent, and the United States began pulling away from Batista by cutting off his arms supply. In the popular revolution that became known as the "26th of July Movement," Castro forced Batista into exile the following January 1959. Within a week the government in Washington extended recognition to the new regime, which had assured democratic elections and freedom of speech and press. To many Americans, Castro became a romanticized revolutionary figure who had risen from the people to institute reform.

But by the spring of 1959 the enchantment had worn off as Castro seemed to have been a communist from the start. To bring changes to the island, he began an agrarian reform program that involved the expropriation of over $1 billion worth of American holdings. Should there be doubt about his intentions, Castro boasted that "we will take and take, until not even the nails of their shoes are left." In the meantime thousands of Cubans fled to the United States: democratic freedoms had not materialized in Cuba and mock trials led to mass executions of Batista's followers. By the summer Castro's need for a broader political base had driven him closer to the communists on the island. The director of the CIA, Allen Dulles, warned President Eisenhower that "communists and other extreme radicals appear to have penetrated the Castro movement." Indeed, two communists had joined his regime: Raúl Castro, Fidel's brother, and Ernesto (Ché) Guevara. Washington's impression was that Cuba threatened to become a propaganda center and training ground for promoting communist revolutions throughout Latin America.

The United States became Castro's particular object of scorn because of its longtime exploitation of the island, and because it protested against the executions and granted asylum to refugees. Washington responded by placing an embargo on nearly all of Cuba's goods and appealing for collective defensive action under the Rio Pact of 1947. But in August, when the American foreign ministers met in Santiago, Chile, the United States failed to arouse full Latin American support against communism in Cuba. Many leftists favored Castro, and numerous other Latin Americans simply enjoyed seeing the United States in an uncomfortable position. The meeting resulted in a vague pronouncement against totalitarian rule that made no reference to Cuba.

Castro soon consorted openly with the Soviets, while intensifying his radio and television attacks on the United States. He demanded America's withdrawal from Guantánamo and gave the American embassy in Havana forty-eight hours to reduce its 300-member staff to eleven. He called Eisenhower a "gangster" and a "senile White House golfer." He extended recognition to Red China, and in February 1960 concluded a treaty with the Soviets by which Cuba agreed to exchange 5 million tons of sugar over the next five years for arms, oil, machinery, and technical advisers. In less than two years Cuba's trade with Soviet-controlled countries grew from 2 percent to 80 percent of its total commerce. Khrushchev bragged of his communist brother and warned that he would rain rockets on the United States if it interfered in Cuban affairs. Though he later claimed the warning was only "symbolic," he pronounced the Monroe Doctrine dead and urged the United States to "bury it, just as you bury anything dead, so it will not poison the air."

By the end of the Eisenhower presidency, the United States had formulated plans for Castro's overthrow. In March 1960 Eisenhower approved a secret $13 million fund for the preparation of a small group of Cuban refugees to invade their homeland and stage a coup. The CIA began training 1,400 Cuban exiles in Guatemala and Nicaragua. In August the American foreign ministers met in San José, Costa Rica, and criticized "extracontinental" intervention in the hemisphere, although they again did not refer to Cuba or suggest remedial measures. On January 3, 1961, the United States and Cuba broke diplomatic relations, leaving a legacy of trouble for the new president.

By the time Kennedy assumed office, Castro's regime had become synonymous with communism, even though America's ambassador to Cuba, Philip Bonsal, attempted to downplay this fear. Though opposed to Castro, Bonsal attributed the dictator's Soviet leanings to America's unbending policies, not to communism. Castro's purpose, Bonsal later declared, "was radically and exclusively nationalistic; it became oriented

Fidel Castro and Khrushchev

A warm embrace at the UN in New York in late 1960. (Wide World)

toward dependence on the Soviet Union only when the United States, by its actions in the spring of 1960, gave the Russians no choice other than to come to Castro's rescue." Bonsal's warnings had no effect on Washington. Kennedy had chastised the Republicans during the presidential campaign for allowing a "communist satellite" at "our very doorstep." Americans would not be "pushed around any longer."

Kennedy had virtually announced his intention to rid the hemisphere of Castro's communism. Senator J. William Fulbright, when asked his opinion by Kennedy, remarked that the Castro regime was "a thorn in the flesh" and "not a dagger in the heart." Yet the new administration continued to treat the regime as a threat to American prestige and security. Shortly after Kennedy's arrival in the White House, the CIA informed him of its invasion plans and assured him that the landing of Cuban exiles would set off a full-scale insurrection against Castro, just as an earlier coup had succeeded in Guatemala and erased another communist menace. The CIA had already helped to establish a Cuban Revolutionary Council to take over the government after Castro's overthrow. The point of invasion, Kennedy learned, was to be Cochinos Bay (Bay of Pigs) located on the southeast side of the island. The date was to be April 17, 1961.

At first Kennedy was hesitant about the invasion plan and approved it only as a "contingency" operation, subject to cancellation at any time. Such blatant interventionism bothered him: not only would it raise widespread criticism both inside and outside the United States, but it might not succeed. And there would be no way, Kennedy realized, to deny complicity, whether direct or indirect in nature. Yet there was the other side of the matter. If successful, his administration would score an early victory in the Cold War and force Moscow to sense the determination of the new leaders in Washington. Kennedy instructed his historian-in-residence in the White House, Arthur M. Schlesinger, Jr., to draft a White Paper justifying America's decision to intervene in Cuba. The Department of State published a pamphlet entitled "Cuba," which outlined Castro's broken promises and labeled his alleged communist regime "a fateful challenge to the inter-American system." Without attempting to open negotiations with Castro and without consulting Congress, the Kennedy administration embarked on a dangerous course that had little assurance of success.

The secret plan was anything but secret. Rumors had spread that American marines were preparing Cuban exiles in Guatemala for an invasion of Cuba. Details were so widely known that two American reporters, working independently of each other, had written stories for national publication that were amazingly accurate and which their journals refrained from releasing only after direct appeals from the White House. At a press conference less than a week before the invasion, Kennedy assured journalists that there would be "no intervention in Cuba by United States armed forces."

Kennedy had told the truth: American armed forces did not intervene in Cuba. The Cuban exiles, sixteen to sixty-one in age and largely inexperienced in military matters, set out by trucks from Guatemala to Nicaragua, where they boarded boats headed for the Bay of Pigs. Everything went wrong. An American air strike on Cuba's air force two days before had not had the softening effect claimed by the CIA, and Kennedy's doubts about the expedition had become so deep that he called off the second air strike scheduled for the day of the invasion. When the landing force hit the beaches, 300 fell victim to Castro's tanks and soldiers, leaving the 1,100 survivors no choice but surrender. In an effort to save them, the president authorized an airborne expedition that failed because no one took into account the change in time zones when arranging the rendezvous of the rescue units. Most of the captives won their freedom nearly two years later, but, in a further embarrassment, only after the United States paid over $50 million ransom in food and medicine. Castro's agents among the rebels had forewarned him of the attack, no massive uprising occurred, and his regime won a great triumph at Kennedy's expense.

With America's prestige reeling, Kennedy accepted full blame for the Cuban disaster, realizing that his greatest task now was to convince the Soviet Union that the Bay of Pigs episode was not indicative of American weakness. "How could I have been so stupid, to let them go ahead?" he moaned afterward. "[A]ll my life I've known better than to depend on the experts." Thus Kennedy held the CIA and the Joint Chiefs of Staff responsible because of their careless planning and clumsy implementation of the operation. One can perhaps attribute part of the blame to his newness in office, and yet the fact remains that the idea of such an invasion was not alien to Kennedy's worldview. The rub was that the plan was ineptly executed by so-called intellectuals, making the youthful president vulnerable to charges of stupidity as well as weakness. Latin Americans intensified their accusations of Yankee imperialism and questioned whether this action was consistent with the UN Charter and the principles of the OAS. "Fair Play for Cuba" rallies in the United States drew numerous Americans disenchanted with the administration for participating in the scheme, and the CIA was sarcastically referred to as the "Cuban Invasion Authority." But even more embarrassed was UN Ambassador Adlai Stevenson, who had not known of the impending attack and went before member nations to deny rumors of an invasion.

The Kennedy administration was especially concerned about image, for even though the Soviets had in reality gained nothing on the United States, they publicly warned Washington to stay out of Cuban affairs, leaving the appearance that a shift was under way in the world balance of power. Attorney General Robert F. Kennedy recognized the danger. "We just could not sit and take it," he warned, for the Soviets would consider Americans to be "paper tigers." White House adviser Walt Rostow tried to assure the president that "we would have ample opportunity to prove we were not paper tigers in Berlin, Southeast Asia, and elsewhere." Thus, in the minds of the administration the methods had aborted—not the objective. In fact, the danger of communist expansion loomed larger than ever.

To restore faith in the United States, the president asserted that the nation's "restraint" was "not inexhaustible," and that it would continue to fight communism "in every corner of the globe." In response to Khrushchev's warnings of war if the United States invaded Cuba, Kennedy insisted that Americans would determine the business of the hemisphere. "In the event of any military intervention by outside force we will immediately honor our obligations under the inter-American system to protect this hemisphere against external aggression." A few days later he told the American Society of Newspaper Editors that America's patience had limitations. "Should it ever appear that the inter-American doctrine of noninterference merely conceals or excuses a policy of non-action—if the nations of this hemisphere should fail to meet their commitments against outside Communist penetration—then I want it clearly understood that this Government will not hesitate in meeting its primary obligations, which are to the security of our Nation."

Cuba remained a major irritant to Washington as Castro used the Bay of Pigs fiasco as propaganda against the United States and swore to spread communism throughout the hemisphere. The Kennedy administration tightened its economic restrictions on the island, continued to withhold recognition, criticized Castro through the United States Information Agency and other means, assisted those in Miami who opposed him, and gave at least tacit support to the CIA's plans for his assassination. Castro meanwhile proclaimed Cuba a "socialist" state under single-party control of the Popular Socialist (Communist) party. "I am a Marxist-Leninist and will be one until the day I die," he insisted over radio and television. Castro's professed socialism caused Colombia and Peru to assemble the American foreign ministers at Punta del Este, Uruguay, in late January 1962, where all delegations except Cuba's pronounced communism alien to the hemisphere and barred Cuba from the Inter-American Defense Board. By a large margin also, the ministers halted the arms trade with Cuba, and when they turned to the question of removing the island from the OAS, the vote was likewise favorable—but by the minimum two-thirds majority. Even then, these measures had little effect because they drew no support from the larger, more populated Latin American states of Argentina, Bolivia, Brazil, Chile, Ecuador, and Mexico. Chastised but not brought under control, Castro accepted Soviet aid and repeated his promise to spread communism into all of Latin America.

THE THIRD WORLD

Kennedy's ordeal with Cuba had repercussions that affected his administration's policies toward the Third World. To prevent other Castrolike revolutions, the president considered it necessary to control the nationalist energies of these emerging peoples by emphasizing calm, orderly development through American aid and advice. Washington's policymakers continued to believe that the Third World's peculiar susceptibility to revolution was an invitation to communism. The remedy was an evolutionary nationbuilding process turned toward democracy.

To bring stability to the new postwar nations, Kennedy had issued an executive order in March 1961 establishing the Peace Corps, which sent Americans to Latin America and Africa to aid in social and economic development. In the autumn, after the Bay of Pigs episode, Congress approved a bill giving the organization permanent standing. Within two years nearly 5,000 Americans worked as teachers, doctors, and agricultural and technical advisers in bringing about flood control, irrigation, and general community development. The goal was to alleviate poverty through economic and social uplift and reduce the attraction of communism, although few recipients converted to American policy in return.

In an even more ambitious attempt to combat unrest in Latin America, the Kennedy administration pushed for a social and economic program known as the Alliance for Progress. Based upon the Act of Bogotá of 1960, the idea of a new aid program first appeared in the president's inaugural address. To Latin American diplomats meeting in the White House, Kennedy praised the hemisphere's revolutions for independence and then asserted that the work was not over: "For one unfulfilled task is to demonstrate to the entire world that man's unsatisfied aspiration for economic progress and social justice can best be achieved by free men working within a framework of democratic institutions." In August 1961, Secretary of the Treasury Douglas Dillon told an Inter-American Economic and Social Conference at Punta del Este that nearly $20 billion of assistance would be necessary over the next decade. The money would come from the United States, Europe, and Japan, although his government agreed to provide a "major part" of the funds. The Charter of Punta del Este established the Alliance for Progress, whose purpose, according to the accompanying Declaration to the Peoples of America, was "to bring a better life to all the peoples of the Continent."

Despite high hopes and considerable publicity, the Alliance for Progress never reached expectations. Within two years the United States had furnished nearly $2 billion for improvements, and yet the program did not achieve the desired economic changes in Latin America. There were several reasons for this failure. Private investors were afraid of the disorder emanating from a program that encouraged such sweeping social and economic changes. Latin America lacked the skilled workers needed to carry out the program, and the money did not reach those who needed it. Landowners were in authority and resisted land reforms, whereas the rest of the people resented American intervention under any name. Within the decade the Alliance for Progress had virtually died out as military coups continued and political democracy remained elusive.

The Congo (now Zaire) in central Africa also concerned the Kennedy administration as a potential breeding ground for communism. As the largest African state, the Congo's political direction would undoubtedly influence others on the continent. Under the threat of racial violence, Belgium had granted independence to the colony in June 1960, but civil war broke out and Moise Tshombe, an anticommunist favored by Belgian mining interests, led the mineral-rich province of Katanga in a separatist movement from the Congo. The United States supported a UN Security Council decision to send a force to the Congo to restore the peace, but not to return Katanga to the central government. The Congo's premier, Patrice Lumumba, bitterly opposed the UN action as a conspiracy against him and turned to the Soviet Union for help. CIA Director Allen Dulles referred to Lumumba as "a Castro, or worse," and won approval from the Eisenhower administration to bring about Lumumba's overthrow. In September 1960 Congolese President Joseph Kasavubu, regarded as conservative and pro-American, overthrew Lumumba and ordered the Soviets out of the country.

When Kennedy became president, he infuriated the Belgians by calling for a "middle-of-the-road government." To prevent a Soviet-American confrontation, he added, the UN had to keep order through a trusteeship until the Congolese could administer the government. In February 1961 Lumumba was assassinated by Katanga authorities, but, according to some writers, encouraged by CIA operatives acting under past orders of former President Eisenhower. Less than six months later a moderate was elected premier and received American support in trying to reunify the country. When continued efforts failed, the UN reversed its stance and authorized its forces to put down the opposition to the government. They succeeded, and in 1963 restored Katanga to the Congo. Though problems lingered for two more years, Americans interpreted the reunification of the Congo as a victory over communism, ignoring the possibility that nationalism was a major victim of their actions. The results of such alienation threatened to have serious ramifications in the UN, where by the spring of 1963 the Afro-Asian nations comprised the majority.

BERLIN

The reverberations from the Bay of Pigs failure became evident during the first meeting between Kennedy and Khrushchev at Vienna in June 1961. The announced purposes of the tense two-day gathering were to discuss a nuclear test-ban treaty and growing problems in Berlin and Laos, but the conference became a grim opportunity for each leader to exchange caustic remarks designed to assess the will of the other. Except for Khrushchev's agreement to seek a negotiated settlement in Laos, neither man retreated on any issue. After the Soviet premier suggested that the United States had exposed a basic weakness by refusing to launch a military invasion of Cuba, he suddenly announced an ultimatum on Berlin that resurrected the crisis of 1958. Berlin should be a "free city," he declared. If Western occupation did not terminate within six months, his government would sign a separate peace with the East Germans, forcing the West to negotiate with them for access to West Berlin. Kennedy was determined to show strength, although newsreels and cameras revealed a nervousness that stood in sharp contrast with the calm and paternalistic bearing of Khrushchev. The president realized that he had lost the battle at Vienna, but he made clear that he was not about to lose the war. "If Khrushchev wants to rub my nose in the dirt," Kennedy disgustedly declared, "it's all over."

By mid-July the Berlin issue had stirred a war scare in the United States, as the Kennedy administration took a stand exactly like that of its predecessor in 1958. The president insisted that his country, along with Britain and France, had "a fundamental political and moral obligation" to West Berlin. Any action endangering the city "would have the gravest effects upon international peace and security and endanger the lives and well-being of millions of people." Over television he proclaimed that "we cannot and will not permit the Communists to drive us out of Berlin, either gradually or by force." Americans "do not want to fight, but we have fought before." He activated 250,000 reserves, asked Congress to expand the country's military forces by 25 percent, and aroused fears of a nuclear holocaust by calling for a civil defense program based on fallout shelters in case of attack. Congress approved the president's requests and added 45,000 troops for assignment to Europe. Meanwhile France and West Germany bolstered their numbers in NATO. "If we don't meet our commitments in Berlin," Kennedy warned, "it will mean the destruction of NATO and a dangerous situation for the whole world. All Europe is at stake in West Berlin."

As escalation fed escalation during the summer of 1961, the Soviets constructed a twenty-eight-mile long wall of concrete and barbed wire between East and West Berlin to stop the exodus of East Berliners into the free section of the city. For the first time the Cold War had a visible symbol of totalitarianism. Whereas the "iron curtain" was abstract and arguable in terms of existence, the Berlin Wall was physical and real. The city, it appeared, would be divided permanently. During the first tense moments of this new crisis in Germany, the United States ordered more soldiers into West Berlin.

At the end of August Khrushchev announced an end to the three-year moratorium on nuclear tests in the atmosphere, which ultimately led to the explosion of a weapon 3,000 times more powerful than the bomb dropped over Hiroshima. Although the United States still had a far superior delivery capability, the impression was that the Soviets had surged ahead in nuclear capacity. Kennedy, under enormous pressure to resume testing, finally agreed to underground tests in September 1961 and in the following April extended them to the atmosphere.

Berlin Wall

Construction of the Berlin Wall around the Brandenburg Gate, November 20, 1961.
(U.S. Army)

As in 1958, however, neither nation wanted war and the problems over Berlin did not graduate beyond mere rhetoric and shows of force. Construction of the wall had mixed results. The United States's inaction proved its reluctance to fight over East Berlin,, while the wall constituted a Soviet admission to repressive tactics that furnished the Free World a superb source of propaganda. Kennedy defused the situation by asking for a negotiated settlement, which in turn suggested his willingness to forgo serious efforts to reunify Germany. Though the tension eased, Kennedy's offer to negotiate over Berlin further weakened NATO's unity by upsetting both Charles de Gaulle in France and Konrad Adenauer in West Germany. The December deadline set by Khrushchev (as during the Eisenhower administration) passed without incident.

THE CUBAN MISSILE CRISIS

The long feared Soviet-American showdown came not in Berlin but in Cuba, where Khrushchev in 1962 had arranged the construction of missile sites to test the resolve of the Kennedy administration. No doubt encouraged by the president's apparent lack of resolution in the Bay of Pigs, Vienna, and Berlin, the Soviet premier knew that if he could place missiles within the Western Hemisphere, the impression would be that his country had achieved nuclear parity or equality with the United States. Furthermore, leverage gained in Cuba could guarantee against American invasion of the island, set examples for allies of both the United States and Soviet Union, force concessions in Berlin and elsewhere, and salvage Khrushchev's position in Moscow, apparently under fire because his calls for "peaceful coexistence" seemed to abdicate communist leadership to Red China. Khrushchev later asserted that he had felt committed to defend his Cuban ally against an American assault. Besides, he declared, the United States had missiles in Turkey, and Soviet missiles in Cuba would show Americans "what it feels like to have enemy missiles pointing at you."

The Cuban missile crisis had its origins in July 1962, when American U-2 flights detected a growing number of Soviet ships in the island's waters. Refugees from Cuba and secret agents from the United States had also noted what might have been missile sites under construction. In August the director of the CIA, John McCone, wanted the president notified of these findings, but a communications breakdown led to delays. Finally, someone in the CIA leaked the information to a reporter for the Buffalo *Evening News*, who aroused little attention with a published account in late August. The following month the president, who was then more concerned about problems in Europe and Southeast Asia, repeatedly assured the press that there was no evidence that the Soviets were establishing offensive military installations in Cuba. But in early October U-2 commanders were ordered to photograph western Cuba, and by the middle of the month had located missile sites close to San Cristóbal. Indeed, the pictures revealed over forty IL-28 [Ilyshin-28] light bombers, the same number of strategic missiles, and nine missile sites in preparation. There was no sign of nuclear warheads. The crucial point was that missiles fired from Cuba could reach Washington, D.C.

President Kennedy, then on the campaign trail, learned of these developments on October 16. Two days later he raised the matter of Soviet military matériel arriving in Cuba with Soviet Foreign Minister Andrei Gromyko and Soviet Ambassador Anatoly Dobrynin. They assured him that the goods were for defensive purposes only. The president decided against confronting them with the photographs until he could decide upon a course of action.

Thus the most serious legacy of the Bay of Pigs fiasco became the supreme test of will during the Cuban missile crisis of October 1962. To deal with the problem, Kennedy established an Executive Committee of the National Security Council ("Ex Comm") that included administration figures along with some from the Truman presidency. Rusk chaired the proceedings, although he allowed them to operate on a free-discussion basis. President Kennedy avoided the meetings as much as possible to

U-2 Photo of Cuban Missile Site in San Cristobal in October 1962

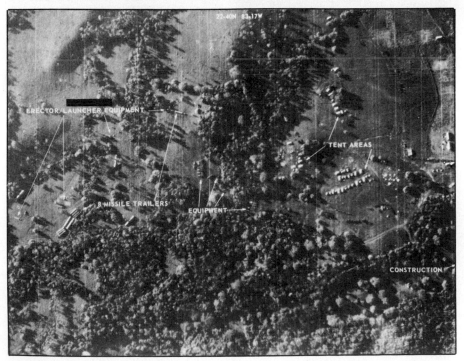

One of the aerial surveillance pictures that helped to set off the "thirteen days" of the Cuban missile crisis that threatened nuclear war between the United States and the Soviet Union. (CIA)

promote a free interchange of ideas among a varied group of individuals that included McNamara, Robert F. Kennedy, presidential adviser Mc-George Bundy, the presiding officer of the Joint Chiefs of Staff, General Maxwell Taylor, speechwriter Theodore Sorensen, former Secretary of State Dean Acheson, and, at intermittent times, UN Ambassador Adlai Stevenson.

During an emotion-packed week in October, Ex Comm met almost continuously to discuss Soviet motives for emplacing the missiles in Cuba and to decide how to resolve the crisis. Khrushchev, the committee members surmised, could not have expected to keep the weapons installation a secret. He was surely aware of the U-2 flights over Cuba and yet made no effort to conceal the arrival of Soviet ships and the construction of the missile sites. Perhaps missiles in Cuba would not have actually changed the world power balance, Sorensen noted, but they would have forced an alteration *"in appearance*; and in matters of national will and world leadership, as the President [himself] said later, such appearances contribute to

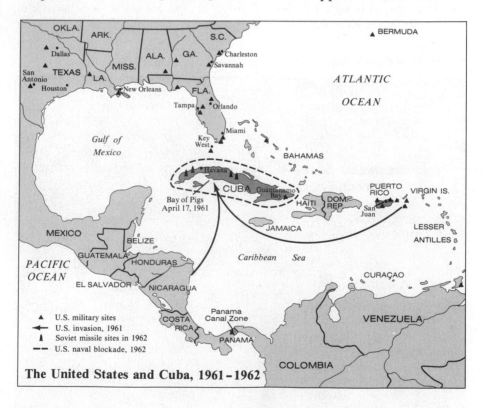

The United States and Cuba, 1961–1962

- ▲ U.S. military sites
- ◄ U.S. invasion, 1961
- ⚑ Soviet missile sites in 1962
- −− U.S. naval blockade, 1962

MAP 34

Cuba became the center of the Cold War early in the Kennedy administration. After the United States failed to achieve the overthrow of Castro, it went to the brink of nuclear war after the Soviet Union implanted missile sites on the island.

reality." The Soviets would leave the impression that they were supporting an ally against invasion, blunting the Red Chinese claim that Khrushchev was reluctant to support "liberation" movements. At the same
time the presence of the missiles in Cuba would damage America's prestige by raising questions about its military power. One truth was certain:
the United States could not allow missiles to remain in Cuba. "The
1930s," President Kennedy observed, "taught us a clear lesson: aggressive conduct, if allowed to go unchecked and unchallenged, ultimately
leads to war."

Ex Comm's discussions of the missile crisis were free and open, as
Robert F. Kennedy's memoir *The Thirteen Days* dramatically attests. Its
members were unclear about Soviet motives but considered them dangerously provocative. Some believed that Khrushchev sought leverage to
force the West out of Berlin, whereas others thought he wanted the
United States to remove its missiles from Turkey. The latter suggestion
brought a sharp reaction from the president, who was aware that they
were outmoded, but who now realized that their retention was more important to Turkey's morale than to its defense. Furthermore, under the
agreement of 1959 allowing the missiles' installation, the Turks owned the
missiles and the Americans the nuclear warheads. Any attempt to remove
the missiles would have inflicted domestic political damage on the
Turkish government while drawing negative reactions from other NATO
members. And now, the president could not take the missiles from Turkey because to do so would give the appearance of capitulation. Khrushchev, several Ex Comm members believed, did not seek a nuclear
showdown, but as the president and his brother realized late one night,
war could come through whim or miscalculation.

After considerable debate, Ex Comm finally focused on whether the
president should order a blockade of the island (advocated by Undersecretary of State George Ball), or approve an air strike against the missile
sites (promoted by Acheson and the Joint Chiefs of Staff). The Joint
Chiefs at one point called for an all-out invasion to rid the hemisphere of
both the missiles and Castro. Opponents countered, however, that this
would lead to a lengthy and costly war with Cuba, while leaving the
Kremlin free to take Berlin. Suggestions for arranging private talks with
Castro or turning the matter over to the UN led to staunch opposition, as
did Stevenson's recommendation that in exchange for withdrawal of the
missiles, the United States should pull out its missiles from Turkey and
Italy and give up its naval base in Guantánamo. Air Force General Curtis
LeMay argued that the Soviets would do nothing if the United States
bombed their missile sites in Cuba. The president strongly disagreed. To
a friend he disgustedly remarked, "Can you imagine LeMay saying a
thing like that? These brass hats have one great advantage in their favor.
If we listen to them, and do what they want us to do, none of us will be
alive to tell them later they were wrong." The air force admitted that it
could not assure total destruction and warned that the missiles left would

be capable of hitting the United States. The air force also allowed that bombings might kill Soviet nationals and lead to full-scale war. "My brother is not going to be the Tojo of the 1960s," Robert F. Kennedy asserted in clinching the argument for a blockade.

Ex Comm decided on a "quarantine" of Cuba, which would deny the island arms and supplies while, as McNamara argued, leaving the administration some flexibility either to escalate or de-escalate the situation. Robert F. Kennedy and others had recommended using the term "quarantine" rather than "blockade" to avoid the language of war, although some warned that in either case the Soviets could retaliate by shutting off Berlin without removing the missiles from Cuba. Proponents of the quarantine pointed out that Article 51 of the UN Charter allowed the use of force in "self-defense if an armed attack occurs," and argued that the emplacement of missiles was tantamount to an attack. The United States had to move quickly and alone. Attempts to work through either the UN or the OAS would lead to interminable delays, although the United States kept its allies informed and got their support along with that of the OAS and the Third World. Though de Gaulle was unhappy that he had been informed rather than consulted, he joined others in realizing that missiles aimed at the United States could also be turned toward Western Europe.

While American air, land, and naval forces prepared for action, President Kennedy appeared over nationwide television on the evening of October 22 to deliver a chilling address on the crisis in Cuba. He first outlined the revelations of the past few days and declared that the Soviet Union's purpose in planting missiles in Cuba was "none other than to provide a nuclear strike capability against the Western Hemisphere." The missiles already there could hit Washington, D.C., Cape Canaveral, and the Panama Canal, whereas others under construction could reach Hudson's Bay in the north and Lima, Peru, in the south. Such Soviet action came under the "cloak of secrecy and deception," and constituted "an explicit threat to the peace and security of the Americas." The United States therefore would "regard any nuclear missile launched from Cuba against any nation in the Western Hemisphere as an attack by the Soviet Union on the United States requiring a full retaliatory response upon the Soviet Union." He called on Khrushchev to "halt and eliminate this clandestine, reckless and provocative threat to world peace and to stable relations between our two nations." To encourage this, the United States would establish "a strict quarantine on all offensive military equipment under shipment to Cuba," effective on the morning of October 24.

The United States adopted other measures as well. It reinforced Guantánamo, evacuated dependents of military personnel, and requested declarations of support from the OAS and the UN. President Kennedy meanwhile approved the State Department's plans to draw up a blueprint for civil rule over the island in the event of occupation. In the UN Stevenson dramatically confronted Soviet Ambassador Valerian Zorin with giant photographs of the missile sites, challenging him to work for a settlement before nuclear war developed. While nearly 200 American ships in the Caribbean prepared to enforce the quarantine, B-52s were already airborne, carrying nuclear bombs.

The minutes seemed to tick loudly during the following days. The day after the president's television appearance, the Council of the OAS met with Rusk and voted nearly unanimous support for a resolution urging "the immediate dismantling and withdrawal from Cuba of all missiles and other weapons with any offensive capability." It also called on member states to use any means necessary to stop a further missile buildup; the Rio Treaty of 1947, the Council pointed out, permitted assistance to any American state threatened by aggression. That same day Washington received a letter from Khrushchev asserting that the blockade was illegal. "The actions of [the] U.S.A. with regard to Cuba," he alleged, "are outright banditry or, if you like, the folly of degenerate imperialism." Kennedy, he charged, was pushing the nations to nuclear war.

October 24 seemed the day of reckoning, for two Soviet ships with a submarine escort were approaching American naval patrols in the Caribbean, only an hour away. The American aircraft carrier *Essex* prepared to contact the submarine by sonar and ask it to surface; upon refusal the American captain was to employ small-scale depth charges. Robert F. Kennedy described his brother's tense waiting:

> His hand went up to his face and covered his mouth. He opened and closed his fist. His face seemed drawn, his eyes pained, almost gray. We stared at each other across the table. For a few fleeting seconds, it was almost as though no one else was there and he was no longer the President. Inexplicably, I thought of when he was ill and almost died; when he lost his child; when we learned that our oldest brother had been killed; of personal times of strain and hurt. The voices droned on.

The Soviet vessels suddenly stopped and turned back.

Still the tension persisted, even while signs of an impending retreat became evident. UN Secretary-General U Thant called for negotiations and Khrushchev sought a summit conference to resolve the question, but President Kennedy insisted that removal of the missiles would have to come first. On October 26 Washington received encouraging news. A high official in the Soviet embassy informed the administration, through ABC news correspondent John Scali, that under UN auspices the Soviet Union would remove the missiles if the United States lifted the quarantine and guaranteed against an invasion of Cuba. That same Friday night Khrushchev sent a long, rambling letter offering similar conditions. "If you have not lost your self-control," he wrote the president, "we and you ought now to pull on the ends of the rope in which you have tied the knot of war." Insisting that he did not want war, Khrushchev appealed to Kennedy to "let us not only relax the forces pulling on the ends of the rope, let us take measures to untie that knot. We are ready for this."

Yet the conciliatory tone of these developments was puzzling because it did not coincide with other events. The FBI discovered the day afterward that Soviet officials in New York City were destroying sensitive papers (which indicated the possibility of war), a Soviet SAM shot down a U-2 over Cuba, and no slowdown had occurred in the construction of the missile sites. Most ominous, a second note had arrived from Khrushchev, more belligerent than the first. The Soviets, the note asserted, would pull out their missiles from Cuba only if the United States withdrew its missiles from Turkey.

Khrushchev's second note threatened to create a new impasse. President Kennedy of course could not agree to this new proposal, but his brother and Sorensen suggested a way out: disregard the second letter and reply to the first with a three-part ultimatum. On October 27 the president notified Khrushchev that in return for removing the missiles from Cuba, America would promise not to invade the island. That same night Robert F. Kennedy met privately with Soviet Ambassador Dobrynin and assured him that even though the president could not immediately remove the missiles from Turkey and Italy, he would do so shortly after the Cuban crisis had passed. Had Dobrynin refused the administration's terms, the president was prepared to make a concession designed to avert war: ask the UN to propose a withdrawal of the American missiles from Turkey in exchange for the Soviet withdrawal of missiles from Cuba. Thus the White House could argue that the UN, not the United States, had made the explicit link between the missiles in Turkey and those in Cuba. But this step never became necessary because Dobrynin was satisfied with the terms and the next day made clear that the Soviet missiles would be withdrawn.

On Sunday, October 28, thirteen days after the first confirmation of missiles in Cuba, the danger was over. Khrushchev accepted Kennedy's assurance against an invasion of Cuba in exchange for the UN's on-site inspection of the withdrawal of Soviet missiles. As events would show, this verification never took place because of Castro's opposition, thereby releasing the United States from the pledge against invasion. But these considerations now seem academic: the United States and the Soviet Union had averted the most serious threat to global peace since before World War II. Rusk later reminded newsman John Scali to "remember when you report this—that eyeball to eyeball, they blinked first." Walt Rostow remarked that Khrushchev had relented when "he felt the knife on his skin."

President Kennedy has received praise for courage under fire; and yet many critics have raised searching questions about whether he might have averted the Cuban missile crisis through careful diplomacy. Castro remarked that "if the United States had not been bent on liquidating the Cuban revolution, there would not have been an October crisis." The Kennedy administration made no effort to open discussions with the Castro regime before approving the disastrous course leading to the Bay of Pigs. Had the invasion succeeded, it is doubtful that the unfavorable publicity surrounding America's involvement would have been worth the victory. Succeeding events do not substantiate the fear that Castro was spreading communism throughout Latin America. In fact, the actions of the Kennedy administration were largely responsible for the new wave of anti-Americanism in the southern half of the hemisphere. Kennedy's critics also note other diplomatic breakdowns in the autumn of 1962. Leaders in Washington made no attempt to talk privately with Cuba before the October confrontation, despite this repeated suggestion during the Ex Comm meetings by former ambassadors to the Soviet Union, Charles E. Bohlen and Llewellyn Thompson. As early as October 25 columnist Walter Lippmann wondered why the president, in his private meeting the week before with Gromyko and Dobrynin, did not reveal the U-2 photos and warn of public disclosure should the Soviets refuse to withdraw the missiles. Finally, the president's televised ultimatum virtually ruled out the chances for compromise.

The irony is that an administration of intellectuals who were determined to change the course of events became themselves captives of the events. The central force in the administration's foreign policy was the Bay of Pigs disaster. President Kennedy was determined not to sustain another loss of prestige. He thus engaged in a policy of brinkmanship much more dangerous than that of the 1950s; fortunately Khrushchev chose to retreat. Economist John Kenneth Galbraith wrote afterward, "We were in luck, but success in a lottery is no argument for lotteries."

The Cuban missile crisis constituted the most dangerous series of events in the Cold War, and for that reason both powers took steps designed to avoid another direct confrontation. To reduce the chances of miscalculation, President Kennedy installed a "hot line," which was a private teletype directly connecting the White House and the Kremlin. He also worked toward an arms limitations agreement with the Soviet Union. To weaken Castro's rule, the United States banned travel to Cuba and prohibited international monetary exchange; the Soviets countered these efforts with increased aid to Cuba. Despite Kennedy's directive against boasting of an American victory in the missile crisis, the fact remained that the Soviet Union had suffered extreme embarrassment. Khrushchev had foolishly challenged the United States in an area vital to its security and where it held conventional military superiority. One Soviet official eerily commented, "Never will we be caught like this again."

The missile crisis had severe repercussions. It exposed Moscow's nuclear inferiority and led to a program of expansion, contributed to a change in Soviet leadership, and encouraged both Moscow and Washington to turn toward indirect policies in Third World scenes of trouble. The Red Chinese ridiculed Khrushchev's capitulation on the Cuban matter, leading the Soviet premier to retort that if the United States was a "paper tiger" it had "nuclear teeth." Khrushchev fell from power in 1964, and the new premier, Alexei Kosygin, was less belligerent than his predecessor, making this an opportune time for the United States to pursue détente or a reduction of tensions and at the same time exploit the growing Sino-Soviet rift. Cuba meanwhile remained a Soviet protectorate, as nearly 17,000 Soviet soldiers and technicians stayed on the island. The Monroe Doctrine was not dead as Khrushchev had earlier remarked, but it had suffered a near fatal blow.

SOUTHEAST ASIA

Cuba monopolized the attention of the Kennedy administration, causing concurrent problems in Laos and Vietnam to pale in importance. Laos, an agricultural country landlocked from the sea, had become independent under the Geneva agreements of 1954 and soon assumed a neutralist position in international affairs. Three years later, under Prince Souvanna Phouma, the nationalists established a coalition regime comprised of neutralists and a former wartime resistance group, now communist, known as the Pathet Lao ("Lao nation"). The Eisenhower administration countered with military assistance to the rightist Laotian army, which was concentrated in the towns, but the money did little to improve its performance in the field and in fact contributed to the country's inflated economy and widespread graft. Yet there seemed no choice. Eisenhower wrote in his memoirs, "the fall of Laos to Communism would mean the subsequent fall—like a tumbling row of dominoes—of its still-free neighbors, Cambodia and South Vietnam and, in all probability, Thailand and Burma. Such a chain of events would open the way to Communist seizure of all Southeast Asia."

In 1958 the CIA worked with rightists in bringing down Phouma and installing a pro-American government clear of Pathet Lao representation. American military advisers soon arrived to stabilize the new government. But trouble continued. The Laotian government asked the UN for help, and the situation calmed when the Security Council sent a team of inquiry. In August 1960 Phouma and the Pathet Lao regained control and soon were receiving Soviet and North Vietnamese aid. But Phouma's regime collapsed again, forcing him to flee to Cambodia. Phouma later lamented: "The Americans say I am a Communist. All this is heartbreaking. How can they think I am a Communist? I am looking for a way to keep Laos non-Communist."

The Kennedy administration was also concerned that problems in Laos would spill into surrounding countries and spread communism throughout Southeast Asia. Guerrilla activities had intensified in both Laos and Vietnam by the spring of 1961, causing White House adviser Walt Rostow to urge the president to use counterinsurgency measures in restoring stability. In line with previous policy, Kennedy attributed Laos's problems to the communists and supported the rightist regime as the basis of "a neutral and independent Laos." He stationed the Seventh Fleet in the South China Sea, had 500 marines helicoptered into Thailand, and ordered American soldiers to Okinawa to be ready for action.

The Cuban fiasco had affected the president's thinking on Asia, for he later remarked that it made him more cautious than he might otherwise have been about intervening in Laos. "I just don't think we ought to get involved," Kennedy told Nixon, "particularly where we might find ourselves fighting millions of Chinese troops in the jungles." Furthermore, he could not justify taking action in Laos, which was thousands of miles away, when he had not done so in Cuba, which was only ninety miles away. The president, however, could not appear weak in Laos while undergoing the criticisms arising from the Bay of Pigs episode. He made a show of force by ordering several hundred American military advisers in Laos to wear military uniforms. That same month of April, the Soviet Union supported the president's call for a cease-fire. But the Pathet Lao refused to follow the Soviet lead. Kennedy asked the Joint Chiefs of Staff if American combat soldiers could deliver a victory in Laos. Though most of the commanders were skeptical, the chairman, General Lyman Lemnitzer, argued that "if we are given the right to use nuclear weapons, we can guarantee victory." When someone asked what "victory" would entail, Kennedy called the meeting to a close.

In May 1961 fourteen governments gathered in Geneva to devise a solution to the Laotian problem. Arguments focused on the guidelines for a coalition government comprised of the three dissident groups—the neutralists, rightists, and leftists. The conference took place against a background of trouble, for the Pathet Lao was forcing the rightists out of Laos and into the neighboring country of Thailand. A believed communist drive in Thailand caused the United States to dispatch the first contingent of 5,000 marines. They would join combat troops from Britain, Australia, and New Zealand, all under the auspices of the SEATO Treaty.

The delegations in Geneva reached an agreement in June 1962, over a year after they had convened. According to terms, Laos would be neutral, it could enter no military pacts and house no foreign military bases, and its government would be a coalition of all three groups with Phouma as premier. The situation was not auspicious. The Pathet Lao held two-thirds of the country and was armed with Soviet weapons, while the Kennedy administration continued to send military matériel to the rightists, justifying the aid on the basis of a believed North Vietnamese infiltration of upper Laos.

Then a strange mixture of events took place: the Kennedy administration's decision to negotiate over Laos seemed to combine with the embarrassment of the Bay of Pigs to elevate Vietnam's importance as a symbol of Washington's stand against communism. "At this point we are like the Harlem Globetrotters," Bundy remarked, "passing forward, behind, sidewise, and underneath. But nobody has made a basket yet." Elections had not taken place in Vietnam in 1956, as stipulated in the Geneva Accords of two years previous, partly because of the Eisenhower administration's reluctance, but perhaps also because of what the North Vietnamese communists later asserted: that Red China had been willing to accept a divided Vietnam, and had cut off military aid to Hanoi to assure compliance. In either case, a succession of terrorist activities developed in the south during the late 1950s that Americans feared were communist-inspired. The United States, it appeared, was about to undergo another test of will.

Controversy still exists over whether the ensuing troubles in Vietnam were due more to Diem's repressive regime than to claimed North Vietnamese aggression. Part of the confusion was attributable to the Kennedy administration's inconsistent policies. The Department of State implied that South Vietnam was a separate nation (contrary to the Geneva Accords of 1954) when it recommended American aid to counter the believed threat from outside forces (in line with the same Geneva agreements). Several French and American writers, however, called it a local rebellion against Diem that Hanoi indeed aided by 1960, but only after Ho Chi Minh's former Vietminh forces in the south sought his assistance against American intervention in Vietnamese domestic affairs. Washington's interpretation of the conflict in Vietnam was vital in justifying assistance to the south, for under the SEATO Treaty of 1954 the White House had guaranteed the Senate that it would not become involved in the domestic troubles of Southeast Asian nations. If the North Vietnamese had intervened in the south as either Peking's or Moscow's agent, of course, this would have constituted a threat from the outside. Rusk was convinced of this. He argued that Red China had incited the war in Vietnam as part of its effort to control all of Asia. Thus, according to this stance, Diem's Army of the Republic of Vietnam (ARVN) had become locked in a guerrilla war with the Chinese-assisted Vietcong (Vietnamese communists), who in December 1960 became the military arm of the National Liberation Front (NLF) in South Vietnam and had gained control over nearly all of its rural areas. The primary threat was therefore external, requiring the United States to honor its assumed SEATO obligations. A recently published history of the war, by the People's Army of Vietnam, tends to support the administration's case. It asserts that Hanoi played an earlier and important part in promoting the military development of the Vietcong in the south. If so, this helps to explain the heightened military activity in the south that Kennedy faced when he became president in 1961.

By early 1961 the Kennedy administration was well under way toward making Vietnam a testing ground of America's will to combat communism. In May the president sent Vice President Lyndon B. Johnson on a fact-finding tour of Southeast Asia. If communism permeated that area, Johnson later reported to Kennedy, the United States would have to "surrender the Pacific and take up our defenses on our own shores." America had to protect "the forces of freedom in the area," even at the cost of deep commitment and sacrifice. In fact, such involvement could lead to "the further decision of whether we commit major United States forces to the area or cut our losses and withdraw should our efforts fail." Johnson urged "a clear-cut and strong program of action" in behalf of Diem. Though never explaining how Diem's collapse would automatically strip the United States of its Pacific bases, Johnson insisted that the choice was either to "help these countries . . . or throw in the towel in the area and pull back our defenses to San Francisco and a 'Fortress America.' " That same month Kennedy sent another 100 military advisers and 400 Special Forces to train the Vietnamese in counterinsurgency warfare. "If we can save Vietnam," Bundy declared, "we shall have demonstrated that the communist technique of guerrilla warfare can be dealt with."

Over the next few months conflicting reports from Vietnam led the president to inquire deeper into the situation. While Rusk and others argued that the south was in danger from the outside, American intelligence agents in October 1961 claimed that nearly 90 percent of the 17,000 Vietcong had come from South Vietnam. In fact, some writers believe that the NLF was an independent organization that received military aid directly from Moscow and Peking, and not through Hanoi. As the Joint Chiefs of Staff and the National Security Council considered sending combat troops, Kennedy dispatched two of his advisers to South Vietnam: Walt Rostow and General Maxwell Taylor. They returned with a dismal report. Diem wanted more technical advisers, not American soldiers. Though the South Vietnamese Army seemed unable to take the offensive, Diem still intended to maintain control over the grim military situation. Rostow called for American bombings of North Vietnam and joined Taylor in recommending an 8,000-man "logistic task force" of engineers, medical personnel, and infantry to assist the ARVN in closing North Vietnam's supply lines to the Vietcong in the south. The introduction of this huge force, Taylor believed, would raise morale in South Vietnam and instill confidence in the United States because the men would be a "visible symbol of the seriousness of American intentions." To conceal their purpose, the Americans could arrive under the title of a "flood control unit."

Kennedy, however, decided against sending fighting forces to Vietnam. Such a move, he feared, would jeopardize the negotiations over Laos and dangerously escalate the war in Vietnam. As Kennedy remarked, "The troops will march in; the bands will play; the crowds will cheer; and in four days everyone will have forgotten. Then we will be told we have to send in more troops. It's like taking a drink," he declared. "The effect wears off, and you have to take another." Instead, Kennedy compromised between negotiations and combat troops by approving Diem's call for more advisers. Yet he realized that a further escalation might be necessary to save South Vietnam. By the end of 1961 over 3,000 United States military advisers were in South Vietnam, more than triple the number there a year before.

In December 1961 America's military presence in Vietnam became increasingly visible. An American carrier brought in more than thirty helicopters, four single-engine training planes, and 400 men for operations and maintenance. Eventually minesweepers and reconnaissance planes would arrive. Meanwhile American military advisers trained the South Vietnamese in guerrilla warfare, and soon convinced Diem to adopt a "strategic hamlet" program designed to undermine the Vietcong's war effort. According to its proponents, the purpose of the program was to isolate the peasants by relocating them in bamboo stake encampments encircled by moats and soldiers, therefore denying the Vietcong any assistance, recruits, and places of refuge. Its greatest effect, however, was negative: it allowed the Vietcong to assume the role of "liberators." Kennedy assured Diem that "the campaign of force and terror now being waged against your people and your Government is supported and directed from the outside by the authorities at Hanoi." North Vietnam's actions had violated the Geneva Accords of 1954, the president explained, and the United States had to "promptly increase" help to South Vietnam.

Despite optimistic reports, the Vietnamese situation continued to deteriorate. McNamara visited Vietnam in the summer of 1962 and declared that "every quantitative measurement we have shows we're winning this war." A few months later Rusk proclaimed that the war was coming to an end. Yet a Senate subcommittee had visited Southeast Asia and warned that a cut in American aid would lead to "upheaval and chaos" and to the establishment of Chinese influence. The South Vietnamese, it appeared, could not win the war by themselves, although the subcommittee cautioned the administration against converting the conflict into "an American war, to be fought primarily with American lives." The United States under *"present circumstances"* had no interests in Vietnam that could justify such involvement.

In the spring of 1963 Diem's long-standing problems with the Buddhists fomented into a crisis that drew the United States deeper into South Vietnamese affairs. His Catholicism had long been a focal point of growing opposition from the Buddhists, who comprised 80 percent of the country's population. But then Diem stirred a wave of angry protests by prohibiting the Buddhists from flying their religious flags in commemorating Buddha's birth, and in May the government's forces turned on the protesters in the city of Hue, killing nine in the melee. Raids on Buddhist pagodas followed, leading to the arrests of more than 1,400 Buddhists, including relatives of Diem's own officials. In June an elderly Buddhist monk doused himself in gasoline and, as an American photographer recorded the event, set himself afire before screaming crowds in the streets of Saigon. Madame Nhu, Diem's vitriolic sister-in-law, dismissed the actions as "Buddhist barbecues," while her husband and cohort of Diem, Ngo Dinh Nhu, callously remarked that if more Buddhists wanted to immolate themselves he would furnish the gasoline and matches. Diem blamed the Buddhist unrest on the Vietcong. The United States, however, was already disenchanted with Diem's domestic failures and began to cut back assistance.

The Kennedy administration still opposed direct military involvement in South Vietnam, but it had come to realize that Diem was not the solution to the problem. The president told CBS newsman Walter Cronkite: "In the final analysis, it is their war. They are the ones who have to win or lose it. We can help them, give them equipment, send our men out there as advisers, but they have to win it." On another occasion, Kennedy explained that "strongly in our mind is what happened in the case of China at the end of World War II, where China was lost. . . . We don't want that." Diem had not instituted reforms in South Vietnam, as Americans had hoped. Instead, he had aroused deep resentment by ending longtime elections in the villages, brutally repressing opposition to his rule, engaging in nepotism, and rejecting American advice as interference in domestic affairs. "No wonder the Vietcong looked like Robin Hoods when they began to hit the hamlets," a civilian American official commented.

America's commitment became nearly irreversible in the autumn of 1963, when the Kennedy administration was identified with a conspiracy against Diem, led by South Vietnamese Army generals. Dissatisfied officers notified the CIA in late August that Nhu intended to have them executed and then negotiate away the independence of South Vietnam. They intended to overthrow Diem and wanted to know what the American reaction would be. In a cable cleared with Kennedy, the U.S. ambassador in Saigon, Henry Cabot Lodge, received instructions to persuade Diem to dismiss Nhu from the regime; should Diem refuse, the United States had to "face the possibility that Diem himself cannot be preserved." In that event, Lodge was to inform the generals that Diem no longer could count on American aid and that they would receive "direct support in any interim period of breakdown of central government mechanism." The cable found a receptive reader. Lodge had been appalled by the raids on the pagodas, and when Diem ignored the recommendation to rid himself of Nhu, the American embassy dispatched a CIA agent to notify the generals of American support should their scheme succeed, and no assistance if it failed. But the generals became uncertain about both internal and American support, and called off the coup.

The next month was a confusing period for the administration in Washington. McNamara was upset that the president seemed willing to participate in Diem's overthrow, and he sent a mission of inquiry to South Vietnam led by General Victor Krulak of the Defense Department and State Department official Joseph Mendenhall. But this effort only underlined the administration's uncertainties. Krulak was optimistic about the war effort, Mendenhall was disenchanted with Diem, and Kennedy was frustrated with both emissaries. "You two did visit the same country, didn't you?" he asked.

By late October the generals had revived their plot to overthrow Diem and this time went through with it. On November 1, again with the tacit approval of the Kennedy administration, they staged their coup, afterward killing both Diem and his brother Nhu. Suddenly the reality of the Vietnamese situation hit the White House. Upon learning of the murders of Diem and Nhu, Kennedy, according to Taylor, "leaped to his feet and rushed from the room with a look of shock and dismay on his face which I had never seen before."

After the coup the United States's promise of support now made it directly responsible for the welfare of the South Vietnamese government. The new regime in Saigon was civilian in form only, for power remained in the military, but it promised elections and a free press, released political prisoners, and made needed changes in the war effort. When the United States extended recognition to the new government, the impression grew that it had been involved in the assassination. The presence of nearly 17,000 military advisers in South Vietnam, along with 8,000 other Americans, seemed proof of a commitment. Shortly after Diem's death the NLF in North Vietnam proposed negotiations with Saigon aimed at a cease-fire, to be followed by "free general elections" to establish a "national coalition government composed of representatives of all forces, parties, tendencies, and strata of the South Vietnamese people." Though some ARVN officials seemed interested, the United States opposed the offer. By November 1963 America's prestige was on the line, for it was now clear that both the successes and the failures of the South Vietnamese government would belong to the United States.

Questions remain about the potential direction of America's Vietnam policy, had Kennedy not been assassinated that same November of 1963. Several signs suggest that he had matured in office because of the Cuban and Berlin war scares, and would have worked for a more cooperative relationship with the Soviet Union that might have curtailed America's involvement in Vietnam. Yet, in one of his last press conferences, he asserted that "for us to withdraw from that effort would mean a collapse not only of South Vietnam but Southeast Asia. So we are going to stay there." Whatever the outcome had Kennedy lived, America's involvement in Vietnam was much more extensive than when he came into office.

The evidence is mixed about whether Kennedy by late 1963 had moved away from his initial foreign policy—built on challenge and response—and toward one emphasizing diplomacy and disarmament. In June he delivered an address at American University, asserting the possibility of all peoples living peacefully, and calling for disarmament and an end to the Cold War. Later that month, however, he tried to revive support for NATO, which was in a state of decline largely because of Europe's fears brought on by the two superpowers' near clash over Cuba. Kennedy was especially worried that France would assert leadership on the continent, based upon its recently developed nuclear device and an alliance with West Germany. De Gaulle had already blocked Britain's membership in the Common Market because, he declared, "it would appear as a colossal Atlantic community under American domination and direction." West Germany's decision to remain closely aligned with the United States was partly due to Kennedy's efforts. In June 1963 he appeared before the Berlin Wall and accepted honorary German citizenship with these words: "Ich bin ein Berliner." ("I am a Berliner.") The following August the United States, Britain, and the Soviet Union negotiated the Nuclear Test Ban Treaty, ending testing under water and in the atmosphere and outer space. Though its prohibitions did not apply to underground testing because of continued opposition to on-site inspection, it was the first arms limitations agreement between the nations after nearly two decades of attempts. Despite Kennedy's declaration that the pact was a great step forward on "the path of peace," the Joint Chiefs of Staff agreed to it only after McNamara assured them of a big program of underground tests and presented them a written promise to begin nuclear tests anew in the atmosphere "should they be deemed essential to our national security." In October the United States sold $250 million of surplus wheat and flour to the Soviet Union and Eastern Europe. Tensions seemed to have eased by the end of 1963.

The rhetoric had receded, and yet it still seems doubtful that Kennedy would have reduced America's commitments in Vietnam. It would have been a sharp reversal indeed for him to have shed the past in favor of a softer approach to foreign policy. His administration had already paid the price of hesitation at the Bay of Pigs. Kennedy's sense of American righteousness remained, and this necessitated the establishment of world order and stability in preventing the spread of totalitarian rule by either the Soviets or the Red Chinese. If his administration never developed a plan for winning the war in Vietnam, it certainly refused to be the one to lose it.

Selected readings

Abel, Elie, *The Missile Crisis*. 1968.

Allison, Graham T., *Essence of Decision: Explaining the Cuban Missile Crisis*. 1971.

Ambrose, Stephen E., *Rise to Globalism: American Foreign Policy since 1938*. 4th ed. 1985.

Baritz, Loren, *Backfire: A History of How American Culture Led Us into Vietnam and Made Us Fight the Way We Did*. 1985.

Berman, Larry, *Planning a Tragedy: The Americanization of the War in Vietnam*. 1982.

Burchett, Wilfred, *Catapult to Freedom: The Survival of the Vietnamese People*. 1978.

Buttinger, Joseph, *Vietnam: A Dragon Embattled*. 2 vols. 1967.

Cate, Curtis, *The Ides of August: The Berlin Wall Crisis, 1961*. 1978.

Chayes, Abram, *The Cuban Missile Crisis: International Crises and the Role of Law*. 1974.

Cohen, Warren I., *Dean Rusk*. 1980.

Detzer, David, *The Brink: Cuban Missile Crisis, 1962*. 1979.

Dinerstein, Herbert S., *The Making of a Missile Crisis: October 1962*. 1976.

Fairlie, Henry B., *The Kennedy Promise*. 1973.

Fall, Bernard, *Anatomy of a Crisis: The Laotian Crisis of 1960–1961*. 1969.

FitzGerald, Frances, *Fire in the Lake: The Vietnamese and the Americans in Vietnam*. 1972.

FitzSimons, Louise, *The Kennedy Doctrine*. 1972.

Gaddis, John L., *Strategies of Containment: A Critical Appraisal of Postwar American National Security Policy*. 1982.

Goodman, Allan E., *The Lost Peace: America's Search for a Negotiated Settlement of the Vietnam War*. 1978.

Gurtov, Melvin, *The United States against the Third World*. 1974.

Halberstam, David, *The Best and the Brightest*. 1972.

Hammer, Ellen J., *A Death in November: America in Vietnam, 1963*. 1987.

Heath, Jim F., *Decade of Disillusionment: The Kennedy-Johnson Years*. 1975.

Herring, George C., Jr., *America's Longest War: The United States and Vietnam, 1950– 1975*. 2d ed. 1986.

Hilsman, Roger, *To Move a Nation: The Politics of Foreign Policy in the Administration of John F. Kennedy*. 1967.

Kahin, George M., *Intervention: How America Became Involved in Vietnam*. 1986.

———, and John W. Lewis, *The United States in Vietnam*. Rev. ed. 1969.

Kalb, Madeleine G., *The Congo Cables: The Cold War in Africa—From Eisenhower to Kennedy*. 1982.

Karnow, Stanley, *Vietnam: A History*. 1983.

Kattenburg, Paul M., *The Vietnam Trauma in American Foreign Policy, 1945–1975*. 1980.

Kennedy, Robert F., *The Thirteen Days: A Memoir of the Cuban Missile Crisis*. 1969.

Kern, Montague; Patricia W. Levering; and Ralph B. Levering, *The Kennedy Crisis: The Press, the Presidency, and Foreign Policy*. 1983.

Kolko, Gabriel, *Anatomy of a War: Vietnam, the United States, and the Modern Historical Experience*. 1985.

LaFeber, Walter, *America, Russia, and the Cold War, 1945–1984*. 5th ed. 1985.

Lewy, Guenter, *America in Vietnam*. 1978.

Maclear, Michael, *The Ten Thousand Day War, Vietnam: 1945–1975*. 1981.

Mahoney, Richard D., *JFK: Ordeal in Africa*. 1983.

Mangold, Tom, and John Penygate, *The Tunnels of Cu Chi: The Untold Story of Vietnam*. 1985.

Miroff, Bruce, *Pragmatic Illusions: The Presidential Politics of John F. Kennedy*. 1976.

Noer, Thomas J., *Cold War and Black Liberation: The United States and White Rule in Africa, 1948–1968*. 1985.

Parmet, Herbert S., *JFK: The Presidency of John F. Kennedy*. 1983.

Rice, Gerard T., *The Bold Experiment: JFK's Peace Corps*. 1985.

Rust, William J., *Kennedy in Vietnam*. 1985.

Schick, Jack M., *The Berlin Crisis, 1958–1962*. 1974.

Schlesinger, Arthur M., Jr., *A Thousand Days: John F. Kennedy in the White House*. 1965.

Slusser, Robert M., *The Berlin Crisis of 1961*. 1973.

Smith, R. B., *An International History of the Vietnam War: The Kennedy Strategy*. 1985.

Sorensen, Theodore C., *Kennedy*. 1965.

Spanier, John W., *American Foreign Policy since World War II*. 9th ed. 1983.

Stevenson, Richard W., *The Rise and Fall of Détente: Relaxations of Tensions in U.S.-Soviet Relations, 1953–84*. 1985.

Summers, Harry G., Jr., *On Strategy: A Critical Analysis of the Vietnam War*. 1982.

Szulc, Tad, and Karl E. Meyer, *The Cuban Invasion: The Chronicle of a Disaster*. 1962.

Truong Nhu Tang, *A Vietcong Memoir*. 1985.

Walton, Richard J., *Cold War and Counterrevolution: The Foreign Policy of John F. Kennedy*. 1972.

Welch, Richard E., Jr., *Response to Revolution: The United States and the Cuban Revolution, 1959–1961*. 1985.

Wyden, Peter, *Bay of Pigs: The Untold Story*. 1979.

Chapter Twenty-Three

Containment in Collapse: Johnson and Vietnam, 1963–1969

"Let us continue," President Lyndon B. Johnson declared, as he assumed his new duties in November 1963. In an attempt to retain the Kennedy effect, the president promised to fulfill his predecessor's domestic and foreign programs and persuaded several members of his staff to remain. McNamara, Rusk, Bundy, Rostow, and others stayed until most of them found it no longer possible to support the policies of the Johnson administration. Part of the reason was personal. The new president was demanding and inflexible. Grounded in the principles of Franklin D. Roosevelt's New Deal program, Johnson implemented an ambitious range of domestic reforms under the label of the "Great Society." He was hardworking, stubborn, egotistic, self-righteous, and extremely sensitive to criticism. As a Texan he lived in the shadow of the Massachusetts-bred Kennedy, never managing to throw off the image of a wheeler-dealer politician, the result of his three decades in the Senate. Yet Johnson's central tragedy was his acceptance of traditional assumptions about containment and Vietnam. Like Truman, Eisenhower, and Kennedy, Johnson was virtually the captive of appeasement and McCarthyism, and like them he was convinced that communism was a threat in nearly every trouble spot in the world. Most social revolutions in the Third World, Johnson believed, were communist-tinged if not inspired, necessitating a rigid stand by the United States for order and stability. Thus he accepted the fundamental precept of the containment policy: America's vital interests lay wherever there was a threat of communism.

As Cuba had been the supreme test of Kennedy's will, Vietnam became that of Johnson's. To establish America's imprint on that small country, Johnson confidently declared that "we can turn the Mekong [River delta] into a Tennessee Valley" and democratize the surrounding area. In fact, however, he turned the country's Vietnam policy toward a greater military orientation than Kennedy had conceived, and by mid-1965 the United States was locked in a major land war in Asia. Johnson meanwhile encountered other issues that often became intertwined with the Vietnam involvement and showed the dangers in overcommitment: problems in the Dominican Republic; secret attempts to reestablish diplomatic relations with Cuba; the timeless Arab-Israeli struggle in the Middle East; the effort to promote détente or a reduction of tensions with the Soviet Union, built on nuclear proliferation treaties and other measures; Soviet repression of an uprising in Czechoslovakia similar to that in Hungary both in causes and results. Yet it was America's war in Vietnam that hampered success in some of the above matters, brought down Johnson's presidency in 1968, and ushered in the Republican party and Richard M. Nixon. Johnson's adherence to containment climaxed in failure and necessitated a search for new directions in foreign policy.

AMERICANIZING THE WAR IN VIETNAM, 1963–1965

The most consuming problem of the Johnson presidency soon became America's deepening involvement in Vietnam. Though the president considered Vietnam a "fourth-rate country," he feared that if the United States failed to "stop the Reds in South Vietnam, tomorrow they will be in Hawaii, and next they will be in San Francisco." Along with advisers retained from the Kennedy administration, he was convinced that Red China sought to control Southeast Asia and that North Vietnam's aggressions were part of that objective. "I am not going to lose Vietnam," Johnson promised soon after becoming the chief executive. "I am not going to be the president who saw Southeast Asia go the way China went." As was the case with the Kennedy administration, Johnson seemed to have no strategy for victory, except to escalate involvement; his objective was to avoid defeat.

Johnson firmly believed that America's military strength would resolve the situation in Vietnam, but he failed to recognize that since the peak year of 1945 the United States had been steadily losing its capacity to control global events. The world's power structure was becoming increasingly diffused as the Soviet Union grew in military strength, as NATO members acted more independently, and as the Third World stepped up demands for a greater voice in international affairs. But the most baffling dilemma, which the administration never resolved, was how North Vietnam could handcuff the United States, denying it a military victory assured by every resource statistic available. After Diem's assassination in November 1963, the pressure had grown for the establishment of a coalition government and a neutral stance for Vietnam in international affairs. But Johnson insisted on victory. The "neutralization of South Vietnam," he declared in a statement forecasting the direction of his administration, "would only be another name for a Communist takeover." To the new South Vietnamese leader, General Duong Van Minh, he wrote: "The United States will continue to furnish you and your people with the fullest measure of support in this bitter fight."

Despite American aid, the situation in Vietnam continued to unravel in early 1964. General Minh fell before a military coup in January that resulted in a long period of political uncertainty complicated by intensification of the war. The South Vietnamese raided North Vietnam and bombed its sources of supplies in Laos, but by April the Vietcong had gained control of most Vietnamese villages. In retrospect, it seems clear that the crucial battle involved winning political support in the countryside rather than military victory in the field. But the emphasis was upon achieving a triumph through superior firepower, which had the potential of alienating the surrounding peoples whose support the South Vietnamese could least afford to lose.

In the autumn a series of incidents in the Gulf of Tonkin placed America's prestige on the line and caused it to take a major step toward direct involvement in the war. The U.S. destroyer *Maddox* was engaged in electronic espionage in the Gulf of Tonkin when, on the morning of August 1, it underwent fire by North Vietnamese torpedo boats. Counterfire aided by American aircraft drove away the assailants, but Johnson was outraged and ordered the *Maddox* to return, accompanied by another destroyer, the *C. Turner Joy*. On the evening of August 4, according to American accounts, North Vietnamese torpedo boats fired on both vessels, then cruising sixty miles at sea. Hanoi had admitted to the first attack on the *Maddox* as retaliation for American collaboration with South Vietnamese commando raids, but it vehemently denied the second incident. Indeed, American commanders were possibly mistaken about whether an attack had occurred. The fog was dense and the night so black that one sailor termed it "darker than the hubs of Hell." The "enemy" had appeared only on sonar and radar, and the captain of the *Maddox* later admitted that both detection systems were unreliable in such bad weather. Since there had been no "visual sightings," he strongly urged a "complete evaluation" before taking action.

But the Johnson administration had already decided to intervene, as later shown in *The Pentagon Papers*, a collection of secret Defense Department documents on Vietnam which were leaked to *The New York Times* in 1971. These materials suggest that the president and his advisers had been frustrated with South Vietnam's war effort and were looking for an

---

MAP 35

America's involvement in Indochina began in 1950 during the Korean War, escalated into troop involvement in 1965, and officially ended with a cease-fire arrangement in 1973 that the Nixon administration termed "peace with honor."

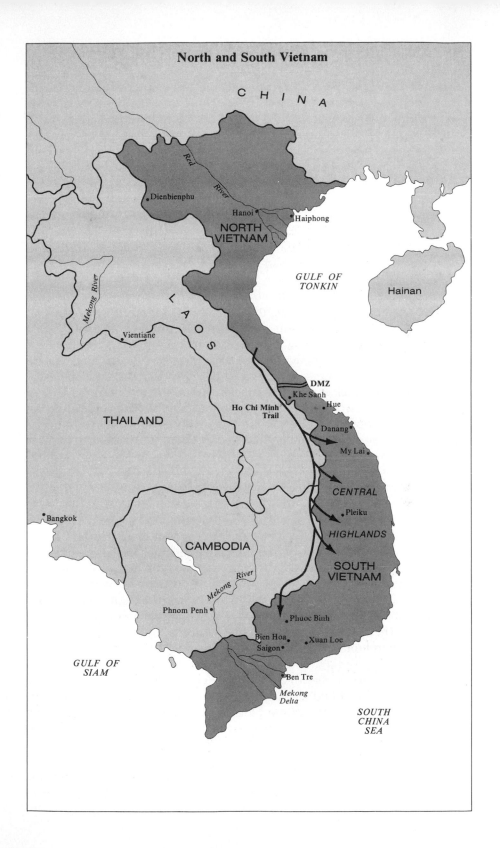

North and South Vietnam

CHINA

Red River

• Dienbienphu

Hanoi •   • Haiphong

NORTH VIETNAM

Mekong River

GULF OF TONKIN

Hainan

LAOS

• Vientiane

THAILAND

DMZ
Khe Sanh •
• Hue

Ho Chi Minh Trail

Danang •

My Lai •

• Bangkok

CENTRAL

• Pleiku

HIGHLANDS

CAMBODIA

Mekong River

SOUTH VIETNAM

Phnom Penh •

• Phuoc Binh

Bien Hoa •   • Xuan Loc
Saigon •

GULF OF SIAM

• Ben Tre

Mekong Delta

SOUTH CHINA SEA

opportunity to justify direct American action. In a matter of hours the administration in Washington, without launching an investigation, authorized a "firm, swift retaliatory [air] attack" on North Vietnamese torpedo boat bases. Johnson appeared on television that same evening of August 4 to inform Americans of recent events in the Gulf of Tonkin and to accuse North Vietnam of "open aggression on the high seas." Though the SEATO Treaty pledged only consultation about military aid, the president asserted that it was the duty of the United States to help any member "requesting assistance in defense of its freedom." In asking Congress for authorization to use military force, he did not reveal that the *Maddox* had been involved in espionage and raiding expeditions, pointing instead to official reports that the vessel had been on patrol in international waters and had not provoked an attack.

After virtually no debate in either chamber, Congress took the first major step toward Americanizing the conflict when it approved American military action through the Gulf of Tonkin Resolution of August 7. By a unanimous vote in the House and the wide margin of 88 to 2 in the Senate (the only negatives being Ernest Gruening of Alaska and Wayne Morse of Oregon), Congress empowered the president to "take all necessary measures to repel any armed attacks against the forces of the United States and to prevent further aggression." A high-ranking official in the State Department called the resolution "a functional equivalent of a declaration of war," although Johnson had no intention of broadening the war effort. He still thought it possible to achieve success in Vietnam through restrained military measures.

The administration believed the Tonkin Resolution would accomplish both foreign and domestic objectives. It would show the North Vietnamese that Americans were determined to uphold their commitments in Southeast Asia. The White House would also appear resolute and in control, which would help Johnson fend off his challenger in the presidential contest of 1964, conservative Republican Barry Goldwater of Arizona. In the heat of the campaign, Johnson attacked Goldwater for wanting to escalate the war by authorizing air strikes on North Vietnam. Such an unreasoned approach could lead to the use of American fighting forces, the president warned. He would not send Americans "nine or ten thousand miles away from home to do what Asian boys ought to be doing for themselves."

Perhaps because of fear of a Goldwater victory or because of the Tonkin Resolution, Hanoi had secretly offered to negotiate; but the president refused since, as a former White House aide later explained, "the very word 'negotiations' was anathema in the Administration." Rostow insisted that "it is on this spot that we have to break the liberation war— Chinese type. If we don't break it here, we shall have to face it again in Thailand, Venezuela, elsewhere." In a statement that undoubtedly expressed the central feeling of the administration, Rostow declared that "Vietnam is a clear testing ground for our policy in the world." There were other considerations. The country's strategic location, some believed, was vital to America's position in Southeast Asia. Neither the Johnson administration nor the ARVN leaders in Saigon were interested in the establishment of a coalition government. Nor would Johnson subject himself to charges of appeasement and the possible loss of Vietnam—especially on the eve of an election.

Johnson won a massive victory in November, and soon afterward members of his administration intensified their earlier discussions of whether to use air power in Vietnam. The objectives were mixed. Some officials thought that bombings would raise morale in South Vietnam; others hoped that aerial attacks would reduce suspected regular army infiltration from the north and perhaps even cause Hanoi to cease its aid to the Vietcong. Though many administration critics rejected the argument that Hanoi had stepped up activity in the south by the autumn of 1964, communist leaders in Vietnam during the early 1980s claimed that they had indeed done so, and that Johnson's advisers had been correct. In any case, intelligence reports in the 1960s warned that air assaults would have minimal effect on the fighting in South Vietnam. The Vietcong were of course an insurgency group with no air force, and bombings would undoubtedly alienate the area's inhabitants and result in political calamity. Some observers pointed out that if the Vietcong's tools were primarily nonmilitary—propaganda, terror, political subversion—then the key to victory was to win the support of the people. Bombings had no potential for that. One American artilleryman noted that in World War II, "there were real targets to aim at—enemy artillery or fortresses or fortified positions or massed enemy-troop formations or even bridges." But in Vietnam such targets did not exist, and artillery fire "did nothing but kill a lot of innocents and alienate us from those we were supposedly trying to help."

By the end of the month the administration had agreed to begin what one adviser called a "carefully orchestrated bombing attack" on North Vietnam. Proponents of the new strategy countered the fears of such an escalation by asserting that restrained bombing raids would not endanger North Vietnam's existence, and thus would furnish no grounds for intervention by China. Air assaults would also allow the South Vietnamese government a "breathing spell and opportunity to improve." China's recent development of a nuclear device seemingly made it imperative to protect South Vietnam, and, according to some in the White House, the use of air power would greatly diminish the chances of having to send American combat troops.

On the night of February 6, 1965, Vietcong forces afforded the Johnson administration a reason for implementing its bombing policy when they attacked the huge American army barracks and air base at Pleiku, in central South Vietnam, inflicting over a hundred American casualties, including nine dead. National Security Adviser McGeorge Bundy, then on an investigatory mission in Saigon, rushed to the scene and joined two others there—the American ambassador to South Vietnam, Maxwell Taylor, and the commander of American forces, General William Westmoreland—in calling for instant retaliation. Bombing raids, they emphasized, were the major assurance against having to send American ground forces. Johnson immediately authorized air strikes on North Vietnam. "We have kept our guns over the mantel and our shells in the cupboard for a long time now. I can't ask our American soldiers out there to continue to fight with one hand behind their backs."

The attack on Pleiku had thus provided the pretext for American bombing operations rather than their cause. Within twelve hours of the Vietcong attack the first of nearly fifty American jets raided military installations above the 17th parallel. Soon known as "Rolling Thunder," the air raids graduated from individual retaliatory missions to a sustained campaign by the summer of 1965. Besides hitting key military targets, the bombs eventually struck Hanoi, Haiphong (with Soviet vessels in the harbor), and the railroad from Hanoi to China, some damage occurring only ten miles outside China's borders. The attack on Pleiku had provided the rationale for bombing the north, which in turn had argued for a greater escalation of the war.

Despite the pilots' claims that they hit military targets with "surgical" accuracy, the bombings ultimately became indiscriminate and included civilian centers. Yet Hanoi held on. To counter the effects of the bombings, the North Vietnamese moved urban civilians to the countryside, spread out industrial and storage centers, often placing them in caves or underground, and dug thousands of miles of tunnels for transportation and living purposes. UN Secretary-General U Thant urged an end to the bombing, French President Charles de Gaulle called it "detestable" for "a great nation to ravage a small one," and the United States became subject to the charge of atrocity as up to a thousand Vietnamese civilians a week were added to growing casualty lists. Within the United States, Americans were shocked by the apparent suddenness of the decision to bomb North Vietnam. The Johnson administration did not fully explain the reasons behind the decision, raising the suspicion that the United States was the aggressor.

The growing emphasis on bombing had an unforeseen and ironic effect: whereas the Johnson administration had counted on the new strategy ruling out the need for ground forces, American soldiers now became necessary to protect air bases from Vietcong assaults. In February 1965 the president gave in to Westmoreland's requests and ordered two battalions of marines to South Vietnam. Their arrival at Danang's air base on March 8 further Americanized the conflict. Though at first restricted to patrol duty, American forces would soon engage in "search and destroy" missions that more deeply alienated the populace and paradoxically diminished chances for winning the war, almost in direct relation to their military success. By the end of the year American troops in Vietnam numbered more than 184,000, a figure which more than doubled a year later.

America's involvement in Vietnam developed out of a strange mixture of the olive branch and the sword. In early April 1965 Johnson delivered a speech at Johns Hopkins University in which he declared that "the appetite of aggression is never satisfied." America's stipulations for peace included "an independent South Vietnam—securely guaranteed and able to shape its own relationships to all others—free from outside interference—tied to no alliance—a military base for no other country." Once peace was restored, he added, the United States would provide $1 billion for the economic development of the Mekong Delta. The next day Hanoi replied with demands for total American withdrawal from South Vietnam, the severing of military ties with Saigon, no "foreign interference" in the unification of the Vietnams, and acceptance of the National Liberation Front's social, political, and economic reform program in South Vietnam. Hanoi later stipulated that the United States had to end the bombing before peace talks could begin. Johnson reaffirmed America's commitment. "Let no one think for a moment that retreat from Vietnam would bring an end to the conflict. The battle would be renewed in one country and then another. . . . We must say in southeast Asia—as we did in Europe—in the words of the Bible: 'Hitherto shalt thou come, but no further.' "

REVOLUTION IN THE DOMINICAN REPUBLIC

While the bombings went on, another problem confronted the Johnson administration, the resolution of which perhaps contributed to the decision to adopt stronger military measures in Vietnam: a leftist revolution in the Dominican Republic. America's goals and methods were the same there and in Vietnam: to halt the spread of communism by intervening with military force to uphold domestic stability. After a dictatorship of over thirty years, Dominican President Rafael Trujillo was assassinated in 1961, and the following year the islanders elected liberal reformer Dr. Juan Bosch as president. Though a military coup forced Bosch into exile in less than a year, his leftist supporters led an insurrection against the military regime in April 1965 that brought on civil war. "Men and women like this," warned the U.S. ambassador to the Dominican Republic, John Bartlow Martin, "have nowhere to go except to the Communists." Action by Washington seemed necessary to prevent the establishment of another Castro-like regime in the Caribbean.

Johnson quickly dispatched over 20,000 troops to safeguard America's interests on the island. Having decided against first consulting either the UN or the OAS, he spoke on television on April 28 to defend his actions. Not only were the soldiers to restore order and bring citizens home, the president explained, but they had to deal with a new menace. The Dominican revolution had taken a communist turn, an argument he buttressed with a dubious list of over fifty "identified and prominent Communist and Castroite leaders" among the rebels. Another Cuba seemed likely. In a statement in May that some referred to as the "Johnson Doctrine," the president pledged that the "American nations cannot, must not, and will not permit the establishment of another Communist government in the Western Hemisphere."

Despite bitter opposition in the United States and Latin America, the American soldiers remained and became enmeshed in the Dominican conflict. Many critics claimed that America's action violated the OAS Charter, which stipulated that "no State or group of States had the right to intervene, directly or indirectly, for any reason whatever, in the internal or external affairs of any other State." Johnson countered with an argument that had no factual foundation: "[P]eople trained outside the Dominican Republic are seeking to gain control." Senator J. William Fulbright, chairman of the Foreign Relations Committee, questioned whether the communist danger was real and denounced the intervention. Americans, he declared, had become "the prisoners of the Latin American oligarchs who are engaged in a vain attempt to preserve the status quo— reactionaries who habitually use the term communist very loosely, in part . . . in a calculated effort to scare the United States into supporting their selfish and discredited aims."

The United States finally turned to the OAS as a way out of the imbroglio. In early May the American foreign ministers' deputies met in Washington, D.C., where after a week of debate the United States narrowly won the two-thirds support needed (the larger states opposed the measure) for the establishment of a five-nation OAS Inter-American Peace Force. Most American soldiers could now leave, although some stayed with the force as it worked toward establishing a new regime comprised of military and civilian leaders.

Though the Dominican intervention had been costly in credibility and prestige, the Johnson administration claimed a victory in blocking the installation of a leftist president. America's unilateral action had violated a number of assurances given to Latin America as long ago as Franklin D. Roosevelt's Good Neighbor policy, and as recently as Kennedy's Alliance for Progress. In June 1966 moderate rightists, led by Joaquín Balaguer, defeated Bosch for the presidency and the following month Balaguer took office, permitting a few of Bosch's followers to join the cabinet. Bosch bitterly asserted that his had been "a democratic revolution smashed by the leading democracy of the world." Johnson was convinced that his actions had prevented a communist takeover in the Dominican Republic and doubtless believed that the same resolute action in Vietnam could achieve similar results.

ESCALATION IN VIETNAM

Meanwhile the war in Southeast Asia threatened to escalate again as both Saigon and Washington adopted harder positions. For nearly a week in May 1965 the United States called off the bombing to encourage negotiations, but with no results. In June Saigon's government came under the control of Air Marshal Nguyen Cao Ky, who had fought with the French against the Vietminh during the First Indochinese War. Ky became premier and his cohort, General Nguyen Van Thieu, became commander-in-chief of the armed forces. Although Americans attested to Thieu's abilities, the CIA dismissed Ky as irresponsible and concerned only about "drinking, gambling and chasing women." It was "absolutely the bottom of the barrel," one of Johnson's advisers recalled. Less than a week before Ky took over, America's soldiers received authority to engage in full combat duty. In July Johnson, without congressional approval, assured Westmoreland of as many troops as he needed to win the war. That same month several key Great Society programs were at critical points in the legislative process, leading some writers to believe that Johnson's major fear was that he was about to lose South Vietnam at precisely the time he needed leverage to force through his reform program at home. Therefore, the argument goes, the president raised the level of involvement in Vietnam out of both domestic and foreign considerations. Whatever the truth, it appears that Johnson, like Kennedy, lacked a planned war effort and simply followed the day-to-day developments, with the central emphasis being a desire to avoid losing the war. Johnson's decision to approve the escalation in Vietnam further converted the conflict into an American war, narrowing succeeding options and making his nation's commitment virtually unlimited.

As the fighting in Vietnam intensified in 1965, the United States defended its involvement on several grounds. First and foremost, its intention was to halt outside "aggression" through military action, while at the same time shoring up a rapidly deteriorating South Vietnam. The Department of State argued that the Tonkin Resolution was an extension of the SEATO Treaty, by which signatory nations agreed to aid members whose "peace and safety" were in jeopardy. The Johnson administration, like that of Kennedy, believed North Vietnam had infiltrated South Vietnam, thus constituting an armed attack requiring protection by SEATO's members. In addition, Article 51 of the UN Charter allowed "collective self-defense" and justified American action. Furthermore, failure to protect South Vietnam would break a moral duty, setting an example injurious to American prestige and security throughout the world. The potentially most dangerous assumption in Washington was that a show of America's military might would shatter the Vietcong and end the war.

Increasing numbers of Americans were questioning the wisdom of widening the nation's commitment to South Vietnam. In view of the growing rift between Moscow and Peking, the traditional argument—halting a Kremlin-directed communist monolith—suddenly rang hollow. Questions arose about containment's open-ended premise that America's vital interests encompassed every area of the world threatened by communism—which meant that America was in danger of overextending itself. The United States also found itself in the uncomfortable position of opposing all social revolutions simply because they opened the door for communist subversion; the only safe situation seemed to be the status quo, which meant upholding stability even at the price of reform. By 1965 the justification for America's involvement in Vietnam, begun by the Truman administration in 1950, had to come from other sources. The United States could not pull out of Vietnam without losing prestige and honor. The first intervention necessitated a deeper commitment, which in turn grew because of the first involvement, and the longer the United States remained in Vietnam the longer it had to stay.

SEEDS OF VIETNAMIZATION, 1966–1969

Continuation of the bombings had serious repercussions inside the United States because it tended to divide Americans into two broadly defined camps: the "doves," a mixed group of liberals and others who wanted a negotiated withdrawal; and the "hawks," mainly right-wing Republicans and conservative Democrats who advocated victory through increased military force. Protest demonstrations grew into a firestorm as America's escalated involvement drained the dollar and fed inflation, threw the nation's budget out of order, forced major cutbacks in foreign aid, and badly damaged the Great Society's domestic reform programs. "Teach-ins" began in 1965 at the University of Michigan and spread to other places of learning, while youths either burned their draft cards and chanted "Hell no, we won't go," or avoided the draft by going to Canada or to jail. "Hey, hey, LBJ, how many kids have you killed today?" drummed demonstrators around the White House, as they called the United States immoral, racist, and imperialist. The American government, they declared, was killing reform at home and innocents abroad. The presidency was becoming imperial in disregarding the wishes of Congress and the people. Involvement in Vietnam, the doves argued, was wrecking the Western alliance and undercutting America's authority and prestige. Furthermore, it was unconstitutional because Congress had not declared war. Withdrawal was the only solution.

Though the hawks accused the doves of being rife with communists, the criticisms of America's Vietnam policies were nationwide and not attributable solely to propaganda. Opponents of the war included Senators Fulbright, Mike Mansfield, and Wayne Morse, containment proponent George F. Kennan, journalist Walter Lippmann, civil rights leader Dr. Martin Luther King, Jr., numerous notables from both major political parties, newspapers including *The New York Times* and the *Washington Post*, "New Left" writers critical of America's alleged capitalist and exploitative "ruling class," and a great number of America's youth. The United States, they declared, was guilty of aggression in a civil war that had no relation to SEATO obligations. In fact, the United States was the only SEATO member that felt a responsibility to South Vietnam, and was in addition helping a repressive government crush a movement of the people. The

United States had not supported the elections called for by the Geneva Accords of 1954, Diem and his successors had released the United States from its commitments by failing to implement reforms, and Johnson had violated his word in sending American soldiers to an Asian war. Moreover, they concluded, "victory" could come only at the cost of annihilating Vietnam; the United States could not win the war through conventional means, and the bombings would devastate the land in the name of peace. The most fundamental failure, some argued, was that the village pacification program had alienated the vast majority of peasants, encouraging the Vietnamese people to hate Americans. The bombings had now underlined the problem. Defeat, the doves admitted, might allow Vietnam to become communist, but that did not mean the country would automatically become Red China's puppet. Ancient hatreds between Vietnam and China dictated against their cooperation. The multiplicity of arguments against the war guaranteed division among the doves, preventing unified resistance and helping the hawks to stay in command.

The hawks' defense of the war was formidable because they based their arguments on the fear of global communism and on America's fictional belief that it had won all of its wars. Americans believed that withdrawal from Vietnam would constitute their first defeat, and Johnson refused to be the first chief executive to lose a war. Furthermore, the hawks declared, the president as commander-in-chief could send American soldiers anywhere, a power confirmed by the passage of the Tonkin Resolution. On the charge of immorality, the hawks declared that the Vietcong were the aggressors, and that South Vietnam had asked for America's help. It was not a civil war any longer—if indeed it ever had been—because the North Vietnamese depended on Chinese and Soviet assistance. The hawks insisted that Johnson's pledge against using American combat forces was no longer applicable, for conditions had deteriorated so rapidly that South Vietnam needed direct assistance. Containment of communism was vital to the security of the United States because failure in Southeast Asia would have a "domino" effect that would ultimately reach Pacific shores. Appeasement in Vietnam, the hawks concluded, would show a lack of American will, inviting direct intervention by Moscow and Peking.

Unrest over the war continued to grow throughout 1966 and 1967. In early 1966 Fulbright chaired a series of televised hearings on America's involvement in Vietnam. Asking probing questions of administration supporters, he could get no satisfactory answer regarding which country's communism the United States was seeking to contain in Southeast Asia. The major spokesman for the administration, Secretary of State Rusk, argued that America was fighting the spread of Chinese communism, ignoring growing reports that by the mid-1960s the Soviet Union had assumed the major burden of aid for North Vietnam. He quoted from the Truman Doctrine of 1947 in explaining the American presence in Southeast Asia: "I believe it must be the policy of the United States to support free peoples who are resisting attempted subjugation by armed minorities or by outside pressures."

Criticisms of the administration's Vietnam policies were steadily intensifying. Kennan asserted that he never intended the containment doctrine to entail the use of military force at virtually any point in the world. There was "no reason why we should wish to become so involved" in Vietnam. The United States should begin a phased withdrawal, he declared, because containment was not the solution to Asian problems as it had been to those of Europe's during the 1940s. Communism was now too diverse and the world's problems too monumental for the United States alone to resolve. In 1967 McNamara resigned from the Defense Department in protest over the administration's policies in Vietnam, joining National Security Council Adviser McGeorge Bundy, Undersecretary of State George Ball, and the president's political adviser and friend Bill Moyers, all of whom had already left Washington.

While the arguments drummed on, the United States slowly sank into what writers later called the "quagmire" of Vietnam. By 1967, after three years of direct military involvement, the situation in South Vietnam had not improved and the United States had sustained great losses, including $6 billion worth of aircraft over North Vietnam. In fact, General Westmoreland was calling for more soldiers. Johnson was reluctant. "When we add divisions," he asked in April, "can't the enemy add divisions? If so, where does it all end?" America's "search and destroy" missions had led to heavy loss of life and property, while not succeeding in rooting out villagers suspected of helping the Vietcong. On television news programs, Americans heard skyrocketing "body counts" of enemy dead that allegedly proved the imminence of victory, and watched their soldiers clear the Vietcong from areas by using napalm, tear gas, flame throwers, saturation bombing, chemical defoliants, and firepower of all kinds. "Pacification" centers were filled and failing, the Vietcong found sanctuary in Laos and Cambodia, and the number of refugees by the beginning of 1968 had soared to 4 million or a quarter of the country's population. The Americanization of the war had reduced the role of the ARVN and made it less effective, and Ky's Saigon government had become increasingly repressive, having imprisoned thousands of political enemies stemming largely from another Buddhist upheaval. And all the while, the political battle over the people's support was being lost as mounting numbers of peasants, including refugees, flocked into the ranks of the Vietcong. The irony was that as the United States's firepower became more effective, its chances for gaining popular support and winning the war seemed to decline correspondingly.

America's relations with most other Asian countries also steadily deteriorated in almost direct proportion to its level of escalation in Vietnam. The United States accused Cambodia of providing sanctuary for the Vietcong, leading that government to break relations with Washington in

America's Longest War

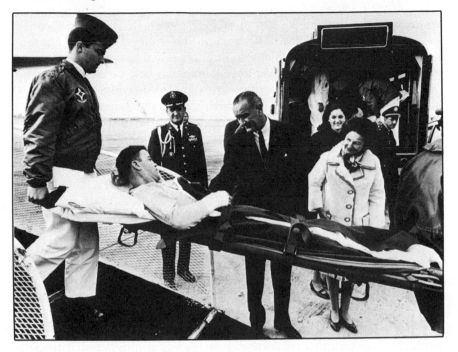

President Johnson meets a wounded member of the armed forces arriving at Andrews Air Force Base, Maryland, from Vietnam, February 1967. (U.S. Air Force)

1965. Americans bombed neutral Laos because that country appeared to be a vital cog in the "Ho Chi Minh Trail" that wound over bicycle paths through the jungles of Laos and Cambodia, permitting goods to reach the Vietcong. Japan increasingly questioned American involvement in Southeast Asia, especially after Okinawa became the headquarters for launching aerial attacks on North Vietnam. Thailand was an exception to the region's growing anti-American feeling; it feared communist guerrillas in the east and permitted the establishment of American military plants and bombing bases. As in the Korean War, Americans comprised the great bulk of fighting men in Vietnam, although 50,000 soldiers from South Korea joined the few contributed by Thailand, Australia, New Zealand, and the Philippines.

Johnson continued his calls for peace while at the same time refusing to condone any appearance of capitulation to aggression. The UN, the Vatican, and Poland offered to mediate an end to the war, and several times the United States authorized bombing pauses to encourage negotiations. During a month-long bombing halt that began on Christmas Eve of 1965, Johnson sent a peace mission to forty capitals to explain the American stand and to seek their help in ending the war. The delegation's membership was impressive—Vice President Hubert Humphrey, UN

Ambassador Arthur Goldberg, and Ambassador-at-Large W. Averell Harriman—but the effort failed and the bombings resumed. The president then instructed Goldberg to take the issue before the Security Council, but that body took no action. The United States stood virtually alone in Vietnam, and yet the Johnson administration still refused to relent. In an interview the president explained in Rooseveltian language, "I deeply believe we *are* quarantining aggression over there, just like the smallpox. Just like FDR and Hitler, just like Wilson and the Kaiser. . . . What I learned as a boy in my teens and in college about World War I was that it was our lack of strength and failure to show stamina that got us into that war."

THE SIX DAY WAR

In the spring of 1967, the danger of America overcommitting itself in Vietnam became evident when in the Middle East, Israeli forces again grappled with those of Egypt's in an abbreviated conflict known as the Six Day War. The region had remained unstable after the Suez crisis of 1956. The United States had continued its two-headed policy toward the Israelis and the Arabs, including the sale of arms to both sides to maintain a power balance, while Nasser received Soviet planes and tanks, worked with other Arab leaders in 1964 in establishing the Palestine Liberation Organization (PLO) to tear Palestine from Israel, and demanded that the UN peacekeeping force withdraw from the Egyptian-Israeli border. When the UN complied with his wishes in May 1967, the two antagonists directly confronted each other for the first time since 1956. Shortly afterward Nasser moved his forces into the Sinai Peninsula and seized Sharm el-Sheikh, a camp overlooking the entrance into the Gulf of Aqaba. His actions closed the gulf and denied Israel its only port.

Nasser seemed to be preparing for an invasion of Israel. His seizure of Sharm el-Sheikh had brought the United States into the matter because in 1956 the Eisenhower administration had secured Israel's withdrawal from the area in exchange for America's promise to support Israel's access to the Gulf of Aqaba. Meanwhile PLO terrorist groups from Syria and Jordan began guerrilla raids on Israel that drew immediate reprisals.

As Egyptian, Syrian, and Jordanian troops massed along Israel's borders, the Israelis decided to repeat their strategy of 1956 by striking first. On the morning of June 5 Israeli planes, averting Egyptian radar by approaching over the Mediterranean, launched a series of devastating strikes on Nasser's air force which was still on the ground, and then did the same with those of Jordan, Syria, and Iraq. Israeli tanks and soldiers crossed the Sinai and within six days had blocked the Suez Canal and were in control of Sharm el-Sheikh, the old city of Jerusalem, the West Bank of the Jordan River, the Golan Heights along Syria's border, and parts of Jordan and Syria. Neither the Soviet Union nor the United States intervened, although their use of the "hot line" between Moscow and

Washington perhaps reduced the chances of a misunderstanding that could have widened the war. With the Arabs defeated, the Soviets recommended a cease-fire, and on June 11 the UN Security Council accepted it. The Six Day War was over.

The UN managed a shaky truce in late November 1967. The vaguely worded document, Security Council Resolution 242, stipulated that in exchange for the Israelis' withdrawal from recently occupied Arab territories, they would receive guarantees of border security and free use of regional waterways. To assure peace, the resolution called for the establishment of "demilitarized zones," the nondiscriminatory use of international waters in the area (the Suez Canal was closed again, for as in 1956 Nasser sank ships at its entrance), and "a just settlement of the refugee problem," which the Palestinians interpreted as the establishment of a homeland. Though the antagonists did not implement the terms of the resolution, the situation was temporarily eased.

In the aftermath of the Six Day War the Middle East remained unstable, further revealing the incapacity of the United States to keep peace all over the world. America's relations with the Arabs plummeted. Nasser broke relations after making erroneous charges that American and British planes had aided the Israeli offensive, and several Arab nations instituted a short-lived oil embargo against the West. Meanwhile the Israelis refused to comply with the Security Council Resolution by continuing to occupy the Sinai Peninsula, the Gaza Strip, and the east bank of the Suez Canal, and by barring access to the waterway until it was open to everyone. The Soviet Union finally broke relations with Israel after warning it to return all Arab lands before negotiations could begin. Though the United States refused to recognize the Israelis' occupation of the old sector of Jerusalem, it understood their need for security and tried to persuade them to return the lands taken, in exchange for guaranteed access to the canal and to the Gulf of Aqaba. But neither the Soviets nor the Americans were able to arouse enough support for their program, and Israel refused to return territories taken during the Six Day War. While several mediation attempts failed, sporadic border incidents and increasing terrorist acts by the rapidly growing PLO underlined the need for permanent settlement. Peace continued to elude the region throughout Johnson's tenure in office.

ATTEMPTED NEGOTIATIONS WITH HANOI AND THE *PUEBLO* INCIDENT

By the end of 1967 the ever imminent hostilities in the Middle East had highlighted the dangers of America's global commitments and given impetus to the search for an honorable way out of Vietnam; indeed, prospects for peace had improved. Earlier that year in June the president had met with Soviet Premier Alexei Kosygin at Glassboro State College in New Jersey, where even though they failed to reach agreements on either Vietnam or the ongoing Middle East crisis, the image was that of a friendly atmosphere conducive to détente. In autumn opinion polls showed that a majority of Americans considered intervention in Vietnam to have been a mistake. That September in San Antonio, Texas, Johnson set out a plan for peace that became known as the "San Antonio formula." "The United States," he declared, "is willing to stop all aerial and naval bombing of North Vietnam when this will lead promptly to productive discussions. We, of course, assume that while discussions proceed, North Vietnam would not take advantage of the bombing cessation or limitation." Thus the United States now only demanded an end to new "infiltration" as a prerequisite to negotiations. Two months later the United States withdrew its opposition to negotiating with the National Liberation Front as a separate organization. North Vietnam had also retreated from some of its conditions for talks. No longer did it demand total military withdrawal by the United States, although it still insisted on a bombing halt. Hanoi also seemed willing to accept a long-range reunification plan.

Yet neither side was willing to concede anything on the premier issue of South Vietnam's future, and that meant a prolongation of the war. That same month of November America's ambassador to South Vietnam, Ellsworth Bunker, joined Westmoreland in assuring Washington that the pacification program was working. "We are winning a war of attrition," Westmoreland declared. Within two years, he asserted, the United States could begin a gradual withdrawal that would allow South Vietnam to take over the war. But even though America's chief diplomatic and military representatives in South Vietnam had discerned a timetable for withdrawal, two more years of fighting seemed interminable to those who wanted out immediately.

Several events in early 1968 suddenly complicated America's struggle to command leverage in Vietnam, none of which was more exasperating than that involving the American intelligence vessel *Pueblo*. An American B-52 disappeared in Greenland carrying four H-bombs; Democratic Senator Eugene McCarthy from Minnesota had entered the presidential race on an antiwar platform; and new troubles developed in Berlin, perhaps necessitating more American troops. Then on January 23 North Korean forces seized the *Pueblo* in the Sea of Japan, charged it with invading their territorial waters, and imprisoned the ship's eighty-two officers and sailors. Though Americans demanded prompt military action, the Johnson administration could not risk a war in Korea while immersed in one in Vietnam. After nearly a year of negotiations the American sailors, clearly under duress, admitted to violating North Korean waters and signed an apology. In a strange twist the American commander had permission from his captors to renounce the confession before and after signing it. The men were freed, although the communists kept the ship and won a major propaganda victory that further underlined the finite nature of America's superpower status.

TET

A week after the *Pueblo* incident, on January 30, Vietcong and North Viet-namese forces violated the long-honored truce during the Tet or lunar new year holiday by launching a surprising, massive offensive against South Vietnam that the communists expected would cause a popular up-rising against the Americans and the ARVN. At 2:45 A.M., nineteen Viet-cong exploded a hole in the thick-walled, eight-feet-tall barricade around the American embassy in Saigon, killing two MPs on duty. Using antitank guns and rockets hidden in the city weeks earlier, the Vietcong entered the courtyard but never managed to seize the embassy, which at the time housed only a few CIA and Foreign Service officers. American forces re-taliated at daybreak. Marines and paratroopers landed by helicopter on the embassy roof and regained control of the grounds a little after 9 A.M. Five Americans died, and all nineteen Vietcong were either killed or seri-ously wounded.

The greatest casualty of the Tet offensive was the Johnson administra-

General William Westmoreland

The leader of American forces in Vietnam (second from left) talks to military personnel in the U.S. Embassy in Saigon after the Vietcong siege during Tet, January 31, 1968.
(U.S. Army)

U.S. Embassy in Saigon, 1968

With their dead comrades lying nearby, these American soldiers held out against the Vietcong attacking the embassy during the Tet offensive. (Wide World)

tion's credibility at home. Americans were shocked to see televised coverage of their embassy grounds being overrun by Vietcong, especially after the president had declared just two weeks before in his State of the Union message that South Vietnam was nearly all "secure." The offensive had surprised the United States and South Vietnam, for both had thought the major North Vietnamese assault was an ongoing siege on the marine garrison at Khe Sanh, located in the northwest section of South Vietnam and close to the Laotian border. Indeed, some observers considered Khe Sanh another Dienbienphu.

Westmoreland was correct in terming the outcome of Tet a victory for the United States, but Americans refused to believe him, particularly when he called it the Vietcong's "last gasp." Johnson labeled the assault a "complete failure," although he admitted that the Vietcong had won a "psychological victory." Westmoreland privately referred to Tet as a "severe blow" to South Vietnam. If true, the offensive also hurt the Vietcong: local television accounts of the stacks of Vietcong bodies in Saigon convinced many villagers in South Vietnam that it would be wiser to send their young males into the local defense units rather than have them forced into the Vietcong. Whatever the final verdict of Tet, most talk of victory came to an end as American leaders moved toward a negotiated

The TV War in Vietnam

A Vietcong guerrilla executed by South Vietnamese national police chief, Brigadier General Nguyen Ngoc Loan, in Saigon on February 1, 1968. Associated Press photographer Eddie Adams took the picture that brought the war home to Americans and others around the world. (Wide World)

peace based on the reality of a stalemate. The Vietcong attack had raised the question that many Americans had been silently asking for some time: if the war was going so well, why was it lasting so long?

The Tet offensive drew a furious counterattack by American and ARVN forces that succeeded in the field but did little to change growing doubts in the United States about the war effort. Using rockets and gas, the combined armies regained control of the city of Hue, but only at the costs of three weeks of fighting, the deaths of 4,000 civilians, and the addition of more than 100,000 refugees to the already bloated list. "[N]othing I had seen during the Second World War in the Pacific, during the Korean War, and in Vietnam," journalist Robert Shaplen wrote, could compare to the "destruction and despair" in Hue. By the middle of March more than 40,000 Vietcong, or half of their forces, lay dead throughout the country, while America's dead numbered 1,000 and the ARVN twice that amount. The war seemed to have reached a new level of atrocity. An NBC news program in February showed Saigon's police chief executing a Vietcong prisoner in the street by a pistol shot to the head. In the provincial capital of Ben Tre, American and ARVN troops killed a thousand civilians while rooting out the Vietcong, causing one American officer to capsulize the new direction of the war in these words: "We had to destroy the town to save it." By March Vietcong units had resumed their earlier attack on Khe Sanh, but even though the Americans held, people in the United States were convinced that their soldiers were now on the defensive. In fact, it now appears that the American and ARVN counterattack was so successful that North Vietnamese regulars had to fill the Vietcong's sharply diminished ranks, finally changing the fighting into a conventional war between North and South Vietnam.

By early 1968 skepticism about America's Vietnam involvement had permeated the top echelons of the Johnson administration. In late February the president asked his new secretary of defense, Clark Clifford, to assess the nation's Vietnam policy. Westmoreland had just called for 206,000 more soldiers to join the 535,000 already there, in preparation for a major offensive. Opposition to escalation had been growing, as more

Robert McNamara and Clark Clifford in the Pentagon on February 7, 1968

McNamara was secretary of defense from 1961 to 1968, when he resigned and Clifford took his place and worked toward America's withdrawal from the war in Vietnam.
(U.S. Army)

members of the administration noted that American goods and purpose were disappearing, and that the real danger in international affairs was the Soviet Union. In March Rusk suggested a cease-fire based upon a bombing halt, while presidential hopeful Eugene McCarthy, calling for an immediate American withdrawal, made a strong showing in the New Hampshire Democratic primary that may have been more the result of unhappy hawks than doves, but nonetheless showed severe displeasure with the administration. Meanwhile, former Secretary of State Dean Acheson assured the president that "the Joint Chiefs of Staff don't know what they're talking about" in asking for more men, and Clifford could get no specific answers from the generals on when and how victory would come and at what cost. In early March Clifford recommended the addition of only 22,000 more American soldiers, the calling up of an undetermined number of reserves, and a "highly forceful approach" to Ky and Thieu to take over more of the fighting. Support for the "Vietnamization" of the war came from the Senior Informal Advisory Group on Vietnam, a collection of diplomatic and military figures of the Truman years who stunned the president by expressing doubt about America's ability to win the war.

Thus by the spring of 1968 misgivings about America's role in Vietnam had reached the White House, where the lack of progress in the war and its tremendous expense soon forced a change both in tactics in Vietnam and leadership in Washington. The ARVN's surprising recovery from the Tet offensive upheld the argument that scaling down America's involvement to its pre-1965 level might be the most feasible way out of the war. Johnson, believing that his generals had misled him in Vietnam, decided against sending the 22,000 men Clifford had recommended, and then ordered Westmoreland home to spare him the blame for America's failure to win the war. Finally, in view of marked domestic restiveness over the war, the president announced in a televised broadcast on March 31 that he would call off much of the bombing of North Vietnam to encourage peace talks. Lest his plea appear to be a political effort to ensure re-election, he surprised the nation by adding that he would neither seek nor accept the nomination of his party for the presidency.

Within a week of the president's withdrawal from the 1968 campaign the North Vietnamese surprised Washington by agreeing to peace talks, which began in Paris on May 13. But snags immediately developed. The American delegation, headed by W. Averell Harriman, encountered resistance from the North Vietnamese, who refused to discuss terms until the United States stopped *all* bombing. The Johnson administration declined on the same ground as earlier: the North Vietnamese might exploit the truce to strengthen their forces and therefore endanger American soldiers. With neither side willing to retreat, the United States and South Vietnam intensified their pacification and Vietnamization programs, apparently leaving the peace talks as the legacy for a new presidential administration in Washington.

THE PRESIDENTIAL ELECTION OF 1968

With Vietnam the major issue of the presidential election of 1968, the Republicans met in Miami Beach in early August and nominated Richard M. Nixon for the office. Trying to walk down the political middle, he offered experience in office, and promised reductions in government spending and no retreat in Vietnam. In a reminder of the Eisenhower strategy of 1952, Nixon assured Americans that he had a "secret plan" designed to "end the war and win the peace." Secrecy was essential, Nixon explained, because of the ongoing Paris negotiations.

The Democrats prepared for battle. With Johnson out of the race, Vice President Humphrey declared his intention to run, as did Senator Robert F. Kennedy of New York, who announced his candidacy on an antiwar platform and took most of McCarthy's supporters from him. Kennedy won the June primary in California, but, like his brother five and a half years earlier, that evening he was assassinated, shocking the nation and leaving the antiwar campaign in disarray. Kennedy's followers had no choice but to shun the campaign in frustration or fall back with McCarthy, for Humphrey was locked into administration policies that called for continued bombing until concessions from North Vietnam allowed peace with honor.

Later that August the Democratic party gathered in Chicago, where a siegelike atmosphere dominated the inside of the convention hall and antiwar protesters were ringed around the outside. Inside, a major political battle developed over the Democratic platform on Vietnam. McCarthy's followers demanded an end to the bombing, immediate negotiations, and withdrawal of American forces. Humphrey's supporters countered with the administration's hardline argument, and after a bitter three-hour debate defeated the peace plank. Violence broke out in the streets of Chicago, where youths carrying Vietcong flags called the police "pigs," sang the popular song "I Ain't Marchin' Anymore," and chanted "Ho, Ho, Ho Chi Minh," "Sieg Hiel, Sieg Hiel, Sieg," and "The Whole World Is Watching." In what an investigatory commission afterward termed a "police riot," club-wielding policemen swarmed into the crowd, injuring hundreds of demonstrators, bystanders, and reporters, and taking many to jail. Humphrey won the nomination of his party.

The political sides had not yet been fully drawn, for a third party entered the contest. The American Independence Party nominated Alabama Governor George Wallace for the presidency on a "law and order" campaign, which many called a euphemism for continued racial segregation and a crackdown on all types of protesters. He demanded victory in Vietnam, while his vice presidential running mate, General Curtis LeMay, lamented America's "phobia" over nuclear weapons and reminded observers that he favored bombing North Vietnam back "into the stone age."

Nixon's candidacy suddenly received a big boost, when on the night of August 20–21 Soviet tanks and troops stormed into Czechoslovakia to put down an uprising similar to that of two decades ago. To justify this action, Soviet General Secretary Leonid Brezhnev asserted in what became known as the Brezhnev Doctrine that the Soviets had the right to intervene in any allied country to defend "proletarian internationalism." Though Johnson protested, he found it difficult to fend off the strong counterattacks pointing to America's recent intervention in the Dominican Republic and its ongoing war in Vietnam. The Soviet intervention in Czechoslovakia seemed to have undermined hopes for détente, for it heightened the Cold War, stimulated a missile and arms buildup that threatened to interfere with the Senate's approval of the nuclear nonproliferation agreement, drew the NATO alliance closer together again, and underscored America's inability to determine world events. The hawks in the United States cited the Czech crisis as evidence of the need to stand up to the communists in Vietnam, and many Americans became convinced that Nixon's long record of fighting communism made him the best choice in 1968.

With Nixon running ahead in the polls, on October 31 Johnson announced that all bombing would end the following day, a move that lifted Humphrey's chances and offered new hope for the staggering peace talks in Paris. On November 5 Nixon won a narrow victory despite Humphrey's rapid surge following the bombing halt. With 302 electoral votes but only 43.4 percent of the popular vote, and both Houses of Congress still Democratic, Nixon prepared to assume the presidency and "win the peace" in Vietnam. Prospects looked good: on January 16, 1969, four days before the inauguration, the Paris conferees agreed to sit at a round table, resolving a bitter dispute by awarding all participants equal status, and the three delegations from South Vietnam, North Vietnam, and the National Liberation Front agreed with the Americans to turn to substantive matters.

The containment policy followed since the Truman era virtually collapsed during the Johnson presidency. All of its assumptions had come into question: that a huge communist monolith existed under the direction of Moscow; that the United States had to define "vital interests" in accordance with whatever area in the world the communists sought, never seeming to doubt either South Vietnam's strategic importance, its viability as a nation-state, or the popularity of its government; that the instability resulting from social revolutions was a breeding ground for communism and had to be resisted with either military or economic means; that America's sense of mission necessitated the establishment of democratic ways of life in every nation in the world; and, above all, that America could leave no indications of a weakened will. Thus, the future of the world appeared to rest in Vietnam, which dictated a total commitment and made the collapse of containment devastating. The consolation was that the new presidential administration seemed to offer a different direction in foreign policy.

Selected readings

Ambrose, Stephen E., *Rise to Globalism: American Foreign Policy since 1938*. 4th ed. 1985.

Baritz, Loren, *Backfire: A History of How American Culture Led Us into Vietnam and Made Us Fight the Way We Did*. 1985.

Berman, Larry, *Planning a Tragedy: The Americanization of the War in Vietnam*. 1982.

Bornet, Vaughn Davis, *The Presidency of Lyndon B. Johnson*. 1983.

Burchett, Wilfred, *Catapult to Freedom: The Survival of the Vietnamese People*. 1978.

Buttinger, Joseph, *Vietnam: A Dragon Embattled*. 2 vols. 1967.

———,*Vietnam: A Political History*. 1968.

Cincinnatus [pseudonym for Cecil B. Currey], *Self-Destruction: The Disintegration and Decay of the United States Army during the Vietnam Era*. 1981.

Cohen, Warren I., *Dean Rusk*. 1980.

Cooper, Chester L., *The Lost Crusade: America in Vietnam*. 1970.

DeBenedetti, Charles, *The Peace Reform in American History*. 1980.

Fall, Bernard B., *Last Reflections on a War*. 1967.

———, *The Two Vietnams: A Political and Military Analysis*. 2d ed. 1967.

FitzGerald, Frances, *Fire in the Lake: The Vietnamese and the Americans in Vietnam*. 1972.

Gaddis, John L., *Strategies of Containment: A Critical Appraisal of Postwar American National Security Policy*. 1982.

Gelb, Leslie H., and Richard K. Betts, *The Irony of Vietnam: The System Worked*. 1979.

Geyelin, Philip, *Lyndon B. Johnson and the World*. 1966.

Goldman, Eric F., *The Tragedy of Lyndon Johnson*. 1968.

Goodman, Allan E., *The Lost Peace: America's Search for a Negotiated Settlement of the Vietnam War*. 1978.

Gurtov, Melvin, *The United States against the Third World*. 1974.

Halberstam, David, *The Best and the Brightest*. 1972.

Hallin, Daniel C., *The "Uncensored War": The Media and Vietnam*. 1986.

Harrison, James P., *The Endless War*. 1982.

Heath, Jim F., *Decade of Disillusionment: The Kennedy-Johnson Years*. 1975.

Herring, George C., Jr., *America's Longest War: The United States and Vietnam, 1950–1975*. 2d ed. 1986.

Hoopes, Townsend, *The Limits of Intervention: An Inside Account of How the Johnson Policy of Escalation in Vietnam Was Reversed*. 1969.

Kahin, George M., *Intervention: How America Became Involved in Vietnam*. 1986.

————, and John W. Lewis, *The United States in Vietnam*. Rev. ed. 1969.

Kalb, Marvin, and Elie Abel, *Roots of Involvement*. 1971.

Karnow, Stanley, *Vietnam: A History*. 1983.

Kattenburg, Paul M., *The Vietnam Trauma in American Foreign Policy, 1945–1975*. 1980.

Kearns, Doris, *Lyndon Johnson and the American Dream*. 1976.

Kolko, Gabriel, *Anatomy of a War: Vietnam, the United States, and the Modern Historical Experience*. 1985.

LaFeber, Walter, *America, Russia, and the Cold War, 1945–1984*. 5th ed. 1985.

Lewy, Guenter, *America in Vietnam*. 1978.

Lowenthal, Abraham F., *The Dominican Intervention*. 1972.

Maclear, Michael, *The Ten Thousand Day War, Vietnam: 1945–1975*. 1981.

Mangold, Tom, and John Penygate, *The Tunnels of Cu Chi: The Untold Story of Vietnam*. 1985.

The New York Times, *The Pentagon Papers*. 1971.

Oberdorfer, Don, *Tet!* 1971.

Palmer, Dave R., *Summons of the Trumpet*. 1978.

Pike, Douglas, *Viet Cong: the Organization and Techniques of the National Liberation Front of South Vietnam*. 1966.

Pisor, Robert L., *The End of the Line: The Siege of Khe Sanh*. 1982.

Poole, Peter, *The United States and Indochina from FDR to Nixon*. 1973.

Schandler, Herbert Y., *The Unmaking of a President: Lyndon Johnson and Vietnam*. 1977.

Schlesinger, Arthur M., Jr., *The Imperial Presidency*. 1973.

Shaplen, Robert, *The Lost Revolution: The U.S. in Vietnam, 1946–1966*. 1966.

————, *The Road from War: Vietnam, 1965–1970*. 1970.

————, *Time Out of Hand: Revolution and Reaction in Southeast Asia*. Rev. ed. 1970.

Spanier, John W., *American Foreign Policy Since World War II*. 9th ed. 1983.

Spiegel, Steven L., *The Other Arab-Israeli Conflict: Making America's Middle East Policy, from Truman to Reagan*. 1985.

Stevenson, Richard W., *The Rise and Fall of Détente: Relaxations of Tensions in US-Soviet Relations, 1953–1984*. 1985.

Summers, Harry G., Jr., *On Strategy: A Critical Analysis of the Vietnam War*. 1982.

Thies, Wallace J., *When Governments Collide: Coercion and Diplomacy in the Vietnam Conflict, 1964–1968*. 1980.

Thompson, James C., *Rolling Thunder: Understanding Policy and Program Failure*. 1980.

Truong Nhu Tang, *A Vietcong Memoir*. 1985.

Turner, Kathleen J., *Lyndon Johnson's Dual War: Vietnam and the Press*. 1985.

Ulam, Adam B., *The Rivals: America and Russia Since World War II*. 1971.

Westmoreland, William C., *A Soldier Reports*. 1976.

Chapter Twenty-Four

Vietnamization through Détente: A New Containment, 1969–1977

DÉTENTE: STRUCTURE OF PEACE

The primary objective of the Nixon administration was to build a structure of peace through détente, which would allow America to end involvement in Vietnam and turn attention to other problems, both at home and abroad. The task would not be easy. The new Republican administration faced a shattered consensus of popular support for the White House, a Democratic Congress, and an American people unhappy with containment. Détente was purported to be an alternative foreign policy. Actually begun during the 1960s, détente aimed to reduce tensions with both the Soviet Union and Red China by avoiding confrontations, urging nuclear nonproliferation, and calling an end to the struggle against monolithic communism. To the United States, détente offered an honorable way out of Vietnam. The growth of a multipolar world order helped to promote détente, for while the forces of nationalism encouraged neutralism among numerous Third World countries, these same forces created a polycentric system within the Soviet bloc that reduced dependence on the Kremlin. If the United States could establish good relations with the Soviet Union and Red China, even by playing one against the other, it might be able to wind down involvement in Asia. "I'm not going to end up like LBJ," Nixon proclaimed, "holed up in the White House afraid to show my face in the street. I'm going to stop that war. Fast."

The president's closest adviser in foreign affairs was Henry Kissinger, who was to be the architect of détente. Partly basing his philosophy of foreign policy upon his doctoral studies in political science at Harvard,

Kissinger sought to erect a balance of power patterned after the Congress of Vienna of 1815. All states had legitimate rights, he admitted, but no state could have "absolute security" because such a situation necessitated "absolute insecurity for all the others." He understood, as did the continental powers after the Napoleonic Wars, that peace could come only through a world order based on recognized shared interests and the determination of the major powers to defuse international troubles. Rather than reconstruct a traditional balance of power system, however, Kissinger wanted to replace ideology with an emphasis on geopolitics designed to achieve what he termed an "equilibrium of strength" conducive to world peace. His plan did not rest on specific, unyielding commitments and treaty terms, but on a general frame of mind or attitude that adjusted to constantly shifting power realities. Thus, détente was an ongoing attempt to find new grounds for agreements. As he told a congressional committee in 1974, it was "a process of managing relations with a potentially hostile country in order to preserve peace while maintaining our vital interests." The underlying stipulation was that the major powers had to renounce the use of nuclear weapons in achieving their objectives.

As national security affairs adviser until 1973, when he became secretary of state, Kissinger enjoyed an independence in foreign affairs that someone tied to the Department of State could not have. This suited the White House, for as the president remarked, "No Secretary of State is really important. The President makes foreign policy." New York attorney William Rogers headed the State Department but had little effect on the nation's foreign affairs. Nixon privately assessed the situation in these words: "Henry thinks Bill [Rogers] isn't very deep and Bill thinks that Henry is power crazy. In a sense they are both right."

For a time Kissinger seemed to dominate foreign affairs. Critics considered the German-born and heavily accented adviser to be arrogant and intensely loyal to "the Establishment," and yet they admitted that his individualism, wit, charm, and personal style of diplomacy allowed him to avert State Department bureaucracy and get things done. Those same critics warned, however, that Kissinger did not formalize many of his agreements and that his word was good only as long as he was in a position of power. By not holding a formal office during the first four years of the Nixon administration, Kissinger took advantage of "executive privilege" to engage in secret diplomacy, approve wiretappings of underlings and journalists, avoid congressional hearings, and answer only to the president. In fact, he seldom consulted his own staff. An observer remarked that "Henry's chief lieutenants are like mushrooms. They're kept in the dark, get a lot of manure piled on them, and then get canned."

Nixon and Kissinger argued for détente for several reasons, the most fundamental being to halt a dangerous arms race. They were aware of certain realities: America's declining prestige, primarily brought on by the war in Vietnam; the Cold War's constant drain on resources; the rapid military expansion of the Soviet Union after the Cuban missile crisis; the

rising importance of the Third World; the fruitlessness of refusing to recognize Red China; and the growing economic and political strength of
Western Europe and Japan. A number of agreements with the Soviet
Union had pointed to better relations, and yet the element of trust was
still missing. In the mid-1960s the United States found that the Soviet
Union supported the development of antiballistic missiles (ABMs), which
if successful would undermine America's deterrence capacity by permitting the destruction of approaching intercontinental ballistic missiles
(ICBMs) and thus reducing the level of Soviet "assured destruction" to an
"acceptable" casualty figure of a few million. In 1969 the Nixon administration pushed for an improved ABM system, called Safeguard, to protect
missile sites. More alarming, both superpowers were trying to develop a
better offensive capability through the Multiple Independently Targeted
Reentry Vehicle (MIRV), a first-strike ICBM carrying up to ten independently fired nuclear warheads and thus able to counteract ABMs by its
sheer number of projectiles. Though each side had a satellite reconnaissance system, neither could determine the number of warheads in a
MIRV and therefore neither could know the other's nuclear capability.
With the two nations approaching strategic parity or equality, détente
was not a choice but a necessity.

Détente carried both advantages and disadvantages. First and foremost, it offered a lessening of international tensions and a way out of
Vietnam. If instituted as policy, the United States could lower arms expenditures and encourage negotiations over cutbacks, reduce the need for
combat forces and end the draft, diminish the assumed need to intervene
in other countries, and build a greater international trade system leading
to world order. Kissinger explained that there were five major areas of
power in the world—the United States, the Soviet Union, China, Japan,
and Western Europe—and that each should have hegemony in its locale.
None would interfere in another's region, and all would cooperate in preventing neutralist nations from manipulating the superpowers. Thus, détente called for a global balance of power in which the leading nations
would discourage aggressions within their own spheres. As Nixon put it
in 1971, the "five great economic superpowers will determine the economic future" as well as "the future of the world in other ways in the last
of this century."

Détente worked better in theory than in application. The Third World
preferred diplomatic nonalignment, increasingly resisting efforts by either
the Soviets or the Americans to dictate its policies. Thus emerging nationalisms in Asia, the Middle East, and Africa continued to cause major
problems for the big powers. Economic troubles stemmed from the Organization of Petroleum Exporting Countries (OPEC), as its oil-producing
members aggravated an energy crisis during the 1970s by raising prices
for consumer nations. At the same time, terrorists and hijackers repeatedly posed dilemmas seemingly incapable of resolution. Critics in the

United States complained that détente was a new form of globalism that would again overextend the nation's foreign involvement. Others wondered what would happen if the Chinese tried to play off the Soviets against the Americans, or if the Soviets attempted the same with the Americans and the Chinese. Yet despite the pitfalls of détente, there seemed to be no viable alternative.

Kissinger used the idea of "linkage" in trying to reduce tensions with the Soviet Union and Red China. By exerting economic pressure on Moscow and Peking, the United States might convince them to halt their arms supply to Hanoi and force Ho Chi Minh into a compromise settlement of the war. Despite the apparent new direction in foreign policy, this approach looked backward because it assumed that the North Vietnamese lacked a will of their own. Another premise of linkage was the indivisibility of peace—that an act of aggression in any part of the world constituted a threat to the overall network of peace. Kissinger hoped that the three major powers might tie all facets together in one magnificent design for peace. According to theory, the United States would furnish economic assistance to the Soviets in exchange for winding down the war in Vietnam and accepting arms limitations. Washington would then open negotiations with Peking to guarantee peace. By linking economic aid to military events in Southeast Asia, the United States would lay the basis for détente by improving relations with the Soviet Union and by inaugurating a new era with China. Military withdrawal from Vietnam would also unite Americans at home and allow the United States to negotiate from a position of strength. Détente and linkage sought to alleviate tensions; distrust and rivalry would remain.

Linkage was laden with questionable premises. It offered little guarantee of success. The idea of tying together seemingly unrelated issues to achieve world order had been tried with minimal effect during the presidency of Franklin D. Roosevelt. Furthermore, the amount of war matériel furnished the North Vietnamese by the Soviets and Chinese was small compared to that given the ARVN by the Americans. In truth, linkage was little different from containment in resting on the assumption that world events depended on the decisions of the major powers. The Nixon administration nonetheless sought a Soviet-American arms control agreement and expanded commercial relations, which it claimed would end the war in Vietnam and ease world unrest. Policymakers in Washington still tried to ignore the central truth repeatedly hammered home by America's ongoing experience in Vietnam: by the 1970s the United States was no longer able to shape the world's events. Though its destructive capacity was greater than in 1945, its leverage over global affairs had steadily declined since the war because of the world's shifting balance of power. Détente and linkage were attempts to deal with these developments, but the central objective of America's foreign policy remained the same—to contain communism.

VIETNAM AND DÉTENTE

Meanwhile the war in Vietnam continued. Vietnamization had assured a scaled withdrawal in proportion to expanded aid to Saigon, or, as one American official cynically put it, "changing the color of the corpses." The scheme rested on the improved fighting skills of the ARVN, which so far had displayed little evidence of an upgraded performance. There was no debate about whether the United States was going to pull out of Vietnam; the question was how to do so without marring America's respect throughout the world. Should the United States appear weak in Vietnam, détente would have little chance for success. President Nixon therefore adopted a nonyielding stance in the Paris peace talks and at the same time resumed the bombing. Both measures, he assured Americans, would further Vietnamization. Like Kennedy and Johnson, Nixon refused to allow the appearance of defeat to cloud his administration, and like those before him, the administration's central goal remained an independent Vietnam, free from communist influence and under the rule of the Saigon government. Above all, there could be no coalition government because it would eventually come under communist control. At the least, Kissinger asserted, there had to be a "decent interval" between the time the United States withdrew its combat forces and when South Vietnam collapsed to the communists—presumably two to three years.

Nixon tried to further the process of peace by exerting more military pressure on the battlefield. Little hope came out of Paris, where the talks had bogged down over procedures, the timing of American and North Vietnamese withdrawals, and Vietnam's postwar political framework. The president feared that premature American withdrawal meant immediate communist victory and decided to exploit his hardline anticommunist image as a bargaining point with the North Vietnamese. As he told an adviser, "They'll believe any threat of force Nixon makes because it's Nixon. We'll just slip the word to them that 'for God's sake, you know Nixon's obsessed about Communism . . . and he has his hand on the nuclear button.' " Yet he realized that the use of nuclear weapons would arouse worldwide condemnation, foment opposition among Americans, and create a situation that could lead to total war. The only alternative was Vietnamization, for it would leave the impression that the United States had fulfilled its objectives in Vietnam while not taking away the option of escalating the war.

The North Vietnamese did not make the problem easy for the United States: in February 1969, a month after Nixon's inauguration, they launched a massive offensive across the demilitarized zone (DMZ) that took a heavy toll among Americans. The end of the war seemed nowhere in sight. Television reporters pointed out that America's forces in Vietnam numbered almost 542,000, the most there during the entire war, and that its death totals were now over 40,000, a figure higher than that of the Korean War. Nixon emphasized that America's withdrawal was dependent on success in Paris and on the behavior of North Vietnamese forces in the field, and yet as Hanoi had earlier baffled Washington by refusing to buckle to America's increasing military strength, it now refused to reduce military actions in proportion to the assumed enticement of America's withdrawal.

The North Vietnamese assault in February evoked a strong response from the Nixon administration, both on the battlefield and at the peace table. The United States began bombing North Vietnam's supply routes out of Cambodia, an action kept secret from Congress and the American people for four years, although *The New York Times* published a story on the campaign which led the White House to order FBI wiretaps on reporters and government officials to plug leaks. As in the earlier phases of the war, the B-52s were unable to stop the transportation of goods by humans and bicycles over jungle trails. In mid-May of 1969 Nixon presented what he termed a "comprehensive peace plan" calling for the reestablishment of the DMZ between the antagonists, and the mutual withdrawal of American and North Vietnamese forces from South Vietnam within a year of a cease-fire agreement. Internationally supervised elections would follow, with South Vietnam's military president, Nguyen Van Thieu, remaining in office during the interim. North Vietnam rejected Nixon's proposals as a "farce" and warned that it was prepared to stay in Paris "until the chairs rot." Hanoi demanded total American withdrawal, the establishment of a provisional coalition regime that would not include Thieu, and the final disposition of Vietnam to be settled by the "Vietnamese parties among themselves." There was still no basis for settlement, which meant that Vietnamization would take longer than expected.

In the summer of 1969 the White House announced the first of several reductions in America's forces in Vietnam and called for a program of greater assumption of international responsibility by the allies that eventually became known as the Nixon Doctrine. The president met with Thieu at Midway Island in June, where Nixon declared that as of August 1, 25,000 combat forces would pull out of Vietnam, followed by more in relation to the ARVN's improved battle performance. Shortly after the announcement, on July 20, the nation's prestige received a huge lift when worldwide television covered two American astronauts from the Apollo 11 mission who became the first human beings to land on the moon. Two days later Nixon was en route to Asia and Europe, stopping at Guam and delivering an address on July 25 that called for a new direction in foreign policy. Speaking within the context of Vietnam, the president asserted that in the future the United States would avoid heavy military involvement in Asian affairs; but he added that the principles he expounded would apply "to all our international relationships." Lest some worry about a return to isolationism, Nixon promised to honor treaty obligations, to provide military and economic aid in combating aggression, and to furnish a nuclear shield to any ally or nation deemed vital to American security. The key point in the Nixon Doctrine was the president's pledge to "look to the nation directly threatened to assume the primary responsibility of providing the manpower for its defense." His administration called for partnerships based on "shared burdens and shared responsibilities."

The Nixon Doctrine did not signal an end to America's global commitments; but it was another step toward détente and a withdrawal from Vietnam, because it constituted an admission to America's power limitations and an invitation to antagonists to wind down the Cold War. Secretary of Defense Melvin Laird explained that "America will no longer try to play policeman to the world. Instead, we will expect other nations to provide more cops on the beat in their own neighborhood." America would rely more on Japan in Asia, Iran in the Middle East, and Zaire (formerly the Belgian Congo), Angola, and South Africa in Africa.

The Nixon administration's program also encompassed massive arms sales by America—with nearly predictable repercussions. The influx of arms encouraged the use of force in the Middle East, Latin America, and Africa, tied the Nixon administration to white regimes in Africa and to the shah in Iran, hurt other nations financially, and endangered relations with Japan, which refused the role the United States wanted it to assume in Asia. The inflated prices charged by arms producers, in fact, encouraged America's Iranian ally to raise oil prices to facilitate the purchase of war matériel. At these heavy costs the United States struggled toward an honorable withdrawal from Vietnam.

While the Nixon administration maintained a strong public position in the war, Kissinger secretly opened new peace talks in Paris with North Vietnam's representative, Xuan Thuy. Virtually ignoring South Vietnam, in August 1969 Kissinger called for a cease-fire, the return of American POWs, and for Thieu to remain as president in Saigon. In exchange the United States would withdraw, implicitly recognizing communist control over much of South Vietnam. The offer aroused no interest. North Vietnam wanted both the United States and Thieu out of the country, and it was in the military position to demand all of the south. Thieu felt betrayed by America's attempt to get out of Vietnam "with honor."

While the secret talks went on, so did the war. Ho Chi Minh died in September 1969, but even this blow did not lessen the resolve of the North Vietnamese. Nixon continued to defend his policies to Americans becoming increasingly impatient with the pace of Vietnamization. Antiwar demonstrations spread during October and November, attracting thousands of participants to "The Vietnam Moratorium" in Boston and Washington, D.C. In a television appearance on November 3, Nixon repeated that the United States would pull out "on an orderly scheduled timetable" that depended on progress in Paris, "the level of enemy activity," and how quickly South Vietnam was able to assume responsibilities. Should North Vietnam step up resistance, he promised, the United States would adopt "strong and effective measures." At the end of his speech, Nixon asserted that "North Vietnam cannot humiliate the United States.

Only Americans can do that." The establishment of a lottery system that month, to determine draft picks, helped to take the fire out of the protest movements by making the system fairer in application.

Nixon cited several reasons for repeatedly insisting that the United States would remain in Vietnam as long as necessary. Moving out too quickly would endanger the lives of America's troops and supporters in Saigon. Defeat in South Vietnam would threaten America's other interests in Asia. The United States had treaty obligations and moral commitments to honor. It had to assure the return of the POWs. To Congress in January 1970, Nixon proclaimed that "when we assumed the burden of helping South Vietnam, millions of South Vietnamese men and women placed their trust in us. To abandon them would risk a massacre that would shock and dismay everyone in the world who values human life."

Suddenly the war seemed to take a turn in South Vietnam's favor. Faced with American troop withdrawals, Thieu had announced a general mobilization that called in all males eighteen to thirty-eight years of age, placing over half of South Vietnam's male population in military service and raising the army's rolls from 700,000 to more than a million. Refugees flocked into the cities, where they worked in the ARVN or for Americans, and added to the outward appearance that the metropolitan centers were thriving. The truth was otherwise. Saigon was only a façade of industrial growth, for the peasants had fled there for safety from the "free-fire zones" denominated by American armed forces trying to root out pockets of help for the Vietcong. American money was the country's sole financial base, and the only industry was the war machine underwritten almost entirely by the United States. If the soldiers pulled out now, the economy would collapse.

The irony was that whereas Americans had not intended to make South Vietnam a colony, its existence had come to depend almost totally on the United States. Though Americans had not drained the country's wealth as had the French, they had established a widespread network of services for themselves that the Vietnamese not only filled through the armed forces but also through household duties, office work, and other menial tasks. The Americans had also failed to encourage the production of rice and other commodities, handing Thieu a government without an economic base. As long as the Americans required services, the Vietnamese people remained in a state of dependency that had nothing to do with patriotism or ideals. In 1969–70 the United States cited statistics allegedly proving Vietnamization a success—climbing Vietcong body counts, an expanded ARVN, increasing supplies of weapons. But the new South Vietnamese soldiers were poor fighters because they were there without choice and lacked morale and a cause. The essential ingredient of American victory—"winning the hearts and minds of the people"—had little chance in this atmosphere.

The chances for détente seemed to brighten with the Strategic Arms Limitations Talks (SALT) with the Soviet Union, which began in Helsinki,

Finland in November 1969 and shifted back and forth between there and Vienna for the next two and a half years. Though the United States's triad strategic force had ICBMs, submarine-launched ballistic missiles (SLBMs), and long-range bombers, the Soviet Union had made rapid advances, passing the United States in ICBMs although remaining behind in the other two categories. Rather than seeking superiority in strategic weapons, Nixon appeared to have become satisfied with parity or equality. Kissinger emphasized that "an attempt to gain a unilateral advantage in the strategic field" was "self-defeating." Yet the policy seemed inconsistent. Nixon had campaigned in 1968 on dealing only "from a position of superiority" and had secured the Senate's narrow passage of the Safeguard ABM system in August, just before he notified Moscow of America's readiness to discuss issues. To assure leverage in the SALT talks, he approved the development of the MIRV. The president nonetheless reaffirmed to Congress in February 1970 that his administration sought a partnership in maintaining world peace. "America cannot—and will not—conceive *all* the plans, design *all* the programs, execute *all* the decisions and undertake *all* the defense of the free nations of the world." Détente was the only way out of Vietnam, and the process began with arms limitations agreements.

Before the SALT talks could make headway, attention dramatically returned to the war in Southeast Asia, when Nixon shocked the nation on April 30, 1970, by declaring that the United States and South Vietnam had expanded the military effort into Cambodia to destroy the enemy bases of operation. The United States had known of the Cambodian sanctuary for some time, he explained over television, but had done little for fear of pushing the neutralist regime of Prince Norodom Sihanouk into the communist camp. But Sihanouk had fallen in a coup assisted by the United States and led by a pro-Western general named Lon Nol, who now sought American help against a possible military takeover by the thousands of North Vietnamese forces inside his country.

Nixon's speech was filled with misleading statements and, according to some critics, deceptions and falsehoods. Should the North Vietnamese overthrow the Lon Nol regime, Nixon warned, "Cambodia would become a vast enemy staging area and springboard for attacks on South Vietnam along 600 miles of frontier." Lon Nol had asked for assistance, and the United States intended to "go to the heart of the trouble" by destroying the enemy's military "nerve center"—the Central Office for South Vietnam (COSVN)—which was "the headquarters for the entire Communist military operation in South Vietnam." This was not an invasion of Cambodia, for the assault force would concentrate only on locations "completely occupied and controlled by North Vietnamese forces. . . . Once enemy forces are driven out of these sanctuaries and their military supplies destroyed, we will withdraw." The military operation in Cambodia, Nixon assured, would further America's withdrawal from Vietnam.

Nixon's speech drew such a furious reaction inside the United States that he felt compelled to impose limits on the new military campaign. Americans were enraged that the administration's way out of Vietnam seemed to lie in taking the war into Cambodia. Demonstrations broke out in hundreds of colleges and universities across the United States, while in the Senate a move began toward prohibiting funds for the effort in Cambodia after June 30. On May 4 an explosive atmosphere at Kent State University in Ohio caused National Guardsmen to fire into a group of students, killing four and injuring nine. The day following the events at Kent State, Nixon promised that America's combat forces would go no farther than twenty-two miles into Cambodia without the approval of Congress, and that they, along with their advisers, would pull out of the country by June 30. In addition, he assured against secret deals with the Lon Nol regime and asserted that America's assistance to Cambodia would consist only of war matériel and air cover. At the same time, however, Nixon directed the FBI and the CIA to intensify their search for connections between radical organizations in the United States and those abroad. "Don't worry about divisiveness," he told aides. "Having drawn the sword, don't take it out—stick it in hard."

After June 30, and with the American troops withdrawn as promised, Nixon pronounced the Cambodian mission a huge success. Thousands of North Vietnamese and Vietcong were dead or held prisoner, great amounts of war matériel had been confiscated or destroyed, miles of jungle had been cleared of the enemy, and South Vietnamese forces had fought well. Yet he did not mention that American and allied units had not closed the supply route and had failed to locate the alleged COSVN. In fact, the Defense Department in Washington was unsure whether there really was a nerve center. The North Vietnamese and Vietcong, it now seems clear, never operated out of major command headquarters comparable to those in the West. Nor did the president point out that the campaign had set off widespread unrest in Cambodia, providing cause for a communist insurgency movement led by the Khmer Rouge and thus breathing life into the domino theory. The invasion widened the war in Southeast Asia by committing the United States to another weak regime, this one in Cambodia.

In the meantime the Senate infuriated Nixon by acting to curb the warmaking activities of the White House. On June 24 it had overwhelmingly voted to repeal both the Eisenhower Doctrine of 1957 and the Tonkin Resolution of 1964, and forwarded the bill to the House. Nixon had not fought these moves because, he argued, his policies in Vietnam and Cambodia were justified by his constitutional duty to safeguard members of the armed forces. But evidence was growing that the Executive Office was becoming isolated from the rest of the country. One of Nixon's aides later recalled that during the summer of 1970 a "siege mentality" was developing "quite unknowingly" inside the White House. "It was now 'us' against 'them.' Gradually, as we drew the circle closer around us, the ranks of 'them' began to swell."

In the autumn of 1970 Nixon asserted that the Cambodian venture had opened new avenues to peace in Vietnam. Both North Vietnam and the National Liberation Front (NLF) had boycotted the Paris proceedings because of the invasion, but in mid-September the North Vietnamese returned to the talks with repeated demands for unconditional American military withdrawal from Vietnam and the assurance of Vietcong participation in a political settlement. Nixon countered with a "major new initiative for peace" that drew bitter reactions in Hanoi and Moscow, and among the Vietcong. On television on October 7, he called for a "standstill" cease-fire and the immediate exchange of POWs; inclusion of Cambodia and Laos in the peace talks, thereby establishing the war in Vietnam as an Indochinese conflict and not a civil war; total American military withdrawal according to a determined schedule; and assurances that Thieu would remain in control until elections took place. Thus neither side would make concessions. Hanoi and the Vietcong refused to consider the proposals and Moscow called them "a great fraud."

A month later the war in Vietnam intensified again as the United States began bombing the DMZ and the Hanoi-Haiphong region, in an extensive campaign that Nixon termed "protective reaction strikes." According to the White House, the bombings would continue until the North Vietnamese stopped firing at America's reconnaissance planes over North Vietnam. This announcement drew a sharp reaction from Hanoi's defense minister, Vo Nguyen Giap, who indignantly declared that North Vietnam was "a sovereign independent country, and no sovereign independent country will allow its enemy to spy freely upon it." Congress also opposed the bombings. The House had meanwhile approved the Senate's bill repealing the Tonkin Resolution, but not the Eisenhower Doctrine, and the measure became law in January 1971. Though Congress refused to go so far as to deny funds to American soldiers, it prohibited the use of money to broaden the war in Vietnam and barred the deployment of American troops in either Cambodia or Laos. Congress, however, did not prohibit the use of planes, and when in February 1971 the ARVN invaded Laos to close the Ho Chi Minh Trail, Nixon authorized air cover. But South Vietnam's field performance was disastrous. In less than two months the North Vietnamese inflicted 50 percent casualties and drove the ARVN out of Laos.

By the spring of 1971 the American people had again mobilized against the war. Nearly 200,000 antiwar activists, including Vietnam War veterans, demonstrated in Washington, D.C., only to draw Nixon's remark that they were "mobs" who did not speak for "the great silent majority." But a Gallup poll in May suggested that the president was wrong. According to the survey, six of ten Americans thought the United States should not be in Vietnam, which was an exact reversal of the opinion expressed in the autumn of 1965. Furthermore, the opposition was bipartisan. Later studies revealed that contrary to popular belief, the war's greatest critics by the early 1970s did not come from America's youths, but from older Americans, females, lower-class Americans, and blacks, the last of whom argued that a disproportionate share of their race was fighting and dying in Vietnam. Other revelations had deepened resentment for the war. In early 1971 a court-martial had found Lieutenant William Calley guilty of "at least twenty-two murders" in the village of My Lai in 1968. Nixon soon added to the widespread indignation by intervening in the case and ordering Calley's release while the decision came under review. Americans had also discovered that their soldiers in Vietnam used drugs and that nearly 15,000 had become heroin addicts. The American economy was hurting from recession, inflation, a steady outflow of dollars from the country, and from an unfavorable balance of trade that found the United States for the first time since the 1890s importing more than it exported. In June 1971 *The New York Times* published *The Pentagon Papers*, selections from a long series of classified documents which government employee Daniel Ellsberg illegally removed from the Defense Department in an effort to halt the war in Vietnam. When the Supreme Court decided against preventing their publication, the White House then used its special task force called the plumbers to halt further leaks and to discredit Ellsberg. The Pentagon materials supported the longtime allegations that Kennedy and Johnson had been less than truthful about America's involvement in Southeast Asia.

HIGH TIDE OF DÉTENTE: RED CHINA, THE SOVIET UNION, SALT I, AND VIETNAMIZATION

To further détente, President Nixon made a stunning announcement in July: he had accepted an invitation from Beijing (new spelling form of Peking adopted by Chinese in 1970s) to visit China to "seek the normalization of relations," broken in 1949. Considerable quiet preparation had taken place for this decision. In early 1969 Nixon had directed Kissinger to reassess the situation with China, for the purpose of restoring relations. That same year the United States eased commercial and travel restrictions with China, pointedly referred to its regime as the People's Republic of China, and terminated the Seventh Fleet's regular patrol of the Taiwan Strait. The following year the United States resumed talks with China in Warsaw, adjourned since early 1968 as a result of friction over Vietnam. When war broke out in 1971 between India (supported by the Soviet Union) and Pakistan (which received help from China), the Nixon administration leaned toward Pakistan. That same year, in April, American table tennis players then in Japan were invited to China, where they lost the match to the world champions, but popularized the term Ping-Pong diplomacy as a breakthrough to détente. Shortly afterward the United States ended its trade embargo on China. Kissinger had secretly traveled to Beijing less than a week before Nixon's announcement, where he made arrangements with Zhou Enlai (formerly spelled Chou En-lai), second only to Mao Zedong (formerly spelled Mao Tse-tung) in the Chinese Communist party. "What we are doing now with China," Kissinger later declared, "is so great, so historic, the word 'Vietnam' will be only a footnote when it is written in history." In August the Department of State announced support for Red China's admission into the UN with the simultaneous membership of the Republic of China. This "Two-Chinas policy" lasted until October, when the UN General Assembly approved the admission of Red China and expelled Taiwan.

There were numerous reasons for this revolution in American foreign policy, but as in all reciprocal arrangements the basic consideration was mutual need. Since 1969 both nations had given subtle indications of interest in establishing relations, based on the common grounds of halting Soviet expansion and promoting trade. China was alarmed over recent clashes with Soviet troops stationed along the nations' common border. It was also concerned about Japan, believing that the establishment of relations with America might either reduce Tokyo's belligerence or perhaps even promote a foundation for Sino-Japanese relations. The United States's prime objective, however, was to widen the rift in Sino-Soviet relations and develop a power balance conducive to détente and world peace. The resulting stimulus to trade might also revive America's ailing economy by securing a greater share of the China market before Japan established a monopoly. As *The New York Times* declared, "The President is in the position of the lovely maiden courted by two ardent swains, each of whom is aware of the other but each of whom is uncertain of what happens when the young lady is alone with his rival."

Nixon also had personal reasons for wanting to normalize relations with China. Such a dramatic move would award him a place in history that only he could occupy because of his staunch anticommunist reputation. The presidential election of 1972 was another factor. Nixon had still not extricated the United States from Vietnam, and peace-minded Democrats led by Senator George McGovern seemed to be making gains, as evidenced in the New Hampshire primary of the previous March. Nixon, however, remained in a strong political position. Right-wing Republicans could not accuse him of being "soft on communism," and liberal Democrats could not be critical because many of them had been advocating recognition of China for some time. Though the powerful China lobby and much of American labor favored Taiwan, Nixon realized that emotions in the United States had calmed considerably. During the mid-1960s about a quarter of the American people had not even known that the Chinese government was communist.

But perhaps the most immediate goal in Nixon's China decision was to promote détente and allow American withdrawal from Vietnam. Relations with Beijing might force Moscow to ease its anti-American stance and cause both communist nations to cut aid to North Vietnam and the Vietcong, permitting the United States to complete the Vietnamization of the war and turn to other matters. If handled correctly, détente would raise concern within the Soviet Union about the consequences of an

American alliance with China. The basic goal was to leave the Thieu regime intact for the "decent interval" that Kissinger had referred to earlier.

Nixon's trip to China in February 1972 received worldwide attention. According to the president as he left the United States, it would "signal the end of a sterile and barren interlude in the relationship between two great peoples." Accompanying him on the 20,000-mile journey were nearly ninety journalists plus almost forty members of the mission, including Secretary of State Rogers, who remained subordinate to Kissinger in determining foreign policy.

Nixon's landing in China on February 21 aroused little outward enthusiasm, although the Chinese had probably staged this quiet reception to suggest that the United States was more eager to establish relations than were the Chinese. Premier Zhou Enlai greeted Nixon with a formal

President Nixon and Premier Zhou Enlai Making a Toast in Beijing in February 1972

The president called his visit to the People's Republic of China "the week that changed the world." (Wide World)

handshake and then welcomed Kissinger as his "old friend." No ceremony took place, although a band played America's National Anthem,
followed by China's "The March of the Volunteers." That same day
Nixon and Kissinger met with Mao and Zhou for nearly an hour, and
later that evening attended a huge banquet in the Great Hall of the People, where numerous toasts to good relations set the tone of succeeding
discussions. "What we do here," Nixon proclaimed, "can change the
world."

The image fostered by the White House and the news media was that
Nixon's visit to China was monumental in importance. As the presidential
party stood before the Great Wall, Nixon remarked before television cameras that "I think that you would have to conclude that this is a great
wall. . . . As we look at this wall, we do not want walls of any kind between peoples." On February 27 in Shanghai the two nations signed a
vaguely worded joint communiqué that offered assurances of normal relations. The United States declared that its goal was peace in Asia with "social progress for all peoples . . . [and] free .of outside pressure or
intervention." After reiterating the desire to withdraw from Vietnam, the
United States affirmed that its "ultimate" goal was "the withdrawal of all
U.S. forces and military installations from Taiwan" to promote "a peaceful settlement of the Taiwan question by the Chinese themselves." China
approved, emphasizing that Taiwan was the "crucial question obstructing
the normalization of relations." The two nations probably aimed this
statement at the Soviet Union: "Neither should seek hegemony in the
Asia-Pacific region and each is opposed to efforts by any other country or
group of countries to establish such hegemony." The United States and
China concluded the Shanghai communiqué with a call for expanded
commerce and cultural interchange. Formal recognition seemed imminent. As Nixon departed for home the next day, he proclaimed this "the
week that changed the world."

Nixon's China visit had mixed consequences for détente. Japan was
stunned about the imminent establishment of Sino-American diplomatic
relations, for it remained technically at war with China since the events of
1937. During the September following Nixon's visit, the Japanese premier
traveled to Beijing to repair relations and soon afterward severed ties with
Taiwan. Both Vietnams felt threatened by the new accord between China
and the United States, the north because it depended upon Beijing for
arms, and the south because the Chinese were its avowed enemy. The
Chinese action, in fact, aroused considerable suspicion among Third
World peoples who were undecided about whom to trust. But if the central purpose of Nixon's China trip was to promote détente by placing
pressure on Moscow, it was successful. Shortly after he had announced
his intention to travel to China, the Soviets invited him to Moscow. The
president decided to go in May 1972, just three months after the trip to
Beijing.

Détente underwent a severe test in late March 1972, when North Vietnamese forces protected by Soviet-made tanks crossed the DMZ and scattered the South Vietnamese. Saigon seemed on the verge of collapse. To counter the huge offensive, Nixon approved the largest bombing expeditions of the war—later called "Linebacker I"—hitting Hanoi and Haiphong for the first time since 1968, and, despite fears of involving Red China and the Soviet Union, he authorized the mining of the port of Haiphong and the imposition of a naval blockade of the north. At the same time Nixon held out the possibility of peace by assuring Hanoi that if it agreed to return all American POWs and accept an internationally supervised cease-fire, the United States would pull out of Vietnam within four months. For the first time Washington had set a timetable for withdrawal and had made no demand that the North Vietnamese leave the south. Furthermore, the long-standing stipulation of Thieu's survival was noticeably missing. But Hanoi, perhaps testing the resilience of détente, turned down the offer. In the meantime, even though the Soviets lost four merchant vessels during the bombardment of Haiphong, they raised no objections—perhaps because of ongoing border problems with China and their desire for détente with the United States. China publicly criticized the Nixon administration, but likewise took no action in behalf of North Vietnam. The reluctance of either communist power to intervene must have put Hanoi into a quandary. Though the new fighting again resulted in a stalemate, the North Vietnamese undoubtedly had become more amenable to a cease-fire.

The Soviets' restraint over the escalated American policies in the Vietnam War suggested that they attached great importance to Nixon's impending arrival in May. Soviet General Secretary Leonid Brezhnev had signaled his readiness for détente a year before, when at the Twenty-fourth Party Congress he spoke of peace measures for the 1970s. The Soviet economy was in dire shape, for the recent failure of a Five-Year Plan had underlined his people's need for grain and technological assistance. Revolutionaries in several communist states were still bitter over the Red Army's heavy-handed tactics in putting down the uprising in Czechoslovakia in 1968. Poland and Rumania, for example, increasingly leaned toward the West for trade. In August 1970 Moscow had signed a nonaggression pact with West German Chancellor Willy Brandt that smoothed the path toward détente with the United States and also allowed the dispatch of additional Soviet troops to the tense Chinese frontier. The treaty terms relieved Soviet fears of a revived, powerful Germany by conceding the reality of two Berlins and two Germanies. Three months later West Germany signed a nonaggression agreement with Poland recognizing the Oder-Neisse River as the common border, and thus restoring Polish control over territories lost in 1945. Finally, in September 1971, Brezhnev signed a pact pledging Western access to Berlin in exchange for West Germany's recognition of Eastern European borders established by the Red Army in 1945. Fear of encirclement was a major Soviet concern, especially after China began negotiations with the United States and Japan.

Nixon's visit to the Soviet Union in May led to agreements more substantial than any reached with China. The atmosphere in Moscow was more cordial than in Beijing, as Nixon was allowed to speak to the Soviet people over radio and television. He and Brezhnev agreed to cooperate in space exploration, environmental protection, medical and scientific research, and other matters of common concern. They also discussed Vietnam, but would only state that small nations should not stand in the way of détente. The major accords related to arms limitations. On May 26 Nixon and Brezhnev signed a document proclaiming their goal of "peaceful coexistence," and then reached an agreement based on over two years of SALT talks. Known as SALT I (Strategic Arms Limitations Treaty), it included two pacts: the Treaty of Anti-Ballistic Missiles Systems, and the Interim Agreement on Limitation of Strategic Offensive Arms. The first agreement, aimed at those systems designed to intercept and neutralize approaching nuclear warheads, initially restricted each party to no more than two ABM systems, but later cut them to one. According to the theory that became known as MAD (Mutual Assured Destruction), both sides' major cities would be vulnerable to attack, assuring that neither would choose to begin war. The second—the Interim Agreement—attempted to establish a five-year ceiling on the construction of offensive missiles. Bombers were not part of these agreements, however, leaving the United States at a distinct advantage. By September 1972 both agreements had received formal approval in the United States by wide margins. The following month the two nations negotiated a commercial pact that included the sale of American grain and the Soviet Union's agreement to pay back its Lend-Lease debt of World War II by the year 2001.

The appearance of compromise in Moscow was deceptive, for the SALT I agreements had actually encouraged an arms race in new weapons—the United States in cruise missiles and the Soviet Union in Backfire supersonic bombers. The ABMs were costly and yet ineffective, thus constituting no concession by either side. The United States seemed to have maintained the upper hand in technology, because the agreements had no bearing on the multiple-headed MIRVs. A single American submarine, of which the United States had thirty, could carry MIRVs capable of delivering the impact of Hiroshima 160 times over. Within a year the United States would have 6,000 nuclear warheads to the Soviets' 2,500, and by the time the SALT I agreements expired as scheduled in 1977 the Americans' weapons would outnumber those of the Soviets' by about a two-to-one margin.

Thus the SALT discussions in Moscow paradoxically stimulated an arms race by placing limitations on older models and diverting attention from the ongoing development of newer, more sophisticated weapons. To prevent interference with the MIRVs, Nixon prohibited his negotiating team from discussing them during the SALT talks in Helsinki. In addition, each side was capable of "overkill" numerous times, and both had satellite surveillance systems that made secret testing a thing of the past. The terms of agreement were forwarded to Helsinki, where the intent of SALT II was to convert the interim agreement into a permanent pact.

The SALT I agreements in Moscow encouraged the image of détente, which in turn had repercussions in Europe. The improvement of Soviet-American relations offered the opportunity to resolve problems in Germany remaining from World War II. In June 1972 the Quadripartite Treaty or Berlin Agreement went into effect when the four occupying powers— the United States, Soviet Union, Britain, and France—extended recognition to East Germany. Two years later the United States established formal diplomatic relations, making divided Germany a fact and ending the wartime goal of reunification. Détente also furthered the Helsinki Accords of 1972, which called for recognition of boundaries in Eastern European communist states in exchange for signatory nations pledging respect for human rights. These agreements likewise endorsed the results of World War II in Eastern Europe by admitting to Soviet domination of the area, a fact resisted since the Truman years.

Détente also affected events in the Pacific, for by the 1970s Japan had stepped up demands that the United States relinquish Okinawa, held by the Americans since 1945. In addition to Tokyo wanting to reestablish control over a million of its people on the island, the return of Okinawa would remove the last reminders of defeat in World War II and would reduce the chances of being drawn into an Asian conflict. In November 1969 the Nixon administration had agreed to return Okinawa and the other Ryukyu Islands sometime in 1972, thereby completing the process begun by President Johnson, when he had given up the Bonin Islands. The official transfer of the Ryukyus took place in May 1972.

Despite these concessions by America, détente had not yet freed it from Vietnam, and as the presidential election of 1972 approached, Nixon stepped up the pressure by approving an air offensive against North Vietnam, Cambodia, and Laos. The use of ground forces was out of the question, for by late 1972 the Vietnamization program had left only 70,000 troops in the country. The outlook still seemed promising. Nixon was a certain winner in the election, the Soviets and the Chinese were interested in détente, and the North Vietnamese were reeling badly from the new assault. Hanoi decided to negotiate. It apparently thought that the administration in Washington might permit better terms before the election than afterward.

CEASE–FIRE IN VIETNAM

Kissinger had meanwhile continued peace talks in Paris with North Vietnam's chief negotiator, Le Duc Tho, and finally, in October, a break seemed imminent. Hanoi expressed willingness to turn over the POWs simultaneously with America's withdrawal sixty days after a cease-fire. An international commission was to supervise elections and implement treaty terms. The North Vietnamese had dropped their demands for Thieu's immediate removal from office, and the Americans had not insisted upon North Vietnam's withdrawal from the south. Nixon accepted a cease-fire at points of present military occupation, and approved an electoral commission, both major concessions from his previous stance.

On October 26, less than two weeks before the election, Kissinger returned from Paris and dramatically proclaimed that "peace is at hand." At almost the same time, North Vietnam published the terms worked out in the talks, probably to prevent Washington and Saigon from making private arrangements. Hanoi set a deadline of October 31 for signing an agreement, a move designed to place pressure on Nixon before the election, but which also had the unintended effect of further undercutting his Democratic opponent, Senator George McGovern, who had promised to end the war as soon as he took office. The president assured Americans that he would accept only "peace with honor."

But South Vietnam sensed a sellout to the communists and blocked the settlement. Thieu vehemently opposed any arrangement which approved America's withdrawal while permitting North Vietnamese forces to remain in the south during the cease-fire period. He also complained that an electoral commission was tantamount to a coalition government. Restoration of the DMZ between the Vietnams, he declared, was vital. Though Kissinger was furious with Thieu, Nixon worried that the South Vietnamese premier might complain of a betrayal and wreck the Republicans' promise of "peace with honor." The president sought more than extrication from Vietnam. He considered Thieu's objections defensible and, based on that stand, would permit a delay in the negotiations until after the election had provided a mandate to press for additional concessions from Hanoi. In the meantime the United States could send more aid to Saigon, eliminate the undesirable parts of the treaty, and further impair North Vietnam's capacity to break the peace. To save face, Nixon announced his refusal to bend to North Vietnam's pressure tactics. The deadline came and passed, and on November 2 he declared that he would sign "only when the agreement is right."

Nixon overwhelmingly won reelection and then, to revive the Paris peace talks, he escalated the war in what became known as "Linebacker II" or the "Christmas bombings." After the election in the United States, each side in Vietnam had moved quickly to expand its holdings before a cease-fire in place went into effect. On December 15 Le Duc Tho walked out of the Paris discussions. Three days later Nixon explained that to promote the release of the POWs he had ordered immediate large-scale bombings on North Vietnamese cities and military points—including Hanoi and Haiphong. For nearly two weeks (save for Christmas Day) American planes thundered over North Vietnam, killing thousands of civilians and destroying military and nonmilitary sites, including the area's largest hospital. During the saturation bombing, nearly thirty B-52s and fighter-bombers were shot down, adding almost a hundred to the POW list and supporting the arguments of the generals in Washington who had warned the administration that the Soviets had effectively safeguarded the North Vietnamese capital against an air attack. The massive civilian casualties in what Kissinger termed "jugular diplomacy" drew bitter protests all over the world. A journalist noted that Nixon privately declared that he "did not care if the whole world thought he was crazy for resuming the bombing." The Soviets and Chinese "might think they were dealing with a madman and so better force North Vietnam into a settlement before the world was consumed into a larger war." The bombings above the 20th parallel ceased on December 30, only after North Vietnam expressed readiness to reopen negotiations.

For several reasons the Nixon administration was also ready to talk. America's generals warned that North Vietnam's air defenses were inflicting long-range damages on the strategic strength of the United States; worldwide revulsion had developed for the bombings; Hanoi's peace conditions seemed the best possible; and the Democrats now controlled Congress and in January would doubtless cut off funds for future bombings. Nixon boasted that the Christmas assault had brought peace, although one of his administration officials disagreed. "We were in an embarrassing situation. Could we suddenly say we'll sign in January what we wouldn't in October? We had to do something," he declared. "So the bombings began, to try to create the image of a defeated enemy crawling back to the peace table to accept terms demanded by the United States." Whatever the truth, the terms were strikingly similar to those of the previous October.

On January 27, 1973, the Paris negotiators signed a cease-fire agreement in the old Hotel Majestic in Paris, twenty-three years after America's initial commitment in Vietnam and eight years following its first assignment of combat troops. In the pact signed by Kissinger, the foreign ministers of North and South Vietnam, and the National Liberation Front (the Vietcong—which called itself the "South Vietnamese Provisional Revolutionary Government")—the antagonists accepted the following terms: an immediate cease-fire at present military positions; American withdrawal of its final 27,000 troops from South Vietnam and the return of all American POWs (nearly 600), both within sixty days; enforcement of treaty provisions through an international commission; general elections carried out through the establishment of a National Council of Reconciliation and Concord; an international conference on Vietnam to convene within thirty days; and authorization for the United States to replace South Vietnam's damaged or worn-out military equipment, but not to add to existing stores. In an unofficial, semi-secret arrangement that was not part of the pact, the United States agreed to furnish Hanoi $4.75 billion of reconstruction assistance. To secure Thieu's compliance with the treaty, the United States threatened to withdraw all aid.

The agreement came with mixed blessings. The atmosphere in Paris was so bitter that the South Vietnamese and the Vietcong refused to sign the same copy of the treaty. Though the Nixon administration had assured Americans of no secret agreements in Paris, the president privately pledged military aid to Thieu if North Vietnam violated the cease-fire. To the South Vietnamese premier, Nixon wrote that if you will "go with us, you have my assurance of continued assistance in the post-settlement period and that we will respond with full force should the settlement be violated by North Vietnam." Indeed, Nixon sent Thieu additional arms that year. Kissinger received the Nobel Peace Prize in 1973 for his role in the Vietnam agreement.

The Nixon administration hailed the events of January 1973 as a victory for détente, although it quickly became clear that America had won neither "peace" nor "honor." Conflict went on in Vietnam, even while people all over the world praised the cease-fire. The treaty had left North Vietnamese forces in the south, without specifying which areas belonged to whom, and Hanoi was more determined than ever to seize control of the entire country. In March 1973 twelve nations met in Paris, including the United States, China, and the Soviet Union, and formally approved the cease-fire agreement. Numerous American military and civilian advis-

National Security Adviser Henry A. Kissinger and Hanoi's Le Duc Tho in Paris during Peace Talks of 1972–1973

Kissinger received the Nobel Peace Prize in 1973 for his efforts to arrange the cease-fire of January of that year. (Wide World)

ers remained in South Vietnam, and the American air force continued bombing Cambodia to protect the Lon Nol regime from the communist Khmer Rouge. When Congress cut off funds for the bombing, Nixon angrily vetoed the measure in late June, but soon had no choice other than to sign a bill requiring an end to all American combat in Indochina by August 15.

The Vietnam War left numerous legacies, many of which were bitter. First and foremost, the United States had not emerged victorious, exploding the myth that it had never failed to win a war and never would. Second, the cost of the war had been heavy in armed forces and matériel, immeasurable in national spirit, and nearly devastating to America's image abroad. More than 57,000 Americans died, 300,000 were wounded, at least 1,400 (including civilians) were missing, and over $150 billion had been expended, much of it in support of corrupt regimes. Third, America's involvement dealt a serious blow to the presidency and gave a corresponding impetus to the power of Congress. Yet at the same time the Vietnam experience aroused widespread distrust for public officials and severely restricted the performance of both branches of government. Fourth, the war encouraged the continued shift in America's foreign policy from its dominating role in containing communism to one calling for partnerships and détente. Vietnam had shaken Americans' confidence in containment, for the war showed the danger of defining every problem as communist in origin and then trying to resolve it, whether or not the region was vital to American interests. On another level, some critics wanted the United States to distinguish between areas capable of being defended and those that were not, whereas others discerned danger in the development of a national security state that concentrated power in an elite, impervious to public opinion and military in character.

The attempt by Congress to reassert its role in foreign affairs contributed to America's subdued global role in the post-Vietnam era. Impeachment proceedings then under way for the president's role in the Watergate scandals may have pushed him into a retreat. But another development was important. That November of 1973, Congress overrode Nixon's veto in passing the War Powers Act, which was an effort to make any armed venture by the United States a joint responsibility of Congress and the Executive Office. It asserted that "in every possible instance" the president was to consult Congress before sending soldiers into combat. Should he intervene outside the country without a formal declaration of war, he must "report" his actions to Congress within forty-eight hours. Unless that body endorsed the intervention, the military forces would have to pull out within sixty days. In effect, however, the president could still react immediately to a crisis and wage war for sixty days without congressional approval—a period so long, critics warned, that the United States might find extrication difficult. But this was not the real problem, Kissinger warned. Congress was too closely tied to public opinion to formulate meaningful, long-range foreign policies. Though severely criticized by Nixon and Kissinger, the War Powers Act illustrated the inseparability of domestic and foreign policy, and was therefore an appropriate epitaph for America's military experience in Southeast Asia.

DISINTEGRATION OF DÉTENTE

At the height of détente's triumphs in Beijing, Moscow, and Vietnam, the new peace was paradoxically eroding from within because of problems with the Western alliance, among Third World nations, and within both the Western Hemisphere and the United States. France and other Western European governments were hurting economically and had become unhappy with America's emphasis on noncontinental affairs and with its insistence on dictating their policies in line with Cold War strategy. Western Europeans joined the Japanese in complaining about America's high balance-of-payments deficits, the decline of the dollar, and its accusations that they were guilty of commercial discrimination. Nixon and Kissinger hoped that détente's umbrella effect would bring peace to countries outside the major power blocs. To patch relations, they heralded 1973 as "The Year of Europe." Yet Italy was becoming communist in orientation, Portugal was angry over criticisms of its African policies, and Greece and Turkey were bitter rivals over the Mediterranean island of Cyprus. In the Middle East, Latin America, and Africa, pressures for social reforms were likewise creating explosive situations. Furthermore, the United States faced deepening recession and spiraling inflation, while the seemingly endless unraveling of the Watergate scandals undermined the Nixon administration's credibility at home, dividing Americans and further undercutting the nation's foreign policy.

The most immediate threat to détente came in the Middle East. As shown earlier, the center of controversy was the Arab-Israeli feud, kept under control only by a series of fragile truces. Three times—in 1948, 1956, and 1967—the Arabs had attempted to destroy Israel, and in every instance had failed disastrously. After the Six Day War of 1967, Jews inside the United States had exerted pressure on Washington to approve the sale of fifty F-4 Phantom jets to Israel. A number of Arab states had responded by severing relations with the United States and opening their ports to Soviet ships. The growing crisis in the Middle East endangered détente because of competing Soviet-American economic and strategic interests in the area.

Conflict had again loomed in the Middle East as the Nixon administration moved into the White House in early 1969. Israel refused to withdraw from areas occupied during the war of June 1967, and in the spring of 1969 Suez again became the troublespot as Nasser brought in heavy weapons and the Palestine Liberation Organization (PLO) promised death to any Arab leader who called for a peaceful settlement of the Israeli dispute. Under the leadership of Yasir Arafat, the PLO intensified demands for a homeland and launched a series of raids on Israel, using Syria and

Jordan as bases. The Israelis retaliated against neighboring states helping the PLO—some of their bombing strikes touching the outskirts of downtown Cairo. Moscow sent troops and anti-aircraft matériel to Egypt, including SAM-3 (surface-to-air) missiles operated by Soviets to counter Phantom jet attacks, and Soviet pilots to fly MIGs earlier furnished to Nasser. As the problems escalated, the Israelis appealed to the United States for help, and in July 1970 President Nixon responded with 125 Phantom and Skyhawk jets. "We will do what is necessary to maintain Israel's strength," he declared over television. "Not because we want Israel to be in a position to wage war—that isn't it—but because that is what will deter its neighbors from attacking it."

By the autumn of 1970 the Arabs and Israelis managed another ceasefire that was again quickly violated. Nasser had visited Moscow in July, and afterward agreed to America's proposal for a UN-supervised, ninetyday armistice. The Israelis accepted, but only after the United States guaranteed their security. Ensuing peace discussions then broke down over charges that Nasser, with Soviet help, had moved missiles into the ceasefire area west of the Suez Canal, exposing Israel to attack along the east bank. The Israelis withdrew from the talks until the Egyptian leader removed the missiles.

The same day that the Israelis left the negotiations, September 6, Palestinian guerrillas began a new wave of terrorism that was followed by the outbreak of civil war in Jordan. The PLO hijacked four commercial airliners, including a Pan American 747 jumbo jet, and after evacuating all on board, destroyed the planes. Nearly sixty people, including Americans, Israelis, British, Swiss, and West Germans, were held hostage to secure the freedom of imprisoned Arab terrorists. Negotiations quickly began with the help of the International Red Cross, but these talks were hampered by the conflict in Jordan between government forces and Palestinians living in the country. As Syrian tanks roared into Jordan to help the guerrillas, the Nixon administration bolstered the Sixth Fleet in the Mediterranean and readied its airborne forces at home and in West Germany. But the Syrians, perhaps as a result of Soviet pressure, suddenly pulled out of Jordan, leaving the Palestinians to defeat and exile to Lebanon, where they became a source of instability. After a cease-fire in Cairo on September 25, the Red Cross soon won the freedom of the hostages in exchange for the release of the Arab terrorists.

The end of both the Jordanian civil war and the hostage crisis once again temporarily eased the situation in the Middle East. But during that same month of September Nasser died, leaving the office of premier to Anwar el-Sadat, who promised to continue Egypt's hardline policies toward Israel. With Soviet backing, he refused to remove the missiles from the cease-fire zone, while Israel built up defenses along the east bank and secured a promise of American military assistance. Israel then returned to the peace negotiations after the United States guaranteed support against excessive Arab demands. Sadat intended to open a new offensive against

Israel, but was unable to persuade the Soviets to furnish more arms because of their desire for détente with the United States. Exasperated with Moscow, he ordered the "expulsion" of thousands of Soviet military advisers and technicians from Egypt in the summer of 1972. Though the PLO continued its terrorist acts—including killing Israeli athletes at the Munich Olympics that same year—Sadat's move again relieved the situation in the Middle East.

The peace was not to last, for on October 6, 1973, the Arabs for the fourth time invaded Israel, this time on Yom Kippur (the Jews' most holy Day of Atonement), and set off what became known as the Yom Kippur War. Egypt, aided by Jordan, Iraq, Morocco, and Saudi Arabia, surprised both Israel and the United States by attacking Israeli armies in the Sinai and at the Golan Heights. The Nixon administration called for an immediate meeting of the UN Security Council, but a series of unfriendly sessions on October 8 and 9 brought no results. Forgetting their differences of the past, the Soviets sent military aid to Egypt and prepared to airlift a ground force into the combat zone, while the United States, reeling from Watergate and other domestic scandals, put its nuclear forces on alert. Doubtless seeking to maintain an image of strength during the crisis at home as well as to help an ally in the Middle East, Nixon approved an airlift of planes, tanks, and war matériel, enabling Israel to hold on.

The Arabs only briefly enjoyed their military successes, for the Israelis once again quickly reversed the fortunes of the war. Soviet Premier Alexei Kosygin traveled to Cairo, hoping to convince Sadat to accept a cease-fire, but instead aroused American fears by giving increased visibility to Soviet sympathies in the war. Meanwhile Arab forces overran the east bank and swept toward Israel across the Sinai desert, where between October 14 and 19 they engaged in the fiercest tank battles since World War II. At the same time, Syrian ground forces aided by tanks advanced across the Golan Heights and toward Israel. The Israelis, however, soon turned back the assault both at the canal and along the Syrian front. Their forces won a stretch of land along the western side of the canal, putting them within seventy miles of Cairo. In doing so, the Israelis surrounded 20,000 Egytian forces on the east bank, cutting them off from the main force and raising the imminence of their mass destruction.

The Israelis' reversal of the war's direction forced new peace talks. Sadat appealed to Brezhnev for help, and on October 20 the Soviet general secretary met with Kissinger in Moscow to draft a peace proposal for presentation to the Security Council. En route home, Kissinger stopped in Israel to assure its leaders that the plan was fair. But the only way he could secure an Israeli cease-fire was to threaten a cutoff in military aid. The following evening the Security Council met in emergency session and early the next morning approved the peace resolution. It called for an immediate cease-fire at present military positions; the implementation of UN Resolution 242, which in 1967 called for Israeli withdrawal from lands occupied in the Six Day War, in exchange for defensible borders; the assignment of a large peacekeeping force comprised of soldiers from non–Security Council member nations; and the promise of negotiations aimed at a permanent peace.

Though Egypt and Israel accepted the truce, the Israelis provided an excuse for direct Soviet intervention when they violated the cease-fire lines, seizing more territory and threatening to crush the Egyptian army. Israel's minister of defense, General Moshe Dayan, later explained to *The New York Times* that had he captured thousands of Egyptian soldiers, "Sadat would have had to admit it to his people. We might only have held them for a day and let them walk out without their arms, but it would have changed the whole Egyptian attitude about whether they had won or lost the war." Kissinger was furious because such a humiliation would abort a negotiated peace. Furthermore, Brezhnev and Sadat proposed a joint Soviet-American military contingent to supervise the cease-fire, which the Nixon administration regarded as a thinly disguised excuse for full-scale Soviet intervention. That evening a Soviet note greatly alarmed the White House, for it declared that if the United States did not join, "we may be obliged to consider acting alone." Israel "cannot be permitted to get away with the violations." Nixon feared a Soviet push into Suez and, without informing NATO allies, placed American armed forces and nuclear strike commands on "precautionary alert." The United States, he asserted, "would not accept any unilateral move" by the Soviets. Two days later, on October 24, the Security Council approved a second peace resolution. Under threat of an American arms embargo, the Israelis honored this one and the crisis in the Middle East soon passed.

As in the earlier Arab-Israeli wars, no one was satisfied with the outcome. The Arabs had not regained territories lost in 1967, and the Israelis did not feel secure. Most Arab nations in OPEC were angry with the United States for aiding Israel and with the Western European nations for allowing the Americans to use NATO bases on the continent. Except for Iran, the OPEC nations stunned America with an oil embargo that lasted until March 1974 and raised prices dramatically for its allies in Japan and Europe. OPEC's oil embargo of 1973–74 caused gasoline shortages in the United States and severely strained the Western alliance, for whereas the United States was committed to Israel and received only 12 percent of its oil from the Middle East, Western Europe and Japan were almost totally dependent on the Arabs. When America's allies chose not to be supportive in the Middle East, Kissinger called them "contemptible."

Kissinger meanwhile tried to arrange a permanent peace in the Middle East by traveling back and forth between Egypt and Israel in a series of visits that became known as "shuttle diplomacy." For two years he attempted to secure a pact that would not include Soviet and Palestinian participation, and that would end the oil embargo by the Arabs. Beginning in November 1973, he left for Egypt, where he arranged the restoration of diplomatic relations with the United States (broken in 1967). In a few days Kissinger helped bring about an Egyptian-Israeli cease-fire, and in May 1974 managed the same between Israel and Syria. In September 1975, after repeated travels between Cairo and Tel Aviv, Kissinger secured the initials of the two antagonists to a settlement of their problems. Israel was to evacuate part of the Sinai to enable it to become a UN-guaranteed buffer area. A detachment of two hundred American "civilian technicians" would be in "early warning" stations to watch for the beginnings of trouble. The United States also made general assurances of military assistance to Israel and Egypt, to maintain a balance. Finally, the oil flow was to resume—at quadrupled prices.

Kissinger's diplomacy had mixed results. Boundaries remained uncertain, for the Israelis remained in the Sinai, the Golan Heights, and the West Bank of the Jordan. The PLO's demands for a homeland were still unfulfilled, and both the Soviets and Palestinians were unhappy over being shut out of negotiations affecting their interests in the Middle East. Kissinger's efforts also widened the gulf between Arab moderates and extremists. Yet there was a saving factor: Sadat was disenchanted with the Soviets and had turned to the United States for help. Washington now assumed the role of mediator in the Middle East, a move offering improved prospects for peace.

Lack of unity within the Western Hemisphere also threatened détente. Canada began to follow policies that were not in line with those of the United States. It opened trade with China and the Soviet Union, established rigid controls on foreign investments, and raised its export prices for oil and natural gas sold to the United States while keeping enough at home to assure cheaper energy for Canadians. The situation in Latin America was more serious. Anti-American feeling remained strong, as exemplified by the unfriendly reception accorded New York Governor Nelson Rockefeller during his fact-finding tour of 1969. Though he recommended more economic help by the United States, the Alliance for Progress was virtually dead and the Nixon administration had shown little interest in reviving it. Mexico was upset over America's economic blockade of Cuba and its intervention in the Dominican Republic in 1965, and Venezuela sought to use its OPEC membership and rich oil deposits to win economic independence from the United States. The Panamanians still demanded a renegotiation of the canal treaty of 1903, and discussions were under way toward formalizing an agreement arranged by Kissinger in 1974. Terrorists and guerrillas meanwhile exploited Latin America's dire economic and political situation, and new regimes increasingly expropriated American holdings without making suitable compensation. Washington's response was to counter the alleged communist influence by selling arms to friendly governments.

Cuba remained a special obstruction to détente. Pressure had grown in the United States for lifting the trade embargo and reestablishing diplomatic relations, despite Castro's continued refusal to compensate Americans for expropriations of their properties. "Skyjacking" incidents grew in number as Castro permitted planes to return to the United States, but granted refuge to perpetrators on the ground that Americans did not return Cubans who hijacked boats and escaped to the United States. In the early 1970s, however, the United States agreed to block attempts by Cuban exiles in America to invade the island, in exchange for Cuba extraditing or punishing hijackers, and returning victimized properties and people. Two years later, with representatives of the Castro regime, Kissinger began secret talks in the United States that were aimed at settling differences between the countries. But in 1975 a Senate committee inquiring into CIA activities in Cuba found evidence of "at least eight" plots in the past to kill Castro—including a box of poisoned cigars—and some wondered if Castro had not countered by arranging the assassination of President Kennedy. In December Castro sent nearly 20,000 soldiers and military advisers to aid a leftist insurrection in Angola, and the United States later found that he had sent thousands more to Ethiopia. Cuba, it appeared, was becoming a base for spreading communism overseas as well as throughout the hemisphere. Détente seemed in more trouble as Americans became convinced that Castro was carrying out the Kremlin's orders.

The Nixon administration's greatest concern in Latin America was Chile, where in the autumn of 1970 Marxist Salvador Allende overcame CIA interference and was elected president. Allende's coalition government, which included communists and soon leaned toward Moscow for help against the Americans, promised constitutional amendments guaranteeing against totalitarian rule, and instituted a reform program designed to free the country from the control of large landowners and of America's multinational corporations. In so doing, Allende nationalized $1 billion of American holdings, although with assurances of compensation. International Telephone and Telegraph (ITT) and other business corporations nonetheless put pressure on the Nixon administration to take action against Allende.

Both Nixon and Kissinger regarded Allende as another Castro and hence a potential ally of the Soviet Union. While the administration in Washington maintained what it called a "cool but correct" stance toward Allende, it worked to destabilize his government. The CIA collaborated with American businesses in halting the flow of credit and other materials, secretly paid the Chilean press and opposing political parties to criticize Allende's rule, sent arms to the military, and cooperated with it in a coup. In September 1973 the Chilean army overthrew Allende's government, killing him in the process. A rightist military regime under General Augusto Pinochet came to power; it was repressive, but anticommunist. When the U.S. ambassador complained about the new government's use of torture, Kissinger instructed him "to cut out the political science lectures." The following year Americans learned that the CIA had participated in the coup that led to Allende's death. Two major investigations into the organization's conduct led to revelations in 1975 that mobilized Congress to restrict CIA activities overseas.

Another serious threat to détente had come from within the United States, for by late 1973 the Watergate scandal had greatly weakened the effectiveness of the Nixon administration in foreign affairs and soon led to a change in national leadership. To turn the nation's attention from Watergate as well as to revive détente, the president appointed Kissinger secretary of state in the autumn of 1973 and soon attended another summit meeting in Moscow. But the political scandals had undermined presidential authority, leading to a virtual abdication of domestic and foreign policy formation to Congress. Faced with certain impeachment, Nixon resigned the presidency in August 1974, leaving Vice President Gerald Ford as chief executive.

Ford and Kissinger continued the struggle for détente, but in the wake of Watergate and Vietnam, the actions of the White House were severely curtailed. As previously mentioned, Congress had restricted the president's authority by the War Powers Act. Furthermore, the Senate stipulated that in exchange for American trade, the Soviets had to respect the human rights of all dissidents—including Jews. The Senate also tried to establish a maximum amount on loans the United States could authorize for the Soviet Union. But these attempts at linkage did not work. The Soviets resented the United States's intervention in their domestic affairs and sharply reduced the number of Jews allowed to leave the country. In fact, the Senate's conditions ultimately blocked Soviet approval of the commercial treaty. To avoid further offense to the Soviet Union, President Ford refused a White House visit to Alexander Solzhenitzyn, a famous Soviet writer who had been exiled for exposing widespread brutality inside his homeland.

In late 1974 Ford and Kissinger tried to revive détente by accepting guidelines for SALT II, begun in Geneva two years earlier. The president met with Brezhnev in Vladivostok in November and tentatively agreed to a ten-year limit of 2,400 each on the total number of ICBMs, SLBMs, and big bombers. Of the 2,400 on each side, a maximum of 1,320 could have multiple warheads. In effect, SALT II blanketed the arms race with legality, assuring drawn-out discussions regarding what kinds of weapons fitted the new ceiling.

Meanwhile in Vietnam, the most damaging blow to détente came as the Thieu regime approached its final days in early 1975. The Third Indochina War had begun in late 1973 with the ARVN's attacks on North Vietnam's holdings in the south, but Hanoi had restricted its response until it was sure the Americans were gone. In January 1975, however, the North Vietnamese launched a crushing offensive that was a huge success primarily because of the rapidly disintegrating ARVN caused by poor leadership and widespread corruption, but also because of the huge cutbacks in American assistance, South Vietnam's excessive dependence on the United States, and, according to communist accounts, the popular support given the advancing forces. Thieu appealed to Ford to deliver the "full force" promised him by Nixon two years before. But the letter Thieu alluded to had not been made public, and Kissinger had earlier told the press that such a pledge did not exist. In the meantime Phuoc Binh, the capital of Phuoc Long Province, collapsed in January, confirming North Vietnam's suspicions that the United States would not reenter the war, and leading Thieu to order a retrenchment policy that turned into a full-fledged rout as terrified ARVN soldiers panicked civilians. America's decision not to intervene in the new fighting meant that the Vietnamese would settle the matter among themselves.

The ensuing collapse of South Vietnam was so sudden that it surprised Hanoi and aroused suspicions of a trap. On March 26 Hue fell, followed by Danang within a week, and on April 21 Thieu resigned, bitterly charging over radio and television that the United States was responsible for the debacle. After he fled with friends and relatives to Taiwan, the government in Saigon eventually went to Duong Van Minh, who had been instrumental in the Diem coup of 1963. The ARVN soon pulled out of Xuan Loc, forty miles east of Saigon, and on April 28 Ford approved emergency helicopter evacuations of Americans in Saigon. Meanwhile Bien Hoa air base fell to the Vietcong, who were now only fifteen miles outside the city. Nearly 150,000 Vietnamese managed to escape the country, many of them by boats or American planes in the days before the fall of Saigon. But not enough transportation was available to save everyone. American marines used rifle butts to fight off panic-stricken Vietnamese outside the gates of the American embassy in Saigon, as Americans and Vietnamese pushed and shoved their way into the helicopters taking off from the embassy roof. The final spectacle was that of angry ARVN soldiers shooting at Americans as they left the country.

On April 30 Saigon fell and the Third Indochina War was over. South Vietnam unconditionally surrendered and the Vietcong renamed its capital Ho Chi Minh City. Twenty-one years after the Geneva Accords of 1954, Vietnam was reunited. Almost simultaneously, the domino theory appeared to become a fact. The Lon Nol regime in Cambodia fell to the communist Khmer Rouge, and soon afterward Laos also came under communist control, ending America's long ordeal in Asia in triple disaster by the spring of 1975.

America's Asian policy lay in shambles. At tremendous costs successive administrations in Washington had fought to preserve the Saigon regime as a symbol of the Free World's resistance to communist takeover. And yet South Vietnam had collapsed. North Vietnam seized $5 billion in American military goods to become the leading military regime in Southeast Asia, although its government, like that of the Khmer Rouge in Cambodia, became repressive, causing thousands to flee the country. There was little unity among the new communist regimes, however. Less than a year after the fall of Saigon, communist Vietnam was at war with communist Cambodia, and in 1978 at war with communist China. Vietnam's

Fall of Saigon, April 1975

A South Vietnamese helicopter pilot and his family, safely aboard the U.S.S. Hancock,
*are escorted by a marine security guard to the refugee area during the evacuation of
Saigon on April 29, 1975.* (U.S. Department of Defense)

invasion of Cambodia led to the collapse of the Khmer Rouge as well as
the onset of a famine that threatened to decimate the population. Japan,
South Korea, and Taiwan were stunned by America's withdrawal from
Vietnam and feared that it might now pull out of South Korea and expose
Japan to communist assault. Thailand told Americans stationed in the
country to leave, for it now had to get along with other Asian nations.

In the face of growing lack of respect for America, the Ford administration took advantage of an incident involving an American merchant
vessel, the *Mayaguez*, to make a show of force. In May 1975 Cambodian
patrol boats seized the *Mayaguez*, then in the Gulf of Siam, for allegedly
violating their country's territorial waters. Occurring barely a month after
the fall of Vietnam, the episode afforded the president a chance to restore
the military credibility of the American government. Without allowing
time for either a full investigation or for Cambodia to respond to his de-

mand for the return of the ship and crew, he called the act piracy and approved military action. Unaware that the captors had already freed the thirty-nine Americans aboard, Ford ordered marines to the islands off Cambodia's coast, while American warships sank three Cambodian gunboats and planes bombed an air base and oil depot. At the cost of forty-one American lives, the Ford administration announced that it had saved both the *Mayaguez* and its men. The American public, as frustrated as the White House over the Vietnam War and other foreign policy failures, praised the president's use of force.

There were other attempts to bolster the staggering policy of détente. In July 1975 Ford joined the representatives of over thirty nations in Helsinki at the Conference on Security and Cooperation in Europe, to tie together the loose ends of World War II. In exchange for Soviet pledges to respect human rights and to allow cultural interchange between East and West, the signatories approved the wartime borders of the Baltic States, Poland, and Eastern Europe. The following September the SEATO Council met in New York and voted to phase out the organization; its central reason for existence, South Vietnam, was gone. Before the UN in September 1976, Kissinger called for "coexistence with the Soviet Union" and for "restraint" to be "reciprocal, not just in bilateral relations but around the globe." Finally, the death of Mao Zedong that same year preceded the installation of a moderate government in Beijing, which was more receptive to establishing formal Sino-American relations.

Another threat to détente came in Africa, where the United States became convinced that the Soviet Union intended to spread communism among the new postwar nations. Angola's recently won independence from Portugal had led to a civil war in which the United States worked with China and South Africa in covertly aiding the rightists, while the Soviet Union helped the leftist MPLA—the Popular Movement for the Liberation of Angola—by sending thousands of Cuban soldiers to Angola in late 1975. Kissinger condemned this new Soviet action as expansion by proxy and asked Congress to appropriate aid. Africa's rich resources, he explained to a Senate committee, made the continent important to the United States. But Congress feared another Vietnam, and the American public had learned that its government had already become secretly involved in Angola. Even though some representatives and senators had earlier known of the intervention and privately concurred, Congress recognized the growing public anger and cut off funds for military assistance. Ford reverted to Cold War language in chiding that body for failing to perceive that "resistance to Soviet expansion by military means must be a fundamental element of United States foreign policy." The MPLA emerged victorious in early 1976, and then surprised Washington by seeking technological assistance from Americans in developing Angola's oil resources. Instead of analyzing whether the Angolans were more concerned about their own welfare than about communism and the Cold War, the

Ford administration rebuked the Soviet Union for the outcome of the civil war and ceased talking about détente.

America's experience in Angola promoted a reassessment of its African policies. Americans had invested nearly $4 billion in Africa, but about 40 percent of the money had gone to projects of the white government of South Africa, which followed the racial segregationist policies of *apartheid* (apartness) against a predominantly black people. The United States had alienated most black regimes in Africa, especially by its decision to trade for the chrome ore of Rhodesia (to avoid dependence on the other chief source of the product, the Soviet Union) despite the UN's economic boycott of that nation's white minority regime. In early 1976 Kissinger visited South Africa, where violence had broken out in Rhodesia, and won concessions for the blacks. The United States, he explained, had reversed its African policies to "avoid a race war" and "to prevent foreign intervention." But Washington's central objective remained that of preventing Soviet exploitation of what Kissinger called "the radicalization of Africa."

Détente seemed even more remote by late 1976 as Ford lost his bid for election to a newcomer on the national political scene, a successful peanut farmer, former governor of Georgia, and born-again Baptist—James Earl Carter, Jr. During the campaign, right-wing Republicans denounced détente so vehemently that Kissinger referred to it as "a word I would like to forget," and Ford dropped it from his speeches in preference for the phrase "peace through strength." The administration's strong showing in the *Mayaguez* affair had only temporarily soothed the national frustration over Vietnam. Furthermore, Ford had alienated many Americans by pardoning Nixon for his role in Watergate, and by making the surprising assertion during his television debates with Carter that "there is no Soviet domination of Eastern Europe, and there never will be under a Ford administration." When Carter challenged this observation, Ford refused to retreat, citing his recent visit to Eastern Europe as proof of his claim. Carter also took advantage of Watergate and America's foreign policy failures to promise an honest administration, freed from Washington's bureaucracy, and one that would restore the nation's global standing. Some of his charges were not consistent. Carter attacked Kissinger's secret diplomacy, his support for repressive regimes, and the Republicans' exorbitant defense spending, and yet at the same time he criticized the Ford administration for conceding too much during arms discussions and for the failure of the Helsinki Agreements to guarantee civil liberties within the Soviet Union. The Soviets, he asserted, had exploited détente to America's disadvantage. Carter's strategy was nonetheless successful. He won a little more than half of the popular vote, defeating Ford by about a 2 percent margin. The effects of Watergate and Vietnam doubtless influenced Americans to choose Jimmy Carter—a president determined to revive faith in the country by expounding idealisms and human rights.

Selected readings

Alexander, Robert J., *The Tragedy of Chile.* 1978.

Ambrose, Stephen E., *Rise to Globalism: American Foreign Policy since 1938.* 4th ed. 1985.

Baritz, Loren, *Backfire: A History of How American Culture Led Us into Vietnam and Made Us Fight the Way We Did.* 1985.

Bell, Coral, *The Diplomacy of Détente: The Kissinger Era.* 1977.

Brandon, Henry, *The Retreat of American Power.* 1972.

Brown, Seyom, *The Crises of Power: Foreign Policy in the Kissinger Years.* 1979.

Burchett, Wilfred, *Catapult to Freedom: The Survival of the Vietnamese People.* 1978.

———, *Grasshoppers & Elephants: Why Vietnam Fell.* 1977.

Butler, David, *The Fall of Saigon: Scenes from the Sudden End of a Long War.* 1985.

Cohen, Warren I., *America's Response to China.* 2d ed. 1980.

DuPuy, Trevor N., *Elusive Victory: The Arab-Israeli Wars, 1947–1974.* 1978.

FitzGerald, Frances, *Fire in the Lake: The Vietnamese and the Americans in Vietnam.* 1972.

Ford, Gerald R., *A Time to Heal: The Autobiography of Gerald R. Ford.* 1979.

Franck, Thomas M., and Edward Weisband, *Foreign Policy by Congress.* 1979.

Freedman, Robert O., *Soviet Policy toward the Middle East Since 1970.* 1978.

Gaddis, John L., *Russia, the Soviet Union, and the United States.* 1978.

Gelb, Leslie H., and Richard K. Betts, *The Irony of Vietnam: The System Worked.* 1979.

Glassman, Jon D., *Arms for the Arabs: The Soviet Union and War in the Middle East.* 1975.

Goldman, Marshall I., *Détente and Dollars: Doing Business with the Soviets.* 1975.

Goodman, Allan E., *The Lost Peace: America's Search for a Negotiated Settlement of the Vietnam War.* 1978.

Harrison, James P., *The Endless War: Fifty Years of Struggle in Vietnam.* 1982.

Harrison, Michael M., *The Reluctant Ally: France and Atlantic Security.* 1981.

Herring, George C., Jr., *America's Longest War: The United States and Vietnam, 1950–1975.* 2d ed., 1986.

Hersh, Seymour M., *The Price of Power: Kissinger in the Nixon White House.* 1983.

Isaacs, Arnold R., *Without Honor: Defeat in Vietnam and Cambodia.* 1983.

Joiner, Harry M., *American Foreign Policy: The Kissinger Era.* 1977.

Kalb, Bernard, and Marvin Kalb, *Kissinger.* 1974.

Karnow, Stanley, *Vietnam: A History.* 1983.

Kattenburg, Paul M., *The Vietnam Trauma in American Foreign Policy, 1945–1975.* 1980.

Kissinger, Henry, *White House Years.* 1979.

———, *Years of Upheaval.* 1982.

Kolko, Gabriel, *Anatomy of a War: Vietnam, the United States, and the Modern Historical Experience.* 1985.

LaFeber, Walter, *America, Russia, and the Cold War, 1945–1984.* 5th ed. 1985.

———, *The Panama Canal: The Crisis in Historical Perspective.* 1978. Expanded ed. 1979.

Landau, David, *Kissinger: The Uses of Power.* 1972.

Larson, Thomas B., *Soviet-American Rivalry.* 1978.

Lewy, Guenter, *America in Vietnam.* 1978.

Lomperis, Timothy J., *The War Everyone Lost—And Won: America's Intervention in Vietnam's Twin Struggles.* 1984.

Maclear, Michael, *The Ten Thousand Day War, Vietnam: 1945–1975.* 1981.

Mandelbaum, Michael, *The Nuclear Question: The United States & Nuclear Weapons, 1946–1976.* 1979.

Morris, Roger, *Uncertain Greatness: Henry Kissinger and American Foreign Policy.* 1977.

Newhouse, John, *Cold Dawn: The Story of SALT.* 1973.

Nixon, Richard, *No More Vietnams.* 1985.

———, *RN: The Memoirs of Richard Nixon.* 1978.

Petras, James, and Morris Morley, *The United States and Chile: Imperialism and the Overthrow of the Allende Government.* 1975.

Pipes, Richard, *U.S.-Soviet Relations in the Era of Détente: A Tragedy of Errors.* 1981.

Podhoretz, Norman, *Why We Were in Vietnam.* 1982.

Porter, Gareth, *A Peace Denied: The United States, Vietnam, and the Paris Agreement.* 1975.

Quandt, William B., *Decade of Decisions: American Policy Toward the Arab-Israeli Conflict, 1967–1976.* 1977.

Rabe, Stephen G., *The Road to OPEC: United States Relations with Venezuela.* 1982.

Reich, Bernard, *Quest for Peace: United States-Israeli Relations and the Arab-Israeli Conflict.* 1977.

Safran, Nadav, *Israel.* 1978.

Schell, Jonathan, *The Time of Illusion.* 1976.

Schlesinger, Arthur M., Jr.,*The Imperial Presidency.* 1973.

Shawcross, William, *Sideshow: Kissinger, Nixon and the Destruction of Cambodia.* 1979.

Sheehan, Edward R. F., *The Arabs, Israelis, and Kissinger.* 1976.

Sigmund, Paul E., *The Overthrow of Allende and the Politics of Chile, 1964–1976.* 1977.

Snepp, Frank, *Decent Interval: An Insider's Account of Saigon's Indecent End Told by the CIA's Chief Strategy Analyst in Vietnam.* 1978.

Spanier, John W., *American Foreign Policy Since World War II.* 9th ed. 1983.

Spiegel, Steven L., *The Other Arab-Israeli Conflict: Making America's Middle East Policy, from Truman to Reagan.* 1985.

Stevenson, Richard W., *The Rise and Fall of Détente: Relaxations of Tensions in US-Soviet Relations, 1953–84.* 1985.

Stockwell, John, *In Search of Enemies: A CIA Story.* 1979.

Stookey, Robert W., *America and the Arab States.* 1975.

Szulc, Tad, *The Illusion of Peace: Foreign Policy in the Nixon Years.* 1978.

Whitaker, Arthur P., *The United States and the Southern Core: Argentina, Chile, and Uruguay.* 1976.

Wills, Garry, *Nixon Agonistes: The Crisis of the Self-Made Man.* 1970.

Chapter Twenty-Five

The New Isolationism: Carter and the Diplomacy of Human Rights, 1977–1981

CARTER AND THE NEW ISOLATIONISM

The Carter administration's foreign policy was more vocal about human rights than any presidency since that of Woodrow Wilson's, even though the underlying objective remained the containment of Soviet expansion. Human rights, the new executive declared, was "the soul of our foreign policy." Indeed, he called on the United States to repent of its past sins. The change in public emphasis partly resulted from the limitations on American power imposed by the recent military growth of other nations, particularly that of the Soviet Union. But the human rights emphasis was also in line with ideas growing during the last four decades, most notably those highlighted in Franklin D. Roosevelt's Four Freedoms of 1941, the UN Charter of 1945, the Universal Declaration of Human Rights of 1948, and the Helsinki Agreements of 1975. To guarantee "no more Vietnams," Carter asserted, the United States would no longer be directed by "an inordinate fear of communism." His administration would concentrate on tying the world together by economic means, including the establishment of a law of the sea. The ultimate objective was to reduce the chances for nuclear war by achieving success in the SALT talks and halting the sale of arms to other countries.

Problems were there from the outset. First, containment of the Soviet Union dictated the development of new weapons, the recognition of China, and aid to noncommunist regimes, whereas the drive for human rights led to the encouragement of nationalism, the establishment of a North-South relationship with the Third World, public denunciations of the Soviets' policies toward dissidents at home, and support for the SALT talks. Second, morality did not always fit with America's strategic and economic interests, and the result was that the president made his country vulnerable to charges of hypocrisy. Carter attacked the repressive tactics of Castro in Cuba and Idi Amin in Uganda, and he angered Brezhnev by criticizing his civil liberties policies at home. But the president ignored harsh practices in countries important to America's interests such as Iran, Nicaragua, the Philippines, and South Korea. Though America's ambassador to the United Nations, Andrew Young, asserted that the human rights program was never "thought out and planned," the administration actually spent an enormous amount of time formulating policies.

The Vietnam experience encouraged the new executive to adopt a diplomacy of restraint. The Asian war and domestic scandals had broken the nation's political consensus, allowing the emergence of special interest groups that often operated independently of Washington. The declining global influence of the United States since World War II added to its inability to steer events. Disillusionment and a sense of national guilt over the war in Vietnam meanwhile fostered disengagement in foreign affairs and bred skepticism over the reality of a communist danger. The new attitude manifested itself in an aversion to foreign intervention, and in a call for cooperation in furthering human rights and helping the poverty-stricken, especially in so-called Fourth World countries having few resources. Washington was confident that Moscow would have to relax its offensive because of the growing aspirations of China, NATO, and the Third World. The United States, it seemed, had accepted the limits of power.

The Carter administration encountered numerous problems in its foreign policy. The new president was a novice in national politics, and was unable to work effectively with a Congress where many Democrats had won by greater margins than had Carter and did not feel bound to him. The domestic political structure was in flux because of shifting alliances, which obstructed the formation of a new national consensus. The economy continued to suffer from recession and skyrocketing inflation, a situation exacerbated by OPEC's periodic raising of oil prices. America's allies meanwhile moved farther away as Washington seemed unable to arrange its own political and economic house. Carter's emphasis on human rights hurt détente, for a return to idealism in foreign affairs not only disrupted Soviet relations, but it caused trouble in Latin America and among the European allies. Moreover, a call for human rights could lead to policies similar to those of President Wilson's: self-righteous interference in other countries' internal affairs. As Carter's policies eventually floundered in indirection and indecisiveness, so did his performance approval plunge in the polls.

Carter at first leaned toward the views of Secretary of State Cyrus Vance, who preferred an orderly, behind-the-scenes formulation of policy through the Department of State. America's foreign policy underwent a change from Kissinger's independent and flashy style of diplomacy to that of patient and quiet negotiations led by experienced diplomats. Vance had been deputy secretary of defense from 1964 to 1967 and had participated in the Paris peace talks of 1968–69. A wealthy New York attorney from West Virginia, he opposed military interventionist policies, refused to hold the Soviets responsible for all of the world's problems, and believed that the Vietnamese War had illustrated that Americans could not "prop up a series of regimes that lacked popular support." With the United States no longer dominant in world politics, he asserted publicly, "there can be no going back to a time when we thought there could be American solutions to every problem." Peace could come only through negotiations and the establishment of economic ties. SALT II became his premier objective.

Vance relied heavily on his chief adviser for Soviet affairs, Marshall Shulman, on leave as professor of Russian studies at Columbia University, who argued that the United States should emphasize "soft linkage"—discreet suggestions to Moscow that American economic aid would be forthcoming only if the Soviets respected human rights at home and allowed international matters to calm. Shulman hoped that "within-the-system-modernizers" inside the Soviet Union—youthful and middle-aged professionals and technicians—would bring internal changes conducive to cooperation with the West. But time and patience were required. He and Vance agreed that troubles in emerging nations were attributable more to nationalist tendencies than to a bipolar crisis with the Soviet Union. Change in Eastern Europe, they continued, would have to come slowly. Otherwise, the Soviets would use military force to settle questions as they had done in Hungary in 1956 and Czechoslovakia in 1968.

But the president's national security adviser, Zbigniew Brzezinski, sharply disagreed with Vance, eventually opening a chasm in the direction of the administration's foreign policy. A political science professor from Columbia University who specialized in Soviet affairs, Brzezinski was born in Poland and was a hardline anticommunist who viewed the world as bipolar and regarded the Soviet Union as the central threat to peace. An early critic of détente, he was skeptical about SALT, especially if the Soviets did not change their aggressive policies in Africa and the Middle East. Furthermore, Brzezinski did not believe "that the use of nuclear weapons would be the end of the human race. . . . That's egocentric," he declared.

Carter seldom succeeded in cutting through these opposing viewpoints and therefore failed to institute a firm and consistent foreign policy. He promised peaceful resolutions of world problems, cooperation with Congress, restraints on the CIA, a more open foreign policy, restrictions on arms sales, gradual military withdrawal from South Korea, and curtailment of foreign aid to nations refusing to respect human rights. Past experiences suggested that these objectives were impractical. But for Carter they seemed attainable on an individual basis. One official noted that the president looked at problems "like an engineering student thinking you can cram for the exam and get an A." To Carter, a graduate of the Annapolis Naval Academy and a nuclear engineer, long hours of studying and mastering details left him with a comfortable impression of understanding the issues. But his approach was virtually meaningless without a corresponding understanding of how the issues were interrelated, and that to deal with them required knowledge of both general strategy and history. In 1979 Carter tried to correct the latter deficiency when he admitted to having read more history since becoming president than at any time in his life. Yet the president's religious views influenced him to adopt a simplified world outlook that led him to regard morality as the primary determinant in foreign policy. Thus, those nations not interested in idealisms rejected Carter's calls for human rights as unwarranted attempts to meddle in their domestic affairs. The president sincerely believed in his calls for human decency, but he was hampered by practical global politics, by his country's lowered prestige in the world, and by advisers pulling in opposite directions.

Perhaps Carter's central difficulty was a lack of vision and direction. A former speechwriter noted that the president "holds explicit, thorough positions on every issue under the sun . . . but he has no large view of the relations between them." Carter "fails to project a vision larger than the problem he is tackling at the moment." The president was doubtless correct in arguing that a "national malaise" had caused a "crisis of the American spirit," but he never seemed to grasp the importance of laying out a general course of action designed to combat the problem.

The Carter administration sought to counter Soviet military expansion in Eastern Europe by tightening the Western alliance and furthering the SALT talks. Moscow had apparently matched Washington in nuclear power, necessitating a greater American reliance on its allies and on arms limitations programs. In January 1977 Carter attempted to draw the allies closer together by calling for a program of "trilateralism"—social and economic cooperation among North America, Western Europe, and Japan that would also help the Third World. Less than a week after the inauguration, Vice President Walter Mondale promoted the idea during his goodwill visit to Western Europe and Japan. This program was no surprise; during the early 1970s Carter and Vance had been members of the Trilateral Commission, a private group of Americans, Western Europeans, and Japanese brought together by Brzezinski and banker David Rockefeller to rebuild economic and political ties hurt by the Nixon administration's willingness to deal with enemy nations. But the commission rarely agreed on anything, and by 1975 Brzezinski argued for the importance of standing up to Moscow. In the spring of 1977 President Carter attended an economic conference in London of seven industrial nations—the United States, United Kingdom, Canada, France, Italy, West Germany, and Japan—who agreed to work toward halting inflation, promoting trade, creating employment, and helping underdeveloped nations. Afterward, he reaffirmed ties with NATO as a basis of America's foreign policy.

The Carter administration spent most of 1977 trying to advance the SALT negotiations in Moscow. Vance led the delegation in late March as it tried to further the principles of November 1974, worked out by Ford and Brezhnev in Vladivostok. Vance offered a well-publicized plan containing several proposals: formal approval of the Vladivostok principles, and a specific program calling for a joint cutback in missile launchers and multiple warheads, a cessation of the development of new weapons, and a freeze on ICBMs at their present level of about 550. Vance also recommended an end to mobile missiles, limits on the scope of cruise missiles, and restrictions against the Soviets' new supersonic "Backfire" bomber. His proposals unleashed a furious reaction in Moscow, for they reversed the Ford-Brezhnev understandings by calling for massive reductions in the areas of Soviet strengths. Vance's plan was preposterous, according to Soviet Foreign Minister Andrei Gromyko in a televised news conference, for it required the Soviets to phase out their largest missiles. Though the two nations agreed to continue studying the problems relating to nuclear materials, they abruptly terminated the SALT talks. SALT I was due to expire in October 1977, although Washington and Moscow agreed to extend its life until SALT II became effective. Soviet-American relations had taken a sharp turn downward.

In an effort to defuse the East-West division, Carter relied upon UN Ambassador Andrew Young to build a meaningful North-South relationship. Young, a black minister, former congressman, and civil rights leader from Georgia, promoted closer relations with the Third World by advancing the Vance-Shulman position that new nations would seek help from the United States as long as Cold War issues did not intervene. But Young had to leave office in 1979 after violating the government's declared policy by initiating communications with the PLO (not recognized by the United States), in trying to arrange its participation in settling the Middle East crisis.

The administration's human rights stance toward the Third World necessitated understandings with the Soviet Union. There seemed little choice by the late 1970s; Americans were weary of foreign policy commitments and had supported recent attacks on the so-called "imperial presidency" that led to the War Powers Act and more controls over the CIA. The Cold War was over, many wanted to believe. Détente was crucial to the success of the "new isolationism," as some writers labeled the post-Vietnam national mood.

The United States thus prepared to deal with the realities of a multipolar political and economic system. Should it oppose international cooperation in resolving global problems, growing instability would lead to more political unrest injurious to trade and investment. The world's economy was in a downspin; Fourth World peoples needed massive assistance to combat droughts, famines, and other natural disasters; the Third World controlled valuable natural resources such as oil; the new postwar nations had become a majority in the UN by the 1970s; the proliferation of nuclear weapons was increasing; the Western alliance was shaky; Latin Americans were increasingly resentful of Washington's exploitative policies; and there was an erosion of respect for America catalyzed by Watergate, Vietnam, and the activities of the CIA and multinational corporations. Carter appeared to recognize these realities, but his rhetorical and often inconsistent appeals to human rights so badly interfered with his positions on events that even America's allies viewed his administration as devious, self-righteous, and undependable.

THE THIRD WORLD: AFRICA AND LATIN AMERICA

The Carter administration made noteworthy strides toward establishing good relations with Third World countries, even while the president remained concerned about the spread of Soviet communist influence. Vance, Young, and others in the administration tried to persuade him to deal with the troubles of the underdeveloped nations on their own merits; not every problem, they argued, was Soviet-inspired. Nationalist upheavals could be indigenous in origin and thus have no relation to great power rivalries. During the first half of Carter's presidency he was open to these arguments, even restraining those advisers who called for interventionist policies designed to curb believed Soviet expansionism. Economic assistance programs, tied to assurances of human rights reforms, became the central thrust of the administration's policies toward the Third World.

Africa was a major concern of the United States. Politically, the representation in the UN was already one-third African, whereas inside the United States blacks pressed for a policy recognizing African nationalism. Economically, the continent was rich in minerals and an excellent source of trade and investment. Nigeria, in fact, had become the second largest supplier of oil for the United States. Strategically, Africa offered airstrips and ports at key points interconnecting the world. Should Washington continue to support white regimes, however, the Soviets would be in the position to exploit black nationalism and become a major force in Africa.

Young ultimately convinced the president that Africans should resolve their own problems. Both the Kennedy and Johnson administrations had told the UN that they disliked white minority rule in Rhodesia and South Africa. But despite Johnson's opposition, Congress had permitted Americans to purchase Rhodesia's chrome, violating a UN embargo that the United States had helped to institute. The Nixon administration had then refrained from criticizing white rule in Africa because it believed that whites would remain dominant for years. But a shift in policy had begun under Kissinger in 1976, which Carter continued. After Young visited black regimes in Africa, Carter denounced the racist policy of *apartheid*, and argued that an independent Africa bolstered by American aid would be a strong obstacle to Soviet infiltration. Congress, under immense pressure from the White House, restored the embargo on Rhodesian chrome. In the meantime the Carter administration worked with the British government in persuading Rhodesia's prime minister, Ian Smith, to approve a gradual change to majority rule. The result was that British negotiations led to an election in April 1980 that installed a government in Rhodesia (now Zimbabwe) headed by a black insurgent and Marxist, Robert Mugabe. In South Africa, however, Washington failed to persuade the white regime to change its policies toward blacks, who comprised 85 percent of the population.

A conflict between the Marxist regimes of Somalia and Ethiopia exposed Soviet-American differences over Africa. In 1977 Somalia, Moscow's closest ally in Africa since 1969, sent soldiers to fight with the insurgent Western Somali Liberation Front in the Ogaden area of Ethiopia, then populated by a number of Somalis. The Soviets had to choose between the antagonists. Though Somalia had a naval base and air facilities along the Indian Ocean, the Soviets leaned toward Ethiopia because it was much larger than Somalia and its location would facilitate Soviet access to the strategically important Horn of Africa on the eastern tip of the continent. In November Somalia's president abrogated his country's friendship with the Soviet Union. Moscow promptly sent Ethiopia $1 billion in military assistance, a thousand advisers, and 20,000 Cuban soldiers to put down the Ogaden insurrection. By March 1978 they had succeeded, forcing Somali regulars out of Ogaden. The Carter administration now feared that if the Soviet Union won greater influence in Ethiopia and went on to seize the southern end of the Red Sea, it would endanger the Suez Canal and Israel, and cut off the oil flow from the Persian Gulf to the West.

Growing division within the Carter administration led to a confused reaction to events in Africa. Brzezinski and the Defense Department wanted to send military assistance to Somalia, whereas Vance and the State Department argued that Africa's problems were internal and that American intervention would alienate the entire continent. Though Ethiopia had invited Moscow's help, Vance and Young argued that Somalia was the aggressor. Carter therefore wavered before lashing out at the Soviet Union and Cuba, hurting détente by warning that if Soviet forces did not withdraw from Africa, SALT II was in danger. The United States did not intervene, but urged a moderate policy in Ogaden and a peaceful settlement of Somali-Ethiopian difficulties. Somalia meanwhile eased the situation by agreeing to keep its soldiers out of Ogaden.

Despite Young's departure from the administration in 1979, America's relations with Africa had improved. Commercial ties were growing, and the United States soon secured port and airfield rights in Somalia. In another part of the continent, the Carter administration airlifted supplies to Belgian and French forces in Zaire (formerly the Congo) during May 1978, after Soviet- and Cuban-aided Katangans had invaded the province through Angola; but that was the extent of Washington's military action.

Its restraint paid off. Numerous African regimes voted with the United States in matters before the UN General Assembly, and while the Soviets and Cubans remained influential in Angola and Ethiopia, the Angolans appeared interested in dealing with the West. Africans, the Carter administration seemed to realize, had one fundamental objective: never again to become colonials.

Latin America likewise continued to be a major source of anxiety for the United States. Persisting problems of poverty and overpopulation had stimulated drives for nationalism that were, in turn, repeatedly squelched by harsh military regimes whose power was often maintained by American arms and matériel. Brazil, Cuba, and Mexico had become more independent, although the majority of Latin Americans still sought American help in securing technological assistance, reduced tariffs, higher prices for their goods, and more controls over multinational corporations. Like Africa, Latin America commanded votes in the UN and was an important source of trade and investment. The United States could no longer ignore the problem.

The Carter administration sought to relieve Latin America's problems by using economic pressures to force right-wing regimes to respect human rights. In a speech before the Permanent Council of the Organization of American States in April 1977, the president called for greater consultation among the American states based on three principles: "a high regard for the individuality and sovereignty of each Latin American and Caribbean nation"; "respect for human rights"; and the intention to resolve "the great issues which affect the relations between the developed and developing nations." Carter urged commercial cooperation in stabilizing prices and building a sound economy, and promised that the United States would stimulate lending through the American Development Bank. These efforts, however, were contingent upon a firm Latin American commitment to human rights.

Carter's first diplomatic offensive in Latin America—his attempt to reestablish formal relations with Cuba—was a failure. As prerequisites for American recognition, Castro first had to guarantee respect for human rights, and second, he had to cease sending troops to Africa. In Havana from April through June of 1977, American and Cuban delegates discussed their countries' difficulties. A short time earlier the Carter administration had lifted the ban on travel to Cuba, while Castro had promised to continue efforts to discourage airplane hijacking. But by the close of the Havana negotiations in mid-1977, the two delegations had succeeded only in creating "diplomatic interest sections" in the nations' capitals. America's trade embargo was still in effect, Cuban troops remained in Angola and Ethiopia, and Soviet military and economic influence was conspicuous in Cuba. In fact, over $20 million of economic aid arrived in Havana every week. Though secret American-Cuban discussions continued through 1980, they did not lead to either the lifting of the commercial embargo or the restoration of diplomatic relations.

The Carter administration's most ambitious effort to build a better relationship with Latin America was a success: the termination of the United States's control over the Panama Canal established by the Hay-Bunau-Varilla Treaty of 1903. A longtime source of resentment, the pact had been the subject of negotiations during the Johnson and Nixon presidencies. By mid-century, controversy focused on a local disagreement over the flying of Panamanian and American flags on high school grounds. In January 1964 American high school students tore down and allegedly desecrated the Panamanian flag. Angry Panamanians stormed the Canal Zone, where American soldiers drove them back at the cost of twenty-six lives, including those of three Americans. The Panamanian government broke relations with the United States and turned for help to the UN and the OAS. An OAS committee tried to mediate the dispute, but Johnson refused the Panamanian government's demand to renegotiate the old Panama Treaty. After his election victory in November, he announced his country's intention to build a sea-level canal through either Panama, Nicaragua, or Colombia. The Panama Canal, he explained, was susceptible to sabotage, unable to service the huge volume of ships passing through daily, and not equipped to accommodate America's large aircraft carriers. But Panamanians objected to America's insistence on controlling the canal and retaining its bases in the area, and the issue remained unsettled. The Nixon administration had pledged support for a new treaty, and now Carter as president promised an agreement combining "Panama's legitimate needs as a sovereign nation" with America's "interests in the efficient operations of a neutral canal, open on a nondiscriminatory basis to all users." His administration had a chance to improve relations with Latin America with one bold stroke—turning over the canal to Panama.

The resulting treaties between the United States and Panama were the work of many people, most notably that of Secretary of State Vance and two senators, Democrat Robert Byrd of West Virginia and Republican Howard Baker of Tennessee. The two pacts, drawn in 1977 and approved in Panama by a two-to-one margin in October of that same year, would abrogate the 1903 treaty, raise Panama's share of the canal tolls, and grant the United States the perpetual right to protect the canal's "neutrality." By the first treaty, the "Panama Canal Treaty," the United States would retain central responsibility for the canal until the year 2000, at which time Panama was to take over all duties associated with the Canal Zone. The second pact, the "Treaty Concerning the Permanent Neutrality and Operation of the Panama Canal," promised "no discrimination" against any country wishing to use the canal. In an attached statement, after the year 2000 the United States could use the canal to move warships and had the right to "defend the canal against any threat to the regime of neutrality."

The ensuing debate in the United States over the canal treaties was nationwide and emotional. Opponents denounced the agreements as another retreat similar to that in Vietnam; the treaties would become monuments to appeasement. The United States owned the canal, others charged. One senator asserted that "we stole it fair and square." Republican Ronald Reagan of California, presidential hopeful in the 1980 election, ignored the historical record in asserting that the Canal Zone was "sovereign United States territory just the same as Alaska . . . and the states that were carved out of the Louisiana Purchase." Loss of the canal, critics charged, would hurt the American economy, undercut the nation's defense, and invite Soviet involvement in the regime of Panamanian President Omar Torrijos, which already seemed to be leaning toward communism. Proponents faced an uphill battle. They concurred with Carter that the canal agreements would establish goodwill throughout Latin America. They also argued that the canal's economic advantages were no longer substantial and that America had a moral obligation to relinquish an area belonging to Panama. Less than 10 percent of America's trade, in fact, depended on the canal. It offered even less in strategic advantages, according to the Joint Chiefs of Staff. The canal was subject to sabotage, aircraft carriers and tankers were too large for the waterway, and nuclear submarines wishing to use it would have to surface and reveal their location. The chairman of the Joint Chiefs emphasized that "the strategic value of the canal lies in its use."

Arguments over canal ownership lay at the heart of the controversy. The head of the North American negotiating team in 1976, Ellsworth Bunker, argued that "we bought Louisiana; we bought Alaska. In Panama, we bought not territory, but rights. . . . It is clear that under law we do not have sovereignty in Panama." Carter underlined this point in a "fireside chat," when he asserted that "we do not own the Panama Canal Zone. We have never had sovereignty over it. We have only had the right to use it." Defenders of the treaties rallied behind the Committee of Americans for the Canal Treaties, which numbered among its membership the noted diplomat W. Averell Harriman, and a former director of the CIA, William Colby. Perhaps more impressive, leading Republicans, including former President Ford and Secretary of State Kissinger, joined America's big businesses in favoring the treaties.

During the spring of 1978 the two Panama Canal treaties won narrow approval in the Senate. On March 16 that body approved the neutrality treaty by a margin of 68 to 32, one vote more than the two-thirds majority needed. To secure its passage, however, supporters attached an amendment reserving America's right to keep the canal open, "including the use of military force *in* the Republic of Panama." Torrijos accepted this amendment only after a special appeal from Carter. In a Statement of Understanding in October that became part of the neutrality treaty, Torrijos agreed to the United States's right after the year 2000 to halt "any aggression or threat directed against the Canal or against the peaceful transit of vessels through the Canal." In addition, he assured the United States that in times of trouble its vessels could "go to the head of the line." Carter in turn guaranteed against any claimed American right to intervene in Panama's internal affairs. By the same margin, on April 18, the Senate approved the other treaty turning over the canal to Panama in 2000.

Thus, after three quarters of a century of disagreement with Panama, the United States had accepted the abrogation of the treaty of 1903. In a single move the Carter administration had taken a major step toward establishing credibility in the southern half of the hemisphere. But succeeding events would show that more than one agreement was necessary to remove the ill will engrained among Latin Americans by the United States's long history of interventionism.

In another part of the hemisphere, the Central American state of Nicaragua, the Carter administration's diplomatic efforts were likewise a mixture of idealism and realism that for a time seemed to approximate an effective foreign policy. Since 1936 the United States had supported the anticommunist dictatorship established by General Anastasio Somoza Garcia. Over the years Americans had ignored the Somoza dynasty's repressive practices and sold it arms, in return receiving Nicaragua's cooperation in America's actions in Guatemala in 1954, Cuba in 1961, and the Dominican Republic in 1965. But while the Somozas thrived, their Nicaraguan people suffered from poverty. Finally, in 1978, a leftist organization known as the Sandinista National Liberation Front (FSLN) rose in rebellion. Named after César Augusto Sandino, who had led insurgents against American forces during the 1920s and 1930s, the Sandinistas picked up widespread support from the people, the Catholic Church, and business interests. The Carter administration at first tried to mediate the dispute, but was unsuccessful. The Sandinistas launched a major offensive in 1979 and captured control of the government. In mid-July Anastasio Somoza, son of the original patriarch, Debayle, fled the country and was later assassinated in Paraguay.

To persuade the Sandinistas to promote reform, Carter asked Congress to appropriate $75 million for economic aid to Nicaragua. In July 1980 that body approved his request over numerous protests that the new regime was communist. The Sandinistas, however, promised open political and economic affairs, and continued to receive assistance from the United States until early 1981. At that time Washington cut off aid after accusing them of helping anti-American insurgents in El Salvador.

Mexican-American relations also remained uneasy. Millions of illegal aliens had made their way into the United States by 1980, many of them young males in search of temporary jobs. American workers complained that Mexicans either took the few jobs available and forced down wages, or failed to find employment and went on welfare. In August 1977 Carter recommended that Congress grant amnesty to illegal aliens already in the United States, and then upgrade border patrols and fine American businessmen who hired illegal aliens. Congress established a study commission.

Economic problems also interfered with America's relations with Mexico. Nationalists in Mexico sought to break America's domination over trade and investment in their country by persuading the United States either to lower tariffs or to place more restrictions on foreign investment. Mexico had won bargaining power as a result of oil and natural gas during the late 1970s. Whereas it was not a member of OPEC and Americans expected to buy at cheap prices, the Mexican government charged higher prices than did Saudi Arabia. After several disputes the United States agreed to Mexico's prices in late 1979. Within a year, oil and natural gas comprised half of Mexico's exports to the United States.

Despite the Panama Canal treaties, Latin Americans continued to regard the United States with suspicion. One act could not erase nearly 160 years of resentment stemming from the United States's assumed role as guardian of the hemisphere. Whether or not the charges of imperialism were just, Washington's southern neighbors believed they were. For too many years the United States had appeared calloused, arrogant, and exploitative, ignoring the plight of Latin Americans while extending massive aid programs to other parts of the world. Critics had warned that if communism was indeed a threat in the Western Hemisphere, that situation was in large part the result of America's own policies of neglect. Rather than interpret every insurrection as communist-inspired, they argued, it seemed wiser to recognize that dire economic problems may have led to desperate political and military actions that the United States might have alleviated through astute diplomacy. Economic assistance was needed—not increased arms sales to military regimes that assured only internal order and opposition to communism. The Panama Canal treaties suggested that Washington had altered its policies toward Latin America; only time and additional bold actions could provide proof.

THE MIDDLE EAST

If the Panama Canal treaties prove monumental in importance, a second breakthrough in the Carter administration's foreign policy appeared to come in the Middle East, where the president's personal intervention seemed to lead to the first major move toward peace. The region was beset with numerous troubles that by the late 1970s were multiplying. Besides the ancient Arab-Israeli feud, civil conflict had continued in Lebanon, PLO terrorist acts had grown in number, unrest had developed in Iran, and the West's needs for oil from the Persian Gulf had spiraled upward. Even Israel's military successes in 1967 came at unexpected expense. The "annexation" of the West Bank imposed severe strains on Israel. Not only did the military occupation program involve heavy financial obligations, but it entailed restrictions on fundamental freedoms that violated Israel's cherished democratic principles. In addition, a refugee problem was growing that was both Palestinian and Israeli in scope. About 900,000 Palestinians had been displaced after the war of 1948–49, leading the UN to establish refugee camps primarily in Egypt, Jordan, Syria, and Lebanon. The Six Day War of 1967 had complicated the refugee

problem, for more than 800,000 Palestinian Arabs inhabited the areas occupied by Israeli forces—the West Bank and the Old City of Jerusalem. By
the late 1970s displaced Palestinians numbered perhaps 4 million, a figure
providing a rich source for PLO recruitment. The Israelis noted another
side to the refugee issue: the near million Jewish refugees who had left
the Arab states, many forced into Israel after the war of 1948–49, and still
holding legitimate claims against Arab governments. There were too
many issues to resolve in the Middle East, according to one European observer. It is "something like playing billiards on a small boat in a rough
sea—and each ball with a shifting center of gravity."

President Carter was convinced that the key to a comprehensive
peace in the Middle East was an Arab-Israeli settlement, and in March
1977 he told reporters that the United States sought a general agreement
based on the establishment of fair boundaries and a resolution of the Palestinian issue. Two months later the chances for peace seemed to diminish when the Israelis elected a new government—a coalition regime led
by Menachem Begin as prime minister, a former terrorist who had long
resisted concessions to the Arabs. In the meantime the Carter administration called for a Palestinian homeland, and in October 1977 joined the Soviet Union in a statement admitting to the "legitimate rights of the
Palestinian people." Carter believed that Kissinger's decision to leave out
the Soviets in a Middle East settlement was a mistake because of their influence with the PLO and the Syrians. But Carter's new line of action
with Moscow did not interest either Israel or Egypt.

In November, propects for peace suddenly brightened when Egyptian
President Anwar Sadat took an unprecedented step toward peace: he visited Jerusalem and delivered a worldwide televised speech to the Israeli
Parliament in which he conceded that "Israel has become an established
fact." Optimism seemed justified because the Israelis had earlier proclaimed that if the Arabs dealt with them directly, this would constitute
recognition and Israel would return the territories occupied during the Six
Day War of 1967. Sadat proposed Israeli withdrawal from these lands, followed by the establishment of a Palestinian state derived from the West
Bank and Gaza. In exchange, Egypt would sign a peace treaty assuring
Israel's security and legitimacy as a nation. But there was an ominous
sign: only one other Arab nation showed interest in Sadat's proposal—
Saudi Arabia, an ally of the United States.

The initial optimism faded as Begin announced that he did not favor
the terms. Though willing to withdraw from the Sinai desert, he refused
to concede self-determination to the Palestinians on the West Bank and in
the Gaza Strip. The Israeli army would remain in the West Bank, Gaza,
and the Golan Heights. Begin did not consider the West Bank (which he
called by its Hebrew names Judea and Samaria) to be occupied and now
to be returned. The West Bank was a liberated area, he proclaimed, now
part of Israel along with Gaza. Begin would only agree to postpone the
issue for five years, and then negotiate the final status of the disputed

areas; but many believed that in the meantime he intended to enlarge Israel's control over them by establishing new settlements.

Not surprisingly the talks stalemated. Sadat complained that Begin's proposal would prolong Israeli occupation of the West Bank and Gaza. There could be no separate peace with Israel unless the Palestinians received self-rule and the Israelis withdrew from all Arab areas. To approve Israel's demands, Sadat declared, would make him a traitor, adding to the widespread condemnation of him in the Arab world caused by his visit to Jerusalem.

When the negotiations broke down, Carter intervened. He had hesitated because of diverging American interests in Israeli security and in Arab oil. But fear of Soviet infiltration became decisive. America's involvement in the matter, however, carried a built-in danger: it exposed Washington's differences with Israel on how to achieve peace. Carter argued that Sadat had offered security to Israel and warned Begin that failure to accept would worsen matters. Western Europeans, the president noted, had long called for Arab recognition of Israel in exchange for the evacuation of lands taken in 1967. After reminding the Israelis that only the United States supported them, he called for the implementation of UN Resolution 242, which stipulated "the withdrawal of Israeli armed forces from territories occupied in the recent conflict." To Carter this meant the return of most Arab territories taken in 1967 (with some adjustments for security reasons), the creation of a Palestinian homeland, and the establishment of diplomatic relations between Israel and the Arab states. Begin, however, interpreted the UN resolution to mean that for security reasons Israel had to retain the West Bank and Gaza, and could not permit the establishment of a Palestinian homeland. As for the Old City of Jerusalem, the eastern sector occupied in 1967 and now inhabited by 43,000 Israelis, it was, according to Israeli decree, "one city indivisible, the capital of the State of Israel."

The settlements issue underlined the differences between Israel and the United States. Since 1967 Washington had considered it illegal for Israel to establish settlements in wartime-occupied lands. Carter now criticized the Israelis' efforts to add to them while negotiations were under way. Though Vance termed the new settlements an "obstacle to peace," the Israelis refused to halt the practice, leading the Carter administration to suspect Begin of using the security argument as a guise for annexation. To show dissatisfaction with the Israelis, the White House approved the sale of fighter planes to Israel but also, for the first time, did the same for Egypt and the Saudis. There was still no break in the situation.

Carter, his prestige already low, took a high risk and arranged a meeting between Begin and Sadat at the presidential retreat in Camp David, Maryland. After nearly two weeks of discussions in which Carter worked as a full partner, the negotiators emerged on September 17, 1978, with a general program aimed at completing a formal treaty before Christmas and Israeli withdrawal from Arab territory within three years.

The president had mediated two major settlements: a Framework for Peace in the Middle East, and a Framework for the Conclusion of a Peace Treaty between Egypt and Israel. According to the agreements, there would be "transitional arrangements for the West Bank and Gaza for a period not exceeding five years." To implement "full autonomy to the inhabitants," Israel was to withdraw "as soon as a self-governing authority has been freely elected by the inhabitants of these areas." Thus, the full autonomy question was to become the subject of negotiations *after* Egypt and Israel had signed a peace treaty. But the accords contained no resolution to the two most explosive issues between the antagonists: the status of Jerusalem, and whether the Palestinians would win self-rule. It was clear, however, that the PLO was the basis of most Arab-Israeli troubles. Should that organization dominate a Palestinian state in the West Bank and Gaza, it would be in a prime position to launch terrorist attacks on Israeli families. Begin refused to approve PLO participation in either the negotiations or the establishment of a homeland; Sadat hoped that the Israelis would withdraw from the West Bank and Gaza and that the Palestinians there would win a governing voice. The first step, Sadat believed, was Israeli withdrawal from the Sinai settlements; the second was a peace treaty between Israel and Egypt; the third was Israeli withdrawal from the Sinai Peninsula. Sadat counted on Jordan entering the negotiations concerning the West Bank, and he hoped that the Saudis would remain supportive. Most of all, he relied upon America to persuade Israel to accept the terms.

But the Arab states bitterly opposed the settlement because Israel, they believed, would gain too much. A separate peace with the strongest Arab state, Egypt, would assure Israeli security by reducing the likelihood of attack by other Arabs. Israel would retain the West Bank, Gaza, and the Golan Heights, and the Palestinians would never gain self-rule. The Saudis, not willing to stand alone among their Arab neighbors, banded together with Algeria, Iraq, Jordan, Libya, and Syria in denouncing Sadat, virtually isolating him and paradoxically making Israel's position even stronger.

At this crucial point Carter again intervened, this time to visit Egypt and Israel and appeal for the treaty. The strategy worked. Less than a month later, on March 26, 1979, Sadat and Begin signed an agreement at the White House. Anxious moments had developed during the intervening days. Sadat had repeated his demands for Palestinian autonomy in the West Bank, and Begin had declared before his country's Parliament that Israel would not retreat to the 1967 borders, that Jerusalem was Israel's "eternal capital," and that the Palestinians would never get a state in the West Bank or Gaza. Though Begin's speech nearly halted the treaty proceedings, Carter convinced the two leaders to sign.

The Egyptian-Israeli Peace Treaty was only the first step toward a general settlement. According to terms there would be a scaled Israeli withdrawal from the Sinai Peninsula, to be completed in 1982; UN forces

Signing the Egyptian-Israeli Peace Treaty of March 26, 1979

Left to right: Cyrus Vance, Anwar Sadat, Jimmy Carter, and Menachem Begin. (Wide World)

were to supervise the boundary, assisted by American air surveillance; diplomatic and economic relations were established between the countries; there was to be free passage through international waterways; Israel could buy oil from the Sinai after the region was returned to Egypt; and negotiations were to begin on Palestinian rights in the West Bank and Gaza. To smooth potential difficulties the United States repeated its pledges to defend Israel and then furnished $5 billion in economic and military aid to the two countries. Critics complained that the United States had bribed the antagonists, whereas proponents countered that any peace was better than continued fighting. Though Carter hailed the pact as "the first step of peace," it only indirectly touched on Jerusalem, the Golan Heights, and the PLO. He had earlier hoped for a sweeping settlement, and yet his recent approach had adopted Kissinger's call for piecemeal procedures. If the antagonists could first settle the less inflammatory issues, they might build a momentum leading to resolution of the other matters and end three decades of bitter unrest.

The Arab states, however, immediately condemned the Egyptian-Israeli Peace Treaty. Jordan's King Saddam Hussein denounced the pact as a "dead horse" because it did not guarantee a Palestinian homeland. Israel's policies, the Arabs contended, were annexationist. The Arab

League expelled Egypt and imposed an economic boycott, while most of the Arab states severed diplomatic relations with Egypt. Israel did not ease the situation. It soon announced the establishment of new settlements in the West Bank, prepared to take additional land from the large number of Arabs in the region, staunchly refused self-determination to the Palestinians, and intensified military measures against the PLO.

The United States nonetheless praised the treaty, even though one of its major allies in the Middle East, Saudi Arabia, had moved deeper into the Arab camp. The Saudis held a quarter of the world's known oil reserves and were pro-West and anticommunist, but they could not support the treaty because it contained no Israeli concessions on the Old City of Jerusalem and failed to provide political autonomy for Palestinians. The Saudis were small in population and depended upon an outside labor force to modernize their country, and the result was that numerous foreigners lived in Saudi Arabia, many of them Palestinians or other Arabs. The Saudis did not want to break with Egypt, nor did they seek to loosen ties with the United States. But they had to avoid charges of treason by fellow Arab states. The Egyptian-Israeli Peace Treaty had shaken the Saudis' faith in American policies, making it questionable whether the pact achieved much if anything.

DECLINING SOVIET–AMERICAN RELATIONS

For several reasons, Soviet-American relations markedly deteriorated throughout 1979. Economically, the Soviets were in trouble. Though leading the United States in the production of cement, coal, oil, and steel, they had added to their own problems by investing too much in Cuba and Vietnam as well as in military improvements, none of which brought profitable returns. Much of the Soviets' land was suited for agriculture, but the process of collectivization had not yielded sufficient food. In fact, nearly half of the Soviet Union's farm products came from privately owned concerns which comprised only 3 percent of the country's agricultural area. Soviet industry meanwhile demonstrated little innovation, and in technology lagged behind the United States, West Germany, and Japan. The Soviets also suffered from an inefficient and poorly managed labor force, as well as from ethnic divisions obstructing the integration of workers outside Greater Russia. Furthermore, a drop in the birth rate during the 1950s and 1960s caused a dip in the size of the labor force by the 1980s. Finally, projections were that the Soviets might have to import oil before the decade was over. Outside the country, problems with China threatened to worsen because of the change in leadership in Beijing, the closer ties between China and Japan, and the imminent establishment of formal diplomatic relations between the United States and China. The Carter administration tried to exploit Moscow's troubles. After the early setbacks in the SALT talks in Moscow, the White House criticized Soviet activities in Africa, implied that American arms sales to China were possible, and warned that Soviet military actions in Eastern Europe would encourage a buildup of NATO.

The Soviets' central concern was the establishment of Sino-American relations. Shortly after Carter's inauguration the United States moved toward completing the process begun by Nixon's visit to China in 1972. Liaison officers had been established soon after the initial contact, and Carter now sought to remove final obstacles. In April 1977 a congressional delegation traveled to China accompanied by the president's son, and in late August Vance visited Beijing to talk with Vice-Premier Deng Xiaoping. Over a year later President Carter announced in a televised speech that the two nations would "establish diplomatic relations" on January 1, 1979. According to the joint communiqué of December 15, 1978, the United States severed relations with Taiwan, agreed to withdraw "its remaining military personnel [about 700 men] from Taiwan within four months," and served the required one-year notice of terminating the Mutual Defense Treaty of 1954 with Taiwan. Though the communiqué asserted that Taiwan was "part of China," the United States maintained "cultural, commercial, and other official relations with the people of Taiwan." The Taiwanese accused the United States of breaking commitments, and right-wing Americans joined a few congressional members in expressing anger over the move, but on January 1, 1979, the United States and the People's Republic of China exchanged ambassadors and announced formal relations.

The establishment of Sino-American relations had many repercussions. Washington's decision must have raised doubts among allies about its commitments and resolve, especially after the outcome in Vietnam in 1975. But Carter emphasized the commercial possibilities and the potential impact of recognition on easing the situation in East Asia. There already seemed to be proof of the latter claim. In December 1978 Vietnamese communist forces invaded Kampuchea (formerly Cambodia) to depose Pol Pot, leader of a repressive communist regime that favored China. The following February Chinese forces invaded upper Vietnam, and even though the Pentagon and other Americans wanted the United States to act, Carter refused. After the Chinese administered what they called "punishment" to the Vietnamese, they withdrew. In the meantime the Soviets had signed an amity treaty with the Vietnamese, demanded an earlier Chinese pullout, and threatened to take military action. The crisis passed without a confrontation, but the Soviet threats aroused more American skepticism about the SALT talks and increased the call for an arms buildup.

The establishment of Sino-American diplomatic relations, along with the Soviet desire to avoid a costly arms race and curb America's development of new weapons, promoted the signing of SALT II in Vienna in June 1979. The treaty established equality in the total number of strategic nuclear delivery missiles by permitting each nation to have 2,400 long-range missiles and bombers, to be cut to 2,250 by 1981. It also set MIRVed ballistic missiles (ICBMs and SLBMs) at a maximum of 1,200, established maximum warhead figures for other launchers, drew up verification procedures, and made clear that SALT III would focus on reducing nuclear stockpiles. The United States secured advantages from the treaty in that the Soviets would have to cut back on 250 delivery vehicles already in existence, whereas the United States could add to its supply of 2,060. Furthermore, the Soviets failed to halt America's development of the MX (missile experimental), a mobile missile capable of carrying ten MIRVs and designed to move ICBMs through a maze of underground tunnels, in an effort to confuse Moscow on their location. Despite Carter's campaign assurances of arms cutbacks, he approved the MX—at nearly $30 billion in cost. SALT II also placed no restrictions on the cruise missile and on the Trident-II SLBM, able to carry fourteen warheads. The Americans, however, were unable to halt Soviet development of the supersonic bomber called the Backfire.

Widespread disagreement was evident inside the United States over the wisdom of SALT II. Some Americans warned that the maximum limits were too high and sought to link the pact with Soviet behavior elsewhere. Many did not trust Moscow and argued that verification was impossible, whereas others accused Carter of appeasement and endangering American security. Still others wondered whether the MX might not cause an arms race. At tremendous costs in dollars and in environmental damage, they declared, the MX would not even be ready until 1990. It seemed wise to continue negotiations aimed at establishing more controls. The president countered that SALT II would stem the Soviets' buildup and benefit the United States because restrictions on its own program were less prohibitive. He added that America's ICBMs were not highly susceptible to destruction because the Soviets were unlikely to achieve the extreme accuracy and timing vital to attack. Besides, the United States would have a twenty-minute warning and could move the ICBMs from their silos to places of safety. Other than land-based ICBMs, Carter noted, the remaining 70 percent of the triad strategic system—the SLBMs and big bombers—would be intact and ready for a counterstrike.

While the national debate went on over SALT II, its approval seemed to be in more jeopardy when the Carter administration announced in the summer of 1979 that American intelligence sources had discovered a Soviet brigade of 2,500 combat troops in Cuba. White House spokesmen asserted that until the Soviet soldiers withdrew from the island, ratification of SALT II was out of the question. The *"status quo* was not acceptable," the president insisted. Moscow argued that the soldiers had been on the island for years solely to train Cubans. Furthermore, it accused Carter of publicizing the matter at a particularly opportune time—when his reelection possibilities were down and he needed an issue.

Whether or not the president had acted too hastily in an effort to rebuild his image, the outcome was damaging both to his prestige and to SALT II. The chairman of the Senate Foreign Relations Committee, Frank

Church, postponed hearings on SALT II and noted that approval was doubtful until the Soviet troops left Cuba. In the meantime it became evident that the Soviet forces were not going to leave, and Carter had no choice but to accept the status quo that he had earlier found objectionable. To save SALT II, he told the American people that "I have concluded that the brigade issue is certainly no reason for a return to the Cold War." The Cuban episode fell from America's attention as the focus of trouble dramatically shifted again to the Middle East.

THE HOSTAGE CRISIS IN IRAN

On November 4, 1979, 400 student militants in Iran stormed into the American embassy in Teheran, seizing sixty-six American diplomats and military personnel as hostages and causing a crisis that staggered the Carter presidency. Americans' frustrations over recent foreign policy failures seemed to culminate in this national humiliation, which *The New York Times* called "a metaphor for American decline." Though most Americans were shocked that Iran would permit such an act, the truth is that relations between the countries had long been in trouble.

By the time Carter became president, Iran had become vital to America's strategic and economic interests in the Middle East. Besides lying just south of the Soviet Union, Iran was second only to the Saudis in oil

The Shah of Iran and President Nixon, October 23, 1969

American assistance to Iran greatly increased during the Nixon administration. Here, President Nixon and the shah shake hands in the Rose Garden by the South Lawn of the White House. Secretary of State William Rogers stands to the president's left. (U.S. Army)

production among noncommunist countries. Over the years the CIA had installed listening devices along the Iranian-Soviet border, designed to detect Soviet nuclear and military activity. To solidify America's ties with Iran, Carter visited Teheran in late 1977 and on New Year's Eve toasted the country as "an island of stability" and praised Shah Mohammed Riza Pahlavi as deserving "the respect and the admiration and love which your people give to you." The Iranian people, however, had an intense hatred for the shah that was magnified by the American aid he continued to receive after the CIA helped his return to power in the early 1950s. Fundamentalist Muslims were appalled by the shah's efforts to improve the place of women in society and to import Western life-styles into Iran; youths detested the absence of civil liberties and wanted a constitutional government; merchants, landowners, and young laborers opposed the shah's "white revolution" that had allegedly modernized the economy. Ethnic rivalries, serious economic problems, and terrorist actions by the secret police (called SAVAK) added to the growing resentment, which was capitalized by foreigners holding good jobs in Iran and the government spending tremendous sums of money on weaponry from the United States that could have gone to help the Iranian people. Some observers argued that the shah's arms purchases alienated more of his subjects than any other act.

Despite Carter's glowing praise for the shah, America's relations with Iran were uneasy. The shah complained that he was not getting enough military aid, and he bought a nuclear reactor from France after the United States turned him down. By the mid-1970s Americans were unhappy that Iran had joined other OPEC nations in raising the price of oil, and in 1976 Congress protested when the Ford administration sold fighter planes to the shah. Thus Carter's adulation for the shah was the result of poor American intelligence sources that were grossly out of touch with reality. SAVAK was hated, the shah was despised, and Iran was on the verge of revolution.

In 1978 violence swept Iran, causing the shah to impose martial law which further fed the revolutionary fervor. Striking groups halted oil production, which hurt the United States, and Carter followed Brzezinski's advice and sent military assistance to the regime. By the end of the year, however, Americans in Iran feared for their lives. In late December the antishah forces had become too powerful to contain. American diplomats in Iran urged the shah to abdicate the throne.

In January 1979 the revolutionaries forced the shah to flee the country, leaving Iran to the victorious Muslims led by their chief religious leader, the Ayatollah Rudollah Khomeini. Eighty-one years old, white-bearded, and in France as part of sixteen years of exile, Khomeini now announced the formation of the Islamic Republic. These events shook Americans' confidence in the Carter administration, for the unexpectedness of the revolution had raised serious questions about both the abilities of intelligence sources in Iran, and the failure of the White House to heed

Ayatollah Khomeini

The Muslims' religious leader who, after the shah's departure, came home from exile in 1979 to proclaim the Islamic Republic of Iran. (Wide World)

warnings. America's ambassador in Iran, William Sullivan, recommended a meeting with Khomeini, but the White House ignored the suggestion and infuriated Sullivan by considering a military coup.

On January 31 Khomeini returned triumphantly to Iran and promptly began criticizing the United States. The new regime, he asserted, would cleanse Iran of the Westernizing and secular influences stemming from the shah's "white revolution." Despite public outcries against the United States, it was evident that the Muslims hated the communists' atheism as much as the West's capitalism and that Sullivan's proposed meeting with the ayatollah had perhaps been worth pursuing. But if an opportune time for negotiations had existed, its hour had passed. The new Iranian regime, a theocracy, lacked governing experience and the country quickly moved to the edge of administrative disintegration. The United States faced the unhappy prospect of having to intervene to safeguard Iranian oil, which Khomeini prepared to cut off from Americans while selling it to Japan and Western Europe. Worse, Marxists were among the antishah groups, causing anxiety in Washington that the Soviets had gained an opening into the Persian Gulf and oil-rich Middle East.

The shah meanwhile traveled from one country to another, not welcome anywhere because of fear of alienating Iran or any Arab state and losing access to the region's oil. Carter had at first invited the shah to the United States, but Vance convinced him to withdraw the offer as it became plain that the United States was the chief source of resentment in Iran. In October 1979, however, the shah was in Mexico, dying of cancer and in need of medical attention. Even though the embassy in Teheran warned that moving the shah to the United States would endanger the lives of Americans in Iran, Carter yielded to the pressure of Brzezinski, David Rockefeller of Chase Manhattan Bank in New York (which had monetary connections with Iran), and Kissinger, whose support the White House valued in securing passage of SALT II. Carter's decision to admit the shah into the country, where he entered a New York hospital, "threw a burning branch into a bucket full of kerosene," according to an embassy worker in Teheran. Two weeks later Iranian students seized the American embassy in Teheran.

The reasons cited for the break-in were many and varied. Khomeini called the embassy a "nest of spies," whereas the militants demanded the shah's wealth and announced that they would free the Americans in exchange for his return to Iran to stand trial for alleged past crimes. Custody of the shah, whom the militants refused to believe was ill, would also prevent his collaboration with the United States in a counterrevolutionary move to regain the throne. Furthermore, taking hostages promoted a diplomatic break with Washington that freed Iran from American domination. Khomeini would be able to exploit anti-American feeling and establish control over the moderates and clerics who had opposed him in the revolution. Whatever the reasons for taking the embassy, it was the first time that diplomats had not been granted immunity in times of trouble. Americans were shocked to see televised coverage of huge crowds of angry Iranians calling the United States the "Great Satan" and yelling "Death to America." They were more appalled to see American hostages blindfolded and apparently undergoing unspeakable treatment by their captors. In television interviews Khomeini and others denounced America's longtime support for the shah and criticized the American naval presence in the Indian Ocean. The ayatollah even accused the United States of planning an assault on the ancient Muslim religious city of Mecca, which set off anti-American demonstrations in Muslim areas stretching from the Middle East to the Philippines, and resulted in the deaths of two Americans in Pakistan.

The Carter administration's reaction to the hostage crisis was a confused mixture of shock and dismay that critics claimed was symbolic of America's declining position in the world. No nation commanding the respect of others could permit such a dastardly act to occur, Americans indignantly complained. Yet as Carter later lamented, the seizure revealed "the same kind of impotence that a powerful person feels when his child is kidnapped." American honor, commitment, and the certainty of execu-

Iranian Hostage Crisis

The U.S. Embassy compound in Teheran as Iranians release some American hostages.
(Wide World)

tion dictated that the president could not send the shah home. Besides, the shah had entered the United States legally, and Carter had no legal right either to deport him or to confiscate his wealth. Nor would the United States apologize for past policies toward Iran and allow a UN investigation of its conduct in those matters. Though many Americans demanded military action to free the hostages, the White House realized that such a course could lead to their deaths, stir more Muslim violence against Americans throughout the Middle East, and cause a war beneficial only to the Soviets.

The United States's initial response was a series of steadily escalating pressures on Iran that failed to force its government to intervene and secure the release of the hostages. First, the visas of 50,000 Iranian students in the United States would undergo examination; those not enrolled in school would be sent home. This approach, however, proved slow and cumbersome because it necessitated deliberation through the courts. Second, the United States froze nearly $8 billion of Iranian assets inside the country. Third, the Carter administration covertly enlisted the aid of PLO leader Yasir Arafat, who convinced the Iranian regime to free thirteen of the hostages, mostly female and black. Fourth, the United States sought the assistance of other nations and private individuals in securing the freedom of the remaining fifty-three. Fifth, it worked through the UN and the International Court of Justice in calling for the hostages' release. Nothing worked. On April 7, 1980, in seeming desperation, the United States broke diplomatic relations with Iran and imposed an economic embargo. These measures likewise had little effect. Western Europe and Japan needed Iranian oil and refused to join the embargo, and by the spring of that year the Iranian cutoff of oil to the United States had led to a 130 percent price rise that resulted in heightened American inflation and unemployment. In the meantime the shah left the United States for Panama in late 1979, and negotiations with the Iranians never got under way. A stable government did not emerge from the revolution, as the Carter administration had hoped, and Khomeini, whether he refused to free the hostages or had no choice, did not intervene in their behalf.

On April 24, 1980, the Carter administration made a daring rescue attempt that ended in a humiliating failure and further underlined the helplessness of the United States. Vance had objected to the idea. Casualties would be certain, he warned, and even if successful, the Iranians could seize other Americans. The president nonetheless directed the Joint Chiefs of Staff to organize a rescue mission. Eight helicopters embarked from the U.S.S. *Nimitz*, a carrier then based in the Arabian Sea, while six C-130 Hercules transports left their Middle East base, both military teams eluding radar detection and heading for a rendezvous in the Iranian desert south of Teheran. The plan called for marine commandos to make their way into the embassy and free the hostages. But everything went wrong. Two helicopters broke down before reaching the desert, and a third developed engine trouble at the meeting place. By now frustrated and disappointed with the initial stages of the operation, Carter called it off. In a final tragic embarrassment one of the C-130s, while in rapid night departure, hit a helicopter in a sandstorm, killing eight crewmen.

Over television the following morning Carter informed the American people of the abortive rescue expedition, his tone suggesting that the administration had recognized that the hostage crisis would last until the Iranians brought it to an end. The hostages were now separated and relocated in different hiding places, making it nearly impossible to consider another rescue attempt, and Khomeini warned that the cost of another such operation would be the hostages' deaths. In the meantime Vance quietly resigned from the administration, partly because of the rescue fiasco but also because of growing dissatisfaction with worsening relations with the Soviet Union. SALT II seemed dead, and the United States and its allies were drifting farther apart. The Carter administration, mired in a crisis over which it had no control, underwent criticism from those Americans who believed it had gone too far in a rescue effort that could have led to the deaths of the hostages, as well as from those Americans exasperated that the president seemed too squeamish to take the hard military actions called for in such a situation. In the meantime another issue arose that took over the front pages of America's newspapers: Soviet military forces invaded Afghanistan in December of 1979 and by the following spring were locked in battle with Afghan resistance groups.

LAST DAYS: CRISIS IN AFGHANISTAN, RESURGENCE OF COLD WAR, AND THE SETTLEMENT OF THE IRANIAN HOSTAGE CRISIS

The Soviets' military invasion of Afghanistan had its roots in a coup of 1978, when they established a Marxist regime that soon began to cave in because of assaults from Muslim rebels unhappy with its antireligious emphasis. Islamic teachings in Iran and Pakistan might sweep across Afghanistan and into the Soviet Union, Moscow seemed to fear. The growing crisis attracted America's attention because Afghanistan bordered China, Iran, and Pakistan, the last of which fluctuated in and out of Washington's graces. Though Afghan revolutionary forces became stronger in 1979, the Soviets at first hesitated to make a military move. There was the imminent possibility of a successor problem in Moscow: Brezhnev was seventy-three years of age and in ill health. The Soviets also were concerned about the effect that military intervention would have on SALT II. But Afghanistan posed such a serious problem to the Soviets that during the Christmas holidays of 1979 the Afghans' Marxist leader was assassinated and a new government installed; two days later, on December 29, 30,000 Red Army troops rolled into the country. Within six months the Soviets had established an occupation force of 100,000 troops. Soviet dissidents at home were imprisoned, including Andrei Sakharov, Nobel Prize–winning physicist who led the human rights movement inside the Soviet Union. Soon the regime in Moscow resurrected the Brezhnev Doctrine, announced after the Soviet military invasion of Czechoslovakia in 1968, which defended the use of force in halting any "deviation from socialism" in Marxist states. The Soviets had used similar tactics in Hungary, but this was the first time they had done so outside Eastern Europe.

The Soviet invasion of Afghanistan shattered the Carter administration's illusions about détente, leading it to adopt stringent measures that succeeded only in again calling attention to America's diminished influence on world events. The act, Carter admitted, had "made a more dramatic change in my opinion of what the Soviets' ultimate goals are than anything they've done in the previous time I've been in office." The Afghanistan invasion appeared to be a "steppingstone to their possible control over much of the world's oil supplies"—including those of Iran's. Brzezinski's hardline, anti-Soviet stance won instant credibility in the White House as Vance lost influence and, as mentioned earlier, soon departed the administration. Carter meanwhile took several courses of action that were more shadow than substance, but that the American people at first favored. He withdrew the SALT II treaty from the Senate and broadened commercial, financial, and military ties with China; cut off sales of grain (which hurt American farmers) and high technology items to the Soviet Union; restricted Soviet fishing rights in American waters and temporarily suspended the opening of new consulates in the United States; sent more arms to Pakistan and approved covert CIA help to the Afghan rebels; supported the establishment of a Rapid Deployment Force to be ready for immediate action in time of crisis; asked Congress to require registration of both men and women for a possible draft; and, in one of the most controversial moves of the time, called for a boycott of the Olympic Games scheduled in Moscow that summer of 1980.

The president's most provocative action was his proclamation of the Carter Doctrine, which revived memories of the Cold War by warning the Soviets to halt their expansion into the Middle East. In his State of the Union address of January 24, 1980, the president warned that "an attempt by any outside force to gain control of the Persian Gulf region will be regarded as an assault on the vital interests of the United States of America, and such an assault will be repelled by use of any means necessary, including military force." Carter declared that the Soviet invasion of Afghanistan threatened the Persian Gulf–Indian Ocean oil supply line, and asserted that the United States would act alone if necessary to protect Middle East oil from Soviet takeover. Thus the administration broke with the Nixon Doctrine, which had called for partnership, in preference to the unilateral approach inherent in the Truman and Eisenhower Doctrines. The United States appeared ready to contain the Soviets by establishing military strongholds in the Indian Ocean, East Africa, and the Middle East.

The Soviet Union must have expected that its invasion of Afghanistan would end hopes for SALT II. Carter warned Brezhnev over the hot line that the Soviet action constituted the most serious threat to world peace since 1945. About a third of America's oil came from the Persian Gulf, but even more important, Western Europe and Japan received the overwhelming bulk of their supplies from that region. The Soviet move, according to Washington officials in a statement reminiscent of the early Cold War, was part of a concerted effort to take over the region. Thus again, regional and national issues threatened to become pawns of big power confrontation.

The Carter administration's reaction to the Afghan crisis was undercut by resistance from allies who refused to support either an economic embargo on the Soviet Union or the Olympic boycott. West Germany and Japan had heavy trade with Moscow and Eastern Europe, and argued that Soviet military action had been predictable because no country could permit trouble along its borders. The Afghan invasion was a localized matter, they insisted. West German Chancellor Helmut Schmidt told *The New York Times* that he opposed "nervousness, war cries, or excited or provocative speeches." The reaction by America's allies in Western Europe was understandable: they were vulnerable to military retaliation by having agreed to allow the United States to deploy nearly 600 Intermediate-

Range Ballistic Missiles (IRBMs) aimed at the Soviet Union. Despite American pressures, European defense allotments had remained distressingly low. Inflation and economic problems were also important considerations, but the fact was that, above all, the Europeans sought to avert a confrontation with the Soviets.

The Carter administration encountered other obstacles. The president had not consulted Congress before announcing his "doctrine." Many Americans chastised him for resurrecting the domino theory, when they believed the Soviets were merely trying to bolster a friendly regime. Others warned that Carter had needlessly revived the Cold War by attempting to force the Persian Gulf states to choose between East and West. Some wanted the White House to pull back and allow Moscow to expend itself in a guerrilla war in Afghanistan that they termed "Russia's Vietnam." Argentina and Brazil took advantage of America's grain embargo to increase their sales to the Soviet Union. Pakistan complained that America's military aid offer was too low, while Saudi Arabia turned down America's request for bases. Furthermore, numerous countries ignored Carter's call for an Olympic boycott and prepared to participate in the games, and the director of the international committee, Lord Killanin, denounced the United States for using athletes "as pawns in political problems that politicians cannot solve themselves." One White House official admitted that the Carter Doctrine had resulted from demands for a presidential statement on the matter, not from a careful assessment of the Middle East situation.

While Carter's policies toward the Afghan crisis settled into failure, several events combined to force a resolution of the Iranian hostage question. First, in July 1980 the shah died in Egypt after having moved there from Panama, thus eliminating the most inflammatory issue between the United States and Iran. Second, the Islamic followers of Khomeini won control over the Iranian Parliament, making the hostages no longer vital to his political fortunes. Third, war had broken out between Iraq and Iran in September 1980, leaving Iran with little outside help, hardly any money, and virtually no income from oil sales after someone sabotaged the pipeline. In addition, Iran fought with American-made planes and tanks and no longer had a source for replacement parts. For the first time America's economic pressures were having an effect, in particular the freeze on Iranian funds in American banks. Fourth, Republican Ronald Reagan, a hardliner who had blasted the Iranians as "barbarians" and "kidnappers," had defeated Carter's bid for reelection to the presidency. Military force to free the hostages, it seemed, was likely after Reagan's inauguration on January 20, 1981.

Numerous signs in the United States had pointed toward a Republican victory in 1980. Many Americans had attributed the country's decline in prestige to the Carter administration. Four years of retreat capitalized by the hostage crisis, they lamented, had underlined the world's lack of respect for the United States. In fairness to Carter, most Americans were unaware of the unalterable changes forcing the United States out of its position in 1945 of unquestioned unilateral world leadership into that of increased cooperation with allies. But whereas the Nixon and Ford administrations had acted in accordance with the new forced guidelines in foreign policy, Carter only briefly adhered to them before wandering into threatening policies that were virtually incapable of enforcement. After initially accepting the new limitations on America's policies, he wavered back and forth between the stances advocated by Vance and Brzezinski until chronic internal division led to frustration and finally the declaration of a hardline position that had little chance for success.

During the spring of 1980 the president's human rights efforts aroused anger among Americans, particularly in Florida, when he welcomed Cuban refugees into the country. Castro had permitted dissident Cubans to leave the island if they secured visas from Peru, and as thousands pushed into the Peruvian embassy and Carter threw open the doors to America, Castro announced that Cubans could leave the island by boat. Soon a "freedom flotilla" of 100,000 Cubans flocked into the United States, creating havoc and riots at processing and detention centers, and posing economic problems to a country already burdened with inflation, unemployment, and lengthening welfare rolls. As Castro emptied Cuba's jails, Miami's mayor moaned that "Fidel has flushed his toilet on us."

Reagan exploited Carter's decline in popularity by pointing to contradictions and inconsistencies in policy. Despite Carter's campaign assurances in 1976, he did not cut back on America's forces overseas, nor did he order military withdrawal from South Korea (partly because of revelations of bribes of congressional members by South Koreans), abide by nuclear nonproliferation, scale down military expenditures, or reduce foreign arms sales. On the human rights issue, the administration was not uniformly critical of allies along with the Soviet Union, and it sold arms to repressive regimes. Inflation and the faltering economy, Reagan charged, were attributable to Democratic fiscal and bureaucratic maladministration. The United States had to adopt a hardline, consistent policy toward the Soviet Union. Carter, Reagan declared, had contributed to the declining respect for America. It was time to expand America's military forces to counter the Soviet Union's global "game of dominoes." Though Carter's popularity had briefly surged upward after his initial Iranian and Afghan policies, it lasted only long enough to contribute to victories in the primaries. With the resolution of these and other difficulties nowhere in sight, Americans elected Reagan to the presidency by a wide margin, and awarded the Senate to the Republicans. Carter's defeat, in a bitter twist of fate, took place on the first anniversary of the hostage crisis.

As a final epitaph to the Carter administration, it was unable to claim fair credit for gaining the release of the hostages in Iran. On January 19, 1981, the day before Reagan's inauguration, Algerian mediators secured an agreement freeing the Americans in exchange for the release of frozen

Iranian assets in the United States. The following day, moments after Reagan took the presidential oath, the Iranians, in a calculated final insult to Carter, freed the final fifty-two hostages (one had been freed for health reasons), after 444 days in captivity. In retrospect, Carter perhaps should have downplayed the hostage issue at its beginning and dealt with it through quiet diplomatic channels, but television and newspaper publicity stirred a national sense of indignation that demanded an immediate resolution that the administration found impossible to achieve. Suspicions of permanent physical injury to the hostages or sexual violations by the Iranian captors were unfounded, but there were mock executions, some instances of solitary confinement, and more than a few cases of physical abuse. The daily insults by Iranian mobs, combined with the continued berating of the Carter administration at home, added to the mood of frustration that helped sweep out the Democrats in 1980.

Selected readings

Ambrose, Stephen E., *Rise to Globalism: American Foreign Policy Since 1938*. 4th ed. 1985.

Bradsher, Henry S., *Afghanistan: Soviet Invasion and U.S. Response*. 1981.

Brezezinski, Zbigniew, *Power and Principle*. 1983.

Carter, Jimmy, *Keeping the Faith*. 1982.

Cornelius, Wayne, *Building the Cactus Curtain*. 1980.

Diederich, Bernard, *Somoza and the Legacy of U.S. Involvement in Central America*. 1981.

Dupree, Louis, *Afghanistan*. 1978.

Erb, Richard D., and Stanley R. Ross, *United States Relations with Mexico*. 1981.

Gaddis, John L., *Strategies of Containment: A Critical Appraisal of Postwar United States National Security Policy*. 1982.

Gaushon, Arthur, *Crisis in Africa*. 1981.

Grayson, George W., *The Politics of Mexican Oil*. 1981.

Halliday, Fred, *Iran: Dictatorship and Development*. 1979.

Hansen, Roger D., *Beyond the North-South Stalemate*. 1979.

Hellmann, John, *American Myth and the Legacy of Vietnam*. 1986.

Hogan, Michael J., *The Panama Canal in American Politics: Domestic Advocacy and the Evolution of Policy*. 1986.

Ismael, Tareq Y., *Iraq and Iran: Roots of Conflict*. 1982.

Jabber, Paul, *Not By War Alone: Security and Arms Control in the Middle East*. 1981.

Khalid, Walid, *Conflict and Violence in Lebanon*. 1980.

LaFeber, Walter, *America, Russia, and the Cold War, 1945–1984*. 5th ed. 1985.

———, *The Panama Canal: The Crisis in Historical Perspective*. 1978. Expanded ed. 1979.

Ledeen, Michael, and William Lewis, *Debacle: The American Failure in Iran.* 1981.

Lenczowski, George, *The Middle East in World Affairs.* 1980.

McLellan, David S., *Cyrus Vance.* 1985.

Newell, Nancy P., and Richard S. Newell, *The Struggle for Afghanistan.* 1981.

Payne, Samuel, Jr., *The Soviet Union and SALT.* 1980.

Pierre, Andrew J., *The Global Politics of Arms Sales.* 1982.

Rotberg, Robert I., *Suffer the Future: Policy Choices in Southern Africa.* 1980.

Rubin, Barry, *Paved with Good Intentions: The American Experience and Iran.* 1980.

Ryan, P. B., *The Panama Canal Controversy.* 1977.

Saikal, Amin, *The Rise and Fall of the Shah.* 1980.

Schoultz, Lars, *Human Rights and United States Policy toward Latin America.* 1981.

Sick, Gary, *All Fall Down: America's Tragic Encounter with Iran.* 1985.

Smith, Gaddis, *Morality, Reason, and Power: American Diplomacy in the Carter Years.* 1986.

Smith, Peter H., *Mexico: The Quest for a U.S. Policy.* 1980.

Spanier, John W., *American Foreign Policy Since World War II.* 9th ed. 1983.

Spiegel, Steven L., *The Other Arab-Israeli Conflict: Making America's Middle East Policy, from Truman to Reagan.* 1985.

Stempel, John D., *Inside the Iranian Revolution.* 1981.

Stevenson, Richard W., *The Rise and Fall of Détente: Relaxations of Tensions in US-Soviet Relations, 1953–84.* 1985.

Talbott, Strobe, *Endgame: The Inside Story of SALT II.* 1979.

Vance, Cyrus, *Hard Choices.* 1983.

Vogelgesang, Sandy, *American Dream, Global Nightmare: The Dilemma of U.S. Human Rights Policy.* 1980.

Walker, Thomas W., *Nicaragua: The Land of Sandino.* 1982.

Wolfe, Thomas W., *The SALT Experience.* 1979.

Wolpert, Stanley, *Roots of Confrontation in South Asia: Afghanistan, Pakistan, India, and the Superpowers.* 1982.

Chapter Twenty-Six

Cold War II: Reagan and the Revival of Containment, 1981–

As the nearly seventy-year-old former Hollywood actor and California governor assumed the presidency, Ronald Reagan pronounced an end to the "era of self-doubt" and called on Americans to reassert the nation's "ideals and interests" throughout the world. In a speech reminiscent of Kennedy's 1961 call for a New Frontier, President Reagan warned of a missile gap, emphasized the lines of bipolarity, and revived the rhetoric of containment. The Soviets, he declared at an early press conference, were "prepared to commit any crime, to lie, to cheat." They were the basis of "all the unrest going on. If they weren't engaged in this game of dominoes, there wouldn't be any hot spots in the world." Americans' disillusionment with détente, he charged, was complete.

The Reagan administration's anticommunist, anti-Soviet thrusts ensured a dramatic upsurge of Cold War tensions, making negotiations secondary to a buildup of America's strategic and conventional military forces. Though numerous critics agreed with George F. Kennan that the president's assessment of Soviet behavior was a sign of "intellectual primitivism," Reagan pointed out that the Soviets had surpassed the United States in ICBMs, SLBMs, and megatonnage (total explosive force carried as warheads). Furthermore, the Soviets could soon forge ahead in numbers and size of the warheads. Skeptics sharply disagreed with the new president and argued that a general nuclear balance existed between the superpowers. Soviet production costs were higher than those of the United States, giving the misleading impression that Moscow's greater military expenditures meant military superiority. Moreover, they added,

President Ronald Reagan at His Desk in Oval Office of White House

Calling the war in Vietnam a "noble cause," he attempted to heal divisiveness by restoring faith in America at home and respect for the nation abroad. (Wide World)

Reagan's evaluation did not take into account NATO defense expenditures, nor did it allow for the proportion of Soviet strength directed at China. Reagan nonetheless called for the largest peacetime defense budget in the country's history, and asserted that America's priority had to go toward safeguarding its Minuteman land-based ICBMs and its B-52 bombers. He also approved massive arms sales around the world. Americans, he declared, had to discard their "no more Vietnams" syndrome and recognize that their effort in Vietnam had been "a noble cause." Reagan's foreign policy forecasted an adversary relationship with Moscow and signaled a heightening of the Cold War. The new administration, some observed, had accepted the challenges of Cold War II.

Despite the new president's intention to restore firmness to foreign policy, the effectiveness of his administration, like that of his predecessor's, was impeded by internal division. Reagan's secretary of state, General Alexander Haig, was the most outspoken member of the new administration, and soon found himself at odds with many of his colleagues, including Secretary of Defense Caspar Weinberger, who like Haig had served in the Nixon presidency and was likewise forthright in views. Haig competed for control of foreign policy with National Security Adviser Richard Allen, who also was a staunch anti-Soviet but soon left

The Vietnam Memorial in Washington, D.C.

On May 28, 1984, veterans form an unofficial color guard at the Vietnam Veterans' Memorial on the day of the state funeral for the Unknown Serviceman of the Vietnam Era. (U.S. Army)

the White House after being charged with using his office for personal gain. Haig was almost obsessed with the Soviets' recent military buildup and growing first-strike capacity, and sought to enhance America's deterrent strength by adding extensively to its strategic and conventional forces. Moscow, he charged, sought influence in the Third World by using proxies such as the Vietnamese in Kampuchea (Cambodia) and the Cubans in Africa, and by supporting a growing band of international terrorists who had connections with the PLO. In an argument consistent with Kennan's analysis of Soviet behavior during the Cold War 1940s, Haig attributed the Soviets' increasingly aggressive foreign policy to rising internal problems. But in a stance not in accordance with that of Kennan's, Haig insisted that America had to contain the Soviets through a major military buildup. He concluded that "there are more important things than peace. . . . There are things which we Americans must be willing to fight for."

By the summer of 1982 Haig had resigned as secretary of state, with the office then going to George Shultz, whose "team player" reputation and calm demeanor exemplified a White House effort to close the breach in the administration's foreign policymaking apparatus. Haig, mercurial in temperament and accused of being a power seeker (critics tagged him CINCWORLD, or "Commander in Chief of the World"), failed in a widely publicized effort to mediate a dispute between the United Kingdom and Argentina over the sovereignty of the Falkland Islands in the South Atlantic. After several reported clashes with other administration members, he departed in June following a disagreement with the president over policies in Europe and the Middle East. Shultz, who had a background in business and economics and a Ph.D. from the Massachusetts Institute of Technology, was also concerned about Soviet expansion, but he was not as brusque and impatient as Haig.

THE SEARCH FOR A SOVIET–AMERICAN ARMS AGREEMENT

To deal from a position of strength, the Reagan administration postponed the SALT talks and made several proposals designed to expand the nation's strategic force. Rejecting an arms freeze, the president called for the development of the MX, as Carter had done. Some of the new missiles, Reagan declared, would be located in old Minuteman ICBM silos in Wyoming and Nebraska; the others would await further decision. Congress rejected this plan on the basis that it would make the MX as vulnerable as the Minuteman. Reagan also proposed the "dense pack plan," which would deploy a hundred MIRVed MX missiles in a fifteen-square-mile area in Wyoming, on the theory that onrushing Soviet attack missiles would enter the small air space above the MXs and destroy each other. Congress likewise rejected this plan. As an option to the controversial MX, Reagan supported the development of a new single-warhead mobile missile which was dubbed "Midgetman" and would be distributed over a wide area to assure its safety against attack. He also ordered a hundred B-1 bombers to be ready by 1986 (revoking their cancellation by Carter), even though experts thought the B-1 expensive and the projected "Stealth" bomber, not as susceptible to radar detection, more effective. Finally, Reagan insisted on the production of cruise missiles, despite warnings that their capacity to avoid verification would escalate the arms race by encouraging the Soviets to develop them too.

Arms control attempts during the 1970s, the president argued, had endangered the security of the United States. Their purpose had been to slow the Soviets' growth in numbers while the United States developed more sophisticated strategic weapons—better MIRVs, longer-range SLBMs, and Air Launched Cruise Missiles (ALCMs). But this approach had not worked. Whereas the United States had dutifully restricted its military growth, the Soviet Union had surged dangerously ahead. It was now time to revamp America's military program. Thus the Reagan administration adopted a course of action that would require a long time for success, and that in the meantime was likely to encourage an arms race.

To replace SALT, the Reagan administration in the spring of 1982 introduced the Strategic Arms Reduction Talks (START), aimed at reducing the stockpile of American and Soviet ICBMs and missile warheads. While the START discussions were under way, the United States would add to its military forces. Though both superpowers had for years sought to avert nuclear war by maintaining a strategic balance based upon the concept of MAD, or Mutual Assured Destruction, the danger now was that each power would strive for superiority. The Reagan administration's insistence upon greater military security and additional limitations on Soviet strategic growth raised fears in Moscow about America's motives. But the president countered that the only way to achieve arms reductions by means of START was through an American military buildup intended first to regain Soviet respect.

In an effort to resolve one of Reagan's greatest problems—that of keeping the NATO alliance intact while securing an arms agreement with the Soviet Union—his administration presented a plan known as the zero option. Called for in late 1981 at the Geneva Conference on Intermediate-Range Nuclear Forces (INF), the plan proposed that the United States deploy none of its planned 572 Pershing II and cruise missiles in Western Europe (a NATO decision in December 1979) if the Soviets agreed to dismantle their 613 INFs aimed at Europe. The Kremlin rejected the plan on the grounds that Soviet missiles lacked the range to strike the United States, whereas the new NATO missiles (Euromissiles) could reach the Soviet Union. America's NATO allies complained that the president's proposal would leave them unprotected.

To ward off a dangerous division between the United States and its allies, the president urged an interim solution requiring the Soviet Union to withdraw a large number of its 351 triple-warhead missiles, in exchange for the United States scaling down the number of missiles scheduled to go into Western Europe in December 1983. The United States would put in enough to match the Soviets, warhead for warhead. In mid-April West German Chancellor Helmut Kohl offered some hope when he commented that the president's interim solution provided "a basis for flexible and dynamic negotiations."

Reagan's interim solution drew bitter opposition from the Soviet Union, which sought to promote a NATO division and to prolong arms discussions that would permit the growing antinuclear movement in Europe to gain more momentum. Foreign Minister Andrei Gromyko called a rare news conference in Moscow to reply to the president's proposal. Gromyko declared that Reagan's interim solution was "absurd." If the United States insisted on such a plan, there was "no chance of an agreement" in the INF proceedings in Geneva. Furthermore, it was ridiculous for Reagan to repeat his earlier argument that French and British missiles should not be counted in agreements on warhead limitations in Europe. If an attack took place on the Soviet Union, "Will a French missile have a stamp on it, 'I am French. I was not to be taken into account?' " Should the United States deploy its missiles in Europe, Gromyko darkly warned, the Soviet Union would "take the necessary measures in order to defend its legitimate interests."

In late March 1983 Reagan unveiled a new defense plan that observers predicted could cause a "Star War." To erase the Soviet Union's "margin of superiority," he called for a massive defense budget that would entail the United States giving up deterrence through MAD in favor of a defensive strategy known as SDI, or the Strategic Defense Initiative, which was dependent on satellites to "intercept and destroy" enemy missile attacks by lasers or particle beams. Confrontations in space, he asserted, offered the attractive prospect of sparing the earth from a nuclear holocaust.

Both the Soviet and Western European reactions were sharply negative. Communist Party Leader Yuri Andropov, who had recently succeeded to the position after Brezhnev's death, warned that the plan "would actually open the floodgates of a runaway race of all types of strategic arms, both offensive and defensive." A push for a major missile defense system could upend the basis of peace—the mutual fear of instant retaliation in the event of attack. But Reagan hoped that the new emphasis on defense would lead to a reduction in offensive weapons. Critics warned that the opposite would occur. Should either the United States or the Soviet Union appear ready to deploy an ABM system, the danger would destabilize the situation, encouraging a frantic search for new offensive weaponry by the other superpower and increasing the likelihood of war. Western Europeans denounced what the *Times* of London called "one of the most fundamental switches in American policy since the Second World War." A British colonel complained that the president's plan would lead to "Fortress America," leaving Europeans "out in the cold" because they would no longer pose a nuclear threat to the Soviet Union. Thus the president's message was disturbing because it called for replacing MAD with an "anti-ballistic missile umbrella." Devised to prevent nuclear attack, the new plan threatened to cause an arms race in space that would dangerously destabilize the present balance of nuclear power.

The situation remained uncertain. SALT II was still not ratified, and the ABM Treaty of 1972, the only binding arms-control agreement in existence, was in jeopardy because of the president's new defense recommendations. The ABM Treaty, based on the fear that defensive systems could upset the nuclear balance, assured that "each party undertakes not to develop, test, or deploy ABM systems or components which are sea-based, air-based, space-based, or mobile-land-based." Despite charges that Reagan's plan for a defensive buildup would violate the above provision against space-based ABMs, the White House countered by saying that mere research into such a project did not constitute a treaty violation. In mid-1983 the president and Congress showed interest in a "build-down" strategy, which guaranteed the destruction of a certain number of nuclear weapons for every new one developed. Reagan also leaned toward the recommendation of a bipartisan commission, which warned against the production of MIRVs because their destructive capacity would increase the likelihood of the United States being hit by a first strike. Some critics argued that a proposed reduction in the number of warheads, rather than in the number of missiles, would move the United States closer to the Soviet Union in the START talks.

More than a few observers hoped that a change in Soviet leadership would enhance the possibility of arms reductions. Andropov died after a long illness in early 1984 and was succeeded by Konstantin Chernenko. But he also was elderly and ill and continued the party's rigid control at home and hardline policies abroad. Upon Chernenko's death in March 1985, Mikhail Gorbachev became the Soviet leader. He was considerably younger (in his early fifties) and had dealt with the West in foreign affairs. In November he and Reagan (reelected a year earlier by a wide margin) attended a summit meeting in Geneva, the first since 1979. Though unable to resolve the nuclear deadlock, they agreed to try again. In the spring of 1986, however, the Soviets declared that they would no longer adhere to the SALT II treaty. The following October Reagan and Gorbachev met in Reykjavik, Iceland, where at one point it seemed that they would reach an agreement that would phase out ballistic missiles over the next ten years. Though such a pact would not eliminate nuclear weapons, it would constitute a first step toward arms reduction. But the two men's differences over SDI obstructed any chance for reconciliation. Indeed, some observers have suggested that this meeting was a lost opportunity for a major breakthrough in the arms race, and an indication of the president's growing ineffectiveness. The chilling prophecy made by Winston Churchill some years earlier was still valid: "Safety will be the sturdy child of terror, and survival the twin brother of annihilation."

POLAND

Soviet-American relations had earlier worsened over a workers' upheaval that broke out in Poland in 1980 and threatened the rule of the Polish Communist party. Civil liberties were virtually nonexistent in the country, its economy was staggering, and political leaders had failed to respond to dire shortages of food and other vital commodities, while doing nothing to curb the special privileges accorded to ruling classes. Polish workers had wanted an independent trade union, along with the right to strike. After a series of strikes threatened to upend the government, that body recognized the Solidarity workers' union led by Lech Walesa, which called itself "the authentic voice of the working class" and promised to help other Eastern European workers establish independent unions. But as the communist regime in Poland conceded some of its economic and political power, including the democratization of a few party offices, Solidarity increased demands and attracted support from Catholics and nationalists who hated the Soviets. The organization soon had 10 million members or about a third of the Polish population, which raised questions about whether the Communist party would have to use force to remain in control.

In a series of events strikingly similar to those in Hungary a quarter of a century earlier, Solidarity risked the possibility of a Soviet military crackdown by pushing for a national referendum on the present government and on the country's future military ties with the Soviet Union. Moscow must have considered the use of force. Poland, bordering the Soviet Union and the pathway for numerous past invasions, was more vital to Soviet interests than either Hungary or Czechoslovakia, and certainly more so than Afghanistan. Solidarity's growing successes could set a dangerous example for workers in other Eastern European countries or in the Soviet Union. Yet the Red Army was engaged in a war in Afghanistan, and a military move in Poland could lead to conflict with the Polish army.

From past experience the Soviets recognized the high costs of occupation. A Soviet takeover would raise the question of assuming Poland's huge monetary debt to the West—at a time when the Soviets faced severe economic problems. Moscow must also have worried about how communist regimes elsewhere, including its allies, would have regarded an invasion; and it doubtless was concerned over the reaction by America's Western European allies. Finally, an invasion would have hurt relations with the United States. Reagan might tighten the NATO alliance and secure more military expenditures from Congress. Solidarity, Soviet leaders realized, was not a narrow trade union movement; it was broadly based and well organized. The unrest caused by its activities threatened to have international ramifications.

In December 1981 Polish military and police forces imposed martial law and imprisoned Walesa and other labor leaders. Harsh actions were necessary, Moscow explained, to put down "antisocialistic" and "counterrevolutionary" forces in Poland. Questions arose about whether the Polish government moved first to prevent the Soviet Union from doing so, or if Moscow put pressure on Polish authorities to act. In any case, Washington announced mild sanctions on Poland and the Soviet Union. Neither the United States nor the other Western nations took steps that would have comprised more than token gestures of protest: they did not call in over $25 billion of late debts, nor did the Reagan administration impose a grain embargo—because such a measure would have hurt American farmers. Washington's criticisms of Moscow's policies in Poland won little support from the NATO countries, which refused to take any action that might bring full-scale Soviet intervention in Poland or damage their own trade with the Soviets and their allies. The Reagan administration came to realize what both Presidents Truman and Eisenhower had learned in Cold War I: the United States was unable to determine the direction of events in Eastern Europe because the region lay within the Soviet sphere of influence.

The situation in Poland was still explosive. The government attempted to discredit Solidarity's leadership by outlawing the union and adopting other measures to break the movement, both of which further embittered the Polish population. In June 1983 Polish-born Pope John Paul II visited his homeland, where he arranged a private meeting with Walesa, and then appealed to General Wojciech Jaruzelski to permit Solidarity to exist and to implement the social reforms promised in August 1980. Jaruzelski announced his readiness to end martial law in Poland as soon as the situation "develops successfully." Indeed, in July he did so.

The end of martial law proved beneficial only in appearance. A demonstrator in Warsaw noted: "The new set of laws legalizes the brutality that we have been subject to, while removing the rallying point, martial law, against which people have been protesting." In October 1983 the morale of the workers was given a boost by the announcement that Walesa had won the Nobel Peace Prize for his "determination to solve his country's problems through negotiation and cooperation without resorting to violence." Tension remained, aggravated during the summer of 1985 by a series of government trials of political activists that Walesa called "an escalation of lawlessness."

THE MIDDLE EAST

The most perplexing problem facing the United States continued to be the Middle East. Despite the efforts of the Carter administration, the Egyptian-Israeli Treaty of 1979 had not resolved the region's difficulties. The pact had strengthened Israel's position in the Middle East by alienating Egypt from the other Arab nations, and at the same time it kept the United States in the awkward posture of having to honor commitments to the Israelis while trying to maintain ties with the Saudis and other Arabs because of the need for their oil. As in the 1970s, the Reagan administration followed what seemed to be the only feasible approach: extend military and economic aid to the major antagonists (the Israelis and the Arabs), hoping to maintain a balance of power designed to avert conflict. Thus the Saudis were permitted to buy American tanks and air-to-air missiles for their F-15 fighter planes, which took away Israel's control of the skies. The new sale angered Congress, for the administration had earlier offered pledges against such an act to win congressional support for the original sale of the F-15s. Furthermore, in response to the Saudis' fear of an Iranian assault during Iran's ongoing war with the Saudis' political ally Iraq, the Reagan administration prepared to sell them Sidewinder missiles and five Airborne Warning and Control System planes (AWACS), which were Boeing 707s equipped with huge disk-shaped radar antennas capable of tracking up to 400 aircraft within a radius of 350 miles. The Reagan administration pushed through the hotly debated AWACS sale by a four-vote margin in the Senate.

The Reagan administration's arms sales to Saudi Arabia exacerbated the precarious Middle East situation. Israel was angry with the United

States over the AWACS deal, further undercutting the hopes of the treaty with Egypt. Though Israel reaffirmed its intention to withdraw from the Sinai in April 1982, uncertainty remained. Then, in October 1981, matters became more complicated. Sadat was assassinated by Muslim extremists in the Egyptian army, forcing his successor, Hosni Mubarek, to try to establish credibility at home by affirming that his loyalties to Egypt were more important than the treaty with Israel, and necessitating an effort by his new regime to restore relations with moderate Arab states.

When Begin visited Washington shortly after the AWACS deal, Reagan recommended a policy called "strategic collaboration," which was an attempt to revive the Camp David accords by offering more security assurances to Israel. The administration in Washington hoped that Begin would thus be more open to compromise on the Palestinian issue and would relax resistance to the AWACS agreement. But Begin remained determined to annex the West Bank, and in December he ordered the virtual annexation of the Syrian portion of the Golan Heights by integrating the area into the Israeli administrative and judicial system. When the Reagan administration reacted by suspending the discussions over strategic collaboration, Begin angrily denounced the United States as anti-Semitic and for treating Israel as a "banana republic." Instead of returning to pre-1967 borders in exchange for promises of security, he intended to win the war by strengthening his country's hold on East Jerusalem, the Golan Heights, the West Bank, and Gaza.

Though the central issue in the Middle East remained the Arab-Israeli conflict, the Reagan administration tried to draw the two peoples together by emphasizing the Soviet threat to the region and calling for a "strategic consensus" against Moscow. If the United States could convince the ancient antagonists that a Soviet menace superseded their own difficulties, it might be able to maintain relations with both the Arabs and the Israelis and keep peace in the region. The Reagan administration undertook the formidable tasks of de-emphasizing Arab-Israeli differences and postponing the Palestinian issue, in hopes of shifting the focus to containing the Soviet Union. Success would bring greater security to pro-Western nations, in turn assuring the West an oil supply. The Arab-Israeli issue was not the major obstacle to peace in the Middle East, the Reagan administration argued; the United States had failed in the past to assume leadership and establish respect for its power.

The policy of strategic consensus was a failure. The Reagan administration had attempted to shift attention to the most basic assumption of Cold War containment—that of Soviet-American rivalry—in an effort to supplant the most emotional antagonism in the Middle East; yet not even the Cold War could overshadow Arab-Israeli hostilities. Reagan's critics insisted that the troubles in the Middle East were due primarily to the Arab-Israeli conflict. Israel's major concerns, they argued, were the Palestinians and America's arms sales to the Arabs. The Arab states declared that the Palestinian problem was the central obstacle to a smooth oil flow to the West. Only the establishment of a Palestinian state would ease anti-American sentiment in the Middle East and improve economic and military ties with the United States. Despite the Reagan administration's efforts to inject the Cold War into the Middle East imbroglio, it could not diminish the overwhelming centrality of Arab-Israeli strife.

Lebanon soon became the focal point of another Middle East crisis. Located north of Israel on the eastern side of the Mediterranean, Lebanon had recently been rocked by a civil war between Christians and Muslims. The Christians, more powerful than the Muslims, had demanded restrictions on the Palestinians in Lebanon, who had grown in number after their forced departure from Jordan during the early 1970s. The Palestinians now posed a threat to Lebanon because they were armed and therefore attractive to left-wing Muslim militants who sought PLO help. Should war result between Israel and a Muslim-controlled Lebanon, neighboring Syria would have to become involved. Syria considered it imperative to keep Lebanon intact, first by mediation and then, failing that, by military force.

The United States made a major effort to mediate the growing dispute—especially after Israeli forces raided southern Lebanon to destroy the PLO centers, and then armed the Christians as the basis for creating a buffer state between Israel and the PLO. Internal conflict erupted, during which the Syrians emplaced ground-to-air missiles in Lebanon. The Israelis destroyed the missiles. War between Israel and Syria, Washington knew, would drive the Arab states into Syria's arms and leave the United States alone with Israel, thus alienating the Saudis. The Soviet Union, which had recently entered an amity pact with Syria, would then be aligned with the other Arab states and gain a major inroad into the Middle East.

As tensions mounted in mid-1982, the PLO assassinated the Israeli ambassador in London, and the Israelis launched a massive invasion of Lebanon in June, ostensibly to cripple the PLO's ability to endanger Jewish settlements in the north, but in reality to destroy the PLO and force the Syrians out of Lebanon. At the same time the Israelis surprised the Reagan administration by bombing Iraq's nuclear reactor recently acquired from France—as a preventative against the production of nuclear bombs capable of destroying Israel. The timing of the attack on Lebanon was embarrassing to the United States. President Reagan was on a goodwill visit in Europe, and his administration was involved in the Middle East peace talks. The widespread impression was that the United States either had been unable to restrain Israel, or had tacitly approved the invasion. The Israeli offensive violated the recent fragile and unwritten ceasefire with the PLO secured by U.S. Special Envoy Philip Habib. Now more problems lay ahead. As a State Department spokesman pointed out, "Israel will have to withdraw its forces from Lebanon, and the Palestinians

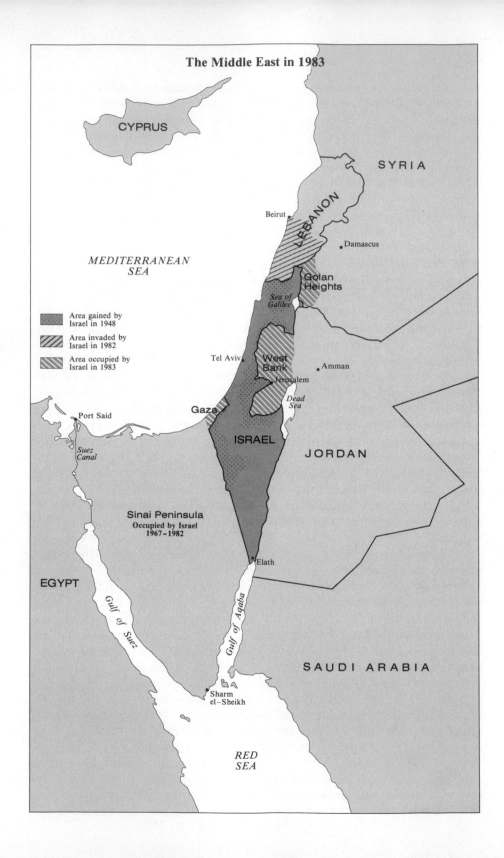

The Middle East in 1983

will have to stop using Lebanon as a launching pad for attacks on Israel." A British diplomat was blunt: Israel was "acting as recruiter in chief for the PLO."

The Israeli military offensive in Lebanon threatened to wreck America's hopes for peace in the Middle East. Israel once more stood alone against the Arab world, restricting Reagan's attempts to build a sweeping consensus to oppose the Soviet Union. The Israeli actions added weight to the charge that Egypt's earlier treaty had been a betrayal of fellow Arab states, made American mediation of the Lebanese dispute more remote, and virtually invited Soviet intervention in the region. Israel's behavior also threw American domestic politics into turmoil. White House support of Israel would alienate the Arabs and stop the oil flow; to do otherwise would cost votes at home. A compromise of sorts was the result. Inside the UN the United States joined Iraq in condemning Israel; but it did not support sanctions, save for a delay in the delivery of seventy-five promised F-16 fighter planes. Even then, these planes were not due for delivery until 1985, and this mild rebuke had no effect. The Arabs remained in an angry mood because America's policies stayed pro-Israel.

The Reagan administration meanwhile hoped for a Labor party victory in the 1982 elections in Israel, for that group had adopted a moderate position toward peace; but it lost and Begin continued as prime minister. For his cabinet he appointed a foreign minister who had resisted the treaty of 1979 with Egypt, and a defense minister who earlier as minister of agriculture had pushed for rapid Israeli settlement of the West Bank. Begin also placed the minister of the interior in charge of the Palestinian autonomy discussions, which was an implication that the issue was internal in nature and that annexation of the West Bank was imminent. Begin's reelection further damaged the Reagan administration's declining hopes for the anti-Soviet strategic consensus in the Middle East; in fact, Begin's renewal in office elevated the Arab-Israeli problem to prominence again. The Arab radicals' position was confirmed, the Palestinians in the West Bank grew more resentful, and the Soviet standing in the Middle East seemed to become stronger in proportion to America's loss of control over the situation.

The Middle East remained a steaming cauldron of trouble. The Israelis' attack on the PLO in Beirut in June 1982 had led to the deaths of numerous civilians, causing the United States to send a small contingent of marines to join French and Italian troops in safeguarding the evacuation of PLO forces from the city's refugee camps. But the trilateral force left too soon. Less than three weeks after its departure, nearly 800 Palestinian civilians in the camps were machine-gunned at the "Beirut massa-

MAP 36

From ancient times to the present, the Middle East has remained almost impervious to a peaceful resolution of its many problems.

cre" of September, leading to the return of American marines as part of another peacekeeping force. Suspicion grew that the Begin ministry had been involved in the act. The main responsibility for the massacre, many argued, lay with the extremist Lebanese Christian Phalangists; but these same observers noted that the killings had occurred in an area under Israel's military control, and that Israeli observation posts were nearby. Furthermore, they believed, Israeli army officers and government ministers knew about the impending act some thirty-six hours beforehand and had done nothing. A stormy session followed in Israel, after which a commission of inquiry eventually called for the resignation of the country's defense minister, Ariel Sharon, who admitted to having permitted Lebanese militia into the camps to clear out Palestinian guerrillas—but only after securing their promise not to harm civilians.

The White House continued its efforts toward peace by first securing the withdrawal of Israeli military forces from Lebanon. Reagan's major proposal was that the 720,000 Palestinians in the West Bank and Gaza should receive self-rule under Jordanian supervision. Begin argued instead for a neutralized Lebanon, free of PLO and Syrian involvement; a government dominated by the Christian Phalangists; a Lebanese special force to patrol the country's southern border; the establishment of a buffer zone policed by an international peacekeeping unit; and the right for Israeli forces to enter Lebanon at any time for searches and arrests. The United States joined Lebanon in rejecting Begin's proposals. The White House then attempted to persuade Jordan's King Hussein to represent the Palestinians in the talks. This plan likewise proved unsuccessful. Besides the PLO's opposition to this arrangement, Hussein refused to act without the support of other Arab leaders. In any case his prior stipulations had not been fulfilled: the United States had not convinced Begin either to withdraw his military forces from Lebanon, or to halt the spread of Jewish settlements on the West Bank. "If the U.S. cannot push the Israelis out of Lebanon," a Jordanian politician asked, "why should anyone believe it can get them out of the West Bank?"

Time was not on the side of the peacemakers. The PLO had no success in supporting the "Fez plan," set out at an Arab Summit conference during September 1982 in Fez, Morocco, which called for an independent Palestinian state in the West Bank and Gaza, with East Jerusalem as its capital. In the meantime the West Bank Palestinians increased pressure for a settlement, for they feared that further delay would promote Begin's goal of settling 100,000 Jews in the area and bringing about Israeli annexation of Jordan and all of the West Bank. As a Jordanian official warned, "If we do not force the Israelis to negotiate about the West Bank now, they will force us to negotiate over the East Bank later."

The Reagan administration continued in its efforts to defuse the Middle East situation. The president called for a freeze on new Israeli settlements in the West Bank that had caused an increase of Jewish inhabitants in the area from 5,000 in 1977 to nearly 30,000 by the summer of 1983.

Beirut, Lebanon

A scene of violence and destruction in the Middle East. (Wide World)

Begin dismissed Reagan's proposal with the observation that "it is as impossible to freeze the settlements as it is to freeze life." The Arabs held President Carter responsible for their troubles because he had failed to insist on a settlements freeze in the Camp David accords. As an Israeli admitted, "Begin started the rapid expansion after Camp David because nowhere does the treaty rule settlements out." With the Middle East talks stalemated, Begin felt no pressure to halt the settlements.

Meanwhile problems erupted again in Lebanon. In mid-April 1983, terrorists blew up a major part of the American embassy in Beirut, killing over fifty people (including several Americans) and injuring more than a hundred others who were in the building at the time. Though the White House gave assurances that this event would not interrupt the peace talks over Lebanon, there was little progress if any. The Israelis and the Lebanese concurred on the need for a security zone in south Lebanon to keep out Palestinian guerrillas and safeguard northern Israel from attack; but the Israelis wanted their soldiers to accompany Lebanese patrols and to have military or police powers, whereas the Lebanese agreed to allow Israeli participation only in "joint supervisory teams" having no such powers. The Syrians opposed any Israeli-Lebanese agreement as an obstruction to their aim of regaining the Golan Heights, taken by Israel in the Six Day War of 1967 and formally annexed in 1981. The biggest threat to peace, the United States feared, was an accidental war caused by the buildup of tensions to the point where neither side could back down gracefully. By mid-1983 there remained in Lebanon 38,000 Israeli and

50,000 Syrian troops, along with perhaps 15,000 PLO commandos—hardly a situation amenable to the control of a peacekeeping force comprised of American, British, French, and Italian soldiers.

The multinational force in Lebanon was soon involved in another terrorist crisis. On a Sunday morning in October 1983, a Muslim suicide mission drove a truck laden with dynamite through the barricade and into the U.S. marines' command center at Beirut International Airport, blowing up the main military barracks and killing 239 marines. Two miles from the U.S. compound, another explosion a few minutes later killed more than fifty French paratroopers. The president refused to withdraw the remaining military personnel; America had vital interests in the region and needed to counter the support that Syrians received from the Soviets. But the hard talk brought no results: the marines were trapped in the garrison, and in February 1984 the president ordered their withdrawal. With their departure, Lebanese groups joined Syria in expressing interest in peace talks.

The war between Iran and Iraq continued to complicate the situation in the Middle East. Long-standing differences had exploded in a conflict in 1980 that imperiled passage through the Persian Gulf and thus affected the oil interests of numerous nations. The Soviets had given planes and ammunition to Iraq, while approving Syria's delivery to Iran of Soviet arms. The result was that neither antagonist trusted the Soviet Union. The United States claimed to be neutral, although its relations with Iraq had improved when the State Department took that government off the list of countries supporting terrorism and thus permitted the extension of export credits. But the United States publicly refused to sell weapons. There was little hope for a negotiated settlement of the war. The president of Iran during the early part of the Khomeini regime, Abolhassan Banisadr, declared from outside Paris that "for us, the war will only end with a general embargo on arms deliveries to both belligerents."

Other problems surfaced over Libya, which, although not part of the Middle East, bordered Egypt and compounded the region's difficulties. In the spring of 1981 the Reagan administration accused Libya's ruler, Muammar al-Qaddafi, of engineering international terrorism with the help of Soviet money, and in May ordered Libyan diplomats out of Washington. The following August American forces on maneuvers in the Mediterranean off Libya's shores were accused by Qaddafi of violating his country's territorial waters, and a brief aerial exchange led to American fighter planes downing two Libyan planes. Relations worsened by the end of the year when the White House announced that Qaddafi had ordered Libyan terrorists in the United States to assassinate Reagan. In early 1982 the administration stopped Libyan oil imports into the country and placed an embargo on all goods to Libya.

Problems intensified between the United States and Libya. In December 1985 terrorist attacks at the Rome and Vienna airports killed 19 (including five Americans and one Israeli) and injured 112. Responsibility seemed to belong to a Palestinian group based in Libya and openly supported by Qaddafi. Sensing danger, he warned the United States and Israel that a strike against his country would cause Libyans to take action against Americans "in their own streets," and would lead to the spread of terrorism throughout the Mediterranean area. In early 1986 American naval forces in the Mediterranean made another show of force off the Libyan coast. When Libyan forces harassed the Americans, U.S. bombers launched retaliatory attacks on Libyan military positions. Then, in April 1986, an explosion rocked a West Berlin discotheque, killing one American serviceman and a Turkish woman and injuring 230, including dozens of off-duty American soldiers. Suspicions grew of Libya's involvement in the bombing, encouraged by electronic eavesdropping by the United States that revealed Qaddafi's intentions to launch more terrorist attacks. At a news conference President Reagan called him the "mad dog of the Middle East."

That same month of April, the White House (with the support of Britain, Canada, and Israel) approved a surprise air raid on the Libyan capital of Tripoli. Using bases in Britain, thirteen F-111s began a 5,600-mile round trip (lengthened by 2,400 miles because France and Spain refused to allow the planes to fly over their territory) and bombed Qaddafi's living quarters and command and communications center. In less than twelve minutes the planes destroyed several military targets; but they also hit some nonmilitary areas and killed a number of civilians, including one of Qaddafi's children. Although the Arabs and many Europeans denounced the action, America's allies on the continent soon exerted diplomatic pressure on the Libyans and the threat of terrorism eased for a few months. But these activities soon picked up again.

The Middle East's problems appeared to be as unsolvable during the 1980s as they had been in the immediate postwar period. All of the issues remained, complicated by international terrorism and by the endemic lack of trust.

CENTRAL AMERICA AND THE CARIBBEAN

Another dangerous foreign policy issue facing the Reagan administration was the ongoing civil war in the Central American country of El Salvador. The matter raised many of the most hotly debated issues during the Cold War years, in particular those issues arising during the latter period of America's involvement in Vietnam. The government of El Salvador, Reagan warned, was threatened by a communist insurgent movement aided by Soviet and Cuban weapons filtered into the country through neighboring Nicaragua. The United States cut off economic assistance to the leftist Sandinista government in Nicaragua in 1981, although Mexico and France lightened the effect by offering aid. Should El Salvador fall to communism, the president explained to reporters and others gazing at a huge map of Central America, the neighboring American states would collapse, one by one, until the entire region became communist and was in a position to endanger the United States. The Soviets must not achieve a victory in the Western Hemisphere, he emphasized to Congress. Though offering assurances that no American combat soldiers would go to El Salvador, Reagan made an unsettling statement when he warned that everything was at stake: "We are the last domino."

Skeptics countered that events in El Salvador were following the same pattern that led to America's military involvement in Vietnam: economic and military aid, followed by advisers (though later referred to as "trainers" by the Reagan administration in an effort to dispel the Vietnam analogy) and administrators, and ultimately by combat troops. The

MAP 37

Whether caused by internal problems or by outside interference—or both—the fighting in Central America continues to divide the United States over what remedies to offer.

Salvadorans' problems were internal in origin, critics declared, and the United States was again extending aid to an unpopular elite opposed to needed reforms. Americans could not accomplish a "victory" for democracy by seeking military solutions to social, political, and economic problems. In fact, administration opponents pointed out, Western Europe and many Latin American countries, particularly Mexico, believed that the guerrillas offered more hope for an improved society. Whether a Soviet threat existed in El Salvador or, as some administration members privately admitted, the United States wanted to use the issue to exemplify a strong course against communist aggression, the cry of "No more Vietnams" became the Reagan administration's chief obstacle to assuming a greater role in El Salvador.

The problems in El Salvador, as in other desperately poor Latin American states, had developed over a long period. Five million people were jammed into the tiny country, mostly in poverty-stricken areas characterized by a high birth rate and rampant disease. Calls for reform had gone unheeded by rightist regimes, which were comprised of a small minority of landowners allied with the army and relying on repressive measures to stay in power. But in October 1979 young, reformist, middle-grade officers in the army won control and installed an anticommunist regime headed by a civilian president, José Napoleón Duarte of the Christian Democratic party (PDC). The Carter administration sent economic and military assistance to Duarte, who in turn assured land reform and other social and political changes. A brutal reaction by the former ruling minority led to a wave of assassinations by "death squads," preventing Duarte from establishing control over the internal security groups within the government. Civil war then broke out after the leftists joined other dissatisfied groups in forming the Democratic Revolutionary Front (FDR) in April 1980 to oppose the regime. According to some estimates, in trying to put down the uprising, government security forces killed 13,000 Salvadorans by the end of that year. The military in El Salvador, complained American Ambassador Robert E. White in *The New York Times,* was "one of the most out-of-control, violent, bloodthirsty groups of men in the world."

The Reagan administration altered Carter's Salvadoran policy by sending more military aid and shifting the emphasis from land reform to victory in the war. The Department of State justified this harder stance on the ground that the situation was a "textbook case of indirect armed aggression by Communist powers." The present regime in El Salvador, the White House insisted, would lead the way to reform, whereas the left-wing guerrillas were Soviet proxies. This was an example of "international terrorism" emanating from the Soviet Union: encouragement to radical groups promoting political changes through violence. Reagan insisted that the United States wanted to help the Salvadoran government because it sought peaceful reforms and was under siege by leftists trying to tear it down. Authoritarian regimes, such as that in El Salvador, had to stamp out criticisms in civil wars, he continued, but were not totalitarian in the sense of seeking to squelch all dissent. Religious beliefs, family

The War in Central America—El Salvador

U.S. Army officer demonstrating map reading to Salvadoran soldiers during field training exercise. (U.S. Army)

matters, cultural pursuits, economic concerns—much latitude remained for individual development in these areas as long as these activities did not grow into political protests. The United States had no choice but to support the military regime, the Reagan administration declared. Whereas authoritarian regimes exercised degrees of repression and thus had the leeway to become more democratic, totalitarian regimes could not change. The best proof was Nicaragua, Reagan asserted. The Carter administration had erred in supporting the Sandinistas over the Somozan government. Once they gained power, the Sandinistas suppressed civil liberties and moved close to the Soviet Union and Cuba. Congress agreed to send economic and military assistance along with advisers, but it staunchly opposed military intervention. Even then, it tied aid programs to improvements in human rights.

During the spring of 1983 the Reagan administration asked Congress to approve more military aid for the war in El Salvador. The year before Americans had met with Mexican emissaries and a short time later, in March 1982, elections took place in El Salvador. Although the insurgents refused to take part, Duarte lost to right-wing leaders and the land reform program came to a halt. The problems, according to the Reagan administration, were attributable to the communists. The Soviets had infiltrated Nicaragua and now El Salvador, and soon would concentrate on Honduras and Guatemala. There was a broader implication in this activity, Reagan warned: "Soviet military theorists want to destroy our capacity to resupply Western Europe in case of an emergency." They intend "to tie down our attention and forces on our own southern border and so limit our capacity to act in more distant places such as Europe, the Persian Gulf, the Indian Ocean, the Sea of Japan." Central America was "simply too close and the strategic stakes . . . too high, for us to ignore the danger of governments seizing power there with ideological and military ties to the Soviet Union." To quiet those Americans who feared "another Vietnam," Reagan explained in March 1983 that he was willing to have Salvadoran troops trained inside the United States. Though repeating his pledge against sending American combat troops to the troubled country, he warned that he would increase the number of advisers if Congress failed to comply with his requests for more military aid. "Two-thirds of all our foreign trade and petroleum pass through the Panama Canal and the Caribbean," the president explained in May. Should a crisis develop in Europe, "at least half of our supplies for NATO would go through these areas by sea." The Caribbean basin was a "magnet for adventurism."

The situation in Central America continued to deteriorate. Charges grew that the United States was secretly aiding the *contras* (an anti-Sandinista force numbering perhaps as many as 2,000 and based in Honduras) in an attempt to overthrow the regime in Nicaragua and ease the alleged communist pressures on El Salvador. The White House denied

The War in Central America—Nicaragua

Contras *standing guard in Matagalpa in eastern Nicaragua in September 1985.*
(Wide World)

the accusation as a "myth," claiming instead that the new fighting was internal in origin and that American aid to the anti-Sandinistas was aimed only at "interdicting" or prohibiting further military assistance to the communists in El Salvador. "The United States isn't invading anybody," UN Ambassador Jeane Kirkpatrick declared. A State Department representative warned congressional committees that the United States might have to escalate its military and political involvement in Nicaragua because of the possible introduction into Central America of either Soviet or Cuban "modern fighter aircraft" or "even Cuban combat troops." Should Soviet and Cuban intervention take place, he asserted, the Reagan administration was prepared to use jets, increase aid to friendly nations, and invoke the Rio Treaty of 1947, allowing the United States to participate in the collective defense of Latin America. The president declared, however, that "we do not view security assistance as an end in itself, but as a shield for democratization, economic development and diplomacy." Shortly afterward the White House announced that a hundred military advisers had left for Honduras to train Salvadoran troops.

Though in the summer of 1983 an American military adviser was assassinated in El Salvador, the United States continued to act with restraint. The Reagan administration adopted a strategy called symmetry, which sought to buy time for democratic development in the Central American country. According to theory, the United States would treat the Sandinista regime in Nicaragua in the same way the Sandinistas treated the U.S.-supported government of President Alvaro Magaña in El Salvador: the United States would help the guerrilla group seeking its overthrow. In late July Reagan appointed former Secretary of State Henry Kissinger to head a twelve-member bipartisan commission to develop a long-range policy on Central America. The president also sent an aircraft carrier battle group to engage in military maneuvers along Nicaragua's Pacific coast as a show of force. Perhaps with these demonstrations of America's interest in Central American affairs, the governments and rebels in both Nicaragua and El Salvador would become amenable to a cease-fire, negotiations, and democratic elections.

The attention of the United States temporarily shifted from Central America to the Caribbean in October 1983, when the Reagan administration warned of a possible communist takeover on the tiny island of Grenada. Four years earlier, in March 1979, leftists led by Maurice Bishop had overthrown the repressive and corrupt but anticommunist government in a bloodless coup. In less than a week a Cuban ship arrived carrying Soviet arms and ammunition. The following November Bishop announced that Fidel Castro would help Grenada build an "international airport." After construction of the airstrip was under way, Bishop signed a treaty with Moscow allowing the Soviets to land their long-range reconnaissance planes. Although the Reagan administration complained that these moves threatened peace in the hemisphere, Bishop visited Moscow in July 1982 and declared that he had received assurances of long-term financial assistance. Over national television in March 1983, Reagan displayed a photograph of the Cuban barracks and airstrip on the island. Grenada had no air force, he declared. "The Soviet-Cuban militarization of Grenada can only be seen as power projection into the region."

An outbreak of violence on the island provided the opportunity for the United States to act. American pressure on Bishop had forced him to ease his criticisms of the United States; but Cuba's insistence on a hardline policy encouraged dissidents on Grenada to seize control in mid-October and place Bishop under house arrest. Bishop's followers soon stormed the building and freed him, whereupon he spoke before a huge rally in the capital city of St. George's. But so-called revolutionary armed forces fired into the crowd, killing several and then executing Bishop. The White House feared that 1,000 Americans on the island, most of them medical students, were in danger.

With the approval of the six member nations of the Organization of Eastern Caribbean States, Reagan resorted to military force. News of the Beirut bombings made the president hesitant about risking more American lives, but he finally gave approval: "We cannot let an act of terrorism determine whether we aid or assist our allies in the region. If we do that," he asked, "who will ever trust us again?" On October 25, a naval task force of 1,900 marines en route for Lebanon was ordered to Grenada. There they encountered brief and surprisingly strong resistance at the airstrip from 800 Cuban workers and troops. Soon, however, about 6,000 American troops secured the island—at a cost of 134 American casualties, including 18 killed. Reagan declared that documents and weapons captured in the assault proved that the Marxist government had become increasingly reliant on Cuba, the Soviet Union, and North Korea—particularly for arms.

Questions remained about the Grenada expedition, even though many observers hailed the outcome a triumph for Reagan's foreign policy. Some wondered if the administration had too readily placed emphasis on the military option. Others were skeptical about the danger and asked embarrassing questions about how efficiently the military forces had performed. British Prime Minister Margaret Thatcher had opposed the invasion as a violation of Grenada's sovereignty and urged economic sanctions, while numerous Latin American governments denounced the action as a return to gunboat diplomacy. The Grenada expedition nonetheless won widespread approval in the United States.

With a pro-American group in charge, the troops began their departure from the island in late December, following seven weeks of occupation.

In early 1984 the Kissinger Commission presented its conclusions: in view of the United States's vital interests in Central America, it had to expand its economic and military commitment. The commission recommended that Congress extend $8 billion in economic aid to the region over the next five years. Most members of the commission took exception with the president's emphasis on the role of private business and urged the United States to condition aid on changes in human rights. Kissinger warned, however, that the United States must not interpret the "conditionality" of aid "in a manner that leads to a Marxist-Leninist victory." To reporters, he declared that it would be "absurd" to cut off military assistance to El Salvador in defense of human rights if the move ensured a communist victory that would lead to more killing. Reagan approved the report but spoke favorably of Kissinger's warning.

The situation in El Salvador meanwhile showed signs of easing in intensity. In May 1984, with the United States supervising election proceedings, Duarte emerged victorious as president. The following year his Christian Democratic party won control over the National Assembly and the military seemed receptive to his moderate policies and assurances of reforms. The death squads decreased their activity, and Duarte met with the rebels to explore the possibilities of a negotiated settlement.

The Reagan administration continued in its efforts to aid the *contras* in Nicaragua. It sent aid, worked to train the army, and tried to bring about land reform. In mid-August 1983 the first of nearly 6,000 army and marine troops had landed in Honduras to begin "training exercises." The CIA meanwhile directed assaults into Nicaragua, flew air missions, and in early 1984 helped to mine the country's harbors. But the mines damaged several neutral vessels and injured ten sailors, causing Congress to stop all aid to the *contras* in late 1984. Colombia, Mexico, Panama, and Venezuela (the "Contadora group") urged negotiations between Nicaragua and El Salvador that would lead to a regional settlement. The White House, however, insisted on maintaining pressure on the Sandinistas in Nicaragua. And while Congress would assist Duarte and El Salvador, it repeatedly turned down the president's requests to aid the *contras*. Private groups of Americans, however, sent $5 million of supplies to them in 1984–85.

The situation continued to deteriorate. The Sandinistas held an election in late 1984 that solidified their control, even though they lost a few seats in the government to opposition groups. When the Sandinistas moved closer to Cuba and the communist bloc, Reagan ordered the *contras* based in Honduras into maneuvers and stationed U.S. warships off the Nicaraguan coasts. He also instituted an economic embargo in 1985. Under the International Emergency Economic Powers Act of 1977, the president could impose sanctions without congressional approval if he declared a "national emergency." Reagan announced that Nicaragua's "aggressive activities" were apparent in its "continuing efforts to subvert its neighbors, its rapid and destabilizing military buildup, its close military and security ties to Cuba and the Soviet Union and its imposition of Communist totalitarian internal rule."

Meanwhile Soviet ties with Nicaragua seemed to grow tighter. Two days before the United States announced the economic sanctions, Nicaragua's president, Daniel Ortega, visited Gorbachev in the Kremlin and, before television cameras, shook hands and talked. In this, Ortega's fourth visit since the Sandinista takeover in July 1979, he was supposedly seeking new economic assistance. The Soviet Union had delayed news of the planned visit until after Reagan's recent *contra* aid defeat in Congress. Soviet news agency TASS announced the establishment of a Soviet-Nicaraguan commission on economic, trade, and scientific-technical cooperation.

In March 1986 Reagan again appealed for congressional money for arms to the *contras*. Three months later Congress (doubtless in reaction to Ortega's visit to Moscow) approved $100 million but in "nonlethal" aid.

In an ironic twist, the issues in the Middle East and Central America suddenly merged in an affair that some called Iranscam. In late 1986 charges spread that the White House had attempted to secure the freedom of American hostages in Lebanon by arranging the sale of arms to Iran through the Israelis, and depositing some of the money in a Swiss bank account earmarked for the *contras*. According to plan, the Iranians would use their influence with the Muslims in Lebanon and win release of the hostages. Accusations came hot and heavy as numerous groups wondered about presidential involvement and drew comparisons with Watergate. Reagan admitted to knowledge of the arms-for-hostages negotiations but professed surprise at the alleged Iran-*contra* connection. In February 1987 a Senate Intelligence Committee reported that it found "no direct evidence" that the president knew of the illegal diversion of funds to the Nicaraguan rebels. But the committee questioned Reagan's defense that the weapons transactions were diplomatic ventures intended to encourage ties with moderates in the Iranian government. The controversy continued as critics declared that the arms-for-hostages deal was tantamount to blackmail.

PROSPECTS

Throughout the 1980s relations between the United States and the Soviet Union continued their uneven course. In September 1983 Soviet planes shot down a South Korean airline passenger plane (KAL 007), killing all 269 aboard (including sixty Americans). When the United States and other nations bitterly complained, Moscow declared that the plane had purposely violated Soviet air space over military installations on Sakhalin Island as part of a U.S. spy mission. The Soviets refused to apologize. In November, when the United States began installing the promised Pershing II and cruise missiles in Britain and Germany, the Soviets broke off the START discussions in Geneva after charging that the missile emplacement left them only ten minutes warning time in the event of an attack. Not until mid-January 1985 did they agree to resume the talks.

As America's defense budget grew, many observers questioned whether the Reagan administration had developed a comprehensive strategy to deal with the Soviets, other than to build more arms and to insist that in a "protracted" nuclear war, the United States would emerge the victor. A high-ranking Pentagon official explained: Americans would "dig a hole, cover it with a couple of doors, and then throw three feet of dirt on top." Another member of the administration blandly assured Congress that in the aftermath of nuclear war, mail would go through "even if the survivors ran out of stamps." He was not taken aback by a member of Congress who noted the difficulty in delivering mail where there were "no addresses, no streets, no blocks, no houses." Scientific studies showed that a nuclear holocaust would cause countless deaths and that it could destroy the chain of life on earth by blackening the skies for a year and disrupting the sun's capacity to provide the basis for food. An escalated arms race seemed likely as the United States continued to push for SDI as an alternative to deterrence theory, while the Soviets made greater efforts at building offensive missiles.

The United States faced a new and more challenging international situation by the 1980s. The bipolar Cold War had receded more into the past, only to be replaced by the virtually unpredictable and uncontrollable tensions caused by a multipolar world. Both the United States and the Soviet Union encountered serious difficulties at home, as well as in areas previously considered part of their spheres of influence. Furthermore, many of the 150 nations in the world exemplified strong feelings of nationalism that encouraged them to be more independent in action. Americans' confidence in their government and culture had been shaken by Watergate and Vietnam, but also by economic problems at home and by the declining respect for their nation throughout the world. America's global dominance, so evident in 1945, was not so evident any more. Part of the explanation rested in the Soviet Union's great advances since World War II, but another consideration was that increasing leverage in world affairs had gravitated into Western Europe, Japan, and the Third World countries, particularly those members of OPEC. Soviet military growth, stimulated especially by the outcome of the Cuban missile crisis of 1962, had brought a precarious balance of power that necessitated arms limitations talks and overtures to Third World nations. No alternatives remained to drawn-out negotiations and big power competition for support from the Third World, which found nonalignment more advantageous to its interests and in that way was able to dictate much of the superpowers' policy.

The Reagan administration, however, was reluctant to accept the growing prominence of the Third World. The White House chose to de-emphasize Carter's attempts to establish North-South relationships based on American economic assistance, in preference for remedies aimed at swelling trade and investment through hard work and private enterprise. It looked with little interest on the recent call for a New International Economic Order (NIEO), which was the Third World's claim for compensation from the West after its long history of exploiting underdeveloped peoples of the world. Within the Western Hemisphere the Reagan administration in early 1982 called for the Caribbean Basin Initiative, which promoted private trade in an effort to help noncommunist governments in the Caribbean and Central America. Globalism again dominated White House policy, causing a growth in superpower rivalry for Third World allegiance and paradoxically allowing the smaller nations to continue to wield an inordinate influence on world events.

The Reagan administration has also drawn criticism on other matters. It claimed some credit in early 1986 for the demise of longtime dictators Jean-Claude ("Baby Doc") Duvalier in Haiti and Ferdinand Marcos in the Philippines. And yet, with regard to the racial violence in South Africa, many Americans believed that the president did not react strongly enough against the white government's segregationist policies of *apartheid*. Instead of calling on American business leaders to "disinvest" from South Africa, Reagan supported "constructive engagement," by which he attempted to build better diplomatic and economic ties in an effort to influence leaders to change their racial policies. Congress imposed mild sanctions on the white South African government in mid-1986—but only after overriding the president's veto.

In March 1979 *Business Week* published an issue entitled "The Decline of U.S. Power," in which the writers pointed out that although the United States was dominant in the mid-1940s, its global position had been the victim of "decay" that by 1980 prevented America's ability to control "radical economic and social change in the Third World." The Suez crisis of 1956, the writers declared, was the turning point because the United States broke with its allies, thereby inviting Soviet intervention in the Middle East and ensuring the West's steady loss of control over oil and thus over the direction of international affairs. The Nixon administration had taken the proper step during the early 1970s by calling for partnerships in combating the world's problems. No single nation could resolve the difficulties resulting from worldwide economic disorder, international terrorism, overpopulation and poverty, pollution and deforestation, threatened nuclear proliferation, and growing numbers of refugees caused by disasters due to natural and human causes in Indochina, the Middle East, South Africa, and Central America and the Caribbean. Perhaps a more accurate assessment would have emphasized a decline in prestige rather than in power, but it is certain that when the two forces are not in balance, a less effective foreign policy results.

Several critics charged that the Reagan administration had ignored the changed realities in the world's power structure and was concentrating on the impossible task of restoring the United States to its former position of leadership. But the military and economic power of the world was now diffused. The United States needed a new direction in foreign policy that accepted a world in which peoples and events were not subject to rigid control. Anticommunism remained a justifiable consideration in policy formation, but many asked whether the forces of nationalism might not be real, rather than based on an ideological connection to either Russia or

China. Military power had again not proved itself the universal remedy to political and economic problems.

Though the White House made economic and military efforts to promote reforms and keep the Western alliance intact, the ideal repeatedly threatened to diverge even farther from the real, causing a further drift from the use of diplomacy and a continuance of a military-oriented foreign policy. Early in his first administration, Reagan asserted that the Soviets were "the focus of evil in the modern world." Not to be outdone, then Soviet Leader Andropov in 1983 called the president's military strategy "not just irresponsible" but "insane." Well into Reagan's second term, arms talks have continued, discussions have resumed about another attempt at a summit conference, and respect has grown for America's military strength and caused a corresponding rise in morale among Americans. And yet, the national debt has reached an astronomical level, and the nuclear arms race has continued. The rhetoric has eased, but one sensed the need for studying the past.

Selected readings

Ambrose, Stephen E., *Rise to Globalism: American Foreign Policy Since 1938.* 4th ed. 1985.

Armstrong, R., and J. Shenk, *El Salvador: The Face of Revolution.* 1982.

Arnson, C., *El Salvador: A Revolution Confronts the United States.* 1982.

Barrett, Lawrence I., *Gambling with History: Ronald Reagan in the White House.* 1983.

Chace, James, *Endless War: How We Got Involved in Central America.* 1984.

Coleman, Kenneth M., and George C. Herring, eds., *The Central American Crisis: Sources of Conflict and the Failure of U.S. Policy.* 1985.

Dallek, Robert, *The American Style of Foreign Policy.* 1983.

Didion, Joan, *Salvador.* 1983.

Diederich, Bernard, *Somoza and the Legacy of U.S. Involvement in Central America.* 1981.

Drew, Elizabeth, *Portrait of an Election: The 1980 Presidential Campaign.* 1981.

Falcoff, Mark, and Robert Royal, *Crisis and Opportunity: U.S. Policy in Central America and the Caribbean.* 1984.

Gardner, Lloyd C., *A Covenant with Power: America and World Order from Wilson to Reagan.* 1984.

Gettleman, Marvin E., et al., eds., *El Salvador: Central America in the New Cold War.* 1981.

Haig, Alexander M., Jr., *Caveat: Realism, Reagan, and Foreign Policy.* 1984.

Hunt, Michael H., *Ideology and U.S. Foreign Policy.* 1987.

Jabber, Paul, *Not By War Alone: Security and Arms Control in the Middle East.* 1981.

Klare, Michael T., and Cynthia Arnson, *Supplying Suppression: U.S. Support for Authoritarian Regimes Abroad.* 1981.

LaFeber, Walter, *Inevitable Revolutions: The United States in Central America.* 1983.

Morris, Roger, *Haig: The General's Progress.* 1982.

Olson, Robert, *U.S. Foreign Policy and the New International Economic Order.* 1981.

Pierre, Andrew J., *The Global Politics of Arms Sales.* 1982.

Rubin, Barry, *Secrets of State: The State Department and the Struggle over U.S. Foreign Policy.* 1985.

Schell, Jonathan, *The Fate of the Earth.* 1982.

Schulzinger, Robert D., *The Wise Men of Foreign Affairs: The History of the Council on Foreign Relations.* 1984.

Spanier, John W., *American Foreign Policy Since World War II.* 9th ed. 1983.

Spiegel, Steven L., *The Other Arab-Israeli Conflict: Making America's Middle East Policy, from Truman to Reagan.* 1985.

Stevenson, Richard W., *The Rise and Fall of Détente: Relaxations of Tensions in U.S.-Soviet Relations, 1953–1984.* 1985.

United States, *Department of State.* Bureau of Public Affairs Publications.

Walker, Thomas W., *Nicaragua: The Land of Sandino.* 1982.

Appendix

MAKERS OF AMERICAN DIPLOMACY

Presidents	Secretaries of State
George Washington (1789–1797)	Thomas Jefferson (1790–1793)
	Edmund Randolph (1794–1795)
	Timothy Pickering (1795–1797)
John Adams (1797–1801)	Timothy Pickering (1797–1800)
	John Marshall (1800–1801)
Thomas Jefferson (1801–1809)	James Madison (1801–1809)
James Madison (1809–1817)	Robert Smith (1809–1811)
	James Monroe (1811–1817)
James Monroe (1817–1825)	John Quincy Adams (1817–1825)
John Quincy Adams (1825–1829)	Henry Clay (1825–1829)
Andrew Jackson (1829–1837)	Martin Van Buren (1829–1831)
	Edward Livingston (1831–1833)
	Louis McLane (1833–1834)
	John Forsyth (1834–1837)
Martin Van Buren (1837–1841)	John Forsyth (1837–1841)
William H. Harrison (1841)	Daniel Webster (1841)
John Tyler (1841–1845)	Daniel Webster (1841–1843)
	Hugh S. Legaŕe (1843)
	Abel P. Upshur (1843–1844)
	John C. Calhoun (1844–1845)
James K. Polk (1845–1849)	James Buchanan (1845–1849)
Zachary Taylor (1849–1850)	John M. Clayton (1849–1850)
Millard Fillmore (1850–1853)	Daniel Webster (1850–1852)
	Edward Everett (1852–1853)
Franklin Pierce (1853–1857)	William L. Marcy (1853–1857)
James Buchanan (1857–1861)	Lewis Cass (1857–1860)
	Jeremiah S. Black (1860–1861)
Abraham Lincoln (1861–1865)	William H. Seward (1861–1865)
Andrew Johnson (1865–1869)	William H. Seward (1865–1869)
Ulysses S. Grant (1869–1877)	Elihu B. Washburne (1869)
	Hamilton Fish (1869–1877)
Rutherford B. Hayes (1877–1881)	William M. Evarts (1877–1881)
James A. Garfield (1881)	James G. Blaine (1881)
Chester A. Arthur (1881–1885)	Frederick T. Frelinghuysen (1881–1885)

(continued)

Presidents	Secretaries of State
Grover Cleveland (1885–1889)	Thomas F. Bayard (1885–1889)
Benjamin Harrison (1889–1893)	James G. Blaine (1889–1892)
	John W. Foster (1892–1893)
Grover Cleveland (1893–1897)	Walter Q. Gresham (1893–1895)
	Richard Olney (1895–1897)
William McKinley (1897–1901)	John Sherman (1897–1898)
	William R. Day (1898)
	John Hay (1898–1901)
Theodore Roosevelt (1901–1909)	John Hay (1901–1905)
	Elihu Root (1905–1909)
	Robert Bacon (1909)
William Howard Taft (1909–1913)	Philander C. Knox (1909–1913)
Woodrow Wilson (1913–1921)	William Jennings Bryan (1913–1915)
	Robert Lansing (1915–1920)
	Bainbridge Colby (1920–1921)
Warren G. Harding (1921–1923)	Charles E. Hughes (1921–1923)
Calvin Coolidge (1923–1929)	Charles E. Hughes (1923–1925)
	Frank B. Kellogg (1925–1929)
Herbert C. Hoover (1929–1933)	Henry L. Stimson (1929–1933)
Franklin D. Roosevelt (1933–1945)	Cordell Hull (1933–1944)
	Edward R. Stettinius, Jr. (1944–1945)
Harry S. Truman (1945–1953)	Edward R. Stettinius, Jr. (1945)
	James F. Byrnes (1945–1947)
	George C. Marshall (1947–1949)
	Dean G. Acheson (1949–1953)

Presidents	Secretaries of State	Assistants to the President for National Security Affairs
Dwight D. Eisenhower (1953–1961)	John F. Dulles (1953–1959) Christian A. Herter (1959–1961)	Robert Cutler (1953–1955; 1957–1958) Dillon Anderson (1955–1956) William H. Jackson (1956) Gordon Gray (1958–1961)
John F. Kennedy (1961–1963)	Dean Rusk (1961–1963)	McGeorge Bundy (1961–1963)
Lyndon B. Johnson (1963–1969)	Dean Rusk (1963–1969)	McGeorge Bundy (1963–1966) Walt W. Rostow (1966–1969)
Richard M. Nixon (1969–1974)	William P. Rogers (1969–1973) Henry A. Kissinger (1973–1974)	Henry A. Kissinger (1969–1974)
Gerald R. Ford (1974–1977)	Henry A. Kissinger (1974–1977)	Henry A. Kissinger (1974–1976) Brent Scowcroft (1976–1977)
Jimmy Carter (1977–1981)	Cyrus R. Vance (1977–1980) Edmund Muskie (1980–1981)	Zbigniew Brzezinski (1977–1981)
Ronald Reagan (1981–)	Alexander M. Haig, Jr. (1981–1982) George P. Shultz (1982–)	Richard Allen (1981) William P. Clark, Jr. (1981–1983) Robert McFarlane (1983–1987) Frank Carlucci (1987–)

Index

X

Y

About the Author

Howard Jones is Professor of History at the University of Alabama, and has also taught at the University of Nebraska and at Maxwell Air Force Base. He has received grants from the American Council of Learned Societies, American Philosophical Society, Earhart Foundation, National Endowment for the Humanities, Franklin D. Roosevelt Library, and Harry S. Truman Library. His books include *To the Webster-Ashburton Treaty: A Study in Anglo-American Relations, 1783–1843; Mutiny on the Amistad: The Saga of a Slave Revolt and Its Impact on American Abolition, Law, and Diplomacy;* and the forthcoming edited work, *The Foreign and Domestic Dimensions of Modern Warfare: Vietnam, Central America, and Nuclear Strategy.* His book on the Webster-Ashburton Treaty was nominated for the Pulitzer Prize and received the Phi Alpha Theta Book Award. He is currently completing a study of the Truman Doctrine in Greece.

A Note on the Type

The text of this book was set in 10/12 Palatino using a film version of the face designed by Hermann Zapf that was first released in 1950 by Germany's Stempel Foundry. The face is named after Giovanni Battista Palatino, a famous penman of the 16th century. In its calligraphic quality, Palatino is reminiscent of the Italian Renaissance type designs, yet with its wide, open letters and unique proportions it still retains a modern feel. Palatino is considered one of the most important faces from one of Europe's most influential type designers.

Composition by P&M Typesetting Company, Inc., Waterbury, Connecticut.

Printed and bound by The Book Press, Brattleboro, Vermont.